Real World SharePoint® 2007

Real World SharePoint® 2007

Indispensable Experiences from 16 MOSS and WSS MVPs

Scott Hillier, Robert Bogue, Adam Buenz, Andrew Connell,
Stacy Draper, Luis Du Solier Grinda, Todd Klindt, Jason Medero,
Dustin Miller, Shane Perran, Joris Poelmans, Heather Solomon,
Nick Swan, Jan Tielens, Mike Walsh, Shane Young

Wiley Publishing, Inc.

Real World SharePoint® 2007

Published by
Wiley Publishing, Inc.
10475 Crosspoint Boulevard
Indianapolis, IN 46256
www.wiley.com

Copyright © 2007 by Wiley Publishing, Inc., Indianapolis, Indiana

Published simultaneously in Canada

ISBN: 978-0-470-16835-6

Manufactured in the United States of America

10 9 8 7 6 5 4

Library of Congress Cataloging-in-Publication Data:

Real world SharePoint 2007 : indispensable experiences from 16 MOSS and WSS MVPs / Scot Hillier...[et al.].
   p. cm.
  Includes index.
  ISBN 978-0-470-16835-6 (paper/website)
  1. Intranets (Computer networks) 2. Web servers. I. Hillier, Scot.
  TK5105.875.I6R43 2007
  004.6'82--dc22
                          2007021319

For general information on our other products and services please contact our Customer Care Department within the United States at (800) 762-2974, outside the United States at (317) 572-3993 or fax (317) 572-4002.

Trademarks: Wiley, the Wiley logo, Wrox, the Wrox logo, Programmer to Programmer, and related trade dress are trademarks or registered trademarks of John Wiley & Sons, Inc. and/or its affiliates, in the United States and other countries, and may not be used without written permission. Microsoft and SharePoint are registered trademarks of Microsoft Corporation in the United States and/or other countries. All other trademarks are the property of their respective owners. Wiley Publishing, Inc., is not associated with any product or vendor mentioned in this book.

Wiley also publishes its books in a variety of electronic formats. Some content that appears in print may not be available in electronic books.

About the Authors

Scot Hillier is an independent consultant and Microsoft Most Valuable Professional (MVP) focused on creating solutions for Information Workers with SharePoint, Office, and related .NET technologies. He is the author of ten books on Microsoft technologies, including *Microsoft SharePoint: Building Office 2007 Solutions in C# 2005 (Berkeley: Apress, 2007)*. When not writing about technology, he can be found presenting at industry conferences such as Microsoft TechEd and SharePoint Connections. Hillier is a former U. S. Navy submarine officer and graduate of the Virginia Military Institute. He can be reached at scot@shillier.com.

Robert Bogue, MCSE (NT4/W2K), MCSA:Security, A+, Network+, Server+, I-Net+, IT Project+, E-Biz+, CDIA+, is the president of Thor Projects LLC, which provides SharePoint consulting services to clients around the country. He has contributed to more than 100 book projects and numerous other publishing projects. He was recently honored to become a Microsoft MVP for Microsoft Office SharePoint Server. Before that, he was a Microsoft Commerce Server MVP, and before that, a Microsoft Windows Servers-Networking MVP. He blogs at http://www.thorprojects.com/blog. You can reach Robert at Rob.Bogue@thorprojects.com.

Adam Robert Buenz is a SharePoint Architect and Developer for ARB Security Solutions, LLC (sharepointsecurity.com). He focuses on security-centric collaboration environments that build off the SharePoint and .NET Framework. Focusing heavily on the security of SharePoint, along with integration of sister Microsoft platforms into SharePoint (such as ForeFront, ISA, MIIS, and DPM), he has developed against several of the largest health care, financial, and federal implementations of SharePoint within the United States. He is co-author of *Professional SharePoint 2007 Development (Indianapolis: Wiley, 2007)* and co-author of 7 Microsoft® Office Business Applications for Office SharePoint® Server 2007 (Redmond, WA: Microsoft Press, 2007). He lives wherever he is contracted, and can be contacted at adam@sharepointsecurity.com.

Andrew Connell is an independent consultant, instructor, and Microsoft Office SharePoint Server MVP with a focus on Web Content Management. He has authored and co-authored numerous books on the subjects of Microsoft Content Management Server and SharePoint, including the first published books on the latest release Windows SharePoint Services (WSS) v3 and Microsoft Office SharePoint Server (MOSS) 2007. Connell has spoken on the subject of Office SharePoint Server 2007 development and Web Content Management at various community events in the southeast United States, as well as national conferences such as TechEd, SharePoint Connections, VSLive, and the Microsoft SharePoint Conference. You can reach him at me@andrewconnell.com or subscribe to his popular SharePoint and Web Content Management focused blog at http://www.andrewconnell.com/blog. He would like to thank his wife, Meredith, for the support and encouragement in all his efforts; his son, Steven, who's always there to put things in perspective (as well as put a smile on his face); and the other SharePoint MVPs who make up the most incredible and diverse group of talented professionals that he has been privileged to be a part of.

Stacy Draper is 37 years old, married, founder of Wild Wires, LLC (a consulting firm based in South Florida), author, and member of PMI. He holds an MCSD certification and MVP award. Being involved with Web development since 1993 has led his life in a very interesting direction. He started out in UNIX and, since 1997, has had a strong concentration in Microsoft technologies. Draper enjoys public speaking and has spoken at conferences, code camps, and user groups. Draper would like to dedicate his contribution to this book to his wife, who is his driving force, and his little bundle of joy, Alicia.

Luis Du Solier Grinda is a Microsoft Office SharePoint Server MVP. He worked a few years ago in one of the top Business Schools in Mexico City (IPADE) as a System Administrator, as well as designing and implementing the corporate SharePoint intranet for the company. After he became an IW and Collaboration expert, he joined one of the best Microsoft Certified Partners in Mexico City (PlexIT Consulting). Since then, he's been working on many projects designing, creating, and implementing collaborative solutions related to the Microsoft Collaboration platform, SharePoint Products and Technologies. He has provided new technology solutions based on SharePoint and Office platforms for many companies. He also helped to manage the User Group from his country, and writes several blogs (English—`http://www.sharepointblogs.com/ldusolier`; and Spanish—`http://sharepointmx.mvps.org/blogs/ldusolier`, `http://geeks.ms/blogs/ldusolier`).

Todd Klindt is an IT Professional working mainly with SharePoint technologies. He currently works at UGS and maintains their internal SharePoint deployment. He has been in the IT field for more than ten years, getting his MCSE in 1996. He has written for Windows IT Pro and TechNet magazines, as well as serving as a presenter at TechEd. Klindt lives in Ames, Iowa, with his lovely wife Jill. You can visit his Web page at `http://www.toddklindt.com`, or email him at `todd@toddklindt.com`.

Jason Medero, MCP, MCT, MVP (WSS) is a systems architect with a concentration in Microsoft Office SharePoint Server and its related Microsoft technologies. He is an employee of B&R Business Solutions, a central New Jersey–based firm specializing in SharePoint and surrounding technologies, infrastructure, real-time communication, and application development. He is an active member of the SharePoint community, contributing as a mentor for both the SharePoint Portal Server (SPS) and Windows SharePoint Services (WSS) forums on `MSD2D.com`, along with many other popular forums. He would like to dedicate his contributions to this book to his family, colleagues, and soul mate, Kate.

Dustin Miller is the President and owner of SharePoint Experts (www.sharepointexperts.com), a leading provider of SharePoint Products and Technologies Training. He authored the first course devoted to SharePoint development and customization, the SharePoint Bootcamp (`www.sharepointbootcamp.com`), and also maintains two popular SharePoint Community sites, SharePoint University (`www.sharepointu.com`) and SharePoint Blogs (`www.sharepointblogs.com`). He lives in the Chicago suburbs with his wife, his son, and his white German shepherd dog. He would like to thank his wife, Julie, for her support and confidence during his crazy-busy work days and hectic travel schedule, and his son, Graham, for his uncanny ability to sniff his feet whenever Dad most needed a laugh.

Shane Perran is a Microsoft MVP for Windows SharePoint Services living in St. John's, Newfoundland and Labrador, Canada. He has been designing online user experiences for more than a decade. His strong passion for visual presentation, Web standards, and usability has paved the way for a successful transition into the SharePoint Products and Technologies world, where he has become well-known in the SharePoint customization space over the past five years. Perran's SharePoint Customization blog (`http://www.graphicalwonder.com`) is a popular stop for customization experts across the globe. He would like to say thanks to his family for their constant support and encouragement, especially his fiancé, Amanda, for her patience and late-night proofreading. He would also like to thank his friends and calming voices of JC, BD, RC, and WN.

Joris Poelmans has more than seven years of experience with Microsoft development. He works at Dolmen (www.dolmen.be), a Belgian IT services company and Microsoft Gold Partner. His main competence area is Information Worker solutions, where he currently focuses on the SharePoint Products and Technologies platform. In October 2005, he was awarded with the Microsoft MVP award for Windows SharePoint Services. He is also one of the founding members of Belux Information Worker User Group (BIWUG at http://www.biwug.be). He regularly posts some SharePoint stuff on his blog at http://jopx.blogspot.com.

Heather Solomon is a Web designer with more than ten years of experience designing and deploying online applications and sites. Specializing in SharePoint branding, layout, and usability, she has extensive experience with SharePoint technologies and Web Content Management. Currently, Solomon works delivering training, branding, and consulting services to help corporations maximize SharePoint's potential through her company, Solomon Creative. She is active in the SharePoint community, speaks at community events and conferences, is a contributing author to books and publications, and is active on her blog at www.HeatherSolomon.com/Blog. She would like to thank her family for their love and support. She says that words can't describe the enrichment they bring to her life. She is also grateful for the chance to be involved in the SharePoint community. Being a part of this group has been one of the more unique experiences in her life.

Nick Swan is a Microsoft Office SharePoint Server MVP who has been developing with Microsoft-based technologies for seven years since completing Software Engineering in college. Having become interested in developing on top of SharePoint, he decided to start the SharePoint User Group UK (http://www.suguk.org). His particular focus recently has been the Business Data Catalog (BDC), which has led to the development of the application BDC Meta Man (http://www.bdcmetaman.com). You can visit his blog, SharePointNick.com, at http://www.sharepointnick.com.

Jan Tielens is currently working for the Belgian company U2U (http://www.u2u.be), which delivers developer-oriented courses focusing on Microsoft technology all around the world. His areas of expertise are Microsoft BizTalk Server, ASP.NET, and especially Information Worker technologies, including SharePoint. He became an MVP for Microsoft SharePoint Portal Server in 2005 because of his work in the SharePoint community. He's known for his blog (http://weblogs.asp.net/jan) and the famous SmartPart Web Part. Tielens is also a frequent speaker on various Microsoft events across Europe. Besides writing code, he also enjoys photography and traveling with his wife and daughter.

Mike Walsh works as a consultant in Finland. Originally from the UK, he has worked in several European countries since 1970—first on mainframes, and from the early IBM PC days, on micros. He first came across SharePoint Team Services (STS) at a Microsoft conference toward the end of 2001, and started asking (and then answering) questions on it in the public STS newsgroup. Later, he started up an FAQ for the newsgroup to cover the usual questions being asked. Walsh became an MVP for STS in October 2002, and has been a SharePoint MVP (now for Windows SharePoint Services) ever since.

Shane Young is a recovering Server Farm Administrator and active SharePoint zealot. From his home base in Cincinnati, Ohio, he travels the country, and sometimes the world, supporting, teaching, and evangelizing for all things SharePoint. He is the founder of his own SharePoint consulting company, and has recently been invited to speak at TechEd on the subject of upgrading SharePoint. When he is not living the glamorous life of a Microsoft MVP, he can be found spending time with his lovely new bride, Nicola, and their dogs, Tyson and Pugsley.

Credits

Senior Acquisitions Editor
Jim Minatel

Contributing Editor
Scot Hillier

Development Editor
Kevin Shafer

Technical Editors
Robert Bogue
Todd Klindt

Production Editor
Angela Smith

Copy Editor
Kim Cofer

Editorial Manager
Mary Beth Wakefield

Production Manager
Tim Tate

Vice President and Executive Group Publisher
Richard Swadley

Vice President and Executive Publisher
Joseph B. Wikert

Project Coordinator, Cover
Adrienne Martinez

Compositor
Craig Woods, Happenstance Type-O-Rama

Proofreader
Sossity Smith

Indexer
Jack Lewis

Anniversary Logo Design
Richard Pacifico

Contents

Contents

Contents

Contents

Contents

Contents

Foreword

This is an extraordinary book written by 16 extraordinary people. All of the authors are Microsoft MVP awardees for either Microsoft Office SharePoint® Server or Windows SharePoint® Services. MVP, in this context, stands for Most Valuable Professional. What makes MVPs so valuable to Microsoft? For starters, MVPs are very early adopters of Microsoft products and technologies, and they consistently provide a significant percentage of feature ideas and bug reports back to Microsoft. Secondly, MVPs have the innate quality of naturally sharing their knowledge in a no-holds-barred manner, and that's exactly what the authors of this book have done.

As the Microsoft SharePoint Product Group lead for the MVP program, I interact with the authors as well as other SharePoint MVPs on a very frequent basis. In fact, during the course of drafting this foreword, I exchanged emails with several of the authors about topics ranging from forms-based authentication (covered in Chapter 2) to customization and branding (covered in Chapter 6) based on real-world scenarios that they're currently dealing with. Every chapter in this book is based less on what SharePoint was designed to do and much more on how SharePoint has been implemented and utilized by the respective MVP in real-world scenarios. I would not hesitate to vouch for any of the authors as being an expert in their respective chapter topics.

I am very proud of how 16 SharePoint MVPs came together so quickly and created this book in such a collaborative way even though a few of them have not yet met each other in person. I am honored that they have asked me to write the foreword for their book. And I am confident that you will find this book to be a valuable resource in helping you understand how to leverage SharePoint in your own real-world scenarios.

If you have questions for or just want to say, "Thank you" to any of the authors, I encourage you to visit his or her blog and leave a comment. If you are interested in learning more about the SharePoint community—how to leverage various resources to find additional information about SharePoint, how to connect with others with similar interests and objectives for SharePoint, or how to become a SharePoint MVP, start by visiting the SharePoint Community Portal at http://MySharePointCommunity.com.

Lawrence Liu
(blog: http://sharepoint.microsoft.com/blogs/LLiu)
Senior Technical Product Manager and Worldwide Community Lead
Microsoft SharePoint Products and Technologies
Redmond, WA

Introduction

Remember the days when you used to get three books in the box with the CD of your favorite Microsoft product? In those days, it seemed that the scope of a technology could easily be contained within those manuals. Sure, you might buy an extra book, but the expectation was that the majority of required knowledge accompanied the product. Not anymore.

The disappearance of product manuals has been driven by the high cost of printing, demand for shorter product life cycles, and an ever-increasing level of product complexity. It is now commonplace for major Microsoft products to ship with almost no documentation initially. Instead, knowledge is distributed through industry conferences, blogs, wikis, and third-party books. Over time, of course, the online Software Development Kit (SDK) does get revised with better examples, but we are just as likely to read a blog as we are to visit the Microsoft Developer Network (MSDN). In short, product documentation has been replaced by a community of technologists working together, innovating, and reviewing content. Though this model can often be frustrating when you are first learning a product or technology, it is incredibly valuable after you understand the fundamentals and are ready to innovate.

Microsoft recognizes key individuals who contribute significantly to the community of technologists through the Microsoft Most Valuable Professional (MVP) award. These individuals are active authors, speakers, bloggers, and innovators. They are also skilled network engineers, developers, trainers, designers, and architects. In the SharePoint community, these MVPs are recognized for their expertise in either Windows SharePoint Services (WSS) or Microsoft Office SharePoint Server (MOSS).

This book represents the efforts of MVPs in the SharePoint community to present core areas of SharePoint 2007 products and technologies seasoned with significant field experience. The idea behind the book is to lower the learning curve for the reader, while providing the insight necessary to avoid common missteps. This book is an extension of the work the authors have done in their own blogs, books, and presentations.

Who This Book Is For

This book is for the community of SharePoint professionals. That means that architects, designers, developers, administrators, and engineers all will find something useful in its pages. As a reader, you will want to focus on chapters that appeal to your areas of expertise directly. Some of the chapters, for example, assume a strong programming background, whereas others are centered on administration or maintenance. All readers should have some prior experience with SharePoint 2007 products and technologies to get the most out of this book, although the book does include an introductory chapter for those who are just getting started. The authors generally assume a working knowledge of SharePoint in an effort to focus the discussion on implementation and best practices.

How This Book Is Structured

This book covers SharePoint 2007 products and technologies. Specifically, you will find topics relating to both WSS and MOSS. The topics were selected based on the authors' capabilities to represent a cross-section of the most important areas within SharePoint. Although the chapters have been arranged in a logical order, they are intended to stand alone as independent articles.

Following is a brief description of each chapter:

Chapter 1: "Introduction to SharePoint"—This chapter provides an introduction to SharePoint using WSS. This chapter is included in the book for those who want an overview of SharePoint, or those who want to install SharePoint for use with the remainder of the book. Readers with significant SharePoint experience may choose to skip this chapter.

Chapter 2: "Configuring Forms Based Authentication"—This chapter provides a review of the steps necessary to implement Forms Based Authentication (FBA) within SharePoint. This chapter examines the different approaches to FBA, along with their strengths and weaknesses. Included in this chapter are some custom solutions to problems such as user and role management.

Chapter 3: "Understanding SharePoint Administration"—This chapter covers all of the basic administration tasks necessary to keep a SharePoint farm healthy. This chapter covers the basics (such as backup and recovery), but also examines more advanced topics (such as command-line utilities and tips). This chapter also presents techniques for managing site templates.

Chapter 4: "Developing Publishing Sites the Smart and Structured Way"—This chapter presents an alternative technique for developing Publishing sites within MOSS. The chapter discusses development with the SharePoint Designer (SPD), but then challenges the conventional thinking with a new structured approach. Readers will learn new ways to ease the management and maintenance of Publishing sites.

Chapter 5: "Using SharePoint Designer 2007"—This chapter covers everything the SharePoint professional should know about SPD. This often-maligned tool can be a powerful part of your SharePoint toolkit, and this chapter shows why. The reader will learn new techniques for using the SPD with WSS and MOSS.

Chapter 6: "Customizing and Branding the SharePoint 2007 Interface"—One of the first tasks in any SharePoint project is branding the use interface. In this chapter, the reader will learn all of the different ways to customize the look and feel of SharePoint using master pages, style sheets, and graphics. This chapter is a must read for all architects and designers.

Chapter 7: "Understanding Web Parts"—This chapter covers all of the information any developer needs to know about creating Web Parts in SharePoint. This chapter walks the reader through the creation and deployment of Web Parts. Readers of this chapter should have a strong C# programming background.

Chapter 8: "Creating Workflows in WSS"—This chapter covers the creation and deployment of workflow solutions in WSS. Readers will learn how to create custom workflows and forms for deployment in WSS. This chapter includes many tips and tricks from actual field experience. Readers of this chapter should have a strong C# programming background.

Chapter 9: "Creating Workflow in SharePoint Server 2007"—This chapter covers creation and deployment of workflow solutions in MOSS. The big difference between WSS and MOSS workflows is the ability to use InfoPath forms. This chapter has extensive coverage of InfoPath forms and how to use them with MOSS workflows.

Chapter 10: "Using the Business Data Catalog"—The Business Data Catalog (BDC) is used to allow MOSS to access line-of-business databases. This chapter covers everything you'll need to set up and use the BDC. Included in this chapter are tips to make the development process easier. Readers of this chapter should be familiar with XML.

Chapter 11: "Using Excel Services"—Excel Services is used to allow MOSS to present spreadsheet data to end users through a browser. This technology is a foundational element in the development of dashboards in the SharePoint Report Center. This chapter is appropriate for any reader who wants to display report data in SharePoint.

Chapter 12: "Securing SharePoint Communication"—This chapter provides full coverage of the various options for securing SharePoint. Readers of this chapter will learn to implement Secure Sockets Layer (SSL), Kerberos security, and other configurations. This chapter also includes coverage of how to use the Microsoft Internet Security and Acceleration (ISA) Server.

Chapter 13: "Using Information Rights Management"—Information Rights Management (IRM) allows document functionality (such as printing and attaching) to be restricted so that sensitive information does not leave an organization. This chapter covers the basics of setting up IRM and using it with SharePoint libraries. Readers of this chapter will learn to secure libraries individually with IRM.

Chapter 14: "Upgrading from SPS 2003 to MOSS 2007 Using the Gradual Method"—One of the biggest trends in the SharePoint community is upgrading from SharePoint Portal Server 2003 (SPS 2003) to MOSS. This chapter examines all of the different upgrade approaches, and then walks the reader through the gradual method for upgrading. This chapter contains a wealth of field experience learned from performing many upgrades.

What You Need to Use This Book

To use this book successfully, readers should have a development or test SharePoint environment where they can work through the chapters. Most of the chapters in the book provide step-by-step examples that require administrator rights to perform. Whereas some chapters only require a WSS installation, others require MOSS.

Conventions

To help you get the most from the text and keep track of what's happening, a number of conventions have been used throughout the book.

> **Boxes like this one hold important, not-to-be forgotten information that is directly relevant to the surrounding text.**

Tips, hints, tricks, and asides to the current discussion are offset and placed in italics like this.

As for styles in the text:

❑ Important new terms and important words are *highlighted* when we introduce them.

❑ Keyboard strokes are shown like this: Ctrl+A.

❑ Filenames, URLs, and code within the text are shown like this: `persistence.properties`.

Code is presented in the following two ways:

```
In code examples, new and important code is highlighted with a gray background.
The gray highlighting is not used for code that's less important in the present
context, or has been shown before.
```

Source Code

As you work through the examples in this book, you may choose either to type in all the code manually, or use the source code files that accompany the book. All of the source code used in this book is available for download at `http://www.wrox.com`. Once at the site, simply locate the book's title (either by using the Search box or by using one of the title lists), and click the Download Code link on the book's detail page to obtain all the source code for the book.

> **Because many books have similar titles, you may find it easiest to search by ISBN; for this book the ISBN is 978-0-470-16835-6.**

Once you download the code, just decompress it with your favorite compression tool. Alternatively, you can go to the main Wrox code download page at `http://www.wrox.com/dynamic/books/download.aspx` to see the code available for this book and all other Wrox books.

Errata

We make every effort to ensure that there are no errors in the text or in the code. However, no one is perfect, and mistakes do occur. If you find an error in one of our books (such as a spelling mistake or faulty piece of code), we would be very grateful for your feedback. By sending in errata, you may save another reader hours of frustration and, at the same time, you will be helping us provide even higher quality information.

To find the errata page for this book, go to `http://www.wrox.com` and locate the title using the Search box or one of the title lists. Then, on the book details page, click the Book Errata link. On this page, you can view all errata that has been submitted for this book and posted by Wrox editors. A complete book list including links to each book's errata is also available at `www.wrox.com/misc-pages/booklist.shtml`.

If you don't spot "your" error on the Book Errata page, go to `www.wrox.com/contact/techsupport.shtml` and complete the form there to send us the error you have found. We'll check the information and, if appropriate, post a message to the book's errata page and fix the problem in subsequent editions of the book.

p2p.wrox.com

For author and peer discussion, join the P2P forums at p2p.wrox.com. The forums are a Web-based system for you to post messages relating to Wrox books and related technologies, and to interact with other readers and technology users. The forums offer a subscription feature to email you topics of interest of your choosing when new posts are made to the forums. Wrox authors, editors, other industry experts, and your fellow readers are present on these forums.

At `http://p2p.wrox.com`, you will find a number of different forums that will help you not only as you read this book, but also as you develop your own applications. To join the forums, just follow these steps:

1. Go to `p2p.wrox.com` and click the Register link.
2. Read the terms of use and click Agree.
3. Complete the required information to join, as well as any optional information you wish to provide, and click Submit.
4. You will receive an email with information describing how to verify your account and complete the joining process.

You can read messages in the forums without joining P2P, but to post your own messages, you must join.

Once you join, you can post new messages and respond to messages other users post. You can read messages at any time on the Web. If you would like to have new messages from a particular forum emailed to you, click the Subscribe to this Forum icon by the forum name in the forum listing.

For more information about how to use the Wrox P2P, be sure to read the P2P FAQs for answers to questions about how the forum software works, as well as many common questions specific to P2P and Wrox books. To read the FAQs, click the FAQ link on any P2P page.

Introduction to SharePoint

by Mike Walsh

When PCs were new, there were two main computer magazines — *Byte* from McGraw-Hill and *PC Magazine* from Ziff-Davis. The older *Byte* covered not just PCs, but also Apples, and was a tough read in parts, whereas *PC Magazine* concentrated entirely on PCs and was placed at the ability level of most of its readers. Ziff-Davis covered the "professional" market with a magazine called *PC Tech Journal,* and despite hardly being able to understand much of it, I subscribed to this because I thought that in time I would. Two years later, I was just about able to start following the articles, so naturally Ziff-Davis then pulled it and that was the end of that.

If you bought this book without having been responsible in some way for any previous SharePoint product, you are roughly at the level with SharePoint where I was with PC computing more than 20 years ago — that is, you have a good knowledge of computing in general, just no specific experience of the SharePoint products. Because I'm assuming that you don't have a couple of years available to you while things click into place, this first chapter is for you. This chapter provides the basic knowledge you need to be able to follow the rest of the book.

> *This chapter is not for people with existing knowledge of SharePoint products. You have the choice of going directly to Chapter 2 or (and this seems most likely) picking and choosing among the chapters that follow. Some chapters will talk about SharePoint areas that are completely new to you, and others will add to your knowledge of other areas.*

I start by briefly showing you how "SharePoint" became the multifaceted set of applications we have to choose from today. I equally briefly outline the differences between the various applications before showing how to install the simplest SharePoint 2007 version in the simplest way possible, so that you quickly will have something concrete to look at when reading the rest of the chapter.

The rest of the chapter goes through what is installed and is available for your use when you do an installation of Windows SharePoint Services (WSS) 3.0 (that "simplest version").

Looking at the Old and New

Let's start by ensuring that you know how we reached the present complicated set of applications and what these are. There are lots of different (and yet similar) names for the various SharePoint products, so this section should make you are aware of both the old and the new names. By the end of this section, you should know at a glance which SharePoint product and version people are discussing when you see some advice on the Internet.

As shown in Figure 1-1, in 2001, there were three "Microsoft" products of what later became SharePoint 2007. One of these, Content Management Server (CMS), was a product that had been acquired by Microsoft during the acquisition of a company. Another product, SharePoint Portal Server 2001 (SPS 2001), started out in the Office team using the Exchange storage engine. A third product, SharePoint Team Services (STS), was something that started off as an internal piece of code written by members of the FrontPage team as a super-set of Front Page Server Extensions. This piece of code was so useful that its use spread like wildfire throughout Microsoft. At some stage, it was decided to make a Microsoft product out of it.

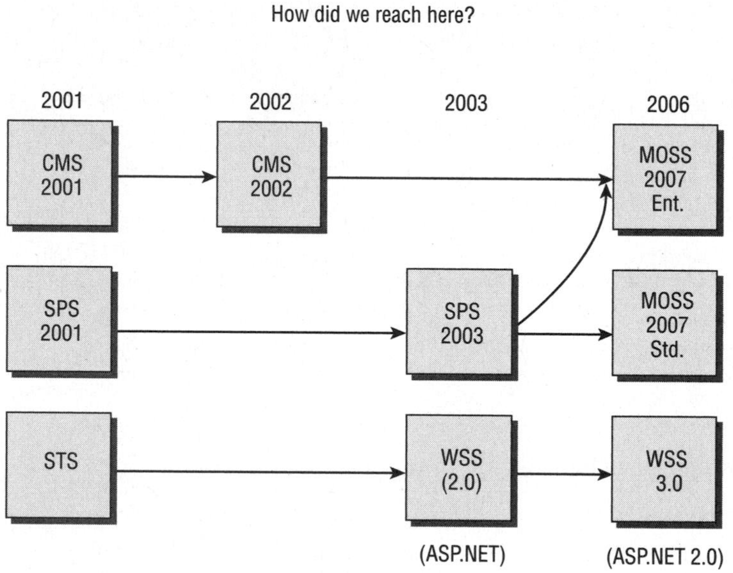

How did we reach here?

Figure 1-1: Product progression timeline

It's important to note that the use of SharePoint in the product name of STS was purely a marketing one. The product and the techniques it used had nothing in common with the slightly earlier released product SPS 2001.

So, by the end of 2001, there were three completely different products, all of which could be used for a server-based Internet or for an intranet. CMS was the big product, because it typically required a set of computers for staging information from test to production. SPS 2001 didn't have staging, but usually needed a set of servers because its design was based heavily on search, and so it needed servers for indexing and search. STS was, by comparison, a small product that could run on a single server, or a single front-end server with a database server back-end, although it, too, was extensible in a limited way (more front-ends; clustered database system).

> **The discussions in this chapter use common abbreviations, including the following:**
>
> *Version 1 (v1) — SharePoint Team Services (STS); SharePoint Portal Server 2001 (SPS 2001)*
>
> *Version 2 (v2) — Windows SharePoint Services (WSS or WSS 2.0); SharePoint Portal Server 2003 (SPS 2003)*
>
> *Version 3 (v3) — Windows SharePoint Services 3.0 (WSS 3.0); Microsoft Office SharePoint Server 2007 (MOSS 2007)*
>
> **Common mistakes are made with the use of SPS 3.0 (which equals MOSS 2007); WSS 2007 (which equals WSS 3.0); and STS (when actually WSS is meant).**

In 2002, CMS was refreshed (and became CMS 2002), but it still had nothing to do with the two "SharePoint" products. In October 2003, the new versions of these products came out after major rewrites. These were SPS 2003 and Windows SharePoint Services (WSS) 2.0.

> *Note that only Microsoft called it WSS 2.0. Most other people called it simply WSS because, after all, it was first called Windows SharePoint Services.*

WSS was a rewrite of STS that moved most of the data that had previously been stored in the file system to the database. Also, by using ASP.NET, SharePoint Web Parts became available.

SPS 2003 was a hybrid product. It had two layers: a *WSS layer* (which was virtually identical to that used by WSS itself), and an *SPS layer* (which looked similar to SPS 2001). The big index/search was still there, but it only worked at the SPS layer, and a simpler search was in use for data in the WSS layer. There was much more additional functionality with SPS 2003 that I won't go into here because it is beyond the scope of this chapter. It is important to note, however, that WSS used SQL DB Full Text Search, whereas now WSS 3.0 uses the same search methods as MOSS 2007.

So, by the end of 2003, there were no longer three different product streams. But there weren't only two either — more like two and a half. These were all still providing server-based Internet access or intranetworks.

What was released at the end of 2006 as a "2007" set of products is finally one stream based on ASP.NET 2.0 and WSS 3.0. In this stream, the difference between the various products is the amount of Microsoft-written code that comes with each product. For example, as you pay more, you get more built-in Web Parts, but you will also get additional functionality provided by Microsoft code that does not come in the form of Web Parts.

> **A *Web Part* is a piece of code that performs a set of functions. Web Parts, once written, can be added to a library (called a *gallery*) in a SharePoint product, and then used in Web pages of that SharePoint product. Writing your own Web Parts is discussed in greater detail in Chapter 7.**

For the version 2 (v2) time frame, the people experiencing the most adjustment problems were those who had been running SPS 2001 and had now moved on to SPS 2003 (because, suddenly, they had a WSS layer to learn). The people experiencing the most adjustment problems for version 3 (v3) products are those who are using CMS and CMS 2002 (who now have to learn some completely new techniques).

So, what are the 2007 products and how do they differ?

> *Microsoft considers WSS 3.0 to be an "application" rather than a product, because it doesn't cost anything. I'm going to use "products" for all different SharePoint 2007 packages because I found when writing this chapter that using "applications" instead was very confusing. The main reason for this confusion is that an IIS Web site that used to be called a "virtual server" in the v2 SharePoint products is now called a "Web application" in the v3 products.*

If you have been to a Microsoft SharePoint 2007 presentation, chances are that at least some of what you have been shown is only available in the most expensive SharePoint 2007 product, which is the *Microsoft Office SharePoint Server 2007 Enterprise Edition* (*MOSS 2007 Enterprise Edition*). Most of what you will have been shown is also in the *MOSS 2007 Standard Edition* (a natural upgrade path for both CMS 2002 and SPS 2003 users — although many will find the additional features of the Enterprise Edition irresistible).

Very little of what you have been shown in the Microsoft presentation will be WSS 3.0, although that is a natural path for WSS users, and it provides many functions users have requested without changing in any way the "size" of the product. If anything, there is now more of a gap in total functionality between WSS 3.0 and MOSS 2007 Standard Edition than there was between WSS (2.0) and SPS 2003 because content management functionality has been added to MOSS 2007 that wasn't present in SPS 2003.

Figure 1-2 is probably what you have been shown. Note that the WSS 3.0 "product" includes the inner circle ("Platform Services") used by all the pieces in the outer ring and also includes the "Collaboration" part in the outer ring. All the other parts of the outer ring are in the various versions of MOSS 2007 only. It's a good idea to try to remember that there is both a WSS 3.0 "technology" (inner circle) and a WSS 3.0 "product" ("Collaboration" plus inner ring) because people tend to say WSS 3.0 without indicating which of the two they mean.

However, there are also a couple of other SharePoint products that are irrelevant in the big picture, and are mainly there to give Microsoft a couple of different price points, so I won't do more than just mention them here. These are "Microsoft Office SharePoint Server 2007 for Search" (which is a subset of the main MOSS 2007 product that provides the MOSS 2007 Search scope without the need to pay for CALs for users) and "Microsoft Office SharePoint Server 2007 for Internet" (which is, in effect, the standard MOSS 2007 product already licensed for use on the Internet).

The rest of this chapter concentrates entirely on the small "free" product — Windows SharePoint Services 3.0. Although usually written off by Microsoft speakers (if they mention it at all) as being for departments (by which they mean a handful of people), even this product can scale up and can be used as the basis of a useful Internet/intranet site. However, the main purpose in using it here is to give you a feel for the basic features that are present in all the SharePoint 2007 products without complicating things with a lot of additional features. In essence, you'll be learning to fly on a small plane, rather than on a Jumbo Jet.

Because the aim of this chapter is to get you off the ground as quickly as possible, I'll be using the very simplest installation of WSS 3.0, which installs on a single server and which uses the default "embedded" database system that used to be called "embedded SQL Server 2005 Express (Windows)," but that now (to our relief) is called simply the "Windows Internal Database." Despite the change of name, it's still a version of SQL Server 2005 Express, but one that, unlike the normal versions, does not have a 4GB limit in database size. However, it does have an additional restriction that it can only be used for WSS 3.0 (and, to be exact, for other "Windows components") databases and also has additional limits on being attached to management tools.

It is possible to upgrade from WSS 2.0 to WSS 3.0. There are three methods, all of which take the full installation (that is, the complete site structure) of WSS 2.0 and upgrade it completely to WSS 3.0. Be grateful that you won't (as new SharePoint users) be doing this, because there are various small differences between sites upgraded in this way and sites in completely new WSS 3.0 installations. (Look at Shane Young's Chapter 14 if you are faced with an upgrade.)

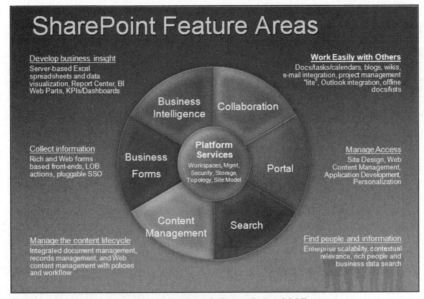

Figure 1-2: A standard view of Microsoft SharePoint 2007

(Diagram: Copyright Microsoft — used by permission)

Installing WSS 3.0

To install WSS 3.0 without problems, you'll need a fresh copy of Windows Server 2003. Whether or not you use the R2 version doesn't matter, but don't make it a Domain Controller (DC). Any version will do, except for Web Edition, so I'd suggest using the Standard Edition. Make sure you have *at least* 512MB memory.

MOSS 2007 will only install if there is a minimum of 1GB or more of memory, and there is very clearly a good reason for that. WSS 3.0 will work faster with more memory, too, but unlike MOSS 2007, it will at least install and work with 512MB. For the small test installation needed for this chapter, that will be enough.

There is a good Microsoft link with complete details of how to install WSS 3.0 on a single server at http://technet2.microsoft.com/Office/en-us/library/6181fe5b-90ca-40cf-aade-abd59cf3c9071033.mspx?pf=true, *but the simple instructions in this chapter are all that you should need.*

The first step is to install IIS. The easiest way to do that is to create the Applications Server role in the "Manage Your Server" window (Figure 1-3), which is the first thing you see after you install Windows Server 2003. Select Add or Remove a Role ⇨ Next ⇨ Custom Configuration. Then, select Applications Server ⇨ ASP.NET. (*Do not select FPSE.*)

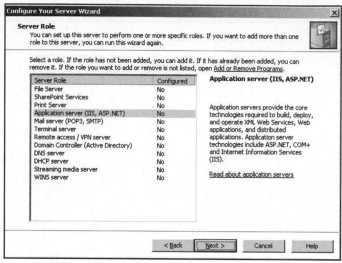

Figure 1-3: Specifying IIS as the Application Server

You'll now see the screen shown in Figure 1-4.

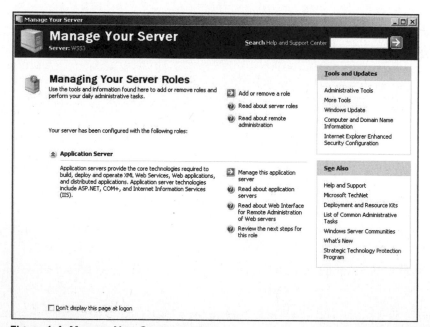

Figure 1-4: Manage Your Server screen

The second thing to do is to install .NET Framework 3.0 from the following link (Figure 1-5):

```
http://go.microsoft.com/fwlink/?LinkID=72322&clcid=0x409
```

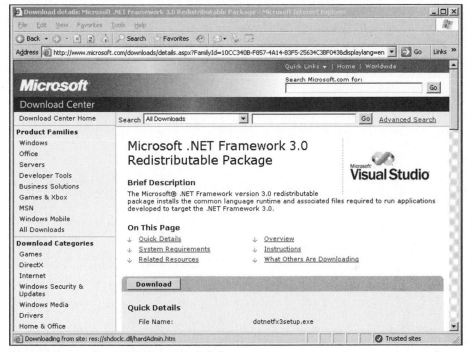

Figure 1-5: Installing .NET Framework 3.0

When this is completed, you must restart before moving on to the final part of this process. This third thing is probably unnecessary, because usually this is the default setting at this point. Just in case, though, go to IIS and ensure that ASP.NET 2.0 is set to Allowed, as shown in Figure 1-6. Just to be 100 percent sure, also go to C:\Windows\Microsoft.Net\Framework\V2.0.50727 and run aspnet_regiis -i to ensure that ASP.NET 2.0 is registered correctly with IIS.

Now you're ready for the WSS installation, which is in two parts. What is called "installation," in fact, only copies the necessary files. The key to this process is the configuration wizard that follows. The wizard takes you through ten steps and performs a lot of work, so don't worry if any step seems to take a while.

WSS 3.0 is available as a free download from the following URL:

```
http://www.microsoft.com/downloads/details.aspx?FamilyID=d51730b5-48fc-4ca2-b454-8d
c2caf93951&DisplayLang=en
```

Run this download. Select the Basic Installation. Then, at the end, select Close and let the configuration wizard do its work.

At the end of all this, you will be asked (R2) to supply a UserName and Password (use the Server Administrator). After a while, you should see a ready-made WSS 3.0 Web site, as shown in Figure 1-7.

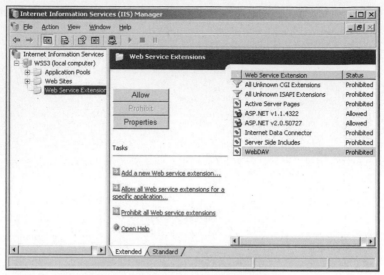

Figure 1-6: Ensuring that ASP.NET is set to Allowed

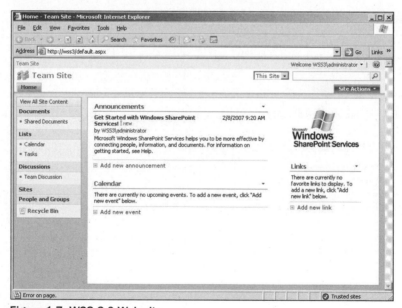

Figure 1-7: WSS 3.0 Web site

My experiences with this installation on a clean machine and performed as described have always been positive. If you do have problems with the configuration wizard phase, first check the Microsoft article referenced earlier to see if it helps you work out what you have missed doing (if anything). If that doesn't help, post a message to the `microsoft.public.sharepoint.setup_and_administration` *newsgroup (at* `msnews.microsoft.com`*) saying that you were doing a WSS 3.0 installation and got the following error at step X of the configuration wizard stage.*

Licensing

Although this copy of WSS 3.0 is being used for test purposes, I should at least mention the licensing requirements. As I mentioned earlier in this chapter, WSS 3.0 is "free." This means that WSS 3.0 can be downloaded for no charge and can be used for no charge. However, to use it, you will need a server running some version of Windows Server 2003 (not the Web Edition) and normal licensing of that Server will apply. (An enterprise license, or a server license plus user CALs, is the usual level.) In addition, if that server is available on the Internet, you will need an "Internet Connection License" (again server-based).

> *The Internet Connection License is connected with the server operating system (Windows 2003) and has nothing specifically to do with WSS 3.0. The situation is different with MOSS 2007, where you need a MOSS-specific Internet license that is much more costly.*

So, WSS 3.0 is free, but in the single-server installation using the built-in (free) database, the server it is running on must be licensed. If a full database system such as SQL Server 2005 is used to store the WSS 3.0 data in (as opposed to the free "embedded" database system), that must be licensed, too.

> *This information is provided as a guideline only. On licensing issues, always contact the local Microsoft office to be sure.*

The Components of the Standard Web Site

Before looking at what is visible on the Home page, let's start off with a few basics.

Libraries and Lists

Information that users add to a site is stored in either *libraries* or *lists*. There are several different types of both provided out-of-the-box, and it is possible to create your own by using a *custom list*. Libraries are actually just a special type of lists. The main distinguishing feature of libraries is that they are used for storing files.

Documents in document libraries were stored in the file system in STS (v1), but since WSS (v2), they have been stored in the database as blobs/images, depending on which terminology you want to use.

I've previously mentioned Web Parts in passing as pieces of code that can be added to Web pages. Each list or library that is available for use in a site has its equivalent Web Part added to the gallery. For example, what you see on the default page for the site just created by the installation of WSS 3.0 called "Announcements" is, in fact, the (equivalent) Web Part of the Announcements list that has been by default added to the page. Click the word "Announcements" and you can see the Announcements list in all its glory.

Another thing that occasionally leads to confusion is the fact that what you have directly after install is not what you must have. If you don't want an Announcements Web Part on that top page, you can remove it. If you want to position it elsewhere on the page, you can move it. But that's less important than the fact that, even though the installation created only one list (plus a Web Part) of each Type (called with two exceptions after the list type — so Announcements, Calendar, and so on), you can create any number of additional lists of the same type, provided you give them different names. Each of these additional lists will then have its own additional corresponding Web Parts.

For example, if you want more than one document library (which is, in my experience, very likely), you can create a second document library called, say, "Final Offers." So, now you will have two document libraries listed on the left pane of the Web page (Shared Documents and Final Offers), and two matching Web Parts. You'll have noted that "Shared Documents" is one of the exceptions to the "rule" that the list created by the installation routine always has the same name as the type of list.

All lists and libraries can be shared, including the new Final Offers library. In fact, at this stage, the only difference between the Shared Documents library and the Final Offers library is the name, because both are empty, both have exactly the same look, and both can be accessed in the same way. It is unfortunate that Microsoft chose this name (Shared Documents) because some people assume that this is the only document library that can be shared. It isn't.

Later in this chapter, you look at how to create a Final Offers library and what you have there. But first, just look at that first page shown in Figure 1-8, in which you'll notice that I already created a Final Offers library from the standard Document Library template. The Final Offers already appears on the left side of the page.

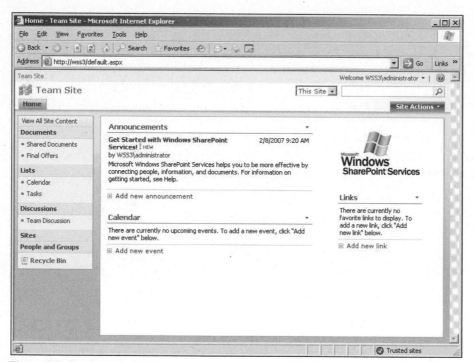

Figure 1-8: Final Offers library

What you see on the left is the "Quick Launch" section. It contains links to five lists — Shared Documents, Final Offers, Calendar, Tasks, and Team Discussion. Notice that the two document libraries are under the heading Documents; Calendar and Tasks are under the heading Lists; and Team Discussions is under the heading Discussions. They are all lists of one kind or another. This is just a way to make this section easier to read.

Web Parts

The main body of the page consists of four Web Parts in two columns. Three of these are the equivalent Web Part for a list (Announcements, Calendar, Links), and the fourth is a Web Part called a *site image Web Part* (which, at the moment, is pointing to the internal address of the WSS logo image).

This main body of the page is actually divided into zones. The setup of these "Web zones" is included in the template for the Home page (`default.aspx`) with one typical setup being a horizontal zone across the top, with two vertical zones under that, and under them, a final horizontal zone at the bottom. Web Parts can be dragged into any of the zones. However, if any zone has no content added to it, the user looking at the Web page will not be aware of those zones at all. For example, if you only have Web Parts in one vertical zone, the user will only see a single column of data taking up the entire main body of the page. The initial zone arrangement can be amended by accessing the site and page with SharePoint Designer 2007 (SPD 2007).

Of the three lists that the first three Web Parts represent, only one (Calendar) is also listed in the left-hand column. When creating a list, you can always choose whether it is to be listed in the Quick Launch pane. You decide (at any time) which Web Parts will be used in the main body and where they will be located there (within the current Web zone setup).

If you want all the lists that the installation routine created to be accessible from this top page, then you should have a total of seven Lists (Shared Documents, Calendar, Tasks, Team Discussions, Announcements, Links, and the Final Offers list that was added). Check this by clicking View All Site Content at the top of the left-hand column, and the screen shown in Figure 1-9 appears. (At this stage, your site will still not have the Final Offers list, of course.)

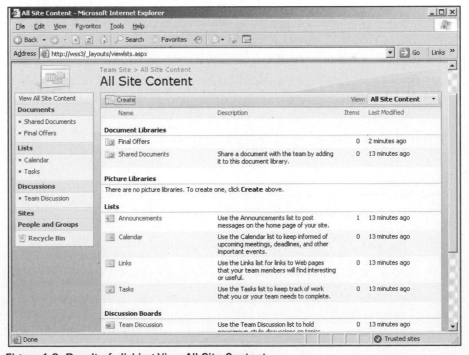

Figure 1-9: Result of clicking View All Site Content

Yes, they are all there (and nothing else).

Within the sections here, the names of the lists are in alphabetical order — so, Final Offers comes before Shared Documents. In the Quick Launch section of the top page, Shared Documents comes before Final Offers. This is because newly added lists are always added to Quick Launch (within the appropriate section) below the existing lists. Typically, the next step after adding a list is to go to go back to the top page and choose Site Actions ⇨ Site Settings. You can select (in the "Look and Feel" column) Quick Launch, where one of the options is Change Order, as shown in Figure 1-10. Note, too, that though I tend to use alphabetic sorts in the Quick Launch section, this isn't necessary — you can have whatever order you want, and can vary this from section to section.

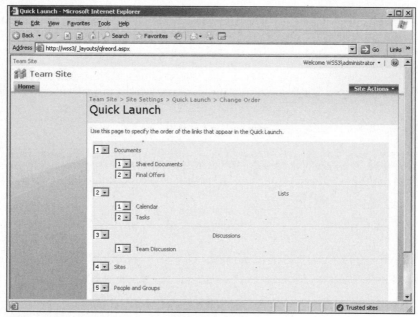

Figure 1-10: Changing the order in Quick Launch

If you don't want a Quick Launch section at all, you need to select Tree View in the same "Look and Feel" column. I mention that here because it isn't exactly an obvious choice for removing Quick Launch!

Options Within Lists

Before you can look further at the Web Parts on that top page, you'll need to first of all have a basic knowledge of what options you have for lists. I'll look at a document library, but the principles apply to other types of lists, too. To do this, you'll need to create a Final Offers list, too.

Select Site Actions ⇨ Create and Document Library (top left). Just type **Final Offers** in the Name field and leave all the other options as they are.

Now, you should have the same site I've been showing you already. Follow the earlier instructions to re-sort the Quick Launch so that Final Offers is listed before Shared Documents.

Click Final Offers and you'll see nothing much. So, first upload a few documents — preferably of different types such as a Word document, a text document, and a PDF document. If you have Office 2003 Pro or Office 2007 installed on your client, you'll be able to use the "Upload Multiple Documents" feature. If you don't (or if you are using a browser such as Firefox that doesn't support ActiveX), you won't see this at all, and you'll be forced to upload documents one at a time if you are using the standard Upload Document page.

There are other ways to get bulk data into document libraries, but in this overview, I'll stick to using the WSS 3.0 User Interface. There's a useful list of alternatives for doing bulk uploads in the "Tutorials" section of the WSSFAQ part of the WSS FAQ site (www.wssfaq.com) These still apply for the WSS 3.0 product.

For a few documents, the list you see is fine, but what if you have a few hundred documents? That's where WSS 3.0 offers two main alternatives to either just have long Web pages or a number of Web pages of, say, 100 documents at a time (which, not by coincidence, is the default value). These two alternatives are Views and Folders.

Before you move on, add a few more documents to the document library so that you have between 10 and 20 documents there. With six documents or less, you won't be able to see the point of some of the discussion that follows. You should now see a screen similar to Figure 1-11.

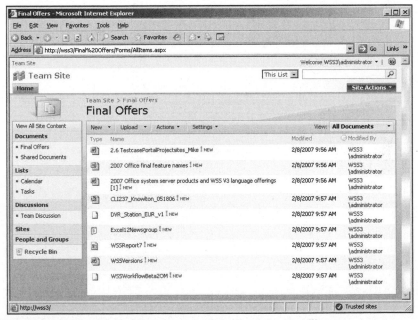

Figure 1-11: Result of adding documents to the document library

Views

A *view* is a selection of documents based on specified criteria. At the moment, the only view is the All Documents view (look at the right-hand edge of the horizontal menu line that appears at the top of the main pane in the Web page). This view, which was created by the installation routine, shows a list of all the documents with a maximum of 100 documents (default value) per Web page. If there are more than 100, there will be a Next button so that the user can access the next 100.

Just because the name of the view is All Documents, it doesn't necessarily mean that it lists all documents. You could change the definition, but in normal cases, it's a good idea to leave this view as it is and create new ones if you want fewer than all the documents listed.

You could create a new view now, but if you did so at the moment, all that you could do would be create a view that selected on the existing information you have about those documents (name, date added, who by, and so on), and that won't be too useful to you. So, first add a column to the document library and then use that column for selection purposes.

Select Settings (in the horizontal menu line that appears at the top of the main pane in the Web page) and Create Column. Give it the name "Document Source" and specify that the field is of Type Choice. Fill in four values (HP, IBM, Microsoft, Other) and make the default value Microsoft (use copy/paste to get the name right!).

Site Columns

If there is already a suitable site column for your needs, it's advisable to use this (Settings ⇨ Document Library Settings ⇨ Add from existing site columns) instead of creating your own new column. If there isn't (which is the case here), first create a site column and then use that site column in your document library. This is especially advisable in the case of a field of type Choice because you must only write the list of alternatives once, and the list is then available wherever that site column is used. What's more, when you need to add, say, Adobe and Sun to the list, you add those names once, and they are immediately available to all document libraries in which you are using the (site) column. (This repeated use is quite likely in this particular case and less likely in others.) This would not be the case if you had specified a new (normal) column for each document library; then you'd have to add Adobe and Sun to the column in each document library that used it.

To create a new site column, go to Site Actions ⇨ Site Settings and under Galleries click "site columns." Check the existing site columns just in case. There's a site column called Category that looks promising (it was the name I used for views in WSS 2.0), but you see that it's a "single line of text" type, so you reject it. (Experience shows that allowing users to write the name will give you "HP," "H-P," and "Hewlett-Packard" at the very least.) Instead, you select Create, and do exactly as previously described for a normal column.

Give it a name "Document Source" and specify that the field is of Type Choice. Fill in the four values (HP, IBM, Microsoft, Other) and make the default value Microsoft. I usually select "Allow Fill-in choices" even if this means checking the document libraries occasionally to see if a non-standard name has been used. The other alternative is to not allow fill-in choices and hope the users will contact you with a request for an addition to the list of choices (rather than them using the wrong one).

By the way, try to avoid using a name for a normal column that is the name of a site column. This is possible, but can only lead to confusion. Similarly, try to avoid using the same name for a new site column as for an existing site column. Once people know that Category is a single line of text column, there's no point in you creating a site column called Category that isn't.

This is the quick-and-dirty method, which adds a column only for this one document library. If you want to use the same column in another document library using this method, you must add it again and re-specify those four values.

However, there is another option (new to WSS 3.0) that allows you more flexibility and, over the course of working with the site, probably time savings for the administrator. This is the use of *site columns*, which are a set of ready-made names and definitions that can be used (when adding a column) throughout a site.

Creating a View

After all that preparation you are now ready to create a view.

Go again to Settings and this time use "Create a View." Select Standard View and call the view "HP." Unselect "Document Source" from the columns section. Sort by "Name" and, finally, in the Filter section, specify that Document Source is equal to HP. Click OK.

Repeat these steps for IBM, Microsoft, and Other.

These are views that you are going to use when you access the document library page. To make this sensible, add some more documents and then, if your client allows you to do so (Office 2003 upward and Internet Explorer 5.5 upward are required), open Final Offers in Datasheet Mode (Actions) and add random HP/IBM and so on values (by using copy/paste). If you don't have Office 2003 or Office 2007, use the drop-down at the right of each name and select Edit Properties. If you are using Firefox, add an Edit icon to each row of the Final Offers library and use that to edit the item by adding a value to the Document Source field. (Make sure you are using the All Documents view when you do this, as shown in Figure 1-12.)

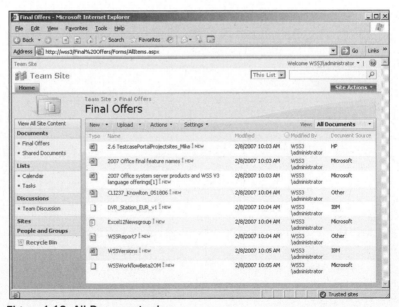

Figure 1-12: All Documents view

Now that you have five sensible views for use in the Final Offers library, you create one additional view that will be used for the Web Part of the Final Offers library.

Again, create a view, only this time call it WebPartView. This time, remove Type, Modified By, and Document Source from the list of Columns. Sort according to Modified (*descending*) and define a second sort by Name. Change the Item Limit from the default 100 to 6. Click OK.

When you open the list/library, possible views will be listed in a drop-down at the top-right of the screen with the name shown for the view being used for the display.

Amending the Home Page

Now, go back to Home to start investigating what you can do with Web Parts on such a page.

In Site Actions, select Edit Page. Have a look at what you can see by clicking the various edit buttons (for Announcements, Calendar, and so on), but don't change anything.

The first thing you're going to do is to add the Web Part of the Final Offers library to the page.

Click the "Add a Web Part" link in the left pane and you'll see a long list of the Web Parts that are available to you. Select Final Offers and Add.

What you'll now see is a very large Final Offers section (with maybe 10 to 20 documents) at the top of the center column that dominates the page. Avoiding this domination is the reason you created a special view called WebPartView. Select "edit" at the top-right of the Final Offers block and then Modify Shared Web Part (Figure 1-13).

Figure 1-13: Editing the view

The present Selected View is <Current view>. It's a pity, but that's what it always shows here. In this case, the Current view is the default view that was available when the installation routine added this Web Part to the Home page. Here it's the All Documents view without the Modified field.

Yes, this is odd. Logically, it ought to be identical to the All Documents view, as was the case with WSS (2.0).

Use the drop-down under the heading Selected View, select WebPartView, and click OK (or Apply). You'll notice that the Final Offers Web Part no longer dominates the Home page — there are fewer fields and only six documents listed.

If you think that you are never going to want to change the view that will be used for this Web Part on this page (and never need it anywhere else), you can delete the WebPartView. The Current view has already been set for this Web Part and the Web Part retains the settings of the view even if the view is deleted. But do this only if you are completely sure and the listing of WebPartView in the drop-down list offends you; otherwise, you will need to re-create the view if you want a different version of it for the Web Part on this page.

Now is perhaps the time to note that you can add the Final Offers Web Part to the Home page twice (or more times) if you want. Both Web Parts are, however, still a representation of the same document library. In other words, if you use the "Add new document" feature of one of those Web Parts to add a document, that document is, in fact, added to the *document library* (not the Web Part) and, thus, will appear in *both* Web Parts, even though you only added it to one.

This is a simplification. Whether the added document will be listed in both Web Parts depends on the views being used in the two Web Parts. But, assuming that there is no reason for it not appearing (for example, that the document isn't filtered out in the view being used in one of the Web Parts), then it will appear in both. What is certain is that it is present in the document library from which both Web Parts get their information.

Typically, there is no point in having two Web Parts on a page that represent the same list/library, but there is one case where this is useful, and I'll cover that soon when explaining what Web Part connections are.

But first, let's get back to lists.

The main alternative to using views to divide information into useful chunks is to use folders.

Folders

Just as in a file system, you can create folders within a document library and you can create subfolders below them, and so on. The main problem with using folders is that they encourage bad habits.

One example is the temptation to copy your existing file system in bulk to a document library when you first install WSS 3.0 or MOSS 2007. Some Microsoft people (typically not those from the SharePoint team) have read up a little on SharePoint and have noticed that the recommended limits for the number of documents you can store in a single document library are 2,000 documents per folder, and 2,000 folders per document library. They then make the mistake of thinking that this means that a SharePoint system is a solution to the age-old problem of how to move files away from the file system — simply copy the file structure of your entire common disk to SharePoint. *Well, don't do it!*

The problems include the fact that there is an overhead of up to 80 percent in the disk space required to store a file as an image in the database compared to storing it in the file system. There's also the fact (compounded by that size increase) that backup processes for SharePoint systems are by no means as simple as those for files in file systems, and they take longer (much longer). Finally, four million documents per document library (if you use folders) is by no means a figure to aim at, and is much more of an "our system can handle XXX" boasting point of little value in the real world.

The real-world recommended process is that you use SharePoint 2007 document libraries for new information, rather than as a thoughtless dumping ground for old information. By all means, transfer key information that is still of considerable value from your file system to a SharePoint 2007 document library. But do this only after a major study that both evaluates the data you already have and specifies a *set of* document libraries to handle it. You'll need to do such an evaluation in any case when creating a set of document libraries for storing your new information, and your old information will give you good guidelines on which document libraries (and sub-divisions of document libraries) you will need.

> *Anyone who wants to read a semi-official Microsoft take on this (from within the SharePoint team) should have a look here:*
>
> `http://blogs.msdn.com/sharepoint/archive/2007/01/02/is-the-file-server-dead.aspx.`

As for the choice of using folders or using views, my own preference is for a number of document libraries to cover completely different topic areas to use views rather than folders to cover the different pieces of data in sections (and sub-sections) within each topic area.

Using again the HP, IBM, Microsoft example, it could be that you have a document library for Quotes and a second document library for Technical Specifications (and later a third for Contracts, perhaps). Though you could keep the relevant information in each document library in HP, IBM, Microsoft folders, views have the advantage that they can be used when specifying the look of a Web Part on a page. So, for example, you could have a Quotes page where there are three Web Parts displaying information from the Quotes Document Library, with one part showing only HP quotes, one IBM quotes, and one Microsoft quotes. You can't do that with folders. There are also other slightly annoying "features" of the way folders are implemented that I'll leave for you to discover.

On the other hand, it is possible to specify that only certain people can access a folder, which isn't possible for a view. So, perhaps it's time for a quick overview of security.

Security

Security in SharePoint is composed of two things: who can access what, and with what rights they can access.

A user can be given rights (through Create User) to access a site/sub-site/document library or list/folder or item. Typically, the user is given rights to access a site or sub-site, and this automatically means that the user has the right to access everything in the site. But in special circumstances (for example, a document library contains personnel information), access rights to a document library/list and to a folder or even an item can be restricted if needed. You cannot give special access rights to a view. Anyone who can access the document library or list can access any view.

Specifying access rights for items in a list/library, even though it is now possible in WSS 3.0 and MOSS 2007, is a pain, and should only be done if really necessary. If the items can be grouped in any way at all, put each group in its own document library/list or folder, and specify access rights for the group of items.

Specifying access rights for folders would perhaps be necessary in similar circumstances (such as for document libraries), but where your design of the site was based on a small number of document libraries plus folders, rather than on a large(r) number of document libraries (with views).

When you create a sub-site, you can specify that it inherits the access rights of the site below which it is being created. This is the default value when creating a sub-site. The value can be changed at a later date, but it is better to think out whether special access rights are needed when doing the design of the SharePoint site structure.

Permission Level

"Permission Level" is the new name for what used to be called a Site Group. You are likely to still see both names being used, but I will use the new name throughout this chapter because it is at least no more confusing than the earlier name.

Each user when being "created" (that is, given rights to access a site and so on) is assigned to one or more (typically only one) *permission levels*. This is a somewhat confusing name for what is just a collection of rights (for example, the right to add information, the right to delete, and so on). There is a long list of rights and the four ready-made permission levels (Reader, Contributor, Site Designer, and Administrator) that Microsoft provides out-of-the-box. Each contains a sub-group of selected rights (logically) as follows:

- ❑ A Contributor has the rights of a Reader and more
- ❑ A Site Designer has the rights of a Contributor and more
- ❑ An Administrator has all rights

This ever-increasing number of rights in the default permission levels is the reason why typically only one permission level is selected when a user is created (that is, a user is given access rights to site/sub-site/list, and so on).

These built-in permission levels are useful in most cases, but a typical request is, "How do I give a user Add rights, but not the right to Delete?"

One method would be to amend the rights specified for the Contributor permission level by removing the cross for Delete. This is, however, not a good idea, because it means that everyone who is a member of the Contributor permission level can from now on only add items and not delete them. So, the people who are allowed to delete items will need to become members of the Site Designer permission level, which will give them too many rights.

Instead, you would create a new permission level with a suitable name — AddOnlyContributor wouldn't be catchy, but would describe the functionality well — and give it the same rights that the Contributor permission level has, minus the Delete right.

It's wise to create a new permission level slightly different from that of the standard Contributor permission level, even if you never intend to use the standard list of rights of the default Contributor permission level. This is because people coming later to administrate the site who have experience from other SharePoint sites will automatically assume that the Contributor permission level has the standard, default rights assigned to it.

In time, as you build up a set of new permission levels, it is probable that there will no longer be the strict hierarchy of permission levels there was at the beginning. This is the reason why, when giving a user access rights to a site (via "Create User") or specifying that a user has rights to access, say, a list, there is the option of selecting one or more rights.

For example, suppose that you wanted only Fred, Jim, and Bert to be able to access a document library. The seemingly easiest way would be to access the document library, select "Modify Settings and Columns" and "Change Permissions for this Document Library," then remove all the existing people/groups with access rights to the library. Then, one by one add Fred, Jim, and Bert. A smarter way, however (and one allowing more flexibility in the future), would be to create a new permission level especially for access to this document library. Fred, Jim, and Bert would, as usual, be created at the site level, but, in addition to being assigned to the normal Contributor permission level, they would also be assigned to this special permission level.

In this case, when changing permissions for the document library, and after all other users have been removed, this special permission level would be specified in the list of what is allowed to access the library. The benefits naturally are that when Wanda also needs to be able to access the document library (and there are possibly other places this group of users needs restricted access to), she only needs (at Site ⇨ Create User level) to be made a member of the additional special permission level (called, perhaps, PersonnelContributors).

All of these explanations talk about users. Typically, in a domain environment, users are members of an Active Directory (AD) group and AD groups (rather than individual users) would be "created" using the Create User function. Thus, these AD groups could be used in the previously described document library restricted access case. However, the permission level approach used here for restricted access to a document library can still be valid, even when using only AD groups, because perhaps more than one AD group needs to be given rights. As with many things in working with SharePoint systems, there are several options, and it might be just that you need to ask someone else to create a new AD group, but you can create a new permission level yourself and, thus, using the permission level method is a faster way for you to solve the problem.

Anonymous Access

One thing that hasn't been mentioned so far is the possibility of having anonymous access to a site.

Typically, this would be an information site open to the Internet where there is no need to keep track of exactly who is accessing the site or, indeed, of who is adding to the site, because usually such sites don't allow anyone other than a few key people to add items to the site. Another of the uses I have come across and recommend is having the Home page specified as anonymous access, while having the site structure below it to be restricted access. This Home page would serve as an advertising page that encourages people to want to be given access rights to the real sites.

When specifying anonymous access for a site, it is important to note that this is a two-step process. First, anonymous access must be made possible by specifying this in IIS. Then (and only then) you can specify anonymous access for a particular site.

Another thing I've not mentioned is the scenario where the user is not a member of a domain (or, indeed, in the test case here, if the server is in a workgroup, not a domain). Then you could use local (on the WSS server) users.

> *To specify that a local user has access rights to the WSS sites, that local user must first be created (Start ⇨ Programs ⇨ Administration Tools ⇨ Computer Management/ Local Users and Groups ⇨ Users ⇨ right-click + "New User" and so on) and given a permanent password that cannot be changed. This local user is then assigned (in WSS 3.0) access rights to a WSS site via Create User — that is, in the case here, two steps rather than the one (Create User) step required when adding an AD user or group.*

> *(Typically I use local users called Reader password Reader, Contributor password Contributor, and Designer password Designer on my test sites.)*

Specifying users local to the server should only be done when you have a single front-end. If you have load-balanced front-ends, there will be potential problems because of the need to keep those front-ends identical. In other words, those local users must be added to all front-end servers. The main problem with local users in a single-server situation is that the password must be permanent because the users don't have the rights to the server to allow them to change it, and this is a major security problem.

There is one last important thing about access rights. In the v2 version of WSS, if you could access a site/page and so on, you saw all the links on that page, even if they led to pages that you have no rights to access. If you then clicked those links, you were asked three times for your name and password (which was to give you the opportunity of using a different name with better rights) before being given an error message. In the v3 products, you see only what you can access.

You still might come across the "three times and you are out" syndrome, however, because you might have the rights to *access* a document library (that is, read), but not the rights to save anything to it. In this case, again you will be asked three times for "better" authorization, and then rejected.

The easiest way to see this "lesser links for lesser rights" working is to log in as a different user and then access Site Settings, first as Administrator and then as a Contributor. Your options will have shrunk.

Finally, here are three common access questions and answers:

Q: *Why isn't Create User working? I've specified a valid domain and username.*

A: In order for Create User to work in this case, it must be possible to access a Domain Controller (DC) of the domain in question. Lack of access could mean that the DC is down at the time of access. But a more normal case is that there is no trust relationship between the domain containing the WSS server and the domain of the user that is not being found.

Q: *I've given "All Domain Users" rights to access my site, but they still need to log on. How do I avoid this?*

A: In the client, specify for the security zone in which the WSS site is located (in Internet Explorer, go to Tools ⇨ Internet Options ⇨ Security ⇨ Custom Level and then to the final User Authorization part). Go to the Logon section and select "Automatic Logon with current user-name and password."

   (This will work, provided the user is logging on to a client with the same domain\username that has been given access rights to the site.)

Q: *After making this change, my users can access the site without the need for logon, but they are requested to log on when opening a Word document. How do I avoid this?*

A: Ensure that the WSS site is in the Trusted Sites zone in your Internet Explorer. If this doesn't work, add the WSS site to the Intranet zone.

The Home Page — Again

Now that the security aspect has been briefly covered, let's go back to the Home page for a few tips on the Web Parts you see there.

The Announcements Web Part is almost always something that you should use as a means of giving the latest information about the site to your users. Use it sparingly so that people will notice it when it's important that they do so.

One thing to watch out for is the standard view (Current view) that is used in the Web Part. This view of the Announcements Web Part is a special view that should not be changed. If you do change it by mistake, recover by adding a new copy of the Announcements Web Part to the Home page and deleting the original one.

The Links list is an odd one. Although there are separate entry fields for URL and Description when you create a new Links item, you'll notice that when you are in a view (such as the default All Links view) and select the URL field, what will be visible in the list will be the Description (which, when clicked, goes to the URL). If you don't have a description, you will see the URL itself, but only then.

Because URL is the only field available to you in a view (and this is shown as a description text linked to the URL), a view can only be sorted by Description (what is visible) and not by the URL itself. If you know that, for some reason, you must sort according to the actual URL (for example, you need to keep track of the numbers of Knowledge Base articles), then create a new text field called URLTxt and copy the URL to that field as well as to the URL field when you create a new item. Similarly, if you see the need to have the text of the Description field available as a pure text field, then add a second new field called Desc and add the text of the Description to that field, as well as to the Description field, when creating a new item.

Both these actions will give you more flexibility at the cost of additional manual actions every time you add a new Links list item.

Whereas you will usually have only one Announcements list (and Web Part), you can have as many Links lists as you like — all, of course, with more specific names than "Links," and, of course, none of them need to include the word "Links" in the name.

There are restrictions in the kinds of URL that you can specify in this field and, most importantly, that "test this link" will accept links that the upload function will not accept. So, http:// *links are fine, provided they are absolute URLs. WSS 3.0 will not accept relative URLs, even though the "test this link" function will, and WSS 3.0 also requires that the whole path is not longer than 260 characters, which again "test this link" has no problems with. Similarly,* "file:///" *will work in WSS 3.0, but things like* ftp:// *will not, even though "test this link" has no problems with them.*

Looking further at the Home page, you'll notice the WSS logo taking up rather a lot of space in the right-hand column. You'll find that it's wise to get rid of this because this space could be used for much more important things (such as useful data). I just close the Web Part so that it's no longer visible, but still available in case I want to resurrect it (even if only to give it a new image). One thing that you must constantly be aware of is that when putting images on your Web pages via this kind of Web Part, make quite sure that all the people accessing the Web page have the rights to see the image. One way to ensure this is to have an image library in a site that has anonymous access, and upload all your site images to that.

Moving on, you'll see that the Calendar is both linked to in the Quick Launch section and is a Web Part in the main section of the page. It's a matter of opinion whether this duplication is a good idea. I tend to have everything listed in Quick Launch, whether or not it appears in the main body. One reason is that if you use the space in the main body of the page, these are important enough for the duplication not to be a problem. Another reason is that I can, at any time, re-adjust what's visible in the main body of the page without the need to fiddle around with adding something to Quick Launch (which requires opening the list and specifying "add to Quick Launch").

However, the main reason for adding everything to the Quick Launch section as well as having them available on the page itself is that the Quick Launch section in WSS 3.0 sites now is repeated on pages lower in the structure (that is, even on pages that don't have that particular Web Part showing on the page), whereas in WSS 2.0 it was only available in the Home page of a site (`default.aspx`). Just make sure the length of the Quick Launch list is not excessive to avoid it dominating all the subsequent pages.

The Calendar itself is of no use for an information-providing Web site of the usual kind because it provides links to documents or Web pages, or even to text information in lists, and dates are of no relevance. Thus, often you can just close the Web Part and leave some free space for something else.

But there will be circumstances where having a Calendar in your face every time you access the Home page will be very useful. Think, for example, of the internal Web site of a company. It would be very useful if there were a calendar showing where all the salesmen were (and were going to be) at any one time. At the very least, it would avoid the disaster scenario of two sales representatives appearing on successive days at the site of a potential customer, or of two support people needing to re-boot the same set of servers at slightly different times on the same day.

> *When thinking about the Calendar Web Part, it's easy to start thinking about using an Outlook calendar on a Web site. This is addressed later in this chapter in a discussion of the integration between WSS 3.0 and the various components of Office 2007 (such as Outlook 2007). Unfortunately, what you'll see there is that in Outlook 2007 you will have the Outlook calendar plus one or more SharePoint calendars.*

One link that is only included in the Quick Launch section and is not in the main body of the page is *General Discussions*. Like Shared Documents, this is misleading. This is an example of creating a list of type Discussions and giving it the name "General Discussions." It is not the only place you can have discussions among yourselves. You can quite easily set up a number of Discussion lists (which, typically, you would give rather more meaningful and specific names than "General Discussions" such as "Outlook Questions," perhaps, if you are going to use Discussions as a way to list and answer user questions).

One reason why you might well have a large number of Discussion lists could be that SharePoint Discussion lists are not of major league/premier division (pick your own sporting metaphor) quality. If you imagine that a Discussion list is like Lotus Notes with many years of development behind it, think again. Discussion lists are a simple way of providing threads of questions, answers, and comments that are little changed in the essentials compared to when they were part of STS back in 2001. So, use them by all means (and I used them in STS, despite their failings for all the questions involved in a major migration exercise), but be aware of their weaknesses and try to use many different Discussion lists to keep each set of discussions relatively small and focused.

There is one final tip on lists and libraries for non-U.S.-based people. The U.S. uses MM/DD/YYYY for the date, whereas most of the rest of the world uses DD.MM.YYYY. It's not easy to find where to change this if you have an installation that is showing you MM/DD/YYYY because you'll be looking for something to do with "date" or "date format" and failing to find it. In fact, the only way, it seems, to change this is to choose (in Site Settings) a Regional Setting (Figure 1-14) that is for a country that has DD.MM.YYYY as standard. This means that you must be careful, because changing the Regional Setting will cause other things to change, too — the 24-hour clock might be standard and you might have a different sort order (both of which can be corrected on the Regional Settings page) and maybe (and much worse) Regional settings mean that you have a decimal comma, not decimal point, which will throw off all your formulae. However, for example, choosing "English(UK)" will probably be a safe way to get a date format change without anything nasty happening.

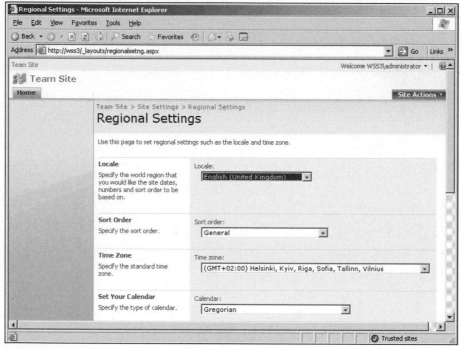

Figure 1-14: Regional Settings screen

Most locations allow you to choose between a 12- and a 24-hour clock, but some don't. This is a "design decision" no doubt, but one that seems overkill to me — I hate Big Brother restricting my options in this way.

That's enough about the lists and libraries. I'll now look briefly at Web Part connections before closing this Home page section by having a look at a few nice improvements compared to earlier versions.

Web Part Connections

Provided two Web Parts on a page have a common field (which may or may not have the same name, but ought to be the same kind of field), they can be linked together. The procedure that uses the drop-down for a Web Part when you specify that you want to Edit the Page is straightforward enough, so I won't go into the details of it, but instead discuss a couple of cases where you might use this.

Let's say you had a picture library containing images of all your business contacts. This would be just a standard picture library with an extra text field for Full Name. You put the Web Part of this picture library on the page so that it shows just one image. You then have a Custom List with company name, department, and fullname. You put a Web Part of the Custom List on the page that consists only of the Full Names from that company. You connect that Web Part via Web Part connections to the picture library using the two Full Name/fullname fields to connect. Then, when the user clicks fullname in the Web Part of the Custom List, the image in the Web Part of the picture library will change.

That's the simple one-to-one version of Web Part connections, but you can chain them, too. In this case, you have three Web Parts of the *same* Custom List on the page, along with a single Web Part of the picture library.

Custom List Web Part 1 (WP1) shows only the companies. Custom List Web Part 2 (WP2) shows only the departments. Custom List Web Part 3 (WP3) shows only the full names. You can connect WP1 to WP2 (using the Company field), WP2 to WP3 (using the Departments field), and, finally, as mentioned previously, WP3 to the Web Part of the picture library (using the Full Name field).

> Note that this is an example of the rare case where using the Web Part of the same list more than once on a page can be beneficial.

Those are the principles of Web Part connections. You need to experiment with when and how they will be useful to you. They can, of course, be used on any pages where there are Web Parts, not just on the Home page.

A Few Nice Improvements

The way to see the first improvement to the Home page is to open the Final Offers library. You'll see it in the section above the main body of the screen — Home ⇨ Final Offers. This is known as a *breadcrumb* and it simply means that wherever you are in the structure of the site, you can jump back to anywhere on the path to it. It's no big deal in this case because there is a Home link available anyway in the main title bar, but in a deep structure, it's a real time-saver. (By the way, earlier versions saw you madly clicking Back, Back, Back, on the browser.)

Another small thing is that, whereas in the version 2 products it was necessary to amend the Links on the Title bar in Front Page 2003, this is now a function that is under Site Settings. So, you can add, amend, and remove links while still in the browser.

But the really big change has probably escaped you newcomers to SharePoint because it's something that obviously has to be there. This is the Recycle Bin at the bottom of the Quick Launch section. In the v2 SharePoint products, if a user deleted a document, it was gone for good — unless that user was the boss, in which case recovery of that single document meant the administrator using a backup of the entire site and using it to create a copy of that entire site on a spare server. This was the only way to recover that single document (if you were lucky and the backup included that document).

So, the WSS 3.0/MOSS 2007 addition of a Recycle Bin is a major plus. This is a Recycle Bin only for data stored in the WSS database and is of two levels. There is one level the user sees and one that I suggest you keep the user unaware of — namely a second-level Recycle Bin (for Administrators only).

There's nothing weird about the concept. Documents deleted by the user move to the Recycle Bin until they are either deleted by the user, or the time limit for such documents runs out (the default is 30 days). From that point on, the user cannot individually recover the deleted documents, and will timidly approach the administrator. In my mind, the administrator should reply that he or she will see what can be done, then go for lunch, and, upon returning, go to the second-level Recycle Bin that only the administrator can see. With one click, the administrator could recover the document.

This second-level Recycle Bin retains documents for a percentage of the Quota Limit, which is set by default to 50 percent (which seems rather high to me). Reducing this and not letting the users know about the second-level Recycle Bin seems a good option to me — experience shows that if users do know about the second-level Recycle Bin, and know, too, that it contains almost everything they've ever deleted, they will be (shall we say) "less responsible."

This is perhaps a good time to use the Recycle Bin as an example of the places that only the administrator can get to.

The user sees his or her own Recycle Bin, as just mentioned, but isn't aware (unless told) that there is a second-level Recycle Bin. This is because the administration of that second-level Recycle Bin is under Site Settings, and as you have learned, for a user, that menu is restricted to things he or she can work with. So, the second-level Recycle Bin link in Site Settings is only visible to a person who is an administrator. All that the administrator can see is a long list of documents that have been deleted; there are no administration settings that can be amended there.

This is fairly normal. If you want to work with an administrator function, go to Site Settings; but if you want to specify the defaults, go to SharePoint v3 Central Administration (also called Central Admin, and discussed in more detail in Chapter 3). In the v3 products, you can either go to the Server (Start ⇨ Administration Tools ⇨ SharePoint v3 Central Administration) or, in the browser, go to your site but use the port that was randomly generated for the Central Administration site when you installed WSS 3.0 (in other words, you access `http://servername:nnnnn` where *nnnnn* is the port name).

Both methods of getting there give you the same Web page and, in the case of amending the Recycle Bin settings, you must go to Application Management and then to Web Application General Settings, where you'll find what appear from the somewhat confusing different default types (number of days / percentage of quota) for the first and second-level Recycle Bins. There is also the option for both of having the Recycle Bin off. Somehow, having been so relieved that v3 finally has a Recycle Bin, I can't see me turning it off in a hurry.

> *Although the rough split just mentioned (Central Administration for specifying settings; Site Settings for routine administration) applies a lot of the time, there are no guarantees. So, the best advice I can give you is to first look in the place that seems most likely to be correct for what you want to do as an administrator. But, if you don't find it there fairly quickly, try the other location. Failing that, search the WSS FAQ to see if it's listed there. Failing that, post a message to a SharePoint newsgroup. Some of these settings are well hidden and not in an obvious location (just think of removing Quick Launch by selecting Tree View that was mentioned earlier).*

Next are the requirements for clients and the effect on what you can do in a site, depending on what software you have installed on a client and which browser you are using there.

Interaction with Browsers and Clients

The browser story is simply told. Browsers that support ActiveX have potentially full functionality, whereas those that don't have ActiveX (such as Firefox or Apple's Safari) don't. (Note that from this point forward, "Firefox" will be used to refer to all such non-ActiveX browsers.) This lack of functionality isn't usually important for a user, but is important for an administrator. So, administrators (even if they regularly use Firefox) should also have a copy of a recent version (6.01 upward) of Internet Explorer (IE) handy.

Firefox seems to be faster in use than IE, and is certainly faster when initially loading the site because it does not load any ActiveX components (which are always the first step for a new IE session). The Web designer must be slightly careful and check that his or her amendments look equally good in both main browsers, but this is merely cosmetic. The main problem is with things such as a drop-down (on or after the filename in a view) followed by a right-click, which works in IE but not in Firefox. In some cases, drop-downs work, but Firefox shows fewer items, as demonstrated in Figures 1-15 and 1-16.

Figure 1-15: Firefox 2.0.0.1

Figure 1-16: IE 7.0

Similarly, multiple uploads of documents can be very useful for the administrator, and this, too, is only available in IE (and also requires a particular Office version — see the discussion later in this chapter).

In the case of a lack of a drop-down, the administrator must provide users (of Firefox and so on) with an alternative to the drop-down for editing an item in a list. In other words, the administrator must provide an Edit icon in the view. In the second case, the user of Firefox is forced (if he or she uses the Web User Interface) to upload one document at a time. Similar to the drop-down on the filename itself (rather than as on the area after the filename) is the way to use "Save As" to save a document to the user's hard disk. In this case, a Firefox user must open the file (read-only) and then, in the application, do "Save As" to save to the hard disk.

The interaction between a client and a SharePoint Web site (apart from the differences caused by a browser) is very much governed by which Office version the client is running.

The basic principle here is that for each version level of SharePoint, there is a corresponding version of Office. So, STS was released as a part of the extended Office XP package, WSS (2.0) was released at the same time as Office 2003, and WSS 3.0 was released at the same time as Office 2007. Because of this, new functionality in the new version of SharePoint is only available if the client is using the corresponding new version of Office.

So, if the client has Office XP, functionality is available that was available with STS, but no more; if Office 2003, functionality is available that was available with WSS 2.0, but no more. (Office 2000 has very limited functionality.)

That is the basic principle, but as you'll see when reading the "WSS 3.0 and Office 2007 Working Together" section later in this chapter, in a few cases, functionality that was available with WSS 2.0/Office 2003 is no longer available with WSS 3.0/Office 2007.

There is a very good Microsoft paper for WSS 2.0 that describes in detail the differences between the use of Office 2000, Office XP, and Office 2003 with WSS 2.0. You can use this paper for details of what functionality you will have with WSS 3.0 if one of these Office versions is installed on your client (and not Office 2007). The paper is called "Good, Better, Best: Windows SharePoint Services Integration with Microsoft Office" and is available here:

```
http://www.microsoft.com/office/sharepoint/prodinfo/officeintegration.mspx.
```

There is a newer version of this document now titled "Microsoft SharePoint Products and Technologies Document: Microsoft Office Programs and SharePoint Products and Technologies Integration—Fair, Good, Better, Best" available at:

```
http://www.microsoft.com/downloads/details.aspx?familyid=e0d05a69-f67b-4d37-961e-2d
b3c4065cb9&displaylang=en&tm
```

One thing to note is that, whereas Office 2003 (and 2007) has support for SharePoint set by default, this is not the default for Office XP. This may well need to be set by amending the user's copy of Office XP (Control Panel ➪ Add or Remove Programs ➪ Select Office XP and specify Change) and going to the Office Shared Features section and selecting SharePoint support there. (In Office 2007, this is in the Office Tools section at the end, and is "Windows SharePoint Services support.")

Another thing to watch out for is that not all versions of the same Office release have the same functionality when used with SharePoint sites. This particularly applies to Office 2003 Standard and Business Editions, which do not, for example, support Datasheet view (unlike Office 2003 Pro Edition), although they do support multiple uploads (if IE is used).

The usual problems for users of back versions of Office lie in two areas. First, they will not (unless they have at least Office XP) be able to create a new document in the browser by using "New Document," and they will not be able to use the "Edit in Microsoft Word" (if a Word document) function and then save the amended document back to the site (this again requires at least Office XP). This is the same problem faced by people who are storing documents from any application other than the main Office products (Word, Excel, PowerPoint) because this "New Document" and "Edit In" problem applies to all non-Office products — even Visio files are only covered with Visio 2003 (or 2007) installed on the client.

The main problem, however, lies in the area of synchronization between SharePoint and Office, which is examined next. There have been considerable improvements in synchronization in SharePoint v3/Office 2007 compared to the limited first attempt at this with SharePoint v2/Office 2003, and all these improvements are lost if the user base is not using Office 2007.

The next section provides an overview of the main ways in which this improved functionality can be beneficial.

WSS 3.0 and Office 2007 Working Together

There are two main ways in which WSS 3.0 and Office 2007 work together.

The first main set of functions is the ability of the user (when using Excel, PowerPoint, and Word) to specify a Document Workspace as the place where a document (that the user is saving) is stored. The other variant of this is with Outlook, where there are two functions where a SharePoint site is used.

First, when a meeting is created, it is possible to specify that a Meeting Workspace is to be created for that meeting (and the people invited to that meeting are given rights to access the workspace). The second is that, when a message is sent with an attachment, it is possible to specify that the attachment is stored in a SharePoint site (so that people always get the latest version of the document when opening email and are told automatically about later versions).

These basic functions were changed little between Office 2003 (where they were introduced along with WSS 2.0) and Office 2007. What improvements have been made for Office 2007 are beyond the scope of this chapter, and for now, the key thing to remember is that both the Document Workspace and the Meeting Workspace are only sites created using a particular site template. The same site templates are also available when creating a normal site or sub-site. The difference here is that those sites would be part of a site structure, whereas Document and Meeting Workspaces are single independent sites. There are often more of them, and they are usually more difficult to administer (in the sense that they are created more or less randomly and often no one bothers to delete them when their use is over) than sites within a site structure. However, there are ways to automatically delete them after a time.

The second main way in which WSS 3.0 and Office 2007 work together is to have lists that are synchronized (or copied) between the two. Two-way synchronization is an area in which functionality has been greatly improved in connection with Office 2007, whereas Office 2003 with WSS 2.0 offered only one-way transfers.

Access 2007

One product that didn't have synchronization before is Access 2007.

There is no built-in function in the SharePoint v3 products for providing quality reports of the contents of SharePoint lists. All you can do is to create a suitable view and hope it will fit into standard letter (or A4) format when it's printed. Thus, one of the ideas of the 2007 products is to provide a couple of alternative methods of creating reports from SharePoint v3 lists. One is to use SQL Server 2005 Reporting Services to extract data direct from the SharePoint databases. The "lighter" version is to synchronize a list between Access 2007 and WSS 3.0, and then use the Access reporting functions to create a report on that SharePoint list.

This latter method is intended to replace the previous usage of transferring data to Excel and manually producing reports there. In Access 2007, it works as follows.

Note that Excel 2007 no longer provides this functionality.

Access 2007 is opened and in the External Data menu bar, "SharePoint List." A WSS 3.0 site is specified in the format `http://servername/sitename` and "link to the data source by creating a linked table." This will provide a list of lists available in that WSS 3.0 site, and you can select one or many by using checkboxes. In this case, let's take a document library with some documents in it. Let's do this by opening the Final Offers document library, and then, using Upload from the menu bar, selecting "Upload Multiple Documents."

Because this is the first mention in this chapter of using the Multiple Documents function, note that there is a limit for the maximum size of an upload of a batch of documents (which also applies as the limit for a single document). This default limit is now 250MB compared to the 20MB it was in WSS 2.0 (where there was also a separate limit for a single document). This limit can be amended if necessary in SharePoint v3 Central Administration ⇨ Application Management ⇨ Web Application General Settings (although, compared to WSS 2.0 where 20MB was far too little, 250MB should be enough in most environments).

Select the document library (in Access 2007) and click Synchronize (top-right section of the menu bar). Then, double-click the document library and you will see (if this is a newly created standard document library) five columns: ID, Checked Out, Name, File Size, and Title. Checked Out typically contains no information and Title typically only sometimes contains information.

Select Create in the menu bar and click Report. Now, select the ID text and delete it; repeat for Checked Out. Now, select Title and drag it to between Name and File Size, and also widen it. Play with the widths of all the columns until they use the full width of the printed page. Finally, sort the list by File Size by selecting "Group & Sort" in the menu bar. Then select "Add a Sort" (it appears below the list), select File Size, and then amend the settings to "from largest to small." Click Done.

Now, you can use Save and it will know that you want to save a report. Give it a suitable name such as "DocLib_SortByFileSize" and click OK. Now, both the document library and the report are saved in the same section in the left-hand column in Access 2007.

This is, of course, a trivial example. However, the idea is for you to see what Access 2007 offers for report creation that WSS 3.0 itself doesn't. Note that there could be several ready-made reports available in the same section as a linked list, and that these automatically receive the latest data from the WSS 3.0 site via synchronization. Note too that "Report Design" (instead of "Report") gives you a more powerful way of creating your report, including creating reports made by linking two or more lists.

Excel 2007

It's logical to move on to Excel 2007 at this point. As stated in the Access 2007 discussion, using Access is Microsoft's solution to what was earlier done with Excel 2003. To ensure that users don't just ignore this and work with Excel 2003 anyway, Microsoft has taken the drastic step of actually reducing functionality between Excel 2007 and WSS 3.0 compared with what was available with Excel 2003 with WSS 2.0.

In Excel 2003, it was possible to connect to (read) and update (write) lists that were located on SharePoint sites. In Excel 2007, this is no longer possible.

Instead, Microsoft has tried to avoid problems for those people who already used this in WSS 2.0 by allowing existing files from Excel 2003 to load. Microsoft has also continued to support update functionality (in connection with WSS 2.0) when files are opened in Excel 2007. However, once these files are saved to the new Excel 12 file formats, even that is no longer possible, and lists that are linked to SharePoint will be converted to read-only tables.

It is still possible to "Publish" an Excel table to WSS 3.0 (by using File ⇨ Document Management ⇨ Server) just as it was in Excel 2003 with WSS 2.0, but this is only a one-time write to SharePoint. It is equivalent to the "Create List from Excel" function in WSS 2.0 with which you could move the contents of an Excel file to become a WSS 2.0 list (or what is now the "Create/Import Spreadsheet" function in WSS 3.0).

Outlook 2007

When talking about Office 2007 and WSS 3.0, interaction with Outlook 2007 is perhaps the area in which the greatest amount of work has been done, and unlike the situation with Excel 2007, this has not been done at the cost of losing existing functionality. You can still send messages in Outlook 2007 where you specify that your attachments should be stored in a WSS site, and this still means that readers of your email message will see the latest version of that document when they access the message and not the version that was current when the message was sent. (Earlier readers will be informed that an attachment they have already accessed has been amended.) You can also still create a Meeting Workspace when creating a message, informing a group of people about an upcoming meeting, and these people will still be automatically granted access to the small site created for the meeting (and be informed by email of how to access it). This site is a good way to have a Web location for a single small project (one typical reason for inviting people to a meeting).

But, back to the newer features, interaction occurs with calendars and contacts. In Outlook 2007, you can administer SharePoint documents, and SharePoint tasks are tracked in the same way as Outlook tasks.

When considering the interaction between SharePoint calendars and contacts and Outlook 2007, one key thing to be aware of is that these are always listed *in addition to* the standard Outlook 2007 calendars and contacts. In other words, in Outlook 2007, you will see a list of both your Outlook calendar *and* one or more SharePoint calendars. The interaction available is that you can administer your SharePoint calendars within Outlook 2007, and you can show your SharePoint calendar(s) alongside or overlaying your Outlook calendar (just as you can do with your Outlook calendar and the Outlook calendar of a colleague). You do not, however, combine the two calendars in a permanent way to become a single calendar.

SharePoint contacts, too, are listed completely separately from your Outlook contacts, and here there is no equivalent to the joint calendar view. Instead, "interaction" between the two consists of the ability to copy and paste contacts between them. Tasks are better. They are tracked in the same way as Outlook tasks and appear on the To-Do bar, for example. Just as in the previous two cases, Tasks deriving from SharePoint can also be administered in Outlook 2007. Here, too, a task can be created in Outlook 2007, and then saved to a SharePoint site, but still with the option of adding the Task to the To-Do bar.

The ability to administer SharePoint documents in Outlook 2007 started out for me as something of a "so what?" bullet point. I didn't see the point of using another system instead of a SharePoint site itself to search for and open/save documents that are located in SharePoint (which are what Microsoft highlights as being better in Outlook 2007 than before) or even — to use an example that Microsoft gives — to have the files from a SharePoint library listed in Outlook 2007 so that you can refer to them there rather than by opening the SharePoint site in a browser. I assumed this was only useful to the user whose life revolves around Outlook, and whose SharePoint needs are limited and occasional. But then I starting investigating this function and found that there were a couple of very good reasons for having the contents of a document library visible in the Outlook 2007 User Interface.

> *To set this up, by the way, open the document library in WSS 3.0 (or MOSS 2007) and click the Actions menu item. If you haven't done this before, you will see a "Connect to Client" option and when you select this, you will be prompted to set up a connection to Outlook (the alternative is that "Connect to Outlook" is listed). Don't be surprised if this process takes quite a while (and perhaps demands re-authorization from you), but in the end, you will have an entry in Outlook 2007 in the "SharePoint Lists" section toward the end and below all the Mailbox entries.*

When you have the SharePoint document library files accessible in Outlook 2007, one thing you can do (that you can't do in SharePoint itself) is to take the files offline to work with them. Then, when you get back, you can update those documents in the SharePoint document library (again via Outlook 2007). For some people, this would be a very valid reason for having a synchronized copy of a SharePoint document library in Outlook 2007.

However, the feature I liked the most was the ability to have a three-pane screen with the Mailbox at the left, the document library in the center, and a pane in the right of the screen that shows the *contents* of the documents (Figure 1-17). This is provided that Outlook 2007 provides Viewer support for them, which it does for Excel 2007, PowerPoint 2007, Word 2007, Visio 2007, and jpg (and other image formats) and text files. (As far as I could see, files saved under older versions of the Office applications also were viewable.) Being able to quickly browse through PowerPoint slides in this manner was, for me, a really nice-to-have. (I needed access to my work Outlook; hence, the slightly different site name in Figure 1-17.)

Be aware that both PowerPoint 2007 and Word 2007 can store their documents in a so-called Document Workspace (or one small site meant for discussions and so on about a single document) that works for documents in the same way that a Meeting Workspace works for Meetings (and small projects).

Ways to See What's New

Now that I have gone through most of the basics of what can be in a WSS site, it's time to move on to what a normal user's needs are.

Most users don't contribute to Web sites. They just want to quickly and easily access information that is important for them. There are several ways for an administrator to ensure that this goal of the user is attainable.

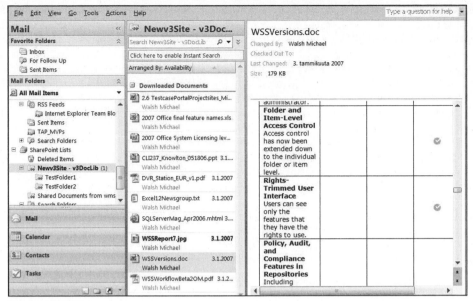

Figure 1-17: Three-pane screen

As I've mentioned already, the first thing is to have pages with Web Parts showing the latest few documents or items. If this is done according to user needs (is he or she is interested in the last few new documents or the last few amended documents — a single Web Part can only show one or the other), then all the user needs to do is to have the URL to that Web page (or those Web pages) in IE Favorites (or similar for another browser). The user can then access the page regularly to see what's happening — for example, to see if a Project Meeting report has been added to the site yet.

This is nice and simple, but a bit haphazard. What happens if the six latest items are listed, and there has been a flurry of action since the last visit? In fact, what happens if seven items have been added since then? It will be there in the list, but not visible in the Web Part in the page. So, you need some other options, which may include the following:

- Alerts
- RSS feeds
- Search functions

Alerts

Alerts are one such option. In the SharePoint 2007 products, it is possible to specify an alert on all levels (site, sub-site, list, folder, item, and even view) and, if anything changes, the user receives an email that can be immediate or accumulated *per alert* on a daily basis.

The ability to be able to create alerts is dependent on the administrator for the SharePoint installation having defined that alerts are supported. However, typically this just means specifying an Exchange Server to handle the emails (or, indeed, any other SMTP mail server).

Even so, there are a couple of snags with alerts. For the administrator, any additional feature adds to the amount of questions he or she will get from users and, with emails being involved, the number of questions increases a lot. For example, there will be questions about the form of the email, with the user wanting more or different information on it. There will be questions about the frequency of alerts, and why isn't a user is getting an alert when that user has amended an item, or why is the user getting an alert to tell him or her that he or she has created an alert (all of which happen). All of these are at the level of "small and irritating," rather than particularly difficult for the administrator to deal with. However, they still provide a reason for an administrator with too much on his or her plate to not implement alerts.

For the user, there are, perhaps surprisingly, downsides as well. If the user sets alerts at too high of a level (the site, say), then the user is alerted to everything that moves on the site. So, there is typically a very long daily message, most of which doesn't interest the user. However, if the user sets alerts at too low of a level (say, the folder level), then there will be a large number of email messages (one per folder) daily. In other words, just as when signing up for free newsletters, care should be taken by users when signing up for alerts.

RSS Feeds

For the user who doesn't like adding to the number of emails received, the SharePoint 2007 products offer something that wasn't in the v2 products — *RSS feeds*. Because you can safely assume that a user is already using email, my feeling is that only users who are already using RSS feeds for other things will bother with adding RSS feeds from WSS 3.0 lists, and that they would be well-advised to consider using both alerts and RSS feeds, depending, in part, on the urgency of the information.

> *I'm assuming here that it is never a good idea to have an alert email sent at once, and so you can divide your warnings of changes into daily batched alerts, and use (immediate) RSS feeds for the really key lists only.*

So, alerts and RSS feeds have their uses, but what about users who don't want to either continually follow developments in a site or to receive alert emails or read RSS feeds? They can rely on the Search functions that WSS 3.0 (and MOSS 2007) includes.

Search Functions

Search in the 2007 SharePoint products is based on the same search technology that Microsoft uses for its MSN site — in other words, it's a Google-level search technology (or at least is close to that). Unlike the situation with the v2 products, the search technology used is the same for both WSS 3.0 and MOSS 2007.

The differences only come in the scope of the search, with WSS 3.0 (like WSS 2.0) being restricted to search data stored in its own databases and, in fact, also being restricted to searching in a single site in an installation rather than over multiple sites in the same SharePoint installation as MOSS 2007 can do. (MOSS 2007 can index and, thus, search file shares, public folders, Web sites, SharePoint sites, databases, structured and unstructured data sources, and so on.)

What can be searched when using the product as delivered is not by any means everything most people will want to search. This is because you can only search what has been indexed, and what can be indexed is dependent on what file formats the indexing system can recognize. As with most Microsoft products, this means the main Office products and the most general neutral file formats such as .txt.

This takes us to the obvious missing format that most people would want to include in their searches — the .pdf file format used by Adobe Acrobat files. Just as with all other missing formats, the way to make sure that the `.pdf` file format is indexed is to install an *iFilter* for `.pdf` files on the server doing the indexing. Microsoft's strategy is to provide iFilters only for their own main products (and for those very widespread neutral formats), and to rely on the software makers to write software that uses their own file formats to provide iFilters for those file formats. Mostly, that type of iFilter is provided free by those vendors because they want the files produced by their software to be searchable in such applications as the SharePoint software, whereas filters for less common (but still neutral) formats are often provided at a cost by small, third-party vendors.

Luckily, an iFilter for a 32-bit SharePoint v2 system will still usually work for a 32-bit SharePoint v3 system, so the iFilter that Adobe has long provided for Acrobat files will still work with WSS 3.0 and MOSS 2007. (Less lucky is the fact that this won't work for a 64-bit system, and Adobe has, as of this writing, not provided a 64-bit version.)

Another thing that is strangely lacking in v3 of SharePoint as it was in v2 is an icon for `.pdf` *files. You may have noticed that in a document library view, the line normally starts with an icon, and that this is a Word icon, or an Excel icon, and so on. All file types that are not recognized are given the same Windows icon. This is, however, easily fixed. There's a* `pdf` *icon available on the Adobe site, and this can be slotted in to a file on* `C:` *to provide even Acrobat files listed in WSS 3.0 with their own icons. (Add the icon to* `C:\Program Files\Common Files\Microsoft Shared\Web server extensions\12\ TEMPLATE\IMAGES,` *and then add an entry for* `pdf` *to* `C:\Program Files\Common Files\ Microsoft Shared\Web server extensions\12\TEMPLATE\XML\DOCICON.XML` *and after saving do* `IISRESTART.`*)*

Additional Areas of Interest

Finally, here are a few words on a few additional areas of interest.

Customizing a Site

There are roughly three different ways you can customize a site. You can customize it using the user interface, you can customize it with SPD 2007, or you can customize it with Visual Studio 2005.

❑   *User Interface changes* — Done in a browser while accessing a WSS site, these affect the look of the site in standard ways. For example, you can apply a new Site theme (Site Settings ➪ Site theme) so that at least the colors used in your site are different from the standard that most people will use when using the product as delivered.

❑   *SPD 2007* — This is typically used to make changes to the code that Microsoft supplies with the SharePoint product. So, to take a trivial example, a heading that Microsoft provides could be amended or removed; other headings could be made larger; or the color changed, or both. A more complicated (and far-reaching) example would be to amend the master page of the installation.

Changes to the 2003 SharePoint products were made using FrontPage 2003. SPD 2007 is really the renamed FrontPage 2007 — renamed because of the much greater amount of functionality it contains and also because of the new concentration on this being a tool only for SharePoint sites. You should not use FrontPage 2003 to amend WSS 3.0 or MOSS 2007 sites and, although you can use SPD 2007 to amend WSS 2.0 and SPS 2003 sites (backward compatibility), I would advise against it, because there will be many functions in SPD 2007 that will not work with the 2003 SharePoint products. The use of SPD 2007 with those products might prove to be confusing.

❑   *Visual Studio 2005* — This is typically used to add functionality to a SharePoint implementation. For example, this could be the creation of a new Web Part offering functionality that the sold product doesn't offer in its Web Parts (or perhaps, that is included in MOSS 2007, but you want to use the same functionality with a WSS 3.0 installation, so you need to write your own). It could be new code that (at the extreme) provides a new customer interface to a SharePoint installation. Typically, such new code would use the many functions that are described in detail in the WSS 3.0 and MOSS 2007 Software Developer Kits (SDKs), which can be downloaded from the Microsoft site.

Virus Checking

One common question is to ask is whether normal server-based virus checkers are enough for SharePoint systems. The answer is that they are not — you will need a special SharePoint virus checker installed on the front-end servers (in the case of a farm), or on the single server (when that's all you have).

After the 2003 SharePoint products were released, it took a while for the main virus checker vendors to provide SharePoint versions of their products, and it looks as we are in the same situation today with the 2007 SharePoint products. The only exception that I know of, as of this writing, is the Forefront product from Microsoft itself ("Forefront Security for SharePoint 2007"). This is an update for WSS 3.0 and MOSS 2007 of a product for the 2003 SharePoint products that was previously sold by Sybaris and, along with other Sybaris products, was acquired by Microsoft when it bought the company. Like that earlier product, it continues to use most of the many third-party scanners that were the strength of the Sybaris software.

Backup/Restore

Here, too, there are special needs for SharePoint products, although typically any backup scenario will also include a standard SQL Server backup of the configuration and (especially) content databases.

This area is covered in Chapter 3 of this book, and is also covered in a chapter of the *Microsoft Office SharePoint Server 2007 Administrator's Companion* by Bill English (Redmond, WA: Microsoft Press, 2007).

Workflow

Workflow wasn't available in the v2 products, and was a major customer request for the v3 products. Chapters 8 and 9 discuss workflow, so for now, this is just a note for you that workflow is based on the Windows Workflow Foundation (WWF) that is installed as part of .NET Framework 3.0.

WSS 3.0 includes only one built-in workflow; otherwise, with WSS 3.0, you create sequential workflows by using SPD 2007. In addition, you can create more complicated workflows (with loops) in Visual Studio 2005.

Wikis and Blogs

These are new functions in the 2007 SharePoint products and, because of this, still only offer basic functionality.

To create a site for a wiki (or a blog), you follow normal procedures to create a site, but when given the choice of which site template to use for the site, you select the wiki (or blog) template. This site is just like any other site created in this way in that it is a sub-site to the site in which it is created, and may (or may not) inherit the permissions of the parent site.

The standard wiki site, when created, includes a link to a Web page, "How to Use This Wiki Site," which gives the basic information that you'll need. Going into details of this and blog sites (which are created in a similar way) goes beyond the scope of this chapter.

For More Information

Apart from the Microsoft SharePoint Web pages starting at www.microsoft.com/sharepoint, there are various private Web pages full of SharePoint information. The two I will mention here are my own WSS FAQ site (www.wssfaq.com) and Ian Morrish's WSS DEMO site (www.wssdemo.com).

As far as other books are concerned, the most complete list of SharePoint 2007 books can be found here:

    http://wss.asaris.de/sites/walsh/Lists/WSSv3%20FAQ/V%20Books.aspx

There are books for all needs, but most administrators will probably find that one book they will definitely need to have will be the *Microsoft Office SharePoint Server 2007 Administrator's Companion* from Microsoft Press, although, if past experience is any judge, several of the chapters from this book may well (at a later date) appear in .pdf form on the Microsoft Web site.

Questions can be asked in the Microsoft public newsgroups at msnews.microsoft.com. There are four newsgroups for different aspects of using the products, and they are for all SharePoint products and versions, so make sure you say which exact product you are using when asking a question there.

❑   microsoft.public.sharepoint.setup_and_administration is for Installation and Administration questions.

❑   microsoft.public.sharepoint.design_and_customization is for questions on amending the code supplied with the product, typically (if WSS 3.0 or MOSS 2007) with SPD 2007.

❑   microsoft.public.sharepoint.development_and_programming is for questions on creating new code such as writing Web Parts or writing code that uses Web services, and this typically uses Visual Studio 2005.

❑   microsoft.public.sharepoint.general is for questions that don't fit in any of the previously mentioned newsgroups.

Microsoft forums are also available. These are listed here, along with their RSS feeds, which is the way I prefer to read them.

❑   *SharePoint General Q&A and Discussion* — http://forums.microsoft.com/MSDN/rss.aspx?ForumID=1200&Mode=0&SiteID=1

❑   *SharePoint Setup, Upgrade, Administration, and Operation* — http://forums.microsoft.com/MSDN/rss.aspx?ForumID=1201&Mode=0&SiteID=1

❑   *SharePoint Design and Customization* — http://forums.microsoft.com/MSDN/rss.aspx?ForumID=1202&Mode=0&SiteID=1

- ❏ *SharePoint Development and Programming* — `http://forums.microsoft.com/MSDN/rss.aspx?ForumID=1203&Mode=0&SiteID=1`

- ❏ *SharePoint Business Data Catalog* — `http://forums.microsoft.com/MSDN/rss.aspx?ForumID=1204&Mode=0&SiteID=1`

- ❏ *SharePoint Business Intelligence* — `http://forums.microsoft.com/MSDN/rss.aspx?ForumID=1205&Mode=0&SiteID=1`

- ❏ *SharePoint InfoPath Forms Services* — `http://forums.microsoft.com/MSDN/rss.aspx?ForumID=1206&Mode=0&SiteID=1`

- ❏ *SharePoint Workflow* — `http://forums.microsoft.com/MSDN/rss.aspx?ForumID=1207&Mode=0&SiteID=1`

- ❏ *SharePoint Excel Services* — `http://forums.microsoft.com/MSDN/rss.aspx?ForumID=1208&Mode=0&SiteID=1`

- ❏ *SharePoint Search* — `http://forums.microsoft.com/MSDN/rss.aspx?ForumID=1209&Mode=0&SiteID=1`

- ❏ *SharePoint Knowledge Network* — `http://forums.microsoft.com/MSDN/rss.aspx?ForumID=1210&Mode=0&SiteID=1`

As of this writing, these RSS feeds only gave links to the first items in each thread, and there were no feeds for replies. Microsoft has promised to fix this by the time this book is published, but check this when you first use these RSS feeds just to be sure.

If you don't like the style of these Microsoft newsgroups or forums, then Dustin Miller's "SharePoint University" has its own SharePoint v3 forums and can be found here:

`http://www.sharepointu.com/forums/default.asp.`

Finally, Microsoft's Product Services Support (PSS) team has as always actively been creating Knowledge Base (KB) articles warning of problems and giving fixes or workarounds. The Knowledge Base can be searched at `http://support.microsoft.com/search?adv=1`, but again, I find the best way to follow developments is to use the relevant RSS feeds, which are the following:

- ❏ *Windows SharePoint Services 3.0 KB Articles:*

  `http://support.microsoft.com/common/rss.aspx?rssid=12200&ln=en-us&msid=232c70a3bb2693499aef676972853630`

- ❏ *Microsoft Office SharePoint Server 2007 KB Articles:*

  `http://support.microsoft.com/common/rss.aspx?rssid=11373&ln=en-us&msid=232c70a3bb2693499aef676972853630`

- ❏ *SPD 2007 KB Articles:*

  `http://support.microsoft.com/common/rss.aspx?rssid=11677&ln=en-us&msid=232c70a3bb2693499aef676972853630`

Even if you are only using WSS 3.0, you will still need the MOSS 2007 feed because the categorization is often random. Similarly, many of the supposedly SPD 2007 feeds will be general Office 2007 feeds and will not apply to SPD 2007 specifically.

If you want to avoid these problems and also see KB articles that are relevant to WSS 3.0 and MOSS 2007, but that have been allocated to, say, Word 2007 or other Office products, check the KB Articles section of the WSS FAQ site where I try to keep track of all relevant KB articles (for WSS 2.0 and for WSS 3.0 and MOSS 2007). The direct address is as follows:

```
http://wss.asaris.de/sites/walsh/Lists/KB%20Articles/V3%20Sorted%20By%20Date.aspx
```

As with all SharePoint lists, you can set an alert on it. (Note, though, that this is still at the moment a v2 site, and so alerts can only be set at the list level, so you get alerts for WSS 2.0 KB articles as well as for the v3 SharePoint products.)

Summary

This chapter provided brief overview of the main SharePoint concepts by helping you to install a copy of WSS 3.0 and taking you briefly through the various items that you will see on the Web page when you create a site based on the standard "Team Site" template.

This chapter has provided a feel for how the SharePoint products have developed over the years, and examined how the functionality provided has evolved with particular notice being given to the additional features that are included in WSS 3.0 compared to WSS 2.0. As part of this, the chapter also discussed the interaction with Office 2007 products.

The chapter concluded with tips on where to get further information, and where to ask further questions on the SharePoint v3 products.

2

Configuring Forms Based Authentication

by Stacy Draper

Forms Based Authentication (FBA) is a technique developers can use for authenticating users into Web applications. As a capability built into ASP.NET 2.0, FBA has become a very popular method for providing authentication functionality. FBA is the technology that challenges users to identify who they are. Once the credentials are obtained, the user identity is cached in a cookie. In its most basic form, an FBA challenge is a Web page that consists of a request of a username, password, and in what manner to persist the cookie. Because the SharePoint 2007 platform is built on top of ASP.NET 2.0, you essentially get FBA for free.

It's "essentially for free" only because there is no money changing hands, but what an investment in time it seems to have been in trying to figure out how to set it up. When you first take on configuring SharePoint for FBA, it seems that it's either the most counter-intuitive process, or it just simply doesn't work. After the community has invested several months collaborating, comparing notes, and working through it, we found out it does indeed work. It's simple, actually, once you know where everything is and how everything works and interacts with each other. This chapter covers the basic assets of FBA by utilizing the following:

❑ *A user store* — In this case, I will use a SQL database. If the application must be migrated to Active Directory (AD) later, using ADAM would be a better approach.

❑ *Modified* `web.config` *files* — There are a few things to remember about SharePoint:

  ❑ Central Administration is a separate site

  ❑ Shared Service Provider (SSP) is a separate site

  ❑ The sites your users access are all separate sites

❑ *Configuring SharePoint and Permissions* — These are discussed in more detail later in the chapter.

This chapter also covers some more complicated techniques, caveats, and ways to work around them where applicable.

Creating a Simple User Store

This chapter uses a common data store that comes for free with ASP.NET 2.0: ASP.NET SQL Server Database running on SQL Server 2005. You might be able to get SQL Express up and running, but it could be more difficult. With SQL Server 2005, you'll have better tools to troubleshoot and examine what's going on in the database.

Creating a Database Using aspnet_regsql.exe

For those who might be unfamiliar with it, there is a tool that comes with the Microsoft 2.0 .NET Framework called `aspnet_regsql.exe`. This tool enables you to create a database for things such as membership, profiles, role management, and personalization, among other things. This is the traditional method for implementing FBA with .NET applications, and is the example used with SharePoint in this chapter. If you've already built the database, all you will need is the database name and a security account with access. If you don't have the database, follow these steps to create one:

1. Run `C:\WINDOWS\Microsoft.NET\Framework\v2.0.50727\aspnet_regsql.exe`. You'll be presented with the ASP.NET SQL Server Setup Wizard, which explains that you are about to create a database to be used with ASP.NET applications. Like any command-line tool, there are many switches that can be passed to `aspnet_regsql.exe`, and the whole process can be completed without the setup wizard.

2. Clicking Next provides a couple of options: creating a new database or removing an existing one. Continue through with creating a new database and be sure that the "Configure SQL Server for application services" radio button is selected. Click Next.

3. After indicating that you want to create a new database, you are presented with a few options: the SQL server where this new database is to live, authentication information, and the database name to be created.

   a. A period (.) represents the local server. If you happened to have SQL and SharePoint on the same server, this will work for you. SharePoint and SQL Server will probably never be on the same box in the real world, and, in that case, you must put in the actual server name.

   b. For the database creation, use "Windows authentication" if you are logged in with an account that has the database creation privileges. Otherwise, enter in a SQL Account with the database creation privilege.

   c. Use a name that everyone will know or recognize so that they will know what the database is used for. Using `<default>` will generate something difficult to decipher like `aspnetdb`, and subsequent creations will add a number after it. For the sake of this walkthrough, use `SharePointFBA` to represent FBA users of SharePoint.

4. Clicking the Next button from the "Select the Server and Database" screen (Figure 2-1), you are asked to confirm your settings. Clicking the Next button again will create the appropriate database.

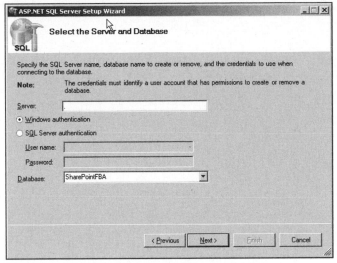

Figure 2-1: "Select the Server and Database" screen

Now you have a database in SQL Server that you can use in your ASP.NET applications, including SharePoint.

Preparing to Use the Web Site Administration Tool

Remember that this database is meant to be used with ASP.NET applications. Most developers use Visual Studio, so that's where Microsoft put one of the management tools for this type of database. As a beneficial side effect, while connecting to the database, you will be generating some of the `web.config` code you'll need to use in the SharePoint sites.

Creating a Project in Visual Studio 2005

Open Visual Studio and create a file-based Web project. Once Visual Studio is open, click File ➪ New ➪ Web Site. You'll be presented with a modal window titled New Web Site.

1. Choose "Empty Web Site."

2. The location should be File System.

3. The default name is usually `website#` where # is the next available Web site. Change the name to something meaningful like `SharePointFBA`. Mine looks like this:

   ```
   C:\Documents and Settings\Administrator\My Documents\Visual Studio 2005\
   Projects\SharePointFBA
   ```

4. Set the language to C# just so you will be on the same page as me and click OK.

At this point, you have an empty Web project.

Connecting to the ASP.NET Application Database

To be able to manage users and roles in the application database, you must let the Web application know how to access the database. That is done in the `web.config` file. In the Solution Explorer in Visual Studio, right-click the project (it's probably `C:\...\SharePointFBA`) and select "Add new item." Double-click Web Configuration File (or you could click it once). Ensure that the name is `web.config` and click Add. The point here is that you want to have a `web.config` file in the project.

For the purposes of this exercise, there are a few things that the Web application must be aware of in order for it to connect to that application database:

❑ *Connection string* — For the sake of simplicity, the connection string tells the system what database to connect to, and what credentials to use. There's more to connection strings than that, but that's all we're really concerned with for this chapter.

❑ *Membership provider* — A membership provider is the conduit between ASP.NET's membership feature and the membership data source.

❑ *Role provider* — A role provider is the conduit between ASP.NET's role service and the role data source.

Simply put, the providers tell the application services how and where to get the data they need to do their respective jobs. Microsoft has already made a few of these available for free:

❑ *Membership provider* — You have `SqlMembershipProvider` for membership data in SQL server and `ActiveDirectoryMembershipProvider` for membership data in SQL server and AD.

❑ *Role provider* — You have `SqlRoleProvider` for accessing SQL or SQL Express ASP.NET application data, `AuthorizationStoreRoleProvider` for accessing AD or Active Directory for Application Management (ADAM) data, and `WindowTokenRoleProvider` for Windows authentication token data.

These providers will get you pretty far until you need to connect to a user store that does not fall into one of these categories. In that case, you'll need to buy or write your own role and membership providers.

If you modify the following connection string, the ASP.NET application will be able to determine where the ASP.NET application database is located and what credentials to use:

```
<connectionStrings>
  <add
    name="connectionName"
    connectionString="Data Source=serverName; ↵
    Initial Catalog=databaseName;Integrated Security=True" />
</connectionStrings>
```

If your application is on the same server as Visual Studio and SharePoint, just enter a `.` or `localhost` to represent the local machine. In a normal environment, you would have to put in the name of the server. Additionally, you may or may not use integrated security. The integrated security will use the credentials of the application pool identity the Web application is running under. When running from Visual Studio, the credentials are those of the logged-in user. However, in the case of Internet Information Server (IIS), it would use the credentials from the application pool that the Web site is associated with.

Finally, set the database name to `SharePointFBA`, the same database that you created earlier. You must give the connection a name so that you can reference it for later use. Call the connection string `aspnetConnectionString`. So, your `connectionStrings` node should look like the following:

```
<connectionStrings>
  <add
name="aspnetConnectionString"
connectionString="Data Source=.;Initial Catalog=SharePointFBA;↵
Integrated Security=True" />
</connectionStrings>
```

Now that you have a connection string written, you must put it in the `web.config` file. Under the configuration node of the `web.config` file, there is a `<connectionStrings />`. Only one of these nodes is allowed.

Your Web application can find the ASP.NET Application Database and what credentials to use to access it. You have just a couple more things to do before you can start getting down to the business of creating users and roles: set the role and membership providers.

The following XML node displays several of the possible values, and though I can't cover all of them, they are shown here for self exploration. There are two attributes that are very important. The first is the `defaultProvider` and the provider `name`. The `providers` node is a collection of providers and the `defaultProvider` attribute tells the Web application which provider to use first. The other important node is the `connectionStringName`, which tells the provider where to get the data and what credentials to use.

```
<membership defaultProvider="aFriendlyName">
  <providers>
    <add
      name="aFriendlyName"
      connectionStringName="NameOfTheConnectionString"
      applicationName="/"
      enablePasswordRetrieval="false"
      enablePasswordReset="true"
      requiresQuestionAndAnswer="false"
      requiresUniqueEmail="false"
      passwordFormat="Hashed"
      maxInvalidPasswordAttempts="3"
      minRequiredPasswordLength="3"
      minRequiredNonalphanumericCharacters="0"
      passwordAttemptWindow="5"
      passwordStrengthRegularExpression=""
type="System.Web.Security.SqlMembershipProvider,System.Web,Version=2.0.0.0,↵
Culture=neutral,PublicKeyToken=b03f5f7f11d50a3a" />
    </providers>
  </membership>
```

You must inform the membership provider that the connection string name is `aspnetConnectionString`. For `aFriendlyName`, you must use a name that you don't mind seeing in your application because users will be prefaced with this name. In your AD environment, you might notice domain/username. A similar behavior will occur with FBA users. In this example, it would be `aFriendlyName:username`. This doesn't happen everywhere in SharePoint, but you want to make the name something that is easy on the eyes and easy to understand. Maybe you could use the word extranet or partner. For this walkthrough, let's name it aspnetMembershipProvider so that you can compare and contrast other connection methods later. So, the connection string should look like this:

```
<membership defaultProvider="aspnetMemebershipProvider">
        <providers>
          <add
            name="aspnetMemebershipProvider"
            connectionStringName="aspnetConnectionString"
            applicationName="/"
            enablePasswordRetrieval="false"
            enablePasswordReset="true"
            requiresQuestionAndAnswer="false"
            requiresUniqueEmail="false"
            passwordFormat="Hashed"
            maxInvalidPasswordAttempts="3"
            minRequiredPasswordLength="3"
            minRequiredNonalphanumericCharacters="0"
            passwordAttemptWindow="5"
            passwordStrengthRegularExpression=""


type="System.Web.Security.SqlMembershipProvider,System.Web,Version=2.0.0.0,Culture=
neutral,PublicKeyToken=b03f5f7f11d50a3a" />
        </providers>
      </membership>
```

This node belongs in the system.web node of the web.config file. Typically, there isn't an existiing membership provider, so put this one just under system.web.

The role provider is nearly identical to the membership provider. Again, you must give the provider a distinct name and assign a default provider, as well as let the provider know where and how to get its data:

```
<roleManager enabled="true" defaultProvider="aspnetRoleManager">
        <providers>
          <add
            name="aspnetRoleManager"
            connectionStringName="aspnetConnectionString"
            applicationName="/"

type="System.Web.Security.SqlRoleProvider,System.Web,Version=2.0.0.0,Culture=neutra
l,PublicKeyToken=b03f5f7f11d50a3a" />
        </providers>
      </roleManager>
```

Now you have a role manager that will use the provider named aspnetRoleManager as the default provider, and that provider is using the connection string you created earlier named aspnetRoleManager. This node also belongs in system.web (put it just below the membership provider).

Altogether, you should have code that looks like this:

```
    <connectionStrings>
        <add name="aspnetConnectionString" connectionString="Data Source=.;Initial
Catalog=SharePointFBA;Integrated Security=True"/>
    </connectionStrings>

    <system.web>
        <!-- membership provider -->
        <membership defaultProvider="aspnetMembershipProvider">
            <providers>
                <add
                name="aspnetMembershipProvider"
                connectionStringName="aspnetConnectionString"
                applicationName="/"
                enablePasswordRetrieval="false"
                enablePasswordReset="true"
                requiresQuestionAndAnswer="false"
                requiresUniqueEmail="false"
                passwordFormat="Hashed"
                maxInvalidPasswordAttempts="3"
                minRequiredPasswordLength="3"
                minRequiredNonalphanumericCharacters="0"
                passwordAttemptWindow="5"
                passwordStrengthRegularExpression=""

type="System.Web.Security.SqlMembershipProvider,System.Web,Version=2.0.0.0,↵
Culture=neutral,PublicKeyToken=b03f5f7f11d50a3a" />
            </providers>
        </membership>

        <!-- role provider -->
        <roleManager enabled="true" defaultProvider="aspnetRoleManager">
            <providers>
                <add
                name="aspnetRoleManager"
                connectionStringName="aspnetConnectionString"
                applicationName="/"
                type="System.Web.Security.SqlRoleProvider,System.Web,Version=2.0.0.0,↵
Culture=neutral,PublicKeyToken=b03f5f7f11d50a3a" />
            </providers>
        </roleManager>
```

Now that you have a Web application with the web.config containing the connection string, membership provider information, and role provider information, you're almost ready to create some users.

Working with the Web Site Administration Tool

The Web Site Administration Tool is used to manage users, roles, and other settings in a Web application. One way you can open this tool is from Visual Studio with a Web application open. This is because it uses the web.config file to know where the database store is and what providers to use. From the menu bar, click "Web site" at the bottom is the ASP.NET Configuration screen, which opens the Web Site Administration Tool. From here, you can manage your users, roles, and other settings.

By default, the Web application is set to use Windows authentication, and you want to use FBA. By clicking the Security tab, you can see a box in the lower left-hand corner indicating that you are currently using Windows authentication, as shown in Figure 2-2.

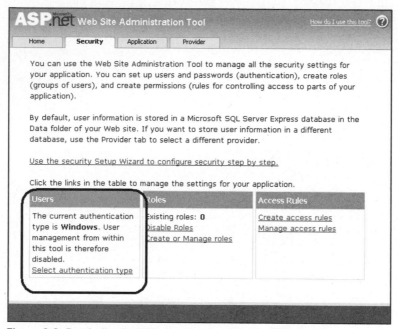

Figure 2-2: Box indicating Windows authentication being used

Click the hyperlink "Select authentication type" and choose the "From the Internet" radio button. Click Done. You are now able to add and remove users. Add an Admins role, a Readers role, and a Contributors role. Then add users aspnetAdmin in the Admins role, aspnetReader in the Readers role, and aspnetContributor in the Contributors role. Normally, you wouldn't prefix this in this way. Users would be instructed to log in with aspnet:username. Later in the chapter, I really want to drive home where these users are stored. If you have two users with the same name, it might be tough to notice the difference.

Creating SharePoint Applications

There are a couple of reasons why you need FBA in the first place. You'll have a specific business or technical problem that says certain customers, partners, or whoever must be able to get to the site, but those users won't have domain credentials. In this chapter, I am simply demonstrating how to get FBA up and running. This would certainly go way off topic talking about firewalls, Domain Naming Service (DNS), and a myriad of other issues that come into play when you are putting a SharePoint application on the Internet. So, let's stay on point and now simulate an environment.

Modifying the Host File

Located at C:\WINDOWS\system32\drivers\etc is a "host" file. The operating system will look to this file first any time it gets a request to translate a domain name into an IP address. Here you can create your own "quasi domain" names and route that traffic back to your Web server, or more specifically, SharePoint sites.

Navigate to `C:\WINDOWS\system32\drivers\etc` and open the host file with Notepad. Add the following:

```
127.0.0.1      intranet
127.0.0.1      aspnet
```

The `intranet` URL represents an intranet site and the `aspnet` URL represents the Internet-facing FBA site. Simply save the host file and close Notepad.

Creating Two Sites that Point to the Same Content

For this demonstration, you will have two sites on two different zones: one for an intranet and the other is an ASP.NET FBA site pointing to the same content database.

Creating the Intranet Site

Follow these steps to create the `intranet` site:

1. Open "SharePoint 3.0 Central Administration" on the SharePoint server.

2. Click the Application Management link on the left, or on the tab (either will take you to the Application Management section).

3. Click "Create or extend Web application."

4. Click "Create a new Web application."

5. In "The IIS Web Site" section, there are Port and Host Header fields. Change the Port to `80` and change the Host Header to `intranet`. IIS can route traffic a couple of different ways. It can route by IP number, or it can be routed by a Host Header. In the case of a Host Header, it will look at the URL of the incoming request and send the traffic to the appropriate Web site.

6. Leave the Security Configuration and Load Balanced URL sections as they are. They are fine with the default values.

7. Select an application pool that has a user with sufficient security to access the database you created earlier. (Or, you could have SharePoint create one, and then change either the user or add the user to the SQL Server as a database owner.)

8. In the Reset Internet Information Services section, mark "Restart IIS automatically" if it's not grayed out. If it is, just restart IIS at the end of these steps.

9. The "Database Name and Authentication" section is a little misleading in its instructions. The fact of the matter is that you can't create a content database with the same name as one that exists already. That is often interpreted as, "Use the default name that is given." This is very cryptic, difficult to use, and the SQL administrators absolutely hate it. Give the database a name that reflects the project you are working on. Name it `Content_FBA`.

10. Click OK to start the site creation process. This process can take a few minutes.

11. Once the site is provisioned, you'll have arrived at the Application Create page. Click the "Create Site Collection" link. The link is in the bottom part of the paragraph.

12. Give the site a title such as FBA Site and a brief description such as Sample FBA Site.

13. Choose a Blank Site or a Team Site.

14. Provide the appropriate Primary Site Collection Administrator account (perhaps whatever you are logged in as now).

15. Click OK to create the site.

16. Click the link to your site (for example, `http://intranet`) and your newly created site will open.

Now, you've just created a site that will be used on the intranet. Let's now create a site that is used on the Internet.

Creating an Internet Site

The Internet site will be an extension of the intranet site. In other words, the Internet site will use the same content database as the intranet site. Go back to the Central Administration Application Management section and once again click "Create or extend Web application." This time, choose "Extend an existing Web application" and follow these steps:

1. In the Web Application section, Microsoft introduces a new user element. Typically, the value is "No selection." Click the drop-down arrow and click "Change Web Application." Choose the `intranet80` site you just created.

2. As before, change the Port and Host Header. Change the Port to `80` and change the Host Header to `aspnet`.

3. This time, let's do something a little different than before in the Load Balanced URL section. Before, you didn't change a thing. This time, ensure that it is set for Internet Zone.

4. Click OK and a new site will be created in IIS. The new site is mapped to the content database that you created before.

5. Open a browser and ensure that you can load the `aspnet` site by navigating to `http://aspnet/`.

Now you have two sites pointing to the same content database. Chapter 3 explains in detail about alternate access mapping and zones. Alternate access mapping will prove useful when you want to allow people to arrive at `aspnet.myCompany.com`. Now, you must point the Internet site to the ASP.NET Application Database and authenticate against that.

Modifying web.config Files

Taking an inventory of what has transpired, you can see that there are many sites in play. You just created two: one for intranet and one for Internet. Central Administration is also a site, as well as the Shared Service Provider (SSP). The SSP is a large topic, but for the purposes of this discussion on FBA, understand that the SSP provides services such as user profiles, audiences, and personal sites (among many other things) to a SharePoint site. In addition to the SSP, you may also have an additional host site for My Site. Simply put, My Site is a personal site that gives users the capability to display their skills, interests, contact information, and other information to other users.

One important thing to realize is that the crawler doesn't understand FBA sites and will have to crawl your Windows authenticated site.

All of these sites must know about the new user store. Earlier in this chapter, you created everything you need to modify the `web.config` files of these sites.

Modifying Central Administration web.config

Let's start at the least-intuitive spot: the Central Administration site. The Central Administration site is a little different because that site needs to continue to use the `AspNetWindowsTokenRoleProvider` as the default role provider. But there's an interesting fact starting to unveil itself. You set the default role provider, but the Central Administration site still knows about the other providers. This is the first indication that you can have more than one provider, and later you will learn about having a third site and set of providers. For now, though, let's focus on just having two sites, one being FBA and the other being the ASP.NET Application Database.

In this case, working with the `web.config` is most easily done through IIS. Follow these steps:

1. Open IIS Microsoft Management Console (MMC) by clicking Start ➪ All Programs ➪ Administrative Tools ➪ Internet Information Services (IIS) Manager.

2. Expand the IIS for the Local Computer.

3. Right-click "SharePoint Central Administration v3" and select Explore from the context menu. Now you're in a position to edit live files. Naturally, you'll need to follow your Standard Operating Procedure (SOP) when it comes to modifying files. In this case, you will simply copy and paste to back up the `web.config` file. Copy and paste the file in the same folder so that you end up with `Copy of web.config`. This copy is only meant as a backup, because you'll be editing the `web.config` file a lot.

4. Open `web.config` with Notepad or Visual Studio. (Right-click `web.config` and choose "Open with" from the context menu. Click "Choose Program…" and select Notepad or Visual Studio from the list.)

5. Copy the `connectionStrings`, `membership`, and `roleManager` nodes from the `web.config` of the Web application you created earlier and paste the nodes into the `web.config` for the Central Administration site.

6. For the `roleManager`, change the default provider from `aspnetRoleManager` to `AspNetWindowsTokenRoleProvider`. This is because you want to be able to log in to the Central Administration site from a Windows account. It's best to always have the Central Administration login be a Windows account.

Editing web.config Files

Editing `web.config` files is very easy with Visual Studio. This is because you get IntelliSense, a feature that provides potential options based on what you've already typed. You can also expand and collapse nodes. In Notepad, you don't even get color, so it can be difficult to read. As with editing any files, always be sure to make a backup of your `web.config` file before making any changes.

Your code should include the following:

```
    <connectionStrings>
      <add name="aspnetConnectionString" connectionString="Data Source=.;Initial
Catalog=SharePointFBA;Integrated Security=True"/>
    </connectionStrings>

    <system.web>
      <!-- membership provider -->
      <membership defaultProvider="aspnetMembershipProvider">
        <providers>
          <add
            name="aspnetMembershipProvider"
            connectionStringName="aspnetConnectionString"
            applicationName="/"
            enablePasswordRetrieval="false"
            enablePasswordReset="true"
            requiresQuestionAndAnswer="false"
            requiresUniqueEmail="false"
            passwordFormat="Hashed"
            maxInvalidPasswordAttempts="3"
            minRequiredPasswordLength="3"
            minRequiredNonalphanumericCharacters="0"
            passwordAttemptWindow="5"
            passwordStrengthRegularExpression=""

type="System.Web.Security.SqlMembershipProvider,System.Web,Version=2.0.0.0,↵
Culture=neutral,PublicKeyToken=b03f5f7f11d50a3a" />
        </providers>
      </membership>

      <!-- role provider -->
      <roleManager enabled="true" defaultProvider="AspNetWindowsTokenRoleProvider">
        <providers>
          <add
            name="aspnetRoleManager"
            connectionStringName="aspnetConnectionString"
            applicationName="/"
            type="System.Web.Security.SqlRoleProvider,System.Web,Version=2.0.0.0,↵
Culture=neutral,PublicKeyToken=b03f5f7f11d50a3a" />
        </providers>
      </roleManager>
```

Modifying My Site Host Site web.config

My Site is an interesting animal because it can be hosted a couple of different ways. One way is that it can be on its own Web application. Another way is that it can be hosted on top of an existing SharePoint site. There are benefits and detriments to each.

When My Site is hosted on its own Web application, it's easier to manage in the long run. If there is a lot of traffic, it can be moved to its own server. In FBA, however, when users go from the SharePoint site to the My Site, it will cause them to go from one URL to another. This will cause users to log in again, or feel as though they must log in twice for what they perceive is that same Web application.

Microsoft best practices dictate that it's best to have My Site hosted separately. You must also consider usability, and FBA may drive you away from the best practice. You'll have to give your situation some careful consideration. In either case, you can find out where your My Site is by actually navigating to one and taking note of the URL. Look in IIS for the Host Header that matches what you see in the URL.

To find out where My Site is located, go to the Application Management section of Central Administration. Under Office SharePoint Server Shared Services, click "Create or configure this farm's shared services." Mouse over your SSP and you'll be able to click a drop-down menu. Choose "Edit Properties" and you'll be able to see the My Site Location section that indicates the My Site URL.

As before, open the `web.config` file of the My Site host and paste in your `connectionStrings`, `membership`, and `roleManager` nodes from the `web.config` you created earlier. The code should look like this:

```
    <connectionStrings>
      <add name="aspnetConnectionString" connectionString="Data Source=.;Initial
Catalog=SharePointFBA;Integrated Security=True"/>
    </connectionStrings>


    <system.web>
      <!-- membership provider -->
      <membership defaultProvider="aspnetMembershipProvider">
        <providers>
          <add
            name="aspnetMembershipProvider"
            connectionStringName="aspnetConnectionString"
            applicationName="/"
            enablePasswordRetrieval="false"
            enablePasswordReset="true"
            requiresQuestionAndAnswer="false"
            requiresUniqueEmail="false"
            passwordFormat="Hashed"
            maxInvalidPasswordAttempts="3"
            minRequiredPasswordLength="3"
            minRequiredNonalphanumericCharacters="0"
            passwordAttemptWindow="5"
            passwordStrengthRegularExpression=""

type="System.Web.Security.SqlMembershipProvider,System.Web,Version=2.0.0.0,↵
Culture=neutral,PublicKeyToken=b03f5f7f11d50a3a" />
        </providers>
      </membership>


      <!-- role provider -->
      <roleManager enabled="true" defaultProvider="aspnetRoleManager">
        <providers>
          <add
            name="aspnetRoleManager"
            connectionStringName="aspnetConnectionString"
            applicationName="/"
            type="System.Web.Security.SqlRoleProvider,System.Web,Version=2.0.0.0,↵
Culture=neutral,PublicKeyToken=b03f5f7f11d50a3a" />
        </providers>
      </roleManager>
```

Now, the My Site host knows where the user store is, and what kind of providers to use.

Modifying the SSP web.config

As mentioned earlier, one SSP provides critical services for many different sites — services such as user profiles, audiences, and personal sites. The SSP must know about the user store as well. You can get to the SSP from the Central Administration. Look for a section on the left titled "Share Services Administration" that contains all of the SSPs. Click yours. The SSP is typically located at a randomly generated port. Use this port number to find the Web application in IIS.

Just as you did with My Site, copy the `connectionStrings`, `membership`, and `roleManager` nodes you created when creating the user store into the `web.config` file of the SSP.

Modifying the aspnet web.config

The `aspnet` URL represents your Internet site, and this is the site you want to be using FBA. As before, modify the `web.config` by replacing the `connectionStrings` node and adding the `membership` and `roleManager` nodes from your original `web.config` when you created the user store.

You have now completed the customization of `web.config` files needed for authentication. But you haven't authorized anybody in the new user store to do anything.

Configuring SharePoint for FBA, Authentication Providers, and Permissions

Your users need permissions to the sites. This is done through Central Administration's Application Management section. There are a couple of steps to this process:

- ❏ First, the SharePoint site must know it should be using FBA and what providers to use.
- ❏ Then, users can be added to the Web application.

Setting FBA and Authentication Providers for Intranet

The first thing you must do is to tell the SharePoint `intranet` site that you want to use FBA, and what authentication providers to use for the sites. Follow these steps:

1. Open Central Administration.
2. Navigate to Application Management.
3. Click Authentication Providers.
4. In the Web application section, be sure that your newly created site of `http://intranet` is selected. If it's not, click the drop-down arrow and select Change Web Application. A modal will appear with an unconventional interface. Here you click the hyperlink of the site you want to select.
5. Click Internet zone.
6. Change the authentication type to Forms.
7. Enter the membership provider name **aspnetMembershipProvider**.

8. Enter the role manager name **aspnetRoleManager**.

9. Ensure that "Enable Client integration" is set to "yes" if you want to be able to use Office products such as Word, Excel, or even SPD. In order for the client integration to work, the user logging in must check the "Sign me in automatically" checkbox. You learn more about modifying the `logn.aspx` later in this chapter.

10. Click Save.

Now, the `intranet` application is totally aware of how to access your new user store, but there are other sites that you must make aware as well.

Setting FBA and Authentication Providers for the Personalization

For the personalization features of SharePoint to work properly for the `intranet` site, the SSP and the My Site host must have the same authentication method and use the same providers.

Following the same steps just outlined, set the SSP default zone to use FBA. Set the "Membership provider name" to **aspnetMembershipProvider** and the "Role manager name" to **aspnetRoleManager**.

Repeating the process for the My Site Host default zone, set the authentication type to Forms. Set the "Membership provider name" to **aspnetMembershipProvider** and "Role manager name" to **aspnetRoleManager**.

Setting Permissions

Now that you've modified all the `web.config` files to point to your user store, and set the Web applications to the appropriate providers and appropriate authentication method, users can be managed like normal. You must to give your ASP.NET Application Database groups the permission to create sites, as well to view them and other documents. Most urgently, you've turned the SSP on its ear and it cannot be accessed at all. You'll have to set the site collection administrator, add users to the intranet site, and, finally set the permissions for the SSP.

Setting Site Collection Administrator

Back in Application Management of Central Administration, click "Site collection administrators" in the Site Collection drop-down. Select the SSP site. In the "Secondary site collection administrator" section, type in **aspnetAdmin** and click OK.

The site collection administrators are users, not groups.

Go back into "Site collection administrators" and choose your My Site host in the Site Collection drop-down. Now, this can get a little tricky because when you select the site collection domain (as it were), you must also select the sub-site, which is `/MySite`. Set the administrator to `aspnetAdmin`. Repeat the process for the root of this site as well. One more time, go back into "Site collection administrators" and choose the site you created earlier (`intranet`) and set the site collection administrator to `aspnetadmin`.

Adding ASP.NET Application Database Users to the Intranet Site

From the Application Management page of Central Administration, click "Policy for Web application." Click "Add Users" and now an "Add Users" page presents itself. The Web application should read `http://intranet/`. If not, change it to the appropriate Web application. Select the Internet zone because you will make your `intranet` site available to the Internet. Add the "`admins`" group and click the Check Names icon. Figure 2-3 shows the mouseover after the Check Names icon has been clicked. Notice the `aspnetRoleManager:admins`.

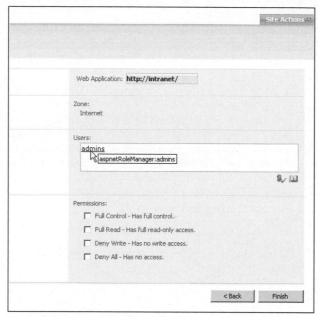

Figure 2-3: Mouseover after the Check Names icon has been clicked

If you were to add a user (say, user `aspnetAdmin`), and mouse over, you would see `aspnetMembershipProvider:aspnetAdmin`. The point here is to show you how to set up FBA so that you can easily see that the difference between the membership and the role provider. This shows you that a meaningful provider name is important. The name of the member provider is what is displayed, so it's important that the name reflect what type of users these are (maybe partner or extranet). `aspnetMembershipProvider` was used to illustrate the name of the provider and where it appears. This technique would be meaningful to users and administrators alike, and avoids a lot of confusion.

Give the Admins role Full Control permissions and click Finish. Repeat the process for Contributors and give them full access as well. Give Readers only full read permissions.

Setting Personalization Permissions

From Central Administration, choose your SSP. (It's the link just above the Recycle Bin.) The SSP now challenges you with FBA. Log in with `aspnetAdmin`. Click "Personalization services permissions" and "Add user/groups" from the menu bar. Add Admins and give them all the permissions (after all, they are admins). Add Contributors and only give them "Create personal site" and "User personal features."

Click "My Site Host Permissions." Once again, you are challenged for credentials because the URL has changed from the SSP to the root of where My Sites is hosted. Click "Site Permissions" on the left menu under Groups. Add Admins and Contributors and give them full access. Give the Readers group only read access.

You now have an `intranet` site that uses Windows authentication and an Internet site (`aspnet`) that uses FBA. For Office integration to work, the user must remember to log in to the site and check the "Sign me in automatically" checkbox. You can create you own `login.aspx` and modify it to remind the users to check the box if they want to use client integration.

Creating a login.aspx

Creating a `login.aspx` page is usually not necessary, but there may be times when you want to control branding or add functionality to the login page. Modifying any of Microsoft's code is not a good idea. Microsoft has benevolent updates that will overwrite shipping code. It's best to assume that everything in the `layouts` folder is shipping code.

So, what you should always do is to copy the pages you'd like to modify and put them in a space that is protected from Microsoft. I like to make a folder with the company name, the site, or application name. This way you can have more than one variation in your system. To do this, follow these steps:

1. Open file explorer and go to `C:\Program Files\Common Files\Microsoft Shared\web server extensions\12\TEMPLATE\LAYOUTS\`.

2. Make a new folder and call it `myCo` (short for "my company").

3. Copy the `login.aspx` from the `layouts` folder to the `myCo` folder. This is where your `login.aspx` page will be kept.

4. In all `web.config` files, change the authentication node of `system.web`. If it doesn't exist, you must add it, as shown here:

   ```
   <authentication mode="Forms">
     <forms loginUrl="/_layouts/login.aspx" />
   </authentication>
   ```

5. Change the URL to `"/_layouts/myCo/login.aspx"` so that the code now looks like this:

   ```
   <authentication mode="Forms">
     <forms loginUrl="/_layouts/login.aspx" />
   </authentication>
   ```

The result of following these steps is that you tell the system not to use the default `login.aspx`, but rather to use your version. Now there is a `login.aspx` that is protected from Microsoft updates and one that you can freely customize. Let this be a rule and guide any time you wish to modify an existing page in SharePoint.

Now you can navigate to `C:\Program Files\Common Files\Microsoft Shared\web server extensions\12\TEMPLATE\LAYOUTS\myCo` and modify how you see fit. Perhaps you could add a friendly reminder that, if users are planning on using an Office client, they must check the "Sign me in automatically" checkbox. Otherwise, the cookie will not be persisted properly for other applications to use it, and the Office clients will not run properly.

Building a Custom Application to Manage Users in the Application Database

This chapter is focused on configuring FBA, but I can't help but throw in a little bit about development. After all, getting FBA set up is just the implementation portion, but what about maintenance? What about when a user must be added to the system or a user must be removed? Or, what about groups, for that matter? Someone must maintain users somehow, and sending them to Visual Studio is probably not the best way to go.

Some have managed to surf the ASP.NET Configuration Application located at `C:\WINDOWS\Microsoft .NET\Framework\v2.0.50727\ASP.NETWebAdminFiles`, but I think I'd rather see people build their own management tool. The Configuration Application was designed to be used in Visual Studio. It's an application separate from SharePoint.

Some community work has started on `http://www.codeplex.com/features`, a site that Scot Hillier has put together. This is rapidly becoming a great starting point for SharePoint Features. There you will find a project that a few of us are working on that will allow you to manage users, groups, and other functionality from an FBA perspective. But, for those who want to build their own, I'm going to outline a few of the objects to get you started.

ASP.NET Objects and Methods

The assumption here is that you have a basic understanding of Web-based applications with ASP.NET. This section is meant to get you started.

The ASP.NET framework has a namespace, `System.Web.Security`, that supports the ASP.NET Application Database. I won't detail the building of a user management application here, but I will cover some of the more basic functionality — such as adding, editing, and deleting users; creating and deleting roles; and understanding the relationship between users and roles (just to give you a rolling start).

Starting with roles, remember that you should never assign a user to any resource, but rather always to a group or a role. It's much easier to remove a user from a role than every resource he or she has been given permission to. Besides, creating a role is really simple. `Roles` is a static class in the .NET Framework. Simply call `Roles.CreateRole(roleName);` (where `roleName` is the name of the role you'd like to create). However, if the role exists, you would get an error indicating so. That is why this class also has the `RoleExists` method, and a snippet might look something like this:

```
if (!Roles.RoleExists(roleName))
    Roles.CreateRole(roleName);
else
    //the users deserves to know the role already exists.
```

The same holds true for `Roles.DeleteRole(roleName)`.

Creating users is a little different. There is no concept of a `userExists` method in the `Membership` object. Instead, there is a `MembershipCreateStatus` object that is passed by reference to the `Membership .CreateUser` method. The `MembershipCreateStatus` then tells you if the action was successful or, if not, why not.

The following code assumes there are ASP.NET textbox controls for username, password, email, and a label, or some other equivalent to display the status message:

```
MembershipCreateStatus status;
Membership.CreateUser(
    username.Text,
    password.Text,
    email.Text,
    "question",
    "answer",
    true,
    out status);
messages.Text = status.ToString();
```

There are some other minor differences that will cause you to spend some time pondering. I'll just spell them out quickly. `Membership` has a method `GetAllUsers()` that returns a `MembershipUserCollection`, where `Roles` has a `GetAllRoles()` method that returns an array of strings. The array is fairly straightforward and the items in the `MembershipUserCollection` are of type `MembershipUser`. The following code demonstrates working with the `MembershipUserCollection` collection:

```
MembershipUserCollection users;
users = Membership.GetAllUsers();
MembershipUser user = users[username];
```

The following code demonstrates how to do the same thing more efficiently, by simply getting a user by username:

```
MembershipUser user = Membership.GetUser(username);
```

A developer can get quite far with the object model provided in the .NET Framework. But there are also some really great shortcuts when it comes to user interface development.

Getting a Head Start with the Toolbox

All of the controls in the toolbox login group in Visual Studio can be used in a SharePoint application. You've been introduced to modifying the `login.aspx`. Once you are sure that you have everything set up for a `PasswordRecovery` control (such as having email properly configured), drop it onto your `login.aspx` page, and now users can comfortably forget their passwords. The `CreateUserWizard` can be useful if you allow users to self-register on your site. The `login` control is especially useful when setting up the `web.config` file for FBA in the first place. By adding a `login` control, you know for certain whether or not the Web application can connect to the Application Database. You might have other third-party controls that are built around ASP.NET Application Database. I would be tempted to say that they would work in the SharePoint environment as well, and it is certainly worth giving a try.

Development Tip

When developing in a SharePoint environment, it's always helpful to be able to see the actual error messages. To do this, set the `CallStack` to `true`. It's a lot easier than it sounds. Open the `web.config` file of your FBA file and set the attribute shown in the following code to `true`:

```
<configuration>
    <SharePoint>
```

```
<SafeMode
        MaxControls="200"
        CallStack="true"
        DirectFileDependencies="10"
        TotalFileDependencies="50"
        AllowPageLevelTrace="false">
```

The custom error node can also be modified to offer a more familiar screen, but the important thing to note is that with the call stack turned on, everyone will always see the error messages. This modification should only be done on development servers. To see the error messages, you can navigate to `C:\Program Files\Common Files\Microsoft Shared\web server extensions\12\LOGS`, or use another one of Scott Hillier's Features found at `http://www.codeplex.com/features` that allows administrators to choose a log file and view the Web interface in Central Administration.

Active Directory for Application Mode as a User Store

This entire chapter has been based on using the ASP.NET Application Database, because it was an easy way to demonstrate some complicated steps. If you are going to consider FBA, consider connecting to an existing data store or creating an Active Directory for Application Mode (ADAM) store. ADAM is an LDAP server that is a bit more flexible to set up than Active Directory. Microsoft has provided an ADAM membership and role provider, and there are a plethora of benefits to using ADAM over ASP.NET Application Database. The biggest benefit is migration. Microsoft Office SharePoint Server (MOSS) is an enterprise application, and AD is an enterprise-level authentication server. It only makes sense that the two work well together.

ADAM is a convenient stepping stone into an AD environment. Migrating ADAM to AD is a breeze, whereas migrating ASP.NET Application Database to AD would be an aggressive undertaking. Several environments already have AD management tools. Usually, these tools can be used on ADAM as well. So, you get the benefits of easy management and maintenance by leveraging your existing investment in management tools. ADAM just makes more sense because it's more closely related to AD. It's a very common model, and makes the context switching of employees who use it much easier. The ASP.NET Application Database seems attractive on the surface.

Developers are familiar with ASP.NET Application Database, but no real management tools are available. I'd hate to see anyone try to give an administrator Visual Studio and say, "Here's what you use to manage your users."

From an FBA point of view, everything is really very similar. The only thing different is the providers to use. Now, let's use the `AuthorizationStoreRoleProvider` for the role manager and the `ActiveDirectoryMembershipProvider` as the membership provider. In this case, `connectionString` doesn't connect to a database, but rather it connects to an LDAP store. After making this change to all of the appropriate Web applications, it's simply a matter of setting the authentication providers and setting permissions. The following is an example of a connection string, role manager, and membership provider:

```
<connectionStrings>
 <add
    name="AzManADAMServer"        connectionString="msldap://localhost:389/
CN=AzManADAMStore,OU=Extranet,O=WildWires,C=US" />
```

```
</connectionStrings>

<membership>
  <providers>
    <add
    name="ADAMMembershipProvider"
    connectionStringName="ADConnectionString"
    enableSearchMethods="true"
    connectionProtection="None"
    connectionUsername="CN=StacyDraper,CN=Users,OU=Extranet,O=WildWires,C=US"
    connectionPassword="StacyDraper"
type="System.Web.Security.ActiveDirectoryMembershipProvider, System.Web,
Version=2.0.0.0, Culture=neutral,  PublicKeyToken=b03f5f7f11d50a3a" />
  </providers>
</membership>

<roleManager>
 <providers>
  <add
   connectionStringName="AzManADAMServer"
   applicationName="/"
   name="RoleManagerAzManADAMProvider"
type="System.Web.Security.AuthorizationStoreRoleProvider, System.Web,
Version=2.0.0.0, Culture=neutral,
publicKeyToken=b03f5f7f11d50a3a" />
  </providers>
</roleManager>
```

> For readability, the container nodes (connection string, membership, and role manager) have been added. These container nodes can take more than one add node. A Web application could then have ADAM and ASP.NET Application Database in the same web.config file.

All configurations have been in the web.config file. This can also be done in the machine.config instead, eliminating the need to update each web.config file individually. The downside to this is that it affects all sites, and though it might keep the maintainability down, it might also decrease your agility. Another thing to consider is connecting to an existing data store.

Custom Providers

There are quite a few companies out there that do not use AD to store information about their people. This could be very difficult with the personalization and membership aspects. Creating your own custom provider can be the solution. Though this chapter is not about creating custom providers, it is important to know that ASP.NET 2.0 has a pluggable provider model.

A pluggable provider simply means that, by inheriting an interface or existing object, a developer could build a role provider and membership provider to anything that ASP.NET can talk to. This way, an organization can easily leverage the data and investment that it has in its existing "people" management application.

Consider Using Internet Security and Acceleration Server

Setting up Internet Security and Acceleration (ISA) Server is well outside the scope of this chapter, because the discussion here only describes how to configure FBA. But that doesn't mean that it should go unnoticed. If you or your organization has the capability to leverage an ISA Server, you might want to consider an ISA Server in your list of options when it comes to alternate authentication. One of the greatest benefits to ISA Server is that no configuration takes place on the SharePoint server. The server simply looks to ISA as it would AD and authenticates against ISA. Many of the problems that have been solved in FBA magically don't even present themselves, because SharePoint natively understands this type of authentication.

Chapter 12 discusses ISA Server in more detail.

Summary

Now you can configure SharePoint to use FBA all the way through to My Site functionality. There are many places that you must configure the `web.config` files for the site you created in this chapter (Central Administration, My Site host, and the SSP). Configuring the authentication providers in the system allowed you to add users. This walkthrough went into great detail, but in many situations, you may not need to bring My Sites to your FBA users. SharePoint's new interface will only show users what they are allowed to do, security-trimmed. In this way, FBA users can still come in, surf the site, and even see employees' My Sites if you want to allow that.

Here are just a few things to know:

❑   If all else fails, use `IISreset`.

❑   SharePoint can only provide personalization functionality for the authentication method of the SSP. FBA and challenge response are two totally different authentication techniques. You can, however, have more than one FBA provider, and they will work together well.

❑   By putting My Site on its own URL, you will have greater scalability, but users will have to log in twice.

❑   By putting My Site on the same URL as the external-facing site, those users will not have to log in twice, but everything will be going into one content database and will be more difficult to maintain.

❑   In regard to SQL server, you can connect to whatever you can write a provider for. Microsoft has created a pluggable authentication provider framework. So, if the users aren't in AD, but are in some accounting package or other system, a provider can be written to connect to those systems and leverage those user accounts in the native system.

3

Understanding SharePoint Administration

by Todd Klindt

SharePoint is fun. SharePoint is great. I started working with SharePoint on a lark years ago when it was still code-named Tahoe, and came bundled with Office 2000. My boss saw it at a Microsoft conference and was smitten. Even then, SharePoint provided us with amazing and much needed collaboration capabilities. When the next version of SharePoint came out in 2003, I was blown away. It had so many more capabilities, and with that came greater complexity. Of course, the 2007 version of SharePoint raised the bar even higher in power, but also complexity.

In this chapter, I cover some of the issues I've encountered in the field as an IT professional moving from Windows SharePoint Services (WSS) v2 to Microsoft Office SharePoint Server (MOSS) 2007/WSS v3. I'll share with you how the tasks I performed in WSS v2 have changed to WSS v3. This includes the new ways that WSS v3 interacts with Internet Information Services (IIS), and how managing WSS is different now. I also cover SharePoint's command-line administration tool, STSADM, and what new functionality it has. Any good SharePoint administrator has to script things from time to time, and STSADM is the way to go for that. Plus, there are a few tweaks to SharePoint you can only do in STSADM. After you read this chapter, your users will thank you.

Central Administration

Although SharePoint v2 was a great product, as an administrator, I saw some places where it could be better. Microsoft listened to our pleas and improved the management of SharePoint immensely in v3. The first radical change was a complete revamp of Central Administration (or Central Admin). One of Microsoft's most heard enhancement requests was for a search inside of

Central Admin. This was a clear indicator to them that something needed to be done to make Central Admin easier for the administrator. Rather than reinvent the wheel, Microsoft made Central Admin a regular SharePoint site — a special type of site, but a site just the same (Figure 3-1). Because of this, Central Admin has a lot features that make it easy to use, and easy to customize.

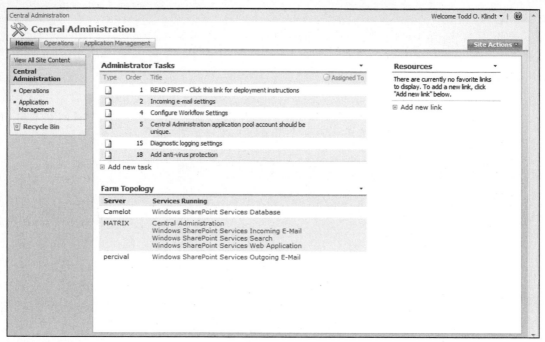

Figure 3-1: The Central Admin site

As you can see from Figure 3-1, Central Admin has a much more dynamic appearance in v3 than it did in v2. If you're reading this book, you've probably seen Central Admin before. You may not have recognized all the features that have been added, because there's a lot of options in there.

First, notice the blue question mark in the upper right-hand corner. This is searchable help that is specific to the Central Admin. If you have a question about content databases, search there for "content databases." If you can't remember where the link is to create a new site collection, search for "create site collection."

Because Central Admin is a SharePoint site, it also uses breadcrumbs to aid navigation, as shown in Figure 3-2.

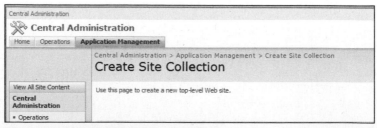

Figure 3-2: Breadcrumbs in Central Admin

You can see from the breadcrumb in Figure 3-2 that the Create Site Collection page is at Central Admin, then Application Management, and then Create Site Collection. Any applications that install on top of SharePoint can take advantage of this and use breadcrumbs to help to integrate themselves into Central Admin. You can also create content in Central Admin. You can add Web Parts to the Central Admin Home page, and you can create lists and libraries in Central Admin. You could use this to save administrative documents for other members of the team, create a wiki for processes, or host a discussion board. The Quick Link bar at the top can be edited, and additional links can be added. Because Central Admin is a site collection, it also has its own content databases that will need to be backed up as well.

Backups

Backups are another new addition to Central Administration. You can back up sites and configurations, and restore them, all within the Central Admin site. On the Operations tab, there are four backup and restore related links, as shown in the lower-right portion of Figure 3-3.

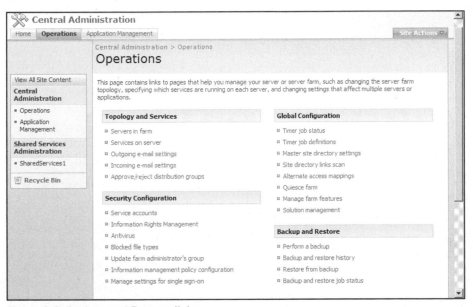

Figure 3-3: Backup and Restore links

Clicking the first link, "Perform a backup," starts the backup process. You can see from Figure 3-4 that Step 1 of the backup process gives you very granular control over what is or is not backed up. You can back up the entire farm, or a single content database.

As shown in Figure 3-5, Step 2 lets you choose what type of backup to do, either a full or differential, and where that backup should be saved. Ensure that the location you specify is accessible by the account your Application Pool and SQL are running as. The backup process uses a combination of SQL to dump tables to disc, and SharePoint to back up objects. If your SQL server is not the same as your Web Front End (WFE), you'll need to specify a Universal Naming Code (UNC) path instead of a local one, because two separate boxes and processes will be writing to it.

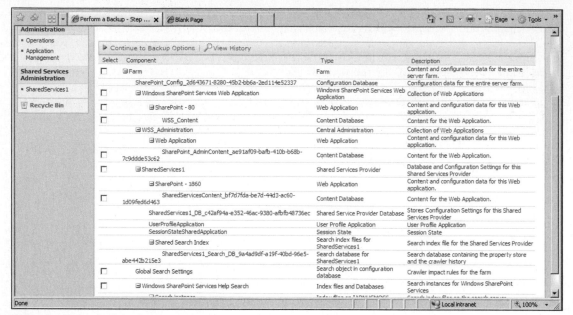

Figure 3-4: Step 1 of the backup process

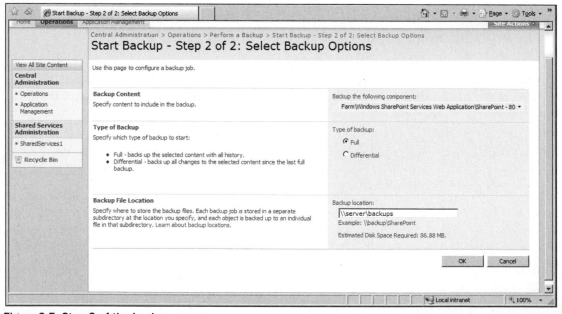

Figure 3-5: Step 2 of the backup process

Once the backup starts, you'll be taken to a screen to monitor the backup job as it runs. SharePoint uses the Timer Service to run this job, so you can also monitor it from the Timer Job Status page at Central Administration ⇨ Operations ⇨ Timer Job Status. If the backup job fails for any reason, you'll need to remove it from the Timer Job Definitions (Figure 3-6) before you can run another backup or restore. You can edit jobs from the Edit Timer Job page (Figure 3-7).

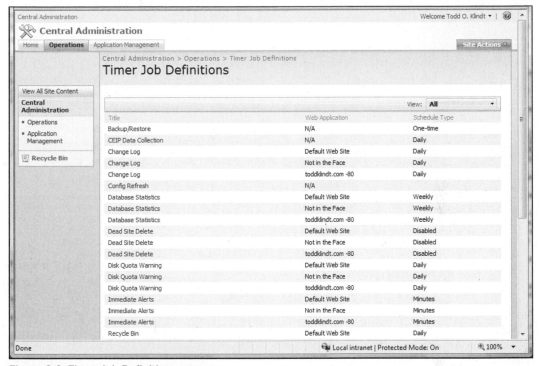

Figure 3-6: Timer Job Definitions page

You'll notice a file in the root of the directory you wrote your backup to, spbrtoc.xml. As the name suggests, this is a "Table of Contents" for your SharePoint Backups and Restores. It's a standard XML file, so feel free to open it up and look around. The backups themselves are stored in directories starting with spbr, followed by an incrementing four-digit number. That directory holds the backup files, as well as a log file and an XML file that describes the backup job and lays out what is contained inside of each backup file. If there are any problems with the backup, you can use the log file to determine what the problem was.

Restore

Of course, backups are no good if you can't restore them. You can use the "Backup and restore history" link on Operations tab to see what backups you've performed, and restore them if you need to. If you click it, you will see the option to change the directory. With this option, you can choose to save your backups in different spots, and point the restore to them as you need. If you do a restore with the "Restore from backup" link, you'll also have the option of loading the backups from a specific directory. You must point it at a directory with a spbrtoc.xml file, because that's what Central Admin uses to determine which backups are available. Once you choose a backup job to restore, you'll be able to decide how much of that backup to restore. The most you can restore is the entire farm; the least you can restore is a single content database.

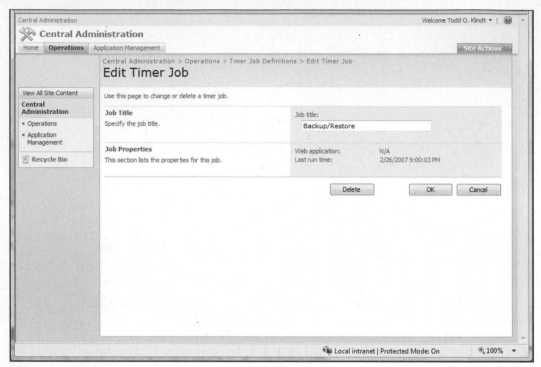

Figure 3-7: Edit Timer Job page

As you can see, using Central Admin to back up or restore your environment is very easy and convenient. It does have a few deficiencies, though, so you should use it to supplement your existing disaster-recovery plan. You cannot use Central Admin to schedule a backup. Backups can only be done interactively. Also, if you need to restore a single document or site collection, you must restore the entire content database to get it back. Later in this chapter in the section, "Backup and Recovery with STSADM," I discuss some other ways to back up and restore your SharePoint content with STSADM.

New Operational Features

Now that you know how to back up your settings, let's dig in and make some changes. In this section, I highlight some of the other operations you can do in the Operations tab in Central Admin. I won't cover everything, but I will cover the functionality that has been improved from WSS v2/SPS 2003, and a couple of new features that are really exciting.

Incoming Email

Under the Topology and Services heading is an interesting link: "Incoming e-mail settings." One of the more requested features for SharePoint was the ability to email content to SharePoint lists and libraries. WSS v2 and SPS 2003 could pull attachments out of Exchange Public Folders, but they couldn't attach the text of the message to the attachment. This didn't meet the needs of most customers who wanted to bring email into SharePoint. With WSS v3/MOSS 2007, incoming email gets completely revamped, and it's pretty impressive. Not all lists or libraries can be email-enabled. Table 3-1 shows a list of which can and cannot receive incoming email.

Table 3-1: Incoming Email Compatibility

Incoming Email Works On	Incoming Email Does Not Work On
Document libraries	Links lists
Announcements	Wikis
Calendars	Blog catagories
Discussion boards	Blog comments
	Surveys
	Tasks
	Project tasks
	Contacts

If you send an email to a calendar list, it must be a .VCS file. In Outlook, send the calendar location a Meeting Request or an Appointment for it to show up correctly.

The first step to using Incoming e-mail is to ensure that the SMTP service is installed locally on your WSS/ MOSS server. I also recommend enabling all the logging for the SMTP service, as shown in Figure 3-8. The logs don't take up much space, and they can be invaluable when it comes time to troubleshoot. They are a good addition to the SharePoint logs found at C:\Program Files\Common Files\Microsoft Shared\ Web Server Extensions\12\LOGS\ when you're troubleshooting.

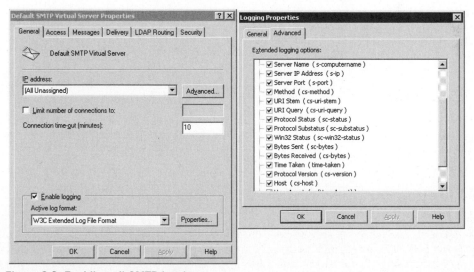

Figure 3-8: Enabling all SMTP logging

Once you've done that, go into Central Administration ⇨ Operations ⇨ Incoming E-mail Settings (Figure 3-9). Incoming E-mail doesn't take a lot configuration. You can get away with just enabling sites to receive mail and setting the display address. You'll also need to ensure that your email environment knows to route email to your server. This may involve setting MX records in DNS, or creating an SMTP connector in Exchange.

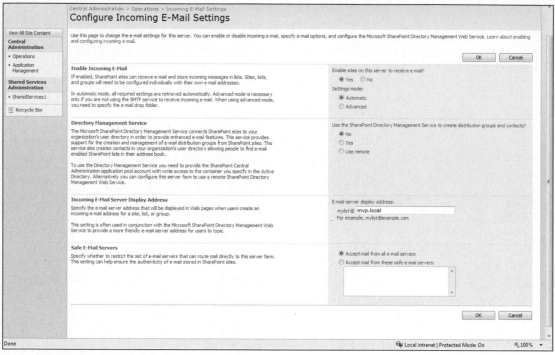

Figure 3-9: Configuring Incoming E-mail Settings screen

If you want, you can use a Directory Management Service to create contacts for your lists automatically in Active Directory. This has the advantage of exposing your SharePoint lists and libraries to Outlook users without any more work on your part. If you choose not to use a Directory Management Service, your users can email the library addresses directly, or you can create contacts in Active Directory manually.

Once Incoming E-mail is enabled in Central Admin, you still need to enable it for the lists and libraries you want to be able to send email to. Follow these steps:

1. Go to the Site Settings for your SharePoint site.

2. Click "Site libraries and lists" under Site Administration.

3. Click the "customize" link for the list or library.

4. Click "Incoming e-mail settings" under Communications.

5. Select Yes under "Allow this list to receive e-mail" and give it an address.

Different types of lists have some additional settings you can tweak here as well. For example, with a document library, you'll also need to decide how you want to handle attachments, and whether you want to restrict who can email to this library or list. If the email comes from an address that SharePoint can resolve, the item will show as being created by it. If SharePoint cannot resolve the address, the item will show up as being created by the System Account. That's it. Now you're ready to start emailing your SharePoint sites.

Web Applications

With previous versions of SharePoint, administrators spent a lot of time switching between Central Administrator and IIS Manager. A lot of SharePoint setup and configuration had to be done in IIS Manager, and there was no way to accomplish those tasks in Central Admin. With WSS v3 and MOSS 2007, that's all changed. Now you can complete almost all aspects of your site creation without leaving the comfort of Central Admin. There still a few things that Central Admin can't handle. For example, if you will be using an SSL certificate with your site, you'll still need to add that in IIS Manager.

In WSS v3 and MOSS 2007, each site hosted on a Web server is called a *Web application* (or *Web app*). In WSS v2 and SPS 2003, these were known as *virtual servers*. That name was changed to avoid confusion with Microsoft's Virtual Server product. To create a new Web app, go into Central Admin ⇨ Application Management ⇨ Create or Extend Web Application. From here, you can create a new Web application (as shown in Figure 3-10), or extend an existing Web application. When creating new content, you'll want to create a new Web application. If you want to publish existing content with different policies or to a different zone, choose Extend Existing Site.

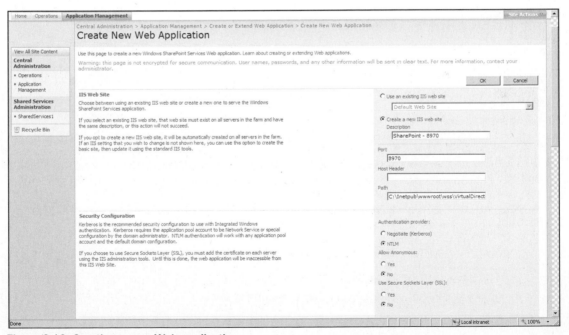

Figure 3-10: Creating a new Web application

In Figure 3-10, you can see the first part of the page where you create a new Web app. If you want to extend an existing IIS Web site with SharePoint, you can, but you can also create a new IIS Web site for SharePoint without having to go into IIS Manager. If you'll be hosting multiple sites on a single WFE, you can choose different ports for each Web app, or use host headers. You can also choose here what kind of authentication to use with your site.

The next settings (Figure 3-11) let you choose a load-balanced URL. This setting sets the Default zone URL for the Web application. You would only change this if you have several WFEs serving up the same content and will be load-balancing them with something like the Windows Network Load Balancing Service. Your application pool settings can be configured here, allowing you to use an existing one or create a new one. Central Admin will also run IISRESET for you. That's a nice change from previous versions, where you had to run IISRESET yourself.

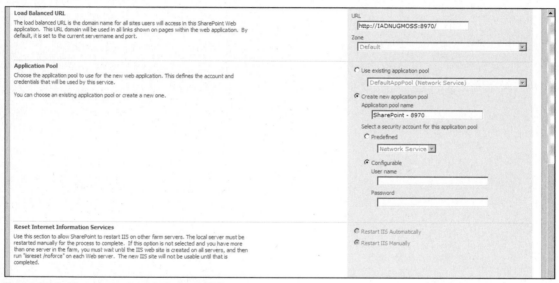

Figure 3-11: Choosing a load-balanced URL

The final part of setting up the new Web app is the database configuration shown in Figure 3-12. Your Web app will need at least one content database to store its content. You can allow SharePoint to name it for you, or you can choose your own name. If you want to use an existing content database, you can put its name in here and SharePoint will use it. You would do this if you were moving a content database from one server to another (for example, in a test environment).

If you do this in a MOSS environment, use the STSADM operation preparetomove to prepare the content database before you detach the database. This will ensure that the synchronization service won't fail when it's attached to the new environment. This way, your users' profiles will keep synchronized and the list of sites they have access to in their My Site will stay accurate.

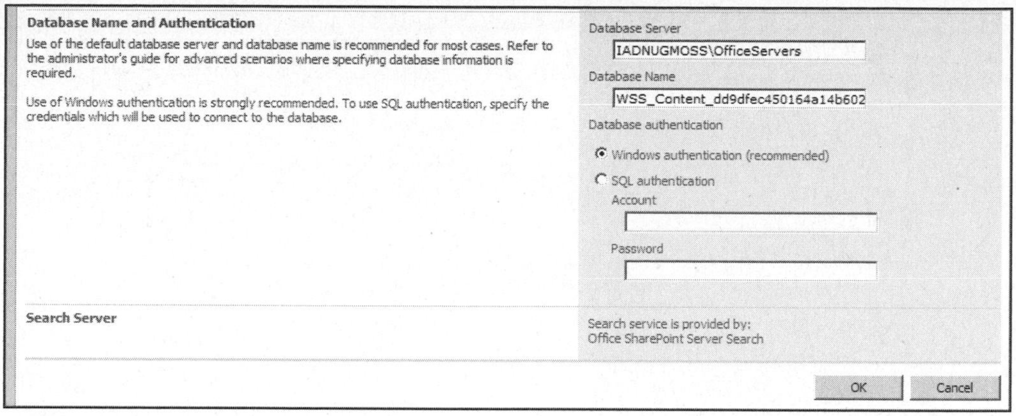

Database Name and Authentication

Use of the default database server and database name is recommended for most cases. Refer to the administrator's guide for advanced scenarios where specifying database information is required.

Use of Windows authentication is strongly recommended. To use SQL authentication, specify the credentials which will be used to connect to the database.

Database Server

`IADNUGMOSS\OfficeServers`

Database Name

`WSS_Content_dd9dfec450164a14b602`

Database authentication

⦿ Windows authentication (recommended)

○ SQL authentication

Account

Password

Search Server

Search service is provided by:
Office SharePoint Server Search

OK   Cancel

Figure 3-12: Database configuration

If you already have a Web app defined, you can create a new Web app and extend your existing one. You would do this if you wanted to have your content published with different policies. For example, you could publish content internally and allow anonymous access, and publish the same content to an extranet and require a login. Let's walk through that.

First, create a Web application by following the previous instructions. This site will represent an internal site. Let's call it "mvp" for ease of demonstration. Because we trust the users on the internal network, we will allow anonymous access to the site. This will allow internal users who are not using Windows or Internet Explorer to access the site without needing to log in. To do this, go to Central Administration ⇨ Application Management ⇨ Authentication Providers. Ensure that the mvp Web application is selected from the drop-down. There should be only one zone listed, Default, as shown in Figure 3-13. Click it to edit its properties. Ensure that the checkbox next to "Enable anonymous access" is checked.

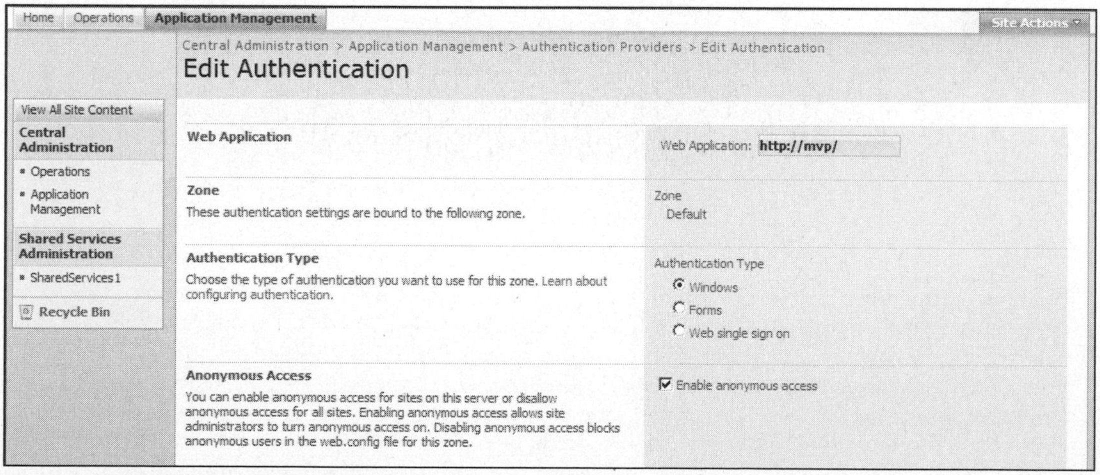

Figure 3-13: Edit Authentication screen

That setting just makes it possible to assign permissions to the anonymous user. It doesn't actually provide the user with access to anything. To do that, go into the Site Settings of the site itself. Go to `http://mvp` in your browser. Navigate to Site Settings ➪ Advanced Permissions. Select Anonymous Access from the Settings button, as shown in Figure 3-14.

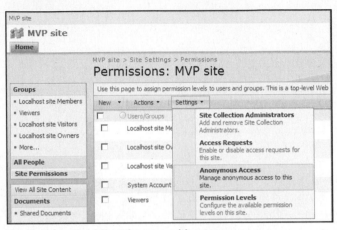

Figure 3-14: Providing the user with access

For this exercise, give the anonymous user access to the entire site. While you're at the site, create some content such as adding an announcement. Do something so that the site doesn't just look like an untouched site. That will make it easier to see what you are accessing when you extend it. To test that anonymous access works, log out of the site by clicking Logout from the Welcome message, as shown in Figure 3-15. Verify that you can access the site without logging in.

Figure 3-15: Logging out of the test site

Now, let's extend the Web application for extranet users. Go back into Central Administration ➪ Application Management ➪ Create or Extend Application ➪ Extend an existing Web application. Choose the mvp Web application from the list. Let's create a new IIS Web site called `www.toddklindt.com`. Change the port to 80 and the Host Header to `www.toddklindt.com`. Make sure that Allow Anonymous is set to No and change the Zone to Internet. Click OK and let SharePoint extend the Web application for you. If you haven't added the name you gave the host header to your DNS zone, you'll need to do that, or add an entry for it in the hosts files of whatever machines you'll be hitting it from. Adding entries to a local hosts file is also a quick-and-easy way to test host headers without having to dig into your DNS server, if you even have access to it.

Once the Web app is extended, browse to `http://www.toddklindt.com`. If all went well, you won't be able to access the site without providing a username and password. After you authenticate, you'll see the same content you were publishing as `http://mvp`. If you go to Site Settings ⇨ Advanced Permissions, you'll notice that Anonymous Access is not an option under the Settings menu. This is because you did not enable Anonymous Access in Central Administration, so SharePoint isn't even providing the option to turn it on in the site. Even though the content is the same, each zone has different settings. What's all this about zones, you ask? Good question; let's take a look at it.

Alternate Access Mappings and Zones

In the discussion in the previous section, you extended an existing Web app and published the same content with a different set of permissions. This was possible through the magic of *zones*. Zones are the different networks that SharePoint knows your users will be coming from. There are five zones defined: Intranet, Internet, Extranet, Custom, and Default.

Default is the only zone that must have a value in it (Figure 3-16). The other four can be populated if you need them. You populate them by creating *Alternate Access Mappings* (AAMs). An AAM is how you tell SharePoint what URLs your users will be using to access it, and which zone it should put those users in. You configure AAMs in Central Admin at Central Administration ⇨ Operations ⇨ Alternate Access Mappings.

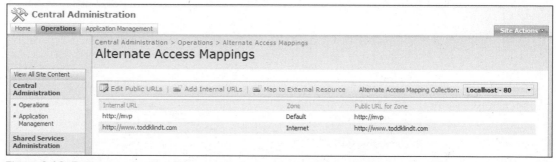

Figure 3-16: Zones

In the context of AAM, there are two types of URLs: Public and Internal. A *Public URL* is any URL that an end user might type or click to get to your SharePoint site. This might be in the form of `http://servername` if it's a server that only people inside your network access. It might also be in the form of `http://www.company.com` if the user is outside your network. Both of those URLs would be considered Public URLs to SharePoint. When SharePoint returns search results, it will base them off the Public URL the user is coming from, and all links to the site will use it as well.

The second type of URL is the *Internal URL*. This is the URL that is being sent to the SharePoint server in the request. This will only be different from the Public URL if your servers are behind something that remaps URLs, like a reverse proxy or a network load-balancer.

Figure 3-17 shows three examples of ways you might set up your Public and Internal URLs. In the first example, the Public and Internal URLs are the same. This is fine, because the firewall between the user and SharePoint does not alter the URL any. In the second example, there is a reverse proxy, such as Microsoft ISA Server 2006, between the user and SharePoint. The user is using the URL `http://www.company.com`

to access SharePoint. When the reverse proxy is fetching the SharePoint content for the user, it is using the Internal URL of `http://mvp` to contact the SharePoint server. You would need to create an AAM mapping `http://www.company.com` to `http://mvp` so that SharePoint will be able to create the links correctly as it builds the page and sends it back to the user. In the last example, there is a hardware load-balancer between the user and SharePoint. The load-balancer spreads user requests between the SharePoint servers in the back-end. It may make requests to `http://wfe01` or `http://wfe02` on behalf of the user. An AAM would need to be created for each of the back-end servers so that SharePoint could correctly map requests back to the end user.

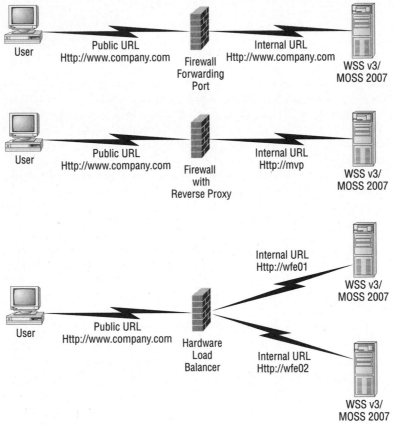

Figure 3-17: Public and Internal URLs

A common problem I've seen administrators make is not creating AAMs for their Internet-facing URLs. The only AAM that SharePoint creates on its own is for the Default zone, and it sets that to the machine's hostname. If you simply make an entry in DNS for your Internet-facing address and point it at your SharePoint server, users who use that address will not be able to access your content. Without an AAM to tell SharePoint how to format the request, requests made to `http://www.company.com` will be transformed to the Default zone, which is inaccessible to your external users. The fix is to create an AMM with your Internet URL as both the Public and Internal URL.

With AAMs set up similar to Figure 3-16, people will be able to browse your site from the Internet without problems.

Now that you have a handle on AAMs, let's move on to zones and put them all together.

Zones and Authentication Methods

As mentioned earlier in this chapter, zones allow you to publish content to different URLs and with different authentication providers. One of the pain points in WSS v2 and SPS 2003 was that they only supported Windows NT LAN Manager (NTLM) and basic authentication. WSS v3 and MOSS 2007 support NTLM authentication, as well as allowing you to take advantage of any ASP.NET authentication providers. This allows you to create a forms-based login to SharePoint, which was something administrators that maintain Internet-facing servers have wanted for years. You can combine AAMs, zones, and authentication providers to meet nearly any authentication need you have.

The example earlier in the chapter showed how to extend a Web application and assign different authentication properties. In the example, the only difference was whether or not anonymous access was available. Using zones, you can cater the authentication method to the network your users are coming from.

A typical scenario would be to publish your content to your internal network and use NTLM authentication, and maybe enable anonymous access, depending on your security plan. As an administrator, one of the complaints I get the most is about users having to log in. It seems most every user must type the password more times than he or she thinks should be necessary. By using NTLM and anonymous access, you lower the number of times your users are prompted, and likely lower the number of angry Help Desk tickets you'll receive.

If you want to make this content also available to the Internet, you'll want different policies. For one, you probably won't want anonymous access enabled, because you don't everyone in the world being able to see your content. Also, NTLM will do Internet users no good, because they are likely not logged in as an account on your domain. In this case, you would extend your existing Web application and use the Internet zone for the new Web app. You have two good options now. You can use a forms-based login with the account information stored in SQL. I won't go into how to do that here. Stacy Draper covers that in Chapter 2. You can also choose to use basic authentication. If you do, be sure you run it over SSL so that your users' passwords aren't sent over the Internet in the clear.

Although most of this was possible in previous versions of SharePoint, SharePoint didn't handle it very well. When it formed the URLs that it sent back the user, they wouldn't consistently have a URL that matched how the user was accessing the site. That problem is now gone when you use AAMs and zones. It's important to note that you can only assume a single authentication provider to any Web application, which is why you must extend it to use a different one. Because it is a separate Web app, the URL namespace will be different. It's not a huge deal, but it's something to keep in mind as you're planning your environment.

STSADM

As a SharePoint administrator who can't program, STSADM has been a ray of sunshine on some of my dreariest days. In this section, I give you an introduction to STSADM and show you some of the ways I use STSADM to make magic on SharePoint.

Introduction to STSADM

STSADM is a command-line tool that is included with SharePoint. It's a command-line administrative tool that dates back to when SharePoint was called SharePoint Team Services (STS). It's located in the `bin` directory of what we SharePoint admins call "The 12 Hive." The full path to the 12 Hive is `C:\program files\common files\Microsoft shared\web server extensions\12`. STSADM is located in the `bin` folder there. That path is quite a mouthful, so I take a few steps to make working with STSADM and other hive-based files less painful. Which ones work best for you is a matter of personal preference and of your environment.

The first thing I do is add `C:\program files\common files\Microsoft shared\web server extensions\12\bin` to my `Path` variable. This means that I can use STSADM from anywhere. Some programs don't handle long `Path` variables well, so there are other options.

Second, you can create a shortcut to `CMD.exe` and put the `bin` folder of the 12 Hive as the "Start in" path. `STSADM.exe` also has an icon you can use, if you don't want to use the standard `CMD.exe` icon. The properties for the shortcut will look like Figure 3-18. This allows quick access to STSADM without requiring your `Path` variable to become obscenely long.

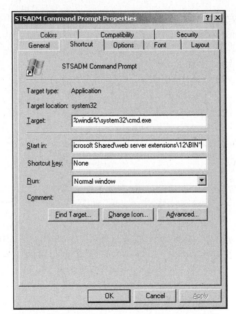

Figure 3-18: Properties for the shortcut

The third option is to create a system variable that points to the `bin` directory. Then you can just `cd` to that variable and you're there, without all the messy typing. I use the variable `hive` and point it at the 12 Hive. Figure 3-19 shows how it looks.

Be sure that you create a system variable so that all your administrators can take advantage of it. Also, be sure that you set it in a way that persists outside of the existing command prompt. If you use SET from the command prompt, it will only work in that window, and will go away when you close that window. Set the variable in Control Panel ➪ System ➪ Advanced.

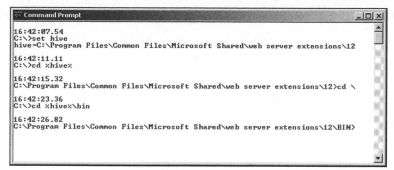

Figure 3-19: Creating a system variable pointing to the `bin` **directory**

Got the Time?

You might have noticed that my command prompt displays the time on the line before the path. I do this to give me an idea when I execute commands, and how long they take. There are a couple of ways to set it up.

The easiest way is to use the PROMPT command. If you use PROMPT /?, you can see the usage. I use the string T_PG to give me the time and path the way it's shown in the figures in this chapter. If you decide that you want your prompt to always look that way, set an environment variable PROMPT to the string. Do this in Control Panel ⇨ System the same way you would set the Hive variable. If you do that, every command-prompt window will have your custom prompt.

Any of these three methods will make it easy to get to and use STSADM. Now that your environment is all set up, let's dig in and start using it.

Using STSADM

STSADM is a tremendously powerful tool. Let's start out by going through some common administrative tasks and show how you accomplish them using STSADM. Normally, you'd perform these tasks in Central Admin. As you read before, I really like the new Central Admin interface, but GUIs can be clumsy for repetitive processes. This is where scriptable command-line interface programs such STSADM really shine.

Let's take a look at a very common administrative task: creating a new site collection. To find out if STSADM can do this, type **STSADM** at a command prompt. When it's passed no parameters, it will give you a list of the operations it supports. It also gives you a few examples of how to use them. You'll find the list is quite long, and will probably scroll past your command-prompt window. When this happens to me, I pipe the output through `find` and search for a word I think will be in the operation, as shown in Figure 3-20.

I see two commands in Figure 3-20 that might create a site for us: `createsite` and `createsiteinnewdb`. There is even an example of how to use `createsite`. To see how to use a command, you can usually provide it with no parameters. If STSADM doesn't get all information it needs to execute an operation, it will return the usage for that command (Figure 3-21). You can also pass the operation name to `-help` to get the usage for it.

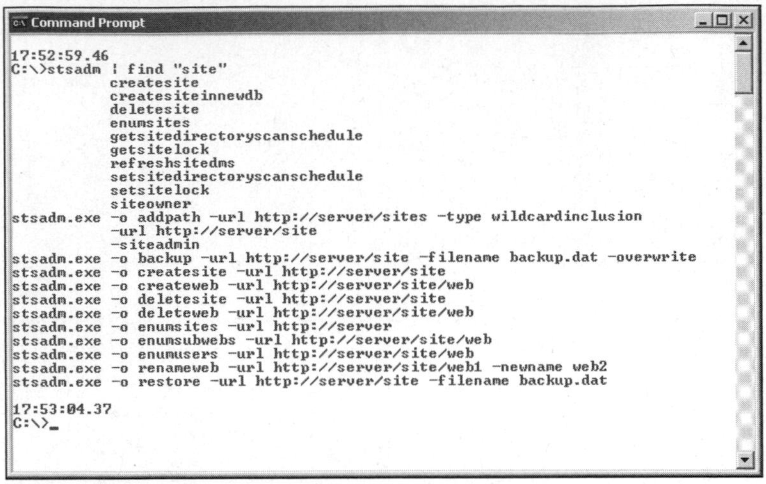

```
Command Prompt                                                    _|□|×|
17:52:59.46
C:\>stsadm | find "site"
            createsite
            createsiteinnewdb
            deletesite
            enumsites
            getsitedirectoryscanschedule
            getsitelock
            refreshsitedms
            setsitedirectoryscanschedule
            setsitelock
            siteowner
stsadm.exe -o addpath -url http://server/sites -type wildcardinclusion
            -url http://server/site
            -siteadmin
stsadm.exe -o backup -url http://server/site -filename backup.dat -overwrite
stsadm.exe -o createsite -url http://server/site
stsadm.exe -o createweb -url http://server/site/web
stsadm.exe -o deletesite -url http://server/site
stsadm.exe -o deleteweb -url http://server/site/web
stsadm.exe -o enumsites -url http://server
stsadm.exe -o enumsubwebs -url http://server/site/web
stsadm.exe -o enumusers -url http://server/site/web
stsadm.exe -o renameweb -url http://server/site/web1 -newname web2
stsadm.exe -o restore -url http://server/site -filename backup.dat

17:53:04.37
C:\>_
```

Figure 3-20: Piping the output and searching for a word

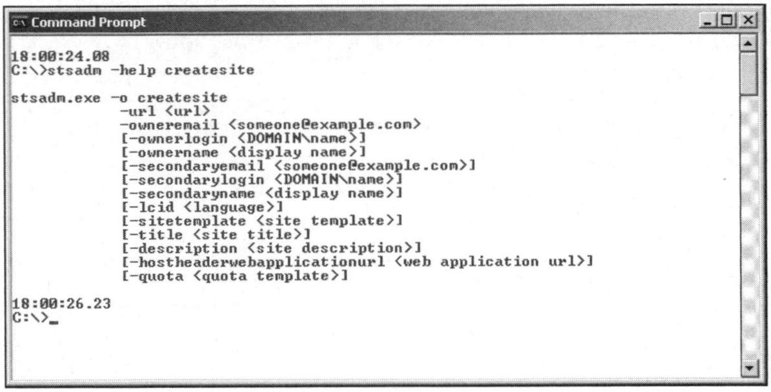

```
Command Prompt                                                    _|□|×|
18:00:24.08
C:\>stsadm -help createsite

stsadm.exe -o createsite
            -url <url>
            -owneremail <someone@example.com>
            [-ownerlogin <DOMAIN\name>]
            [-ownername <display name>]
            [-secondaryemail <someone@example.com>]
            [-secondarylogin <DOMAIN\name>]
            [-secondaryname <display name>]
            [-lcid <language>]
            [-sitetemplate <site template>]
            [-title <site title>]
            [-description <site description>]
            [-hostheaderwebapplicationurl <web application url>]
            [-quota <quota template>]

18:00:26.23
C:\>_
```

Figure 3-21: Getting usage for a command

Here you can see what information STSADM needs to create a new site for you with -o createsite. For the most part, this is all the same information you provide when you create a new site collection in Central Admin. You can assign a site template, set the owner, all the normal stuff. If you want to create an empty site collection to restore into, simply don't specify a site template when you create the site. One option that is only available via STSADM is to create a new site in its own content database. Use the operation createsiteinnewdb to do this. It is very similar to createsite, but it accepts parameters that allow you to create a content database at the same time the site is created.

You can also create a Web with the createweb operation. Once again, the information needed is very similar to what you would provide if you were creating the Web in the UI. The advantage, of course, is that it can be scripted. If you need to create many sites or Webs at the same time, or need to create the same type of site frequently, it can easily be done with a script. If you wanted to create a large number of sites quickly, you could use a for loop and a text file to do it. Create a text file that has the information you need to create your sites. It would look something like Figure 3-22.

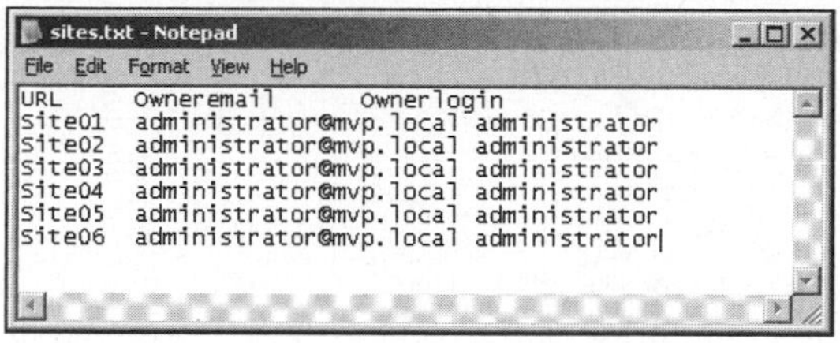

Figure 3-22: Creating a text file with information for your sites

The least information you need to create a site is the URL and the OwnerEmail. If you're not running in Active Directory Creation mode, you must provide the Ownerlogin as well. Once you have a text file with that information, you can use a for loop to walk through that file and create the sites, as shown here:

```
for /f "skip=1 tokens=1-3" %a in (sites.txt) do @stsadm -o createsite -url
http://server/sites/%a -owneremail %b -ownerlogin %c
```

That's all you need. That command will walk through sites.txt and create sites based on the information in there. The skip=1 option tells for to ignore the first line so that you can put headers and remember what each column is. Tokens=1-3 tells for to use the first three columns it finds. If you want to read in additional columns, like secondarylogin, you'll need to make sure that number matches the number of columns.

If you don't specify a site template, the owner will be prompted to add one the first time he or she goes to the site. This gives you some flexibility in creating sites in that you don't have to assign a template to each one, and users are given flexibility. You'll also want to create a site with no template if you want to restore a site with STSADM to this new site collection. If you assign a template, you won't be able to restore into it. There is a complementary operation, deletesite, to remove sites you no longer want.

After you've gone crazy creating sites and Webs, it's easy to lose track of what's out there. If you're using MOSS, you can use features like the Site Directory to keep track of your sites. If you're using WSS, you don't have as many options. STSADM comes to the rescue once again. It has two operations, enumsites and enumsubsites, which are perfect for this. If you run enumsites against a Web application, STSADM will report back all the site collections in that Web app, as well as some pertinent information about each. The output will look something like this:

```
<Sites Count="12">
  <Site Url="http://mvp" Owner="MVP\administrator" ContentDatabase="WSS_Content"
StorageUsedMB="28.4" StorageWarningMB="0" StorageMaxMB="0" />
  <Site Url="http://mvp/MySite" Owner="NT AUTHORITY\network service"
SecondaryOwner="MVP\administrator" ContentDatabase="WSS_Content"
StorageUsedMB="0.2" StorageWarningMB="0" StorageMaxMB="0" />
  <Site Url="http://mvp/personal/administrator" Owner="MVP\administrator"
ContentDatabase="WSS_Content" StorageUsedMB="0.4"
StorageWarningMB="80"StorageMaxMB="100" />
  <Site Url="http://mvp/sites/One" Owner="MVP\administrator"
ContentDatabase="WSS_Content" StorageUsedMB="1.1" StorageWarningMB="0"
StorageMaxMB="0" />
  <Site Url="http://mvp/sites/Script01"
Owner="MVP\
administrator"ContentDatabase="WSS_Content" StorageUsedMB="0.1"
StorageWarningMB="0" StorageMaxMB="0" />
  <Site Url="http://mvp/sites/Script02"
```

```
Owner="MVP\
administrator"ContentDatabase="WSS_Content" StorageUsedMB="0.1"
StorageWarningMB="0" StorageMaxMB="0" />
  <Site Url="http://mvp/sites/Script03"
Owner="MVP\
administrator"ContentDatabase="WSS_Content" StorageUsedMB="0.1"
StorageWarningMB="0" StorageMaxMB="0" />
  <Site Url="http://mvp/sites/Script04"
Owner="MVP\
administrator"ContentDatabase="WSS_Content" StorageUsedMB="0.1"
StorageWarningMB="0" StorageMaxMB="0" />
  <Site Url="http://mvp/sites/Script05"
Owner="MVP\
administrator"ContentDatabase="WSS_Content" StorageUsedMB="0.1"
StorageWarningMB="0" StorageMaxMB="0" />
  <Site Url="http://mvp/sites/Script06"
Owner="MVP\
administrator"ContentDatabase="WSS_Content" StorageUsedMB="0.1"
StorageWarningMB="0" StorageMaxMB="0" />
  <Site Url="http://mvp/sites/Test01" Owner="MVP\administrator"
ContentDatabase="WSS_Content" StorageUsedMB="1.8" StorageWarningMB="0"
StorageMaxMB="0" />
  <Site Url="http://mvp/sites/Test2" Owner="MVP\administrator"
ContentDatabase="WSS_Content" StorageUsedMB="0.5" StorageWarningMB="0"
StorageMaxMB="0" />
</Sites>
```

That output is regular XML formatting. This means that you can manipulate it with any readily available XML utility. I primarily work with WSS, and I'm often asked by my users for a list of sites. In v2, it was very difficult to do this. To give my users a mostly current list of sites, I would pipe the output of createsites to an XML file. Then I pointed a Data View Web Part at that XML file. I used FrontPage to clean it up a bit and add links to the sites. It was very popular. With v3, you can also get a list of site collections in Central Admin at Central Administration ➪ Application Management ➪ Site Collection List.

STSADM has a few tricks up its sleeves when it comes to Webs too. Many of the operations that work with sites have similar operations for Webs. You have createweb, deleteweb, and enumsubwebs to perform common administrative tasks. My favorite Web operation is renameweb. You can use this operation to rename a Web. This one has been used when business units or projects change names. Unfortunately, there is not a corresponding operation to rename sites.

STSADM is just as happy working with users as it is working with sites. It has standard operations such as adduser and deleteuser for adding or removing users from a site. It also has an enumusers operation to tell you all the users who have been given access to a particular site. You can use the userrole operation to grant or remove roles to a site user.

The user-based STSADM operation I use the most is migrateuser, which was designed to facilitate migration of users from one domain to another. The operation would ensure that the user's account in the destination domain has the same permissions as that user's account in the original domain. The usage would look like this:

```
stsadm -o migrateuser -oldlogin olddomain\jsmith -newlogin newdomain\jsmith
```

This would give `jsmith`'s login in `newdomain` the same access it had in the `olddomain`. On the surface, it would seem like this would have a pretty limited use, because once you do a migration, you won't need it anymore. On the contrary, it has one more bit of usefulness. WSS v2 doesn't actively sync itself with Active Directory (AD). If a user is renamed in AD, you can get into a complicated situation where the user cannot be authenticated by WSS v2. `migrateuser` can migrate permissions from the old username to the new username, once the user has been renamed. WSS v3 and MOSS handle this more intelligently, but if you're still maintaining any WSS v2 installations, this little gem is a lifesaver.

Backup and Recovery with STSADM

Earlier in this chapter, I discussed Central Administration and all the functionality that's been added to it. STSADM has kept up, and you can accomplish all the same tasks I mentioned before with it. I talked about backup and restore through Central Administration first, so it makes sense to start there.

STSADM has a number of operations that deal with backups and recovery. The first thing to discuss is backups. If you execute `stsadm -help backup`, you'll get the following output for a site collection backup:

```
stsadm.exe -o backup
    -url <url>
    -filename <filename>
    [-overwrite]
```

You'll get the following output for a catastrophic backup:

```
stsadm.exe -o backup
    -directory <UNC path>
    -backupmethod <full | differential>
    [-item <created path from tree>]
    [-percentage <integer between 1 and 100>]
    [-backupthreads <integer between 1 and 10>]
    [-showtree]
    [-quiet]
```

Like Central Admin, STSADM can do farm-level backups. Let's examine them first. These backups are compatible with the Central Admin backups, so you can back up with one and recover with the other, should the need arise. Because they're compatible, you can point STSADM at an existing backup directory when you use it, and it will integrate the backup it does with the ones that already exist in the `spbrtoc.xml` file. It uses the same facilities to do its backup, so you can monitor the backup either from the command line or from Central Admin under Central Administration ➪ Operations ➪ Backup and Restore Job Status just like you would if you had started the backup in Central Admin. The command you would use would look like this:

```
stsadm -o backup -directory \\server\backup -backupmethod full
```

This would do a complete farm-level backup using STSADM. You can use the following command to verify that the backup is integrated with any previous backups you did:

```
stsadm -o backuphistory -directory \\server\backup
```

You should see the backup you just did at the top of the list. A backup is no good if you can't restore it, so let's delete some content and restore it using STSADM. I used STSADM -o enumsites to get a list of site collections on one of my Web apps, then STSADM -o deletesite to delete one. Go ahead and delete a site collection and use -o enumsites to verify that it is gone.

Now, let's walk through restoring that site collection. When you ran the -o backuphistory, you got the backup ID for the backup job you just ran. Now let's see what you can restore from that. Use the backup ID for your job in the following command:

```
stsadm -o restore -showtree -backupid 7ea8e17a-27f2-09a3-d07d-481e018a9101
-directory \\server\backup -quiet
```

The output you'll get will look like this:

```
Farm\
    [SharePoint_Config_2d643671-8280-45b2-bb6a-2ed114e52337]\
    Windows SharePoint Services Web Application\
        Localhost - 80\
            WSS_Content_localhost\
    [WSS_Administration]\
        [Web Application]\
            [SharePoint_AdminContent_ae91af09-bafb-410b-b68b-7c9ddde53c62]\
    SharedServices1\
        [SharePoint - 1860]\
            SharedServicesContent_bf7d7fda-be7d-44d3-ac60-1d09fed6d463\
        [SharedServices1_DB_c42af94a-e352-46ac-9380-afbfb48736ec]\
        [UserProfileApplication]\
        [SessionStateSharedApplication]\
        [Shared Search Index]\
            [SharedServices1_Search_DB_9a4ad9df-a19f-40bd-96e5-abe442b215e3]
\
        Global Search Settings\
        Windows SharePoint Services Help Search\
            [Search instance]\
                [WSS_Search_MVP]\

        [ ] - item cannot be selected.
          *  - not selected to be restored.

To start the backup or restore process, run the command again omitting the
-showtree option.
```

From here, you can decide how granular of a restore you want to do. Because it was a site collection that was deleted, all you really need to restore is the content database for that Web application. Of course, restoring the entire farm would get you the same results, but it carries some consequences.

First, it takes longer. Your users will want their data back as soon as possible, and recovering as little data as possible helps that. Second, if you restore additional Web apps or content databases, you'll lock users out of them while they're being restored, and will potentially lose data if it were added after the backup was run. Restoring as little as possible decreases the amount of collateral damage.

For this exercise, the site collection I want to restore is in `"Localhost - 80."` It only has one content database, so I know exactly which one to restore. My `restore` command looks like this:

```
stsadm -o restore -backupid 7ea8e17a-27f2-09a3-d07d-481e018a9101 -directory
\\server\backup -item "Localhost - 80" -restoremethod overwrite
```

STSADM will show you what it's doing while it's restoring your content database. You can also watch in Central Admin. Once the restore job is finished, SharePoint has a little cleaning up to do, but you should be able to get back to the site collection you deleted. For small environments, this would work well, and unlike Central Admin, you can schedule STSADM to do backups. However, if you have multiple site collections in a content database, you risk losing changes made to one while restoring the database to recover another.

Here's where STSADM goes above and beyond. You can use it to back up discrete site collections or Webs. Let's cover site collections first. Using `-o enumsites`, let's pick one to back up individually. Use a command like the following to back it up:

```
stsadm -o backup -url http://mvp.local/sites/recovery -filename recovery.stsadm
```

Pretty easy. You can choose any filename or extension to write your backup out to. Most people seem to use the BAK extension. I avoid that, because other backup files use it (such as SQL backups). Giving it an extension like STSADM means that there will be no confusion when tensions are high and a site needs to be restored. That backup file encompasses everything in that site collection — all the content, all the subwebs, the permissions, everything. It is full fidelity.

However, for it to work correctly when you restore it, the environment must have all the features installed that it uses, and it must be running the same version of SharePoint right down to the patch level. Like the farm backups, these backups can be restored back to the environment they came from originally, or a completely different environment.

Let's walk through a restore. First I'm going to use `-o deletesite` to remove the site, then `-o restore` to restore it:

```
stsadm -o restore -url http://mvp.local/sites/recovery -filename recovery.stsadm
-overwrite
```

The syntax is similar to `-o backup`. `restore` also supports an overwrite switch, if you don't want to delete the existing site before restoring it. You can use backup and restore to make a copy of your site collection if you'd like, but there is one caveat. If more than one instance of a site collection exists in the same Web app at the same time, they must exist in different content databases. For example, if you did the commands shown in Figure 3-23, you would receive the error if you only had one content database for your Web app.

Figure 3-23: Error produced when content database does not match

You can see from Figure 3-23 that I backed up the site `Recovery` and then tried to restore it as `Recovery-copy`. The error I received makes it sound like my content databases have hit the maximum number of sites, and there's no place to put the restored site collection. In reality, there's plenty of room in the content databases. The site won't restore because it would exist in the same database as another copy of itself. That's a problem, because each content database uses GUIDs to keep track of the Webs, lists, and other objects inside of them.

When `STSADM` backs up a site collection, it maintains those GUIDs. When it tries to restore, it cannot create lists with those GUIDs because there are already lists with those GUIDs there. To get around this, create another content database for your Web app and make sure the restored site goes into it instead. You can also use `-o import` and `-o export` to get around this.

`STSADM` will allow even more granular backups than at the site collection level. You can also export and import individual Webs. When you do imports and exports, Web and list GUIDs are regenerated, so you can get around the issue of conflicting list GUIDs.

Here's how you would use `-o export` and `-o import` to make a copy of a site inside of one content database export the site collection.

First, make sure the site has some content in it, distinguishing it from a fresh site. You could even create a subweb or two. Next, export the site with a command like this:

```
stsadm -o export -url http://mvp.local/sites/recovery -filename recovery.export
-versions 4 -includeusersecurity
```

`export` provides a lot more options than `-o backup` does. That command is telling `STSADM` to back up all versions of the files and to include user security. Next, you must create someplace to put the site. `import`, unlike `restore`, doesn't create a new site, so you must do that manually, as follows:

```
stsadm -o createsite -url http://mvp.local/sites/recovery-copy -owneremail
administrator@mvp.local -ownerlogin mvp\administrator -sitetemplate STS#1
```

This command creates a new site collection called `Recovery-Copy`. It sets the local administrator as the owner and applies the Team Site template.

After the site collection is created, you can import the contents of the old site into it. Use a command like this one:

```
stsadm -o import -url http://localhost/sites/recovery-copy -filename
recovery.export -includeusersecurity
```

That command will merge all the content that was exported from the original site into the newly created one. It's not an exact restore, so you may notice some oddities, such as duplicate "Getting Started…" announcements. This is why I used a blank template in the example, so that there would not be any duplicate content. `import` and `export` also do individual Webs, so they can be used to copy and move Webs from one site collection to another.

Site Templates

STSADM has an operation that enumerates Site Templates. However, it will not show you the Site Templates that are included with SharePoint, only templates you add with -o addtemplate. If you tried to do STSADM -o enumtemplates to see where I got the template name "STS#1," you'll be disappointed. I had to pull that out of an XML file and from scouring the Internet. Here's a partial list of the built-in Site Templates and their names:

- ❑ STS#0 — Team Site
- ❑ STS#1 — Blank Site
- ❑ STS#2 — Document Workspace
- ❑ MPS#0 — Basic Meeting Workspace
- ❑ MPS#1 — Blank Meeting Workspace
- ❑ MPS#2 — Decision Meeting Workspace
- ❑ MPS#3 — Social Meeting Workspace
- ❑ MPS#4 — Multipage Meeting Workspace
- ❑ BLOG#0 — Blog Site
- ❑ WIKI#0 — Wiki Site

Managing Web Applications and Zones with STSADM

You can manipulate Web applications and zones handily with STSADM. It has several operations to administration of Web applications. When looking through STSADM operations, keep in mind that they are still referred to as "vs" for Virtual Server. That's a holdover from earlier versions of SharePoint. You can use STSADM to create a Web app with -o extendvs. Like Central Admin, STSADM will take care of all the IIS side portions of the Web app creation process. You can also extend a Web app to an existing Web app. Figure 3-24 shows a comparison of the two operations.

Much like Central Admin, the two are very similar. To remove a Web app, use the unextendvs operation.

After your Web apps are created, you can use STSADM to add and remove zones as well. You can use -o enumszoneurls to see what zones a particular Web app has. addzoneurl will allow you to assign a new zone and AAM to a Web app. deletezoneurl will remove it. Finally, if you have a URL and aren't sure what zone it's from, -o geturlzone will report back the zone a URL is in. If you wanted to add a URL of http://www.company.com to the Internet zone of http://mvp, the command would look like this:

```
stsadm -o addzoneurl -url http://mvp -urlzone internet -zonemappedurl
http://www.company.com
```

You could verify the zone was added by using either of the two commands shown in Figure 3-25. Both will show you that the zone was added correctly. You could also see it in Central Admin at Central Administration ⇨ Operations ⇨ Alternate Access Mappings.

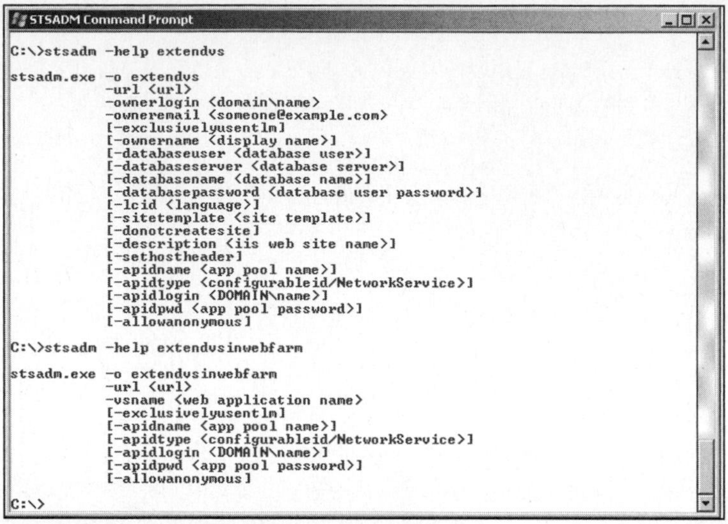

```
STSADM Command Prompt                                              _ □ x

C:\>stsadm -help extendvs

stsadm.exe -o extendvs
              -url <url>
              -ownerlogin <domain\name>
              -owneremail <someone@example.com>
              [-exclusivelyusentlm]
              [-ownername <display name>]
              [-databaseuser <database user>]
              [-databaseserver <database server>]
              [-databasename <database name>]
              [-databasepassword <database user password>]
              [-lcid <language>]
              [-sitetemplate <site template>]
              [-donotcreatesite]
              [-description <iis web site name>]
              [-sethostheader]
              [-apidname <app pool name>]
              [-apidtype <configurableid/NetworkService>]
              [-apidlogin <DOMAIN\name>]
              [-apidpwd <app pool password>]
              [-allowanonymous]

C:\>stsadm -help extendvsinwebfarm

stsadm.exe -o extendvsinwebfarm
              -url <url>
              -vsname <web application name>
              [-exclusivelyusentlm]
              [-apidname <app pool name>]
              [-apidtype <configurableid/NetworkService>]
              [-apidlogin <DOMAIN\name>]
              [-apidpwd <app pool password>]
              [-allowanonymous]

C:\>
```

Figure 3-24: Comparison of two operations

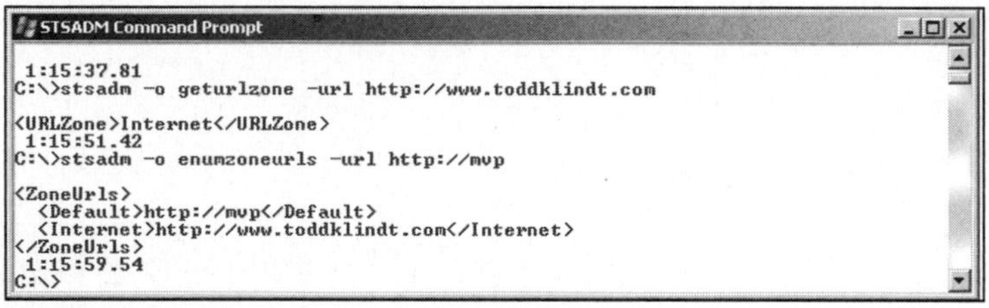

```
STSADM Command Prompt                                              _ □ x

 1:15:37.81
C:\>stsadm -o geturlzone -url http://www.toddklindt.com

<URLZone>Internet</URLZone>
 1:15:51.42
C:\>stsadm -o enumzoneurls -url http://mvp

<ZoneUrls>
   <Default>http://mvp</Default>
   <Internet>http://www.toddklindt.com</Internet>
</ZoneUrls>
 1:15:59.54
C:\>
```

Figure 3-25: Verifying the zone was added

Feature Management with STSADM

New to WSS v3/MOSS 2007 are *Features*, which are bundles of functionality that you can add and activate to your SharePoint installation. Features can be Web Parts, event handlers, site definitions, any number of things. You can use STSADM to install a new Feature. Use the installfeature operation to install the Feature:

```
stsadm -o installfeature -filename C:\Program Files\Common Files\Microsoft
Shared\web server extensions\12\TEMPLATE
\FEATURES\featurename\feature.xml
```

This will install the Feature for you. After it's installed, you can activate the Feature with -o activatefeature. There are the complementary operations of deactivatefeature and uninstallfeature. Once you've installed a Feature you can also activate or deactivate it from the UI. Farm Features are managed in Central Admin under Central Administration ➪ Operations ➪ Manage Farm Features. Features with a Web app scope are managed at Central Administration ➪ Application Management ➪ Manage Web Application Features. Site Collection and Site scoped Features are managed in their respective Site Settings page. If you don't see a Feature listed that you know is installed, check to see if it's hidden by looking for the Hidden tag in its feature.xml file. If Hidden is set to TRUE, you can set it to FALSE to make it show up.

Tricks with STSADM

There are a few tricks that I've picked up with STSADM that really don't fit into any other category, so I'm going to present them here. These are basically responses to questions I get in the form of "How do I...?" Here are a few:

Q: *How do I change how long the !New icon shows up on announcements?*

A: Use STSADM -o setproperty. You want to set the days-to-show-new-icon property to however long you want the !New icon to show up. To set it to 10 days, use this command:

```
stsadm -o setproperty -pn days-to-show-new-icon -pv 10
```

To remove the !New icon completely, set the Property Value (pv) to 0.

Q: *I don't like the port that Central Admin is on and I'd like to change it. What can I do?*

A: Use STSADM -o setadminport. You might be tempted to just go into IIS Admin and change the port there. That kind of works, but the Central Admin port is also in the Config Database as well as a shortcut in Administrative tools. Because it's so easy in STSADM, do it that way.

```
stsadm.exe -o setadminport -port 8176
```

Q: *I've got a timer job definition and I don't want to wait up to 15 minutes for it to run. What can I do?*

A: Use STSADM -o execadmsvcjobs to force the Time Job Service to execute your job immediately.

Q: *I want to create a new site collection, and I want it to be in its own content database. What's the easiest way to do this?*

A: Use STSADM -o createsiteinnewdb instead of the regular -o createsite.

Q: *My users complain that their Immediate Alerts aren't nearly immediate enough. What can I do?*

A: Use STSADM -o setproperty -pn job-immediate-alerts to change the amount of time between Timer cycles when SharePoint sends out immediate alerts. The default is 5 minutes.

Summary

The 2007 version of SharePoint has a greatly improved administrative experience. Central Administration has been completely overhauled. It is now a SharePoint site, meaning that content can be added to it and it can be backed up like a regular SharePoint site. Administrators have many more options for disaster recovery. The options range from backing up the entire farm from inside of Central Admin, to backing up individual Webs with STSADM.

Central Admin wasn't the only administrative component that was improved. STSADM has been given a host of new features as well. Increased support for reverse proxies and extranets has been added.

As SharePoint administrators, we have many options available to us. Hopefully this chapter has provided more tools to add to your SharePoint administrator's toolbox.

4

Developing Publishing Sites the Smart and Structured Way

by Andrew Connell

The latest release of the SharePoint platform, Microsoft Office SharePoint Server (MOSS) 2007, introduces new capabilities to the SharePoint platform: hosting content-centric Web sites on SharePoint and providing a robust publishing infrastructure. This publishing infrastructure enables site owners to delegate to certain individuals the creation and management of content on the site. Other users have rights to approve and publish content for readers to see. Interwoven in this process is a robust controlled publishing infrastructure founded on the Windows Workflow Foundation (WFF). Combined with significant performance enhancements and improvements to the underlying foundation of MOSS, Windows SharePoint Services (WSS) v3, SharePoint is now capable of hosting content-centric Internet sites! This component of MOSS 2007 is commonly referred to as *Web Content Management* (WCM), and sites utilizing the WCM features are called *Publishing sites*.

A major component to Publishing sites is the development story: the process behind constructing a content-centric site. Most development concepts surrounding Publishing sites are really SharePoint concepts, because a Publishing site is just another WSS site with some extra functionality. So, how are you supposed to develop a Publishing site? To date, only one approach has been the leader in the WCM community. This is the approach you will find in virtually all documentation, every whitepaper, every Webcast, every conference or trade show presentation, and every magazine article. However, this approach poses certain challenges in the real world when many organizations have a strict change control process.

An alternate development process is presented in this chapter. It addresses many of the pitfalls associated with the conventional approach. Though many of the concepts in this chapter are tailored to work specifically with Publishing sites, they will also work with little or no modifications in general

WSS v3 sites. Before any concerns arise from the process outlined in this chapter, rest assured everything is 100 percent supported by Microsoft. In fact, this is the process Microsoft's out-of-the-box site templates (Collaboration Portal and Publishing Portal) utilize to create the site infrastructure and layout files to implement the default sites!

Conventional Approach to Developing a Publishing Site

What guidance is provided when approaching a new Publishing site project? Most of the documentation comes from the MOSS 2007 Software Development Kit (SDK), from various Webcasts, blog posts, presentations, and so on. Collectively, the guidance from all of these sources is generally the same.

First, identify the different types of pages that will be used across a site. These types of pages help in identifying the different content types that must be defined. In the process of defining all the content types used in a Publishing site, common site columns are identified that can be shared across two or more content types (such as "First Name"). This process of identifying the content types and site columns for a Publishing site defines the schema of all pages in the site.

Once the schema of the pages in a Publishing site is defined, the site columns and content types must be created. MOSS provides three options to creating site columns and content types:

1. Via the SharePoint browser interface

2. Writing custom code to create site columns and content types using the SharePoint object model

3. Creating XML files containing `<Field>` and `<ContentType>` nodes included in element manifest files within SharePoint Features

The first option is by far the most commonly used and documented approach to creating site columns and content types. Because of its widespread popularity, it is referred to as the *conventional approach* in this chapter.

The next step is to scope out the various rendering options for each of the content types, or page schemas. The deliverable of this exercise is a list of all the page layouts (also known as *page templates*) that will be created for each content type.

Next, the project designer(s) will create mock-ups of each page layout, giving the Publishing site a user interface. Once the mock-ups have been created and the site has a user interface, common elements are identified. These include elements such as the site logo, common branding (page headers and footers), global navigation, and search controls, to list the more common ones. These common elements are abstracted out of the page layouts into one or more ASP.NET 2.0 master pages to enforce consistency and ease the maintenance burden once the site is in production. Obviously, part of this process involves incorporating any necessary images, cascading style sheets (CSS), and script files that are needed to support the user interface into the Publishing site's appropriate lists (such as the styles, documents, and images libraries).

Just like site columns and content types, developers have a few options for creating page layouts and ASP.NET 2.0 master pages in a Publishing site:

1. Use Office SharePoint Designer 2007 (SPD 2007) to create the page layouts and master pages against a live Publishing site.

2. Create page layouts and master pages outside of the live Publishing site with SPD 2007, Visual Studio 2005, or another editor, and upload the files to the Master Page Gallery through the SharePoint browser interface.

3. Create page layouts and master pages using the same tools listed in the previous option, but add these files to the Master Page Gallery using XML files containing `<Module>` nodes included in element manifest files within SharePoint Features.

As with site columns and content types, the first option listed (using SPD 2007) is the most documented and commonly used approach to creating page layouts and master pages. Because of its popularity, it, too, is referred to as the *conventional approach* in this chapter.

At this point, the infrastructure of the content pages has been defined, and the layout files have been created and added to the Publishing site. Typically, this is where the available documentation ends. Although this is enough information to get a site created, it stops well short of what is needed in the real world. Unfortunately, developers, designers, and project owners are left to figure out the best way to move all this work from the developer's workstations to a central development build server, and then progress through the typical development environment: from build to user acceptance testing to staging and, ultimately, to production.

Challenges Presented by the Conventional Approach

The conventional approach, as the previous section outlined, leaves those with the responsibility of creating and managing Publishing sites to craft their own policies and procedures to move the infrastructure components (site columns and content types) and layout files (page layouts, master pages, images, CSS, script files, and so on) in a project between developers and environments. Unfortunately, the conventional approach has many challenges associated with it. This section examines the most significant challenges.

Creating the Site Infrastructure with the SharePoint Browser Interface

Content types are used in a MOSS Publishing site to define the schema (or the type of content that can be saved) on a specific page layout. Each content type contains site columns that define the individual kinds of content the content type supports. The site columns and content types make up the core Publishing site infrastructure.

As previously discussed, the conventional approach to creating and managing content types and site columns is by using the SharePoint browser interface. This is by far the easiest and quickest way to manage site columns and content types. This method is fine when developing a Publishing site in a development environment, but what happens when the content types and site columns must be moved into another environment (such as another project team member's development machine, or the central development machine)? What happens when the content types and site columns must be implemented in the test, staging, or production environment?

One option is to re-create the site's infrastructure components manually using the SharePoint browser-based interface. This is obviously not ideal, because it is tedious, error-prone, and not automated. Another option would be to use the content deployment capabilities in Publishing sites to move the infrastructure to another environment. This is not an ideal option either, because content deployment is not intended to move site columns and content types between environments; its primary purpose is to move content from staging environments to production environments.

Another option is to write custom code that uses the SharePoint object model to analyze one Publishing site's infrastructure, and dynamically either create or modify another Publishing site's infrastructure. Although this option offers the most granular control over implementing changes to different environments, it is also potentially the least desirable because each implementation creates more custom code that must be tested and maintained.

Clearly, though the conventional approach of creating a Publishing site's infrastructure is very easy using the provided SharePoint browser interface, it has its downsides.

Creating Site Layout Files with Office SPD 2007

With the site columns and content types created, the next step is to build the user interface part of a Publishing site. The user interface component of a Publishing site is implemented with page layouts, master pages, images, CSS, client-side script files, and other types of media files (Flash, Windows Media, and so on).

As previously discussed, the conventional approach to authoring page layouts and master pages (including the ancillary supporting media files) promotes the use of SPD. Using SPD, developers can author and preview master pages and page layouts in a rich designer, similar to the ASP.NET designer in Visual Studio 2005. Developers can easily create new master pages and page layouts, drag-and-drop field controls from associated content types from a tool window onto a page layout, create new Web Part zones and add default Web Parts to zones, and utilize rich navigation and preview functionality when editing CSS or inline styles.

Just like the site infrastructure issue, this method will work just fine in a development environment, but what happens when the layout files must be migrated to another environment? How are changes to the layout files migrated from development to testing, then to staging and, ultimately, into the production environment?

The conventional approach promotes the use of SPD to make the changes to each file manually, live in each environment. This is not ideal, because developers and designers will need to have contributor-level access in each of the environments, including production, to implement the changes. Such access is typically not permitted in most organizations because of the inherit risks and lack of a strict change control process.

Another challenge with the conventional approach is that making changes using SPD customizes pages. It is important to understand how SharePoint stores pages, and what the terms *customized* and *uncustomized* mean when referring to pages in SharePoint.

Uncustomized and Customized Pages

For those familiar with the *ghosted/unghosted* concept in WSS v2 and SPS 2003, the terms have been changed in WSS v3 and MOSS 2007 to *uncustomized/customized* because the terms ghosted and unghosted do not translate to all languages. Ghosted pages in WSS v2 are referred to as uncustomized pages in WSS v3, and unghosted pages in WSS v2 are referred to as customized in WSS v3.

Page files in SharePoint are virtualized across multiple sites — in other words, the same file is used across many sites, eliminating the need to create a new set of page files every time a new site is created. However, developers and designers can modify pages on a site-by-site basis and save those changes using a tool such as SPD (or FrontPage 2003 in WSS v2 / SPS 2003) without affecting any other sites. Therefore, Microsoft needed a way for each site to retain its own modified version of the file without adding hundreds of additional files to the file system on each SharePoint Web Front End (WFE) server each time a page was modified.

The way this challenge was overcome is that the default file used by all new sites is left on the file system. When someone makes changes to a page using SPD and saves those changes, the source of the changed page is saved in the database.

So, in WSS v3, pages exist in one of two states: customized or uncustomized. An uncustomized page is one that is listed in the site's content database, but the actual source of the page (the file) resides on the file system, and the content database simply contains a link pointing to the file. A customized page is also listed in the content database, but the source of the page is also stored in the database. Future requests for that page (in the context of a specific site) will be served from the database, not from the file system.

Customized pages can pose a challenge in a production environment for a large organization. For example, consider if an organization wants to implement a rebranding campaign. If pages have been customized, this means that each customized page on each and every site must be updated using SPD, or using the SharePoint Application Programming Interface (API) to update the page in each site's content database. A rebranding campaign would be much easier to implement if the files resided on the SharePoint WFE server's file system where it is easier to deploy multiple modified files to various locations at once, just like a typical ASP.NET application.

As in the site infrastructure discussion, moving layout files between environments can also be achieved using MOSS's content deployment capabilities. However, just as in the site infrastructure discussion, this is not ideal, because content deployment is not intended to move files between environments; content deployment is ideally used to move content (such as page instances and images) between environments.

Although the challenges outlined in this section may make it seem as if there are not any good options when it comes to developing a Publishing site the proper way, this is certainly not the case. In the remaining sections of this chapter, an alternate method is presented, as well as guidance on how to implement it in your Publishing site development environment. Though it may seem a bit tedious at first, consider the gains over the long-term life of your project, and the time and manageability savings will be evident.

A Better Approach to Developing Publishing Sites

So far, this chapter has covered the challenges associated with developing a Publishing site using the conventional approach, which involves using the SharePoint browser interface to create and manage the site infrastructure (site columns and content types), as well as using SPD to create and manage layout files (master pages, page layouts, images, CSS, and so on). Though the conventional approach is by far the most documented and advocated approach to developing a Publishing site, it is not the only option, nor is it the best option. Another (and arguably better) option is to leverage the Feature and solution framework, a new addition in WSS v3.

Before diving into the solution, it is important to have an understanding of the Feature and solution framework.

The Feature and Solution Framework

Before explaining what Features and solutions are, it helps to understand why they were introduced in WSS v3. When a site was created in WSS v2, it was not easy to add new functionality to the site at a later date without writing some custom code to implement the changes. In addition, when some sort of functionality was reused across multiple site definitions or site templates in WSS v2, the functionality was literally copied to each site definition or site template. This meant there was no such thing as code reuse in WSS v2 when it came to site definitions and site templates.

A classic example of this is a list definition. Many site templates used the Tasks list definition. However in WSS v2, to make this work, Microsoft had to copy the Tasks list definition into each site template configuration. In addition, if a site was already created, there was no easy way to add a new (or updated) list definition to previously provisioned (created) sites.

Another challenge in WSS v2 was the deployment of custom code and files. The deployment of Web Parts was handled by creating *.CAB files and adding them to each site using the SharePoint command-line administration utility STSADM.EXE. Web Part developers could also package custom Web Parts into a *.MSI using the WPPackager utility, but this utility had known issues and Microsoft pulled support for it even before WSS v3 was released. However, there was no method other than copy-and-paste to deploy new site definitions, site templates, or list templates, to name a few.

Understanding Features

Microsoft introduced the concept of Features in WSS v3 to address a few issues in previous versions of SharePoint. Put quite simply, a Feature reduces the need for duplicating functionality or site customizations across multiple site definitions and templates. In addition, Features can be activated or deactivated on specific sites after they have been created, adding or removing functionality or customizations at any point in the site's lifetime. WSS v2 had no such included vehicle to add functionality to existing sites.

Features can be used to add various types of functionality to a site, as well as implement site customizations. Table 4-1 lists the various ways Features can be used in WSS v3.

Table 4-1: Feature Capabilities

Use	Description
Content Type	Define a content type that can be applied to list definitions or existing lists. Features can also bind content types to existing list templates.
Controls	Define and register user controls in an already defined delegate control on a Web page. Used to replace existing controls, such as the out-of-the-box search control with a custom user control.
Custom Actions and Groups	Create (or hide) new menu items within one of many predefined menus: site actions, Content Type settings page, Site Settings page, Edit Control Block menu (ECB menu, the drop-down menu actions that appears on items in a list), toolbar buttons on New/Edit/Display toolbars, and so on. Also enables the creation of custom action groups.
Event Receivers	Register an event receiver with a specific event on SharePoint lists and sites.
Document Converter	Define an executable that takes a file from one list and creates a different file in another list.
Feature Receivers	Define and register custom code to handle Feature events such as installed, activated, deactivating, and uninstalling.
Field	Define a new field definition (also known as a *site column*) that can be used in new or existing lists and content types.
List Templates and Instances	Register a new list template definition, or create an instance of a list based on an existing template definition.
Module	Provision files into SharePoint lists, libraries, or other files that are simply added to a site.
Site Definition or Template Association	Bind a Feature to a specific site definition or template (also known as *stapling*). Once a Feature is bound to a site definition or template, it is automatically activated when a site is created, based on the definition or template.
Workflow	Register a custom workflow in the Workflow Gallery to be used in new or existing lists.

As Table 4-1 outlines, SharePoint developers now have a very powerful tool to implement new functionality and site customizations not only to new sites, but also to existing sites that have already been provisioned using Features. This chapter does not go into granular detail on all the capabilities of Features. Rather, it focuses on a select few: content types, fields, and modules.

Understanding Solutions

To address the issue with deploying custom code, files, and other components to SharePoint implementations, Microsoft added the solution framework to WSS v3. Using the solution framework, developers can deploy custom components such as Web Parts, Features, site definitions and templates, custom code access security (CAS) policies, and assemblies to a specific SharePoint site's BIN directory or to the global assembly cache (GAC).

A solution file, called a *Windows SharePoint Package* (WSP) file, is essentially a cabinet (*.CAB) file with a *.WSP extension. The solution framework is based on similar functionality that was included in WSS v2: *.STP files. As previously mentioned, WSPs also now serve the same purpose as Web Part Package (*.WPP) files as well in WSS v3.

Each solution file is composed of a single manifest file and one or more content files. The *manifest file* (manifest.xml located in the root of the *.WSP file) contains a list of everything included in the solution (such as Web Parts, resource files, Features, site definitions and templates, and assemblies). The solution framework uses this file to determine what to do with all the files included in the *.WSP file.

Once a solution is created, the SharePoint farm administrator adds it to the farm's solution store. This can only be done using the SharePoint command-line utility STSADM.EXE. If the solution package were named Sample.wsp, the command to add it to the SharePoint farm's solution store would be the following:

```
stsadm.exe -o addsolution -filename sample.wsp
```

With the solution package added to the SharePoint farm's solution store, it can now be deployed. Deployment can be triggered in one of two ways:

1. *Central Administration* — SharePoint administrators can deploy solutions from Central Administration. Open Central Administration, select the Operations tab, and under the Global Configuration section, select Solution Management to deploy, retract, and remove solutions.

2. *Command line* — Administrators can also deploy solutions using the STSADM.EXE command-line utility with the following command (this command deploys a solution to all SharePoint sites in a farm):

```
stsadm.exe -o deploysolution -name sample.wsp -allcontenturls
```

Finally, if a SharePoint farm has multiple load-balanced WFEs, the solution framework will deploy the solution package to each WFE that is hosting the SharePoint site the solution is deployed to. In addition, SharePoint solutions are easily retracted once a solution has been deployed.

Benefits of Features and Solutions

Features and solutions each individually bring many benefits and improvements to the WSS v3 platform, but when used together, they provide an entirely new set of capabilities that can be used to solve common SharePoint development challenges.

Using Features and solutions, SharePoint developers can package multiple SharePoint components into a single portable file that can be easily shared with developers on the same team, as well as deploying the new application or functionality to a central build server, or user acceptance environment, or, ultimately, into production. These solutions can be as big or as small as desired, and not all solutions must be used in all environments on a project. Some solutions may be small enough to simply serve the purpose of sharing a few new files with the rest of a development team. In a way, the combination of the Feature and solution frameworks acts as SharePoint's own installer infrastructure.

Using Features and Solutions to Deploy Site Infrastructure and Layout Files

Going back to the discussion on the conventional approach to creating the site infrastructure (site columns and content types) and layout files (master pages, page layouts, images, and so on), remember that most of the issues associated with the conventional approach are centered around many manual steps. If the combination of Features and solutions can be thought of as an installer infrastructure for SharePoint, could these same frameworks be used to eliminate many of those manual tasks in the conventional approach? They sure can!

Remember from the earlier discussion about the conventional approach that both site infrastructure and layout files can be implemented with XML files in Features. Among their various capabilities, Features can be used to create site columns (also known as *fields*), content types, and provision files. Using these capabilities, developers can create a Feature (or multiple Features) that create the site infrastructure (site columns and content types) and layout files (master pages, page layouts, and so on), package up the Feature(s) into a solution file, and share it with other development team members, or hand it off to environment administrators to implement the changes to the production systems.

The ideal way to implement a Publishing site's site columns, content types, and add files (also called *file provisioning*) is using a Feature(s) and deploying the Feature(s) with solutions. Quite simply, it offers developers the most granular control and the easiest way to implement the necessary elements in various environments.

Creating a Feature

> *All files used in the following demonstration are available for download from* www.wrox.com.

The first step in this alternate approach is to create a Feature. To create a Feature, create a new directory named `AlternativeApproach` in the following location:

```
C:\Program Files\Common Files\Microsoft Shared\web server
extensions\12\TEMPLATES\FEATURES.
```

All Features must contain a Feature definition file, so create a new XML file in Visual Studio 2005 named `feature.xml` and save it in the `AlternativeApproach` directory.

With `feature.xml` open in Visual Studio 2005, add the following code to the file to create the Feature definition. (Table 4-2 contains a list of the most common attributes used in the `<Feature>` node.)

```
<?xml version="1.0" encoding="utf-8"?>
<Feature xmlns="http://schemas.microsoft.com/sharepoint/"
         Id="6B0480D2-009A-49c1-9DCB-EBF5F7358873"
         Title="Alternative Approach Feature"
         Description="Creates site columns, content types, a master page, and page
layouts for a Publishing site."
         Scope="Site"
         Hidden="FALSE">
</Feature>
```

Table 4-2: Feature Element's Attributes

Attribute	Description
Id	Unique ID (a GUID without brackets) of the Feature. This is required.
Title	Name of the Feature to be displayed on the Site Features or Site Collection Features pages linked from a site's Site Settings page. This is optional and limited to 255 characters.
Description	Description of the Feature to be displayed on the Site Features or Site Collection Features pages linked from a site's Site Settings page. This is optional.
Scope	One of four values: Farm (applies to all sites in the entire SharePoint farm), WebApplication (applies to all SharePoint sites within the Web application it was activated in), Site (applies to all sites within a site collection), or Web (applies to the specific Web it was activated in). This is required.
Hidden	If True, the Feature is not displayed in the Site Features or Site Collection Features pages linked from a site's Site Settings page. This is optional (default value is False).
Version	This optional value can be used to version the Feature. The format to use is: [#.#.#.#].

Only one attribute needs to be highlighted here: Scope. When creating site columns and content types, Scope can be Site or Web. However, when provisioning files, it should be Site.

For more information on the <Feature> node schema, refer to the following MSDN documentation: http://msdn2.microsoft.com/en-us/library/ms475601.aspx.

Creating Site Columns with Features

With the shell of a Feature created, the next step is to create an element manifest file that will create a site column. Create a new XML file in Visual Studio 2005 named SiteColumn.xml and save it in the AlternativeApproach directory.

Then, add the element manifest file to the Feature by adding the following code between the <Feature></Feature> tags in the feature.xml file:

```
<ElementManifests>
  <ElementManifest Location="SiteColumn.xml"/>
</ElementManifests>
```

Next, add the following code to SiteColumn.xml that will create the site column when the Feature is activated. (Table 4-3 contains a list of the most common attributes used in the <Field> node.)

```
<?xml version="1.0" encoding="utf-8"?>
<Elements xmlns="http://schemas.microsoft.com/sharepoint/">
```

```
<Field ID="{C3AA9C21-81F7-41d7-B5A5-CBEB40768C46}"
       Name="AlternateApproachColumn"
       DisplayName="Alternate Approach Column"
       Group="WROX"
       Type="Text" />
</Elements>
```

Table 4-3: Field Node's Attributes

Attribute	Description
ID	Unique ID (a GUID with brackets) of the site column. This is required.
Name	Unique name for the new site column. This is the internal name used by SharePoint to uniquely identify the column within a list. This value will never change. This is optional. If not specified, the Name is automatically generated based on the DisplayName of the column.
DisplayName	The user-friendly name of the column that appears in the SharePoint browser-based interface, such as the column name when a list is displayed in table format. This is optional.
Group	Specifies the site column group that the site column will be added to. This is optional.
Type	The data type of the field.

For more information on the <Field> node schema, refer to the following MSDN documentation: `http://msdn2.microsoft.com/en-us/library/ms437580.aspx`.

Creating Content Types with Features

The next step is to add a content type to the Feature. Create a new XML file in Visual Studio 2005 named `ContentType.xml` and save it in the `AlternativeApproach` directory.

Then, add the element manifest file to the Feature by adding the following code between the `<ElementManifests></ElementManifests>` tags, just after the existing `<ElementManifest>` tag in the `feature.xml` file:

```
<ElementManifest Location="ContentType.xml"/>
```

Next, add the following code to `ContentType.xml` that will create the content type when the Feature is activated. (Table 4-4 contains a list of the most common attributes used in the `<ContentType>` node.)

```
<?xml version="1.0" encoding="utf-8"?>
<Elements xmlns="http://schemas.microsoft.com/sharepoint/">
  <ContentType
ID="0x010100C568DB52D9D0A14D9B2FDCC96666E9F2007948130EC3DB064584E219954237AF3900213
FEEC23C37400bBEC425C10E76F37F"
            Name="Alternate Approach Content Type"
            Group="WROX">
```

```
    <FieldRefs>
      <FieldRef ID="{C3AA9C21-81F7-41d7-B5A5-CBEB40768C46}"
                Name="AlternateApproachColumn" />
    </FieldRefs>
  </ContentType>
</Elements>
```

Table 4-4: ContentType Node's Attributes

Attribute	Description
ID	Unique ID of the content type. This is required. *For more information on content type IDs, refer to the note following this table.*
Name	The name of the content type. This is required.
Group	Specifies the content type group that the content type will be added to. This is optional.

For more information on the `<ContentType>` *node schema, refer to the following MSDN documentation:* `http://msdn2.microsoft.com/en-us/library/aa544268.aspx`.

Two things need some explanation in the preceding code snippet.

First, the *content type ID* is a unique ID that every content type requires. Every content type must inherit from another content type; no content type can exist without a parent. The first part of the content type ID (up to the third instance of 00) represents the ID of the content type's parent. In the preceding code snippet, this is the Page content type that is created by MOSS when provisioning a new Publishing site. The latter part of the content type ID (00213FEEC23C37400bBEC425C10E76F37F) is what makes this content type unique from other content types.

For more information on content type IDs (a complex subject), refer to the following MSDN documentation: `http://msdn2.microsoft.com/en-us/library/aa543822.aspx`.

Second, note that the `<FieldRef>` node's ID and Name attributes are the same as the site column previously created. This is how a site column is added to a content type.

Provisioning Files with Features

Now that the site infrastructure components have been created and added to the Feature, the next step is to create the element manifest file that will provision the master page and page layout, each using a specific preview image. Create a new XML file in Visual Studio 2005 named `ProvisionFiles.xml` and save it in the `AlternativeApproach` directory.

Then, add the element manifest file to the Feature by adding the following code between the `<ElementManifests></ElementManifests>` tags, just after the existing `<ElementManifest>` tag in the `feature.xml` file:

```
<ElementManifest Location="ProvisionFiles.xml"/>
```

Next, add the following code to `ProvisionFiles.xml` that will provision the files when the Feature is activated. (Table 4-5 contains a list of the most common attributes used in the `<Module>` node, and Table 4-6 contains a list of the most common attributes used in the `<File>` node.)

```xml
<?xml version="1.0" encoding="utf-8"?>
<Elements xmlns="http://schemas.microsoft.com/sharepoint/">
  <!-- provision master page -->
  <Module Name="WROXMasterPages"
          Url="_catalogs/masterpage"
          Path=""
          RootWebOnly="TRUE">
    <File Url="ACminimal.master"
          Type="GhostableInLibrary">
      <Property Name="ContentType"
                Value="$Resources:cmscore,contenttype_masterpage_name;" />
      <Property Name="PublishingPreviewImage"
                Value="~SiteCollection/_catalogs/masterpage/Preview
Images/wrox.jpg, ~SiteCollection/_catalogs/masterpagePreview Images/wrox.jpg" />
      <Property Name="Description"
                Value="Provisioned from the AlternativeApproach Feature. "/>
    </File>
  </Module>

  <!-- provision page layout  -->
  <Module Name="WROXPageLayouts"
          Url="_catalogs/masterpage"
          Path=""
          RootWebOnly="TRUE">
    <File Url="AltApproachPageLayout.aspx"
          Type="GhostableInLibrary">
      <Property Name="ContentType"
                Value="$Resources:cmscore,contenttype_pagelayout_name;"/>
      <Property Name="PublishingAssociatedContentType"
Value=";#$Resources:cmscore,contenttype_articlepage_name;;#0x010100C568DB52D9D0A14D
9B2FDCC96666E9F2007948130EC3DB064584E219954237AF3900242457EFB8B24247815D688C526CD44
D;#"/>
      <Property Name="PublishingPreviewImage"
                Value="~SiteCollection/_catalogs/masterpage/Preview
Images/wrox.jpg, ~SiteCollection/_catalogs/masterpagePreview Images/wrox.jpg" />
      <Property Name="Description"
                Value="Provisioned from the AlternativeApproach Feature"/>
    </File>
  </Module>
  <!-- provision preview image -->
  <Module Name="WROXPreviewImages"
          Url="_catalogs/masterpage"
          Path=""
          RootWebOnly="TRUE">
    <File Url="wrox.jpg"
          Name="Preview Images/wrox.jpg"
          Type="GhostableInLibrary"/>
  </Module>
</Elements>
```

Table 4-5: Module Node's Attributes

Attribute	Description
Name	Name of the file set. This is required.
Url	Address of the folder, relative to the top-level Web in the site collection, where the files in the set will be provisioned. This is optional.
Path	Address of the folder, relative to the Feature, where the files to be provisioned reside. This is optional.
RootWebOnly	When set to True, the files in the set are installed only in the top-level Web within the site collection. This is optional.

Table 4-6: File Node's Attributes

Attribute	Description
Url	Path to the file. This is combined with the Path attribute in the parent <Module> node to determine the physical location of the file in the Feature. This is required.
Type	When provisioning files, this should always be set to GhostableInLibrary. The other option, Ghostable, applies only to files that are not added to SharePoint libraries. This is optional.

In the preceding code snippet, notice that the master page is provisioned, followed by the page layout, and finally the preview image used by both files is added to the site. Each <Module> node contains at least one <File> node, which contains optional <Property> nodes.

Module Node Overview

The <Module> node, signifying a file set, contains a few attributes that define the common aspects of the file set. The Url attribute specifies the target SharePoint library where the files in the set should be provisioned. Path is the local, Feature-relative path where the files are located. In the case of the Feature in the preceding code, because all files are in the root directory, no path is necessary. If the master page and page layout were in the LayoutFiles directory within the Feature, Path would be set to LayoutFiles. The last attribute, RootWebOnly, specifies that the files are provisioned only in the top-level Web of the site collection the Feature is activated in. In the case of Publishing sites, RootWebOnly should always be set to True.

> *For more information on the <Module> node schema, refer to the following MSDN documentation:* http://msdn2.microsoft.com/en-us/library/ms434127.aspx.

File Node Overview

Modules are essentially file set groupings. Each <Module> node contains one or more <File> nodes. All files in a set will follow the directives set in the set they belong to, defined in the <Module> node. The Url attribute specifies the location of the file in the feature. This is combined with the Path attribute defined in the <Module> that contains the <File> node.

Although optional, the other attribute that should always be included in the <File> node is Type, which, when specified, dictates the file should be cached in memory on the SharePoint WFE server, regardless of the value. There are two possible values for Type: Ghostable and GhostableInLibrary. Ghostable is used when files are not stored in a library or gallery. In the case of a Publishing site, when provisioning files, this value should never be used because master pages, page layouts, images, CSS — they will all reside in a library in the top-level Web of the Publishing site collection. Therefore, always specify GhostableInLibrary here.

> *For more information on the <Module> node schema, refer to the following MSDN documentation:*
> http://msdn2.microsoft.com/en-us/library/ms459213.aspx.

Property Node Overview

<Property> nodes are contained within <File> nodes. These elements are used to specify the value of the fields within the SharePoint library the file is provisioned into. For example, for the master page and page layout files in the previous code snippet, three properties are specified:

- ❑ ContentType — This value specifies the content type of the item. For master pages and page layouts, developers should use localized values. The master page localized value is $Resources:cmscore,contenttype_masterpage_name; and the page layout localized value is $Resources:cmscore,contenttype_pagelayout_name;.

- ❑ PublishingAssociatedContentType — This is the content type that is associated with the page layout. The associated content type is the content type that defines the schema of the page. The value contains a delimited string, which includes the name of the content type as well as the content type ID.

- ❑ PublishingPreviewImage — This is the value where the preview image can be found. The field type of the PublishingPreviewImage field is of type URL. This explains why the preview image value is specified as a comma-delimited string with two values. One value is used as the description for the URL, and the other is used for the target. In the previous code snippet, the same address was used for both values, so content owners and administrators can easily identify where the image is located.

> *The address of the preview image is pointing to the image that is provisioned at the end of the code snippet.*

- ❑ Description — This field is used to enter a user-friendly description of the file.

Notice that no properties are specified for the preview image provisioning. None are required, and in this demonstration, none were specified to simply add variation to the code snippet.

Testing the Site Infrastructure and Layout File Feature

At this point, the Feature is ready for deployment. The following test assumes a Publishing Portal site has been created with the URL of http://wrox.

First, the Feature must be installed. Open a command prompt and navigate to the following directory:

```
C:\Program Files\Common Files\Microsoft Shared\web server extensions\12\BIN
```

Now, install the Feature by entering the following in the command line:

```
STSADM.EXE -o installfeature -name AlternativeApproach
```

STSADM.EXE should have returned the message Operation completed successfully. The next step is to activate the Feature. This can be done in one of two ways.

First, the user can browse to the top-level Web in the site collection, browse to the Site Settings page, and select Site Collection Features from the Site Collection Administration group. From the Site Collection Features page, click the Activate button for the specific Feature.

The other way to deploy the Feature is with STSADM.EXE:

```
STSADM.EXE -o activatefeature -name AlternativeApproach -url http://wrox
```

Again, STSADM.EXE should have returned the message Operation completed successfully. To verify everything worked correctly, navigate to the Site Settings page for the top-level Web in the site collection. First, verify the site column was created by selecting site columns from the Galleries group. Use the Show Group selector to filter on the group WROX. The single site column specified in the Feature should be listed, as shown in Figure 4-1.

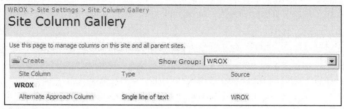

Figure 4-1: Single site column specified in the Feature

Next, verify the content type was created by selecting "Site content types" from the Galleries group on the top-level Web in the site collection's Site Settings page. Use the Show Group selector to filter on the group WROX. The single content type specified in the Feature should be listed, as shown in Figure 4-2.

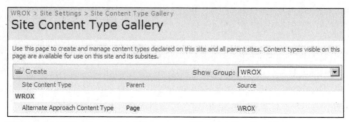

Figure 4-2: Single content type specified in the Feature

Select the content type by clicking its name. The list of columns should contain many columns coming from the source System Page. However, there should be one more column with no source listed: Alternate Approach Column Type — the one created in the Feature!

Finally, verify that the three files were successfully provisioned. Select Content And Structure under the Site Administration group on the top-level Web in the site collection's Site Settings page. Navigate to the Master Page Gallery. Most likely near the bottom of the list, the master page and page layout should be listed, as shown Figure 4-3.

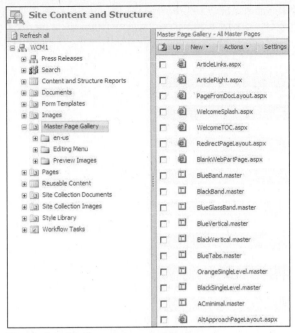

Figure 4-3: Master page and page layout

Notice there is a new subfolder in the Master Page Gallery: Preview Images highlighted in Figure 4-3. This did not exist prior to activating the Feature. Because the Feature specified the preview image should be placed the `Preview Images` directory within the Master Page Gallery, SharePoint automatically created the folder for you!

This concludes the demonstration that has shown how to use Features to create site columns, content types, and provision layout files into a Publishing site.

As with any process, there are advantages and disadvantages to using Features and solutions to implement a Publishing site's infrastructure and layout files. Regardless of the advantages and disadvantages of this approach, this is still the most preferred method in the development of a Publishing site. Before walking through a demonstration of this approach, let's cover the positives and negatives when following the guidance outlined in this chapter. The following two sections extrapolate the disadvantages and advantages to this approach.

Disadvantages to Using Features and Solutions for Deployment

Even though the approach of using Features and solutions for implementing a Publishing site's infrastructure and layout files is recommended, it does have a few drawbacks.

Tedious to Build

First and foremost, Features are tedious to build. At a minimum, all Features must live in a subdirectory within the directory where all SharePoint Features reside (`C:\Program Files\Common Files\Microsoft Shared\web server extensions\12\TEMPLATES\FEATURES`) and contain a definition file (`feature`

.xml) that specifies the ID, name, description, and scope of the Feature, as shown in Figure 4-4. Typically, the Feature definition file also contains references to element manifest files that define the actions to perform on the Feature. The element manifest file is where the site column, content type, and provisioning of files is defined.

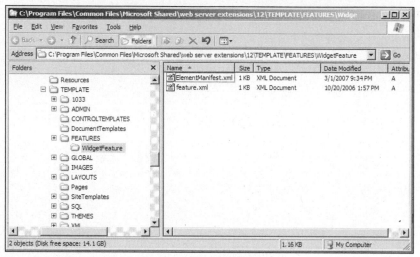

Figure 4-4: Required subdirectory and definition file

Features are also nearly all XML, with exception of the resource files that are referenced by the Feature such as an assembly. Unfortunately, no Feature or solution designer is available, so all XML files must be created by hand. The same is true for the solution manifest.xml file required in all *.WSP files. This drawback is somewhat mitigated because Microsoft provides an XML schema file that adds IntelliSense when editing files in Visual Studio 2005. Enabling IntelliSense for SharePoint-based XML files in Visual Studio is covered in the section, "Tips, Tricks, and Traps," later in this chapter.

No Debugging Support

Once a Feature has been deployed to the SharePoint Features directory, the next step is to install and activate it. If there are any syntax errors in the XML files or other random problems, SharePoint will fail to install/activate the Feature and return an error message. Many times, this error message does not provide enough detail to effectively troubleshoot the problem. Unfortunately, no mechanism exists that allows you to perform rich debugging when installing or activating a Feature (such as applying breakpoints and watches that are familiar to .NET developers in Visual Studio). The same is true when adding solutions to the SharePoint farm's solution store.

When encountering troubling errors in solutions and Features, you should cut out pieces of XML, and then repeat the installation or activation of the Feature or solution. Eventually, the error will disappear, providing a hint to the problem area. Once the error has been resolved, add the cut-out sections of XML back to the files and repeat the installation/activation process. This process is also referred to as *Pac-Man Debugging* because sections of XML are removed until the error disappears, then they are added back one piece at a time.

Provisioning Files Requires Double Development

Provisioning files into a Publishing site has its drawbacks as well. First, a developer must create a user interface for the site and pull everything together, adding images to master pages and page layouts, incorporating CSS, and writing any custom client-side script necessary to implement the user interface. Only after the site has been completed can the Feature(s) be created that will provision the files. This introduces a bottleneck into the process, because one step cannot be implemented until the previous step is complete.

In addition, this requires that files be created in one environment (SPD and a live Publishing site), then saved locally to the developer's workstation to create the file-provisioning Features. This results in a pseudo-double development because files are created in one environment, then duplicated in another environment.

Feature Deactivation and Solution Retraction Leaves Artifacts

When activating a Feature that provisions files, creates site columns, and creates content types, each of these different actions adds information to the specified Publishing site. Conventional wisdom would be that when these Features were deactivated, everything they added to the site would be removed. Unfortunately, conventional wisdom does not prevail in this case.

Generally speaking, SharePoint does not remove data that was added to a site via Feature activation when that Feature is deactivated. This means that simply deactivating a Feature does not remove all the master pages and page layouts that were added to the Master Page Gallery. The files are not locked where they were provisioned. Files can still be removed manually via the SharePoint browser interface, or by writing custom code that utilizes the SharePoint object model.

The same is true for site columns and content types under certain circumstances. For example, if a content type has not been added to any lists, it will be removed. However, if the content type has been added to a list, deactivating the Feature that created it will not remove it from the site because the content type is technically in use. Site columns work the same way. If they are used in a list or in a content type that has been added to a list, they will not be removed when the Feature that created them is deactivated. However, if the site column is not used anywhere on the site, it will be removed when the Feature is deactivated.

Advantages to Using Features and Solutions for Deployment

With the negatives out on the table, let's take a look at some of the advantages this approach carries with it. Arguably, the advantages outweigh the disadvantages when you consider the productivity gains and, more importantly, the maintenance of a Publishing site well beyond the "go-live" milestone.

Keep Layout Files Uncustomized

When files are provisioned into a Publishing site using Features, they are added to the various lists and libraries as GhostableInLibrary (this is one option, defined in the element manifest file within the Feature). This creates an entry in the target list or library for the file, but it tells SharePoint that the contents of the file are actually on the file system, not in the database. Therefore, the file is added to the Publishing site as an uncustomized file.

What if someone wants to open the file in SPD and make changes to it? No problem, that is completely supported and possible. The only difference between editing files using SPD when the file has been provisioned with a Feature and when a file is originally created in SPD is that SharePoint will switch the

...sioned file from uncustomized to be customized instead of the SPD-created file, which started out ...tomized. To the developer, there is no difference.

Uncustomized files are preferred in most cases. Consider a single master page that is used by three different sites. If the master page were created using SPD, it will exist as three different instances within SharePoint (one copy in each Publishing site's content database). However, if the master page was provisioned to each site using a Feature, three records would exist (one in each Publishing site's content database), but all would be pointing to the same physical file in the Feature. In the future, if the organization needs to update the master page, in the first case, developers would need to update three different files using SPD. In the latter case, only one file would need to be updated in the feature.

> *A common misperception with uncustomized files is they are much faster than customized files because they live on the file system rather than in a SharePoint site's content database. Thus, the misperception continues that uncustomized files eliminate the need to hit the database. This is not true, because SharePoint must go to the database to determine if the file is customized (and lives in the database) or uncustomized (and lives on the file system) regardless.*

Easy Deployment to Multiple Sites

An obvious benefit to packaging files, assemblies, and Features into solutions is that it is very easy to deploy these grouped files to multiple sites with a single operation. Once the solution has been added to the SharePoint solution store, farm administrators can deploy the solution to one or all SharePoint sites in the farm very easily via SharePoint's Central Administration site.

Another added benefit is that the solution deployment mechanism is smart enough to deploy the solution to all Web applications if a specific site collection has been extended to multiple zones using Alternate Access Mappings (AAMs).

> *Once a site collection is created, administrators can extend the existing Web application where the site collection resides with a new Web application. This new Web application is assigned a specific zone (such as Internet, Intranet, Extranet, or Custom). Each zone is then accessible using a different URL. The benefit to using multiple zones and AAMs is that each zone can leverage unique authentication providers. The Default zone can be configured to only permit authenticated users, authenticating against Active Directory, whereas the Internet zone would leverage Forms Based Authentication (FBA) and allow anonymous users. Both zones would point to the same site collection, meaning the site is now exposed to two types of users, as well as anonymous users!*

When a solution is deployed to a Web application that leverages multiple zones via AAM, SharePoint will automatically deploy the solution to each Web application. Why is this important? Consider if the solution contained a Web Part with an assembly deployed to the site's BIN directory. If the Web application has been extended to more than one zone, the solution deployment mechanism will deploy the assembly to both Web applications' BIN directory, add the <SafeControl /> entry to both Web applications' web.config file, and add the Web Part's *.webpart file to the wpcatalog directory in both Web applications. If this were not the case, either manual steps would be necessary to avoid errors on one of the zones, or the solution would need to be deployed twice.

Easy Deployment to Multiple Environments

Files, assemblies, and Features packaged into solution files make it very easy to quickly distribute multiple changes to an environment. This approach is beneficial for moving custom solutions from a developer's workstation to a central, shared development environment, a user acceptance testing environment, a staging environment, or eventually into the production environment.

In addition, if the development team subscribes to the isolated development model (where each developer works against an individual copy of the environment) rather than a shared development environment, solutions make it much easier for one developer to share the latest updates with the rest of the development team. One developer can share a solution package with other developers on the team, and everyone can quickly incorporate the changes by either adding the solution to the solution store, or upgrading it if the solution is an update to a previously deployed version.

Using a solution to share project and code updates is much easier than sending multiple files in a ZIP, or as a loose collection with a long and detailed installation script.

Fully Utilize Source Control Management

The conventional approach to building a Publishing site does not yield itself to being incorporated into a source control management (SCM) solution such as Microsoft's Visual Source Safe (VSS), Microsoft Team Foundation Server (TFS), or the Open Source Subversion, to name a few of the more popular options. The tasks that are typically implemented using the SharePoint browser interface (such as creating site columns and content types) have no source or version control built in. There is no way to make batch changes to multiple content types at once, nor is there a facility to revert back to a previous version of the site column or content type.

Creating layout files using the conventional approach also does not allow for easy SCM integration. When a master page or page layout is modified in SPD, a new version is created. Though this does allow developers to view or revert to previous versions and track who made the changes, as well as when those changes were made, this is not true *source control* — it is simply *version control*. Version control does not offer things such as *branching* and *labeling* (also known as *tagging* in some SCM implementations), or *atomic commits* (committing multiple files as a single check-in, all adopting the same check-in comment) — things that are included as core functionality in SCM implementations.

The development approach outlined in this chapter is founded on using Features to do all the work of creating the site infrastructure and layout files. Because Features are just a collection of files and folders, they can be added to any source control solution and fully leverage atomic commits, branching, labeling/tagging, and all the other capabilities of today's robust SCM solutions. Putting the source for creating site columns, content types, and provisioning files in an SCM facilitates increased collaboration and control between development team members.

Full Control of Site Column and Content Types

When creating site columns and content types using Features, developers have full control over the IDs and names of each component created. This is a huge advantage over creating these same components using the SharePoint browser-based interface.

For example, if a new site column called Street Address is created using the browser interface, the field is assigned an internal name of Street_x0020_Address. Any custom code that references this field must do so using this name, not Street Address. However, if the same site column were created using a Feature, the developer would have the option to specify the internal name of the site column as StreetAddress, a value much easier to remember and type.

Tips, Tricks, and Traps

After absorbing the development process outlined in this chapter, the advantages and disadvantages associated with it, and walking through a demonstration, it may look like a significant amount of additional work is required when compared to the conventional approach. Much of the additional work, and topics highlighted in the disadvantages section of the chapter, can be addressed with a few tips and tricks. However, this approach also introduces a few nuances that developers should be aware of.

This section introduces a few tips and tricks that developers can leverage to eliminate some of the additional work, as well as a few traps to watch out for.

Trick: Visual Studio 2005 XML Schema Cache

One of the disadvantages previously covered is that the XML files that make up Features and solution package manifests are tedious to build. In addition, because of the lack of a designer and debugging support, typos can pose quite a problem.

Thankfully, Microsoft has shipped a fairly well flushed-out XML schema that, when added to XML files in Visual Studio 2005, adds IntelliSense to most SharePoint-related XML files. There are two ways to add IntelliSense to SharePoint-related XML files (such as the Feature definition file `feature.xml` or solution manifest file `manifest.xml`) in Visual Studio 2005:

❑   Adding the SharePoint XML schema one file at a time

❑   Adding the SharePoint XML schema to the Visual Studio 2005 XML Schema Cache

Adding the SharePoint XML Schema One File at a Time

The first option is to add the SharePoint XML schema to an individual XML file. With an XML file open in the Visual Studio 2005 Code Editor, open the Properties tool window by selecting Properties Window from the View menu, or by pressing F4. Select the ellipsis for the Schemas field to open the XSD Schemas dialog, as shown in Figure 4-5.

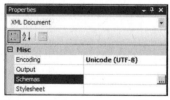

Figure 4-5: Selecting the ellipsis for the Schema field

In the XSD Schemas dialog, click Add… and browse to the SharePoint WSS.XSD file in the following location:

```
c:\Program Files\Common Files\Microsoft Shared\web server
extensions\12\TEMPLATE\XML\wss.xsd
```

Click Open in the Open XSD Schema dialog, and then click OK in the XSD Schemas dialog. Now, the SharePoint XML schema has been added to the file. This is demonstrated by typing an opening XML bracket (<), which should trigger the IntelliSense to appear, as shown in Figure 4-6.

Figure 4-6: IntelliSense indicating successful addition of the file

The downside to this approach is that it must be repeated for every single file.

Adding the SharePoint XML Schema to the Visual Studio 2005 XML Schema Cache

The second option is to add the SharePoint XML schema to the Visual Studio 2005 XML Schema Cache. Every time Visual Studio 2005 loads, it loads the schemas defined in the XML Schema Cache automatically, eliminating the need to attach a schema for each and every file. To implement this preferred method, the SharePoint XML schema must be added to the Visual Studio 2005 Schema Cache.

Using Windows Explorer, navigate to the following directory that contains the Visual Studio 2005 XML Schema Cache:

```
C:\Program Files\Microsoft Visual Studio 8\Xml\Schemas
```

Create a new file named `sharepointcatalog.xml` and open it in a text editor (such as Visual Studio 2005). Add the following code to the file:

```
<SchemaCatalog xmlns="http://schemas.microsoft.com/xsd/catalog">
  <Schema href="file://%ProgramFiles%/Common Files/Microsoft Shared/web server
extensions/12/TEMPLATE/XML/wss.xsd"
          targetNamespace="http://schemas.microsoft.com/sharepoint/"/>
</SchemaCatalog>
```

This file tells Visual Studio 2005 where the XML schema file is, and the namespace that utilizes it. If Visual Studio 2005 is open, close and reopen it because it only loads the XML Schema Cache when it starts up. Create a new XML file in Visual Studio 2005. To use the schema, a root node must exist that contains the XML namespace specified in the file added to the XML Schema Cache. This requires the developer know the root node for the SharePoint XML file that the developer is working in, and represents the only loss in functionality this method provides when compared to adding the XML schema to each file individually.

For example, if a Feature definition file were being created, enter the root node and specify the XML namespace, as shown in Figure 4-7.

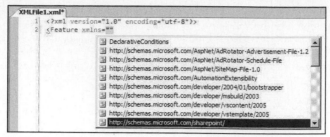

Figure 4-7: Entering the root node and specifying the XML namespace

Once the namespace is selected, the XML file will now have complete IntelliSense, as demonstrated in Figure 4-8.

Figure 4-8: IntelliSense resulting after selecting of the namespace

Trick: Leveraging MSBuild with MakeCab.EXE to Create Automated Solution Packages

WSP solutions are simply cabinet (*.CAB) files with a *.WSP extension. How do you build a cabinet file? Unfortunately, it is not as easy as it seems. Visual Studio 2005 includes a setup project template that you can use to include another project's output, but it has two limitations, one of which is very big:

❑   The project will only generate *.CAB files. Even if the output has renamed the settings, it will always generate a *.CAB file.

❑   The project doesn't allow the creation of subdirectories in the *.WSP, which localized deployments require.

Cabinet creation is not limited to the project template provided in Visual Studio 2005. Another option is to use MakeCab.EXE, included in the Microsoft Cabinet SDK, to generate WSP files (yes, the output filename can be specified using MakeCab.EXE).

The Microsoft Cabinet SDK is available for download at the following address:
http://support.microsoft.com/default.aspx/kb/310618.

`MakeCab.EXE` is a command-line utility that takes a few arguments. One argument is the name of a file containing the instructions for `MakeCab.EXE` (such as how to compress the files, subdirectories that should be created in the cabinet file, and the files that should be included in the cabinet, as well as which subfolders to add the files to). This file is a *diamond directive file* (`*.DDF`). Other arguments passed into `MakeCab.EXE` are parameters for things such as the name of the cabinet to create and where the file should be created.

Creating a cabinet file sounds tedious, and it is if you do it by hand. However, it can be automated by leveraging `MSBuild`, the workhorse behind the build process of Visual Studio 2005. Once a Visual Studio 2005 project is created, add a custom `MSBuild` targets file (which contains the instructions for `MSBuild`) to the project.

> *Entire books have been written about `MSBuild`, and it warrants that, but details about it are beyond the focus of this chapter. For more information on `MSBuild`, refer to the documentation on MSDN (`http://msdn2.microsoft.com/en-us/library/0k6kkbsd.aspx`) or the official `MSBuild` wiki on Channel9 (`http://channel9.msdn.com/wiki/default.aspx/MSBuild.HomePage`).*

The first step is to create a new C# Empty Project in Visual Studio 2005. Next, add all files to be included in the Feature to the project (Figure 4-9). In this case, I'll use the Feature built previously in this chapter.

**Figure 4-9: Adding all files
to be included in the Feature**

Every SharePoint solution file (`*.WSP`) must contain a manifest file, so add the manifest file to the project. This file includes all information about the solution, such as the location of the Feature definition file and all files required by the Feature. The next step is to create the diamond directive file (`*.DDF`) that contains the instructions for `MakeCab.EXE` to build the project and add it to the project. The following code snippet represents the contents of the `*.DDF` file for this project:

```
.OPTION Explicit
.Set DiskDirectoryTemplate=CDROM
.Set CompressionType=MSZIP
.Set UniqueFiles=Off
.Set Cabinet=On
;***************************************************
manifest.xml

.Set DestinationDir=AlternativeApproach
feature.xml
SiteColumn.xml
ContentType.xml
ProvisionFiles.xml
ACminimal.master
```

```
AltApproachPageLayout.master
WROX.jpg

;***End
```

Now, the custom MSBuild targets file must be added to the project. The following code snippet represents the contents of the *.targets file for this project:

```
<?xml version="1.0" encoding="utf-8" ?>
<Project DefaultTargets="BuildSharePointPackage"
xmlns="http://schemas.microsoft.com/developer/msbuild/2003">
  <PropertyGroup>
  <!-- assumes MSFT Cab SDK extracted to the following directory -->
    <MakeCabPath>"C:\Program Files\Microsoft Cabinet
SDK\BIN\MAKECAB.EXE"</MakeCabPath>
  </PropertyGroup>

  <Target Name="BuildSharePointPackage">
  <!-- execute MakeCab from the command line, specifying necessary arguments -->
    <Exec Command="$(MakeCabPath) /F BuildSharePointPackage.ddf /D
CabinetNameTemplate=$(MSBuildProjectName).wsp /D DiskDirectory1=$(OutputPath)"/>
  </Target>
</Project>
```

The last step is to modify the project file to tell MSBuild to call the custom targets file. Right-click the project name in the Solution Explorer tool window in Visual Studio 2005 and select Unload Project. Now, right-click the project name in the Solution Explorer tool window and select Edit [project name].csproj. Make the following changes:

1. Change the DefaultTargets attribute in the opening node from Build to SharePointFeaturePackage.

2. On (or about) line 31, change the node's Project attribute to BuildSharePointPackage .Targets. This tells MSBuild to use the targets file, not the C# targets file (usually used for compiling).

That's it! Save all changes, right-click the project in the Solution Explorer tool window, and select Reload Project. (If you are prompted with a security warning, select Load Project Normally and click OK.) Build the project (Shift+Ctrl+B). When the build is finished, in the project's \BIN\DEBUG directory, there should be a file named [project name].wsp.

For more information on this trick, including more in-depth information on the custom MSBuild targets file and diamond directive file, read the following article on my blog: http://www.andrewconnell .com/blog/articles/UsingVisualStudioAndMsBuildToCreateWssSolutions.aspx.

Tip: Use the SharePoint API

The development approach outlined in this chapter advocates using Features to create site infrastructure and layout files. This requires the creation of multiple XML files. Each XML file can grow to be quite large, increasing the probability of a typo or specifying an incorrect value. Compounding the problem is the fact that Feature installation and activation includes no debugging support, and this can turn into quite a daunting task. Another challenge is knowing which values to specify, and, as of this of writing, the SharePoint (both WSS v3 and MOSS 2007) SDK does not include granular detail on this (such as every attribute for the `<Field>` node when creating site columns or the `<ContentType>` node when creating content types).

Fortunately, SharePoint includes a very robust API that developers can use to obtain references to existing SharePoint objects as a point of reference. Developers can even create utilities that leverage the SharePoint API to make their lives easier, which provides a nice transition to the next trick!

Trick: AC's WCM Custom Commands for STSADM.EXE

The lack of a designer for the various XML files used in Features presents a challenge to creating element manifests that create site columns, content types, and the provisioning of files. XML files are not the only way to create site columns or content types, as covered in the overview of the conventional approach at the beginning of this chapter.

The SharePoint browser-based interface can be used to create site columns and content types. As the previous tip explained, SharePoint comes with a very robust API that enables developers to write custom code to obtain references to SharePoint objects — including site columns and content types! This means that developers are provided with a designer for creating the site infrastructure components right out of the box!

Now, all that is needed is a utility that can obtain a reference to a site column or content type, and create the XML element files used in Features to create the site infrastructure components. Instead of writing a new utility from scratch, why not leverage an existing one that every SharePoint installation already has out-of-the-box?

Microsoft extended the capabilities of the command-line utility STSADM.EXE to allow for custom commands in the WSS v3 release. Developers can now extend STSADM.EXE by adding custom commands to address specific administrative functions required by their organization.

Taking this approach, I've started a project called *AC's WCM Custom Commands for STSADM.EXE*. The goal of this project is to create a suite of commands targeted to SharePoint Publishing site developers that generates the XML element files used to create the site infrastructure. This allows developers to leverage the SharePoint browser interface to "design" the site infrastructure.

> *AC's WCM Custom Commands for STSADM.EXE is a free, Open Source project, available on my blog. The following URL contains links for downloading the latest release, as well as the source code and documentation for all the commands included in the project:* http://www.andrewconnell.com/ blog/articles/MossStsadmWcmCommands.aspx.

Once site columns and content types are created using the browser, use the custom commands to generate the XML used in the element files within a Feature. The commands do not address every possible scenario; instead the approach of the project is to generate as much valid XML as possible. Developers would then use these files as starting points and edit them for their specific needs. Think of the project as following the 80-20 rule, where 80 percent of the work is automated, leaving only 20 percent for developer involvement.

Following this 80-20 rule, two of the custom commands in *AC's WCM Custom Commands for STSADM .EXE* generate the XML that can be used as a starting point for constructing a Feature that creates site columns (command: `GenSiteColumnsXml`) and content types (command: `GenSiteContentTypesXml`). Again, the XML generated by these commands is not intended to be dropped into a Feature right away. The contents of the XML must be inspected and tweaked to the desire of the developer. Not all code in the XML files is necessary, but it is certainly easier to cut code out than it is to write it; therefore, this is the approach I took with this project.

The project is by no means complete. It is in a constant state of revision and tweaking because I have many plans for future commands that will become part of the project.

Trap: Publishing Field Types

When using the SharePoint API to analyze the properties of site columns, or using *AC's WCM Custom Commands for STSADM.EXE*, be aware that fields created using one of the Publishing field types do not expose their underlying type.

Site columns are represented as the object `SPField` in the SharePoint object model. The read-only property `SPField.Type` returns the underlying type of the field using the `SPFieldType` enumeration. The `SPFieldType` enumeration contains named constants for each of the out-of-the-box WSS v3 field types. Unfortunately, this list does not include the Publishing field types added when MOSS 2007 is installed.

When a site column is created using one of the Publishing field types, the `SPField.Type` property returns `SPFieldType.Invalid` because the actual field type is not an option in the enumeration. However, developers can obtain the actual field type. The public properties `SPField.TypeAsString` (the actual Publishing field type name) and `SPField.TypeDisplayName` (the display name of the Publishing field type) contain all the information needed to deduce the Publishing field type of the site column.

A list of all Publishing field types added to SharePoint when MOSS is installed can be found in the following file:

```
C:\Program Files\Common Files\Microsoft Shared\web server extensions\12\TEMPLATE\
XML\fldtypes_publishing.xml
```

Each `<FieldType>` listed in the Publishing field types definition file contains the values contained in the `SPField.TypeAsString` and `SPField.TypeDisplayName` properties. The `SPField.TypeDisplayName` is actually obtained from a resource file installed when MOSS is installed. Table 4-7 displays the value in the `SPField` object, the value from the Publishing field types definition file, and the corresponding values for the Publishing HTML field type.

Table 4-7: SPField Object, Publishing Field Types, and Publishing HTML Field Values

SPField Property	SPField Property Value	Publishing Field Type Definition Node Name	Publishing Field Type Definition Value
Type	Invalid	TypeName	HTML
TypeAsString	HTML	TypeName	HTML
TypeDisplayName	Publishing HTML	TypeDisplayName	$Resources:cmscore, fieldtype_HTML_name;

Trap: *Site Column Updates Don't Take Effect*

As is always the case in the process of developing an application, changes must be made to some of the objects created. To update a site column, the Feature should be deactivated, the element manifest is modified with the desired changes to the site column, and, finally, the Feature is reactivated.

However, at times, the changes to the site column are not reflected when the Feature is reactivated, even when using the optional `-force` switch to force all updates. It appears that, even though the Feature was deactivated and the site column was removed from the site, SharePoint has left an artifact or orphaned site column in the system, and future changes will not take effect, even though it does not appear anywhere on the site.

To get around this issue, add the attribute `DisplaceOnUpgrade=TRUE` to the `<Field>` node. This way, SharePoint will update the existing site column the next time it is activated.

Another method is to change the site column's ID, a GUID, when making other changes to the site column so that the next time the Feature is updated, SharePoint will see it as a brand new site column. Note that any content types referencing this site column must have their references updated as well. This is lesser preferred of the two options.

Trap: *Content Type Updates Don't Cascade*

Once a Feature containing content types is activated, developers can update the Feature and reactivate it to make changes to the created content type. However, changes are not pushed down to other content types that inherit from the one being inherited, nor are the changes pushed onto lists where the content type has been added. The only content types updated are those that are not in use.

Unfortunately, this is a big hang-up for this approach. However, this limitation only exists when updating content types using Features. The SharePoint object model provides a method for updating content types, and forcing updates to cascade to other child content types and lists that contain the content types. Regardless, content type changes can still be implemented using the object model or via the SharePoint browser-based interface. This approach has an optional flag the individual can set if updating child content types and lists is desired.

Parting Thoughts

After a comprehensive discussion on the conventional approach, the alternative development process, an examination of the advantages and disadvantages of this alternate process, as well as identifying some tips, tricks, and traps associated with it, you may be left wondering, "OK, so is this really a good idea?" I'm convinced this alternate development approach is how all Publishing sites should be created. Though there are some disadvantages to this approach as well as some pitfalls, the advantages mitigate virtually all of them.

How do I use this approach to developing a new Publishing site? Today, I use the SharePoint browser-based user interface to create all the site columns and content types necessary for a new site. Then, I leverage SPD to create all master pages and page layouts that will be used in the site. The most common question I hear when I describe this approach is, "Why do you use SPD for the creation of your master pages and page layouts?" Quite simply, it is much easier to drag-and-drop field controls, Web Part zones, and Web Parts onto page layouts, edit the CSS, and view the files in a live preview of the site using SPD. So, I'm effectively using the conventional approach for the first part of my development, and I stay in this phase for quite a while — until I feel my master pages and page layouts are essentially complete (minus a few tweaks here and there).

Next, I use my *AC's WCM Custom Commands for STSADM.EXE* utility to generate the site column and content type element manifest files for the site infrastructure components. I never use the full generated XML files. I edit them before adding them to a Feature for deployment. Then, I save all layout files, including master pages, page layouts, images, CSS, media files (movies or animations), and client-side script files, locally into a Feature that will provision all of them. Finally, I package both Features into a single SharePoint solution for deployment.

I recommend you use two different Features to create the site infrastructure and layout files. This way, you can be assured that the dependency that page layouts have on content types is addressed by first activating the Feature containing the site infrastructure, then activating the Feature containing layout files. This is the same approach Microsoft takes when creating a new Publishing site using the Publishing Portal site template. When the site is created, it activates a Feature (PublishingWeb) that does nothing but activate two other Features (PublishingSite and Publishing), both of which are hidden from the SharePoint browser interface. The PublishingSite Feature then activates four more Features, one of which contains the site infrastructure (PublishingResources) and another which creates the layout files (PublishingLayouts).

Summary

This chapter has presented an alternative approach to developing Microsoft Office SharePoint Server 2007 Publishing sites than that of the generally accepted conventional development approach. The conventional approach advocates using the SharePoint browser-based interface to create site infrastructure components (such as site columns and content types), and using Office SPD 2007 to create layout files (such as master pages and page layouts). Development teams usually run into challenges with this approach while implementing it in real-world projects when first attempting to replicate the site infrastructure and layout files from the development environment. After covering the challenges with the conventional approach to developing a Publishing site, a better approach is proposed.

The approach covered in this chapter advocates using Features to create site infrastructure components and layout files when developing Publishing sites. Arguably, there is more work associated with this approach, and much of it was outlined when the disadvantages were covered, specifically regarding double deployment and cleaning up artifacts left around after deactivating the Feature(s). However, the advantages covered provide enough proof that this process is worth the drawbacks. After a demonstration of the process, some tips, tricks, and traps associated with the proposed development approach were covered, arming developers with all the knowledge necessary to implement the process on their next Publishing site projects.

Finally, I offered some prescriptive guidance on how to best leverage this approach in your own development environment.

Using SharePoint Designer 2007

by Dustin Miller

In this chapter, I'm going to take you on a whirlwind tour of some of the most interesting features of SharePoint Designer. Now, I can cover only so much in the space allotted, so don't be upset if *your* favorite feature doesn't get covered. I tend to be a very visual person, so you'll see screenshots of the important things along the way. I hope, above all, that this chapter inspires you to experiment and explore SPD, and try to create new and unique solutions based on that product we all know and love: Windows SharePoint Services!

What's in a Name?

I use the word "SharePoint" in my writing, rather than the full platform title "Windows SharePoint Services." So, whenever I mention a "SharePoint site," I'm actually referring to a site using the "Team Site" site definition on a server running Windows SharePoint Services 3.0 (WSS v3.0).

Appreciating SharePoint Designer

Okay, let's just get this out of the way right now. You have baggage. You've been carrying it around for years, and nothing that anyone says will make you put it down. When someone says that magic word, "FrontPage," you grumble and mutter to yourself, "I would rather write my Web pages in Notepad." Whenever you see its built-in templates used on a Web site, your blood pressure rises. You suffer from the condition I like to call "FrontPage Avoidance Disorder."

It's okay; you don't have to explain it to me. I feel your pain. In years past, FrontPage was known to occasionally mess with your code, insert unnecessary tables, and generally mess up your day. I've been there. Well, those days are over! FrontPage is history, and in its place is a new and triumphant product: Microsoft Office SharePoint Designer 2007 (SPD 2007). Well, there are actually two products designed to replace FrontPage — Expression Web Designer is the other half of the equation, but SPD can do everything that Expression Web Designer can do. So, stick with me on this one. Besides, this is a SharePoint book you're holding in your hands right now.

Back to the story: SharePoint Designer has come a long way from its FrontPage roots. After one Web design session, you'll see that it was created for Web developers and designers alike.

At this point, you may have the following reactions:

❑ *I prefer to write code; give me Notepad any day* — No problem. SPD includes is a great code editing environment complete with real developer-friendly features such as IntelliSense (shown in Figure 5-1), which auto-completes statements as you type them in Code view, and helps ensure standards compliance.

Figure 5-1: IntelliSense on a `<script>` **element**

❑ *I like to customize my development environment; cookie cutter applications aren't for me* — I hear you, loud and clear. That's one of the great things I like about SPD. There are dozens of panes that can be docked, tabbed, or floated above your work environment, as shown in Figure 5-2 — even on multiple monitors. It's not quite as pretty as Visual Studio, but it's a great option for Web developers who like to customize their development environments to suit their own personal workflows.

❑ *I write XHTML sites, thank-you-very-much, so WYSIWYG applications don't really help me there* — Whoa, hold your horses there, partner! SPD can do everything that Expression Web Designer can do. That includes Web sites with table-free layouts written with "XHTML 1.0 Strict" compliance. Don't believe me? Look at this *built-in* template shown in Listing 5-1 and Listing 5-2. Your eyes aren't deceiving you. It's XHTML 1.0 Strict, and there aren't any tables in there. In Design view, it looks like Figure 5-3.

Listing 5-1: untitled_1.htm

```
<!DOCTYPE html PUBLIC "-//W3C//DTD XHTML 1.0 Strict//EN"
"http://www.w3.org/TR/xhtml1/DTD/xhtml1-strict.dtd">
<html xmlns="http://www.w3.org/1999/xhtml">

<head>
<title>Untitled 1</title>
<meta http-equiv="Content-Type" content="text/html; charset=utf-8" />
<link rel="stylesheet" type="text/css" href="Untitled_1.css" />
```

```
  </head>
  <body>
  <div id="container">
    <div id="left_col">
    </div>
    <div id="page_content">
    </div>
  </div>
  </body>
  </html>
```

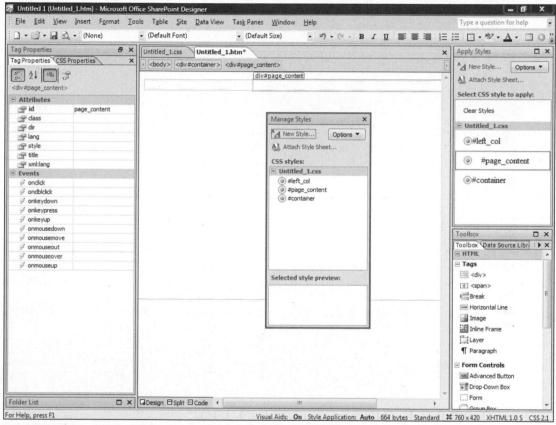

Figure 5-2: Some of SharePoint Designer's task panes and dialogs, customized just for you

Listing 5-2 untitled_1.css

```css
/* CSS layout */
#left_col {
  width: 200px;
  position: absolute;
  left: 0px;
```

```
    top: 0px;
}
#page_content {
  margin-left: 200px;
}
#container {
  position: relative;
  width: 100%;
}
```

Figure 5-3: Look ma, no tables!

As you can see, SPD has come a long way. As this chapter progresses, I will give you a crash course on some of the great features of SPD, from designing accessible sites to building SharePoint Web Parts that pass parameters to (and capture data from) a Web service.

Using SPD for Web Design

The WYSIWYG (what-you-see-is-what-you-get) capabilities of SPD are, as of this writing, unmatched by any other Web designer or Web developer tool. Even complex Web sites based on Cascading Style Sheets (CSS) are rendered in Design view with nearly perfect accuracy when compared to their rendering in

Internet Explorer (IE) or even — hold on to something — Firefox! I use SPD to build standards-compliant sites, and I've historically been a "code only" kind of guy. SPD has become a must-have tool in my Web design toolbox, even for sites that don't use SharePoint under the hood.

Standards Compliance

SPD (and its little brother, Expression Web) were created to build Web pages that were standards-compliant, no matter which standard was preferred by the developer wielding the tool. If your sites are HTML 1.0 Transitional, that's no problem. XHTML 1.0 Strict? Got you covered there, as well.

SPD is capable of building sites that honor the following standards:

- ❑ HTML/XHTML:
  - ❑ HTML 4.01 Frameset
  - ❑ HTML 4.01 Strict
  - ❑ HTML 4.01 Transitional
  - ❑ XHTML 1.0 Frameset
  - ❑ XHTML 1.0 Strict
  - ❑ XHTML 1.0 Transitional
  - ❑ XHTML 1.1
- ❑ CSS:
  - ❑ CSS 1.0
  - ❑ CSS 2.0
  - ❑ CSS 2.1
  - ❑ CSS "IE6"

Throughout this chapter, I use step-by-step processes (or walkthroughs) to provide hands-on examples of key SPD features. These walkthroughs are progressive in nature (one walkthrough may build from another walkthrough).

To that end, here is a step-by-step walkthrough for creating your first XHTML 1.0 Strict, CSS 2.1–compliant Web page, with no tables and no inline CSS. These steps assume you have SPD opened, and, if you're attempting these exercises on a remote server, connected to your destination Web site.

1. First, SPD must be told that you prefer designing with the XHTML 1.0 Strict standard. To do this, find the current HTML/XHTML schema declared in the right side of the status bar, as shown in Figure 5-4.

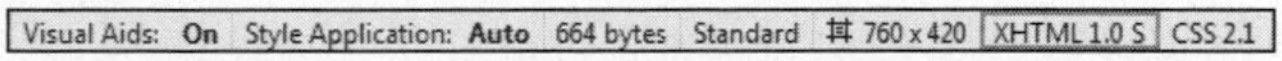

Visual Aids: **On** Style Application: **Auto** 664 bytes Standard 760 x 420 XHTML 1.0 S CSS 2.1

Figure 5-4: The current HTML/XHTML schema as seen in the status bar in SPD

125

2. Once you've found the current schema, double-click it to open the Page Editor Options dialog, as shown in Figure 5-5.

Figure 5-5: The Page Editor Options dialog

3. On the Page Editor Options dialog, pull down the drop-down list box titled Document Type Declaration (on the left side, toward the bottom of the dialog), and select XHTML 1.0 Strict.

4. Click OK.

5. Next, go to File ⇨ New. You will see the New dialog, as shown in Figure 5-6.

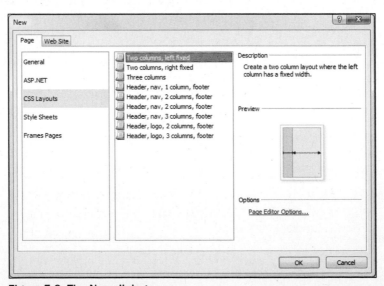

Figure 5-6: The New dialog

6. In the New dialog, select CSS Layouts. Then, choose a layout style from the list shown in the second list box in the dialog (shown in the middle pane of Figure 5-6). In this example, let's choose the first option: "Two columns, left fixed." Then, click OK.

7. You'll see that SPD created two files: a CSS file and a blank HTML page that is (temporarily) using XHTML 1.0 Transitional as its DOCTYPE.

8. Select the tab to edit the .HTM file created by SPD, and then go to the Code view of the page by clicking the Code button at the bottom of the design pane, as shown in Figure 5-7.

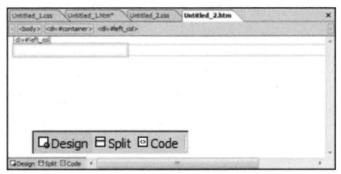

Figure 5-7: The view selector for the current page

9. The default DOCTYPE for this template is XHTML 1.0 Transitional. For this example, change the DOCTYPE to XHTML Strict by using the built-in DOCTYPE snippets. First, drag-select the first line of code that reads as follows:

```
<!DOCTYPE html PUBLIC "-//W3C//DTD XHTML 1.0 Transitional//EN"
"http://www.w3.org/TR/xhtml1/DTD/xhtml1-transitional.dtd">
```

10. To open the snippet menu, hold down your control (CTRL) key and press Enter.

11. From the snippet menu that appears, select "dtx1s XHTML 1.0 Strict DOCTYPE," as shown in Figure 5-8.

Figure 5-8: Code Snippets list

12. The first line of code should now read as follows:

```
<!DOCTYPE html PUBLIC "-//W3C//DTD XHTML 1.0 Strict//EN"
"http://www.w3.org/TR/xhtml1/DTD/xhtml1-strict.dtd">
```

13. Go back to Design view using the view selector shown in Figure 5-7.

14. You are now visually designing a fully XHTML 1.0 Strict–compliant Web page.

Designing for Accessibility

SPD has features designed to create Web pages compliant with common Web accessibility standards, such as "Section 508" or Web Content Accessibility Guidelines (WCAG). Built-in wizards and accessibility checkers ensure that your Web pages (even those written with XHTML as a DOCTYPE) are accessible to browsers that may be using alternative input/output devices (such as a screen reader).

Let's look at how you can check your page for accessibility. This walkthrough assumes that you have a blank XHTML 1.0 Strict page open in Design view, such as the one just created in the previous walkthrough. During this step-by-step exercise, you'll see how SPD helps you to create accessible Web pages.

1. Insert an image into the "left_col" <div> element:

    a. Go to Insert ⇨ Picture ⇨ Clip Art.

    b. Search the clip art gallery for "person." If asked to include online sources, select Yes.

    c. Click the image you want to insert.

2. Once you have clicked the image you want to insert, SPD will prompt you to enter accessibility information for the image, as shown in Figure 5-9. Give the image some alternate text by filling in the "Alternate text" box. In this dialog, you can also enter text in the "Long description" for the image, or you could browse to the URL of a page that describes the image. When you have finished entering the text, click OK.

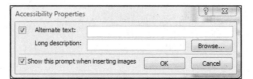

Figure 5-9: The Accessibility Properties dialog

3. Check the rest of the page for accessibility guidelines:

    a. Go to Tools ⇨ Accessibility Reports.

    b. The Accessibility Checker dialog shown in Figure 5-10 appears, and allows you to configure the type of report you want to run. Under the "Check where" heading, select Current Page. Select all the checkboxes under the "Check for" and "Show" headings to get a verbose report on any issues (if any issues exist).

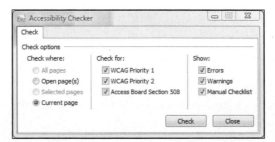

Figure 5-10: The Accessibility Checker dialog

4. The resulting report (shown in Figure 5-11) contains more information than you would typically need. Much of this is generated by the Manual Checklist option selected in Step 3b under the Show heading. There is also a warning regarding pages that include a link to a CSS file. Be sure your pages will work if CSS is turned off!

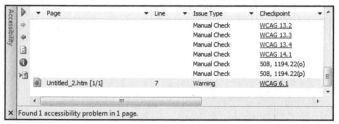

Figure 5-11: The accessibility report for your simple page

5. Double-click the last warning, the one suggesting that you should be sure your pages will work if CSS is turned off. SPD goes to the Code view, and pre-selects the code that triggered the warning, in this case, the referenced stylesheet.

As you can see, SPD is able to provide rich reports capable of walking you through the creation of accessible Web pages, as well as prescriptive "as you go" guidance for ensuring accessibility of your content.

IntelliSense for JavaScript and CSS

SPD is an excellent visual designer for Web pages, but is also a capable JavaScript editor. The JavaScript IntelliSense feature in SPD not only provides member lists for common JavaScript objects, but is also able to read declared functions and provide jump-to capabilities, similar to Visual Studio.

CSS gets first-class treatment in SPD as well. Not only is there a robust graphical CSS management system (the "Manage Styles" dialogs for applying and managing CSS styles), but Code view has some rich CSS editing capabilities as well.

Interacting with JavaScript in Code View

This walkthrough assumes that you have a simple XHTML 1.0 Strict page open in Design view, perhaps with an image (if you're doing these walkthroughs in order). During this step-by-step exercise, you'll see how SPD's Code view helps Web developers write and interact with JavaScript.

1. Change to Code view for the current page. You can use the view selector at the bottom of the design pane (shown in Figure 5-7), or go to View ➪ Page ➪ Code.

2. Immediately after the opening `<body>` element, add the `<script>` block shown here:

```
<script>
  function AnnoyingWarning() {
    window.alert("This is an annoying warning.");
  }
</script>
```

3. As you type the `window.alert` line, notice that SPD pops up an IntelliSense window (Figure 5-12) as you type.

Figure 5-12: IntelliSense
for JavaScript

4. Before the closing `</body>` element, add the `<script>` blog shown here:

```
<script>
  AnnoyingWarning();
</script>
```

5. Once you've entered this code, the function call `AnnoyingWarning` will automatically be hyper-linked by SPD. If you control-click the function call, SPD will jump to (and highlight) the function declaration, as shown in Figure 5-13.

```
<!DOCTYPE html PUBLIC "-//W3C//DTD XHTML 1.0 Strict//EN" "http://www.w3.org
<html dir="ltr" xmlns="http://www.w3.org/1999/xhtml">

<head>
<title>Untitled 2</title>
<meta http-equiv="Content-Type" content="text/html; charset=utf-8" />
<link rel="stylesheet" type="text/css" href="Untitled 2.css" />
</head>

<body>
<script>
    function AnnoyingWarning() {
        window.alert("This is an annoying warning.");
    }
</script>
<div id="container">
    <div id="left col">
    <img alt="Person" src="file:///C:/Users/Dustin/AppData/Local/Microsoft/
    <div id="page content">
    <script>
        AnnoyingWarning();
    </script>
    </div>
    </div>
</div>

</body>
```

Figure 5-13: Code hyperlinks in SPD

Interacting with CSS in Code View

This walkthrough assumes that you have a simple XHTML 1.0 Strict page open in Design view, with CSS declared in an external file. If you followed these walkthroughs in order, you're all set.

1. Change to Code view for the current page. You can use the view selector at the bottom of the design page (shown in Figure 5-7), or go to View ⇨ Page ⇨ Code.

2. Control-click the filename shown in the following code:

```
<link rel="stylesheet" type="text/css" href="Untitled_2.css" />
```

3. Notice that SPD loads the file (if it's not already loaded) and jumps to the tab containing the CSS file referenced in the clicked code hyperlink.

4. Switch back to the Web page tab and control-click a CSS ID selector for one of the elements. For example, control-click the text "container" in the following code:

    ```
    <div id="container">
    ```

5. Notice that SPD not only loads the CSS and switches to its tab, but highlights the portion of the CSS file referenced by the selector you control-clicked.

Using SPD for SharePoint Sites

Now we're talking! Though SPD is a capable Web design tool for non-SharePoint sites, when you first open a site from a WSS-enabled Web application, you'll see quite a bit more power at your fingertips. SPD is capable of customizing the look and feel of SharePoint sites (via ASP.NET master pages), creating new pages, and even building Web Parts that download data from a database.

Master Pages

An ASP.NET master page dictates the general presentation of a Web page by defining shared controls and placeholders, CSS, navigational elements, and other such design elements, often referred to as "chrome." Because it's based on the .NET Framework, WSS v3.0 benefits from this technology built into ASP.NET. This master page is used by every "page instance" on your SharePoint site. Changing the master page will affect any page that uses that master page as its base template. It's an easy way to brand your SharePoint sites.

Publishing Sites and Master Pages

Publishing sites, or sites using the Web content management features available in Microsoft Office SharePoint Server 2007 (MOSS 2007), utilize an additional page structure element called a "page layout." In Publishing sites, master pages typically contain the CSS declaration and navigational elements used on the page, and page layouts are the templates that define what Web Parts appear on that particular content type. You'll find more information on master pages and page layouts in Chapter 6.

Every SharePoint site has one or more master pages that define the look and feel of non-administrative pages on that site (in other words, pages that don't include _layouts in the URL).

Modifying the default.master for a Team Site

This walkthrough assumes you have a default SharePoint team site opened in SPD, and you have the Folder List task pane open on the left side of the SPD window. As with all the walkthroughs you may find in this book, be sure you're working in a development environment, and that you're not running these experiments on a production server!

1. In the folder list on the left side of the SPD window, expand _catalogs and then expand master page (Master Page Gallery). Your folder list should look similar to Figure 5-14.

**Figure 5-14: The folder list
showing the Master Page Gallery**

2. Double-click the `default.master` file in the `masterpage` directory.

3. Click in the very bottom of the design area for the page, under all the placeholders, where there is nothing but blank white space, as shown in Figure 5-15.

**Figure 5-15: The blank space at the bottom of the page where
you should click**

4. Type the text **Copyright (c) 2007, My Web Design Company, All Rights Reserved**. You'll notice that SPD automatically inserts a new paragraph for your text — this is expected.

5. Save the page. You'll see the following warning that you're about to customize this page:

   ```
   Saving your changes will customize a page from the site definition. Are you
   sure you want to do this?
   ```

   I'll provide more on this later; for now, click Yes.

6. Open your SharePoint site in your favorite Web browser, and look around. Notice that every page now has the copyright notice on the bottom of the page, with the exception of administrative pages (pages with _layouts in the URL).

Now that you've modified the master page, every non-administrative page on your site will inherit the look and feel of the changes you made to that master page. Although this example created a simple change (the addition of a simple footer), you are limited only by your imagination (and patience!). There is so much more you can do with master pages, including modifying CSS, adding custom imagery, and so on.

Important Warning

SPD is a powerful tool, and like any tool, when wielded improperly, it can cause significant damage. One way to wreak untold havoc on your SharePoint sites is to use SPD on the SharePoint Web Front End (WFE) servers themselves, editing pages on the file system. Take it from me, editing the file system templates with SPD will break your SharePoint sites. SPD is meant to access SharePoint sites from your client desktop via HTTP, and not via any other method.

The Data View Web Part

SPD is home to one of the most powerful Web Parts known in the SharePoint world: the Data View Web Part. This one Web Part is able to do a myriad of wondrous things, including the following:

❑   Show data stored in SharePoint lists and libraries, even on other sites

❑   Connect to a database and display data stored in a table

❑   Show custom views of external XML scripts (such as RSS feeds)

❑   Pass parameters to Web services

The capabilities of this Web Part are better experienced than explained.

Connecting to a SharePoint List

This walkthrough assumes that you have a default SharePoint team site opened in SPD.

1. Create a blank Web Part page with a single Web Part zone:

    a. Go to File ➪ New ➪ Create from Master Page.

    b. Accept the default option on the "Select a Master Page" dialog and click OK.

    c. Find the placeholder known as "PlaceHolderMain (Master)." Click it to select it, and click the small right-facing arrow on its right side to open the Common Content Tasks menu for the placeholder, as shown in Figure 5-16.

    d. Select "Create Custom Content" from the Common Content Tasks menu.

    e. Click inside the PlaceHolderMain (Custom) placeholder.

    f. Go to Insert ➪ SharePoint Controls ➪ Web Part Zone.

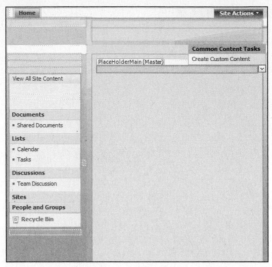

Figure 5-16: Common Content Tasks for the target placeholder

2. Add a data view displaying data stored in the Announcements list:

    a. Go to Data View ➪ Manage Data Sources.

    b. Find the Data Source Library task pane on the right side of SPD's main window.

    c. If necessary, expand SharePoint Lists.

    d. Drag the entry for Announcements and drop it over the Web Part zone, directly over the text "Click to insert a Web Part."

3. Save the page (using the CTRL+S key combination) using a filename of your choice, as long as it ends with the extension .aspx.

4. Preview the page in your browser by pressing F12.

You should now have a Data View Web Part on your page, showing data stored in the default Announcements list from the SharePoint team site. Immediately after placing the part, a new menu called Common Data View Tasks (Figure 5-17) appeared on the screen.

Figure 5-17: The Common Data View Tasks dialog

This menu provides easy access to the common tasks you'll typically perform on a Data View Web Part. Table 5-1 provides a brief definition of these tasks.

Table 5-1: Common Tasks Performed on a Data View Web Part

Option	Description
Filter	Filters the data provided to the Data View Web Part before it is rendered.
Sort and Group	Sorts the data provided to the Data View Web Part, and optionally enables group-by headers.
Paging	Sets paging properties for the Data View Web Part, including options to display everything, limit the number of rows displayed, or display rows in sets of a given size.
Edit Columns	Displays a simple dialog to select which fields get displayed by the Data View Web Part.
Change Layout	Offers a choice of built-in layout templates for the Data View Web Part.
Data View Preview	Selects how much data is shown in the design mode preview of the Data View Web Part. This is a great way to improve design-time performance.
Show with sample data	Pre-fills the Data View Web Part with "dummy" data.
Conditional Formatting	Opens the conditional formatting task pane, where you can apply formatting to the Data View Web Part based on the value(s) of the underlying data.
Web Part Connections	Starts the Web Part Connections Wizard.
Parameters	Allows you to define additional parameters that may be used by the Data View Web Part, including references to query string parameters passed in a GET request.
Refresh Data View	Refreshes the preview of the Data View Web Part with updated data from the server.
Data View Properties	Opens the general Data View Properties dialog, where you can enable different toolbars, turn on column heading features for sort and filter, modify the header and footer, and change the text displayed if the data source does not contain any records.

Conditional Formatting

This walkthrough assumes that you have a default SharePoint team site opened in SPD, and that the site's default Tasks list has several tasks added to it, some of which are past due.

1. Create a new, blank Web Part page (follow Steps 1a through 1f from the previous walkthrough).

2. Add a data view displaying data stored in the Tasks list:

> **a.** Go to Data View ➪ Manage Data Sources.
>
> **b.** Find the Data Source Library task pane on the right side of SPD's main window.
>
> **c.** If necessary, expand SharePoint Lists.
>
> **d.** Drag the entry for Tasks and drop it over the Web Part zone, directly over the text "Click to insert a Web Part."

3. Customize the Tasks list to show Title, Due Date, Priority, and Status:

> **a.** On the Common Data View Tasks menu, select Edit Columns.
>
> **b.** Remove Modified By and Modified. Add Due Date, Priority, and Status.
>
> **c.** Click OK.

4. Conditionally format the task status cell "RED if it is past due":

> **a.** Select the cell to which you want to apply the conditional formatting. In this case, click inside one of the task status cells, next to the status text, and then click the "handle" with the text `td.ms-vb`, as shown in Figure 5-18.

Figure 5-18: The Data View Web Part with the TD element selected

> **b.** Right-click inside the `td.ms-vb` "handle" and choose Conditional Formatting.
>
> **c.** In the Conditional Formatting task pane that opens on the right, click the Create button to open the Create menu. Select "Apply formatting."
>
> **d.** A dialog appears, which allows you to define the condition for this conditional formatting exercise. Using this dialog, create two clauses for past-due tasks: due date less than the current date, and status not equal to completed (Figure 5-19).

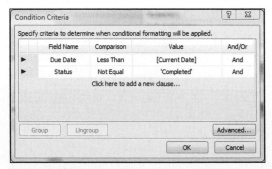

Figure 5-19: The Condition Criteria dialog

e. Once you have defined the condition using this dialog, you may wish to examine the XPATH notation that SPD created to represent the condition. Click the Advanced button to see this dialog.

f. Click OK.

g. Using the Modify Style dialog that appears (Figure 5-20), set the font color to a light color (such as yellow), and set the background color to a darker color (such as red).

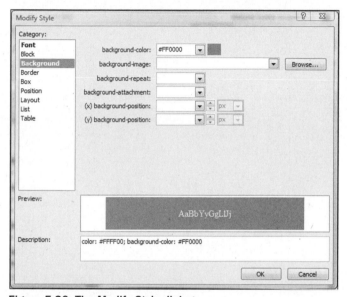

Figure 5-20: The Modify Style dialog

h. Click OK. The Data View Web Part should now highlight past-due tasks by coloring the status cell of the past-due task red, with yellow text.

5. Save the page (using the CTRL+S key combination) using a filename of your choice, as long as it ends with the extension .aspx.

6. Preview the page in your browser by pressing F12.

Connecting to an RSS Feed and Passing Parameters

This walkthrough assumes that you have a default SharePoint team site opened in SPD, that you've created a blank Web Part page on that site (see Steps 1a–1f from the earlier section, "Connecting to a SharePoint List"), and that the blank Web Part page is currently open in Design view.

1. Add an entry to the Data Source Catalog that references the Google News RSS feed after searching for "SharePoint":

a. Go to Data View ⇨ Manage Data Sources.

b. Find the Data Source Library task pane on the right side of SPD's main window.

c. If necessary, expand "Server-side Scripts."

> **d.** Click "Connect to a Script or RSS Feed."
>
> **e.** Enter the following URL in the text box titled "Enter the URL to a server-side script":

```
http://news.google.com/news?q=sharepoint&scoring=d&output=rss
```

> **f.** Press the Tab key and notice that the URL parameters (query string parameters) get copied to the "Add or Modify Parameters" section, as shown in Figure 5-21. Also notice that each of them is marked as capable of being set at run-time.

Figure 5-21: Data Source Properties for an RSS feed

> **g.** Select the General tab. Name this connection something memorable, such as "Google News via RSS."
>
> **h.** Click OK.

2. Drag the entry for "Google News via RSS" and drop it over the Web Part zone, directly over the text "Click to insert a Web Part."

3. Customize the Web Part to show news headlines with a link to the story:

> **a.** Open the Common Data View Tasks menu by clicking the small right-facing arrow at the top of the Data View Web Part.
>
> **b.** Select Edit Columns.
>
> **c.** Remove everything except "title."
>
> **d.** Click OK.
>
> **e.** Right-click one of the news stories (the "title" element) and select Hyperlink.
>
> **f.** If prompted to confirm that you're using a trusted environment, click Yes.

      g.   On the right side of the Edit Hyperlink dialog that appears, click the Parameters button.

      h.   Click Insert Field Value and select "XSL: link."

      i.   Click OK, and then click OK again.

4. Add a form Web Part to allow user-entered search terms:

      a.   Go to Insert ⇨ SharePoint Controls ⇨ Web Part.

      b.   Drag a Form Web Part and drop it just above the "Google News via RSS" Data View Web Part.

5. Add a Web Part connection between the two parts to pass a parameter to Google News' RSS feed:

      a.   Right-click the Form Web Part and select Web Part Connections.

      b.   In the first step of the wizard, confirm that the action is "Provide Form Values To" and click Next.

      c.   Confirm that "Connect to a Web Part on this page" is selected and click Next.

      d.   Confirm that "Google News via RSS" is selected as the Target Web Part.

      e.   Change the Target action to "Get Parameters From."

      f.   Click Next.

      g.   Find the q parameter under "Inputs to Google News via RSS" and click in the empty space to its left.

      h.   Open the drop-down list box and select "T1." Then click Next.

      i.   Click Finish.

6. Save the page (using the CTRL+S key combination) using a filename of your choice, as long as it ends with the extension .aspx.

7. Preview the page in your browser by pressing F12.

The page that appears in your browser is your own custom Google News search page. By default, it will return the last ten news stories with the word "SharePoint" in them. By entering your own search term, you instruct SharePoint to re-fetch an RSS feed from Google News, searching for your custom term.

Connecting to a Web Service

This walkthrough assumes that you have a default SharePoint team site opened in SPD, that you've created a blank Web Part page on that site (see Steps 1a–1f in the earlier section, "Connecting to a SharePoint List"), and that the blank Web Part page is currently open in Design view.

1. Add an entry to the Data Source Catalog that references the current site's built-in "Lists" Web service:

      a.   Go to Data View ⇨ Manage Data Sources.

      b.   Find the Data Source Library task pane on the right side of SPD's main window.

      c.   If necessary, expand "XML Web Services."

      d.   Click "Connect to a web service."

e. For the "Service description location," enter the URL to the Web Service Definition Language (WSDL) file for the Web service you want to consume. For this example, enter the base URL to your current site (without the `default.aspx`), followed by `_vti_bin/lists.asmx`. For example, if the URL of your current site is `http://www.myserver.com/mysite/default.aspx`, you would enter `http://www.myserver.com/mysite/_vti_bin/lists.asmx`.

f. Click Connect Now.

g. Next to Operation, expand the drop-down list box and select GetListCollection.

h. Click OK.

2. Drag the entry for "Lists on <servername>" and drop it over the Web Part zone, directly over the text "Click to insert a Web Part."

3. Customize the Web Part to show a nicely formatted list of the lists on the current SharePoint site:

a. Open the Common Data View Tasks menu by clicking the small right-facing arrow at the top of the Data View Web Part.

b. Select Edit Columns.

c. Configure the selected fields so that only `ImageUrl` and `Title` are listed in the Displayed Columns list box, then click OK.

d. Single-click one of the repeating `ImageUrl` fields.

e. Click the right-facing arrow that appears next to the URL to open the "Common xsl:value-of Tasks" menu.

f. Expand the drop-down list box next to "Format as" and select Picture.

g. If prompted to confirm that you're using a trusted environment, click Yes.

h. Right-click one of the list titles (such as "Announcements") and select Hyperlink.

i. On the right side of the Edit Hyperlink dialog that appears, click the Parameters button.

j. Click Insert Field Value and select "XSL: DefaultViewUrl."

k. Click OK, and then click OK again.

4. Save the page (using the CTRL+S key combination) using a filename of your choice, as long as it ends with the extension `.aspx`.

5. Preview the page in your browser by pressing F12.

The page that appears in your browser should show you an up-to-date list of all the lists on the current site, along with the list's standard icon next to the list title. You can take this page back into SPD and further customize it, adding filters to remove unneeded list entries (such as "fpdatasources" and "Master Page Gallery").

As you can see, SPD is a powerful tool, capable of creating heavily customized no-code solutions — even solutions that integrate with RSS feeds and Web services. That's just the tip of the iceberg.

Customized (Unghosted) and Uncustomized (Ghosted) Pages

Before I close this chapter, I would be remiss to bring one last topic into the limelight. You see, there is a big fuss out there about ghosted versus unghosted pages (now called uncustomized and customized pages, respectively — I'll stick with the more colorful and outdated terminology). Why does it matter, and how does it affect you when you're using SPD?

To understand the terms, first you should understand what happens when you request a page from a SharePoint site — for example, the default home page, `default.aspx`.

As shown in Figure 5-22, when you request a page, SharePoint has to (among other things) determine if that page has been customized using SPD. If it has been, SharePoint retrieves the customized version from the database. If it hasn't been, SharePoint retrieves a shared version the file from the file system. This shared version (part of the site definition) is used by all the team sites on the server. It's "ghosted" (or "uncustomized"), and because it's shared by everyone, it's faster than retrieving single one-off copies from the database. It can be cached, and you can even effect sweeping changes to your SharePoint implementation's look and feel by modifying this root, shared template. Modifying this template, as you might imagine, is not actually supported by Microsoft. That's not to say that they won't help you if your site breaks, but if modifying these base templates is what broke your site, you will need to roll back your changes.

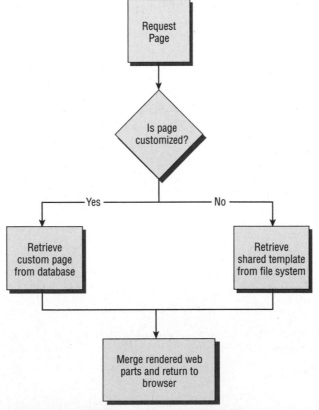

Figure 5-22: Simplified page request life cycle

Customized (or "unghosted") pages are slightly slower to execute, because they must be fetched over the network from the database, rather than from the local hard drive of the WFE server. In reality, however, caching improvements in ASP.NET reduce the typical performance impact of unghosted pages to less than 10 percent, according to my own stress testing.

Though using unghosted pages prevents you from modifying the base templates to change every site on your server (because some sites could have their own, customized, in-database version of the page you would be changing), you shouldn't be modifying those pages in the first place — not when there are sites deployed against them. If you want to make wide-reaching visual changes to your sites, that's what master pages and CSS modifications are for. Don't brand your sites by modifying dozens (or even hundreds!) of base template pages. Brand your sites by using master pages or by changing some CSS files around.

Branding is discussed in more detail in Chapter 6.

If you follow that advice, you'll see that you're not really losing much by "unghosting" your pages. You're gaining a great deal, however. By using SPD and adding features like the Data View Web Part to your pages, you are able to create powerful, deeply connected no-code solutions. Don't leave that behind just because the page goes into the database!

There's So Much More

There is a great deal more that SPD brings to the table. I always tell my students to "experiment and explore" SPD as they use the product to build custom SharePoint solutions. The investment you make in experimentation and exploration will pay significant dividends in the future. And, remember: It's a powerful tool, capable of great destruction if wielded improperly. So, back up your pages before you edit them in SPD!

Summary

SPD is a rich and complex application. The big brother to Expression Web, SPD is capable of creating standards-compliant Web sites using XHTML and CSS, if that's your preference. Borrowing features from more powerful IDEs such as Visual Studio, SPD offers IntelliSense, tag completion, and a Code view that enforces standards compliance.

SPD is not just a capable Web editor. It is an important part of any SharePoint solution development. With SPD, you can create custom XSLT-based views of data stored in SharePoint lists, syndicated via RSS feeds, even connect to Simple Object Access Protocol (SOAP) Web Services, all without writing a single line of code.

Concerns about "unghosting" or "customizing" SharePoint pages are largely unnecessary, because caching improvements in ASP.NET 2.0 provide improved performance over similarly modified pages in WSS v2.0.

6

Customizing and Branding the SharePoint 2007 Interface

by Shane Perran and Heather Solomon

The benefits of customizing a user interface run deep, with many layers, each as unique as they are important. From standard brand recognition, to ensuring a user experience that will promote healthy adoption, there is much more to customization than meets the eye.

The 1990s failed to deliver a long-promised usable Web experience, leaving the world weary of doing business online. The expectations in the new world of work have increased significantly.

A seamless and connected experience across applications in which technology is borderline transparent (a term dubbed "Web 2.0" by the global marketing machine) is not only expected, it's demanded.

SharePoint is certainly no exception to this rule. Being a Web-based platform, the expectations are high, and the need to deliver has never been stronger.

In this chapter, SharePoint MVPs and customization experts Shane Perran (www.graphicalwonder.com) and Heather Solomon (www.heathersolomon.com) have teamed up for the first time to share real-world field experience and guide you through some of the least-documented and understood aspects of SharePoint, user interface customization.

To begin, Shane Perran guides you through a basic overview of each customization option at a high level before moving on and sketching out several realistic business scenarios based on real-life experience in the field, helping you to logically match customization options with business problems. Next, the discussion takes a deep dive into the mechanics of each option as they apply directly to the solutions, giving you step-by-step instructions, trips, tricks, and best practices sure to make your next customization project a success.

In the latter half of the chapter, Heather Solomon focuses solely on a major component of any SharePoint customization, cascading style sheets (CSS). By the end of this part of the chapter, you will be able to identify, edit, and create your own styles, and fully customize SharePoint for your unique branding.

Have you been fretting the interface customization of SharePoint? This chapter will give you a clear view of what to do, how to do it, and how to be successful at it.

An Overview of SharePoint 2007 Customization Options

This section guides you through the process of identifying the available options, matching them with organizational requirements, and, finally, guiding you step-by-step through a set of customization best practices as used in the field to address real-world scenarios.

Assume, for a moment, that you have been tasked with transforming your organization's newly acquired Microsoft Office SharePoint Server 2007 (MOSS 2007) site into an intuitive and brand-aware user interface where employees can interact, store data, and share information.

Several customization options are available. Your unique requirements as an organization will help you to decide on the specifics of a particular option, or combination of options, that are discussed later in this chapter.

SharePoint customization can be categorized into two main groups, each containing several sub-topics:

❑   Out-of-the box customization

❑   Developer-focused customization

Each type offers slightly more advanced extensibility and, subsequently, varying levels of development knowledge and time are required.

Out-of-the-Box, "No Code Required" Customization

Out-of-the box customization refers to customizations that can be completed without code, using the user interface. Some of the most popular forms of out-of-the box customization include the following:

❑   Adding Web Parts to a Web Part page and moving them from zone to zone

❑   Changing the properties of a Web Part (things such as the title or border) using the tool pane

❑   Adding metadata columns to a list or site

❑   Creating filtered views

❑   Applying a site theme

❑ Applying an alternate out-of-the box master page

❑ Creating sites, Web Part pages, and Web content-managed pages

❑ Creating list or site templates

Although these types of customization are a great addition to the product, and help you to extend portions of your sites, they are somewhat limiting when it comes to branding because you are confined to a set of predefined templates, colors, images, and the like. This chapter focuses on the more advanced customization options.

Organizations able to fill their requirements using only options from the previous list of items are an exception to the rule. The majority of customization jobs will require a combination of the items appearing in the preceding list, and one or more developer-focused customizations.

Developer-Focused Customizations

Developer-focused customizations are the more advanced customizations that require the use of code and tools, such as Microsoft Office SharePoint Designer 2007 (SPD 2007) or Microsoft Visual Studio 2005.

There are several types of developer-focused customizations, each slightly more advanced, and in the end, the sky is the limit when it comes to solutions that use custom code.

The following are the more popular forms of developer-focused customization discussed in this section:

❑ Master pages

❑ Page layouts

❑ Cascading style sheets (CSS)

❑ Role-based site templates

❑ Site definitions

Master Pages

A product of ASP.NET 2.0, *master pages* are used to define the common elements of your site (such as navigation menus, headers, or footers). These elements are often referred to as the *chrome* of your Web site, and remain consistent throughout all pages.

Master pages force consistency across all pages within a site, a great usability benefit. At the same time, master pages greatly reduce development cycles. By modifying a single master page, the effect is rippled out to all pages in a site that inherit it.

Master pages work in conjunction with other pages known as *content pages,* which actually inherit the master page via a declaration at the top of the page similar to the following example:

```
<%@ Page language="C#" MasterPageFile="~masterurl/default.master"
Inherits="Microsoft.SharePoint.WebPartPages.WebPartPage,Microsoft.SharePoint
,Version=12.0.0.0,Culture=neutral,PublicKeyToken=" %>
```

Because master pages are used to define the chrome of a page rather than the content, they contain special placeholders where content can be "plugged in" later from a content page. A *content placeholder* is defined using syntax similar to the following example:

```
<asp:ContentPlaceHolder id="PlaceHolderMain"
runat="server"></asp:ContentPlaceHolder>
```

Likewise, a content page has content controls that can be plugged into the master page when requested. A *content control* is specified using syntax similar to the following example:

```
<asp:Content ContentPlaceHolderId="PlaceHolderMain" runat="server"></asp: Content>
```

When a user requests a page in the browser, the content page first looks to see what master page it must inherit based on the declaration at the top of the page. Finally, the content controls in the content page that match the IDs of the placeholders in the master page are merged together, presenting a single rendered page to the user. This process, of course, is invisible to the user, taking place in the background, as shown in Figure 6-1.

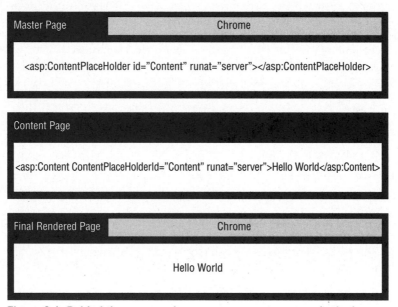

Figure 6-1: Behind the scenes when a user requests a page in the browser

Content controls that exist in a content page must have matching placeholder IDs in the master page that it inherits. Requesting a page that has a content control with no matching content placeholder in the master page will produce an error, and, as such, it is extremely important to ensure that you do not remove content placeholders from the default master pages.

Master pages are stored in the Master Pages and Page Layouts library, accessible via the Site Settings option of the Site Actions menu.

Page Layouts

A common joke surrounding SharePoint products and technologies is that the best thing about the product is that it is so easy to use, but the worst thing about the product is also that it is so easy to use. What people mean by this is that, although it's great that the average non-technical information worker can easily create content, the worker may not have the experience or savvy required to properly maintain it.

Page layouts, specific to MOSS 2007 and a product of Web Content Management (WCM), help to address this issue by offering a flexible and powerful way to control exactly what content can be created on a page, and how it is presented. Much like a master page defines the chrome, a page layout defines the content area.

Working in conjunction with other SharePoint 2007–specific technologies (such as content types, site columns, and master pages), site administrators can finally allow more users to create content and still maintain a level of control over it.

When the Publishing Feature is enabled on a site, page layouts are accessible and applicable via the dialog exposed by selecting the Create Page option from the Site Actions menu.

Page layouts are stored alongside master pages in the Page Layouts and Master Pages library. These are the pages you can choose after selecting the Create Page option from the Site Actions menu, as shown in Figure 6-2.

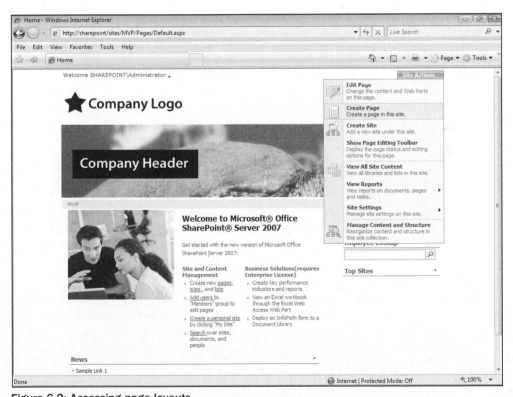

Figure 6-2: Accessing page layouts

Cascading Style Sheets

Cascading style sheets (CSS) offers an easy way to separate the presentation of content from the markup. CSS drastically reduces the amount of inline code required to style content, and, hence, significantly reduces the size and load time of your pages.

Style sheets are comprised of a collection of selectors known as *classes* or *IDs* that have special properties used to change the appearance of content contained within HTML elements such as a `<div>`.

Style sheets can be specified in a variety of ways, from standard linking, to importing, to just inline. Depending on the situation, you may require a more advanced style sheet specification that uses a relative path. Using SPURL, an option available only to Publishing sites, it is possible to specify relative paths. Later in this chapter, you learn about the ways in which you can use SPURL.

Like its predecessor, SharePoint 2007 makes extensive use of style sheets in several forms. In fact, every new site you create makes use of CSS to control the look and feel of the basic fonts and background colors or images.

The following custom style sheet options are available to you:

❑   *SharePoint Themes* — This is available for Windows SharePoint Services (WSS) sites only. This is a reusable file system–based collection of style sheets and images that can be applied via Site Settings to modify the color scheme.

❑   `AlternateCSS` — This is a property available via the interface in MOSS 2007 that allows you to override the default styles by uploading an alternate style sheet, which is placed last in line to render. The default behavior of CSS is that the last style sheet (or properties within a style sheet) takes precedence. In more advanced situations, the `AlternateCSS` property is also applicable via a site definition configuration.

Each style sheet contains a collection of classes and IDs known as *contextual selectors* that are referenced throughout the pages of a SharePoint site. Changing the properties of a class will, in turn, change the appearance of the contents of the HTML element the class is applied to.

By using tools such as the Internet Explorer Developer Toolbar, to identify what classes are applied to each area of a site, customization is fairly easy.

> *Editing default files can lead to issues during service packs or upgrades, because it is not a supported scenario by Microsoft. Because of this, you should not edit any default style sheets and instead, where possible, the best method is to create new files based on existing ones, or to override styles based on their placement in the page.*

Because style sheets are used in multiple ways, they are also stored in multiple locations both on the server's file system and in document libraries. The `_layouts` folder can be referenced relatively to where you are in the site; it is common practice to store style sheets and images there.

The `_layouts` folder is located on the server's file system at the following path:

```
C:\Program Files\Common Files\Microsoft Shared\web server
extensions\12\TEMPLATE\LAYOUTS
```

Site Templates

The idea behind a *site template* is that you create a site, add content, customize it, and then template it so that it becomes a benchmark that can be reused to create identical sites in just a few seconds.

Just as every organization is unique, so are the corporate cultures and business processes. To operate at maximum efficiency, it is important that organizations be able to easily identify these unique business processes and the roles associated with each. For example, the Sales and Marketing Department would have much different business processes than the Finance Department.

SharePoint offers an out-of-the-box method to create, package, and reuse site templates to better allow you to easily deploy and reuse simple customizations that you implement to support your various business units and processes.

These site templates, commonly referred to as *application* or *role-based templates,* are actually a collection of lists, document libraries, metadata, filtered views, and, at times, workflow. Collectively, these templates streamline business processes by connecting people with common roles with the information they need to perform day-to-day tasks (such as updating sales projections). Several of these templates have been released by Microsoft to provide a starting point for many common business processes and roles. They can be downloaded from the Microsoft Web site at `http://www.microsoft.com/technet/windowsserver/sharepoint/wssapps/templates/default.mspx`.

Site templates can be created and selected using the browser. Once created, templates are stored in the site template gallery with an `.STP` extension. When creating new sites, site templates will be accessible from the Custom tab on the site template selection screen, as shown in the lower-right of Figure 6-3. The templates displayed in this figure are available as part of the Microsoft download mentioned earlier.

Figure 6-3: Accessing site templates

Site Definitions

Much like site templates, *site definitions* are available to select from the list of available templates when creating a new site.

The most complex and powerful of the available customization options, site definitions are file system–based configurations consisting of a collection of pages, images, style sheets, and XML, which, when called on, define how a new site is provisioned.

By default, all SharePoint sites start their life cycle from a site definition. When a new site is created, SharePoint reads the XML configuration file for the matching site definition and provisions the pages, lists, libraries, and customizations accordingly.

Many SharePoint designers and developers will use site definitions to implement their customizations rather than customizing via SPD to avoid issues with deploying a large number of sites or more advanced customizations. When a page is customized in SPD, it may pose risks when upgrading to newer versions of the product. Because of technology changes and the introduction of Features, there are some differences in the way site definitions work in SharePoint 2007.

Site templates are located on the server's file system at the following path:

```
C:\Program Files\Common Files\Microsoft Shared\web server
extensions\12\TEMPLATE\SiteTemplates
```

One common area of confusion while working with site definitions has been their location on the file system in a folder called SiteTemplates. *Though site definitions and site templates are similar, they should not be confused as being the same. Site definitions offer distinct advantages over the standard out-of-the-box site templates (*.STP *files), which any site can be packaged as and stored in the sites template gallery.*

Each type of site that you can create in SharePoint has its own site definition folder within the one previously listed. Inside the definition folder, you will find an XML folder containing the XML configuration file for that site definition known as the ONET.XML. The ONET.XML file is the magic behind the scenes during site creation, broken down into several important parts that specify what files to create and where to place them, as well as any lists, libraries, or customizations. As a standard practice, it is a good idea to register each site definition with SharePoint via its own WEBTEMPsite-defintion-name.XML.

Choosing Customization Options that Are Right for Your Organization

Each organization's corporate culture and needs are unique and very personal to it. Organizations make significant investments of both time and money to ensure that their corporate brands are known, and that their business processes effectively allow them to deliver quality products and services as determined by their business models.

Going into any customization project, it is important to understand that the biggest hurdle you must overcome is making change as transparent as possible. People already have a set way of doing things, which they have no intention of changing. The more familiar an experience you can deliver via user interface (UI) customization and branding, the better the odds are of your overall project being adopted by the masses.

The following short story has been pieced together based roughly on a real project as experienced in the field. This story has been selected because it combines a majority of customization options into a single solution.

Matching Business Needs with Customization Paths

It's early November and the community is buzzing with rumors of MOSS 2007 Release to Web (RTW) getting set to launch. The product team doesn't disappoint, and on November 16, Joel Oleson announces both the RTW and several upgrade paths generously created and donated by the community on the SharePoint Team Blog.

Within a week of receiving notice of the release, the phone was ringing and customers were eager to get started. First up was a reputable retailer that wanted to replace an existing file-management application that connected its globally dispersed employees with important digital assets.

Of course, no *real* project is free of challenges, and almost all have a catch. In this case, there were several child companies that would inherit the same basic functionality, but required unique content. On top of that, though they technically could and, by default, would fall under the master corporate brand of the parent company, it was requested that they be able to present their own unique brand if desired. Finally, like any good solution, it should easily scale and, in the event of a merger or acquisition, it was important that they be seamlessly integrated into the portal system.

After numerous meetings to determine the details of the expected deliverables, we were able to get started with the most important portion of any project: the planning.

Taking a step back to assess the requirements, we were able to break the customizations down to the following set of separately manageable modules:

❑ To address the need for a seamless transition from one application and technology to the next, master page customization can be leveraged to create an interface that is both usable and familiar to the user base — not only masking the change, but actually building a better experience on top of what is already known and used.

❑ Page layouts, though not always required, offer an easy value-add to any solution, and, as such, it would be considered best practice to introduce a few varieties.

❑ To address the need for the possibility of multiple brands across child sites, a combination of techniques and options is required. The master page that defines the familiar UI can also be set to inherit an alternate style sheet used to define the color scheme, which, by default, should be the parent company's brand.

❑ Using the SPURL technique of specifying paths relative to site or site collection files (such as style sheets or images), it is possible to create page elements that assume a default brand, but still remain flexible to change.

❑ To support the use of SPURL, a site-specific resource library is required to store the images and style sheets. The reason for using a site-specific library versus the more popular site collection library was to address the need for separate brands when requested. The general idea here is that when a new site is created, the administrator has the option of overwriting styles and images specific to the site to quickly transform the brand.

❑ The out-of-the box site template system lends support to both scalability and flexibility of the solution. After implementing all of the preceding techniques and options to create a custom UI, a site snapshot (complete with resources and content) can be taken and stored in the site template gallery.

The end result was a mix of custom master pages, techniques, style sheets, and images that were combined to deliver a single site template consisting of a custom and familiar UI, as well as a resource library where brand assets (such as the parent company logo, header image, and style sheet) are stored.

Creating new child sites based on a site template takes just a few seconds, meeting the scalability requirements. Because of the SPURL technique used, uniquely branding a site is as simple as overwriting a couple of images and modifying a few CSS properties.

The untold story of customization is that creating an interface that is familiar means less reaction to change, and subsequently faster and easier user adoption. Leveraging carefully planned techniques to maximize scalability and flexibility also drastically reduces the maintenance overhead for many years to come.

This exercise was designed to offer a different perspective on SharePoint customization, one that logically maps business value and need directly to the options available. Based on common business needs (as experienced in the field) and best practices for customization (as defined by Microsoft and subject matter experts), Table 6-1 will help you to select the best customization options and techniques for your next project.

Table 6-1: Choosing Customization Options

Business Need	Recommended Customization	Recommended Tools
No custom UI or brand required. Used only to store and find role/user-specific content.	Basic metadata customization and filtered views. No code required.	Browser only
No custom UI required. A single branded set of colors only.	Custom style sheet customization using either our preferred method AlternateCSS or themes.	Browser, SPD 2007
Custom UI and single brand required.	A combination of custom master page and style sheet customization.	Browser, SPD 2007
Custom UI and multi-branded site hierarchy required.	A combination of custom master pages, which leverage the SPURL technique, style sheets, and site templates.	Browser, SPD 2007
Custom content restrictions and branding.	Custom page layouts	Browser, SPD 2007

Practical Customization Solutions that Work in the Real World

Fire up SPD 2007 and get ready. In this section, you take the driver's seat and get hands-on experience as you are guided step-by-step through customizing and branding the SharePoint UI.

Using the solution outlined previously as a rough guide, we will dive deep under the covers to transform a standard SharePoint 2007 Publishing site into an application interface that will both meet specific requirements as outlined previously, and leave a positive, lasting impression on the user base.

Getting Started

Getting back to the basics for just a moment, the first thing required is a site collection to customize. Because many of the techniques I will leverage are unique to the Publishing Features of MOSS 2007, the Publishing Portal site template should be selected when creating the site collection. The remainder of this section assumes a Publishing Portal site collection has been created.

> *One caveat for Publishing sites is that they cannot be turned into a template using the out-of-the-box, Save as Site Template method. They can, however, use the Content Migration Package (.CMP) available in SPD 2007.*

Understanding Custom Master Pages

As mentioned earlier in the chapter, master pages control the UI, often referred to as the chrome of a page. This includes items generally shared across all pages in the site (such as a navigation menu, header, or footer).

A master page also contains a variety of content placeholders used by content controls on other pages (known as content pages or page layouts), which are used to control the presentation of the content of the page. When a page is requested, the two are merged to form a single page.

> The default master page for a SharePoint site has many content placeholders, *all* of which are required for various reasons. Removing any required content placeholder will result in an error being generated when you attempt to view a page inheriting that master page, so it is incredibly important that they all remain on the page. It's also important to note that a content placeholder being in the master page does not mean it will render on every page. They will render the default contents of what is in the master page, which can be empty, or they will be overwritten by the contents of a matching content control.

Now, let's take a look at a hands-on example of creating and specifying a custom master page.

Creating and Specifying a Custom Master Page

Because modifying a master page is a long, risky, and tedious process, it is recommended that you start with a base minimal master page, such as the one provided on the MSDN Web site at `http://msdn2.microsoft.com/en-us/library/aa660698.aspx`.

The purpose of the minimal master page is to remove the majority of the presentation from the page. Removing the styling and positioning of elements gives you a blank starting point. The idea is that you create your own interface using `<div>` or `<table>` elements, then the controls (such as search, navigation, and breadcrumbs) where you want to display them, before finally styling them with CSS.

Creating and specifying a custom master page is easy. You can get started by following these steps:

1. Connect to your site using the SPD 2007 File ⇨ Open Site option.

2. From the folder list on the left, locate and click the `_catalogs/masterpage` library. This is where all master pages and page layouts are stored. Subsequently, you will want to create your custom master page here.

3. From the File menu in SPD 2007, Select New ⇨ Page.

4. Select the Page ⇨ General ⇨ Master Page option before clicking OK.

5. Download the file `custom.master` from the resource location.

6. Open and copy the entire contents of the `custom.master` page.

7. Paste the contents into the new master page you created in Step 4.

8. Save the file, naming it customnew.master.

9. Visit the same site in the browser.

10. From the Site Actions menu, select Site Settings ⇨ Modify all Site Settings.

11. From the Look and Feel column, select Master Page.

12. From the Site Master Page section, select the radio button for "Specify a master page to be used by this site and all sites that inherit from it" to expose the `.master` pages available in the `_catalogs/masterpage` folder in a drop-down menu, as shown in the lower right of Figure 6-4.

13. From the drop-down menu, select the `customnew.master` page.

14. Scroll to the bottom and click OK. You will notice that your site has transformed significantly.

By default, all master pages and page layouts are stored in the Master Pages and Page Layouts library. Adding master pages to this library makes them available to be applied to the site using the drop-down menu in the Site Master Page Settings page. This gives you an easy way to dynamically change the UI of your site.

Changing the selected master page will ultimately change a token in the default page layout, telling it to inherit the new master page, subsequently changing the chrome, which, in this case, is a skeletal page that you can now work with.

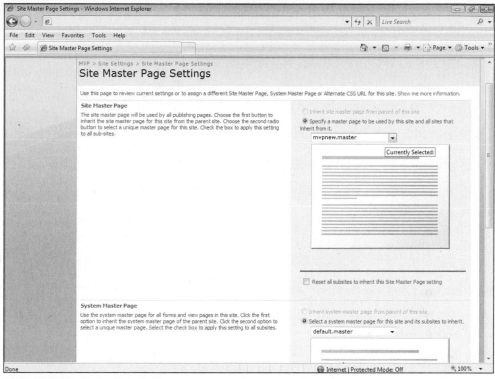

Figure 6-4: Viewing a list of all `.master` **pages**

Using SPURL to Specify Site or Site Collection Relative Paths

SPURL (which is available only in the MOSS 2007 Publishing Feature) is the magic key for specifying paths to files as being relative to the site, or collection. Specifying relative versus hard-coded paths is considered a general best practice because it is the most flexible and it is adaptable to change in the event of a site migration.

Let's take a look at a hands-on example of specifying site and collection relative paths with SPURL.

Specifying Site and Collection Relative Paths with SPURL

SPURL can be used to specify two specific path references: `~site` (which is relative to the current site) and `~sitecollection` (which is relative to the top level of the site collection).

Using SPURL to specify relative paths is easy. You can get started by following these steps:

1. Visit your site in the browser and select View all Site Content from the Site Actions menu.

2. Select Create from the toolbar.

3. From the Libraries Column, select Document Library.

4. Name it **Resources** and click Create.

5. Upload the images `companylogo.gif` and `companyheader.gif` from the `resources` folder to the library.

6. Connect to your site using the SPD 2007 File ⇨ Open Site option.

7. From the folder list on the left, locate and click the `_catalogs/masterpage` library and open the `mvpnew.master` page for editing in Code view.

8. Locate the following code:

```
<img alt="" src="/sites/MVP/images/companylogo.gif">
```

9. Replace it with the following code:

```
<asp:Image runat="server" id="Logo" ImageUrl="<% $SPUrl: ~site/resources/
companylogo.gif %>"/>
```

10. Locate the following code:

```
<img alt="" src="/sites/MVP/images/companyheader.gif">
```

11. Replace it with the following code:

```
<asp:Image runat="server" id="Header" ImageUrl="<% $SPUrl: ~site/resources/
companyheader.gif %>"/>
```

The minimal master page you started with contained hard-coded paths to an `images` directory for the site. Because this path is not relative, depending on where you are in the site, it is possible the hard-coded path will be incorrect and, as a result, a broken image would display.

By replacing the hard-coded paths with site-specific paths using SPURL, you have ultimately told SharePoint that regardless of where you are in the site, display the images located in the site images library.

Specifying an Alternate Style Sheet

As mentioned earlier in the chapter, by default, all SharePoint sites make extensive use of style sheets to control site branding (such as background colors, images, and fonts).

Because of the cascading nature of style sheets, the last style sheet specified in the page (or the last class/property in the style sheet) will take precedence over any that precede them.

SharePoint 2007 takes advantage of this fact by offering the `AlternateCSS` property, which ultimately places the specified style sheet last in line to be read, meaning any duplicate classes or properties will take precedence.

You should use the Internet Explorer Developer Toolbar to find what class is applied to what element of the page. You can download the Internet Explorer Developer Toolbar free from Microsoft at the following location:

```
http://www.microsoft.com/downloads/details.aspx?FamilyID=e59c3964-672d-
4511-bb3e-2d5e1db91038&displaylang=en
```

Now, let's work on a hands-on example of specifying and modifying an alternate style sheet.

Specifying and Modifying an Alternate Style Sheet

Because SharePoint 2007 has an out-of-the-box mechanism for specifying an alternate style sheet, the process is easy. You can get started by following these simple steps:

1. From the SPD 2007 File menu, select New ⇨ CSS.

2. From the Folder List on the left, select Style Library. If the folder list is not visible, select ALT+F1 to display it.

3. Select File ⇨ Save As and save the file as `custom.css`.

4. Visit the same site in the browser.

5. From the Site Actions menu, select Site Settings ⇨ Modify all Site Settings.

6. From the Look and Feel column, select Master Page.

7. Scroll to the Alternate CSS URL section at the bottom and select the radio button for "Specify a CSS file to be used by this publishing site and all sites that inherit from it," as shown in the lower right of Figure 6-5.

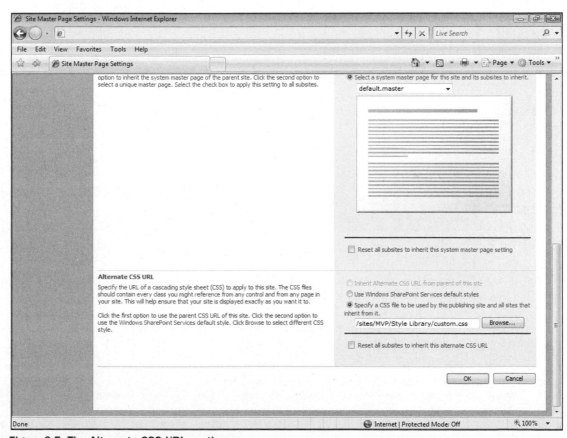

Figure 6-5: The Alternate CSS URL section

8. Select Browse.

9. From the dialog box, select the option in the left for Top Level Site ⇨ Style Library.

10. Select the `custom.css` and click OK, as shown in Figure 6-6.

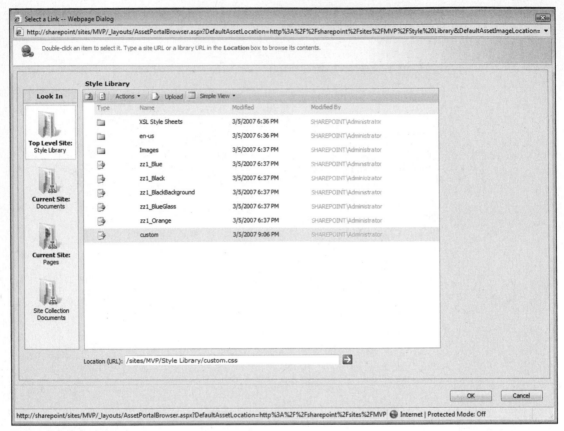

Figure 6-6: Selecting `custom.css`

11. With an alternate style sheet specified, all that is left to do is override some of the default styles that are pulled from the CORE.CSS style sheet located at: `Drive\Program Files\Common Files\Microsoft Shared\web server extensions\12\TEMPLATE\LAYOUTS\1033\STYLES`. This section will take advantage of the Internet Explorer Developer Toolbar.

12. After installing the Internet Explorer Developer Toolbar, select View ⇨ Toolbars ⇨ Developer Toolbar.

    If you are using Internet Explorer (IE) 7, you may need to press the ALT key to expose your File menu.

13. From the Developer Toolbar menu at the top of the screen, select View Dom to open the bottom properties window.

14. From the bottom menu, select Find ⇨ Select Element by Click.

15. After turning on Select Element by Click, you should notice a blue border around elements of the page as you move your mouse around, hovering over different sections of the page. Click an item such as the Site Actions tab to view its properties, as shown in Figure 6-7.

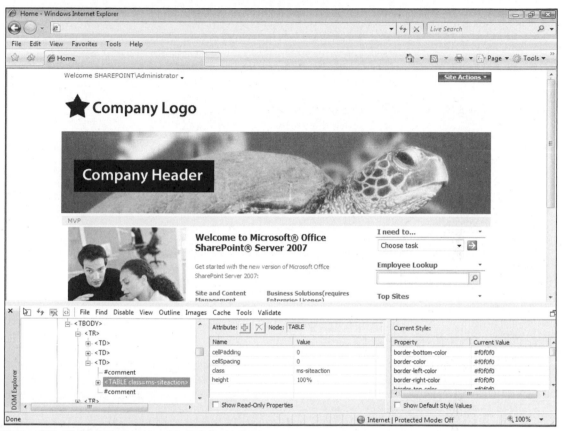

Figure 6-7: Clicking an item to view its properties

16. To change the properties, add them to the `custom.css` style sheet, which was specified as the `AlternateCSS` as seen in the following example that removes the background image and changes the background color to gray:

```
.ms-siteaction {
Background-image:none;
Background-color:#CCC;
}
```

17. Repeat the process of locating elements and overriding styles until you are pleased with the outcome.

The nature of style sheets dictates that the last style sheet in the page takes precedence, just like the last of duplicate properties take precedence and the last of duplicated classes, as well.

SharePoint utilizes this attribute, allowing you to override the default style sheets by placing the alternate style sheet last in the page, after the CORE.CSS specification, similar to the following:

```
<link href="_layouts/1033/styles/core.css" rel="stylesheet" type="text/css" />
<link href="custom.css" rel="stylesheet" type="text/css" />
```

When using SPD 2007, try control-clicking on an underlined item in the code. Underlined items are shared resource files such as style sheets. Control-clicking one of them will open the file and take you to the appropriate section, which is another great tool for customizing style sheets.

Controlling Content Creation with Page Layouts

Unique to Publishing sites, page layouts are one of the most powerful features of WCM sites, offering a vehicle for controlling the type of content that can be created and the way it is presented, much the way master pages control the chrome of the site.

Page layouts are actually associated with a content type. Just as you can create special types of content (such as a Word or Excel template for a document library), you can also create site content templates using page layouts.

The idea behind a page layout is that the columns of its associated content type are actually content fields that can be placed on a page via SPD 2007. This allows you to create multiple page layouts from a single content type by exposing only the fields required for each unique layout.

To get a better handle on page layouts, let's take a look at a hands-on example.

Creating a Custom Page Layout

Page layouts (covered in Chapter 4) allow you to specify unique areas of content that can be created on a page (such as a header, image, or body text). It is important to understand the mechanics of page layouts because they ultimately control how the final page is rendered. This walks you through the steps of creating a new page layout from scratch.

Getting started with custom page layouts is easy. You can get started by following these easy steps:

1. From the Site Actions menu, select Site Settings ⇨ Modify all Site Settings.
2. Select Site Content Types from the Galleries column.
3. Select Create from the toolbar.
4. Name your content type **Generic Page**.
5. From the Parent Content Type drop-down menu, select Page Layout Content Types.
6. The other items can be left at the default setting. Click OK.

The columns associated with a content type are actually the types of content that can be created on the page layout. When creating new columns for a content type, don't forget to choose the publishing field types whenever possible.

7. In SPD 2007, connect to your site using the File ⇨ Open Site option.

8. Select File ⇨ New ⇨ SharePoint Content.

9. From the SharePoint Content tab, select SharePoint Publishing.

10. From the Content Type Group, select Custom.

11. From the Content Type Name, select Generic Page.

12. Type **Generic Page** for the URL and for the Title before clicking OK, as shown in Figure 6-8.

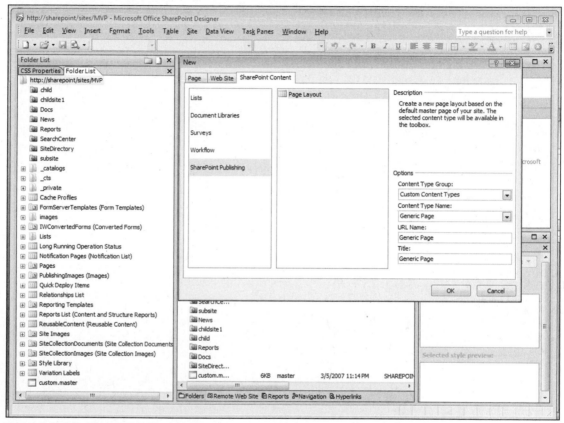

Figure 6-8: Specifying the URL and Title

13. You will notice that you are presented with a basic page that inherits the custom master page. The main area of focus for this page will happen inside the following placeholder, which happens to control the entire content area:

```
<asp:Content ContentPlaceholderID="PlaceHolderMain" runat="server"></asp:Content>
```

14. For basic positioning, add the following table structure inside the PlaceHolderMain content placeholder:

```
<table style="background-color:#F1F1F1; width:95%">
<tr>
<td></td>
```

```
</tr>
<tr>
<td></td>
</tr>
</table>
```

15. As mentioned earlier, each time you create a new column for the content type that the page layout is associated with, a corresponding content control exists that can be placed on the page.

16. From the Task Pane menu, select Toolbox to expose the Toolbox.

17. Scroll down and locate Content Fields.

18. Drag the Article Date control to the first column in the first row of the table.

19. Drag the Byline control to the first column in the second row.

20. Drag the Page Content control to the third row.

21. Save the page and go back to the browser and visit the site.

22. From the Site Actions menu, select Create Page.

23. Notice that included in the list of available page layouts is "Generic Page," as shown in Figure 6-9.

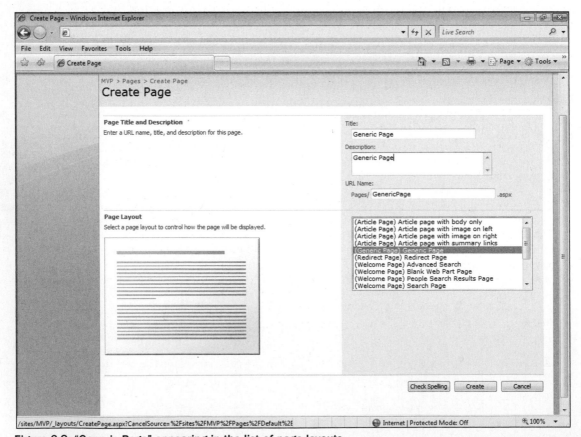

Figure 6-9: "Generic Page" appearing in the list of page layouts

Page layouts are based on content types. Content types have columns representing the content that can be created on a page when the corresponding content control is dragged onto a page.

After creating a page based on your new page layout, you will notice that the fields are displayed in the content area, and the master page customizations manage the chrome.

CSS and SharePoint

Now that Shane has just given us an excellent overview of customization options within SharePoint and taken us into a deep dive about master pages and page layouts, let's take a look at the other major component of branding SharePoint: CSS.

Understanding the Relevance of CSS

You can really do a lot with CSS. SharePoint heavily utilizes it to style the user controls, and you will have to edit CSS to brand certain elements of SharePoint. Whether you have been handed a mock-up, pre-written HTML, or you are the designer yourself, any custom code you write for SharePoint will utilize CSS as well.

This latter half of this chapter first takes a look at what CSS is, and covers some core concepts. With a solid CSS foundation, you will be able to better utilize and leverage CSS in your SharePoint sites. Next comes walking step-by-step through how to add, edit, and override styles to affect the SharePoint page components. At the end of the chapter, a sample master page and CSS deployment is considered and broken down into easy steps for completion.

What Is CSS?

CSS is a language used to describe how elements on a Web page should be formatted. CSS can control the display of many page elements (such as fonts, tables, backgrounds, and positioning). The CSS code can be stored in a separate file (my preferred method), or added to the Web file either in the <HEAD> tag or inline in the code.

CSS was first created by the World Wide Web Consortium (W3C) as a way to manage and curb the growing set of HTML tags that were being created by Web browser providers. HTML tags were being introduced to provide many formatting aspects that people wanted to have available to them. CSS was a compromise, and provided page layout features by adding CSS formatting elements to HTML tags. CSS does not, however, control any behavior of Web page elements. CSS can change the look of features of the page, but it does not create the functionality behind it. CSS essentially creates a separate design layer.

The benefit to this approach is that the CSS can be stored in a single location, and updates can then affect countless numbers of Web pages. This central storage makes updating sites and adding new styles an easy effort.

Utilizing CSS with SharePoint

SharePoint uses CSS in two ways. First, it uses CSS to style the UI code available in all of the out-of-the-box master pages. Second, it uses CSS to style the user controls in SharePoint. Some common user controls you will want to rebrand are controlled through CSS:

❑ Web Part title bars

❑ Toolbars and menu bars

❑ Font, forms, and borders

❑ Navigation (global, top, left, Site Actions, Quick Launch, tree view, Recycle Bin, breadcrumbs)

❑ Consoles

❑ Search

❑ Page titles and text

❑ Calendar control

SharePoint styles are stored in numerous files, but luckily they only have to be looked at every now and again, and the files shouldn't be edited. In fact, I highly recommend against it. How best to handle editing styles is covered later in the chapter.

Personally Utilizing CSS

In regard to SharePoint, there are two categories of styles you will deal with: styles you create, and overriding styles that SharePoint creates.

Most customizations will involve the creation of a master page. As a part of that, you will be creating CSS for your master page code. If you are creating a custom site definition, you will be creating CSS for your custom master page or ASPX files.

Next, you will be overriding SharePoint styles that are already a part of the product. Otherwise, you will end up with a branded site with the default SharePoint coloring and images in several prominent areas (such as Web Part title bars, toolbars, and navigational elements). The styles are pulled into every SharePoint Web page. You get around that by creating styles that are referenced after the SharePoint styles. These new styles override, or rewrite, the formatting for the Web page elements.

If you are creating a theme for a WSS v3 site, you will be working with a custom Theme.css file, which is the style sheet used to apply overriding styles on top of a WSS site.

Understanding Where the Styles Are Stored

All totaled, there are 26 CSS files in SharePoint. Gak! Luckily, most of these you will never even open. CSS files are stored in three places. First, the bulk of the styles referenced in a SharePoint site are located on the Web server:

```
Local Drive:\Program Files\Common Files\Microsoft Shared\web server
extensions\12\TEMPLATE\LAYOUTS\1033\STYLES
```

A subset of CSS files is located in the content database for each site collection:

```
http://site/Style Library/
```

Within this directory, there are CSS files for the various out-of-the-box SharePoint master pages, and there is a language directory (for example en-us) where additional CSS files are kept in a `Core Styles` subdirectory. Additionally, note that .`XSL` files are stored in the Style library. The `XSL` files are used to style other SharePoint components, such as the Content Query Web Part. Figure 6-10 shows a sample of the Style library.

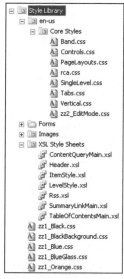

**Figure 6-10: The SharePoint
Style library, viewed from SPD**

And, if you are working with themes (WSS v3 sites only), styles are stored in each `Theme` folder on the Web server:

```
Local Drive:\Program Files\Common Files\Microsoft Shared\web server
extensions\12\TEMPLATE\THEMES\[Theme Name]
```

CSS Core Concepts

Before dipping into re-styling SharePoint, here are the core CSS concepts. All of these concepts are used in the default styles, and I recommend using them in your custom styles to streamline your code and cut down on the repetitive nature that CSS code can create. Already a CSS pro? I recommend you skim this section anyway as a general refresher, and because I point out where each concept comes in handy in regard to SharePoint.

The CSS Statement

CSS statements (or rules) have two components: the selector and the declaration. The selector specifies what will be styled, and the declaration outlines how it will be styled. The selector can be an HTML tag or an ID. It can optionally be further defined by a name, which is a class. Figure 6-11 shows a visual indication of the components of a CSS statement.

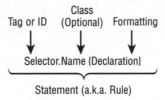

Figure 6-11: CSS statement with selector and declaration notated

Consider the following example:

```
<style>
p {
   color: red;
}
</style>

<body>
   <p>This text is red.</p>
</body>
```

The selector is P (paragraph) and the declaration is color: red.

Now, take a look at this example:

```
<style>
td.MyStyle {
   width: 100%;
}
</style>

<body>
   <table><tr><td class="MyStyle">This table cell has a 100% width</td></tr></table>
</body>
```

The selector is td (table cell) with a class name of MyStyle. The declaration is width: 100%.

For unique instances of an object, an ID can be used instead of a class name, as shown in the next example:

```
<style>
#Header {
   background: green;
}
```

```
<style>

<body>
  <div id="Header">This area has a green background</div>
</body>
```

The selector is `#Header` (which is an ID) and the declaration is `background: green`. When using IDs, the # is required.

Also note that when using names, the use of a selector is optional. Consider this example:

```
<style>
.MyStyle {
  width: 100%;
}
<style>

<body>
  <div class="MyStyle">This DIV has a 100% width</div>
  <table><tr><td class="MyStyle">This table cell has a 100% width</td></tr></table>
</body>
```

Any HTML tag that references the `MyStyle` class will use this style.

You can additionally omit a selector or name entirely:

```
<style>
* {
  font-family: sans-serif;
}
</style>

<body>
  This text is sans-serif.
  <div>This text is sans-serif.</div>
</body>
```

The asterisk (*) refers to all HTML tags.

Class and ID names are case-sensitive. The case used in the class or ID name in the HTML tag must match the name in the statement.

Grouping

Grouping is a CSS concept that helps simplify CSS statements by combining several rules into a single statement. Grouping can be used for both selectors and declarations. Grouping is a very valuable tool that can help shorten your CSS file, and is particularly useful when creating several color palettes for a single branding instance within any site, including SharePoint. Following are some examples of grouping.

Grouping the Selectors

Consider this example:

```
p, h1, h2, td {
    font-family: sans-serif;
}
```

Every p (paragraph), h1 and h2 (headings), and td (table cell) instance will have a sans-serif font applied to the text. Note that the selectors are separated with commas.

Grouping the Declaration Properties

Consider this example:

```
p {
    font-family: sans-serif;
    color: red;
}
```

Every p (paragraph) instance will have red sans-serif font applied to the text. Note the declarations are separated with semicolons.

Inheritance

CSS properties can inherit the display properties of parent HTML tags. Declarations made in child tags are added on to the declarations already set forth in the parent styles. This can often be frustrating when re-styling or debugging CSS code. You can restyle an item in the code, and then have no or a partial effect in the rendered page. Because of the mass of SharePoint CSS statements, this can happen often. Usually the culprit lies in parent declarations located elsewhere in the code. This is an example of how inheritance works:

```
<style>
body {
    font-family: sans-serif
}
div {
    color: red
}
p {
    font-style: italic
}
</style>

<body>
Sans serif text
    <div> Red sans serif text
        <p> Italic red sans serif text</p>
    </div>
</body>
```

Note the formatting in each HTML tag. The children HTML tags inherit properties outlined in the parental declarations.

Contextual Selectors

Contextual selectors can selectively apply CSS formatting rules based upon the context in which the elements appear on the Web page. For example, if you only want to style a child element within a particular parent element instead of all instances of that child, you would use contextual selectors. They can also be used in lieu of, or in conjunction with, class or ID names referenced in HTML tags. Here's an example:

```
<style>
Body div p {
  font-family: sans-serif;
  color: red;
  font-style: italic
}
</style>

<body>
Unformatted text
  <div> Unformatted text
    <p> Italic red sans serif text</p>
  </div>
</body>
```

In this example, all instances of a p (paragraph), when nested in a div tag within the body, will have red, italic, sans-serif font applied to the text. This is the equivalent to only using a class name on the p tag, but it will apply to every nested p in a div without assigning a class name to each instance.

Names can also be used with inheritance:

```
<style>
Body div p.MyStyle {
  font-family: sans-serif;
  color: red;
  font-style: italic
}
</style>

<body>
Unformatted text
  <div> Unformatted text
    <p class="MyStyle"> Italic red sans serif text</p>
    <p>Unformatted text</p>
  </div>
</body>
```

With this instance, only p (paragraph) tags with a class of MyStyle nested within a div will have red, italic, sans-serif font applied to the text.

In regard to SharePoint, contextual selectors are a good feature to have in your bag of tricks. Often, several elements of the SharePoint Web page share the same selector and/or name. If your design requires changes to one, but not the other, you can use contextual selectors to single out the instance you need to update.

Cascading

Cascading is a core feature of CSS that allows for multiple styles to be included in the rendering of a Web page. The Web page "cascades" down the order of referenced styles and applies declarations accordingly. Basically, what comes last is applied last. Here is a list of theoretical rules for the cascade effect:

❑ If both the parent and the child elements have statements assigned to them, the parent statement will overrule the child.

❑ Subsequently, the statements are sorted by explicit importance, which is tagged in the statement with !IMPORTANT. Note that this is not often used.

❑ Styles imported or listed in the <HEAD> are followed in the order listed.

❑ Any styles imported into the file or listed in the <HEAD> tag will be overruled by styles listed inline in HTML elements.

❑ More-specific CSS statements will overrule more-general CSS statements.

❑ If two statements are referenced and are of equal specification, the last statement referenced will be applied to the element.

I say these are "theoretical" rules because, like all things, styles can act unexpectedly. These times leave you trying to find hacks, scratching your head, and generally cause you to yell at your computer. But in most of these cases, you can work around issues by reordering your styles, adding in a contextual selector, or by walking up the style chain to identify problems in parent styles.

Cascading is key in SharePoint. You must reference your custom CSS in just the right spot, or your custom CSS will be pulled before primary SharePoint style sheets, resulting in your changes having no effect on the rendered page. Also, in a handful of places, SharePoint uses inline styles. In these cases, your only option is to edit the ASPX file that is rendering the Web page, or to edit files within the given Feature. Luckily, you aren't likely to run into this issue.

The style changes that you will create to override SharePoint styles will rely solely on the cascade effect in order to work. Essentially, SharePoint will style an item, and then your custom style will rewrite the declarations used for the selector. So, a style will be applied twice to the same element, but because your styles will be referenced last, yours will stick.

Multiple Classes for a Single Element

Within the class specification for any HTML tag, you can specify multiple styles. Each separate style will be applied to the element, in the order they are referenced:

```
<style>
.MyFont {
  font-family: sans-serif;
}
.MyStyle {
  color: red;
}
</style>
```

```
<body>
Sans serif text
  <div class="MyFont MyStyle">Red sans serif text</div>
</body>
```

Note the two classes listed in the DIV tag.

SharePoint uses this method often, and it is handy to use in your own styles. One style can specify common properties (such as font or font color), and other styles can specify specific properties (such as link behavior or background). You can then mix and match these in your code to apply generic properties, as well as specific ones, without repeating declarations in your style statements.

Location, Reference, and Override Order

It is true what they say about real estate and CSS: it is all about location, location, location. Because of cascading, CSS location in your SharePoint site is key. This section provides an overview of where to put your files and how (and in what order) you should reference them.

When you choose to store the CSS code in a separate file, you create a .CSS file. This file does not contain any code except for the CSS statements. You then reference this file in the <HEAD> tag of your Web file or master page.

Where to Store Your CSS Files

You have a couple of options for the location of your CSS files. The CSS files can be stored on the Web server or in the content database of the SharePoint site.

On the Web Server

I would recommend putting the CSS files in a custom directory so that the files are separate from the default SharePoint files. For example, the path to your custom directory would be as follows:

```
Local Drive:\Program Files\Common Files\Microsoft Shared\web server
extensions\12\TEMPLATE\LAYOUTS\1033\STYLES\Custom
```

The benefit to storing the files on the Web server is that you can reference them from any site on your server farm. The drawback is that you need access to the Web server to add and update the files, or it may require a request to your SharePoint administrator to add and update the files for you.

In the Content Database

The second option is to store the CSS file(s) in the content database. This can be done by either storing the files in the Style library provided, or by creating your own document library for the files. There really isn't a benefit to doing it one way over the other. It comes down to personal preference. In fact, you can place the CSS file anywhere you like, but for a cleaner file structure, place the files in the Style library or a document library specifically created for style sheets. Note that if you are utilizing the Document Center and you create a document library for your CSS files, you will need to remove the library from the navigation in Document Center.

The benefit to storing the styles in the content database is that anyone with Designer permission rights in the SharePoint site will be able to access, add, and edit the files. The organizational aspect of keeping styles with their respective sites may work better for your environment as well.

You can add files and directories through the SharePoint UI, or by using SPD.

Follow these steps to add files using the SharePoint UI:

1. Open your SharePoint site in a browser. Select Site Actions ➪ Manage Content and Structure.

2. In the left pane, navigate to Style library. If you want the new directory or the CSS file in a particular subdirectory, navigate to that folder. From this location or from the root of the Style library, hover over the directory name and select the arrow that appears.

3. Mouse over New, select Folder for a new directory, or select Item for a new CSS file, as shown in Figure 6-12. For adding a CSS file, skip to Step 6. For adding a new directory, proceed with Step 4.

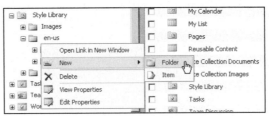

Figure 6-12: Creating a new directory in the Style library in the SharePoint user interface

4. The New Folder screen loads. Name your folder appropriately. Click OK.

5. The Manage Content and Structure screen reloads. Navigate to your new directory. Select the directory. In the right pane, select New ➪ Item in the toolbar. The Upload Document screen loads.

6. Select Browse to navigate to your CSS file. If you don't have a CSS file yet, in an IDE editor or in Notepad, create a blank file and save the file with a .css extension. Once loaded, click OK.

Follow these steps to add files using SPD:

1. Open your site in SPD.

2. Using the Folder List task pane, optionally create a CSS file or directory in any location of your choice, or navigate to the Style library. To create a new directory or style sheet, right-click the directory where you want to place the new directory or file. For a new directory, select New ➪ Folder, as shown in Figure 6-13. For a new CSS file, select New ➪ CSS. For adding a CSS file, skip to Step 5. For adding a new directory, proceed with Step 3.

3. Name the directory appropriately.

4. Right-click the directory and select New ➪ CSS.

5. Name the CSS file appropriately.

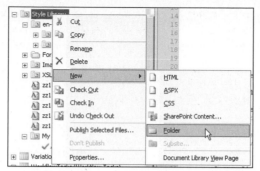

Figure 6-13: Creating a new directory in the Style library in SPD

How to Reference the CSS Files in Your Code or in the Site

Once the CSS files have been created and added to the Web server or content database, the files must be referenced. There are a few ways to do this, all dependent on what other customizations you are doing with your site and how you want to store your styles.

For custom site definitions, you can reference the styles in the ASPX files or in the master page the ASPX files are referencing. Either way, the following instructions for master pages apply to adding CSS styles in a custom site definition. A CSS file can also be referenced in the Site Settings, and you can optionally never create or reference the styles from an ASPX or a master page. Refer to the end of this section for instructions on how to accomplish this.

Including Styles in the Master Page

CSS styles can be added directly, imported, or linked to from the master page. With any of the three options, it is important that you add the code after the SharePoint:CssLink user control that SharePoint uses to pull the default styles, and before the PlaceholderAdditionalPageHead content placeholder. Each example will reference how to do this.

The SharePoint:CssLink user control includes the default CSS files in the Web page. The custom styles need to be referenced after this so that it can override the defaults.

The PlaceholderAdditionalPageHead content placeholder includes any custom page header information that may be specified in a page layout. The custom styles must be placed before this in the master page so that any page level styles included in a page layout can override both the SharePoint site level styles and the custom site level styles created.

Adding Styles Directly to the Master Page

Styles can be added directly to the master page in the <HEAD> tag by using a <STYLE> tag set. If you directly add styles to the master page, you won't have to deal with a separate file for styles, but it can also become cumbersome to work with the file as it grows in line length because of the number of styles located at the top. To reference styles in the <HEAD> tag, complete the following steps in your master page file:

1. Open the master page file (.master).

2. Locate the HEAD section (<head runat="server">).

3. Locate the `SharePoint:CSSLink` user control (`<SharePoint:CssLink runat="server"/>`) and the `PlaceholderAdditionalPageHead` content placeholder (`<asp:ContentPlaceHolder id="PlaceHolderAdditionalPageHead" runat="server"/>`). There will likely be other lines of code between these two.

4. Between these two tags, add a `<Style>` tag set. Insert the CSS statements in the Style tags. See the following for a code example:

```
<SharePoint:CssLink runat="server"/>

<style type="text/css">
p {
  font-style:italic;
}
</style>

<asp:ContentPlaceHolder id="PlaceHolderAdditionalPageHead" runat="server"/>
```

Importing Styles into the Master Page

A style sheet can be imported into a file through a URL reference. This is particularly helpful if you need to reference styles that are located on another server, or in another SharePoint site collection. A file can import in numerous style sheets, and a CSS file can import in other style sheets. Simply add an `@import` statement to your CSS file to additionally add styles from other files and sites.

The process to import styles in your master page file is very similar to adding styles directly in the `<HEAD>` tag, but instead, you use a CSS statement that references the external CSS file. You can also use this method to import style sheets located in the same site if you wish. To import styles, follow these steps in your master page file:

1. Open the master page file (`.master`).

2. Locate the HEAD section (`<head runat="server">`).

3. Locate the `SharePoint:CSSLink` user control (`<SharePoint:CssLink runat="server"/>`) and the `PlaceholderAdditionalPageHead` content placeholder (`<asp:ContentPlaceHolder id="PlaceHolderAdditionalPageHead" runat="server"/>`).

4. Between these two tags, add a `<Style>` tag set. Insert an `@import` CSS statement in the `Style` tags that points to the external CSS file. See the following for a code example:

```
<SharePoint:CssLink runat="server"/>

<style type="text/css">
@import url{http://www.site.com/style.css};
</style>

<asp:ContentPlaceHolder id="PlaceHolderAdditionalPageHead" runat="server"/>
```

Linking Styles to the Master Page

Finally, the easiest way to include your custom styles is to create a link to the file in the <HEAD> tag. If you need to link to several files, add links to each file in the desired cascade order. To link styles, follow these steps:

1. Open the master page file (.master).

2. Locate the HEAD section (<head runat="server">).

3. Locate the SharePoint:CSSLink user control (<SharePoint:CssLink runat="server"/>) and the PlaceholderAdditionalPageHead content placeholder (<asp:ContentPlaceHolder id="PlaceHolderAdditionalPageHead" runat="server"/>).

4. Between these two tags, add a <link> tag and specify properties for REL, TYPE, and HREF. See the following for a code example showing how to link to styles stored on the SharePoint Web server:

```
<SharePoint:CssLink runat="server"/>

<link rel="stylesheet" type="text/css"
href="/_layouts/1033/styles/custom/styles.css">

<asp:ContentPlaceHolder id="PlaceHolderAdditionalPageHead" runat="server"/>
```

5. To link to styles located in the Style library, use the following HREF in the LINK tag:

```
<link rel="stylesheet" type="text/css" href="/Style Library/en-us/Custom
Styles/styles.css" >
```

Using Site Settings to Reference a CSS File

If don't want to create a master page and only want to update the styles in a site, or if you want to apply a second style sheet on any given site separate from the master page, you can specify a single alternative CSS file in the Site Settings. This is especially useful if you need to apply multiple variations of a design to a series of subsites that all use a single master page. Follow these steps:

1. Navigate to the site. Select Site Actions ⇨ Site Settings ⇨ Modify all Site Settings.

2. Under the Look and Feel column, select Master page.

3. Scroll to the bottom of the screen to the Alternate CSS URL section. Choose the option for "Specify a CSS file to be used by this publishing site and all sites that inherit from it."

4. Select Browse and locate the file in the dialog provided, or enter a path to a CSS file stored on the Web server (/_layouts/[language ID]/styles/custom/MyStyles.css), or another Web site.

5. Click OK and navigate back to your site.

Testing Your Styles in the Browser

Now that the styles have been referenced in a master page file or in the Site Settings, test to make sure this is working. An easy way to see if a CSS file is indeed being included in the rendered page is to add a drastic CSS statement.

In the style sheet or between the `<Style>` tags, add the following code:

```
body {
    Background: red;
}
```

Save and refresh the site in the browser. A bright red area should appear behind the site title. Figure 6-14 provides an indication of where the change should be appearing.

Figure 6-14: Adding a drastic CSS statement changes the background of the SharePoint site to red, clearly showing the CSS file is successfully being referenced

If the background doesn't show red, check the following:

❑ If stored in the content database, has the CSS file been published? Unpublished files will not show to all SharePoint site users.

❑ Is your CSS statement syntax correct? Carefully recheck the code against the examples provided to ensure that you have the right tags and statement syntax.

❑ If you are linking to a file, is the path to the file correct? Try some path variations, or move your file to a more directly accessible location.

Once you are finished testing your CSS change, remove the statement that was added to change the background color to red.

You Are Ready to Start Styling!

At this point, what CSS is, core CSS concepts, and how to get CSS files on your server/site and referenced in the code have all been covered. Now you are ready to actually start changing how SharePoint looks. From here on, the focus is on overriding existing SharePoint styles to affect the look and feel of SharePoint user controls. I will, however, touch on some organizational tips that can help with both your custom styles for your code and the overriding styles for SharePoint user controls.

When you initially look at the 26 SharePoint CSS files, it seems like an enormous and daunting task to figure out how to change the styles to reflect your branded images and colors. But honestly, it isn't all that bad. Here is why:

❑ 85 percent of what you need is in `Core.css` (`Local Drive:\Program Files\Common Files\ Microsoft Shared\web server extensions\12\TEMPLATE\LAYOUTS\1033\STYLES\ Core.css`).

❑ Another 10 percent of what you need is in `Calendar.css` (`Local Drive:\Program Files\ Common Files\Microsoft Shared\web server extensions\12\TEMPLATE\LAYOUTS\ 1033\STYLES\Calendar.css`).

❑ The last 5 percent of what you need is scattered in a handful of files, including `DatePicker .css`, `Portal.css` (located on the Web server at `Local Drive:\Program Files\Common Files\Microsoft Shared\web server extensions\12\TEMPLATE\LAYOUTS\1033\ STYLES`) and `PageLayout.css`, located in the Style library in the content database for the site (`http://www.site.com/Style Library/[language ID]/Core Styles`).

❑ Nearly every image on the Web page is referenced in the styles, making it very easy to update it to pull in custom images.

❑ You only need to override a fraction of the styles listed in the default files to update the user controls. You will *not* be re-creating every style SharePoint has.

❑ There are ways! Stay tuned in this chapter for ways to quickly locate styles being used by SharePoint user controls.

Are you still looking to save some time? Consider these tips to trim down time spent on overriding SharePoint styles:

❑ *Stick with the font provided* — The font specifications are listed in numerous styles in SharePoint, so if you feel like you have to change the default font faces (Verdana in some places, Tahoma in others), you will be looking at re-creating a lot of styles. If you must do this, I would suggest running a search on the 26 SharePoint CSS files for all instances of the `font-family` declaration, and pulling out all the selectors into a single grouped style that lists the selectors and names in a group, with a single declaration for a new font.

Don't forget to search for "`font:`" as well. `Font` is the shorthand version of the declaration and can include font family properties.

❑ *Keep your color palette light with pastel colors* — Though you can certainly introduce bold and dark colors in your header, another time-saver is to keep the color palette of your Web Part title bars, toolbars, menu bars, and consoles a light shade. That way, you only have to override background colors and images, and not go into overriding text font colors. Adding in dark backgrounds will require you to change the font color to white or another light color.

❑ *Delete gradations and go solid* — You can skip the step of re-creating gradation or background images for toolbars, menu bars, and navigation buttons by just using a solid background color and setting the background image declaration to None.

Note that to rebrand the many gradations used in a site, you don't need as many images as the SharePoint CSS files use. You can create the same background effects with just a fraction of the images by creating a few variations and using the same image over and over in the style statements.

How to Override SharePoint Styles

There are some key things you need to understand about overriding styles. First, as stated earlier, to override a style, a new style is created using the same selector and declaration as the original. But this is not as easy as just grabbing the selector, class, or ID, adding it to the style sheet, and writing new declarations. You must find the style in the CSS file where it is stored, copy the statement, and paste that into your custom CSS file. Then you can change the properties of the declaration as you need to, optionally group selectors together, optionally add a contextual selector to specify which instances of the style should change, and so on. *But what you don't change will still be applied to the page element.* Just creating another instance of the selector will not wipe out all previous declarations that were set. All you can do is update the declaration, and add new ones. Let's step through an example.

How to Identify Selectors, IDs, and Class Names for a SharePoint Style

In this example, a style used in the global links at the top of a collaboration (intranet) site will be modified to change the appearance of the inactive state of the link. Figure 6-15 shows where this style is applied on the page.

Figure 6-15: Location of the global
toolbar for the sample style work

First, the styles being used for the link must be determined. This information can be determined in one of many ways. The following explanations show the steps for each method.

Follow these steps to locate selectors, classes, and IDs via View Source:

1. Open your site in a browser. Look at the area where you need to identify the style. Select nearby text that you know will be near the style in the rendered code. For the example, select Welcome. Copy this to the clipboard.

2. Right-click anywhere in the browser window where there is not an image. In the menu that appears, select View Source.

3. The source will load in Notepad or a browser window. Select to run a search and paste the copied text (Welcome) into the Find field. The first instance of the text should be the Welcome text used in the global link.

4. Change the Find text to "class," change the direction of the search to "up," and run another search in the code.

5. The Find should locate the following line:

```
<div  id="zz7_Menu_t" class="ms-SPLink ms-SpLinkButtonInActive"
onmouseover="MMU_PopMenuIfShowing(this);MMU_EcbTableMouseOverOut(this, true)"
hoverActive="ms-SPLink ms-SpLinkButtonActive" hoverInactive="ms-SPLink
ms-SpLinkButtonInActive" onclick=" MMU_Open(byid('zz3_ID_PersonalActionMenu'),
MMU_GetMenuFromClientId('zz7_Menu'),event,false, null, 0);"
foa="MMU_GetMenuFromClientId('zz7_Menu')" oncontextmenu="this.click(); return
false;" nowrap="nowrap">
```

6. By looking at the code, the following can be determined:

   a. The text is wrapped in a DIV with a class of ms-SPLink ms-SpLinkButtonInActive.

   b. Hovering over the link calls ms-SPLink ms-SpLinkButtonActive.

   c. Moving the mouse off the link reinitiates ms-SPLink ms-SpLinkButtonInActive.

   d. In total, this DIV is referencing three style statements: ms-SPLink, ms-SpLinkButtonInActive, and ms-SpLinkButtonActive.

7. With the knowledge of what styles are being used, you can now locate selectors, classes, and IDs in the SharePoint style sheets.

If you don't want to spend time analyzing the View Source code, you can add a helpful JavaScript to your file that will show you the styles being accessed in the browser window as you move your mouse around the page. This tool should only be used on non-production sites. You can either add it to your master page (my recommended method) and have it available to you for nearly every Web page in the site, or you can selectively add it to any Web Part zone Web page by adding the code into a Content Editor Web Part. Adding it to your master page will give you more coverage of all of the elements in SharePoint you must update.

Follow these steps to locate selectors, classes, and IDs via a CSS Helper tool:

1. Open your master page file. Select a location to place the code. I suggest in the content area of the page.

2. Go to the book resource site and download the `CSS_Helper_Tool.html` file. The resource site is located at `www.wrox.com` as described on page xxii of the Introduction.. The file includes JavaScript code and a table. This script will add the table to your Web page and display CSS information as you hover over areas of the Web page. The table will display HTML tag and CSS information, including tag, ID, name, and class. Figure 6-16 shows a visual example.

Figure 6-16: CSS Helper tool display in the browser window

3. Save your file. Navigate to your site in a browser to see the tool. Mouse around the browser and the CSS Helper tool will show you the information appropriately. Mouse over the global link in the upper right and it will display similar information that was discovered while looking at the View Source.

This is a fantastic tool that is very helpful. There will still be times, however, where you will still need to use the View Source method to clear up any confusion regarding what type of HTML tags use the parent classes, to see more clearly the chain of styles affecting the element on the page, or to pick up inactive style states for links. Because you are hovering over elements in the Web page, you will only be able to get active hover states for link styles. Luckily, in most cases, the inactive state is the same style name with an "`in`" in the name immediately before the "`active`".

The new SharePoint editing tool, Microsoft Office SPD, has some handy CSS tools that will tell you what style and what declarations are being used for a particular area of the page. This will work particularly well for some styles used on the master page, but as you need to dig deeper into the site, you will need either to open the various `ASPX` files for that page (which means figuring out what those are), or resort to another location method listed. Also, some styles won't display properly in the tool panes (for example, when you try to extrapolate style information for links, it won't show you the information you need).

For the global link example, this method will not work. Instead, for this case, the following example will look at the styles being used for the site title. Follow these steps to locate selectors, classes, and IDs via SPD:

1. Open your master page file in SharePoint Designer.

2. Look for the CSS Properties task pane. If it is not visible, go to Task Panes and select CSS Properties.

3. Select an item in the master page. The CSS Properties task pane will show what rules are being applied to the element, and the properties for each.

4. Alternatively, you can use an abbreviated version of the CSS Properties task pane. Go to View ⇨ Toolbars and select Style.

5. Select an item in the master page. The Style toolbar will show the class and ID of the item. Figure 6-17 shows a sample of these tools.

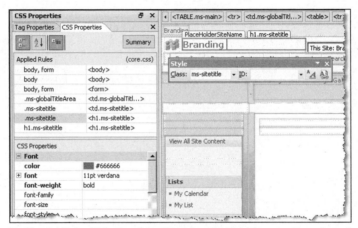

Figure 6-17: In SPD, the Branding site title has been selected, and the CSS Properties task pane shows rules and properties to the left, and the Style toolbar shows Class name immediately under where site title has been selected

Another way to locate styles is to use the resources that others have created. The Internet, blog sites, and articles are other ways to locate which styles do what on a SharePoint site. I have posted a CSS chart online for SharePoint styles that is free to use and reference for your needs. You can find this chart at http://www.heathersolomon.com/content/sp07cssreference.htm.

How to Find Declarations for a SharePoint Style

Once the selectors have been identified, the declarations must be discovered for each selector. Two of the previous methods can help you out with the declarations: viewing the CSS Properties task pane in SPD, and using external resources such as a CSS chart. But SPD can't show all styles, and online resources may not have the style you are looking for. So, it is good to know the following steps for finding SharePoint style declarations:

1. Create a copy of the CSS files from the Web server and from the content database of a sample site that has not been customized. You must create a local copy of all 26 SharePoint CSS files for

your own reference. Refer to earlier sections of this chapter detailing where the styles are located on the Web server and in the content database.

2. Using an IDE Editor with global search capabilities or using SPD, open all of the CSS files.

3. In the application, run a global search for the SharePoint selector/class/ID you need to find. In SPD, select Edit, then Find. In the Find and Replace dialog, enter the search criteria in the "Find what" field, and select the Open page(s) option under "Find where." Select Find All. For the example, the search criteria would be one of the three styles identified earlier (ms-SPLink, ms-SpLinkButtonInActive, ms-SpLinkButtonActive), but don't run a search for all three; only look for one at a time.

4. The editor will return a list of results from all the CSS files, giving you an exact view of where styles appear in the CSS files, as shown in Figure 6-18.

Figure 6-18: SharePoint Designer search results for "ms-SpLinkButtonActive" across the 26 SharePoint CSS files

5. Double-clicking a search result will jump you to the location in the code where it appears. You can continue down the list until you locate the statement that has the properties you want to change. For this example, line 2583 in CORE.CSS has the following statement:

```
.ms-HoverCellActive,.ms-SpLinkButtonActive {
  border:#6f9dd9 1px solid;
  vertical-align:top;
  background-color:#ffbb47;
  background-image:url("/_layouts/images/menubuttonhover.gif");
}
```

6. Congratulations! You have located the CSS selector and declaration for the SharePoint element you want to change. Copy this style to your custom CSS file.

How to Change the Declarations of Your Copy of the SharePoint Style

Through one of the many methods listed thus far, you can gradually create a style sheet of all the SharePoint styles that control the user controls that you need to change. I recommend organizing these styles by area of the page so that you can quickly identify what the various styles alter. Following is an example of how SharePoint styles can be organized in a custom CSS file, along with your styles for the master page:

```
/* --- --- --- Navigation --- --- --- */
/* --- Top Toolbar - Global Links (Welcome...Menu) --- */
/* - Custom Styles -*/
Place styles here

/* - Core.CSS Style Overrides - */
```

```
.ms-HoverCellActive,.ms-SpLinkButtonActive {
  border:#6f9dd9 1px solid;
  vertical-align:top;
  background-color:#ffbb47;
  background-image:url("/_layouts/images/menubuttonhover.gif");
}
```

In this example, there is a master category of Navigation, and a subcategory for Top Toolbar - Global Links. Next is a specification for the custom master page styles, and then for style overrides, noting what CSS file the original statements are from. Organizing a file like this makes it very easy to identify styles that affect the areas of the page, and separates out the styles you created for your master page from the styles you are changing for SharePoint user controls.

Returning to the sample for the global navigation, in the default SharePoint look and feel, this bar has a light blue background when you hover over the link, and a yellow gradation appears with a darker blue border. Additionally, the style specifies a solid background color behind the image. This provides a color background while the image is loading, or in case the image link becomes broken. The solid background color is yellow, to match the gradated image.

To demonstrate how to update a statement, change this style to a green background, dark green border, and a green gradation. The new graphic is stored in the content database in the images folder for the site. The two HEX colors are #22622D for the border and #90C899 for the background. Using these new elements, the updated copy of the code is as follows:

```
.ms-HoverCellActive,.ms-SpLinkButtonActive {
  border:#22622D 1px solid;
  vertical-align:top;
  background-color:#90C899;
  background-image:url("/images/custom/mymenubuttonhover.gif");
}
```

Save the file and test the changes in the browser. Next, clean up unnecessary declarations in the style. In this example, the unnecessary declaration is vertical-align:top. Leaving this line in the code doesn't do any harm; it will just lengthen the code and add unnecessary clutter to the custom CSS file. If there is a declaration you don't want to update from the default SharePoint styles, there is no need to leave it in the file. Delete the line, and the finished code looks like this:

```
.ms-HoverCellActive,.ms-SpLinkButtonActive {
  border:#22622D 1px solid;
  background-color:#90C899;
  background-image:url("/images/custom/mymenubuttonhover.gif");
}
```

That's it! You have successfully updated the SharePoint look and feel with your own branding, without editing a single default SharePoint CSS file. Continue in this manner updating all of the user controls that require changes.

It is very important that you override the CSS declaration properties by just changing the values of the properties. Don't rewrite the CSS declarations as you see fit for cleaner code. For example, assume that the CSS statement specifies the following:

```
.SampleStyle {
  Border-top: red;
  Border-right: red;
  Border-bottom: red;
  Border-left: red;
}
```

Don't replace the declaration with this:

```
.SampleStyle {
  Border: blue;
}
```

Often, the original declarations will appear on the page despite your changes. It is a good rule of thumb to avoid rewriting the user control style statements for this reason. Additions can be made, but existing declarations need to be preserved.

It is also a good idea to apply CSS core concepts to your code to improve code management and length. For example, if items share the same image, border, or background colors, group the selectors together and list the changes only once, as shown here:

```
/* --- Calendar --- */
/* - Calendar.CSS Style Overrides - */
.ms-cal-topday-today, .ms-cal-wtopday-today, .ms-cal-topday-todayRTL, .ms-cal-wtopday-
todayRTL {
  background-color:#DAE6F1;
  border:solid 1px #04407D;
}
```

In this example, several Calendar controls are grouped together and the background and border color are set once, applying to all of the selectors in the rendered page.

If you need to further define a style change for a particular SharePoint user control, add a contextual selector:

```
/* --- --- --- Search --- --- --- */
/* - Core.CSS Style Overrides - */
.Custom-SearchBar td.ms-sbcell {
  border-color: transparent;
}
```

In this example, a custom class name (Custom-SearchBar) was added as a contextual selector for td.ms-sbcell to directly specify when the border will be changed to transparent. If this had not been set, all other instances of this element in the Web page would have been set to a transparent border.

183

Navigation

All this chatter about CSS and changing styles, but what about navigation? Fortunately, you can change the styles referenced in the code used for the various navigation elements, such as the Quick Launch, Tree View, Site Actions, and the Recycle Bin. You don't have to hunt down all the various styles in the SharePoint CSS files and override them. You can simply insert your own classes and then create the styles accordingly. You do this in the master page.

For example, look at the SharePoint code for the horizontal navigation bar in `default.master`. Figure 6-19 shows where this navigation is located on the Web page.

Figure 6-19: Location of the top horizontal navigation bar in a default SharePoint site

Here is the code for the menu:

```
<SharePoint:AspMenu
  ID="TopNavigationMenu"
  Runat="server"
  DataSourceID="topSiteMap"
  EnableViewState="false"
  AccessKey="<%$Resources:wss,navigation_accesskey%>"
  Orientation="Horizontal"
  StaticDisplayLevels="2"
  MaximumDynamicDisplayLevels="1"
  DynamicHorizontalOffset="0"
  StaticPopoutImageUrl="/_layouts/images/menudark.gif"
  StaticPopoutImageTextFormatString=""
  DynamicHoverStyle-BackColor="#CBE3F0"
  SkipLinkText=""
  StaticSubMenuIndent="0"
  CssClass="ms-topNavContainer">
    <StaticMenuStyle/>
    <StaticMenuItemStyle CssClass="ms-topnav" ItemSpacing="0px"/>
    <StaticSelectedStyle CssClass="ms-topnavselected" />
    <StaticHoverStyle CssClass="ms-topNavHover" />
    <DynamicMenuStyle  BackColor="#F2F3F4" BorderColor="#A7B4CE"
BorderWidth="1px"/>
    <DynamicMenuItemStyle CssClass="ms-topNavFlyOuts"/>
    <DynamicHoverStyle CssClass="ms-topNavFlyOutsHover"/>
    <DynamicSelectedStyle CssClass="ms-topNavFlyOutsSelected"/>
</SharePoint:AspMenu>
```

Copy this code and use it in the custom master page, and then update the style properties to include custom styles:

```
<SharePoint:AspMenu
  ID="TopNavigationMenu"
```

```
        Runat="server"
        DataSourceID="topSiteMap"
        EnableViewState="false"
        AccessKey="<%$Resources:wss,navigation_accesskey%>"
        Orientation="Horizontal"
        StaticDisplayLevels="2"
        MaximumDynamicDisplayLevels="1"
        DynamicHorizontalOffset="0"
        StaticPopoutImageUrl="/_layouts/images/menudark.gif"
        StaticPopoutImageTextFormatString=""
        DynamicHoverStyle-BackColor="#CBE3F0"
        SkipLinkText=""
        StaticSubMenuIndent="0"
        CssClass="ms-topNavContainer">
          <StaticMenuStyle/>
          <StaticMenuItemStyle Cssclass="Custom-TopNav" ItemSpacing="0px"/>
          <StaticSelectedStyle Cssclass="Custom-TopNavSelected" />
          <StaticHoverStyle Cssclass="Custom-TopNavHover" />
          <DynamicMenuStyle Cssclass="Custom-TopNavFlyOuts"/>
          <DynamicMenuItemStyle Cssclass="Custom-TopNavFlyOutsItem"/>
          <DynamicHoverStyle Cssclass="Custom-TopNavFlyOutsHover"/>
          <DynamicSelectedStyle CssClass="Custom-TopNavFlyOutsSelected"/>
      </SharePoint:AspMenu>
```

Note that for `DynamicMenuStyle`, a class was added in lieu of the inline styles specified in the original code.

Navigation is generally a design element that is included in the site design provided to you, or that you create. Now you can create styles and images appropriately for your design and not bother with the SharePoint styles.

Applying What You Have Learned

Whew! You have made it to the end of the branding chapter! Putting all the skills together, the knowledge and techniques can be applied to a real-world situation. Here is the scenario.

Mega Oil & Gas, Inc. has contracted out a Web page design for its corporate intranet, and the design firm has delivered a snazzy concept that upper management fell in love with. It consists of a Home page design and different colored sub-page designs for each division of the intranet (such as Human Resources, Training, Accounting, and Sales). The Home page design is blockier and flashier, whereas the sub-page design is more content-focused. Each division has been assigned a color palette in different hues, and each needs custom images that are associated with that division. What do you do?

I can show you how to do this with seven files: two master pages and five CSS files. All of these are configurable through the user interface.

Step One: Master Pages

Create two master pages, one for the Home page design and another for the sub-page design. The master page for the Home page will have a different layout to create more visual interest. This can be accomplished by arranging components on the page differently, incorporating graphic components, or hiding unnecessary navigation elements. The sub-page design, on the other hand, will compact the navigation and header in order to create more space for the page content. Next, create each division of the intranet as a subsite. Do this both for taxonomy purposes, and so you can apply a different master page and CSS file to the subsite. Once both the sites and the master pages have been initially created, publish the master pages and apply each one to the appropriate site. Test the sites to verify the master pages are working properly.

Now you can create the custom code for your master page that will format the content placeholders and add your branding and design. Keep in mind that you need to swap out images easily, so be sure to code your HTML to have images pulled via CSS as backgrounds.

Step Two: Master CSS File

For both your custom styles and the SharePoint styles that you need to override, create a new CSS file for the site. If you include everything in this file you will be able to better manage and leverage the CSS statements, but this is optional. Things such as fonts and navigation can more than likely be grouped together and referenced once for both master pages, instead of using a CSS file per master page. Base your CSS file off a single color palette.

Step Three: Division-Specific CSS Files

In the master CSS file, identify the CSS statements that are setting colors and images that should change from division to division. Look for border colors, background colors and images, colors used in the calendar control, and elements such as the Web Part title bar.

For example, the following SharePoint style is used to control the hover state of the Welcome User menu in the global breadcrumb navigation. Notice the border color, the background color, and the background image that is set for the hover state of the menu:

```
.ms-HoverCellActive, .ms-SpLinkButtonActive {
  border:#6f9dd9 1px solid;
  vertical-align:top;
  background-color:#ffbb47;
  background-image:url("/_layouts/images/menubuttonhover.gif");
}
```

Copy all the style statements that control colors and images into a new division-specific CSS file. For each statement, delete declarations that don't have changing elements (such as widths, fonts faces, margins, and padding). In the example, the vertical alignment declaration can be deleted as well as the non-color information for the border:

```
.ms-HoverCellActive, .ms-SpLinkButtonActive {
  border:#6f9dd9;
  background-color:#ffbb47;
  background-image:url("/_layouts/images/menubuttonhover.gif");
}
```

The style declarations can be altered to change the color and image, as shown here:

```
.ms-HoverCellActive, .ms-SpLinkButtonActive {
  border:#000000;
```

```
        background-color:#FFFFFF;
        background-image:url("/_layouts/images/custom/MyHoverImage.gif");
    }
```

In the master CSS file, delete the declarations where the colors and images are specified. This is required because of the order in which SharePoint includes the CSS files. An alternate CSS file specified in the Site Settings will be called before the master CSS file in the master page, so if the color and image-related declarations are left in the master CSS file, the division CSS file with the custom color palette will have no effect. The resulting trimmed style in the master CSS file would resemble the following:

```
    .ms-HoverCellActive, .ms-SpLinkButtonActive {
        border: 1px solid;
        vertical-align:top;
    }
```

After making all the necessary color and image changes, analyze the CSS statements in the new file and identify where you can condense the color and image changing statements via grouping. In the following example, several styles are grouped and the border color is set once:

```
    .CustomTable, .ms-pagebreadcrumb, .ms-WPHeader TD {
        border-bottom: red;
    }
```

Once all of the styles have been created in the division-specific CSS file, it can be copied and used to create three more CSS files, one for each division. Update only the colors and images for each.

Step Four: Alter Subsite Settings

In the Site Settings for each subsite, set the Alternate CSS URL to the appropriate CSS file. See the earlier section, "Using Site Settings to Reference a CSS File," for instructions.

Step Five: Sit Back and Relax!

In a matter of hours, you have created a multi-dimensional SharePoint site collection with different color schemes and images for the various divisions in the site. Your files are centrally organized and, when the site has to be rebranded in six months, you will easily and quickly be able to propagate the new design across the growing site collection in no time!

Summary

This chapter began with a basic overview of user-interface customization. The discussion described several realistic business scenarios based on real-life experience in the field. The mechanics of each customization option have been examined as they apply directly to the solutions, along with step-by-step instructions, trips, tricks, and best practices to assist you with your next customization project.

CSS plays an important role in SharePoint design and branding. CSS is used in both the custom code created for the individual site or master page, as well as used for all of the common SharePoint functions and features. Creating a completely rebranded site requires alteration of both types of CSS.

Understanding key CSS concepts will help you create streamlined and efficient CSS code, thus decreasing site download times and greatly improving the ease of maintenance for the site both now and going forward. All of the concepts have been covered in this chapter, along with examples showing each concept in action.

CSS code must be referenced properly in SharePoint to be effective. CSS code can be stored in the content database or the Web server. Once stored, the CSS code can be referenced one of many ways in the master pages. Once everything is set up, you can begin locating and updating SharePoint styles, as well as adding in your own styles for your design. After covering several techniques for accomplishing this in this chapter, you are well-prepared to fully rebrand the SharePoint look and feel.

SharePoint branding and customization is a large and subjective topic that depends on your particular installation and site requirements, but the information in this chapter can help you start in the right direction and clear up confusion surrounding options and methods for accomplishing common branding tasks.

7

Understanding Web Parts

by Jan Tielens

Web Parts are the building blocks of pages in SharePoint sites. Users of SharePoint sites can make use of those building blocks to determine what should be displayed on a specific page in a particular SharePoint site.

When you install SharePoint, you can make use of some out-of-the-box Web Parts straight away. Depending on whether you have Windows SharePoint Services (WSS) or Microsoft Office SharePoint Server (MOSS) as your SharePoint installation, you'll have more or less. Additionally, every SharePoint list and document library will have a Web Part counterpart that can display the contents of the corresponding list or document library.

Of course, the out-of-the-box Web Parts are not the only ones that you can use! Developers can build their own Web Parts as well and deploy them to the SharePoint server. End users won't notice the difference between the custom Web Parts and the out-of-the-box Web Parts, so Web Parts are a great way to extend SharePoint.

This chapter takes you through the basic steps to create your own Web Parts in various ways, and discusses some more advanced Web Part topics as well.

> The techniques and technologies described in this chapter are applicable both to Windows SharePoint Services (WSS) and Microsoft Office SharePoint Server (MOSS), unless mentioned otherwise. So, in this chapter, when SharePoint is mentioned, it should be interpreted as Windows SharePoint Services 3.0 or Microsoft Office SharePoint Server 2007.

Web Part History

The concept of Web Parts is not unique to SharePoint or Microsoft. Other companies are making use of similar techniques as well. Different portal-style applications have used this concept. So, if you hear talk about Web Parts, portlets, widgets, or gadgets, it's probably more or less the same thing as a Web Part in SharePoint.

Web Parts were already available in the previous versions of SharePoint, and they became really interesting in the SharePoint 2003 release. Developers could now build the building blocks for SharePoint sites in managed .NET code, making use of the brand new .NET 1.1 Framework. This inspired the market, and lots of companies developed third-party Web Parts to extend SharePoint, as both commercial and free Web Parts.

When version 2.0 of the .NET Framework was released, things got a little confusing. In ASP.NET 2.0, developers also could develop Web Parts and Web Part pages without making use of SharePoint technology. The concepts were the same, but the underlying classes were completely different. Web Parts developed for SharePoint 2003 could not be used in ASP.NET 2.0 Web Part pages, and vice versa.

So, before the SharePoint 2007 release, there were different incompatible platforms to make use of Web Parts. The good news, however, is that SharePoint 2007 can run both the SharePoint 2003 Web Parts and the ASP.NET 2.0 Web Parts. One of the obvious advantages is, of course, that Web Parts developed for SharePoint 2003 can run without any problems in SharePoint 2007. The guideline for creating new Web Parts is to make use of the ASP.NET 2.0 Web Part framework.

> **Although you can create Web Parts making use of the SharePoint 2003 classes, and use those Web Parts in SharePoint 2007 sites, you should make use of ASP.NET 2.0 Web Parts for your new projects.**

The following list shows all Web Part types that can be used in SharePoint 2007:

❑ *SharePoint 2003 Web Parts* — These Web Parts inherit from the `WebPart` base class in the `Microsoft.SharePoint.WebPartPages` namespace, which can be found in `Microsoft.SharePoint.dll`. These Web Parts are compiled by making use of the .NET Framework version 1.1.

❑ *ASP.NET 2.0 Web Parts* — These Web Parts inherit from the `WebPart` base class in the `System.Web.UI.WebControls.WebParts` namespace, which can be found in the `System.Web.dll`. These Web Parts are compiled by making use of the .NET Framework version 2.0.

❑ *Hybrid Web Parts* — Basically, hybrid Web Parts are SharePoint 2003 Web Parts, so they inherit from the base `WebPart` class coming from `Microsoft.SharePoint.dll`, but they are compiled by making use of the .NET Framework version 2.0. Hybrid Web Parts can only be used in Windows SharePoint Services version 2 (2003) together with Service Pack 2.

Key Concepts of Web Parts

Because SharePoint 2007 is completely built on top of ASP.NET 2.0, and SharePoint is making use of the ASP.NET 2.0 Web Part infrastructure, the key concepts are almost identical for both platforms.

First of all, if users should be able to fully make use of the Web Parts, they must be put on special areas of a page. They can only be put in dedicated areas called *Web Part zones*. Every page that should be able to host Web Parts should have at least one Web Part zone.

The second required item on a Web Part page is a *Web Part manager*. The Web Part manager serves as the central class of the Web Parts control set, managing all the Web Parts controls, functionality, and events that occur on a Web page. I usually describe the Web Part manager as the "guy that's doing all the hard work," although its name suggests otherwise! The Web Part manager is a control that doesn't have any user-interface elements. This means that end users will not see the Web Part manager on a page; it just needs to be there to handle the plumbing of the Web Part page.

Figure 7-1 shows the structure of a Web Part page in ASP.NET 2.0. The first control on the page is an instance of the WebPartManager class. The other two controls on the page are instances of the WebPartZone class.

In theory, a Web Part page in SharePoint is the same as a Web Part page in ASP.NET 2.0. The only thing the SharePoint team changed is the fact that they created their own versions of the WebPartManager and WebPartZone classes: the SPWebPartManager and SPWebPartZone classes. Actually, they inherited the SPWebPartManager class from the ASP.NET WebPartManager class, and the SPWebPartZone class is inherited from the ASP.NET WebPartZone class. Luckily, they didn't try to reinvent the wheel!

Figure 7-2 shows a Web Part page in SharePoint 2007. This is also the reason why you can't just use an ASP.NET 2.0 Web Part page in a SharePoint site. However, you can, of course, make use of the same Web Parts either in SharePoint or in ASP.NET 2.0.

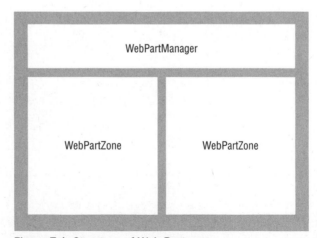

Figure 7-1: Structure of Web Part page

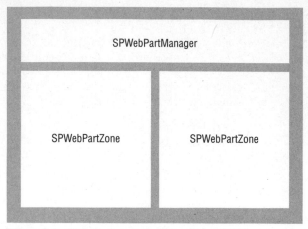

Figure 7-2: Web Part page in SharePoint 2007

Your Development Environment

Before diving into the code used to create Web Parts, let's first get the development environment set up. Actually, the only thing that's really needed to develop Web Parts is the .NET Framework version 2.0 — that is, if you don't mind writing code in Notepad, for example. Obviously, writing code in a professional development environment is more productive than Notepad. A good choice is Microsoft Visual Studio. Because the code that will be written should target the .NET Framework version 2.0, the version of Visual Studio that should be used is Visual Studio 2005.

In some development scenarios, it is necessary to make use of one or more SharePoint assemblies (DLLs) — for example, the `Microsoft.SharePoint` assembly if you want to make use of the SharePoint object model in your code. In this case, you will need a local copy of those DLLs. You can find them on the SharePoint server in the following folder (Figure 7-3): `C:\Program Files\Common Files\Microsoft Shared\web server extensions\12\ISAPI`.

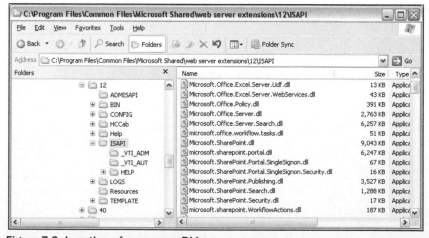

Figure 7-3: Location of necessary DLLs

Thus, it is not necessary to run SharePoint on your development machine. It's perfectly possible to write code on Windows XP or Windows Vista, and later on deploy that code to a SharePoint server. Actually, as of this writing, the only support is to run SharePoint on Windows 2003 Server, so even if you wanted to, you can't run SharePoint on Windows XP or Vista. Alternatively, you can make use of Windows 2003 Server as your development platform. This has the advantage of being able to possibly run SharePoint locally on the computer that you use to write code.

> **My development machine runs Windows Vista, so I can't install SharePoint locally. But for my SharePoint development tasks, I make use of Microsoft Virtual PC. It allows you create a virtualized environment — in this case, a virtual Windows 2003 Server running SharePoint and Visual Studio.**

Besides Visual Studio, and, in some cases, a copy of the SharePoint assemblies, there are no further requirements for your development environment. However, there are some tools and templates available that can make you more productive as a Web Part developer (for example, the Visual Studio 2005 extensions for WSS). The use and advantages of those tools are discussed later in this chapter.

The Traditional Hello World Example

Now that the development environment is set up, it's time to start writing some code. The first example will be the traditional Hello World example. Why start with this boring example? Well, it will become clear that writing code for a Web Part is only a part of the work. The Web Part also must be deployed to the SharePoint server. The Hello World example allows you to focus on the basic concepts and the deployment before the more advanced topics are discussed.

Writing the Code

A Web Part in code is just a normal .NET class, nothing more, nothing less. In Visual Studio, you can make use of the Class Library project template to write code for the Web Part class. This code will be compiled into a .NET assembly, in this case a DLL that is exactly what you need. When Visual Studio is started, create a new project and select the Class Library template (Figure 7-4). The name of the new project is important, so think carefully when you choose a project name. Your project name should be unique on the server where you would like to deploy your Web Parts. Additionally, the project name will be used later when the Web Parts are deployed. Also, be aware that names in .NET are case-sensitive!

> **A common practice to ensure unique names in .NET environments is using namespaces. If the project name is, for example, MVP.Book.WebParts, by default, all the code will be sitting in the namespace with exactly the same name.**

Every Class Library project in Visual Studio can contain any number of Web Part classes, so think of the project as the container of your Web Parts.

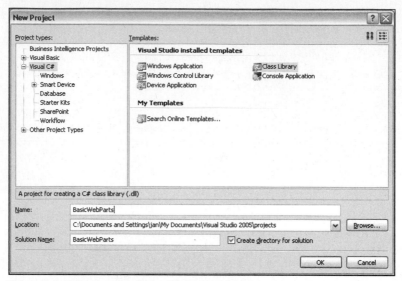

Figure 7-4: Selecting the Class Library template

When the new project is created, there will be one class already available: `Class1.cs`. In general, `Class1` is not a good name for a Web Part, so rename the class to `HelloWorld`. The special thing about a Web Part class is the fact that the class inherits from a specific base `WebPart` class. This base `WebPart` class is available in the `System.Web` assembly (Figure 7-5). By default, the Class Library project doesn't contain a reference to this assembly, so you should add it yourself. Right-click the project node in the Solutions Explorer window and choose Add Reference. Next, select the `System.Web` assembly from the list.

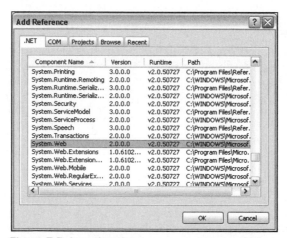

Figure 7-5: Locating the `System.Web` assembly

Now the `HelloWorld` class can inherit from the `WebPart` that is available in the `System.Web.UI`
`.WebControls.WebParts` namespace class.

To avoid having to type the full namespace of the WebPart base class (and other classes as well), it's a common practice to add using statements on top of your code. In this chapter, the common namespaces won't be prefixed.

The resulting code is probably the most basic Web Part that can be created. It's a Web Part that doesn't do anything. But because the HelloWorld class inherited from the base WebPart class, the HelloWorld Web Part already has a title bar and a border, as shown in Figure 7-6.

Figure 7-6: HelloWorld
Web Part with title bar
and border

All Web Part classes must be scoped public. A Web Part class that is not marked as public can't be used in SharePoint Web Part pages. In C#, when a new Class Library project is created, the default class Class1 is automatically set to the public scope. Unfortunately, classes that are added to the project are not scoped public automatically; the developer must add the public keyword manually!

A Web Part developer must only focus on what should happen inside the Web Part. The contents displayed inside the Web Part should be generated in the Render method of the Web Part class. This method is already implemented in the base WebPart class, so it should be overridden in the HelloWorld WebPart class. This is the default implementation:

```
protected override void Render(System.Web.UI.HtmlTextWriter writer)
{
    base.Render(writer);
}
```

The only parameter of the Render method is the writer parameter, which is of the type HtmlTextWriter. You should use this parameter to write HTML that will be rendered inside the Web Part. It's important to write valid HTML with the writer parameter, because invalid HTML is accepted as well, so it could break the Web Part page. The HelloWorld Web Part should display fixed text, which is formatted as a title:

```
protected override void Render(System.Web.UI.HtmlTextWriter writer)
{
    writer.Write("<h1>Web Parts Rock!</h1>");
}
```

> It's not recommended to write HTML tags in plain strings as displayed in the previous example. Later in this chapter, I discuss the proper way to generate. The purpose of this example is to show the real basics. See the section, "Using HTML and Controls in Web Parts," later in this chapter for more information.

For now, the code is sufficient. It is a Web Part that displays fixed text. Before you can deploy this Web Part, the project must be built. So, the assembly (DLL) is generated. There are many ways to trigger the build process in Visual Studio, such as with the Build menu, using the Ctrl+Shift+B key combination, and so on.

The complete contents of the `Class1.cs` looks like this:

```
using System;
using System.Collections.Generic;
using System.Text;
using System.Web.UI.WebControls.WebParts;

namespace BasicWebParts
{
    public class HelloWorld: WebPart
    {
        protected override void Render(
                        System.Web.UI.HtmlTextWriter writer)
        {
            writer.Write("<h1>Web Parts Rock!</h1>");
        }
    }
}
```

Deploying the Web Part

For a Class Library project in Visual Studio (including the type of the `BasicWebParts` project), you cannot simply press F5 to start debugging. To test the HelloWorld Web Part, it must be hosted in either a SharePoint or a Web Part page in an ASP.NET 2.0 Web site. This discussion describes how Web Parts can be deployed manually to a SharePoint server.

> Manual deployment is not recommended to deploy, for example, to a production SharePoint server. Actually, in SharePoint 2007, the Features framework is the more appropriate way to package and deploy any SharePoint customizations, including Web Parts. The Features framework and SharePoint solutions are discussed in detail in Chapter 4.

Once the project has been built in Visual Studio, the assembly is generated. This assembly should be accessible for the SharePoint site on which the Web Part should be used. There are two places that it can be used: the BIN folder and the Global Assembly Cache (GAC).

Deploying to the BIN Folder

Every Web application in SharePoint is mapped to a physical folder on the local hard disk of the server. The location of this folder is determined when the Web site is created in Internet Information Services (IIS). In SharePoint 2007, this can happen either through the SharePoint 3.0 Central Administration site, or by manually creating a new Web site in IIS Manager. When the Web site is created by using the SharePoint 3.0 Central Administration site, the default location of this folder is `C:\Inetpub\wwwroot\wss\VirtualDirectories\<hostheader><port number>`. If the Web site is manually created in IIS Manager, the folder can be anywhere, because you can point to any location on any local drive of the server.

If the location of the folder mapped to the Web site is unknown, it is always possible to open IIS Manager to figure it out. Just select the Web site in the list, and in the properties window, select the Home Directory tab, as shown in Figure 7-7. In this tab, the location of the folder can be read in the Local Path textbox.

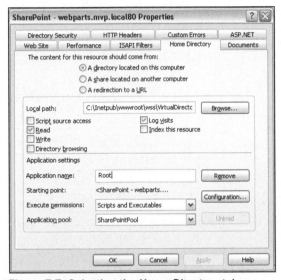

Figure 7-7: Selecting the Home Directory tab

The assembly containing the Web Part code should be placed in the `BIN` folder of the local path, so the location could look like `C:\Inetpub\wwwroot\wss\VirtualDirectories\<hostheader><port number>/bin`. Typically, the `BIN` folder is already created. If not, it can be created manually. In the local path, there is also a folder `_APP_BIN`. Although you could deploy the assembly to that folder, you should not do so, because this folder is reserved for use by Microsoft.

The actual "deployment" of the assembly is just copying the file to that `BIN` folder. In the case of the `BasicWebParts` sample project, the file `BasicWebParts.dll` should be copied.

Deploying to the Global Assembly Cache

The Global Assembly Cache (GAC) also can be used to deploy the assembly containing the Web Part code. The GAC is the location for shared assemblies for the complete server. Before any assembly can be deployed to the GAC, it should have a *strong name*. To assign a strong name to an assembly, you must select a *strong name key file* in the Signing tab of the project properties in Visual Studio, as shown in Figure 7-8.

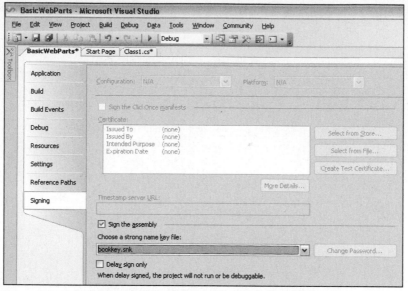

Figure 7-8: Selecting a strong name key file in the Signing tab

> If an assembly is signed, the name of the assembly changes as well. The assembly name will contain, for example, the PublicKeyToken.

Once a strong name key file is selected, you should build the project again so that the assembly is signed with a strong name. After that, it can be deployed to the GAC by dragging the assembly in Windows Explorer to the special C:\Windows\Assembly folder. Alternatively, you could also use the GACUTIL command-line utility.

Differences Between the GAC and the BIN Folder

The first difference between deploying the assembly to the GAC versus the BIN folder of the Web site is the scope of the deployed assembly. If the assembly is deployed to the GAC, it can be used by any SharePoint Web application. If the assembly is deployed to the BIN folder of a Web application, it can only be used in that Web application. If you need to make use of the same assembly from different SharePoint Web applications, the GAC has, of course, the advantage, because the assembly must be deployed only once.

Another difference between using the GAC and the BIN folder is the fact that the GAC can contain multiple versions for the same assembly. Suppose one Web application should be able to make use of multiple versions of an assembly. Once again, the GAC deployment is the preferred way.

A third difference is related to the updating of the assembly deployed to the GAC or the BIN folder. When an assembly file is overwritten in the BIN folder, it's automatically reloaded, so the new version can be used in the SharePoint sites. An assembly deployed to the GAC is cached, so if the assembly is rebuilt and redeployed to the GAC, the SharePoint sites won't automatically pick up the new version. To force SharePoint to reload the assembly, you must execute the IISRESET command-line utility or manually stop and start the IIS service. Technically getting the application pool of the SharePoint Web site to recycle is sufficient, but there is no standard command-line utility that can do that, so although the IISRESET command is "overkill" it's the most used technique.

> **To force SharePoint to pick up assemblies from the GAC, even after rebuilding and redeploying the assembly without using the IISRESET command, you must change the version number of the assembly in the properties pages of project in Visual Studio.**

A final difference between using the GAC and the BIN folder has to do with the Code Access Security (CAS) context in which the assembly is running. Assemblies deployed to the BIN folder will run with the CAS permission level specified in the web.config file. By default, the CAS permission level used in SharePoint sites is WSS_Minimal, which is a very low permission level. Assemblies deployed to the GAC will run with the Full CAS permission level by default.

The Assembly Name

By default, assembly name will be the same as the name of the project in Visual Studio (the name that's specified in the New Project dialog window), but it can be changed afterward. The assembly name is configurable in Visual Studio in the Application section of the project properties, as shown in Figure 7-9.

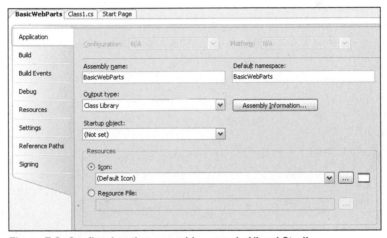

Figure 7-9: Configuring the assembly name in Visual Studio

The full assembly name also includes some additional metadata: the culture and the version number of the assembly. Both properties can be set in the Assembly Information dialog in the Application properties in Visual Studio, as shown in Figure 7-10. The version used in the full name is the Assembly Version of this dialog. If the Neutral Language is set to "none," that culture in the full assembly name will be set to "neutral."

The final piece of information included in the full assembly name is the public key token. This information depends on whether or not the assembly is strong-named. If the assembly doesn't have a strong name, the public key token is empty. If the assembly is strong-named, the public key token is not empty. For more information about adding a strong name, see the section, "Deploying to the Global Assembly Cache," earlier in this chapter.

Figure 7-10: Assembly Information dialog

Following is an example of an assembly name for an assembly that does not have a strong name:

```
BasicWebParts, Version=1.0.0.0, Culture=neutral, PublicKeyToken=null
```

If an assembly is not strong-named, the assembly name can be shortened by leaving out the Version, Culture, and PublicKeyToken attributes, as shown in the following example:

```
BasicWebParts
```

Following is an example of an assembly name for an assembly that has a strong name:

```
BasicWebParts, Version=1.0.0.0, Culture=neutral, PublicKeyToken=357e8569eecdc846
```

> **Assembly names contain lots of information that is very important later on in the deployment of the Web Part assembly. Additionally, the assembly name is case-sensitive, so it's very important that the exact assembly name is known. A very good free tool that can be used for this task is Lutz Roeder's Reflector. You can download it for free from this location:** http://www.aisto.com/roeder/dotnet/.

Trusting the Web Part

Just making sure that SharePoint sites can access the assembly that contains the Web Part code is not enough. Actually, SharePoint considers all "external" code as potentially dangerous — external code is not trusted. So, from SharePoint's point of view, your custom code will not be trusted to be executed by default. To ensure that "external" code will be executed in SharePoint, a change to the web.config is necessary.

The section in the `web.config` file that's responsible for trusting assemblies containing Web Parts is the `SafeControls` section in the SharePoint element:

```
<configuration>
  <configSections>
    <section name="SafeControls"
type="Microsoft.SharePoint.ApplicationRuntime.SafeControlsConfigurationHandler,
Microsoft.SharePoint, Version=12.0.0.0, Culture=neutral,
PublicKeyToken=71e9bce111e9429c" />

    ...
  </configSections>
  <SharePoint>

    ...

    <SafeControls>
      ...
    </SafeControls>
  </SharePoint>

  ...
</configuration>
```

Out-of-the-box, a SharePoint site's `web.config` file already contains a bunch of elements in the `SafeControl` section:

```
...
<SafeControl Assembly="System.Web, Version=2.0.0.0, Culture=neutral,
PublicKeyToken=b03f5f7f11d50a3a" Namespace="System.Web.UI.WebControls"
TypeName="XmlDataSource" Safe="False" AllowRemoteDesigner="False" />
<SafeControl Assembly="System.Web, Version=2.0.0.0, Culture=neutral,
PublicKeyToken=b03f5f7f11d50a3a" Namespace="System.Web.UI.WebControls"
TypeName="ObjectDataSource" Safe="False" AllowRemoteDesigner="False" />
<SafeControl Assembly="Microsoft.SharePoint, Version=11.0.0.0, Culture=neutral,
PublicKeyToken=71e9bce111e9429c" Namespace="Microsoft.SharePoint" TypeName="*"
Safe="True" AllowRemoteDesigner="True" />
<SafeControl Assembly="Microsoft.SharePoint, Version=11.0.0.0, Culture=neutral,
PublicKeyToken=71e9bce111e9429c" Namespace="Microsoft.SharePoint.WebPartPages"
TypeName="*" Safe="True" AllowRemoteDesigner="True" />
<SafeControl Assembly="Microsoft.SharePoint, Version=11.0.0.0, Culture=neutral,
PublicKeyToken=71e9bce111e9429c" Namespace="Microsoft.SharePoint.WebControls"
TypeName="*" Safe="True" AllowRemoteDesigner="True" />
...
```

The default elements in the `SafeControls` section register some ASP.NET 2.0 controls and the out-of-the-box Web Parts of SharePoint itself. For every assembly containing Web Parts, there must be at least one line in the `SafeControls` section for that assembly. An empty `SafeControl` element looks like this:

```
<SafeControl Assembly="" Namespace="" TypeName="" Safe="" />
```

The `Assembly` attribute should contain the name of the assembly that should be registered as a `Safe`. The `Namespace` attribute should determine the .NET namespace of the code that contains the Web Part class. The `TypeName` attribute is used to specify the `Class` name of the Web Part. And finally, the `Safe` attribute (which tells SharePoint if it's safe to execute the assembly or not) can contain `True` or `False`.

The `SafeControl` element for the HelloWorld Web Part reads like this:

```
<SafeControl Assembly="BasicWebParts" Namespace="BasicWebParts" TypeName="*"
Safe="True"/>
```

Alternatively, you could use the following:

```
<SafeControl Assembly="BasicWebParts" Namespace="BasicWebParts"
TypeName="HelloWorld" Safe="True"/>
```

If the assembly doesn't have a strong name (that is, it is not signed), the `Assembly` attribute's value can be retrieved from the project properties in Visual Studio, but it defaults to the name of the project specified at project creation. The `Namespace` attribute's value is, by default, the same as the project name, so it's the same as the `Assembly` name. The namespace of the Web Part class can be retrieved or changed from the code file (`*.cs`). The `TypeName` attribute's value can be set either to an asterisk or to the class name of the Web Part. Finally, the `Safe` attribute is set to `True`, of course.

> Remember, the assembly name contains the version, culture, and public key token if the assembly contains a strong name! For more information about the assembly name that should be used in the SafeControl element, see the section, "The Assembly Name," earlier in this chapter.

To apply the settings made in the `web.config` file, typically just saving the `web.config` file is enough. ASP.NET will automatically refresh the new values when it notices the `web.config` file has been updated. This is also the reason why, after an update of the `web.config` file, it can usually take a little bit longer before the site loads in the browser. This only happens for the first users who hit the SharePoint site with a Web browser.

Advertising the Web Part

Now, everything is set to be able to use the Web Part in the SharePoint site, but you don't have the capability yet to add the newly created Web Part to a Web Part page. First, the Web Part must be advertised. When you want to add a Web Part to a page, you can select from a list of Web Parts displayed in the Add Web Parts dialog, as shown in Figure 7-11.

First of all, in this dialog there is a distinction between the Web Parts connected to a SharePoint list or library, and the Web Parts not connected to a list or library. If the site that contains the Web Part page on which the Web Part should be added contains a list (for example, a Contact list, Task list, and so on) or a document library, those Web Parts will be displayed in the "List and Libraries" section.

The second section, All Web Parts, contains the Web Parts not connected to a list or library. Custom-built Web Parts will be displayed here. The section is divided into groups (for example, Business Data, Default, Miscellaneous, and so on) so that you can find the Web Parts more easily. When a custom Web Part is advertised, the group in which it should be placed can be specified.

To start advertising the Web Part, navigate to the Site Settings command in the Site Actions menu on the top-right of the SharePoint Web page, as shown in Figure 7-12.

On the Site Settings page, there is a link to navigate to the Web Part gallery (the Galleries section). If you don't see the link to the Web Part gallery, it means you are not on the top-level Web site of the site collection. The Site Settings page of a subsite doesn't display the Web Part gallery link, but it shows a link to navigate directly to the top-level site settings in the Site Collection Administration section, as shown in Figure 7-13. The top-level site's Site Settings page does display the Web Parts gallery, as shown in Figure 7-14.

Figure 7-11: Add Web Parts dialog

Figure 7-12: Selecting Site Settings from the Site Actions menu

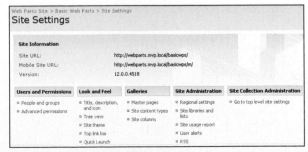

Figure 7-13: Site Collection Administration section containing link to the top-level site settings

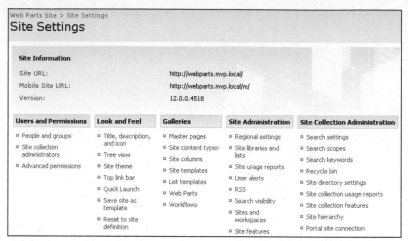

Figure 7-14: Galleries section of Site Settings page showing Web Parts link

The Web Part Gallery page shown in Figure 7-15 displays a list of all the Web Parts that have already been advertised. To add a new Web Part to the gallery, click the New button on the toolbar of the list.

Figure 7-15: Web Part Gallery page

When you click the New button, the New Web Parts page shown in Figure 7-16 loads and shows all Web Part classes that are found in all the assemblies located in the BIN folder, as well as in the GAC. If a Web Part is not displayed in the list, the Web Part is probably not registered correctly as a safe control in the web.config. Additionally, Web Parts can only be loaded if the assembly is either deployed to the BIN folder or the GAC.

To add the new Web Part, all you have to do is to check the checkbox in front of the Web Part class name. Additionally, a filename can be specified. The only important thing about this filename is that it should be unique per site collection.

When you are finished, click the Populate Gallery button to add the selected Web Parts to the Web Part gallery. This list is sorted on the Web Part Type Name, which is the namespace of the Web Part class, concatenated with the class name.

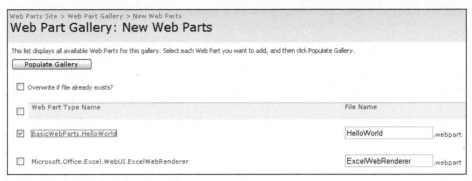

Figure 7-16: New Web Parts page

When the Web Part Gallery page loads again (Figure 7-17), the newly created Web Part will be listed as well. The new Web Part will probably be sitting somewhere between the other Web Parts, because this list is sorted by the name of the Web Parts, not including the class name. A small trick to easily find the newly added Web Part is to sort the list by the Modified timestamp in descending order. The newly added Web Part will be displayed as the first item.

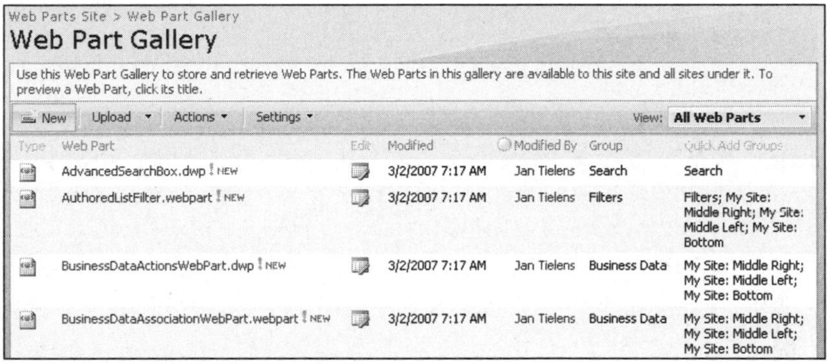

Figure 7-17: New Web Part Gallery page

From now on, the Web Part can be used in all the pages of all the sites of the site collection in which the Web Part was advertised. By default, the Web Part will be displayed in the Miscellaneous group of the Add Web Part dialog.

It's a good idea to add additional metadata to the Web Part by clicking the Edit icon (located in the third column on the Web Part Gallery page) for the newly added Web Part. Once you click the Edit icon, you will see the page shown in Figure 7-18. You should give the Web Part a title and description. These fields will be shown in the Add Web Part dialog. Additionally, the Web Part can be put in one of the existing groups, or it can be put in a new group, the name of which can be filled out on the textbox. In this example, I have placed the Web Part in a new group called MVP Book. Finally, the Web Part can be added to one or more Quick Add Groups. The Quick Add Groups are used to suggest Web Parts for specific types of sites.

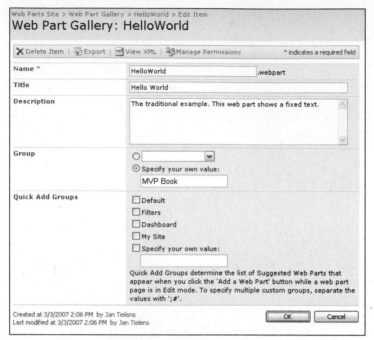

Figure 7-18: Editing the properties for the newly added Web Part

> When changing the metadata of a Web Part, actually an XML file is edited in the background. Instead of using the Edit Item functionality, it's also possible to create this XML file manually and upload it directly to the Web Part Gallery.

Testing the Web Part

Once you have completed all the previous steps, you can test the Web Part. The Web Part can be put on any Web Part page in any site of the site collection that contains the Web Part gallery in which the Web Part has been advertised. The Add Web Part dialog will display the newly created Web Part in the MVP Book group, and it will show both the title and the description entered in the previous step (Figure 7-19).

If everything went OK, the Web Part is displayed on the Web Part page of the SharePoint site (Figure 7-20). The Web Part title is automatically copied from the Web Part's properties in the Web Part gallery. If the mouse cursor is hovered above the Web Part title, the description coming from the Web Part gallery is displayed as a tooltip. These values can be changed in the properties of the Web Part for the current page by clicking Modify Shared Web Part from the Web Part's drop-down menu.

Debugging the Web Part

The Web Part built during the previous steps is, of course, a very simple Web Part, but Web Parts can contain complex logic as well. When something doesn't work as expected in a Web Part, and the developer doesn't have a clue as to what's wrong, debugging the Web Part can be a solution.

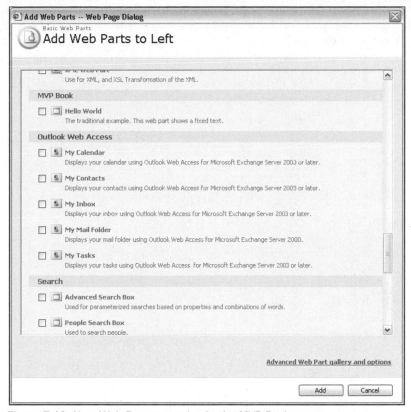

Figure 7-19: New Web Part appearing in the MVP Book group

Figure 7-20: New Web Part displayed on the Web Part page of the
SharePoint site

Debugging Web Parts follows the same techniques and rules as debugging any other .NET application.
The only difference with SharePoint Web Parts is that the Web Part code is executed by the SharePoint
site. The SharePoint site is running in IIS, so to be able to debug the Web Part, the debugger should be
attached to the process of IIS. The process name of the IIS WWW Worker Process is W3WP.EXE.

In Visual Studio, it's very easy to attach a debugger to any process. In the Debug menu, click the "Attach to Process" menu item to produce the page shown in Figure 7-21. The "Show processes from all users" checkbox should be selected so that the IIS worker processes are displayed as well. You may have multiple W3WP.EXE processes running, so every Application Pool will result in a process like that. It is very difficult to figure out which one of them is running the SharePoint site with the Web Part that you want to debug. Luckily, it's also possible to debug multiple processes at the same time simply by selecting all of them and clicking the Attach button.

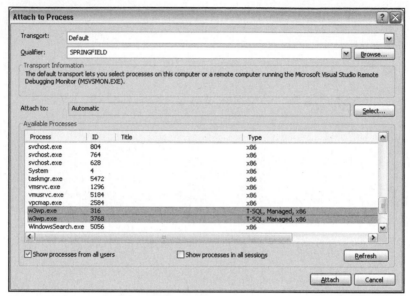

Figure 7-21: "Attach to Process" page

Visual Studio will start a debug session for the selected processes. If any breakpoints in the project's code are hit, Visual Studio will pause the process and switch to break mode, as shown in Figure 7-22. Once Visual Studio has started a debug session, and the breakpoints are set, a page refresh of the Web Part page running the Web Part will force the code to be executed again so that the breakpoint is hit.

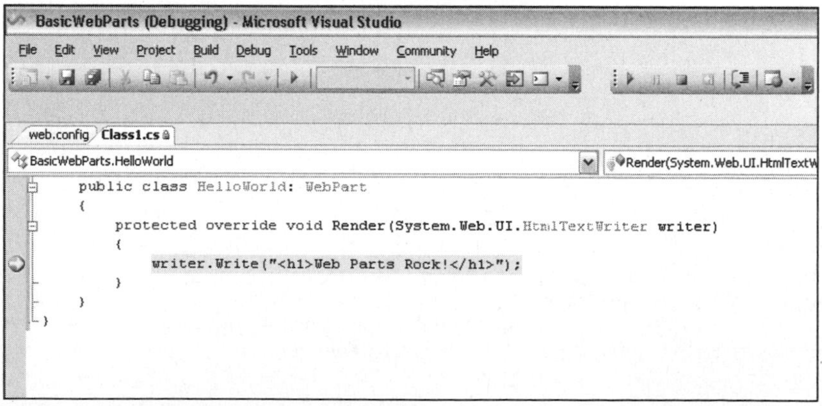

Figure 7-22: Break mode in Visual Studio

Process of Building, Deploying, and Testing

Building, deploying, and testing a new Web Part can be summarized in the following steps:

1. Create a Class Library project in Visual Studio. Add a reference to the `System.Web` assembly and inherit a class from the base `WebPart` class.

2. Override the `Render` method of the base `WebPart` class so that it writes some HTML code.

3. Build the project so that the assembly (DLL) is created.

4. Deploy the assembly either to the `BIN` folder of the SharePoint site or to the GAC so that the SharePoint site can load it.

5. Register the Web Part as a `Safe` control in the `web.config` file.

6. Advertise the Web Part in the Web Part gallery of the site collection.

7. Add the Web Part to a Web Part page to test it.

Now, let's take a look at using HTML and other controls in Web Parts.

Using HTML and Controls in Web Parts

In the previous HelloWorld Web Part example, the Web Part code generated HTML by using a string. It is quite obvious that generating HTML for more complex user interfaces can be complicated. This section examines two techniques to simplify the generation of HTML code in Web Parts:

❏ Building HTML in Web Parts
❏ Using controls in Web Parts

Building HTML in Web Parts

The one and only parameter in the overridden `Render` method in the previous example is of the type `HtmlTextWriter`. This class can be used to very easily build HTML without worrying about opening and closing all those angle brackets. For a full description of the `HtmlTextWriter` class, consult the MSDN library. Only the most important members are discussed here.

Rendering Opening Tags

Instead of generating HTML by using a string, you should use the `HtmlTextWriter` capabilities to render HTML. This class has lots of members that can be used to generate HTML. Let's start with the `RenderBegingTag` method that can write an opening markup element. For example, consider the following code snippet:

```
writer.RenderBeginTag("table");
```

The resulting HTML will be as follows:

```
<table>
```

Instead of using the element as a string for the parameter in the `RenderBeginTag` method, it is also possible to use the following:

```
writer.RenderBeginTag(HtmlTextWriterTag.Table);
```

Rendering Closing Tags

To close the tags opened with the `RenderBeginTag` method, you can use the `RenderEndTag` method. This method doesn't require any parameters. The last tag that was opened will be closed, so the `RenderEndTag` also takes into account nested tags.

```
writer.RenderBeginTag("i");
writer.RenderBeginTag("b");
writer.Write("test");
writer.RenderEndTag();
writer.RenderEndTag();
```

The preceding code snippet will result in following HTML:

```
<i><b>test</b></i>
```

The first time the `RenderEndTag` method is called, the b tag will be closed, because it was the last one that was opened. The second call to `RenderEndTag` will close the i tag.

Writing Attributes

Some HTML markup tags can make use of attributes — for example, to specify styles, alignments, and so on. Attributes can be rendered by using the `AddAttribute` class, which should be called before the `RenderBeginTag` if the actual tag is called. Also, for the `AddAttribute` class, it is possible to use either the attribute name as a string value, or `HtmlTextWriterAttribte` enumeration.

```
writer.AddAttribute("border", "1");
writer.AddAttribute(HtmlTextWriterAttribute.Width, "100%");
writer.RenderBeginTag(HtmlTextWriterTag.Table);
```

The preceding code snippet will result in the following HTML:

```
<table border="1" width="100%">
```

An Example: The TableDemo Web Part

The following Web Part code makes use of the methods just discussed to build a table in HTML. In every cell of that table, the coordinates are shown. The code of this Web Part can be added to the `BasicWebParts` project created in the beginning of this chapter, because every assembly can contain any number of Web Parts.

```
using System;
using System.Collections.Generic;
using System.Text;
using System.Web.UI.WebControls.WebParts;
using System.Web.UI;
```

```
namespace BasicWebParts
{
    public class TableDemo: WebPart
    {
        protected override void Render(
            System.Web.UI.HtmlTextWriter writer)
        {
            writer.AddAttribute(
                HtmlTextWriterAttribute.Border, "1");
            writer.AddAttribute(
                HtmlTextWriterAttribute.Width, "100%");
            writer.RenderBeginTag(
                HtmlTextWriterTag.Table);

            for (int i = 0; i < 5; i++)
            {
                writer.RenderBeginTag(HtmlTextWriterTag.Tr);
                for (int j = 0; j < 5; j++)
                {
                    writer.AddAttribute(
                        System.Web.UI.HtmlTextWriterAttribute.Align,
                        "center");

                    writer.RenderBeginTag(HtmlTextWriterTag.Td);

                    writer.Write(
                        string.Format("{0}, {1}",
                        i.ToString(), j.ToString()));

                    writer.RenderEndTag();
                }
                writer.RenderEndTag();
            }
            writer.RenderEndTag();
        }
    }
}
```

To deploy the new version of the assembly, simple copy the assembly to the BIN folder. The web.config file doesn't need to be changed anymore because the TypeName attribute was set to an asterisk. So, all the classes in the BasicWebParts namespace in the BasicWebParts assembly are considered as Safe controls. Of course, the new TableDemo Web Part should be advertised in the Web Part gallery as well.

The code uses two nested for loops to render an HTML table. Inside every cell, the coordinates are displayed. At run-time, this Web Part will result in the following HTML:

```
<table border="1" width="100%"
    <tr>
        <td align="center">
            0, 0</td>
        <td align="center">
            0, 1</td>
        <td align="center">
            0, 2</td>
```

```
            <td align="center">
                0, 3</td>
            <td align="center">
                0, 4</td>
    </tr>
    <tr>
            <td align="center">
                1, 0</td>
            <td align="center">
                1, 1</td>
            <td align="center">
                1, 2</td>
            <td align="center">
                1, 3</td>
            <td align="center">
                1, 4</td>
    </tr>
    ...
</table>
```

On a Web Part page in a SharePoint site, the Web Part is rendered as shown in Figure 7-23.

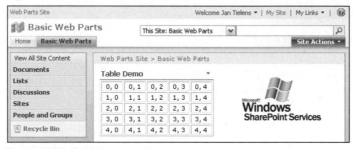

Figure 7-23: TableDemo Web Part

Using Controls in Web Parts

Generating HTML in code is not the way to go. To overcome this issue, it is possible to use Web controls in Web Parts. The .NET Framework has lots of Web controls that can be used, including `Button`, `Textbox`, `Label`, and so on. Most of those user controls are residing in the `System.Web.UI.WebControls` namespace. The advantage of these ASP.NET Web controls is that they can generate HTML for themselves. You as a developer don't have to focus on writing HTML to render a button, for example.

Simple Calculator Example

To illustrate the use of Web controls in Web Parts, let's write a very basic example that nicely shows how to make use of a couple of Web controls, including server-side code for the event handlers of those controls. The example used will be a basic Calculator Web Part: just two textboxes for entering two numeric values, two buttons for adding and subtracting those values, and a third textbox to display the result. The focus of this Web Part won't be how to validate the entered values, and so on, but rather to just show how to build the user interface and the server-side code.

Getting Started with the SimpleCalculator Class

A Web Part using Web controls is still a normal Web Part. So, in the `BasicWebParts` Visual Studio project, add another class named `SimpleCalculator`. First, add the following `using` statements on top of the code:

```
using System.Web.UI.WebControls.WebParts;
using System.Web.UI.WebControls;
using System.Web.UI;
```

The `using` statements allow you to make use of the `WebPart` base class and all the ASP.NET Web controls without including the full namespace.

The second (and very important) addition to the code that must be made is the public keyword for the `SimpleCalculator` class. By default, in a Visual Studio 2005 C# Class Library project, the Class template doesn't include the public keyword. If the Web Part class doesn't have this public keyword, SharePoint won't be able to make use of it, so it must be added. The complete `SimpleCalculator` class looks like this now:

```
using System;
using System.Collections.Generic;
using System.Text;
using System.Web.UI.WebControls.WebParts;
using System.Web.UI.WebControls;
using System.Web.UI;

namespace BasicWebParts
{
    public class SimpleCalculator: WebPart
    {
    }
}
```

Declaring the Web Control Variables

For every Web control on the Web Part, a variable of that Web control should be declared as a member field. For the sample SimpleCalculator Web Part, there must be five variables registered (three textboxes and two buttons):

```
public class SimpleCalculator: WebPart
{
    TextBox tbA;
    TextBox tbB;
    TextBox tbResult;
    Button btnAdd;
    Button btnSub;
}
```

Overriding the CreateChildControls Method

The next step to build the SimpleCalculator Web Part is to override the `CreateChildControls` method from the base `WebPart` class. In this method, you first create of all new instances for all the Web control variables.

Additionally, properties for those Web controls can be set as well. Lastly, all the Web control instances should be added to the `Controls` collection of the base `WebPart` class so that ASP.NET knows about them, and, thus, the server-side events (if they exist) will be handled correctly. Of course, it doesn't matter where the variables are instantiated and added in the `CreateChildControls` method. It can be in the beginning, but it can be at the end as well; they can be added even dynamically in code. Personally, I prefer to structure my code as displayed here:

```
protected override void CreateChildControls()
{
    tbA = new TextBox();
    tbB = new TextBox();
    tbResult = new TextBox();
    btnAdd = new Button();
    btnSub = new Button();

    tbResult.ReadOnly = true;
    btnAdd.Text = "+";
    btnSub.Text = "-";

    this.Controls.Add(tbA);
    this.Controls.Add(tbB);
    this.Controls.Add(btnAdd);
    this.Controls.Add(btnSub);
    this.Controls.Add(tbResult);
}
```

In the SimpleCalculator Web Part example, the `ReadOnly` property for the results textbox is set to `true`, so end users won't be able to change anything in that textbox. This is done from code. Also the text properties of the buttons are set to `"+"` and `"-"`.

The order in which the controls are added to the `Controls` collection of the base `WebPart` class will determine how they are rendered later on in the Web Part. For this example, the two input textboxes should be rendered first, the two operation buttons should be rendered second, and, finally, the textbox that should display the result should be rendered.

If the controls are added like this, one after another, all of them will appear on one line. If the controls should be displayed on multiple lines, HTML break tags (`<br>`) can be added in between, as shown here:

```
this.Controls.Add(tbA);
this.Controls.Add(new LiteralControl("<br>"));
this.Controls.Add(tbB);
this.Controls.Add(new LiteralControl("<br>"));
this.Controls.Add(btnAdd);
this.Controls.Add(btnSub);
this.Controls.Add(new LiteralControl("<br>"));
this.Controls.Add(tbResult);
```

Alternatively, HTML tables, layers, and so on can be used as a more flexible way to add layout to the Web Part.

Adding Event Handlers

At this point, the code doesn't do anything except render some Web controls. The goal, of course, is to execute code when one of the operation buttons is clicked. This can be accomplished by adding event handlers for the corresponding events. These event handlers can be added in the `CreateChildControls` method as well.

```
btnAdd.Click += new EventHandler(btnAdd_Click);
btnSub.Click += new EventHandler(btnSub_Click);
```

The implementation of the event handlers can be done as follows. The `btnAdd_Click` and `btnSub_Click` methods are members of the `SimpleCalculator` class as well.

```
void btnAdd_Click(object sender, EventArgs e)
{
    int a = int.Parse(tbA.Text);
    int b = int.Parse(tbB.Text);
    int c = a + b;
    tbResult.Text = c.ToString();
}

void btnSub_Click(object sender, EventArgs e)
{
    int a = int.Parse(tbA.Text);
    int b = int.Parse(tbB.Text);
    int c = a - b;
    tbResult.Text = c.ToString();
}
```

> **Once again, the focus of this Web Part is not on how to validate the input of the textboxes before the calculations are done. When this code is used in a real-life scenario, adding validation code is obviously required.**

The Full SimpleCalculator Code

Now, the `SimpleCalculator` class is finished, and the complete combined code could look as follows:

```
using System;
using System.Collections.Generic;
using System.Text;
using System.Web.UI.WebControls.WebParts;
using System.Web.UI.WebControls;
using System.Web.UI;

namespace BasicWebParts
{
    public class SimpleCalculator: WebPart
    {
        TextBox tbA;
        TextBox tbB;
        TextBox tbResult;
        Button btnAdd;
        Button btnSub;
```

```
        protected override void CreateChildControls()
        {
            tbA = new TextBox();
            tbB = new TextBox();
            tbResult = new TextBox();
            btnAdd = new Button();
            btnSub = new Button();

            tbResult.ReadOnly = true;
            btnAdd.Text = "+";
            btnSub.Text = "-";

            btnAdd.Click += new EventHandler(btnAdd_Click);
            btnSub.Click += new EventHandler(btnSub_Click);

            this.Controls.Add(tbA);
            this.Controls.Add(new LiteralControl("<br>"));
            this.Controls.Add(tbB);
            this.Controls.Add(new LiteralControl("<br>"));
            this.Controls.Add(btnAdd);
            this.Controls.Add(btnSub);
            this.Controls.Add(new LiteralControl("<br>"));
            this.Controls.Add(tbResult);
        }

        void btnAdd_Click(object sender, EventArgs e)
        {
            int a = int.Parse(tbA.Text);
            int b = int.Parse(tbB.Text);
            int c = a + b;
            tbResult.Text = c.ToString();
        }

        void btnSub_Click(object sender, EventArgs e)
        {
            int a = int.Parse(tbA.Text);
            int b = int.Parse(tbB.Text);
            int c = a - b;
            tbResult.Text = c.ToString();
        }
    }
}
```

Using the SimpleCalculator Web Part

To deploy the SimpleCalculator Web Part, follows the steps described earlier in this chapter in the section, "Deploying the Web Part." The SimpleCalculator looks like Figure 7-24 at run-time.

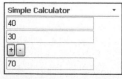

Figure 7-24: SimpleCalculator
Web Part

Manually Rendering the Web Controls

The user controls of the SimpleCalculator Web Part are rendered automatically on the Web Part's user interface because the default implementation of the `Render` method renders all items in the `Control` collection of the base `WebPart` class. It's also possible to override this method so that you are in full control of the rendering process. For every Web control, the `RenderControl` method can be called to render the corresponding HTML.

```
protected override void Render(HtmlTextWriter writer)
{
    this.EnsureChildControls();

    tbA.RenderControl(writer);
    writer.Write("<br>");
    tbB.RenderControl(writer);
    writer.Write("<br>");
    btnAdd.RenderControl(writer);
    btnSub.RenderControl(writer);
    writer.Write("<br>");
    tbResult.RenderControl(writer);
}
```

If the preceding code is used, the HTML break tags don't have to be added to the `Controls` collection. The `CreateChildControls` method could look as follows:

```
protected override void CreateChildControls()
{
    tbA = new TextBox();
    tbB = new TextBox();
    tbResult = new TextBox();
    btnAdd = new Button();
    btnSub = new Button();

    tbResult.ReadOnly = true;
    btnAdd.Text = "+";
    btnSub.Text = "-";

    btnAdd.Click += new EventHandler(btnAdd_Click);
    btnSub.Click += new EventHandler(btnSub_Click);

    this.Controls.Add(tbA);
    this.Controls.Add(tbB);
    this.Controls.Add(btnAdd);
    this.Controls.Add(btnSub);
    this.Controls.Add(tbResult);
}
```

Let's now examine connectable Web Parts.

Building Connectable Web Parts

Very simply stated, *connectable Web Parts* are Web Parts that can exchange data. The data communicated between Web Parts can be anything — text, numbers, or even complete objects.

When discussing connectable Web Parts, a distinction can be made between two types of connectable Web Parts:

❏   *The provider Web Parts* — The provider Web Parts are the Web Parts that can send data.

❏   *The consumer Web Parts* — These are the Web Parts that can receive data sent by the providers.

Typically, a Web Part is either a provider or a consumer, but a Web Part can also be both a provider and a consumer at the same time.

A provider Web Part can't just communicate with any consumer Web Part. Both the consumer and the provider must agree upon the type of data that is sent across. This definition of the type of data sent from the provider to the consumer is the only thing that's shared between them. So, provider and consumer Web Parts can be developed independently from each other, as long as they respectively send and consume the same type of data. This degree of separation is also the base for building Service Oriented Applications (SOA) and, in general, this approach is called "contract-driven development." First, parties agree upon a "contract," then they start independently to build their pieces.

SharePoint provides a framework to use connectable Web Parts. When a provider Web Part and a compatible consumer Web Part are placed on a page that's running Web Parts, the end user can tell SharePoint to make a connection between them. So, the actual connection between the provider and the consumer is triggered by the end user. The developers of those connectable Web Parts can only provide the mechanism to be able to connect them. It's the end user who needs to define the connection.

Connectable Web Part Scenarios

Connectable Web Parts have many scenarios. Here is a (non-limiting) list of the most common scenarios:

❏   *Parent-child relationships* — Relational databases often have parent-child relationships defined in their data model. A typical example is the relationship between an `Invoice` and an `InvoiceLine` table. Every `Invoice` record can have zero or more `InvoiceLine` records. In every `InvoiceLine` table, there should be a column referring to a record from the `Invoice` table. Relational databases can make use of relational integrity mechanisms to enforce that only `InvoiceLine` records can be added when there is a corresponding `Invoice` record as well.

These parent-child relationships illustrate the use of connectable Web Parts. Let's say that there is an Invoices Web Part displaying a list of `Invoice` records, and there's an Invoice Lines Web Part displaying a list of `InvoiceLine` records. When those two Web Parts are connected, it could be possible to select an invoice from the Invoices Web Part so that the Invoice Lines Web Part would display the corresponding invoice lines.

❏   *Master-detail views* — Another scenario for connectable Web Parts is the master-detail view and, once again, it's easier to explain in combination with a relational database. Suppose there is a table in a database containing product details. For every product, there are lots of values stored (name, price, color, weight, and so on). If this products table is shown in a grid in a Web Part, for example, it wouldn't be feasible to display all the columns in the grid because the grid would become too wide.

That's when the master-detail view can come into play. Instead of displaying all the columns for the product table, only the most important columns are shown, so the grid fits nicely on the page. But there's also a second Web Part that displays the details of one single product record (for example, all fields fitting nicely beneath each other). If the Products Web Part and the Product Details Web Part are connected, the end user once again can select a product that he or she is interested in. The Product Details Web Part will show all the details for the selected product.

❑ *Filtering* — The filtering scenario is not as common as the previous two scenarios, but can be quite useful, too. The idea is that there's a Web Part that allows the end user to enter some kind of filtering criteria (such as part of the name). A second Web Part can display a list of all the items that meet the terms of the selected criteria.

The scenarios described here are not the only scenarios that can be accomplished by making use of connectable Web Parts. The flexibility of connectable Web Parts allows virtually endless opportunities for Web Part developers to create customizable, dynamic user interfaces.

Using the Out-of-the-Box Connectable Web Parts

Many of the Web Parts available in SharePoint out-of-the-box are connectable, so it's possible to make use of connectable Web Parts without writing a single line of code. To illustrate this, let's look at an example where there are two SharePoint lists on the same site: Employees (based on the Contact list template) and Departments (based on the Custom list template). The Departments should have at least the title field. The Employees list should have an extra column, the Department column, which is a lookup column to the Departments list (Figure 7-25).

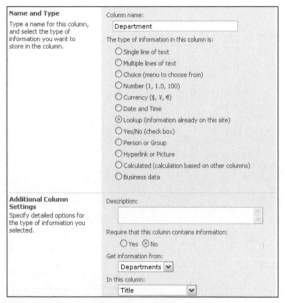

Figure 7-25: Specifying a lookup column to the Departments list

To get this example working, put an instance of the Departments Web Part and the Employees Web Part on a page of a SharePoint site. Make sure the Employees Web Part also displays the `Department` column. This can be done by modifying the view of this Web Part. Select "Modify shared Web Part" from the Web

Part's menu and choose "Modify current view." In this example, the Departments Web Part will be the provider and the Employees Web Part will be the consumer.

1. Switch the page that displays the two Web Parts into edit mode. In the Site Actions menu select Edit Page.

2. In the Edit drop-down menu of the Employees Web Part, select Connections ⇨ Get Sort/Filter From ⇨ Departments, as shown in Figure 7-26. Alternatively, the connection can also be made starting from the Departments Web Part; the end result is exactly the same.

Figure 7-26: Making the connection

3. In the Web Page Dialog window (Figure 7-27), select the Title field of the Departments list and click Next.

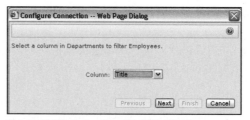

Figure 7-27: Selecting the Title field

4. In the next Web Page Dialog window (Figure 7-28), select the Department field of the Employees list and click Finish.

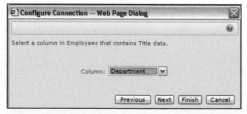

Figure 7-28: Selecting the Department field

5. Now you can close the Edit mode of the page. Notice that the Departments Web Part displays a radio button in front of every department, as shown in Figure 7-29. When you select a department by clicking any of the radio buttons, the Employees Web Part will display only the employees who have the value of the Department set to the selected department.

Figure 7-29: Radio buttons in front of every department

Text Communication Example

Of course, building custom connectable Web Parts is much more fun than using the out-of-the-box Web Parts of SharePoint. To illustrate the necessary code, let's create the following two Web Parts: the SimpleProvider and SimpleConsumer Web Parts. Once again, this is an example of two very basic Web Parts that will clearly show how Web Part connections can be provisioned in code. The SimpleProvider Web Part will display a textbox and a button; the SimpleConsumer Web Part will display only a textbox. When you enter some text in the consumer and click the button, the entered text is sent to the consumer Web Part and displayed in the textbox.

Defining the Connection Interface

Remember, the only thing connectable Web Parts share is the type of data that is communicated between them. This "type of data" is defined by making use of an interface. Because this example should communicate a string (text) between the two Web Parts, the interface looks like this:

```
using System;
using System.Collections.Generic;
using System.Text;

namespace BasicWebParts
{
    public interface ITextCommunication
    {
        string Text
        {
            get;
        }
    }
}
```

Notice that the interface is marked with the `public` keyword for the same reason as the `WebPart` classes should be using that same keyword. The `ITextCommunication` interface only defines a read-only property called `Text`. The type of this property is a basic `string`.

If Web Parts should communicate more complex data than a string value, this complex data must be described in the same interface. Simply add more properties, or change the data type of the properties. Those properties don't have to be read-only, and the interface can also contain other members (such as methods and functions).

The SimpleProvider Class

As described previously, the SimpleProvider Web Part's user interface contains only a button and a textbox. The code for this Web Part, without the connection functionality, looks like this:

```
using System;
using System.Collections.Generic;
using System.Text;
using System.Web.UI.WebControls.WebParts;
using System.Web.UI.WebControls;

namespace BasicWebParts
{
    public class SimpleProvider: WebPart
    {
        TextBox tb;
        Button btn;

        protected override void CreateChildControls()
        {
            tb = new TextBox();
            btn = new Button();

            btn.Text = "Send data";

            this.Controls.Add(tb);
            this.Controls.Add(btn);
        }
    }
}
```

To add connection functionality, the first thing you must do is implement the connection interface that was created previously. When the Text property is retrieved, the current value of the textbox is returned.

```
public class SimpleProvider: WebPart, ITextCommunication
{
    ...

    public string Text
    {
        get
        {
            return tb.Text;
        }
    }
}
```

Finally, the ConnectionProvider attribute should be applied to a function that returns an instance of the ITextCommunication interface. During rendering, SharePoint will interrogate the WebPart class and it will be checked to see if the class has this attribute. If so, SharePoint will render the user interface to create the connection. Otherwise, the end user won't see the menu item to create the connection.

The `string` parameter of the `ConnectionProvider` attribute contains the text that will be shown in the SharePoint user interface when the end user wants to add a connection starting from this Web Part. (The name of this method is not important; it's not required to name it `ReturnProvider`.)

```
[ConnectionProvider("Text Value")]
public ITextCommunication ReturnProvider()
{
    return this;
}
```

The complete SimpleProvider Web Part class looks like this:

```
using System;
using System.Collections.Generic;
using System.Text;
using System.Web.UI.WebControls.WebParts;
using System.Web.UI.WebControls;

namespace BasicWebParts
{
    public class SimpleProvider: WebPart, ITextCommunication
    {
        TextBox tb;
        Button btn;

        protected override void CreateChildControls()
        {
            tb = new TextBox();
            btn = new Button();

            btn.Text = "Send data";

            this.Controls.Add(tb);
            this.Controls.Add(btn);
        }

        public string Text
        {
            get
            {
                return tb.Text;
            }
        }

        [ConnectionProvider("Text Value")]
        public ITextCommunication ReturnProvider()
        {
            return this;
        }
    }
}
```

The SimpleConsumer Class

Just like the provider Web Part, the SimpleConsumer Web Part has a very basic user interface — just one single textbox. The following code will render this user interface, without the connection functionality:

```
using System;
using System.Collections.Generic;
using System.Text;
using System.Web.UI.WebControls.WebParts;
using System.Web.UI.WebControls;

namespace BasicWebParts
{
    public class SimpleConsumer: WebPart
    {
        TextBox tb;

        protected override void CreateChildControls()
        {
            tb = new TextBox();

            tb.ReadOnly = true;

            this.Controls.Add(tb);
        }
    }
}
```

The consumer Web Part also must have a method that is decorated with a specific attribute: the `ConnectionConsumer` attribute. SharePoint will verify which `WebPart` classes have this attribute, so the end user can make connections to or from the appropriate Web Parts.

The string parameter of the `ConnectionConsumer` attribute once again is the text value that will be shown to the user to make the connection. The name of the method that is decorated with this attribute doesn't matter. The only requirement for this method is to have a parameter of the type of the interface that defines the connection data. This parameter will contain a reference to the Web Part that acts as the provider, which is the instance returned in the `ReturnProvider` method of the SimpleProvider Web Part. This instance should be stored on class level so that the other Web Part code has access to it as well. This is typically done by adding a variable on the class level of the type of the communication interface, in this example `textProvider`.

```
[ConnectionConsumer("Text Value")]
public void ReceivesProvider(ITextCommunication provider)
{
    textProvider = provider;
}
```

Once there is a connection made, the `textProvider` variable will contain a reference to the provider Web Part. This reference can only be used *after* the `ReceiveProvider` method is called by SharePoint. A good place to do this is in the `Render` method.

```
protected override void Render(System.Web.UI.HtmlTextWriter writer)
{
    if (textProvider != null)
```

```
        {
            tb.Text = textProvider.Text;
        }

    base.Render(writer);
}
```

If the textProvider is not a null reference, the Text property is retrieved and put in the Text property of the textbox. The textProvider is a null reference if the end user hasn't made a connection to from this Web Part. The complete SimpleConsumer Web Part code looks like this:

```
using System;
using System.Collections.Generic;
using System.Text;
using System.Web.UI.WebControls.WebParts;
using System.Web.UI.WebControls;

namespace BasicWebParts
{
    public class SimpleConsumer: WebPart
    {
        TextBox tb;
        ITextCommunication textProvider;

        protected override void CreateChildControls()
        {
            tb = new TextBox();

            tb.ReadOnly = true;

            this.Controls.Add(tb);
        }

        [ConnectionConsumer("Text Value")]
        public void ReceivesProvider(ITextCommunication provider)
        {
            textProvider = provider;
        }

        protected override void Render(
                System.Web.UI.HtmlTextWriter writer)
        {
            if (textProvider != null)
            {
                tb.Text = textProvider.Text;
            }

            base.Render(writer);
        }
    }
}
```

Using the SimpleProvider and SimpleConsumer Web Parts

Deploying connectable Web Parts is exactly the same as deploying normal Web Parts, as described earlier in this chapter. Once the Web Parts are deployed, they can be put on a Web Part page, as shown in Figure 7-30.

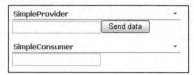

Figure 7-30: Web Part displayed on page

At this point, when you enter some text in the SimpleProvider Web Part's textbox and click the "Send data" button, no data will be sent to the consumer, because there hasn't been a connection made on the Web Part page in SharePoint.

To do so, switch the page to edit mode (Site Actions ➪ Edit page). In the Edit drop-down menu of the SimpleProvider, choose to connect this Web Part to the SimpleConsumer Web Part, as shown in Figure 7-31.

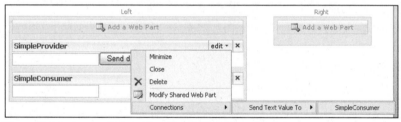

Figure 7-31: Connecting to the SimpleConsumer Web Part

The connection can be made starting from the provider or the consumer Web Part; the end result is exactly the same. Notice that the menu item Send Text Value To contains the Text Value string value that was specified in the `ConnectionProvider` attribute in the code of the Web Part.

Now, you can switch the page to normal mode again. You can enter some text in the provider, and this text will be sent to the consumer, as shown in Figure 7-32.

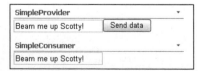

Figure 7-32: Text to the consumer Web Part

Notice that the SimpleProvider Web Part doesn't contain an event handler for the click event of the button, although the Web Part seems to be working correctly. Actually, the button on the provider Web Part is only there to force a postback of the page. Any other control that will cause a postback of the page will also cause the Web Parts to exchange data.

Building Web Parts the Smart Way

Developing custom Web Parts is great. It is a fantastic opportunity for developers to enhance and extend the out-of-the-box SharePoint functionality. However, developers who are spoiled by the incredible Visual Studio designers for building Windows applications or Web applications may be somewhat disappointed. The big difference between developing Windows or Web applications in Visual Studio and developing Web Parts is the fact that Web Part development requires writing lots of code. There is no designer that allows you to drag-and-drop controls from the toolbox onto the design surface of a Web Part. Developers must write code, even to build a user interface.

This section introduces another way of developing Web Parts by combining the best of both worlds: building Web Parts, while making use of the Visual Studio designers to generate the user interface.

Introducing the Web User Control Technique

Way back in the SharePoint 2003 time frame, some smart people in the SharePoint community (including my distinguished colleague Patrick Tisseghem) came up with a technique to use the Visual Studio designer to build Web Parts. This technique is still applicable in SharePoint 2007. The idea is as follows.

In Visual Studio, you create a Web User Control (an ASCX file with the corresponding code-behind) by making use of the normal Visual Studio designer for Web applications. Afterward, a wrapper Web Part is created that loads and renders the Web User Control. This wrapper Web Part only contains a couple of lines of code, so it's really easy to build. The beauty of this solution is, of course, the fact that the main part of the code can be created with the help of the Visual Studio designer.

Building the Web User Control

To illustrate the Web User Control technique, the SimpleCalculator Web Part will be re-created, but now with the help of the Visual Studio designer. So, in Visual Studio create a new Web Site project named BasicControls (the name doesn't really matter).

The Web Site template in Visual Studio automatically adds a Web page to the project named default.aspx. The Web User Control technique needs a Web User Control, of course, so the default.aspx page is not used. It can be closed or deleted.

The next step is to add a Web User Control named SimpleCalculator to the project. By default, in a C# Web Application project, the Web User Control is shown in Source view. But, by making use of the Design tab page at the bottom-left of the page, the control can be viewed and edited in the WYSIWYG editor (Figure 7-33). Now the textboxes and buttons can be dragged-and-dropped from the toolbox to build the user interface of the control.

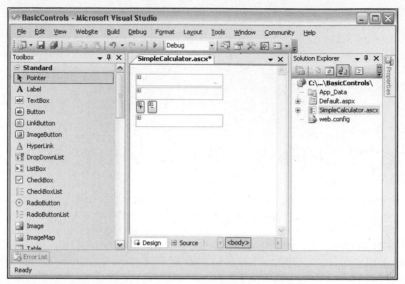

Figure 7-33: Viewing the control in the WYSIWYG editor

From the designer, the properties for the controls can be set as well. In this example, the following properties are set:

❑   Text property for Button1 — +

❑   Text property for Button2 — -

❑   ReadOnly property for TextBox3 — true

Adding event handlers for the "+" and "-" buttons is as easy as double-clicking the controls. The code for the default event handler (in this case, the Click event) is generated as follows:

```
using System;
using System.Data;
using System.Configuration;
using System.Collections;
using System.Web;
using System.Web.Security;
using System.Web.UI;
using System.Web.UI.WebControls;
using System.Web.UI.WebControls.WebParts;
using System.Web.UI.HtmlControls;

public partial class SimpleCalculator : System.Web.UI.UserControl
{
    protected void Page_Load(object sender, EventArgs e)
    {

    }
    protected void Button1_Click(object sender, EventArgs e)
    {
```

```
        int a = int.Parse(TextBox1.Text);
        int b = int.Parse(TextBox2.Text);
        int c = a + b;
        TextBox3.Text = c.ToString();
    }
    protected void Button2_Click(object sender, EventArgs e)
    {
        int a = int.Parse(TextBox1.Text);
        int b = int.Parse(TextBox2.Text);
        int c = a - b;
        TextBox3.Text = c.ToString();
    }
}
```

While editing the control in design mode, Visual Studio is generating markup code in the background for the user interface and event handlers of the control:

```
<%@ Control Language="C#" AutoEventWireup="true"
    CodeFile="SimpleCalculator.ascx.cs" Inherits="SimpleCalculator" %>
<asp:TextBox ID="TextBox1" runat="server"></asp:TextBox><br />
<asp:TextBox ID="TextBox2" runat="server"></asp:TextBox><br />
<asp:Button ID="Button1" runat="server"
    OnClick="Button1_Click" Text="+" />
<asp:Button ID="Button2" runat="server"
    OnClick="Button2_Click" Text="-" /><br />
<asp:TextBox ID="TextBox3" runat="server" ReadOnly="True"></asp:TextBox>
```

Deploying the Web User Control

To ensure that the wrapper Web Part can access the user control later on, the Web User Control must be "deployed." This deployment comes down to copying the user control files (SimpleCalculator.ascx and SimpleCalculator.cs) to a location accessible by SharePoint. Typically, this is done by creating a folder in the folder that has been mapped to the Web Site in IIS that's running the SharePoint site:

```
C:\Inetpub\wwwroot\wss\VirtualDirectories\<hostheader><port
number>/usercontrols.
```

Notice that the code-behind (cs) file is also copied to the server. This can be an issue if it's not preferable to deploy the source code (for example, when the Web Part is a part of a packaged commercial solution). To overcome this issue, it is possible to make use of the ASP.NET 2.0 technique called *precompilation*. The idea is to precompile the source code in an assembly and, instead of deploying the source code, the assembly is deployed just like in the ASP.NET 1.x days. Precompilation can be accomplished by making use of the aspnet_compiler.exe command-line utility, or it can be triggered from Visual Studio's Build menu by using the Publish menu item. You can find more information in the MSDN documentation, "ASP.NET Web Site Precompilation" (http://msdn2.microsoft.com/en-us/library/399f057w.aspx).

Building the Wrapper Web Part

The wrapper is, once again, just a normal Web Part, so it's a public class inheriting from the base WebPart class. The "magic" of the wrapper happens in the overridden CreateChildControls method. The LoadControl method of the underlying ASP.NET Web page is used to load the Web User Control based on the filename of the ASCX file. By making use of the tilde character ("~") in front of the /usercontrols folder name, the path will point to the usercontrols folder of the Web Site's IIS folder.

```
using System;
using System.Collections.Generic;
using System.Text;
using System.Web.UI.WebControls.WebParts;
using System.Web.UI;

namespace BasicWebParts
{
    public class CalculatorWrapper: WebPart
    {
        Control control;

        protected override void CreateChildControls()
        {
            control = this.Page.LoadControl(
                        "~/usercontrols/SimpleCalculator.ascx");

            this.Controls.Add(control);
        }
    }
}
```

Introducing the SmartPart

Building wrapper Web Parts for loading user controls is not very difficult, but it can be tedious work. For every user control that is created, a corresponding wrapper Web Part must be created as well. To overcome this problem, a more generic wrapper Web Part can be created, making it possible to set a property, for example, that indicates which Web User Control should be loaded.

But you don't have to create this Web Part yourself. I have created the SmartPart! The SmartPart is a generic SharePoint Web Part that can host any ASP.NET Web User Control. So, the only thing smart Web Part developers need to focus on is the creation of Web User Controls.

The SmartPart is an Open Source project, nowadays hosted on the Microsoft CodePlex site (www.codeplex .com). This means you can download the SmartPart for free and use it without paying any licenses whatsoever. For more information, visit www.smartpart.info or www.codeplex.com/smartpart.

Using the SmartPart

The first step to be able to use the SmartPart is getting the SmartPart installed and activated on the SharePoint site in which it should be used. Detailed installation instructions are available in the downloadable package, but it comes down to deploying the SmartPart solution and activating the feature on a site collection.

The second step is to create a Web User Control that will be hosted in an instance of the SmartPart. This Web User Control can be built as a normal Web User Control, as described in the section, "Building the Web User Control," earlier in this chapter. By default, the Web User Control files (one ASCX and CS file per control) are loaded from the \usercontrols folder, which should be created in the folder that is mapped to the IIS Web site running the SharePoint site. This is typically `C:\Inetpub\wwwroot\wss\VirtualDirectories\ <hostheader><port number>/usercontrols`.

Once the Web User Control files are deployed, an instance of the SmartPart Web Part should be placed on the page on which the user control should be displayed. By default, the SmartPart will be empty, because it should be configured for which control to show (Figure 7-34).

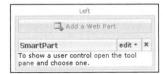

Figure 7-34: Empty SmartPart

To configure which Web User Control should be shown in the SmartPart, click the link to open the tool pane, or, in the edit drop-down menu, select the Modify Shared Web Part item. Both actions will open the SmartPart's tool pane in which a drop-down shows all available Web User Controls that are found in the `/usercontrols` folder. Optionally, other properties can be set at this point as well. It makes sense, for example, to set the Title property, because, by default, the SmartPart will have the title set to "SmartPart" (Figure 7-35).

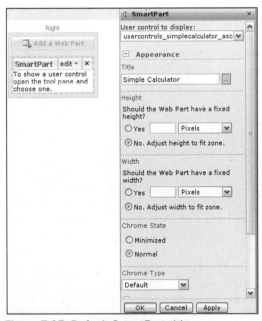

Figure 7-35: Default SmartPart title

When you click the OK or Apply button to apply the settings, the SmartPart will load the selected Web User Control and display it on the SharePoint page (Figure 7-36). The end user doesn't notice that the Web Part that he or she is seeing actually is a control hosted in the SmartPart.

231

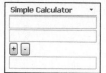

Figure 7-36: SmartPart
displaying on the
SharePoint page

Connectable Web User Controls

As discussed earlier in this chapter, building connectable Web Parts is a great way for the Web Part developer to create flexible, customizable user interfaces in SharePoint sites. When using the SmartPart to create Web Parts, creating connectable Web Parts is even easier!

Of course, the basic concepts of connectable Web Parts still apply. Typically, there is a provider Web Part and there is a consumer Web Part; if they are connected, they can exchange data. Translated to the SmartPart context, this means that there is a provider Web User Control and there is a consumer Web User Control.

To illustrate this, let's make use of the Northwind demo database to build a master detail relationship view. In the AdventureWorks database, there is a view called vEmployees, which is related to the table Orders. So, the provider Web User Control will be the EmployeeGrid, and the consumer Web User Control will be the OrderGrid.

Building the EmployeeGrid Control

Building the EmployeeGrid control will be very easy. When a DataGridView control is dragged onto the designer of the control, Visual Studio 2005 allows you to specify data binding settings by going through a wizard, as shown in Figure 7-37.

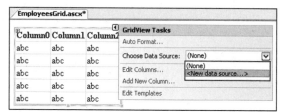

Figure 7-37: Using the wizard to specify data
binding settings

Besides going through the wizard (which will generate the data binding properties), you should also check the Enable Paging and Enable Selection properties in the GridView Tasks. The one and only property that should be set through the properties pane in Visual Studio is the Width. If it's set to 100 percent, the grid will nicely fill all the available space in the Web Part. The resulting Web User Controls can look like Figure 7-38 in the Design view of Visual Studio.

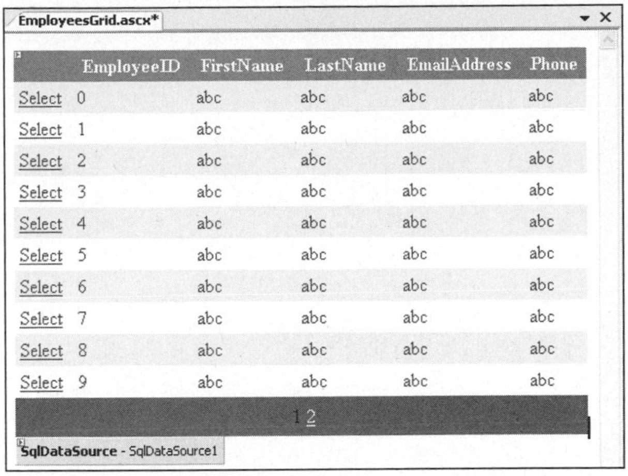

Figure 7-38: Web User Controls in Design view of Visual Studio

So far, the EmployeeGrid Web User Control will display all the Northwind employees and allow the user to select one. But the control is not yet connectable. To identify that this user control should be connectable in SharePoint, you must implement the IConnectionProviderControl interface in code. This interface is defined in the SmartPart assembly, so before the interface is found by Visual Studio's IntelliSense, a reference to the SmartPart DLL should be made. The SmartPart assembly can also be found in the downloadable SmartPart package.

The IConnectionProviderControl interface defines two members: a property to specify the label to display in the SharePoint interface, and a function that is called by SharePoint to retrieve the connection value.

```
using System;
using System.Data;
using System.Configuration;
using System.Collections;
using System.Web;
using System.Web.Security;
using System.Web.UI;
using System.Web.UI.WebControls;
using System.Web.UI.WebControls.WebParts;
using System.Web.UI.HtmlControls;

public partial class EmployeesGrid : System.Web.UI.UserControl,
        SmartPart.IConnectionProviderControl
{
    protected void Page_Load(object sender, EventArgs e)
    { }

    public object GetProviderData()
    {
        if (GridView1.SelectedIndex > -1)
            return GridView1.SelectedValue;
        else
            return -1;
```

```
    }

    public string ProviderMenuLabel
    {
        get { return "Sends an employee to"; }
    }
}
```

In the Source view of the ASCX file, the generated markup shows all the settings made by the data binding wizard:

```
<%@ Control Language="C#" AutoEventWireup="true"
    CodeFile="EmployeesGrid.ascx.cs" Inherits="EmployeesGrid" %>
<asp:GridView ID="GridView1" runat="server" AllowPaging="True"
            AutoGenerateColumns="False"
    CellPadding="4" DataKeyNames="EmployeeID" DataSourceID="SqlDataSource1"
    ForeColor="#333333"
    GridLines="None" Width="100%">
    <FooterStyle BackColor="#507CD1" Font-Bold="True" ForeColor="White" />
    <Columns>
        <asp:CommandField ShowSelectButton="True" />
        <asp:BoundField DataField="EmployeeID" HeaderText="EmployeeID"
            ReadOnly="True" SortExpression="EmployeeID" />
        <asp:BoundField DataField="FirstName" HeaderText="FirstName"
            SortExpression="FirstName" />
        <asp:BoundField DataField="LastName" HeaderText="LastName"
            SortExpression="LastName" />
        <asp:BoundField DataField="EmailAddress"
            HeaderText="EmailAddress"
            SortExpression="EmailAddress" />
        <asp:BoundField DataField="Phone" HeaderText="Phone"
            SortExpression="Phone" />
    </Columns>
    <RowStyle BackColor="#EFF3FB" />
    <EditRowStyle BackColor="#2461BF" />
    <SelectedRowStyle BackColor="#D1DDF1" Font-Bold="True"
        ForeColor="#333333" />
    <PagerStyle BackColor="#2461BF" ForeColor="White"
        HorizontalAlign="Center" />
    <HeaderStyle BackColor="#507CD1" Font-Bold="True"
        ForeColor="White" />
    <AlternatingRowStyle BackColor="White" />
</asp:GridView>
<asp:SqlDataSource ID="SqlDataSource1" runat="server"
    ConnectionString="Data Source=webparts.mvp.local;Initial
Catalog=AdventureWorks;User ID=sa;Password=secret"
    ProviderName="System.Data.SqlClient"
    SelectCommand="SELECT EmployeeID, FirstName, LastName, EmailAddress, Phone FROM
HumanResources.vEmployee">
</asp:SqlDataSource>
```

Building the OrderGrid Control

The first step to create the `OrderGrid` Web User Control is the same as for the `EmployeeGrid` control. When a `DataGridView` control is dragged onto the designer, you can use the data binding wizard to data bind to the `PurchaseOrderHeader` table. The query to fetch the data should contain one parameter to be able to fetch all orders for an employee.

```
SELECT PurchaseOrderID, EmployeeID, OrderDate, SubTotal FROM Purchasing
.PurchaseOrderHeader WHERE (EmployeeID = @empid)
```

In the code-behind for the `OrderGrid` control, the `OrderGrid` class should this time implement the `IConnectionConsumerControl` interface defined in the SmartPart assembly. The `ConsumerMenuLabel` property should return the text that will be displayed in the SharePoint user interface when the connection is made. The `SetConsumerData` method is called by SharePoint to pass the data received from the provider. Additionally, the `Selecting` event of the `SqlDataSource` should be handled, so the received employee ID from the provider is used to fetch the data.

```csharp
using System;
using System.Data;
using System.Configuration;
using System.Collections;
using System.Web;
using System.Web.Security;
using System.Web.UI;
using System.Web.UI.WebControls;
using System.Web.UI.WebControls.WebParts;
using System.Web.UI.HtmlControls;

public partial class OrderGrid : System.Web.UI.UserControl,
        SmartPart.IConnectionConsumerControl
{
    int empID;

    protected void Page_Load(object sender, EventArgs e)
    {

    }

    protected void SqlDataSource1_Selecting(object sender,
SqlDataSourceSelectingEventArgs e)
    {
        e.Command.Parameters["@empid"].Value = empID;
    }

    public string ConsumerMenuLabel
    {
        get { return "Receives an employee from"; }
    }

    public void SetConsumerData(object data)
```

```
        {
            if (data != null)
            {
                empID = (int)data;
                GridView1.DataBind();
            }
        }
    }
}
```

Following is the corresponding source of the ASCX file:

```
<%@ Control Language="C#" AutoEventWireup="true" CodeFile="OrderGrid.ascx.cs"
Inherits="OrderGrid" %>
<asp:GridView ID="GridView1" runat="server" AllowPaging="True"
AutoGenerateColumns="False"
    CellPadding="4" DataKeyNames="PurchaseOrderID" DataSourceID="SqlDataSource1"
    ForeColor="#333333" GridLines="None" Width="100%">
    <FooterStyle BackColor="#507CD1" Font-Bold="True" ForeColor="White" />
    <Columns>
        <asp:BoundField DataField="PurchaseOrderID" HeaderText="PurchaseOrderID"
InsertVisible="False"
            ReadOnly="True" SortExpression="PurchaseOrderID" />
        <asp:BoundField DataField="EmployeeID" HeaderText="EmployeeID"
SortExpression="EmployeeID" />
        <asp:BoundField DataField="OrderDate" HeaderText="OrderDate"
SortExpression="OrderDate" />
        <asp:BoundField DataField="SubTotal" HeaderText="SubTotal"
SortExpression="SubTotal" />
    </Columns>
    <RowStyle BackColor="#EFF3FB" />
    <EditRowStyle BackColor="#2461BF" />
    <SelectedRowStyle BackColor="#D1DDF1" Font-Bold="True" ForeColor="#333333" />
    <PagerStyle BackColor="#2461BF" ForeColor="White" HorizontalAlign="Center" />
    <HeaderStyle BackColor="#507CD1" Font-Bold="True" ForeColor="White" />
    <AlternatingRowStyle BackColor="White" />
</asp:GridView>

<asp:SqlDataSource ID="SqlDataSource1" runat="server" ConnectionString="Data
Source=webparts.mvp.local;Initial Catalog=AdventureWorks;User ID=sa"
    ProviderName="System.Data.SqlClient" SelectCommand="SELECT PurchaseOrderID,
EmployeeID, OrderDate, SubTotal FROM Purchasing.PurchaseOrderHeader WHERE
(EmployeeID = @empid)">
    <SelectParameters>
        <asp:Parameter DefaultValue="-1" Name="empid" />
    </SelectParameters>
</asp:SqlDataSource>
```

The Connectable Controls in Action

When both the EmployeeGrid and OrderGrid Web User Controls are hosted in two instances of the SmartPart, and the connection between those instances is made, end users will be able to select an employee so that the order grid will display the corresponding orders (Figure 7-39).

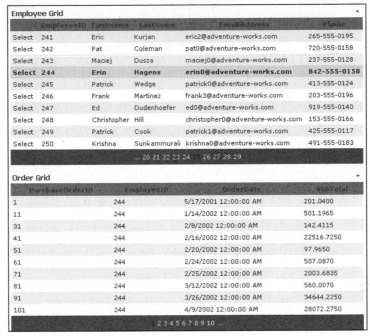

Figure 7-39: Order grid displaying the corresponding orders

Summary

In my opinion, developing Web Parts is one of the nicest ways to customize WSS v3 and MOSS 2007, both from the developer point of view and from the end-user point of view. Building custom Web Parts allows developers to encapsulate logic in building blocks that can be used by end users to quickly "click together" a SharePoint site, according to their needs and without the need of a developer and/or system administrator.

As discussed in this chapter, developing Web Parts completely relies on ASP.NET 2.0 developer skills. Developers can reuse their knowledge and quickly get started with SharePoint development.

Creating Workflows in WSS

by Robert Bogue

Wow! That's all you can say when you look at the capabilities of Windows SharePoint Services 3.0 (WSS 3.0) and Microsoft Office SharePoint Server 2007 (MOSS 2007) — particularly when you evaluate the product's capability to facilitate, coordinate, and track business processes in your enterprise. Although the "SharePoint Vision" has always been about providing more connectivity with Office documents between people, between steps, and between systems, SharePoint has made significant progress in this regard with the latest release compared to previous releases, and when compared to competitive products.

This chapter covers a lot of ground as I help you to understand the options for creating workflows, the fundamentals of workflow, the limitations of workflow, and some ways to make workflow work for your organization.

Largely, this chapter won't be covering how to use Microsoft's Windows Workflow Foundation (WF), upon which SharePoint's workflow functionality is based. Some essential topics are covered only enough to place the SharePoint implementation of WF into perspective. If you need a comprehensive reference to WF, you'll want to pick up another book on workflow, such as *Professional Windows Workflow Foundation* by Todd Kitta (Wiley Publishing, Inc., 2007).

What Is a Workflow?

A *workflow* is a set of reactions to a set of external stimuli. The first stimulus is "start," but there may be many more stimuli during the workflow that control how the workflow responds. Approval workflows respond to the request to start an approval process, and then each approval (or rejection) causes the workflow to flow down a different path.

Inherent in the WF perspective of workflows is that they have built in long (in computer terms) delays. The fundamental assumption is that workflows are connecting systems to humans, or humans to humans. This means a relatively large number of workflow instances (*individual workflows*), and that they may be running for days, weeks, or months. As a result, workflows (from a WF perspective) must be the following:

❑   *Serializable* — They may be taken from memory when a server reboots, a process ends, or some finalizing event occurs. This requires converting the memory representation of the workflow into a persistable stream that can be written out and saved for later. This is sometimes called *dehydration*.

❑   *Resumable* — Capable of being resumed based on new stimuli. When the file is updated, users indicate that they want to interact with the workflow. Or, if a timer expires, the workflow must be reserialized into running memory and activated with the event. This is sometimes called *rehydration*.

Though it's possible to work with workflows that do not need to be serialized or resumed because they consume only a single, start stimuli, these sorts of workflows do not capture the true power of the WF.

Workflow Options

Perhaps the greatest opportunity with SharePoint technologies and workflow exists within the flexibility you have to create *workflow solutions*. Specifically, you can create workflow solutions by:

❑   Using Microsoft Office SharePoint Designer 2007

❑   Customizing out-of-the-box (included) workflows

❑   Utilizing manual processes

❑   Writing event receivers with Visual Studio (VS)

❑   Writing custom workflows with VS

Each of these is a valid option when developing solutions with SharePoint that "require" a workflow. Some options are repeatable and reusable, whereas others are quick to get up and running, and don't replicate well. Let's investigate each one in enough detail that you can make an appropriate decision about which solution is correct for your situation.

Manual Workflow

Manual workflows are just that — manual. In other words, you didn't implement any of SharePoint's workflow features. Users are expected to manage the flow of information themselves. It may seem odd to start off a discussion about workflow features by suggesting that you don't use them — and it is. However, it may be a reality in your organization. Workflows are useful for generating highly repeatable processes. This may or may not be necessary for the business need that you're seeking to use workflow for. If the need for consistency doesn't have a strong business driver, it may make sense to use out-of-the-box features such as alerts to alert people that action needs to be taken, rather than creating a more formal workflow.

Obviously, the benefit to this solution is that there's no workflow development time. The downfall is that it doesn't provide much (if any) support for the process.

Out-of-the-Box Workflows

WSS 3.0 ships with one workflow (Three-State) and MOSS 2007 ships with several more. These workflows are what would be considered *data-driven workflows*. That is, the way that they work is fundamentally based upon the data that they are provided. In this case, the way that you set up the workflow when it is associated with the list (or document library) controls the people who are involved with the workflow — and, to some limited extent, how the workflow operates.

The opportunity here is to use these out-of-the-box workflows with your custom data (such as who will perform approvals) to solve your workflow needs. This is a great option if you want the power of a workflow, but aren't able to develop (or interested in developing) your own.

The benefit of this approach is that it doesn't require development of your own custom workflow. However, it is severely constrained by the fact that your flexibility is limited to the flexibility specifically designed in the out-of-box workflows that Microsoft shipped with the product. This is definitely the first option to pursue, if you can find a workflow that you can customize to your needs.

SharePoint Designer 2007

With a clear focus on being the information worker's way to customize SharePoint, SharePoint Designer (SPD) takes the best of customizing SharePoint with the FrontPage 2003 product, and rolls in new functionality around the creation of workflows and management of SharePoint in general. From a workflow perspective, SPD provides a simplified "rules-based" workflow editing tool, much like you'll find while working with Outlook rules for your mail. This simplified view makes it ideal for workflows that information workers are creating.

SPD-developed workflows are good solutions in many ways, because information workers can be trained on how to create their own workflows. These workflows generally can be done very quickly by IT professionals. As a result, they require the least amount of time to develop of any custom workflow solution option that SharePoint supports. However, this ease of use comes with two costs.

First, the workflows created with SPD don't have the same options that a complete custom workflow might have. Only workflow activities that are marked as safe for SPD use are available in this context. Though these limits may not be felt with simple workflows, any truly complex workflows that are designed to support a business process may find the restrictions to be limiting.

Second, SPD workflows cannot be reused from one list to another — or one site to another. The one way around this is to template the list on which the workflow is based. Lists created from that template will inherit the workflow. Although this is certainly a workable solution in some situations, the limit that the workflow can't be applied to an existing list may be too restrictive for your organizational needs.

Event Receivers

When reading the earlier discussion about what a workflow is, you learned that workflows must be serializable and resumable. They must be able to start and stop, and start again, based on their need for new stimuli. Sometimes, however, workflows can be used when this is not the case. All of the responses from the workflow take place because of the initial start stimuli. Though this is a perfectly acceptable use of the WF that underpins SharePoint, these sorts of workflows are equally suited to be handled by *event receivers*.

Event receivers (which were present in WSS 2.0) have been radically improved for WSS 3.0. WSS 2.0 supported only asynchronous events — that is, events that occurred after the event had completed. It only supported those events for document libraries. WSS 3.0 supports both synchronous (occurring before the operation is complete) and the asynchronous events supported in WSS 2.0. Furthermore, these events are supported for every list — not just document libraries.

Event receivers are a good option for workflows that don't need to respond to multiple stimuli because there is less you need to know to write an event receiver than you need to know to effectively create custom workflows. Of course, event receivers aren't suitable for situations that require multiple interactions with a single item in the context of one larger workflow because they aren't workflows, but rather simple responses to events.

Custom Workflows with Visual Studio

When the other options won't work and you're willing to make the investment to learn the WF infrastructure and how SharePoint interacts with that infrastructure, you're ready to create custom workflows with Visual Studio (VS) that you can deploy to SharePoint. The advantage of developing workflows with VS is that you have substantially fewer barriers preventing you from creating the precise workflow that the business needs. You have full access to every built-in workflow activity, as well as the ability to add code into the workflow as a separate activity, or to respond to events raised by the workflow activities. In addition, you can purchase third-party activities, or even write your own activities that plug directly into the VS design surface.

The negatives to developing custom workflows with VS are primarily that they are more complicated to get right and require more time to develop. However, the reward for the effort is a reusable workflow that can be attached to any list or library on any site where the workflow has been installed and activated. That means that an approval process that you design in the United States can be applied to your offices in the United Kingdom or wherever the workflow is needed. Custom workflows in VS are, in fact, the way that the out-of-the-box workflows were developed.

Because custom workflows (or, more precisely, custom workflow templates) developed in VS are so powerful, the rest of this chapter is dedicated to getting you what you need to know to develop custom workflows with VS.

SharePoint Background

Before I can effectively walk you through creating a custom workflow, you must understand what you can associate a workflow with, and how SharePoint's core features mesh with workflows.

Lists and Libraries

Perhaps the most common way to use a workflow is to associate it to a list or library in SharePoint. In fact, all libraries in SharePoint are themselves lists. Thus, the most common way to use workflows in SharePoint is to associate the workflow with a list (even if that list happens to be a library). Workflows can also be associated with content types.

Content Types

Back in SharePoint Portal Server 2001 (SPS 2001), you had the ability to define different types of documents that were stored in a document library. Each document type had its own fields — metadata about the document. WSS 2.0 and Microsoft Office SharePoint Portal Server 2003 (SPS 2003) removed this functionality from the product because of the effort to re-platform against SQL Server instead of the Web Storage System (essentially the Exchange data store). This brought a great deal of angst from customers as they tried to store different kinds of documents in their document libraries — each document type requiring a few different fields, some of which were required only for certain document types.

WSS 3.0 solves this need by reestablishing the idea that you can store different kinds of data in a list (and, therefore, a library). Each type of data is given a content type. The content type bundles the fields as well as the workflows to be associated with that kind of data. Multiple content types can be bound to a single list and, therefore, it's possible to have different rules for different types of data, both in terms of the fields that are included and the workflows the item goes through.

Content types are essential to understanding how SharePoint implements workflow because when SharePoint creates an item from a workflow, it does so via the content type. In particular, tasks created by SharePoint (whether through the `CreateTask` or `CreateTaskwithContentType` activities) are assigned a content type. This is used to control what fields are available and what fields are displayed to users when they display or edit the item.

Universal Logging Service

The SharePoint Universal Logging Service (ULS) is a centralized spot where all of SharePoint's internal operations log their successes and failures. The log files are created on each member of the farm in their local `C:\Program Files\Common Files\Microsoft Shared\Web Server Extensions\12\LOGS` directory. Each individual log file is created with the format of `SERVERNAME-DATE-TIME`, where `SERVERNAME` is the name of the server the log file was created on and for which events were captured. `DATE` is the date the log file was created in the format of the four-digit year, the two-digit month, and the two-digit day. The final element is `TIME` in 24-hour format, with a two-digit hour, followed by the two-digit representation of the minutes past the hour.

Because workflows don't interact directly with the user and there is often not a place to surface exceptions to the user interface, you'll find a large number of helpful (and not so helpful) exceptions end up here for you to review. The question isn't whether you'll need to look at the ULS log files while developing a SharePoint workflow; it's a question of when you'll need to do it and how often.

These files are much like most other log files you've seen in your career — with one exception. The individual entries may be split across multiple lines. Longer messages, particularly those containing exception details, get split into multiple lines within the file after just shy of 1,000 characters.

The Feature Mechanism

There's actually a mechanism in SharePoint called a *Feature*. That is, you create features that are deployed as a Feature to SharePoint. Are you confused yet? The key to this concept is understanding that there's a specific thing in SharePoint called a Feature, and it's used to "light up" new functionality within a site, site collection, Web application, or SharePoint farm. Chapter 4 provides more information about Features.

Filling the Toolbox

To develop workflows with SharePoint, you'll need two key pieces in addition to WSS and VS 2005 Professional:

❑ *Visual Studio Extensions for .NET 3.0 (Windows Workflow Foundation)* — This package includes the extensions to VS to allow for the design and debugging of workflows that use the Windows WF. It's available for download at `http://www.microsoft.com/downloads/details .aspx?familyid=5D61409E-1FA3-48CF-8023-E8F38E709BA6&displaylang=en`.

❑ *Windows SharePoint Services SDK* — The WSS SDK includes the additional SharePoint activities, snippets, and project templates to make it easier to build and deploy SharePoint workflows. It's available at `http://www.microsoft.com/downloads/details .aspx?familyid=05e0dd12-8394-402b-8936-a07fe8afaffd&displaylang=en`.

If you're working with MOSS 2007, you can download that SDK instead of the WSS SDK. It is available at `http://www.microsoft.com/downloads/details.aspx?familyid=6D94E307-67D9-41AC-B2D6-0074D6286FA9&displaylang=en`. Note that if you do use the MOSS 2007 SDK instead of the WSS SDK, you'll find that it creates a completely different deployment model for workflows. Because of this, in the sections that follow, the steps walking you through how to modify the deployment of your workflow won't work. If you want to follow along step-by-step, you'll need to use the WSS SDK.

Before leaving the things that you need in your toolbox, you should definitely get a copy of Fiddler from `www.fiddlertool.com`. Fiddler is a transparent HTTP proxy that allows you to see and break apart the HTTP traffic between the browser and the Web server. If you start working with Workflow Association and Workflow Instantiation forms, it will be invaluable in making sure that the form-posted variables are correct.

Creating a Workflow

That's enough of the theory and background. It's now time to start developing a workflow.

In this example, you build a student Grades workflow. The Grades workflow is designed to activate whenever a document is uploaded to a specific document library. A task is added to the task list that the students don't have access to. The workflow can add to this list because it runs as a special system account. Instructors and assistants subscribe to alerts on the task list and, in that way, are informed that a new assignment is ready to be graded. When the instructor or assistant has reviewed the assignment, they enter a numeric score, as well as notes on the score, into the task. This is copied back into the document in a set of fields that cannot be modified. In a real-life situation, you might add integration to a grade book program to add the grades. However, this example demonstrates the following core concepts with workflows:

❑ *Content Types* — I illustrate the use of content types to create a custom task type, as well as creating fields that cannot be edited.

❑ *Task Creation* — Creating a task in a SharePoint workflow isn't as easy as dropping an activity on the design surface. Because this workflow relies upon tasks to take instructor input, I walk you through the creation of tasks step-by-step.

❑ *Property Modification* — I show you how to make changes to the workflow item while the workflow is running.

Content Types

As mentioned previously, every piece of information in SharePoint has a content type. The content type defines the fields that are associated with the content. It is possible, as is the case in lists, to add additional fields beyond the base content type. However, the best way to ensure that a field is present is to define a content type and activate it in the list you want your content in.

A content type can also inherit from other content types. For example, the default workflow task, which is used by default to create tasks from a workflow, derives from the standard task content type. In this example, I derive from the workflow content type for the content types.

The definition of content types consists of three basic pieces: field definitions, field references, and the Feature that you deploy them in. Let's start by defining two fields in XML. These will go into a file used in the Feature that I discuss later in this chapter.

```
<Field ID="{0116A5FF-6FB7-43e1-B3E3-30A58B40349C}"
    Name="GradingScore" Group="Grading" DisplayName="Score"
    Type="Number" Sealed="FALSE" ReadOnly="FALSE" Hidden="FALSE"
    DisplaceOnUpgrade="TRUE"/>
<Field ID="{81792580-6F97-4960-84C2-7A8A926D1DCE}"
    Name="GradingNotes" Group="Grading" DisplayName="Notes"
    Type="Text" Sealed="FALSE" ReadOnly="FALSE" Hidden="FALSE"
     DisplaceOnUpgrade="TRUE"/>
```

Let's walk through each of the attributes:

❑   ID — A unique GUID for the field. You can generate a GUID from VS by selecting Tools ➪ Create GUID. The Create GUID application will launch. From there, you can click the Copy button to copy the GUID. The GUIDs in the preceding code snippet were created in precisely this way.

❑   Name — This is the internal name of the field in SharePoint. Care must be taken when naming fields so as not to collide with an internal name already used by SharePoint, or with the names of other fields on the system. Note that the fields in the preceding code snippet were prefixed with Grading for this reason. These names should not contain spaces or special punctuation.

❑   Group — This is the grouping that will be used to organize fields in the user interface. This name can be anything that makes sense for the application.

❑   DisplayName — This is the name that will be displayed to users when they see the field. This field may contain spaces and the special punctuation to make the field easy for users to understand.

❑   Type — This is the type of the field to be created. Here I am using the Number and Text values but Boolean, Choice, Computer, Currency, DateTime, URL, and other field types can be used as described at http://msdn2.microsoft.com/en-us/library/ms437580.aspx.

❑   Sealed — If true, then no one will be able to change the field in list settings. These fields are set to be modifiable.

❑   ReadOnly — The field itself can be written to. If you don't set this to false (or omit it to accept the default), the field won't show up in the user interface.

❑   Hidden — This determines whether or not the field is hidden. You might hide a field if you want to use it internally, but you don't want users to be able to see it.

❑   DisplaceOnUpgrade — This setting indicates that, if the field definition already exists, you want to overwrite it with the values in this XML fragment.

With the fields created, the next step is to create the content type and add references to the fields. To add the content types, you must know how to derive from an existing content type. There's a base content type hierarchy in MSDN at `http://msdn2.microsoft.com/en-us/library/ms452896.aspx`. This shows us the content IDs for existing types. Unlike other IDs in SharePoint (which are either an integer or a GUID), the content type ID is a special hexadecimal string that represents not only the content type itself, but also its parent — sort of like a human's surname, except in more detail.

There are two mechanisms for creating a content type. The first mechanism is appending a two-digit ID after the existing content type. The two-digit ID can be anything except 00. This is generally reserved for content types derived from your own content types because the potential for collision is so high.

The other mechanism (which is recommended) is to use 00 followed by a GUID that has had all of its punctuation removed. This creates a longer content type ID, so it's recommended only for the first level that you derive from a system type. Thereafter, you should use the two-digit mechanism described previously in order to minimize the overall length of the content type, which is capped at 512 bytes (in other words, 1,024 hexadecimal characters). You can learn more about content type IDs in the Content Type IDs entry in MSDN available at `http://msdn2.microsoft.com/en-us/library/aa543822.aspx`.

The content type for the Grades workflow task looks like this:

```
<ContentType ID="0x01080100B7336179CFFE43e59B86E241C767010E"
    Name="GradingTask" Group="Grading" Description="Grading Task"
    Version="0" Hidden="FALSE" >
  <FieldRefs>
  <FieldRef ID="{0116A5FF-6FB7-43e1-B3E3-30A58B40349C}"
        Name="GradingScore" DisplayName="Score" />
  <FieldRef ID="{81792580-6F97-4960-84C2-7A8A926D1DCE}"
        Name="GradingNotes" DisplayName="Notes"/>
  </FieldRefs>
</ContentType>
```

Here, the "00+Guid" method of creating the content type was used because it's the first level from a system content type. The workflow task content type is `0x010801`, thus that is how this content type begins. The XML fragment also contains `<FieldRef>` nodes that correspond to the fields defined earlier — both the `ID` and the `Name` fields match exactly.

The next content type is the content type for the document that will have the same score and notes fields, but this time they won't be editable. The document content type is as follows:

```
<ContentType ID="0x010100ADEC125AC3C74c1bA7E3A50731525809"
    Name="GradingDocument" Group="Grading" Description="Grading Document"
    Version="0" Hidden="FALSE" >
  <FieldRefs>
  <FieldRef ID="{0116A5FF-6FB7-43e1-B3E3-30A58B40349C}"
        Name="GradingScore" DisplayName="Score" ShowInDisplayForm="TRUE"
        ShowInFileDlg="FALSE" ShowInListSettings="TRUE" ShowInEditForm="FALSE"
        ShowInNewForm="FALSE" ReadOnlyClient="TRUE" />
  <FieldRef ID="{81792580-6F97-4960-84C2-7A8A926D1DCE}"
        Name="GradingNotes" DisplayName="Notes" ShowInDisplayForm="TRUE"
        ShowInFileDlg="FALSE" ShowInListSettings="TRUE" ShowInEditForm="FALSE"
        ShowInNewForm="FALSE" ReadOnlyClient="TRUE" />
  </FieldRefs>
</ContentType>
```

This document type is derived from a document (0x0101) with the same GUID method used earlier — but not the same GUID. The content type also includes the same fields as the task by creating `<FieldRef>` nodes that match ID and Name attributes to the `<Field>` nodes created earlier. In this case, however, the fields should not be able to be written to. There is a ReadOnly attribute for the `<FieldRef>`, but it causes the field to become hidden as well, so you can't use it. Instead, the field is prevented from displaying on the new and edit forms. Following are descriptions of the new attributes:

- ❑ ShowInDisplayForm — The display form is the form that is displayed when the user elects to view the item, or view properties of a document. It is set to TRUE so that it will be displayed.

- ❑ ShowInFileDlg — When an Office application saves the document, does the field show? It is set to FALSE, because the user isn't supposed to manipulate the value directly.

- ❑ ShowInListSettings — Show the field in the list settings. If this is set to FALSE, the field will not be visible when changing the list. This value is TRUE so that the field will be displayed.

- ❑ ShowInEditForm — The edit form is the one that a user gets when editing an item or editing properties on a document. Because the user shouldn't change the value, the attribute is FALSE.

- ❑ ShowInNewForm — The new form is the one that the user gets when trying to create a new item. Because the user shouldn't ever set this value, the attribute is FALSE.

- ❑ ReadOnlyClient — This attribute indicates that the client shouldn't be able to set the value of the field. This is TRUE to prevent client-side changes.

The content types are done. To deploy them, a SharePoint Feature is needed. Because the workflow will automatically create a Feature, let's use the workflow Feature to deploy content types at the same time.

Creating a Workflow Project in Visual Studio

As mentioned previously, you must install a few components to develop workflows with SharePoint and WF. Once those pieces are installed, an option to create a SharePoint Sequential workflow will appear, as shown in Figure 8-1. The Grades workflow will perform a few basic steps. It will create a task, wait for the task to change, change the document with some code, and delete the task.

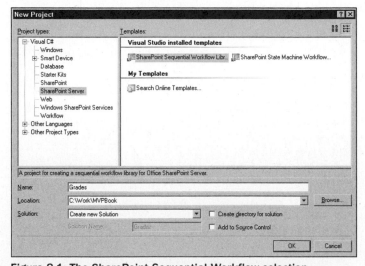

Figure 8-1: The SharePoint Sequential Workflow selection

To create the outline for the Grades workflow, follow these steps:

1. Create a sequential workflow by selecting the `SharePoint` (for WSS) or `SharePoint Server` (for MOSS) folder under Visual C#. Give the project a name of Grades, and select a folder to put the project in.

2. Once the project has been created, double-click the `Workflow1.cs` file from the Solution Explorer to show the workflow that was automatically created. Figure 8-2 shows what the workflow looks like as soon as it's created. VS has automatically created the workflow and added the required `onWorkflowActivated1` activity as the first activity.

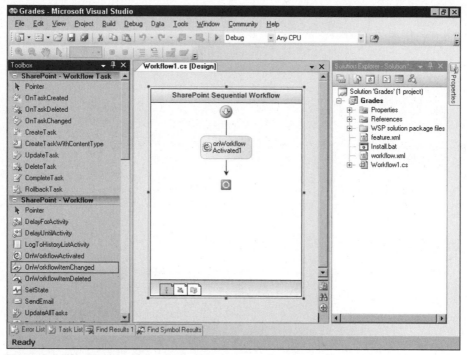

Figure 8-2: The blank workflow template

3. From the toolbox, drag a `CreateTask` activity, an `OnTaskChanged` activity, a `Code` activity, and a `DeleteTask` activity (in sequence) to the design surface, as shown in Figure 8-3.

You may notice that there are little red exclamation points next to each of the four activities that you added to the design surface. That is because they all failed validation. The design interface is warning you that it knows, based on the current settings on the activities, that they won't work. Let's fix those errors and complete the workflow.

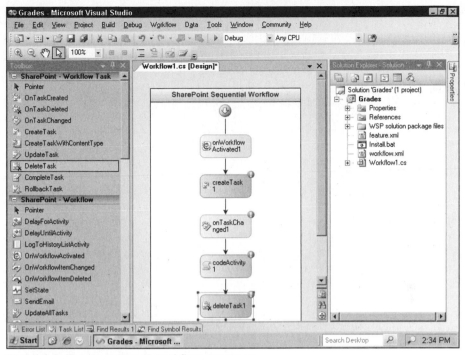

Figure 8-3: The "completed" workflow on screen

Completing the Create Task Activity

To get a `CreateTask` activity working, three things are needed: a correlation token, a task properties object, and a task guide. The easiest of these to take care of is the correlation token, which can be created with the following process:

1. Click the `createTask1` activity, then right-click and select Properties.

2. In the Properties pane, select the `CorrelationToken` box, type in **taskToken**, and press Enter.

3. Now, click the plus sign to the left of `CorrelationToken` and, in the `OwnerActivityName` line that appears, select `Workflow1`. VS has created a correlation token for you. Note that each item that will receive events must have its own correlation token. Thus, the task correlation token you created is different than the workflow correlation token that was created automatically when the project was created.

4. Defining the task properties and the GUID are a bit more challenging. For that, you'll need to right-click the activity and select "view code." You need to add two lines underneath the lines that define the `workflowId` and `workflowProperties`. The lines will define the `taskId` and `taskProperties` like this:

```
public Guid taskId = default(System.Guid);
public SPWorkflowTaskProperties taskProperties =
    new SPWorkflowTaskProperties();
```

5. Switch back to the Design view, which appears in the tabs as Workflow1.cs [Design].

6. Click the createTask1 activity, right-click, and select Properties from the context menu.

7. In the properties for createTask1, select TaskId, and then clicks the ellipsis (…) button that appears. This will raise a Bind dialog, as shown in Figure 8-4.

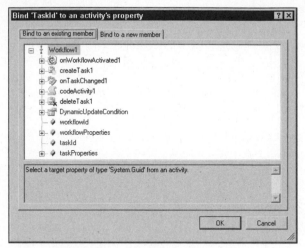

Figure 8-4: The TaskId **property becomes bound to the** taskId **variable**

8. Select the taskId property and click the OK button. You've just bound the taskId property to the taskId that you created.

9. Perform Steps 7 and 8 again on the TaskProperties activity property and taskProperties workflow property.

10. Next is setting the taskId correctly. To do this, code will be added to the MethodInvoking event. Double-click the createTask1 activity so that it creates the default event handler, which is MethodInvoking. Methods that end in "ing" happen before the main work of the activity, so you can use this method to set the taskId. You need to do this because, when you defined it earlier, you didn't give it a unique ID — you just gave it the default for a GUID (all zeros). Add the following line to the createTask1_MethodInvoking method that was created when you double-clicked:

```
taskId = Guid.NewGuid();
```

11. To set the task title to something meaningful, add the following line immediately following the line added in Step 10:

```
taskProperties.Title = "Task for " + workflowProperties.Item.Name;
```

12. Switch back to the Design view. You're finished with the createTask. The red exclamation point that was on it should be gone now. (Actually, it was gone early in the process when you set the correlation token.)

Completing OnTaskChanged

For the onTaskChanged1 activity, you have essentially the same properties to set. However, because they are already created, the process is much easier. In this case, the correlation token must be set, as well as the TaskId property. In addition, taskProperties is bound to AfterProperties so that the taskItemId value will be set.

1. Select the onTaskChanged1 activity, right-click, and select Properties from the context menu.

2. In the CorrelationToken field, click the drop-down list box arrow and select taskToken.

3. Click the TaskId property field and then the ellipsis.

4. Select taskId from the binding dialog and click the OK button.

5. Select the AfterProperties field and click the ellipsis.

6. Select taskProperties from the binding dialog and click the OK button.

The onTaskChanged activity is done. The red exclamation point should be gone for this activity, too.

Completing the Code Activity

The final activity is the code activity where you will copy the fields from the task back to the document.

Double-click the codeActivity1 activity to create a handler for ExecuteCode. In this method, add these five lines:

```
SPListItem item = workflowProperties.Item;
SPListItem task =
workflowProperties.TaskList.GetItemById(taskProperties.TaskItemId);
item["GradingScore"] = task["GradingScore"];
item["GradingNotes"] = task["GradingNotes"];
item.SystemUpdate(false);
```

These five lines get the item for which the workflow was started, the task that was created, and then copy two fields from the task into the item. Finally, the code performs a system update to update the fields without changing the modified information for the item.

Completing the Delete Task Activity

Completing the Delete Task activity is the same as completing the OnTaskChanged activity. You must set the CorrelationToken and the TaskId properties of the deleteTask1 activity so that the workflow will compile, and so that the task will be deleted. You can refer to the earlier section, "Completing OnTaskChanged," for the steps to bind these two properties.

The workflow is done. It should now build successfully. It's time to move on to deploying the workflow.

Modifying the Feature to Deploy the Workflow

When VS created the project, it automatically added the following three files that will help in the deployment process:

❑   `Feature.xml` — This file is a Feature file that SharePoint needs to define the Feature.

❑   `Workflow.xml` — This is an element manifest file that defines the workflow itself.

❑   `Install.bat` — This is a batch file that can be used to install the Feature.

The following sections walk you through the creation of each of these files, and making the updates necessary to install the Feature containing the Grades workflow.

feature.xml

Upon opening `feature.xml`, you'll notice that there isn't much there besides a note telling you to use the snippets functionality with VS to add the nodes necessary in the `feature.xml` file. To create the `feature.xml` for the Grades workflow, follow these steps:

1.   Add the feature from the WSS SDK by right-clicking, selecting Insert Snippet ➪ Windows SharePoint Services Workflow ➪ Feature.xml Code. Figure 8-5 shows what you'll see when you add the snippet. Once the snippet is added, the green highlighted sections must be changed. Specifically, the `Id`, `Title`, and `Description` must be changed. The default value for the `<ElementManifest>` `Location` attribute is correct. First up is changing the `Id`.

> **If, for some reason, you don't see the Windows SharePoint Services Workflow snippets when you try to insert the snippets, you can manually add them by opening the Code Snippet Manager (Tools ➪ Code Snippet Manager). To do this, click the Add button. In the dialog that appears, find the path** `C:\Program Files\Microsoft Visual Studio 8\Xml\1033\Snippets\Windows SharePoint Services Workflow` **and click the Open button. Click OK to close the Code Snippet Manager. You will now have the missing snippets.**

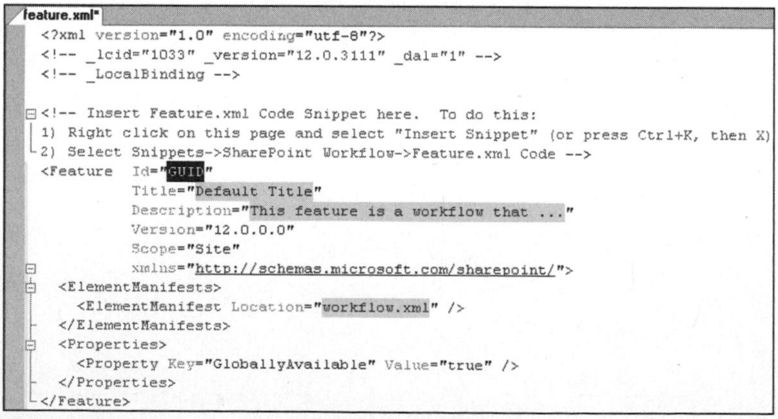

```
feature.xml*
    <?xml version="1.0" encoding="utf-8"?>
    <!-- _lcid="1033" _version="12.0.3111" _dal="1" -->
    <!-- _LocalBinding -->

    <!-- Insert Feature.xml Code Snippet here.  To do this:
     1) Right click on this page and select "Insert Snippet" (or press Ctrl+K, then X)
     2) Select Snippets->SharePoint Workflow->Feature.xml Code -->
    <Feature   Id="GUID"
               Title="Default Title"
               Description="This feature is a workflow that ..."
               Version="12.0.0.0"
               Scope="Site"
               xmlns="http://schemas.microsoft.com/sharepoint/">
       <ElementManifests>
          <ElementManifest Location="workflow.xml" />
       </ElementManifests>
       <Properties>
          <Property Key="GloballyAvailable" Value="true" />
       </Properties>
    </Feature>
```

Figure 8-5: `Feature.xml` **with the inserted snippet**

2. Select Tools ⇨ Create GUID from the Visual Studio menu.

3. Verify that the Create GUID application has the radio button for "4. Registry Format (ie. {xxxxxxxx-xxxx … xxxx })" selected.

4. Click the Copy button in the Create GUID application.

5. Switch back to Visual Studio and the `feature.xml` file.

6. Select the text in the quotes behind the `Id` attribute and paste in the GUID using the Ctrl+V key sequence.

7. Strip the leading and closing braces from the GUID that was pasted in.

8. Enter a descriptive name for the Feature and for the description. For the Grades workflow, the Feature is going to be called "Grades" and the description is "Enable assignment grading."

Because `workflow.xml` is the correct name of the element manifest that you want to create, you are finished with `feature.xml`. Save it and let's move on to `workflow.xml`.

workflow.xml

When `workflow.xml` is opened, you'll find the situation very similar to the `feature.xml`. `workflow.xml` is a mostly empty file with a few instructions on how to add the content to the file. Let's follow a similar procedure as you did with the `feature.xml` file. To customize `workflow.xml` for the Grades workflow, follow these steps:

1. Right-click and select Insert Snippet ⇨ Windows SharePoint Services Workflow ⇨ Workflow.xml Code. This will result in a `workflow.xml` file that looks like the one shown in Figure 8-6.

2. The next step is entering the name and description for the workflow. For the Grades workflow, use "Grades" and "Enable assignment grading," respectively, for the name and description. It isn't required that you enter either the same or unique names in here versus the values that are used in the `feature.xml` file.

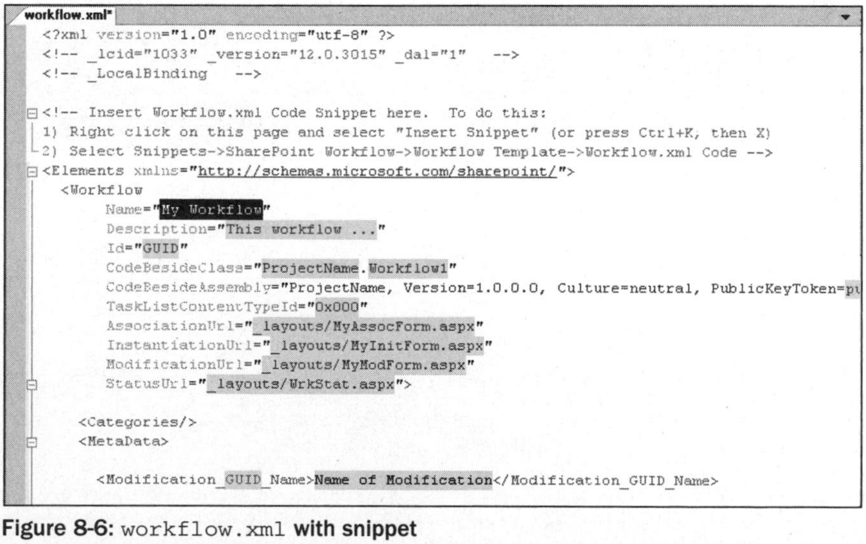

Figure 8-6: `workflow.xml` **with snippet**

3. Use the Create GUID tool to create a new GUID. (See Steps 2–4 of the `feature.xml` procedure if you don't remember how.)

4. Switch back to VS and the `workflow.xml` file.

5. Paste the GUID into the `ID` attribute's value and delete the extra braces.

6. The next step is the code-behind class. In this case, the project name is "Grades," so the namespace is `Grades`. For the `CodeBesideClass`, enter **Grades.Workflow1**. `Workflow1` is the name of the workflow that was created by the Visual Studio SharePoint Sequential Workflow project.

7. Next, you must get the correct assembly name. The first part of the `CodeBesideAssembly` is `ProjectName`. This is the name of the DLL for the project. In this case, Grades, so replace `ProjectName` with `Grades`.

8. The last part of the `CodeBesideAssembly` is the `PublicKeyToken`. For this, the assembly must be strong-named. This is a requirement for all workflow DLLs because they must be installed into the Global Assembly Cache (GAC). In VS, right-click the project name (Grades) and select Properties. On the properties page that appears, select the Signing tab (the last tab on the left). The result will be similar to the page shown in Figure 8-7.

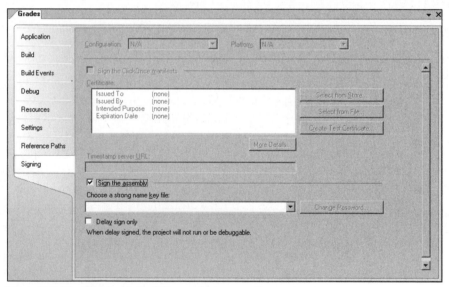

Figure 8-7: The Signing tab of the project properties page

9. Drop down the "Choose a strong name key file" drop-down box and select New. A Create Strong Name Key dialog will appear.

10. Enter a key file name of **Grades**.

11. Uncheck the "Protect my key file with a password" checkbox and click the OK button.

12. To get the public key token, you'll need to build the solution, so build the solution now. (Use the key sequence Ctrl+Shift+B to build the solution.)

13. Next, open a VS 2005 command prompt. This can be done by selecting it from the Start menu. The entry is located under Visual Studio 2005 ⇨ Visual Studio Tools and is named Visual Studio 2005 Command Prompt.

14. Navigate to the directory where the project DLL is created. In this example, I created the solution in `C:\Work\MVPBook\grades`. The debug DLL is created under `bin\debug` by default, so the command to change to the correct directory is `CD \work\MVPBook\grades\bin\debug` to change to that directory.

15. Type the command **SN — T Grades.DLL.** The response to this command shows the public key token for the file, as shown in Figure 8-8.

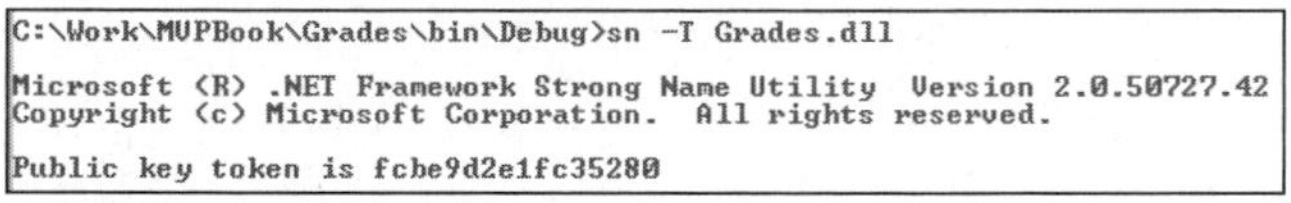

```
C:\Work\MVPBook\Grades\bin\Debug>sn -T Grades.dll

Microsoft (R) .NET Framework Strong Name Utility  Version 2.0.50727.42
Copyright (c) Microsoft Corporation.  All rights reserved.

Public key token is fcbe9d2e1fc35280
```

Figure 8-8: Public key token

16. Right-click in the window and select Mark.

17. Click and drag across the public key token. When you're finished, release the mouse and press Enter.

18. Switch back to VS and to the workflow.xml tab.

19. Select the green highlighted `publicKeyToken` and then press Ctrl+V to paste the key.

20. One final edit for the `CodeBesideAssembly` attribute is to change the version number from `1.0.0.0` to `3.0.0.0`.

21. Next, set the `TaskListContentTypeId`. This is the `Id` shown in the content type section. In this case, the value was the `0x01080100B7336179CFFE43e59B86E241C767010E` value from the content type tag that defined the content type for the task.

22. Delete the `AssociationUrl`, `InstantiationUrl`, `ModificationUrl`, and `StatusUrl` attributes, because the Grades project doesn't implement any of these Features.

23. Delete the whole `MetaData` node and the modification element under it because the Grades workflow doesn't implement a workflow modification either.

24. If you were just doing the workflow in this file, you would be finished. However, let's simplify things a bit and add our fields and content types to the top of this file. So, copy the field and content type nodes above the `<Workflow>` node you've been modifying. Figure 8-9 shows what the completed file should look like. Note that the formatting was changed and extraneous comments removed to get everything to fit on the screen.

```
workflow.xml
<Elements xmlns="http://schemas.microsoft.com/sharepoint/">
   <Field ID="{0116A5FF-6FB7-43e1-B3E3-30A58B40349C}" Name="GradingScore" Group="Grading"
          DisplayName="Score" Type="Number" Sealed="FALSE" ReadOnly="FALSE" Hidden="FALSE"
          DisplaceOnUpgrade="TRUE"/>
   <Field ID="{81792580-6F97-4960-84C2-7A8A926D1DCE}" Name="GradingNotes" Group="Grading"
          DisplayName="Notes" Type="Text" Sealed="FALSE" ReadOnly="FALSE" Hidden="FALSE"
          DisplaceOnUpgrade="TRUE"/>
   <ContentType ID="0x01080100B7336179CFFE43e59B86E241C767010E" Name="GradingTask "
                Group="Grading" Description="Grading Task" Version="0" Hidden="FALSE" >
      <FieldRefs>
        <FieldRef ID="{0116A5FF-6FB7-43e1-B3E3-30A58B40349C}" Name="GradingScore" DisplayNam
        <FieldRef ID="{81792580-6F97-4960-84C2-7A8A926D1DCE}" Name="GradingNotes" DisplayNam
      </FieldRefs> </ContentType>
   <ContentType ID="0x01010400ADEC125AC3C74c1bA7E3A50731525809" Name="GradingDocument"
                Group="Grading" Description="Grading Document" Version="0" Hidden="FALSE" >
      <FieldRefs>
        <FieldRef ID="{0116A5FF-6FB7-43e1-B3E3-30A58B40349C}" Name="GradingScore"
                  DisplayName="Score" ShowInDisplayForm="TRUE" ShowInFileDlg="FALSE"
                  ShowInListSettings="TRUE" ShowInEditForm="FALSE" ShowInNewForm="FALSE"
                  ReadOnlyClient="" />
        <FieldRef ID="{81792580-6F97-4960-84C2-7A8A926D1DCE}" Name="GradingNotes"
                  DisplayName="Notes" ShowInDisplayForm="TRUE" ShowInFileDlg="FALSE"
                  ShowInListSettings="TRUE" ShowInEditForm="FALSE" ShowInNewForm="FALSE"
                  ReadOnlyClient="" />
      </FieldRefs> </ContentType>
```

Figure 8-9: The content type fragment of the completed `workflow.xml`

With `workflow.xml` finished, there's only one more file to finish: the `install.bat` file.

install.bat

When you double-click it in the Solution Explorer, the `install.bat` file opens to reveal quite a few commands and instructions. It's a nice change from the `feature.xml` and `workflow.xml` files that you saw before. The changes you need to make to the `install.bat` file are basically two global searches and replaces. To customize the `install.bat` file, follow these steps:

1. The first step is to search for `MyFeature` and replace it with what you want to name your Feature — in this case, `Grades`. To perform the search and replace, start by pressing Ctrl+H.

2. Enter **MyFeature** in the "Find what" box and **Grades** in the "Replace with" box. Make sure that the "Look in" drop-down list is set to Current Document. Click the Replace All button.

3. Click OK in the message box indicating 14 replacements were made.

4. The next step is to search for `http://localhost` and replace it with the name of your server. In my case, the server name is `w2k3server`, so I'm replacing `http://localhost` with `http://w2k3server`.

5. Click the OK button in the message box indicating three replacements were made.

Once you've made all of the replacements, select Save All in Visual Studio (File ⇨ Save All) and open a command prompt. (The VS 2005 command prompt you used earlier will work fine.) Navigate to the project directory and run install by typing **install** and pressing Enter at the command prompt.

Associating the Workflow to a Document Library

Now that the workflow and associated content types are created, it's time to associate those content types and the workflow to a set of lists in SharePoint. For these instructions, you'll need a blank team site. I've created one called `Grades` under the root of my server. You can use the root site of your installation, or create a site underneath the root site to associate the content types and workflow.

To associate the content type for the grading document (which has the score and notes field) to the document library and remove the default content type, follow these steps:

1. Open up the document library and then, from the Settings menu, select the Document Library Settings entry.

2. The first step is to activate the content type. You do that by clicking the Advanced Settings in the General Settings section. The top item on the Document Library Advanced Settings page is "Allow management of content types." Select the Yes radio button and scroll down to the bottom of the page and click the OK button.

3. Back on the Customize Shared Documents page, in the Content Types section, click "Add from existing site content types."

4. On the Add Content Types page in the "Select site content types from:" drop-down list, select Grading. Click the Add button to move the `GradingDocument` to the "Content types to add:" box. Click the OK button to finish.

5. The next step is to remove the Document type so that all documents that are created in the document library will be the `GradingDocument` type. Click on the Document link under the Content Types heading.

6. From the List Content Type page, click the "Delete this content type" link.

7. Click the OK button on the popup dialog that asks if you're sure.

With the content type in place, it's time to associate the workflow. That can be done by following these steps:

1. From the Customize Shared Documents page, in the Permissions and Management column, click the Workflow Settings link.

2. On the Add a Workflow page in the "Select a workflow template:" list box, scroll down and select the Grades workflow template.

3. Enter a name for this workflow association, **Grades**.

4. Scroll down to the Start Options section and check "Start this workflow when a new item is created" checkbox. Click the OK button. The grades workflow is added to the document library.

All of the plumbing is done. All that is left is to test the workflow and ensure that it works.

Testing the Workflow

Now that the workflow is associated with a document library and set to activate on new items, all that needs to happen is that a document be uploaded. When this happens, the Grades workflow will kick off and add a new task to the workflow. Figure 8-10 shows the task created when the `feature.xml` file from the Grades project was uploaded to the Shared Documents library.

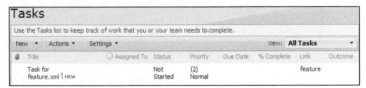

Figure 8-10: The new task created by the Grades workflow

If you update the task to include a score and notes, you'll notice that the task doesn't always go away immediately. Sometimes when you first refresh the task list, the task will appear, and sometimes it won't. Because the workflow and the refresh of the task list page occur at the same time, it's possible you'll see or not see the task, depending upon which thread executed quicker. Refreshing the task list page will definitely make the task disappear.

Switching back to the Shared Documents list, you'll see that there is a column called Grades — which matches the association name you provided when you associated the workflow with the list — and that it has a value of Completed. Figure 8-11 shows the completed Grades workflow.

Figure 8-11: Completed Grades workflow

The properties of the document were, in fact, updated, based on what was entered in the task. Figure 8-12 shows that the student got a score of 100 and a note of Good Work!

Figure 8-12: The results of the Grades workflow

Debugging Workflows

Without a doubt, you're going to need to debug your workflow. With the scant documentation, and the odd little quirks, there are going to be issues that are unanticipated. In this section, you learn some debugging techniques that you can use with SharePoint to find defects quicker and with less pain.

Fault Handlers

One of the key techniques for making the workflow debugging process easier is to add a fault handler to your workflow that logs the exception that caused the error to the history log for the workflow. This gives you a way to capture exceptions in your code wherever they occur.

Not all exceptions are caught by the fault handler. Some exceptions are so core to the workflow that they are only caught in the ULS log. The fault handler is a great way to capture errors in your code that don't relate to core workflow operations.

Adding a fault handler isn't that complicated. To demonstrate how easy it is, the following procedure shows how to add a fault handler to the Grades workflow created earlier:

1. Open the Workflow1.cs [Design] page in VS by double-clicking `Workflow1.cs` in the Solution Explorer.

2. Right-click in the white space to the left or right of the workflow activities and select View Fault Handlers.

3. Drag the `FaultHandler` activity from the toolbox into the horizontal area under the `faultHandlersActivity1`, as shown in Figure 8-13.

4. Right-click the `faultHandlerActivity1` that you just created and select Properties from the context menu.

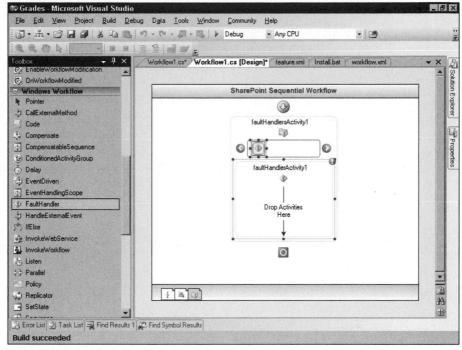

Figure 8-13: Adding a fault handler

5. Click the `FaultType` property and then the ellipsis button.

6. Enter **System.Exception** in the Type Name box and press Enter. In .NET, all exceptions derive from `System.Exception`, thus this type will be a part of all exceptions and will be caught by this fault handler.

7. Drag the `LogToHistoryListActivity` into the main area of the workflow surface where it says Drop Activities Here.

8. Right-click the `LogToHistoryListActivity1` that you just dragged into the design surface and select Generate Handlers from the context menu.

9. Add the following code to the `logToHistoryListActivity1_MethodInvoking` method:

```
LogToHistoryListActivity log = (LogToHistoryListActivity)sender;
log.HistoryDescription = faultHandlerActivity1.Fault.ToString();
log.OtherData = faultHandlerActivity1.Fault.ToString();
```

This code places a string representation of the exception into `HistoryDescription` and into the `OtherData` field. This is because `HistoryDescription` is visible in the workflow history, but is limited to 255 characters. `OtherData` doesn't have a limit, but is only visible by navigating to the hidden `HistoryList` table.

10. Switch back to Workflow1.cs [Design].

11. Right-click the white space to the left or right of the fault handler and select "View SharePointSequentialWorkflowActivity" from the context menu.

With the fault handler in place, you can create an intentional error in the Grades workflow to cause the fault handler to execute. When I changed the `codeActivity1_Execute` code to the code in the following box, and ran the workflow again, the workflow history showed the Null Reference Exception, as seen in Figure 8-14.

```
private void codeActivity1_ExecuteCode(object sender, EventArgs e)
{
    SPListItem item = workflowProperties.Item;
    SPListItem task = null;/* =
    workflowProperties.TaskList.GetItemById(taskProperties.TaskItemId);
    */
    item["GradingScore"] = task["GradingScore"];
    item["GradingNotes"] = task["GradingNotes"];
    item.SystemUpdate(false);
}
```

That's a great start on the exception, but in reality, the entire text of the exception didn't fit. To see the entire text of the exception, including the full call stack, you'll need to view the Workflow History list directly. The Workflow History list was created as a hidden list, so you won't find it by navigating the user interface. However, you can directly enter the URL by appending `Lists/Workflow%20History` to the end of the site name. Thus, if the site name is `http://w2k3server/grades`, the full URL is `http://w2k3server/grades/Lists/Workflow%20History`. Figure 8-15 shows the extra data that you stored into `OtherData` — that wasn't displayed in the Description field.

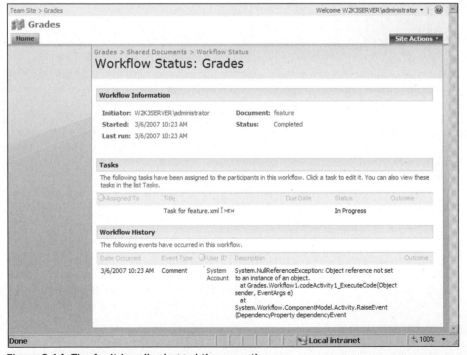

Figure 8-14: The fault handler logged the exception

Figure 8-15: The Description and OtherData columns of the History list, respectively

Logging Messages

Perhaps logging messages isn't the most glamorous way to debug something — but it's effective. Ever since the first programmers started adding PRINT statements to their code to dump out important variables at key times, we've been using the PRINT statement (or its updated equivalent) to gain insight to the inner workings of the code we write. SharePoint is no different. The PRINT statement in SharePoint workflow land is a LogToHistoryList activity. You've already seen it in use in the fault handler. You can just as easily add it to the mainline part of the workflow to drop yourself notes about where the workflow is — and what the values of key variables are.

Breakpoints and Attaching to a Process

Interactive debugging has made the need for logging statements nearly obsolete for most technology platforms. Though you can use interactive debugging with SharePoint, the process is still somewhat painful and, in some cases, inserting LogToHistoryList activities may be a simpler way to understand what is going on with your workflow.

Interactive debugging with SharePoint and workflows must be done by attaching to the IIS worker process (W3WP). Once attached to the process, you can set breakpoints, step through code, and inspect variables, with the following caveats:

❑ *First chance exceptions* — Interactive debugging offers the capability of receiving an exception before the code gets it. This is useful when you want to run the interactive debugger at full speed until a problem occurs, and then stop and tear it apart. Although you can turn on first chance exceptions in VS, they won't be caught while debugging SharePoint workflows.

❑ *Processor utilization* — If you use the workflow debugging template (explained later in this chapter), your machine's processor will go to and stay at 100 percent utilization the entire debugging session. This normally isn't a problem, except that some internals of .NET (the garbage collector) will not run when the system is under a 100 percent load, until it's out of memory.

❑ *Step carefully* — If you attempt to step over an activity that causes a serialization (dehydration) and deserialization (rehydration) event, the code will resume running at full speed. This makes sense, because the execution context ends and a new one is created when the triggering event occurs. However, it makes stepping through a workflow challenging at times.

❑ *Sometimes breakpoints* — Breakpoints don't always fire. This is particularly true for activities immediately following serialization/deserialization events.

Other than these caveats, debugging SharePoint workflows in VS isn't much different than debugging managed code. The Visual Studio Extensions for .NET 3.0 (Windows WF) does add a new code type that you can attach to — Workflow — as shown in Figure 8-16. By selecting this code type for debugging, you can set breakpoints on the activities in a workflow. Unlike other code types, the Workflow code type is mutually exclusive with the Managed code type. This isn't a problem in practice, however, because the Workflow code type allows you to debug managed code as well.

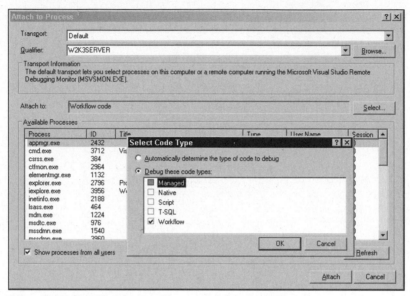

Figure 8-16: The Workflow code type to debug workflows

Common Exceptions

Knowing what the status codes, exceptions, and messages in the log file typically mean can certainly be enlightening on the problems. As mentioned earlier, the SharePoint log files, called Universal Logging Service (ULS) files, are located in `C:\Program Files\Common Files\Microsoft Shared\Web Server Extensions\12\LOGS`. They are the primary place that SharePoint will log internal exceptions to — particularly the workflow area of the product.

Table 8-1 shows a set of workflow statuses, messages, and resolutions that may help you locate your problem.

Table 8-1: Workflow Statuses, Messages, and Resolutions

Workflow Status	Exception / ULS Log Entry	Problem and Resolution

Failed on Start	`[ULS] Load Workflow Assembly: System.IO`
	`.FileNotFoundException: Could not load file`
	`or assembly...`
		SharePoint cannot locate the workflow assembly that you've listed in the `<Workflow>` node in your elements XML. Correct the entry or GAC the assembly.

Error Occurred	`[ULS] Unexpected System.Reflection`
	`.TargetInvocationException: Exception has been`
	`thrown by the target of an invocation. -->`
	`System.NullReferenceException: Object reference`
	`not set to an instance of an object.        at`
	`Microsoft.SharePoint.Workflow.SPWinOETaskService`
	`.CreateTaskWithContentTypeInternal(Guid taskId,`
	`SPWorkflowTaskProperties properties, Boolean`
	`useDefaultContentType, SPContentTypeId ctid,`
	`HybridDictionary specialPermissions)       at`
	`Microsoft.SharePoint.Workflow.SPWinOETaskService`
	`.CreateTask(Guid taskId, SPWorkflowTaskProperties`
	`properties, HybridDictionary specialPermissions)`
		You added a `CreateTask` activity to the workflow, but didn't initialize the `taskId` or `taskProperties` properly. Create a new instance of `SPWorkflowTaskProperties` and bind it to the `TaskProperties` property of the `CreateTask` activity. Create new `taskId` GUID and initialize it to a new GUID in the `MethodInvoking` event or before.

Error Occurred	`[Exception] System.NullReferenceException: Object` `reference not set to an instance of an object`	When using the `CreateTaskWithContentType` activity on a task list that doesn't have content types enabled, set the `.ContentTypesEnabled = true` and add the content type referenced in `CreateTaskWithContentType`.

Continued

Table 8-1: Workflow Statuses, Messages, and Resolutions *(continued)*

Workflow Status	Exception / ULS Log Entry	Problem and Resolution
Error Occurred	`[Exception] SPException: This task is currently locked by a running workflow and connot be edited.`	Tasks for a SharePoint workflow can only be modified by the user while in an `OnTaskChanged` activity and by the workflow itself within an `UpdateTaskActivity`. When updating the task in an `UpdateTaskActivity`, it must be updated through the `SPWorkflowTaskProperties` object.
Error Occurred	`[Exception] Microsoft.SharePoint.SPException: The security validation for this page is invalid.`	`SPWorkflowManager .StartWorkflow()` cannot be called from a HTTP GET — it must be called from an HTTP POST. Setting the `SPWeb.AllowUnsafeUpdates` won't help.
Error Occurred	`[ULS] System.InvalidOperationException: The event receiver context for Workflow is invalid.`	For the `CreateTaskActivity`, the `taskID` must be set to a unique GUID and the `TaskProperties` must be set to a `SPWorkflowTaskProperties` object.

Summary

When you put together all the pieces presented in this chapter, you have a powerful array of workflow options, including a nearly limitless platform for custom workflow development. The simple workflow created in this chapter shows the power of being able to control the fields that are used in the workflow and, more importantly, a method that users can interact with the workflow to change or add data once it's running. Couple that with debugging techniques and common problems discussed here, and you're ready to develop workflows with WSS.

9

Creating Workflow in SharePoint Server 2007

by Joris Poelmans

In the mid 1990s, the Workflow Management Coalition (WFMC) published its first definition of workflow:

"The automation of a business process, in whole or part, during which documents, information, or tasks are passed from one participant to another for action (activities), according to a set of procedural rules. A participant can be a person or a system, local or in a remote organization."

This focus on business processes explains why workflow is so important. Well laid-out and efficient business processes differentiate companies from one another. This is why you have probably heard about such methodologies as Continuous Process Improvement (CPI) and Business Process Re-engineering (BPR). Both BPR and CPI are process-centric methodologies that can be supported by a workflow management system.

> *CPI is part of the Total Quality Management (TQM) approach and focuses on optimizing processes by continuous, incremental improvements, instead of seeking a radical breakthrough. For more information on BPR, see the book Reengineering the Corporation: A Manifesto for Business Revolution by Michael Hammer and James Champy (New York: HarperCollins, 2003).*

Workflow in SharePoint Server 2007 is built on top of the Windows Workflow Foundation (WF) framework, which is part of .NET 3.0. WF was introduced because Microsoft noticed that many people were all re-inventing the wheel when trying to implement workflow. Even its own products such as Microsoft Customer Relationship Management (CRM), Exchange Server, and Microsoft Content Management Server (CMS) each used a different workflow framework. There was no real platform on which to build workflow applications.

On the other hand, Biztalk Server had been around for quite a while and provided a solid foundation for building system-to-system workflow. Unfortunately, Biztalk is not a very good platform for building systems that are human-oriented, especially with regard to the unpredictability of this behavior. However, you will notice some similarities between Biztalk and WF.

Basically, WF consists of a number of assemblies (which use the `System.Workflow` namespace) and a Workflow Runtime (which is the execution environment for your workflow programs). The WF Runtime should, however, be instantiated by a host application that can be any .NET program. The core WF Runtime uses a number of services that are referred to as WF Runtime Services defined in the `System.Workflow.Runtime.Hosting` namespace.

The timing for the development of WF was just right to implement it straight away in the 2007 Office System. As a matter of fact, Windows SharePoint Services 3.0 acts as such a host application for WF and provides the core platform on top of which Microsoft Office SharePoint Server 2007 (MOSS 2007) adds some specific workflow templates for enterprise content management scenarios.

Standard Workflow Templates in MOSS 2007

MOSS 2007 contains a number of out-of-the-box workflow templates. All of these workflow templates are developed as SharePoint Features and can be activated or deactivated on a specific site collection.

To do this, open your portal and navigate to Site Settings using the Site Actions ➪ Site Settings menu. Click the Site Collection Features link in the Site Collection Administration category on the right of your Site Settings screen. In the Features list, you will find the different workflow Features, as shown in Figure 9-1.

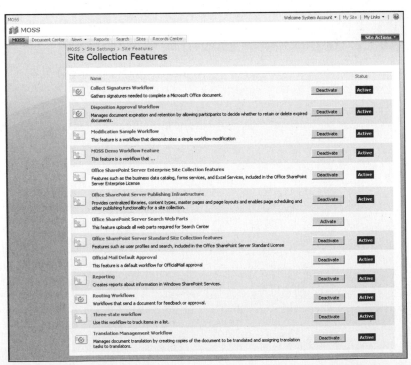

Figure 9-1: Site Collection Features — available workflow templates

Features provide a modular provisioning framework to deploy your own customizations on top of MOSS 2007. They allow you to add functionality such as lists, libraries, workflows and event handlers, and administrative and user interface elements to SharePoint. MOSS 2007 also uses this same Feature framework (for example, all the standard built-in list types are created as separate Features). You will find them at `C:\Program Files\Common Files\Microsoft Shared\Web Server Extensions\ 12\Templates\Features\`. Each of the subfolders in this directory contains a `Feature.XML` file that defines the metadata of the Feature, and also points to other XML files called *manifest files*. These manifest files define the actual functionality of the deployed Features.

Following are the out-of-the-box available workflow Features and their associated workflow templates:

❑ *Collect Signatures* — This workflow allows you to add digital signatures to Word 2007 or Excel 2007 documents. This workflow can only be started from within an Office client application for documents that contain one or more Microsoft Office Signature lines.

❑ *Disposition Approval* — This manages document expiration and retention by allowing participants to decide whether to retain or delete expired documents.

❑ *Translation Management* — This manages document translation by creating copies of the document to be translated, and assigning translation tasks to translators. This workflow can only be linked to a Translation document library.

❑ *Routing Workflows Feature* — This contains the Approval workflow that allows you to add persons or groups of persons who can approve or reject a document. Whenever a user needs to provide feedback, a task is added to a task list. This workflow template also allows you to reassign approval tasks, send email notifications, and specify due dates. The Collect Feedback workflow for document reviews is also part of the Routing Workflows Feature. People can provide feedback that is compiled and sent to the document owner when the workflow has completed.

❑ *Three-state workflow* — This manages the issue tracking process by creating tasks for active issues assigned to a user. When the task related to an issue is complete (hence, resolving the issue), the creator of the issue is assigned a Review task so that the issue can be closed. This is the workflow template that is also available in Windows SharePoint Services (WSS).

Let's take a look at how you can use the Collect Feedback workflow. First, you will need to link this workflow template to a list, library, or content type. In this example, you will see how you can link a workflow to a specific document library. You should start by creating a new Team Site called Wrox Workflow. Open the Shared Documents library and go to the Document Library Settings. (In the Library toolbar, select Settings ⇨ Document Library Settings.) Look for the Workflow Settings link and select it. This will open the page where you can associate your workflow with the document library, as shown in Figure 9-2.

The available workflow templates in the selection list depend on the workflow Features that have been activated for the current site collection. The Collect Feedback workflow has been defined in the ReviewWorkflows Feature, which you can find in the `ReviewWorkflows` subfolder at `C:\Program Files\Common Files\Microsoft Shared\Web Server Extensions\12\Templates\Features\`. This folder contains the Feature definition files. If you take a look at `Feature.XML`, you will notice that it references two different manifest files: one for the Approval workflow and one for the Feedback workflow.

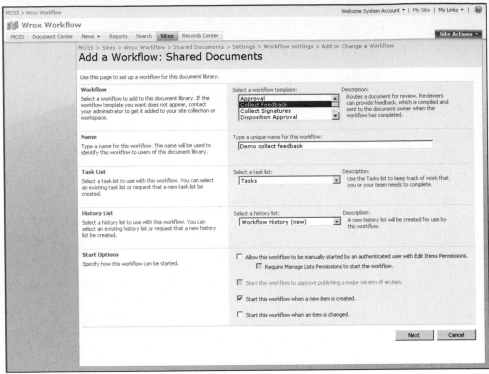

Figure 9-2: Workflow association page — Add or Change a Workflow screen

In this first screen, you must specify a unique name for the workflow template, as well as the task list and the workflow history you will use. The task list is used to provide the user with a way to interact with a running workflow, and the workflow history list is used to track changes in your workflow. Finally, you define the different start options for your workflow. In this example, use the "Start this workflow when a new item is created" option and click Next. This will update the `WorkflowAssociation` table in your SharePoint content database.

Next, you must specify some additional association parameters (Figure 9-3) that are used within the workflow. This specific configuration simply specifies that two reviewers are used for the tasks that are being created. The reviewers will review the document in parallel, after which a feedback email is sent to the person who created the document.

The association page shown in Figure 9-3 is actually an InfoPath form that is using one of the out-of-the-box InfoPath Host pages that come with MOSS 2007. These `aspx` pages contain an `XMLFormView` control that is used to render the InfoPath form. The Host pages make all the necessary object model calls to implement the workflow functionality. Later in this chapter, you see how you can create your own custom workflow and use InfoPath forms as well.

> Using InfoPath forms as workflow forms is only possible with MOSS 2007 Enterprise Edition. You will not be able to use them even when you install WSS v3.0 together with Forms Server.

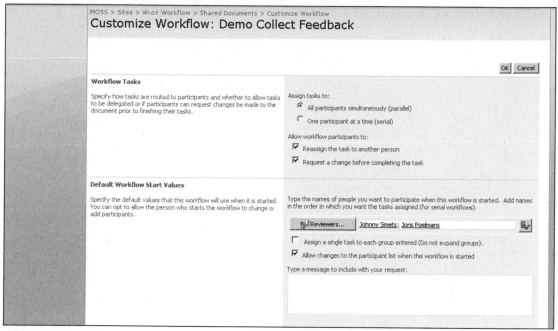

Figure 9-3: Specifying an association parameter using an InfoPath Host page

When you create a new document within the document library, you will notice that a new column appears in the document library with the workflow status information. When you click the workflow status hyperlink, you are redirect to the workflow status page (Figure 9-4) where you get an overview of the tasks that have been created and the events that have been logged to the workflow history list.

When you click a task link, a task screen will open to allow you to provide your feedback, as shown in Figure 9-5. You will probably notice that this is not a standard task edit screen. This screen is using an InfoPath form loaded in the `WrkTaskIP.aspx` host file. (Take a look at the OffWFCommon Feature.)

> There are four types of workflow forms that you can specify: association, initiation, task edit, and modification. Each of these forms is specified in the `workflow.xml` file. Each of these forms can be implemented as an `aspx` page or as an InfoPath form if you are using MOSS 2007. The InfoPath forms are the fastest option, and can also be used in Office 2007 client applications. If you are only using WSS v3.0, your only option is using `aspx` pages.
>
> So, if you take a look at the `ReviewFeedback.xml` for the Collect Feedback workflow, you will notice that it points to the standard InfoPath Host pages:
>
> ```
> TaskListContentTypeId="0x01080100C9C9515DE4E24001905074F9
> 80F93160" AssociationUrl="_layouts/CstWrkflIP.aspx"
> InstantiationUrl="_layouts/IniWrkflIP.aspx"
> ModificationUrl="_layouts/ModWrkflIP.aspx"
> ```

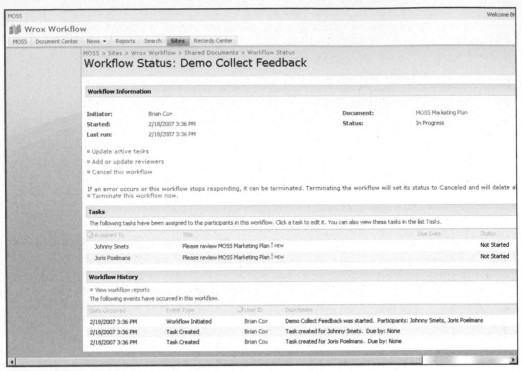

Figure 9-4: Workflow Status screen

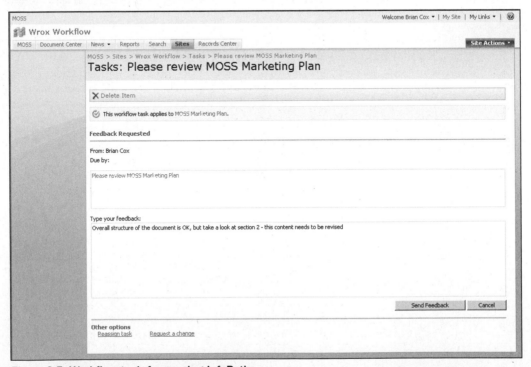

Figure 9-5: Workflow task form using InfoPath

The Task Edit screen is not directly referenced in the workflow node of the element manifest file. Instead, you will specify the task content type. In the definition of a content type, the linked view and edit ASP.NET pages are specified. `0x01080100C9C9515DE4E24001905074F980F93160` is the ID of the base workflow task content type.

Most of these workflows are very document-oriented. However, by combining MOSS 2007 workflow capabilities with InfoPath 2007, you can also use these workflows to automate more data-driven business processes. So, let's first take a look at what InfoPath 2007 is capable of.

Using InfoPath 2007

InfoPath 2007 allows you to design forms without writing any code and still include features such as data validation, conditional formatting, and connections to external data sources. In conjunction with Forms Services (part of MOSS 2007 Enterprise Edition) or Forms Server, you can provide users with the capability to fill in these InfoPath forms without having InfoPath installed on their computers. Forms Services provides multiple browser support, including Internet Explorer (IE), Firefox, Netscape, and Safari.

The following steps show how you can use InfoPath to create an expense report. You will use this same example throughout this chapter while using more advanced options such as external data connections, digital signatures, and managed code data validation.

1. Open InfoPath 2007 and choose "Design a Form Template." Choose "Design a new form template based on a Blank template."

2. In the Design Tasks pane you will see the different available design options. Choose Layout in the Design Tasks task pane. Insert a Table with Title.

3. Choose Controls in the Design Tasks pane and add three section controls within this layout table by dragging them from the Design Tasks Pane and dropping them on the design surface.

4. Double-click the "section" label and change the "field or group name" for each section (from top to bottom) into `ExpenseInfo`, `Remarks`, and `Attachments`.

5. Some sections (parts of the forms) can be hidden. You can do this by defining them as Optional sections. The Attachments and Remarks sections must be converted.

6. To convert a section, double-click the "section" label. Select "Do not include the section in the form by default" and check the "Allow users to insert the section" and "Show insert button and hint text." Change the hint text into "Insert *xxx*" (replace *xxx* with the name of your section). Click OK to convert the section into an Optional section, as shown in Figure 9-6.

7. Add a custom layout table at the top of your form within the first section that you added earlier: 8 rows, 2 columns.

8. Add the title "Employee Information" to the custom layout table in the first column of the third row. Format the title so that it uses bold, font size 12, and a blue color. Do the same in the seventh row, but use "Manager Information" as the title.

9. Drag and drop a `Date Picker` control in the first row and column. Precede it with a label "Expense Report Date." Double-click the `Date Picker` control and change the field name to `ReportDate`. In the Validation and Rules section, you need to check "cannot be blank." Also, change the default value to today's date.

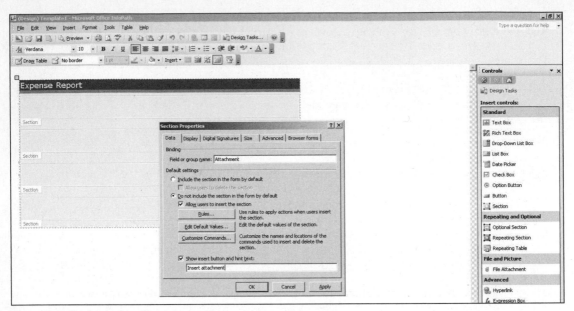

Figure 9-6: Converted section

10. Modify the fourth and fifth row. Add in the necessary labels and textbox controls for the following fields: `EmployeeName`, `EmployeeID`, `EmployeeEmail`, and `EmployeeDept`. Mark them all as required fields.

11. Leave a blank row and add two fields, `MgrName` and `MgrEmail`, beneath the row with the "Manager Information" title.

12. In the `ExpenseInfo` section, you will need to be able to add multiple expense items. Go to Design Tasks ➪ Controls and add a `Repeating Table` control. Specify that it needs to use 4 columns. This will insert a table with 4 columns and a header on top of each row. Change the header titles to "Expense Date," "Description," "Category," and "Cost." Next, you specify the controls you want to use for data entry within your repeating table.

    a. Remove the Text Box control in the first column. Replace it with a `Date Picker` control. Change the field name to `ExpenseDate`.

    b. Replace the `Text Box` control in the third column with a `Drop-down List Box` control. Double-click the control and modify the field name to `Category`. Within the List Box entries section, you leave the option "Enter list box entries manually" checked and add four possible list box entries: "Dinner," "Parking," "Public Transport," and "Other." "Parking" should be marked as the default option.

    c. Change the field names for the other two textboxes to `ExpenseDescription` and `ExpenseCost`. Change the data type for the `ExpenseCost` to `Decimal(Double)` and apply a currency format.

    d. Open the Repeating Table Properties and navigate to the Display tab. Check the "Include footer" checkbox. Add a textbox to calculate the `TotalCost` in the footer of the repeating table. Change the Data Type to `Decimal(Double)` and the value to `Sum(ExpenseCost)` (use the formula builder). Mark this textbox as read-only on the Display tab.

13. Add a Scrolling Region underneath the Attachments title in the "Attachments" section. Add a Horizontal Repeating Table to the Scrolling Region control (Number of rows:1). InfoPath will insert a table with 1 row and 2 columns. The first column is the header and the second column contains the value. Resize the width of the first column to 20 pixels.

    a. Right-click in the table cell and select Table Properties.

    b. Go to the Column tab.

    c. Change the Width property (of Column A) into 20 pixels.

    d. Click OK to close this window.

14. You won't need a header for the Horizontal Repeating table, so clear the border for this cell. To do so, you will need to complete the following steps.

    a. Right-click in the space between the borders. Select Borders and Shading.

    b. Click in the Presets Section on "None" to remove all borders.

    c. Click OK to apply the changes.

15. Remove the current `Text Box` control in the Horizontal Repeating Table and add an `Attachment` control in column 2, cell 1 (into the cell that contains a border). Rename the Repeating Section to `AttachmentList` and the File Attachment control to `Attachment`.

16. Add a `Rich Text Box` control in the last Remarks section.

After you have completed the previous steps, switch to preview mode. Your InfoPath template should look like the template shown in Figure 9-7.

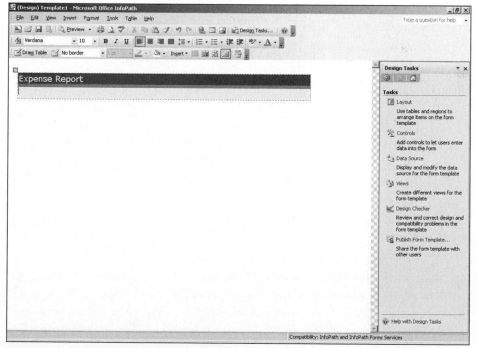

Figure 9-7: Expense Report InfoPath template

Deploying InfoPath Templates to SharePoint 2007

You must publish your InfoPath template to make it available for your end users. This publishing process has gone through some changes in InfoPath 2007. To start the Publishing process, select File ⇨ Publish. This will open the Publishing Wizard, as shown in Figure 9-8.

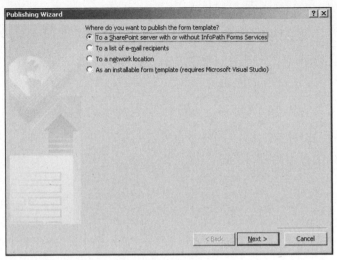

Figure 9-8: InfoPath Publishing Wizard

In InfoPath 2007, you have the following options from which you may choose where you want to publish the form template:

❑   *To a SharePoint server with or without InfoPath Forms Services* — This is the default option and is explained in detail in the next sections.

❑   *To a list of e-mail recipients* — This allows you to send the InfoPath form template as an email. This option was also available with InfoPath 2003 SP1 underneath the File menu as "Send form as attachment." However, one of the key differences between InfoPath 2003 and InfoPath 2007 is the complete integration with Outlook 2007. The InfoPath form will be treated similar to an email message in Outlook 2007 and can be directly viewed, edited, and forwarded.

❑   *To a network location* — This allows you to publish the InfoPath form template to a network location or a Web server.

❑   *As an installable form template (requires Microsoft Visual Studio)* — This can be either Visual Studio 2005 or Visual Studio 2003, and will create a Windows Installer (.msi) file that is stored on a network share. Users can then download and run the installable file to register the form template on their computers.

After you have chosen the option to publish to a SharePoint server, you will need to specify the URL of the SharePoint server to which you want to publish a copy. If you started from the form template, you will have the three available options for publication, as shown in Figure 9-9 (with the third option grayed out):

❑ Document library

❑ Site Content Type (advanced)

❑ Administrator-approved form template (advanced)

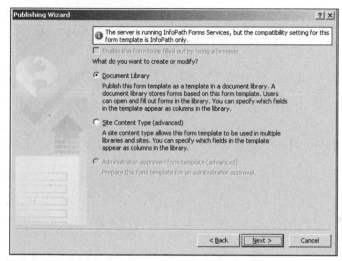

Figure 9-9: Publish to a SharePoint server

Notice the following warning: "The server is running InfoPath Forms Services, but the compatibility setting for this form template is InfoPath only." Later in this chapter, you see how you can enable your InfoPath form template to be filled in by using a browser.

When you choose to deploy the InfoPath template as a Site Content Type, you can assign this form template to multiple document libraries within a specific site collection. You would choose to publish your InfoPath template as a Site Content Type when you wanted to reuse the same form template in multiple sites.

A *site collection* is a set of Web sites on a virtual server that have the same owner and share the same administrative settings. Each site collection contains a top-level Web site and can contain one or more subsites. There can be multiple site collections on each virtual server.

A *site content type* (or simply *content type*) is a reusable collection of settings that you want to apply to a specific type of information. Content types enable you to manage the metadata and behavior of a document or item in one central location — the Site Content type Gallery — which is a system list (or gallery) located on the top-level site of a site collection. A content type includes the columns for your document or item, as well as other settings such as the document template, workflow settings, information management policies, and even the custom forms to use. It is possible to assign multiple content types to a single document library or list.

For the moment, choose the Document Library option. In the next screen that appears, choose to create a new document library. After you have published the form template to the document library, it will be used as the template for all of the documents that users fill out in that specific document library.

Next, you can also specify which InfoPath fields you want to display as columns within your document library, as shown in Figure 9-10. This feature is called *property promotion*. There is also something called *property demotion* where the column values are copied from the SharePoint document library back into the InfoPath field. The property promotion screen in the Publishing Wizard allows you to specify these promoted fields, but it is also possible to specify this beforehand from the Tools ➪ Form Options ➪ Property Promotion menu in InfoPath.

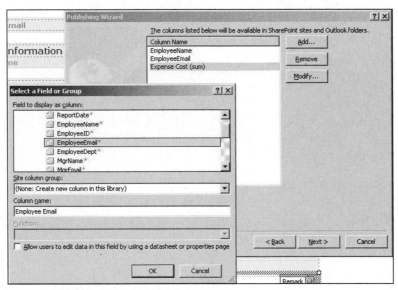

Figure 9-10: Property promotion screen

Remember to remove the spaces from the `ColumnName`, because this isn't very handy to work with when you need to access these columns using the SharePoint object model (it will translate spaces into `_x0020_`).

You will receive a confirmation screen for the settings you added during the publication process and, finally, a screen that displays the publishing status. Now you can navigate to the SharePoint document library where you published the form template and fill in a number of InfoPath forms by selecting New in the document library toolbar, as shown in Figure 9-11. This will open the InfoPath client application, which will load the form template that is linked to this document library.

The necessity of having to deploy InfoPath 2003 on client machines was one of the things that impeded a widespread adoption of InfoPath solutions, because the deployment cost was considered too high. In the next section, you see how you can browser-enable an InfoPath form so that it can be filled in without an InfoPath client installed.

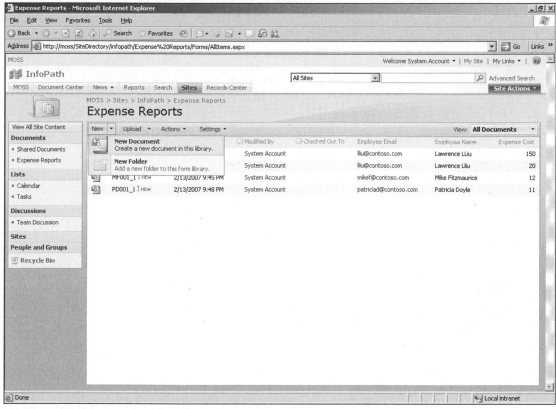

Figure 9-11: Filling in a new InfoPath form

Using Browser-Enabled InfoPath Forms

The key tool to use when you want to browser-enable an InfoPath form is the Design Checker. The Design Checker displays errors and messages about controls in your form template that will not work in a browser-enabled form. You can select the Design Checker option from the Design Task Pane. Next, you will need to click the "Change Compatibility Settings" and check the Browser compatibility checkbox.

> *If you know beforehand that you will need to browser-enable your form, you can select the "Enable browser-compatible features only" checkbox in the Design a Form Template dialog box when you starting creating a new form template. This will hide or disable controls or features that won't work in browser-compatible form templates.*

On the right of Figure 9-12, you can see that you currently have two major issues when you want to deploy this form as a browser-compatible form template. You must resolve these issues before you can deploy this form. If you want a complete report on the compatibility, you must check "Verify on server" on the bottom of the right side of the screen shown in Figure 9-12.

To resolve the indicated issue with the Rich Text Box, go to the Properties pane of the textbox and mark "Enable browser-compatible settings only" on the Display tab. (This option is only visible when you changed Compatibility settings to "InfoPath and InfoPath Forms Services.")

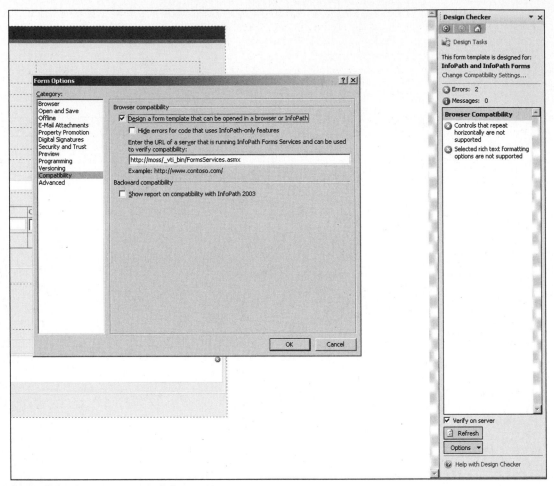

Figure 9-12: Browser compatibility settings

You will also need to replace the horizontal repeating control with a standard repeating control, as well as remove the horizontal scrolling region. To do this, open your InfoPath form in design mode and delete the horizontal scrolling region. Open the Controls section in your Design Task Pane and drag and drop a Repeating Section in the Attachments region. Within this Repeating Section, you can now add your Attachment control.

Some of the other unsupported controls are the combo box, multiple-selection list boxes, master/detail controls, bulleted, numbered, and plain list controls, picture and ink picture controls, vertical labels, scrolling regions, horizontal regions, horizontal repeating controls, horizontal repeating tables, choice group, repeating choice group and choice section controls, repeating recursive sections, and ActiveX controls.

After you have made these changes, you will be able to publish the form in the same way as you did before. Remember to check "Enable this form to be filled out by using a browser" in the Publishing Wizard (refer to Figure 9-9).

When you publish this browser-enabled form to SharePoint, and you fill in a new form on a client with InfoPath 2007 installed, you will see no differences because the InfoPath client will open by default. You can, however, force your form to be opened within the browser. Go to Form Library Settings ⇨ Advanced Settings and, underneath "Browser-enabled Documents," mark "Display as Web page." This will force your InfoPath form template to open in the browser (even when you have the InfoPath client installed), as shown in Figure 9-13.

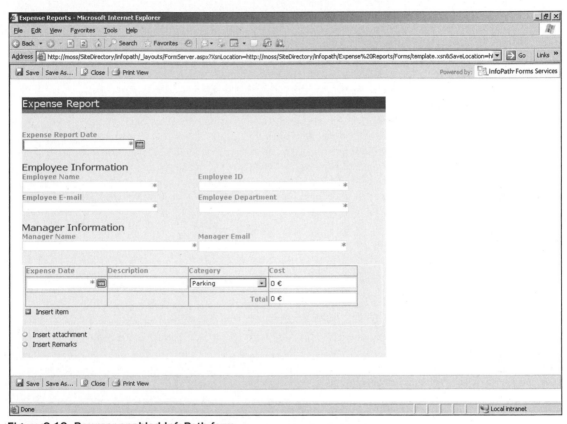

Figure 9-13: Browser-enabled InfoPath form

Before you publish your InfoPath form as a browser-enabled form, you must decide what different menu options (Save, Save As, Close, Print View, and so on) you want to show in your browser. If you fill in an InfoPath form using the full client, you will have the full InfoPath user interface available. When you fill in a browser-enabled InfoPath form, you are provided with an alternative for the default InfoPath user interface, which shows Forms Server toolbars at the top and the bottom of the browser-enabled InfoPath form. You can customize these toolbars by changing the settings in the Form Options dialog (go to Tools ⇨ Form Options) underneath the Browser category.

Using External Data Connections in InfoPath Forms

It is quite easy to use data from an external data source (such as a Web service, a database, or a SharePoint list) within your InfoPath form. InfoPath supports both receive and submit connections.

New in InfoPath 2007 is the integration with Data Connection Libraries (DCLs). With InfoPath 2003, data connections were stored within the form template itself, which was not always very convenient. InfoPath 2007 can store its connection settings in a DCL, which is a new type of SharePoint document library that can be used to store data connection settings in Universal Data Connection (UDCX) files. Using DCLs has a number of important advantages, including the following:

❑   It allows you to streamline your forms development, because you can update your connections without having to update the form templates.

❑   Transitioning forms between your test and production environment will become easier.

❑   It allows you to make cross-domain data connections in browser-enabled InfoPath forms with domain security.

❑   It offers multi-tier authentication.

When you go to the Form Options of your InfoPath form, you will notice that there are three trust options that you can use: restricted, full trust, or domain. Full trust InfoPath forms must be deployed by an administrator. However, most forms that you deploy with the Publishing Wizard are using the domain trust. So, when you access a Web service outside of the SharePoint context from a browser-enabled InfoPath, IE considers this to be a cross-domain call, which is not allowed according to standards. So, your InfoPath form may work correctly when opening with the InfoPath client, but will give the following error when opening in the Web browser and when not configured correctly: `An error occurred accessing the data source in the browser.`

The next example shows you how to create a receive data connection that uses a SharePoint list as a data source, and how you store these data connection settings in a DCL. First, create a custom list where you can specify a number of Expense Categories. You will use this custom list as a data source.

1.   Open your InfoPath form in Design view.

2.   Select Tools ➪ Data Connections and click Add to open the Data Connection Wizard.

3.   Select "Create a new connection to" ➪ "Receive data." Click Next .

4.   Select the source of your data. For this example, select the option to use a SharePoint library or list.

5.   Specify the URL of the site where your custom list is located. Click Next.

6.   Select the "ExpenseCategories" list and click Next.

7.   Select the fields that you are using as a data source. Only check the "Title" field and click Next.

8.   In the next screen of the Data Connection Wizard, you see that it is also possible to store a copy of the data inside the InfoPath form. This allows you to fill in InfoPath forms in Offline mode. Leave the checkbox "Store a copy of the data in the form template" unchecked and click Next.

9.   After you have created your data connection, you must change the data source for the drop-down list in the repeating table. Double-click it and change the data source for the list box entries. Select "Look up values from an external data source" and the data connection you have just created in the previous steps.

Let's first create a DCL within the same site where you are using your InfoPath forms. To create a DCL, select the Create option in the Site Actions menu. Underneath the Libraries category, you will see the Data Connection Library option. After you have created your DCL, you can convert your Data Connection settings into a UDCX file. Go to Tools ➪ Data Connections, select the Data Connection you want to convert, and click Convert. This will open the dialog box shown in Figure 9-14. Here you will need to specify the URL (for example, `http://[servername]/sitedirectory/[sitename]/[dcl]/categories.udcx`) to the UDCX file that you are creating in the DCL. Choose to convert your data connection using the "Relative to site collection" link type. This will create a UDCX file and upload it to the DCL.

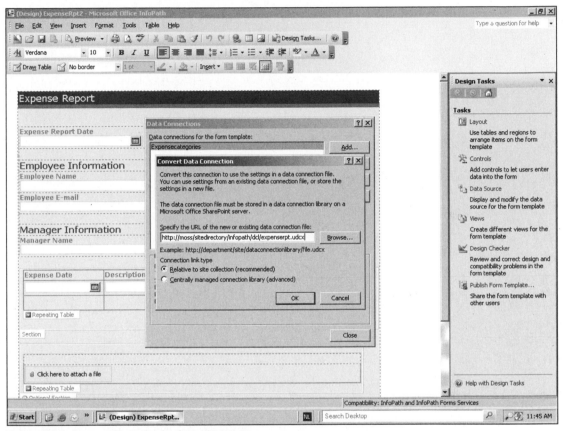

Figure 9-14: Convert Data Connection dialog box

Notice that you actually have two different options for storing the Data Connection files in a DCL: within the site collection or in a centrally managed connection library. Most of the time, you will use the "Relative to site collection (recommended)" option. The site for the "Centrally managed connection library (advanced)" option is located underneath the SharePoint Central Admin site. If you want to use this option, you must first upload the UDCX file to the central connection library. This is the most secure option, because only administrators can access this location.

Choose to convert your data connection using the "Relative to site collection" link type. This will create a UDCX file and upload it to the DCL. As shown in Figure 9-15, you must still approve this connection file; otherwise, only the owner who uploaded the file can use it for his or her data connections.

Because there is another tier present, these browser-enabled InfoPath forms may suffer from a phenomenon commonly referred to as a *double hop issue*. This means that when a user fills in an InfoPath form using NTLM authentication, and the form requires access to a remote database, the NTLM authentication token cannot be delegated. You can use a number of ways to overcome this issue, including (among others) using Kerberos, basic authentication, embedded SQL credentials, and so on. These different authentication options can be configured in the UDCX file. Because this UDCX file is basically an XML file, the InfoPath team has provided an UDC File Authoring Tool on the blog located at `http://blogs.msdn.com/infopath/archive/2007/02/12/udc-file-authoring-tool.aspx`.

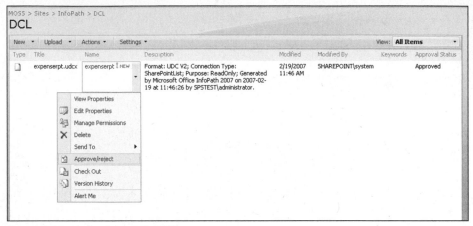

Figure 9-15: Approving a UDCX file

Extending Your InfoPath Templates with Code

With the initial release of InfoPath 2003, developers only had the option to extend their forms with JScript or VBScript. InfoPath 2003 Service Pack 1 (SP1) also allowed developers to use .NET code. InfoPath 2007, however, offers the following three options to extend your form templates with code:

❑ *Microsoft Scripting Editor (MSE)* — This allows you to use either JScript or VBScript to add business logic to your forms. You can open MSE from within design mode by pointing to Programming on the Tools menu, and then clicking Microsoft Script Editor.

❑ *Microsoft Visual Studio Tools for Applications (VSTA)* — This programming environment is included with InfoPath 2007.

❑ *Visual Studio 2005 Tools for the 2007 Microsoft Office System* — This option is available when you have a full version of Visual Studio 2005 installed.

VSTA can be added as an installation option for InfoPath 2007 (.NET Programmability Support ⇨ .NET Programmability for .NET Framework version 2.0 ⇨ Visual Studio Tools for Applications). VSTA requires that Microsoft .NET Framework 2.0 and Microsoft Core XML Services 6.0 are installed.

When you install Visual Studio 2005 Tools for the 2007 Microsoft Office System (also known as Visual Studio 2005 Tools for Office Second Edition, or VSTO SE), you will no longer need to switch back and forth between Visual Studio 2005 and InfoPath Designer. After installing this add-on to Visual Studio 2005, you will be able to create a new project type called an *InfoPath form template*. In the next example, you use VSTA to create an InfoPath solution using managed code.

> When you use VSTA, you can define the programming language of your choice
> (C# or VB.NET) by going to Tools ⇨ Form Options. Here you can specify the "Form
> template code language," as well as the default project location.

The following code sample shows how you can query data connections using the new InfoPath 2007 object
model. It uses a custom Web service that retrieves the user's email address, name, and department from
Active Directory. First, create a new ASP.NET Web service project. Within the business logic of this project,
you will see some code that is retrieving the information directly from Active Directory. When I create a
new ASP.NET Web service project, I typically choose File System in the location box. Add a new class to
your ASP.NET Web service project called `EmployeeInfo` and mark it as `Serializable`. Define six properties for the information that you want to return through the `Serializable` class.

```
[WebMethod]
    public EmployeeInfo GetEmployeeInfo(string accountname)
    {
        EmployeeInfo empInfo = new EmployeeInfo();

        DirectorySearcher objsearch = new DirectorySearcher();
        string strrootdse = objsearch.SearchRoot.Path;
        DirectoryEntry objdirentry = new DirectoryEntry(strrootdse);
        objsearch.CacheResults = false;

        objsearch.Filter =
String.Format("(&(objectClass=user)(objectCategory=person)(sAMAccountName={0}))",
accountname.Split(new char[] { '\\' })[1]);
        SearchResult objresult = objsearch.FindOne();

        if (objresult != null)
        {
            empInfo.UserDepartment =
objresult.Properties["department"][0].ToString();
            empInfo.UserEmail = objresult.Properties["mail"][0].ToString();
            empInfo.UserName = objresult.Properties["cn"][0].ToString();
            empInfo.UserID = accountname.Split(new char[] { '\\' })[1];

            string sMgrDN = objresult.Properties["manager"][0].ToString();
            DirectoryEntry managerEntry = new DirectoryEntry("LDAP://" + sMgrDN);
            empInfo.MgrName = managerEntry.Properties["cn"][0].ToString();
            empInfo.MgrEmail = managerEntry.Properties["mail"][0].ToString();
        }

        return empInfo;
    }
```

After having tested your code, you can publish this Web service to Internet Information Server (IIS). In this
scenario, publish your Web service to `http://[yourservername]:77/`. (Obviously, you will first need to
set up a Web site at this port in IIS.) Now, you can create a new data connection in InfoPath that will consume this Web service. Do not set the value of the input parameter for the `GetEmployeeInfo` Web service
while setting up the connection. This value will be provided in the business logic (custom code) within the
`Form_Loading` event. Remember to uncheck the checkbox for "Automatically retrieve data when form is
opened" in the last screen of the Data Connection Wizard. Next, you must bind the value of the different
InfoPath fields to the data fields returned from the `GetEmployeeInfo` data connections.

Now, open your InfoPath form in design mode. Go to the Tools menu and select Programming ➪ Loading event. This will start up VSTA and add in the `Loading` event. Notice that there is a difference in the InfoPath-managed object model, which is now completely based upon the `System.XML` namespace in .NET 2.0.

```
public void FormEvents_Loading(object sender, LoadingEventArgs e)
{
  XPathNavigator nav = this.DataSources["GetEmployeeInfo"].CreateNavigator();
  XPathNavigator wsnav =
nav.SelectSingleNode("/dfs:myFields/dfs:queryFields/tns:GetEmployeeInfo/tns:account
name", this.NamespaceManager);
  wsnav.SetValue(System.Environment.UserName);

  DataConnection conn = this.DataConnections["GetEmployeeInfo"];
  conn.Execute();
}
```

The XPath expression is used as an input parameter for the `SelectSingleNode` method of the `XPathNavigator` object. Learning how to work with the `XPathNavigator` object is essential for building InfoPath-managed code solutions.

> To get the correct XPath expression, you should go to Data Sources underneath Design Tasks within InfoPath. Here, you can find the XPath expression for every node by selecting the node and clicking Copy XPath. You can also do this for input and return parameters for Web services by switching the data source at the top of the task pane.

Form templates that contain business logic (custom code) requiring full trust (or that use administrator-managed data connections) must be deployed as an administrator-approved form template. So, when you start up the Publishing Wizard, you will notice that you can no longer directly publish the InfoPath to SharePoint. You must publish it to a network location and provide this location to your administrator so that he or she can upload the form template to the Managed Form templates gallery.

So, open your SharePoint Central Administration Web site and navigate to the Application Management tab. Click Upload Form Template. To be on the safe side, verify your form before uploading it.

> You can also upload and verify a form with the `stsadm.exe` command-line utility. To verify the form, use the command `stsadm.exe -o verifyformtemplate -filename <Path\FileName>`. To upload the form to the server, use the command `stsadm.exe -o uploadtemplate -filenmae <Path\FileName>`.

Although the form is uploaded to the server, it is not available to your users just yet. Next, you must activate it on the site collection where you want to use it. So, go back to the Application Management tab and select "Activate to a Site Collection" for the form template that you uploaded. (Be sure to wait until the status of the form template is Ready, as shown in Figure 9-16.) The site collection can only be activated by a farm administrator with site collection administration rights.

After you have activated the form template to a certain site collection, the template will become available as a site content type. So, open the form library where you want to use this content type. Go to Form Library Settings ⇨ Advanced Settings and select "Allow management of content types." You will notice afterward that the columns section on the Form Library Settings page now has a section where you can add a content type. So, select "Add from existing content type" and select the ExpenseRpt form template that you have uploaded.

Notice that when you fill in the form using the InfoPath client, a number of fields are filled in with information retrieved from Active Directory. However, when you try to open the form from within the browser, you will probably get an error stating An error occurred accessing the data source in the browser. This happens because of the cross-domain call issue discussed earlier. To resolve this, use a data connection file (a UDCX file) for the Web service that you created, and also ensure that the option "Allow cross-domain data access for user form templates that use connection settings in a data connection file" is checked (in SharePoint Central Administration ⇨ Application Management Tab ⇨ Configure InfoPath Forms Services).

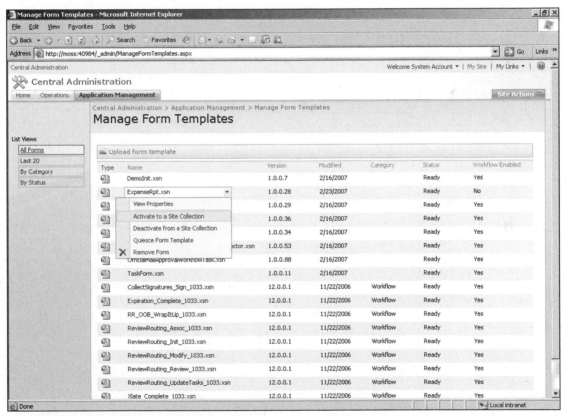

Figure 9-16: Activating a managed form template

Building Custom MOSS Workflow Solutions with Visual Studio 2005

MOSS 2007 shipped with a number of out-of-the-box workflow solutions. Most of these target document scenarios (focusing on review and approval scenarios), but also included are workflows for translating documents. There is also a workflow for the issues list in SharePoint, as well as some workflows that are targeted at specific MOSS Features (such as the Publishing Approval workflow and the Document Expiration workflow).

New in the 2007 Office System is the addition of SharePoint Designer 2007 (SPD 2007), which can be used as a workflow authoring tool. SPD allows information workers to create workflows using "no code" authoring with a wizard-based user interface.

Some of the workflow solutions will need more flexibility and extensively customized workflow templates. This is where the Visual Studio 2005 Extensions for .NET Framework 3.0 (WF) come into play. These extensions include a Windows Workflow Designer tool embedded into Visual Studio 2005 that allows you to create your own workflow solutions using your favorite .NET development language. You will also need to install the WSS (or MOSS) SDK to get the necessary Visual Studio templates to build workflow solutions.

SPD Workflow Authoring versus Visual Studio 2005 Workflow Development

SPD and Visual Studio 2005 both allow you to create workflow solutions, but each is targeted at a different audience, as shown in Table 9-1.

Table 9-1: Comparison of SPD and Visual Studio 2005

	SharePoint Designer (SPD)	Visual Studio 2005
Target audience	Power users	Developers
Activities	Reuse out-of-the-box or custom deployed activities	Reuse out-of-the-box activities, as well as building your own activities
Forms	Auto-generated forms (ASP.NET pages)	Designed forms (both ASP.NET and InfoPath forms)
Deployment	Workflow authored directly against live environment	Use SharePoint solution package to install workflow templates

SPD only allows you to use a number of predefined activities. It does not allow you to create new activity blocks. However, this is possible with Visual Studio 2005, as the following discussion explains.

Forms provide the link between your users and the Office workflow system. They are used for linking workflows to lists and document libraries, starting workflows, modifying existing workflows, and completing workflow tasks. Workflow in Office 2007 supports both ASP.NET forms and InfoPath forms.

ASP.NET forms can be used for workflows in Windows SharePoint Services (WSS) or MOSS 2007. Using InfoPath forms for workflow development can only be used with MOSS 2007 Enterprise Edition. One of the key benefits of using InfoPath is that the same form can be rendered both on MOSS and in the Office client application.

The fact that workflows are directly authored against a live environment is both a strength and a weakness of SPD. Development should be done in a controlled environment with a clear separation between development, test, and production. Unfortunately, this is not possible with SPD, because it is not possible to export the workflow definition created by SPD.

In Visual Studio 2005, a developer can use the WF graphical designer to build a workflow that consists of activities. You can use the workflow activities that ship with WF, as well as the ones that WSS provides.

Extending the Actions within SPD

SPD 2007 contains 23 predefined activity blocks that you can use to build workflows. These activities are defined in `C:\Program Files\Common Files\Microsoft Shared\web server extensions\12\TEMPLATE\1033\Workflow\WSS.ACTIONS`.

Notice that this is for an English version. You should replace the English Locale Identifier (LCID) `1033` *with another LCID for installations using another language.*

This file contains two types of content: the conditions you can use within SPD 2007 and the different actions. The following code sample shows one of the predefined conditions in the `WSS.ACTIONS` file:

```
<Condition Name="Modified by a specific person" FunctionName="ModifiedBy"
    ClassName="Microsoft.SharePoint.WorkflowActions.Helper"
Assembly="Microsoft.SharePoint.WorkflowActions, Version=12.0.0.0,
Culture=neutral, PublicKeyToken=71e9bce111e9429c"
AppliesTo="list"   UsesCurrentItem="true">
        <RuleDesigner Sentence="modified by %1">
            <FieldBind Id="1" Field="_1_" DesignerType="Person"
Text="specific person"/>
        </RuleDesigner>
        <Parameters>
            <Parameter Name="_1_" Type="System.String, mscorlib"     Direction="In" />
        </Parameters>
</Condition>
```

The `ClassName` and `Assembly` attributes of the `Condition` node define which is the associated .NET assembly.

Next, you see the `RuleDesigner` section that is responsible for the interaction between SPD and the connected assembly. The `Sentence` attribute is the text that is shown within the SPD workflow wizard. Here, it uses one input parameter defined with `ID=1`. The `%1` is shown as a customization link. This corresponds to the ID of the `FieldBind` element.

Within the `FieldBind` element, you see the `DesignerType` (which reflects the type of the field) and the `Text` attribute (which contains the value that is shown when no person is filled in yet). Within the `Parameters` section, you see how the `FieldBind` elements are passed to the connected assembly. The value for a `Name` attribute of a `Parameter` must correspond with the `Field` attribute of the `FieldBind`.

Take a look at the following section of the WSS.ACTIONS file:

```
<Action Name="Set Content Approval Status"
ClassName="Microsoft.SharePoint.WorkflowActions.SetModerationStatusActivity"
      Assembly="Microsoft.SharePoint.WorkflowActions, Version=12.0.0.0,
      Culture=neutral, PublicKeyToken=71e9bce111e9429c"
      AppliesTo="list" ListModeration="true" Category="Core Actions"
      UsesCurrentItem="true">
      <RuleDesigner Sentence="Set content approval status to %1 with %2">
          <FieldBind Field="ModerationStatus" DesignerType="Dropdown"
          Id="1"  Text="this status">
              <Option Name="Approved" Value="Approved"/>
              <Option Name="Rejected" Value="Denied"/>
              <Option Name="Pending" Value="Pending"/>
          </FieldBind>
          <FieldBind Field="Comments" Text="comments" Id="2"
        DesignerType="TextArea" />
      </RuleDesigner>
      <Parameters>
          <Parameter Name="ModerationStatus"  Type="System.String,mscorlib"
           Direction="In" />
          <Parameter Name="Comments" Type="System.String, mscorlib"
      Direction="Optional" />
          <Parameter Name="__Context"
      Type="Microsoft.SharePoint.WorkflowActions.WorkflowContext,
      Microsoft.SharePoint.WorkflowActions" />
          <Parameter Name="__ListId" Type="System.String, mscorlib"
          Direction="In" />
          <Parameter Name="__ListItem" Type="System.Int32, mscorlib"
          Direction="In" />
      </Parameters>
      </Action>
```

Notice a similar structure for the actions section. The Action XML node also contains a ClassName and Assembly attribute for the linked workflow assembly. AppliesTo describes the types of lists the activity can be used for with possible values being list, doclib, or all.

Notice that the Parameters section contains the parameters for the defined FieldBind as well as some extra parameters:

❑   _Context — The context of the workflow
    (Microsoft.SharePoint.WorkflowActions.WorkflowContext)

❑   _ListId — The GUID for the associated list

❑   _ListItem — The ID for the current listitem

> If you want to add your own custom activities to SPD, you should not modify the WSS.ACTIONS file, because this is one of the SharePoint system files. Instead, you should create a new file with the .ACTIONS extensions in the same folder.

In the next example, you will write a custom activity that will make a document read-only for all users by changing the security settings of the file. Complete the following steps to create a custom activity that you can use in SPD 2007:

1. Build a custom activity library in Visual Studio 2005.

2. Deploy the assembly to Global Assembly Cache (GAC) and mark it as safe for SPD to load in the `web.config`.

3. Create a new `.ACTIONS` file to allow SPD to use the assembly.

In the next sections, I describe each of the aforementioned steps.

Building a Custom Activity in Visual Studio 2005

In this first step, you will create custom workflow activity that will set a document to read-only for all users by changing the SharePoint security settings. To develop this custom activity, you will need to open your Visual Studio 2005 and create a new custom workflow activity project using the Visual Studio Workflow Activity Library template.

Drag and drop a code activity onto the design surface, and set the `ExecuteCode` property to `ModifySecuritySettings`. This will open the code-behind of your activity, and automatically create the method that will execute. Before you can implement this method, you must find a way to pass information from the workflow into the activity, and back. You do this using `DependencyProperty`.

You must define dependency properties for the extra system parameters shown in the previous discussion (`__Context`, `__ListId`, and `__ListItem_`). Use the `Dependency` code snippet shown in Figure 9-17 to generate the getter and setter code for the different properties.

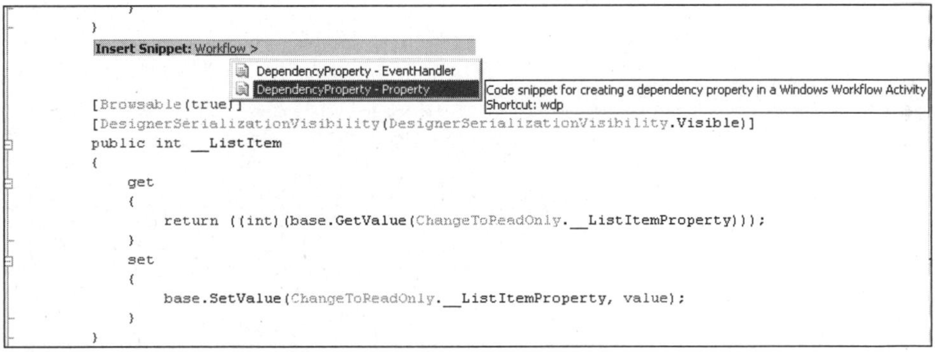

```
        }
Insert Snippet: Workflow >
         DependencyProperty - EventHandler
         DependencyProperty - Property          Code snippet for creating a dependency property in a Windows Workflow Activity
[Browsable(true)]                               Shortcut: wdp
[DesignerSerializationVisibility(DesignerSerializationVisibility.Visible)]
public int __ListItem
{
    get
    {
        return ((int)(base.GetValue(ChangeToReadOnly.__ListItemProperty)));
    }
    set
    {
        base.SetValue(ChangeToReadOnly.__ListItemProperty, value);
    }
}
```

Figure 9-17: `DependencyProperty` **code snippet**

Next, you must implement the `ModifySecuritySettings` method. This method will change the permissions for the current item. It will give all authenticated users read permissions, and the user you specify in SPD Contributor access, except when the document already has unique permissions. Here, you can use the `WorkflowContext` object to access the current `SPWeb` and `SPSite`. This is necessary, because the `SPContext.Current` returns `null` within the activity.

```
private void ModifySecuritySettings(object sender, EventArgs e)
{
    try
    {
        SPWeb site = __Context.Web;
        SPList list = site.Lists.GetList(new Guid(__ListId), false);

SPListItem item = list.GetItemById(__ListItem);

        if (!item.HasUniqueRoleAssignments)
        {
            item.BreakRoleInheritance(false);
            SPUser contributeuser = site.AllUsers[UserWithAccess];

    SPRoleAssignment roleasscont = new
SPRoleAssignment((SPPrincipal)contributeuser);

roleasscont.RoleDefinitionBindings.Add(site.RoleDefinitions.GetByType(SPRoleType
.Contributor));

            item.RoleAssignments.Add(roleasscont);

            SPRoleAssignment roleassreadonly = new
SPRoleAssignment(SPUtility.GetAllAuthenticatedUsers(site), "", "All authenticated
users", "");
                    roleassreadonly.RoleDefinitionBindings.Add(site.RoleDefinitions
.GetByType(SPRoleType.Reader));
            item.RoleAssignments.Add(roleassigreadonly);
        }
    }
    catch (Exception ex)
    {
                EventLog.WriteEntry("ExpenseWorkflowActivities.ChangeToReadOnly",
ex.ToString(), EventLogEntryType.Error);
    }
}
```

SharePoint security rights are managed using permission levels. A *permission level* consists of a collection of rights corresponding to the values of the `Microsoft.SharePoint .SPBasePermission` enumeration. If you need to manipulate security rights, you must use the methods and permissions defined by the `ISecurableObject` interface. In the first line of the previous code section, you use the `BreakRoleInheritance` method to create unique role assignments for the objects, supplying a Boolean parameter that specifies that you don't want to copy the parent's permissions.

To add a user with specific rights, you must create a `SPRoleAssignment` object, and set the user — here, both "All authenticated Users" and "ContributeUser" (the user with the login specified in SharePoint Designer). Add the appropriate role definitions (`SPRoleType.Reader` and `SPRoleType.Contributor`) and add the object to the collection of role assignment for the item.

Deploying the Activity Assembly

The next step is to deploy the assembly to the GAC and to mark the assembly as safe in the `web.config` file. There is a specific section in the `web.config` file where all the assemblies that are loaded by SPD must be defined. Here you must add your own assembly as an `authorizedtype`.

```
<System.Workflow.ComponentModel.WorkflowCompiler>
 <authorizedTypes> <authorizedType Assembly="ExpenseWorfklowActivities,
Version=1.0.0.0, Culture=neutral, PublicKeyToken=29ca332943a56652"
Namespace="ExpenseWorfklowActivities" TypeName="*" Authorized="True" />
 </authorizedTypes>
```

Making the Assembly Available for SPD 2007

Create a new file called `modifysecuritysettings.ACTIONS` in `C:\Program Files\Common Files\Microsoft Shared\web server extensions\12\TEMPLATE\1033\Workflow`. (The name does not really matter, as long as you use the `.ACTIONS` extension.) The content of this file provides the link between SPD and your workflow assembly. This file should look like this:

```
<?xml version="1.0" encoding="utf-8"?>
<WorkflowInfo Language="en-us">
  <Actions>
    <Action Name="Changetoreadonly"
ClassName="ExpenseWorfklowActivities.ChangeToReadOnly"
Assembly="ExpenseWorfklowActivities, Version=1.0.0.0, Culture=neutral,
PublicKeyToken=29ca332943a56652" AppliesTo="all" Category="Custom">
<RuleDesigner Sentence="Change to readonly but give %1 contributor rights">
    <FieldBind Field="UserWithAccess" Text="User" Id="1" DesignerType="TextArea" />
</RuleDesigner>
<Parameters>
<Parameter Name="UserWithAccess" Type="System.String, mscorlib" Direction="In" />
<Parameter Name="__Context"
Type="Microsoft.SharePoint.WorkflowActions.WorkflowContext,
Microsoft.SharePoint.WorkflowActions" />
        <Parameter Name="__ListId" Type="System.String, mscorlib" Direction="In" />
        <Parameter Name="__ListItem" Type="System.Int32, mscorlib" Direction="In"
/>
</Parameters>
</Action>
  </Actions>
</WorkflowInfo>
```

After you have performed an `IISRESET` (or recycled the SharePoint application pool), the custom activity will be available to use in SPD 2007, as shown in Figure 9-18.

Building a Custom Workflow with Visual Studio 2005

Before you can start developing your own custom workflows, you must have the following software installed on MOSS 2007. (Development is done on the server itself.)

❑ Visual Studio 2005 extensions for .NET Framework 3.0 (WF) — You can download this from
   http://www.microsoft.com/downloads/details.aspx?FamilyId=5D61409E-1FA3-
   48CF-8023-E8F38E709BA6&displaylang=en.

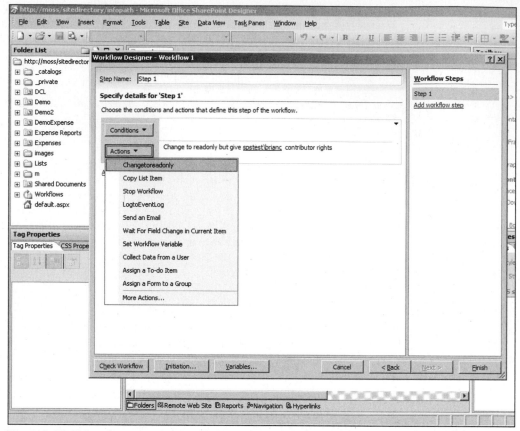

Figure 9-18: Using the `ChangeToReadOnly` **activity in SPD 2007**

- ❑ SharePoint Server 2007 SDK Enterprise Content Management (ECM) Starter Kit — You can download this from `http://www.microsoft.com/downloads/details` `.aspx?familyid=6d94e307-67d9-41ac-b2d6-0074d6286fa9&displaylang=en`.

After installing the ECM Starter Kit, you will get two new Visual Studio project templates: SharePoint Server Sequential Workflow and SharePoint Server State Machine workflow. In this example, you use the SharePoint Server Sequential Workflow template.

Structure of a Workflow Project

Open Visual Studio 2005 and create a project using the SharePoint workflow template (installed with the MOSS SDK). You will notice a number of different files:

- ❑ `Feature.xml` and `workflow.xml` (in `DeploymentFiles` ➪ `FeatureFiles`) — A workflow is deployed as a Feature, so you will need a `Feature.xml` file that points to a number of Feature manifest files defining the actual functionality of the Feature. In this case, `workflow.xml` is the manifest file that defines the workflow functionality.

❑   Manifest.xml and wsp_structure.ddf (in DeploymentFiles ⇨ ProductionDeployment) —
These files are used to create a SharePoint solution file, which is basically a cabinet file with the wsp
extension. This wsp file is used to deploy your workflow. The data directive file (DDF) tells make-
cab.exe how to structure your cabinet file. You will need to use makecab, because you will need a
folder structure within your cabinet file (similar to the structure you see underneath the "12" hive).
The manifest.xml file specifies the different elements that will be deployed.

❑   Postbuildactions.bat (in the DeploymentFiles folder) — This batch program will help
you to deploy the workflow.

❑   Workflow1.cs — This file contains the actual workflow activities and their associated code.

> **SharePoint Solution files (or WSP files) can also be used to deploy Web Parts,
> template files, assemblies, code access security policies, site definitions, or Features.
> After you have created the solution, you must deploy it to the solution store, which
> is a central location within SharePoint Central Administration for all solution files.
> After you have deployed the solution, the SPTimer service will synchronize/deploy
> the solution automatically to the other servers in your farm.**

Building a Simple Workflow

First, let's build a very simple workflow without any forms and just one activity. Double-click Workflow1
.cs to open the Workflow Foundation Designer. You will notice that the first activity of a SharePoint workflow must be the OnWorkflowActivated activity. This event handler activity is triggered when a new
SharePoint workflow is initiated.

> **Building SharePoint workflows with Visual Studio 2005 takes some practice. So, start
> development with a simple workflow and from there, take it a step further each time.**

The workflow template also added some code for you. You can use the workflowProperties variable
object to retrieve things such as the workflow instance ID, as well as custom properties that you defined
in a custom workflow initiation form. (For the sake of clarity, I'm not adding a custom initiation form.)

```
public sealed partial class Workflow1: SharePointSequentialWorkflowActivity
    {
        public Workflow1()
        {
            InitializeComponent();
        }

    public Guid workflowId = default(System.Guid);
    public Microsoft.SharePoint.Workflow.SPWorkflowActivationProperties
workflowProperties = new
Microsoft.SharePoint.Workflow.SPWorkflowActivationProperties();
```

Now, drop a `CodeActivity` onto the designer surface and set the `ExecuteCode` property to `WriteToLog`. Add a `using` statement for the `System.Diagnostics` to your code, and then add the following code snippet to the `WriteToLog` method:

```
private void WriteToLog(object sender, EventArgs e)
{
    EventLog.WriteEntry("ExpenseWorkflow", "Testing expense workflow",
EventLogEntryType.Information);
}
```

Your workflow assembly must be deployed to the GAC, so sign the assembly with a strong name key file. Build your solution and deploy your assembly to the GAC.

Now, let's start with modifying the other required files for deployment. Open `Feature.XML` and use the SharePoint Workflow ⇨ `Feature.xml` code snippet to insert the required elements.

> **Visual Studio 2005 has a Code Snippet Manager for managing different code snippets. If you don't see it, you can make it visible from Tools ⇨ Customize ⇨ Switch to command tab. Underneath the Tools category, you will see the Code Snippet Manager. You can now drag this command onto the toolbar where you want to use it. Next, you may need to activate the SharePoint workflow snippets. If the code snippets are not showing up in Visual Studio, go to Tools ⇨ Code Snippet Manager. Change the language to XML and add** `C:\Program Files\Microsoft Visual Studio 8\Xml\1033\ Snippets\SharePoint Server Workflow` **to your snippets.**

Your `Feature.xml` should look like the following code snippet. The `Id` should be replaced with a valid GUID that you can generate with a tool such as `GUIDGEN.exe`.

```
<Feature   Id="{A54FDF74-2368-4e2c-B6B1-FF5E6F459607}"
            Title="Expense Report workflow"
            Description="ExpenseReports"
            Version="12.0.0.0"
            Scope="Site"
            ReceiverAssembly="Microsoft.Office.Workflow.Feature, Version=12.0.0.0,
Culture=neutral, PublicKeyToken=71e9bce111e9429c"
ReceiverClass="Microsoft.Office.Workflow.Feature.WorkflowFeatureReceiver"
xmlns="http://schemas.microsoft.com/sharepoint/">
    <ElementManifests>
        <ElementManifest Location="workflow.xml" />
    </ElementManifests>
    <Properties>
        <Property Key="GloballyAvailable" Value="true" />
        <Property Key="RegisterForms" Value="*.xsn" />
    </Properties>
</Feature>
```

Next, you must modify the `workflow.xml` file. Create a new GUID for the ID and specify the correct `CodeBesideClass` and `CodeBesideAssembly`. You can also remove the references to the forms, because they will not be used in this first simple workflow. To find the correct `PublicKeyToken` for the `CodeBesideAssembly`, you can first add the DLL to the GAC and retrieve the value from there (right-click the selected assembly and select Properties). Another way to find the correct name is to use a little utility called .NET Reflector (http://www.aisto.com/roeder/dotnet/).

```
<Elements xmlns="http://schemas.microsoft.com/sharepoint/">
<Workflow
    Name="Expense Report workflow"
    Description="This workflow is used to approve expense reports"
    Id="{9E778B0B-012F-43b9-A783-FF83C89AA736}"
    CodeBesideClass="ExpenseWorkflow.Workflow1"
    CodeBesideAssembly="ExpenseWorkflow, Version=1.0.0.0, Culture=neutral,
PublicKeyToken=70c99ed3a3700cf4"
```

The `TaskListContentTypeId` referenced here is the default workflow task content type. You can decide to either leave it in or remove it.

```
    TaskListContentTypeId="0x01080100C9C9515DE4E24001905074F980F93160"
```

The `AssociationUrl`, `InstantiationUrl`, and `ModificationUrl` can be left out as well, because they are not used in the simple example. You can't leave out the `StatusUrl` — this one is required.

```
    AssociationUrl="_layouts/CstWrkflIP.aspx"
    InstantiationUrl="_layouts/IniWrkflIP.aspx"
    ModificationUrl="_layouts/ModWrkflIP.aspx"
    StatusUrl="_layouts/WrkStat.aspx">
    <Categories/>
    <!-- Tags to specify InfoPath forms for the workflow; delete tags for forms
that you do not have -->
    <MetaData>
        <AssociateOnActivation>false</AssociateOnActivation>
    </MetaData>
</Workflow>
</Elements>
```

Right-click your Visual Studio workflow project and select Properties. On the Build Events tab, you will notice that the post-build steps in the Visual Studio project are used to call postbuildactions.bat, which allow you to easily deploy your workflow. Change NODEPLOY to DEPLOY in the post-build events so that it looks like the following:

```
call "$(ProjectDir)\DeploymentFiles\PostBuildActions.bat"
"$(ConfigurationName)" "$(ProjectDir)" "$(ProjectName)" "$(TargetDir)"
"$(TargetName)" DEPLOY
```

Now, you can build your Visual Studio solution. Behind the scenes, your workflow feature will be installed and activated by the `PostBuildActions.bat` file. Now, your custom workflow will appear in the list of available workflow templates and it can be used.

Troubleshooting and Debugging SharePoint Workflows

If your workflow reports `Failed on start`, this usually means that the workflow code could not be loaded. `Error occurred` tells you that the workflow started OK, but that there is an error somewhere within the code.

A lot of information can be found in the SharePoint Unified Logging Service (ULS) logs. You can find the configuration for these logs in SharePoint Central Administration (in the Operations tab, underneath Diagnostic Logging). Here you can change at what severity level something is logged for a specific category. For workflow, there are two important categories: Workflow Features and Workflow infrastructure.

The ULS logs aren't very readable when you open them with Notepad, though, and there is no out-of-the-box viewer available for these log files. Fortunately there is a Feature project on Codeplex (`http://www.codeplex.com/features`) that includes a ULS log viewer. When you install and activate the LogViewer Feature, you get an extra link within SharePoint Central Administration (on the Operations tab) that will direct you to a page to view the existing logs.

You can actually debug a workflow live by adding breakpoints and attaching your Visual Studio to the `W3WP.exe` process. Select Debug ⇨ Attach to Process in Visual Studio to debug your workflows and attach to the `W3WP.exe` process. When you attach to the `W3WP.exe` process, ensure that you only attach to Workflow or Managed Code; otherwise, Visual Studio might crash.

Adding Custom InfoPath Workflow Forms

As mentioned previously, there are four different workflow forms that you can customize (Table 9-2). These workflow forms collect data from the user and must call specific SharePoint object model code. If you are using ASP.NET pages, you must create the user interface, as well as add the specific SharePoint workflow object model code.

Table 9-2: Workflow Forms

Form Type	Description	Workflow Host Page
Association form	Collects information to create the association (`SPWorkflowAssociation`) between a list (`SPList.AddWorkflowAssocation`) or content type (`SPContentType.AddWorkflowAssocation`) and the workflow template. These parameters include the title of the association, when to start a workflow (automatically or manual), and other custom workflow settings.	`layouts/CstWrkflIP.aspx`
Initiation form	Collects information to create a new workflow instance from an association (`SPWorkflowManager.StartWorkflow(SPListIte, SPWorkFlowAssocation, string)`).	`layouts/IniWrkflIP.aspx`
Task form	Gather feedback from users and change the workflow task information (`SPWorkflowTask.AlterTask()`).	`layouts/WrkTaskIP.aspx`
Modification form	Allows you to modify a running workflow instance (`SPWorkflowManager.ModifyWorkflow`).	`layouts/ModWrkflIP.aspx`

However, MOSS Enterprise Edition also contains a number of workflow host pages that contain an `XMLFormView` control that loads the InfoPath form template and that also makes the required object model calls for you.

Modifying the Workflow Assembly

To modify the workflow assembly, you must add workflow activities to create a new task and assign it to the manager (`CreateTaskActivity`), wait until the expense report is approved or rejected (`While` and `TaskChanged` activity), and finally mark the task as complete (`CompleteTaskActivity`). In this section, you also see how you can create a custom InfoPath form that you will be using as a task form.

First, drag and drop a `CreateTask` activity onto your workflow designer surface. Double-click the blue icons to open the Bind <Variable> to Activity Property dialog box. To create and bind a variable to the `TaskId` property, select "Bind to a new member." Fill in `taskId` and choose "create field." Do the same for the `TaskProperties` property. Ensure that all required properties are set as shown in Figure 9-19.

Figure 9-19: `CreateTask` **Activity properties**

By filling in the `MethodInvoking` property, you specify an event handler when the activity executes. Type **CreateTask** into the `MethodInvoking` property and press Enter. You will see that it automatically generates the event handler and switches to Code view, as shown here:

```
private void CreateTask(object sender, EventArgs e)
{
 try
 {
    SPListItem item = workflowProperties.Item;

    //Required - all other lines are optional
    taskId = Guid.NewGuid();
    taskprops.Title = "Please approve - " + item.Name.ToString();
    SPUser user = workflowProperties.Web.Users.GetByEmail(item[item
.Fields["MgrEmail"].InternalName].ToString());
    taskprops.AssignedTo = user.LoginName;
```

You will notice that the ExtendedProperties property of the SPWorkflowTaskProperties task object is used in the next code segment. This property is a hash table that allows you to store key-value pairs, which are passed from the InfoPath form into the workflow assembly and back.

```
    taskprops.ExtendedProperties["instructions"] = "When reviewing the expense
approval make sure that necessary evidence is attached.";
    taskprops.ExtendedProperties["applicant"] =
item[item.Fields["EmployeeName"].InternalName].ToString();
    taskprops.ExtendedProperties["expenseamount"] =
item[item.Fields["ExpenseCost"].InternalName].ToString();
    }
  catch (Exception ex)
  {
    EventLog.WriteEntry("ExpenseWorkflow", ex.ToString(), EventLogEntryType.Error);
  }
}
```

The correlationtoken is used to tell the workflow engine how to map events and actions to a specific object. So, later on when you need to add an OnTaskChanged and CompleteTask activity, you must use the same correlationtoken so that the workflow knows these activities are linked to the same SharePoint task.

Notice that you can access the SPListItem as well as the SPWeb object for which the workflow is running through the workflowproperties object variable. You may also think that I use a strange way to access the InfoPath's promoted fields. The problem is that you can't use the initial names anymore because you published the InfoPath form as an administrator-approved template. When you do this, the promoted fields are converted into site columns, and their values are only accessible through the internal name. To access the values in these columns, you could also use the internal name directly, which would look more or less like this (which is not quite readable):

```
item["_x007b_952854e0_x002d_f783_x002d_4820_x002d_8e26_x002d_5636e26cc517
_x007d_"]
```

If you need to set custom properties on a task, you can use the ExtendedProperties property of the SPWorkflowTaskProperties object, as shown with the instructions field.

Next, add a While activity to wait until the user completes the task you just created. Specify that it uses a Code condition and fill in notCompleted for the condition subproperty. This is the name of the method that is executed to determine if the loop can be exited. (The method is automatically created in code.) Child activities of the While activity will run as long as the condition equals true.

Declare a boolean variable that will be used to check if the workflow has completed and implement the notCompleted method:

```
private bool isCompleted;
private void notCompleted(object sender, ConditionalEventArgs e)
{
    e.Result = !isCompleted;
}
```

The `isCompleted` property is set in the `onTaskChanged` event handler.

Next, drag and drop an `onTaskChanged` activity into the `While` activity. Here you will need the same `correlationtoken` as for the `CreateTask` activity. Every time the workflow task is edited, the code condition will check if the `codecondition` returns `false` (meaning that the task is completed). Specify the `AfterProperties`, and bind it to a new member called `afterprops`. Also, bind the `BeforeProperties` to a new member field `beforeprops`. Add the `onTaskChanged` method to the `Invoked` property. In this method, you can check the task properties. Figure 9-20 shows what the properties should look like for `onTaskChanged`.

Figure 9-20: `onTaskChanged` **properties**

Within the `onTaskChanged` method, you can use the `afterprops` object variable to retrieve the task properties after the task change event has occurred. Finally, you can add a `LogToHistoryList` activity and bind a new member field `histDescription` to the `HistoryDescription` property. The description will be set at the moment that the task gets completed. You can also set the `EventId` for specifying the `Event` log type (`Workflowstarted`, `workflowcompleted`, `taskdeleted`, and so on).

```
private void onTaskChanged(object sender, ExternalDataEventArgs e)
{
    isCompleted = bool.Parse(afterProps.ExtendedProperties["isCompleted"]
.ToString());
    if (isCompleted)
    {
        histDescription = "Workflow has been completed at " +  DateTime.Now();
    }
}
```

After you have finished, your workflow design surface will look like Figure 9-21.

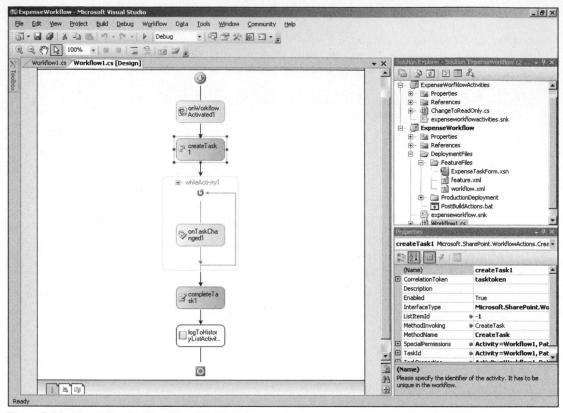

Figure 9-21: Visual Studio Workflow Designer

> Remember that when you want to write out a lot of data to the history list, you must use the `OtherData` property of the `LogToHistoryListActivity`, because the `HistoryDescription` property is limited to 256 characters. This property is not shown on the default workflow status page, but can be read out with custom code. Remember also that the workflow history list is just a hidden list — which you can access using the following URL:
>
> ```
> http://[servername]/sitedirectory/[sitename]/Workflow%20History/
> AllItems.aspx
> ```

Design the Task Form

Now you can design the InfoPath form that is used as a task form. Open InfoPath and select "Design a blank form template." Check "Enable browser-compatible features only." Open the Design Task pane and add the fields to the main data source as shown in Figure 9-22. Change the fields collection name from `myFields` to `ExpenseForm`.

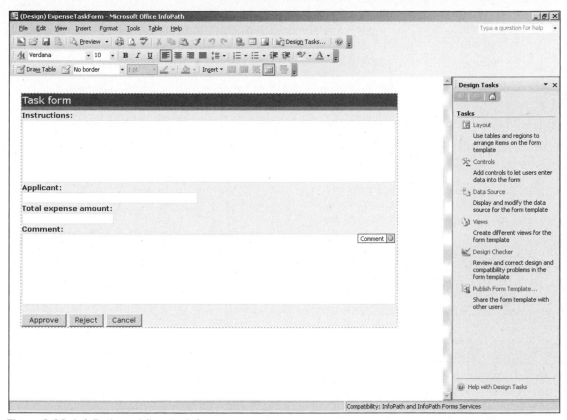

Figure 9-22: InfoPath workflow task form

Ensure that when you click the buttons, the form will be submitted to the SharePoint server. Double-click the Approve button to open the Properties dialog. Click the Rules button and then add the submit using a data connection action. You must create a new submit data connection with a destination "To the hosting environment, such as an ASP.NET page or a hosting application." Then, add another action to close the form.

SharePoint needs a way to pass information from within the workflow to the task form. This is done by creating a secondary data source to load the task data. You do this by creating a file called `ItemMetadata.xml`. In this file, you define every property that you want to use in your task form, as shown in the next code snippet. Simply add an attribute with prefix `ows_` followed by the name of the task property.

```
<z:row xmlns:z="#RowsetSchema" ows_instructions="" />
```

You will need to add this task schema information file as a receive data connection. So, open InfoPath, select Data Source in the Design pane, and select Manage Data Connection. Create a new Receive Data data connection. Select "XML document" as the data source and add the `ItemMetadata.xml` file. Select "Include the data as a resource file in the template" and click Next. Ensure that the data connection name is `ItemMetadata` and that the "Automatically retrieve data when form is opened" checkbox is selected.

> The filename `ItemMetadata.xml` is case-sensitive. If you do not use the correct name, no error will be shown, but your fields will not display the expected values.

Now you can bind your controls to this secondary data source. Double-click the textbox and fill in the Default Value using the Insert Formula dialog. In the "Select a Field or Group" dialog box, select your `ItemMetadata` data connection and select the value you want to bind to.

Next, modify the form options. Ensure that browser compatibility is enabled and that the form uses domain level trust.

As a last step, you must publish your workflow form. Choose "Publish to a network location" and click Next. Publish the InfoPath form to the DeploymentFiles ⇨ FeatureFiles subfolder where your `feature.xml` and `workflow.xml` are also found.

> Leave the alternate access path blank; otherwise, your workflow will not install. The alternate access path is filled in by default, so you must explicitly clear it. Ignore the warning message that is displayed.

Change workflow.xml

It's now time to modify the `workflow.xml` file. Here you should add the Uniform Resource Names (URNs) to the `MetaData` section of the InfoPath task form that you created earlier. You can find the URN by opening the InfoPath form in design mode and choosing Properties from the File menu.

So, open your `workflow.xml`. Position your pointer in the `MetaData` section and use the SharePoint Server Workflow snippets to insert the `Task Form Tag` snippet. Your workflow form should now look like the following code snippet:

```
<Elements xmlns="http://schemas.microsoft.com/sharepoint/">
    <Workflow
          Name="Expense Report workflow"
          Description="This workflow is used to approve expense reports"
          Id="{9E778B0B-012F-43b9-A783-FF83C89AA736}"
          CodeBesideClass="ExpenseWorkflow.Workflow1"
          CodeBesideAssembly="ExpenseWorkflow, Version=1.0.0.0, Culture=neutral,
PublicKeyToken=70c99ed3a3700cf4"
          TaskListContentTypeId="0x01080100C9C9515DE4E24001905074F980F93160"
          AssociationUrl="_layouts/CstWrkflIP.aspx"
          InstantiationUrl="_layouts/IniWrkflIP.aspx"
          ModificationUrl="_layouts/ModWrkflIP.aspx"
          StatusUrl="_layouts/WrkStat.aspx">
        <Categories/>
        <!-- Tags to specify InfoPath forms for the workflow; delete tags for
forms that you do not have -->
        <MetaData>
              <Task0_FormURN>urn:schemas-microsoft
-com:office:infopath:ExpenseTaskForm:-myXSD-2007-02-24T15-08-38</Task0_FormURN>
<AssociateOnActivation>false</AssociateOnActivation>
```

```
        </MetaData>
    </Workflow>
</Elements>
```

Workflow Tips and Tricks

This section provides some tips and tricks for working with workflows.

Parsing Information from a Custom Initiation or Modification Form

If you need to retrieve information from a custom InfoPath initiation form, you must access the InitiationData property of the SPWorkflowActionProperties object variable workflowProperties. The InitiationData property is an XML string that you can either parse using objects in the System .XML, or that you can deserialize using the XML Schema Definition (XSD) of your InfoPath form.

Setting Custom Status Information for a Workflow

The values in the workflow status column are integer-based. To access the workflow status, you refer to this integer value in code. The values 0 to 14 are the ones used by WSS and MOSS 2007. The maximum status value is represented by SPWorkflowStatus.mMax. If you want to add your own custom information, you must modify the workflow definition file (workflow.xml). You must modify the MetaData section by adding in an extendedstatuscolumnvalues element, as shown in the following code snippet:

```
<MetaData>
      <AssociateOnActivation>true</AssociateOnActivation>
      <<Task0_FormURN>urn:schemas-microsoft-com:office:infopath:ExpenseTaskForm:
-myXSD-2007-02-24T15-08-38</Task0_FormURN>
      <ExtendedStatusColumnValues>
        <StatusColumnValue>Approved</StatusColumnValue>
        <StatusColumnValue>Rejected</StatusColumnValue>
      </ExtendedStatusColumnValues>
    </MetaData>
  </Workflow>
</Elements>
```

For example, to set the status in your workflow to the first custom value (in this case, Approved), change the workflow state property to SPWorkflowStatus.Max + 1. The Setstate activity allows you to set the workflow status at completion of your workflow.

Adding Multiple Approvers

If you need to add multiple persons who must approve the document, you will probably need to use ReplicatorActivity, which allows you to add a child activity that will be executed a number of times, depending on the InitialChildData collection. The ExecutionType property dictates whether execution of these child activities will happen in parallel or in a sequential manner. You can find an example of the ReplicatorActivity in ReplicatorContactSelectorSample in the ECM Starter Kit.

Workflow Security Considerations

The task and history list are not secured by default. So, if you want to avoid tampering, you must add your own security. These are, however, standard lists that can be secured as any other type of list. The `CreateTask` activity also has a `SpecialPermissions` property that can be used to secure the workflow task item. For more information, take a look at the `ConfidentialApprovalSample` in the ECM Starter Kit.

Summary

This chapter offered an overview of how you can use InfoPath 2007 and the new capabilities of Forms Services in MOSS 2007. You saw how to implement a custom workflow with both SPD 2007 and Visual Studio 2005.

However, this chapter only scratched the surface of what is possible with the combination of InfoPath and SharePoint workflow. With the new Forms Services, you can also integrate InfoPath in your own custom applications with the `XMLFormView` control. I also expect a lot of samples and more guidance about workflow development to be forthcoming in the near future. WF is clearly still in its infancy, but shows great promise to becoming the most important framework for developing applications in the future.

Remember, you should think of SharePoint as an application platform to build your own solutions by tweaking, tuning, customizing, and branding the out-of-the-box experience.

10

Using the Business
Data Catalog

by Nick Swan

I was initially drawn to SharePoint 2003 because of the promise it offered people in terms of productivity gains through working in a collaborative way. This not only would make their jobs easier, but also would allow them to do more each and every day.

I was first drawn to the Business Data Catalog (BDC) for the same reason. SharePoint 2003 allowed a portal so that your staff could see information from many different systems in your business, whether from an Oracle, SAP, or Siebel system. The problem was that custom Web Parts had to be written to pull this data back from the database and display it on a page. Also, each data source required its own API for developers to learn. SharePoint developers had to spend many hours developing, debugging, and administrating these very similar Web Parts that, for the most part, were simply selecting data from a data source. Although these Web Parts took up a significant portion of a SharePoint developer's life, displaying the data in the Web Part was all that could be done with it. The data was not searchable, and if you wanted to use this data in another custom SharePoint solution, you had to manually create data access code to read from the data source again.

The BDC, which is a part of Microsoft Office SharePoint Server 2007 (MOSS 2007) Enterprise Edition, offers a new way of being able to display your data within your SharePoint environment — without your developers having to write a single line of code. By creating XML application definition files that describe your data source, you can import these into the BDC, which opens up a wealth of opportunities for your organization to use business data within MOSS 2007. BDC supports simple access to any ADO.NET data source (such as SQL Server and Oracle). Even if your legacy data store is not supported by BDC out-of-the-box, you can still allow the BDC to access your data via Web services.

Creating application definition files is an important (and time-consuming) part of making use of the BDC. However, a great deal of information is available on the Web and in books that teach you how to create these files to describe your business data stores. The best place to start is the MOSS 2007 SDK BDC section, which you can find here:

```
http://msdn2.microsoft.com/en-us/library/ms544518.aspx
```

The SDK does a great job of explaining how to create application definition files, so I'm not going to cover the same ground in this chapter. I will, however, explain key parts of the files, and things to consider when you are creating them.

The examples provided in this chapter are mainly based off the AdventureWorks 2000 database that is commonly used by Microsoft examples. You can download the sample database from Microsoft at http://www.microsoft.com/downloads/details.aspx?FamilyID=487C9C23-2356-436E-94A8-2BFB66F0ABDC&displaylang=en.

An application definition file is required to be imported to your Shared Service Provider (SSP) so that you can use the AdventureWorks 2000 database via BDC. This application definition file is available from Microsoft as part of the SharePoint Server 2007 SDK: Software Development Kit at http://www.microsoft.com/downloads/details.aspx?familyid=6d94e307-67d9-41ac-b2d6-0074d6286fa9&displaylang=en.

This chapter begins with an examination of entities and how they relate to your application definition files. Once you have a grasp of what entities are, crafting application definition files is easy. The chapter then looks at how I have been using such BDC out-of-the-box features as Web Parts, search, and business data in lists and libraries. The later discussions in the chapter are dedicated to more advanced topics, such as creating Web services to supply your back-end data to the BDC, and the options available to you to complete the data cycle, or reading, displaying, and writing to your back-end store.

At the end of the chapter, I introduce an application that is available called BDC Meta Man. The aim of this software is to allow you to create application definition files in a visual way (such as dragging and dropping tables from SQL Server onto a design surface).

It's All About Entities

The application definition file describing your data source is something that may need to be written only once. The main concept behind the application definition files is an *entity*, which can be thought of as a real-world object. An entity could be a customer, a product, an order, or perhaps an address. An entity can have many different methods, each of which will have its own way of selecting data from the source. This can be a SQL SELECT statement, a stored procedure, or a Web service call. Within each method, you must describe any input parameters required by your SELECT method, and also a single output parameter. This output parameter must describe each entity field that is being returned.

Each method is also required to have MethodInstances assigned to it. This is simply a way of letting the BDC know which method is being used for which purpose. A method can be decorated with the following MethodInstances:

❑ Finder — An entity can have only one method decorated with the Finder MethodInstance. This method is used by the Business Data List Web Part.

❑ SpecificFinder — An entity can have only one method decorated with the SpecificFinder MethodInstance. This method is used if you want to search across your business data, and also within lists and document libraries that make use of business data. When an entity has a SpecificFinder method defined, something called a *profile page* is automatically created for each entity. This profile page is what will be crawled and linked to by search results. It is a page that can be used by BDC Web Parts to give more detailed information on a record when that particular record is clicked.

❑ IdEnumerator — Again, an entity can have only a single method with the IdEnumerator MethodInstance. This method is only used in regard to search. It simply has to return a list of the of the entity record IDs that you want to be crawled and returned by MOSS.

❑ GenericInvoker — An entity can have as many methods as it wants that are marked with the GenericInvoker MethodInstance.

Finally, if a method is not assigned any MethodInstances, you can presume that it is a method being used as part of an association relationship.

Let's walk through the various elements that make up an entity in your application definition file. Take a look at the following:

```
<Entity EstimatedInstanceCount="1000" Name="Products">
  <Properties>
          <Property Name="Title" Type="System.String">Name</Property>
  </Properties>
  <Identifiers>
          <Identifier Name="ProductID" TypeName="System.Int32" />
  </Identifiers>
  <Methods>

  </Methods>
<Entity>
```

The EstimateInstanceCount is the number of records you expect your methods within your entity to return, and the Name is a unique name that you want your Entity to have. Choosing a name that describes your entity well is important because your users will be using this name in their SharePoint environment to set up Web Parts and lists.

The only property set for this entity is the Title. This sets which column in the Business Data List Web Part will have the drop-down box to perform actions, as well as link to a profile page.

The final part of the main entity definition is the Identifiers. Here, you can set which values are primary keys that are being returned from the query. Setting the Identifiers is an important part when you want to be able to search against business data.

The next part of the entity is the methods. As already mentioned, an entity can have many methods, with each method being given a specific purpose by having a MethodInstance value (or values) set in it. Take a look at the following:

```
<Method Name="GetProducts">
    <Properties>
    <Property Name="RdbCommandText" Type="System.String">Select ProductID,
```

```
Name,ProductNumber,ListPrice From Product Where (ProductID&gt;=@ MinProductID) and
(ProductID&lt;=@MaxProductID)</Property>
    <Property Name="RdbCommandType" Type="System.Data.CommandType">Text</Property>
    </Properties>
<FilterDescriptors>
     <FilterDescriptor Type="Comparison" Name="ProductID" />
    </FilterDescriptors>
    <Parameters>

</Parameters>
<MethodInstances>

</MethodInstances>
</Method>
```

Each method used within the entity must have a unique name. The BDC does not require any specific naming convention, but remember it is a good idea to use a name that makes sense to you in case you have to go back and edit this file later. Here, the method is simply called GetProducts.

Within this method, you must set some properties. The first one is the RdbCommandText, which is the SQL SELECT statement that you want to execute against the back-end data source. The second property, RdbCommandType, describes the value of RdbCommandText. This will, in fact, be text, which is what the SQL SELECT statement is judged to be. If you called a predefined stored procedure from the data source, the RdbCommandType would have a value of StoredProcedure and the RdbCommandText value would be the name of the stored procedure you are calling.

Filter descriptors are used so that users can filter the results that are being returned to them. The most common place to see this in action is with the Business Data List Web Part where users can filter on the number of records they want to be returned. The actual filtering must be done by either the SQL SELECT statement you provide or the stored procedure. However, you must also mark in your application definition file the filters so that they are created in the Web Part user interface. In this simple FilterDescriptor, you filter on ProductID.

The next part of the entity is the parameters. Take a look at the following:

```
<Parameters>
    <Parameter Direction="In" Name="@MinProductID">
  <TypeDescriptor TypeName="System.Int32" IdentifierName="ProductID"
AssociatedFilter="ProductID" Name="ProductID">
     <DefaultValues>
        <DefaultValue MethodInstanceName="ProductFinder"
Type="System.Int32">0</DefaultValue>
        <DefaultValue MethodInstanceName="ProductSpecificFinder"
Type="System.Int32">0</DefaultValue>
  </DefaultValues>
    </TypeDescriptor>
    </Parameter>
    <Parameter Direction="In" Name="@MaxProductID">
  <TypeDescriptor TypeName="System.Int32" IdentifierName="ProductID"
AssociatedFilter="ProductID" Name="ProductID">
  <DefaultValues>
    <DefaultValue MethodInstanceName="dbo.ProductFinder"
Type="System.Int32">9999999</DefaultValue>
```

```
        <DefaultValue MethodInstanceName="dbo.ProductSpecificFinder"
Type="System.Int32">9999999</DefaultValue>
    </DefaultValues>
    </TypeDescriptor>
        </Parameter>



<!-- Return Parameters Coming -->



</Parameters>
```

There are two distinct sets of parameters to look at: *input parameters* and *return parameters*. The first section in the preceding code snippet is the input parameters. You can see that for each of the parameters described in the WHERE clause of the SELECT statement, you must create an input parameter in the parameters collection. If you want to pass in parameters as well, you may also want to execute the SQL statement with default values. This is why each input parameter has default values set for each MethodInstance that this method will be described as.

With the @MinProductID having a default value of 0 and @MaxProductID being 9999999, if no parameters are passed in the SQL SELECT statement, the code will behave as a SELECT without any parameters because it will return all product records.

Now, consider the following:

```
<Parameter Direction="Return" Name="Product">
      <TypeDescriptor TypeName="System.Data.IDataReader, System.Data,
Version=2.0.3600.0, Culture=neutral, PublicKeyToken=b77a5c561934e089"
Name="ProductDataReader" IsCollection="true">
      <TypeDescriptors>
    <TypeDescriptor TypeName="System.Data.IDataRecord, System.Data,
Version=2.0.3600.0, Culture=neutral, PublicKeyToken=b77a5c561934e089"
Name="ProductDataRecord">
        <TypeDescriptors>
          <TypeDescriptor TypeName="System.Int32" IdentifierName="ProductID"
Name="ProductID" />
          <TypeDescriptor TypeName="System.String" Name="Name" />
          <TypeDescriptor TypeName="System.String" Name="ProductNumber" />
          <TypeDescriptor TypeName="System.Decimal" Name="ListPrice" />
        </TypeDescriptors>
        </TypeDescriptor>
    </TypeDescriptors>
    </TypeDescriptor>
</Parameter>
```

The XML here describes what is being returned by the SQL SELECT statement, and is, therefore, marked as a RETURN parameter. A lot of the attributes of the Type Descriptors described earlier (such as IDataReader) are describing .NET classes that will be used by the BDC. So, ensure that your return parameter has this detailed, but understanding what it means is not necessary. The only thing that is important is to make sure the DataReader and DataRecord Type Descriptors have nice unique names. In this example, the DataReader and DataRecord names are ProductDataReader and ProductDataRecord, respectively.

The rest of the Type Descriptors in the return parameter are a collection of elements describing what is actually returned in each `ProductDataRecord` (that is, the fields that were chosen to be returned in the `SELECT` statement). Each field must be described individually by detailing the type of the field and the field name.

The final parts of the entity are the `MethodInstances` that describe what this method can be used for:

```
<MethodInstances>
    <MethodInstance Name="ProductFinder" Type="Finder"
ReturnParameterName="Product" ReturnTypeDescriptorName="ProductDataReader"
ReturnTypeDescriptorLevel="0" />
    <MethodInstance Name="ProductSpecificFinder" Type="SpecificFinder"
ReturnParameterName="Product" ReturnTypeDescriptorName="ProductDataReader"
ReturnTypeDescriptorLevel="0" />
</MethodInstances>
```

As you can see, this entity has been described so that is can be used as both a `Finder` and `SpecificFinder` method. It can be used as both of these methods because of the `Parameter` that is being used and the `WHERE` clause. If no parameter is passed in, the default values of the `IN` parameters are used, and the method executes as a `Finder` method (that is, returning all results from a table). If a `ProductID` is passed in as a parameter, the same value is used for both the `@MinProductID` and `@MaxProductID` and, therefore, only returns a single record.

Describing the Application Definition File for AdventureWorks 2000

Let's take a look at the application definition file for `AdventureWorks 2000` (again, which you can download from the Wrox site).

The first part of the application definition file shown in Figure 10-1 is the `LobSystemInstance`, which simply describes the type of back-end data system that the BDC will be connecting to, along with various parameters that are used to connect to that data source.

```
- <LobSystemInstances >
  - <LobSystemInstance Name="AdventureWorksSampleInstance ">
    - <Properties>
        <Property Name="AuthenticationMode " Type ="System.String ">PassThrough</Property >
        <Property Name="DatabaseAccessProvider " Type ="System.String ">SqlServer </Property >
        <Property Name="RdbConnection Data Source " Type ="System.String ">EnterYourAdventureWorks2000ServerNameHere </Property >
        <Property Name="RdbConnection Initial Catalog " Type ="System.String ">AdventureWorks2000 </Property >
        <Property Name="RdbConnection Integrated Security " Type ="System.String ">SSPI</Property >
        <Property Name="RdbConnection Pooling " Type ="System.String ">false</Property >
      </Properties>
    </LobSystemInstance >
  </LobSystemInstances >
```

Figure 10-1: `LobSystemInstance` in the application definition file

The first entity described within the `Entities` element is the `Product` entity, as shown in Figure 10-2. This entity has two methods, `GetProducts` and `ProductIdEnumerator`. Because of the parameters that are passed into `GetProducts`, this method can be used as a `Finder` and a `SpecificFinder` type method. This is why, toward the end of the method within the `MethodInstances` tags, you'll see entries for both of these types. So, `MethodInstances` are a great way of being able to describe how a method can be utilized for multiple uses.

```
- <Entity EstimatedInstanceCount="10000" Name="Product">
    <!-- EstimatedInstanceCount is an optional attribute -->
  + <Properties>
  + <Identifiers>
  - <Methods>
    + <Method Name="GetProducts">
    + <Method Name="ProductIDEnumerator">
    </Methods>
    <!-- Enter your Action XML here -->
  + <Actions>
  </Entity>
```

Figure 10-2: `Product` **entity in the application definition file**

The `IdEnumerator` method of the `Product` entity simply returns a list of `ProductIds` in the SQL `SELECT` statement.

The second entity in the example application definition file is for `SalesOrder`, as shown in Figure 10-3. This entity has a single method that, again, acts as a `Finder` and `SpecificFinder` method.

```
- <Entity EstimatedInstanceCount="10000" Name="SalesOrder">
  + <LocalizedDisplayNames>
  + <Identifiers>
  - <Methods>
    + <Method Name="GetSalesOrders">
    </Methods>
  </Entity>
```

Figure 10-3: `SalesOrder` **in the application definition file**

The third and final entity described is `Customer`, as shown in Figure 10-4. This has two methods in it. The first is the same as `Product` and `SalesOrder`, a method acting as both a `Finder` and `SpecificFinder`. The second method, called `GetSalesOrdersForCustomer`, does not have any `MethodInstances` assigned to it. This must mean that this method is used for an association that has been created between two entities, which from the name of the method, appears to be between `SalesOrders` and `Customers`.

```
- <Entity EstimatedInstanceCount="10000" Name="Customer">
  + <Properties>
  + <Identifiers>
  - <Methods>
    + <Method Name="GetCustomers">
    + <Method Name="GetSalesOrdersForCustomer">
    </Methods>
  + <Actions>
  </Entity>
```

Figure 10-4: `Customer` **entity in the application definition file**

Sure enough, if you look at the end of the application definition file, after all the entities have been described, you can see an association described, as shown in Figure 10-5. An association can be thought of as a parent-child relationship. So, for this association, you would be able to retrieve all `SalesOrders` for a specific `Customer`.

```
- <Associations>
  - <Association AssociationMethodEntityName="Customer" AssociationMethodName="GetSalesOrdersForCustomer"
    AssociationMethodReturnParameterName="SalesOrders" Name="CustomerToSalesOrder" IsCached="true">
    <SourceEntity Name="Customer" />
    <DestinationEntity Name="SalesOrder" />
  </Association>
</Associations>
```

Figure 10-5: Associations in the application definition file

Now that you have seen in the application definition file what is included in the AdventureWorks 2000 database, let's see how to use that back-end data once it has been imported into an SSP.

Using Out-of-the-Box Business Data

Figure 10-6 shows how the BDC is an abstraction layer above your back-end data source. The application definition files describe to the BDC how to access your data source, and what queries should be executed to return data. A common misconception with the BDC is that once you import an application definition file, the data is actually transferred into MOSS 2007 as well. This would, of course, lead to a huge duplication of data because it would then reside in MOSS and in your back-end system. When an application definition file is imported to the SSP, it is broken down and parsed to ensure that it is syntactically correct, and then the details it contains (such as property values, SQL SELECT statement, and so on) are placed into the Metadata Database.

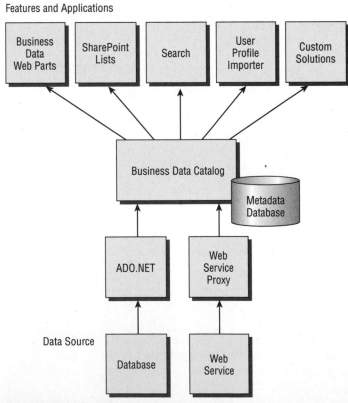

Figure 10-6: Out-of-the-box uses for the BDC

When a user wants to view BDC data in MOSS 2007, MOSS will access the Metadata Database to retrieve the correct SELECT statement and any other necessary properties. It executes this statement against the back-end datastore. The data being displayed in the BDC Web Parts, for example, is therefore live data from the back-end system.

Figure 10-6 also shows how any ADO.NET-compliant data source can be easily integrated directly into the BDC. This includes SQL Server, Oracle, plus any ODBC-compliant system. If you want to make use of data via the BDC that is from a legacy system, or maybe a remote data store, it is also possible to import application definition files that describe Web services. The Web services will then be called by the BDC when data is being retrieved, with the Web service executing queries against the database.

Business Data Web Parts

The way most people will begin displaying their data in MOSS 2007 via the BDC will be with the out-of-the-box Web Parts. These can be found in the top category of the Web Part gallery, as shown in Figure 10-7. The box highlights the Web Parts that you can make use of with the BDC.

Once you add a BDC Web Part to your page, you must open the Web Part toolbar to select which entity defined in your application definition file you should bind to. The BDC Web Parts at their simplest level are Data View Web Parts. This means their look and feel can be easily customized with the use of an Extensible Stylesheet Language Transformation (XSLT).

Figure 10-7: Out-of-the-box Web Parts

Most people will get started with the Business Data List Web Part. To be able to use your entity with this Web Part, the entity must have a `Finder` method defined. If your `Finder` method has any parameters defined, you can enter values to filter the returned results, as well as select which columns you want displayed. If you want to seriously get into modifying the look and feel of this Web Part, you can apply a custom XSLT style sheet to change the way it looks.

As previously mentioned, it is possible in your application definition file to define associations between entities. This allows you to describe parent-child type relationships such as `Customer-SalesOrders`. This relationship just described is the one that has been included in the `AdventureWorks 2000` sample application definition file. By making use of the Business Data List Web Part and the Business Data Related List Web Part, you can select a parent record in the data list, and all the related records be displayed in the related Web Part.

If your application definition file has a `SpecificFinder` method defined for an entity, the entity will automatically get a profile page created for it that makes use of the Business Data Item, the Business Data Actions, and the Business Data Item Builder Web Parts. The Item Builder Web Part is displayed in page design mode, but is not visible to users because it provides a non-visible action. The ID of the entity that is to be displayed in the profile page is passed via a query string parameter in the URL, as shown here:

```
http://servername/ ssp/admin/Content/Product.aspx?ProductID=1
```

The Item Builder grabs the query string parameter and is able to supply it to other BDC Web Parts by connecting them together. From the Web Part options menu, you can choose where to send the value the Item Builder Web Part obtains (Figure 10-8).

Figure 10-8: Choosing where to send the value that the Item Builder Web Part obtains

Once the Business Data Item Web Part gets the ID of the entity record to display, it simply shows the data to the user. The Actions Web Part is very similar in the fact that it needs to get the ID of the entity being displayed on the profile page from the Item Builder Web Part. Once it has this, it displays the actions that are available to perform on that entity.

Because the BDC is part of the Shared Services architecture, this profile page by default is a page from the shared service that the BDC application has been created in. Therefore, the profile Web page is part of a separate Web application to your SharePoint portal, and, thus, a different URL.

If you are using MOSS 2007 to host your public Internet presence site, and you are using the BDC to display information to your site visitors, you will probably not want a profile page with a different URL to be used. The following simple steps show you how to create a profile page for your entities within your main site. Before doing this, remember to ensure that your entity has a `SpecificFinder` method defined for it. For this example, I will use the `Product` entity from the `AdventureWorks 2000` sample.

1. Create a new page within your MOSS public-facing Web site that has at least one Web Part zone defined. (It doesn't necessarily need to be a public-facing Web site. For this example, you can create the page in any portal you want the scenario to work.) Give the page a URL of `product.aspx`.

2. Edit your new Web page and add the following three Web Parts:
    - ❏ Business Data Item Builder
    - ❏ Business Data Item
    - ❏ Business Data Actions

3. Modify the properties of the Data Item and Data Actions Web Parts. From the Business Data Type Picker, select `Product` to be the type of entity you will use for these Web Parts.

4. Once you have selected the type of entity you want to display, connect the Data Item and Data Actions Web Parts to "Get Item" from the Item Builder.

5. Upon exiting the edit mode of the page, you will get an error in the Data Item Web Part that says `Item not found in AdventureWorks 2000`. This is because the URL in the browser does not have a query string parameter attached to it. Enter a URL similar to the following:

    `../product.aspx?productId=1`

Now, you should have the `product.aspx` page displaying the single entity correctly, along with the relevant actions for that entity.

There's a slight problem that you must fix. The entity `Product` still thinks that its profile page is the Web page that resides within the Shared Services Web application. This is because it is using the link to the profile page that was automatically generated when you imported the application definition file. This means that if you click the View Profile Action, or you click a record in the Business Data List Web Part, that is where you will be redirected. Also, if the entity is crawlable, and is being returned within search results, the page users will be directed to when clicking a search result link will again be the Shared Service profile page.

This is something that must be changed in the Shared Services Administration page (where you upload your BDC application definition files):

1. On your `product.aspx` page that you created earlier, select and copy the URL that you are currently pointing at with a correct query string parameter.

2. In a separate browser, navigate to the Shared Service Administration page into which you imported your application definition file. Within the BDC menus, choose View Applications.

3. Select the `AdventureWorks 2000` application, and then the `Products` entity.

4. On the View Entity page, you should see a section for actions. The action you are interested in is the View Profile one. Click that.

5. In the URL section, the value entered in the textbox is the URL that MOSS will use as the profile page. Here you should paste in the URL you copied from your browser in Step 1. One very important change you must make to that link is to the value of the query string parameter. That is, it

must be changed from `product.aspx?productId=1` to `product.aspx?productId={0}`. When MOSS 2007 is piecing together the URL to be used in Web pages, it will then enter the value of Parameter Property selected in the URL Parameters Section.

6. Click OK at the bottom of the page to save the changes you have made to that entity.

Now, if you go to a page with a Business Data List displaying records from the `Product` entity, and click a link to view the entity's profile, you will be taken to the new page, rather than the one belonging to the SSP Web application.

> *An important point to remember for search results is that the new profile page will not be picked up until a full crawl is completed by MOSS 2007 across the BDC data. I provide more detail on searching business data later in this chapter.*

Business Data in Lists and Libraries

Once the application definition file is imported into the BDC, another way in which you can make use of the data stored in a back-end system is through the `Business Data` column type. This is a column type that can be added to any MOSS 2007 list or document library.

In order to illustrate this, let's say that you have imported the `AdventureWorks 2000` application definition file. The Marketing department at your company is working on new documents and ideas to use with each product in the `AdventureWorks` back-end. Therefore, it would be a great idea to be able to associate metadata to relate each Marketing document produced to the actual product stored in `AdventureWorks 2000`.

This could be accomplished by creating a custom list in SharePoint and then adding a linked column in your document library. However, that means duplicating all the product data from `AdventureWorks` into the new list, and also manually updating it if any changes in the back-end system are made. By using the `Business Data` column, you are able to reuse the data in the back-end system in your lists and document libraries. Let's walk through an example of this:

1. Create a new document library where you can put the `AdventureWorks` Marketing documents.

2. Within the document library, click Settings ⇨ Create Column.

3. Give the new column a name such as `Products`, and select the column type to be of `Business Data`.

4. Check the radio box so that this column is a required field. This means that users won't be able to save a Marketing document to this library unless they have selected a product to reference it against.

5. For the type, click the Browse icon and, from the Business Data Type Picker that opens, select the `Products` entity.

6. In the "Display this field of the selected type" field, select a value of ID from the drop-down box. The `Business Data` column will use the `SpecificFinder` method of the entity to bring back information, so for this example, you will only be able to select products by their IDs.

7. Once you have a correct ID, however, you can bring back other columns of data from the back-end `AdventureWorks` system. Select these by clicking the checkboxes in the "addition fields" section. For this demo, select List Price, Name, and Product Number.

8. Click OK to add this new column to the library.

You should now be able to see in your document library the newly added document columns, as shown in Figure 10-9.

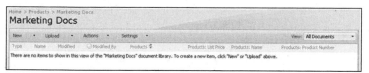

Figure 10-9: Seeing any newly added document columns

When you click New, Microsoft Word 2007 should open up and, below the ribbon, you should see the document information panel (DIP) displayed. It is worth noting that the document information panel will only show if the InfoPath 2007 client is installed on the machine. InfoPath 2007 can be purchased as a separate license, or comes with the Office Pro Plus or Office Ultimate licenses. Because you selected the new `Business Data` column as a required field, the DIP should open automatically. However, if you do not see it, from the new Office button in the top-left of Word, select Prepare ➪ Properties.

In the Products textbox in the DIP, enter an ID of a product in the `AdventureWorks 2000` database. A good example would be `ID = 8`. Click the Check Item button to the right of this textbox. This ID is now validated against the back-end data source, and if it matches up correctly, the List Price, Name, and Products Number will all be displayed to you within the DIP, as shown in Figure 10-10.

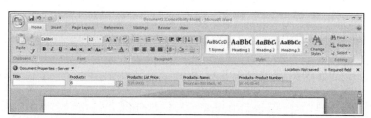

Figure 10-10: List Price, Product Name, and Product Number displayed within the DIP

Enter some great marketing text into the body of the Word document, save it, and exit Word. Now, back in the Marketing document library, you can see the document you created with the product data added to the `Business Data` columns. Just to the left of the "Products: List Price," there is a little icon that looks like a menu item. If you click the drop-down icon that appears while you hover over the menu item, you'll see menu items to "Search on MSN" and "View Profile," which should be recognizable as the actions that you can use in your Business Data List Web Parts.

When business data is stored against documents in a document library, the data is not a direct link to the information from the back-end system. This means that if the back-end system updates product information, the product metadata stored for each document may become out of date. Updating the data stored against each document must be done manually by clicking the Refresh icon that is to the left of the "Products: List Price" column name. You will get a warning explaining that updating this with the latest data may take a long time, which, of course, depends on how many documents you have in the document library. Once you have clicked OK, the Business Data columns will be refreshed with current data from the back-end system with an "Update Successful" screen presented to you when this has been completed.

Now that your documents have business data associated with them, you can make use of this metadata as you would any other metadata added to a document library with functionality such as custom views and workflow.

Custom Views

Using the Business Data you have stored against each document, you can create custom views to filter and sort the library items to complete any daily tasks in an easier way, rather than be presented with a list of hundreds of items. To create a custom view based on Business Data, complete the following steps:

1. In the document library, click Settings ➪ Create View.

2. On the Create View page, click Standard View.

3. Give the view a descriptive name such as **Products above $100**.

4. Navigate down to the Filter section, and select the radio button to "Show items only when the following is true," as shown in Figure 10-11.

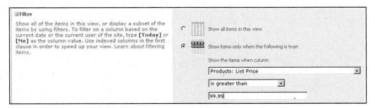

Figure 10-11: Configuring values in the Filter section

5. Select the column "Products: List Price" from the first drop-down list.

6. Select "is greater than" in the middle drop-down list.

7. Enter a value of **99.99** in the third textbox.

Upon clicking OK to create the new view, you'll be taken back to the document library with the new view implemented and selected. You can switch between views by using the drop-down toward the top-right of the document library that is displaying the name of the currently selected view.

Workflow

With SharePoint Designer (SPD), you are able to create sequential workflows attached to lists and libraries that can be designed to act differently, based on what metadata is stored for each list or document item. To illustrate this example, let's imagine that the marketing documents need actions to be completed on them when they are first created. Who is required to complete this action depends on the List Price of the product that the marketing document is related to.

Upon opening SPD and navigating to the site where you created the Marketing document library, you can create a new workflow from the main SPD by following these steps:

1. Select File ⇨ New ⇨ Workflow. You are presented with the first screen of the workflow wizard, as shown in Figure 10-12. You are required to give the workflow a unique name, and set which document library you want it to be assigned to. Ensure that the document library chosen is the one you created when you created a `Business Data` column. Choose from the various options for when you would like the workflow to start. Click the Next button to move to the next screen of the wizard.

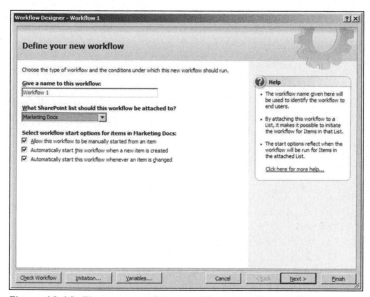

Figure 10-12: First screen of the workflow wizard

2. The next step in the wizard is where things get interesting. This is where you can set various conditions, and what should happen upon a condition evaluating to be `true`. Click the Conditions button and select "Compare *Marketing Docs* field" where *Marketing Docs* is the name of your document library.

3. From the line entered into the condition, click the field link. This brings back all the columns of data from your document library. Scrolling down, you will be able to find the column "Products: List Price." Select this one.

4. Click the equals link and select "is greater than."

5. Click "value" and enter **99.99**. So, from this condition that you have set, when a workflow is started on a document, if the product selected has a list price of more than $99.99, the following action that you are about to set will occur. This action will be a simple To-Do action.

6. Click the Actions button and select "Assign a To-do Item" from the drop-down list of actions.

7. Click the "a to-do item" link and step through the simple wizard to create a To-Do item.

8. Click the "these users" link and select a user from your list of possible people to assign a task to. I have chosen a user called Steve (Figure 10-13).

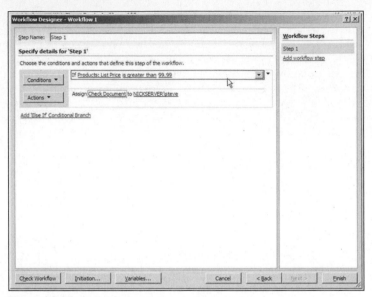

Figure 10-13: Assigning a user

That is all that is needed within this workflow to demonstrate how the `Business Data` column can be utilized. To check that the workflow is correctly configured, you can click the "Check Workflow" button. As long as nothing is reported as being wrong with the workflow, deploy it to your site and document library by clicking the Finish button.

That's a quick example of how you can make use of the `Business Data` with the workflow designer in SPD. Of course, you can test this with your document library by creating a new document and picking a product that has a list price of more $99.99. If you set the workflow to start whenever a new item is created, upon saving the new document, you should be able to go to the task list of your site and see Steve with a To-Do item assigned to him.

Searching Business Data

Being able to display data from your back-end data system through the MOSS 2007 user interface is just the first part of integrating Business Data. MOSS 2007 also allows you to search on the data returned by the BDC. This extends the reach of a search to all the data in your enterprise.

Thankfully, this is now possible. All that is required is ensuring that your entity implements the following two specific method types when creating the application definition file:

❑   IdEnumerator — The `IdEnumerator` is a method that is required solely for the use of search. All it should return is a list of IDs that should be indexed by SharePoint search.

❑   SpecificFinder — Each ID that is returned by the `IdEnumerator` method is then used as a parameter for the `SpecificFinder` method. This is how the search indexer is able to retrieve all the fields of an entity that can be searched upon. If you want a field to be searchable, make sure it is returned as a type `string`.

You can check whether your entity implements these methods even if you have already imported the application definition file. You do this by going to the Shared Service Administration page, viewing the particular application, and then the entity. The third property down in the View Entity page will mark whether the entity is available to be crawled, as shown in Figure 10-14.

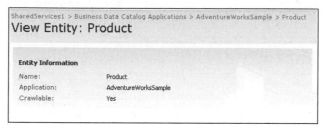

Figure 10-14: View Entity page

To populate the search index with the BDC data, you are required to set this BDC application as a content source by following these steps:

1. At your Shared Services Administration Home page, click Search Settings.

2. Click "Content sources and crawl schedules" to create a new content source.

3. From the Manage Content Sources screen shown in Figure 10-15, click to add a New Content Source.

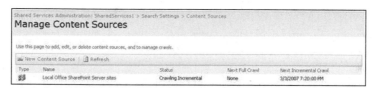

Figure 10-15: Manage Content Sources page

4. Enter a descriptive name for your new content source.

5. Choose the content source to be of `Business Data` type.

6. Optionally, choose which particular `Business Data` applications to crawl, and also set up crawl rules for when the content should be re-indexed.

7. Click the checkbox that indicates to start a full crawl upon clicking OK.

8. Click OK.

This will take some time because MOSS is now indexing all your Business Data. Once the content source has finished crawling, you can head back to your MOSS site and attempt to search for something. If you have used the `AdventureWorks 2000` sample, you can try searching for the term "bike." You should get a number of results returned, as shown in Figure 10-16.

If you followed the steps previously in this chapter describing how to change the location of your entity profile page, clicking a link should take you to your new page.

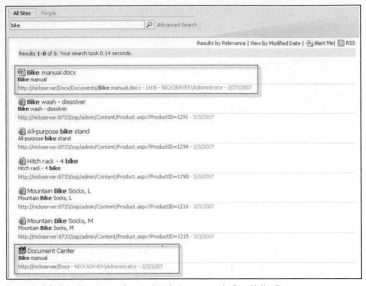

Figure 10-16: Returned results for a search for "bike"

If you look at Figure 10-16, however, you'll also see returned in my search results are some documents, a site, and some tasks that I've created with the word "bike" located somewhere in them. How do you only get products returned in the search results?

To accomplish this, you must map a metadata property to enable you to perform more advanced search queries. This operation is again performed in the Shared Service Administration site.

1. Select Search Settings from the Shared Service Administration page.

2. Click the link to "Metadata property mappings." On this page, you can see all the properties that have already been mapped to default SharePoint fields filled out from lists and document libraries.

3. Click New Managed Property.

4. Enter a property name. Choose this carefully, because, as you'll soon see, this value is what you'll be prefixing your search terms with.

5. Move down and click the Add Mapping button.

6. A new form opens up entitled "Crawled property selection." To reduce the number of properties you can choose from (believe me there's a lot!), select Business Data from the category drop-down list and click the Find button.

7. Select which field you would like to have mapped. If you are working with the AdventureWorks 2000 sample, the property to select is AdventureWorksSampleInstance.Product.Name(Text). Click OK once you have made your choice.

8. Back in the New Managed Property screen, click OK.

And that's it! Your property is now mapped. However, you won't actually be able search any differently until the Business Data content source is re-indexed. To do this, go back to the search settings page, click to view your content sources, and from the list of content sources, click the drop-down list on your Business Data source to begin a full crawl.

Once a full crawl has finished on your content source, head back to MOSS. Now you can perform some more advanced searching by making use of the mapped property. If you want to search for products with the word "bike" in the title, and only get information from the back-end data source, you would simply search for "product:bike," as shown in Figure 10-17.

Figure 10-17: Searching for "product:bike"

User Profile Importer

Very often, personnel data for employees (such as mobile phone numbers) within your company may be held in a separate system or database. Organizations may now want to make use of this data because it can be viewed and accessed through users' My Sites. If this information is stored in Active Directory, it can be imported into SharePoint directly from there. However, if it is stored in a different data source, the Human Resources department will not want to have to re-key this data back into Active Directory for it to appear in SharePoint.

Thankfully, the profile importer can make use of data imported via the BDC and use this data, together with Active Directory, to populate a user's My Site.

Custom Solutions

Before MOSS 2007 and the BDC, if you wanted to write a Web Part that queried a different line of business systems (such as Oracle and SQL Server), you needed to know how to pull data back from both separately. This meant knowing both connection strings, differences in SQL syntax between the systems, and so on. Now, with the BDC, you can integrate both systems together using the BDC object model. Rather than writing queries directly against SQL Server or Oracle, you can use the entities and methods defined in your application definition file. Because the BDC knows how to get data back from these different systems, the only object model a Web Part developer needs to be aware of is the BDC one.

A good example of where this could be used is a warehouse system that uses SQL Server, and a sales system that uses Oracle. A Combo Box could be populated with all the products from the warehouse system, and, when a product is selected, the necessary sales could be bought back from Oracle. The developer could use the same code to call both systems. The BDC object model abstracts the back-end system so much that the developer may not even be aware of what type of database he or she is pulling data from.

Full information on using the BDC object model to return data using C# or VB.NET is available in the MOSS SDK.

Application Definition File Hints and Tips

During the course of creating a number of MOSS 2007 implementations, I have picked up a number of hints and tips along the way that I will share with you now.

❑   It's possible to only have one of each of the following methods implemented in each entity:

    ❑   `Finder`

    ❑   `SpecificFinder`

    ❑   `IdEnumerator`

❑   With your `SpecificFinder` method, you should return all the columns that you are ever going to want to search across. If you are looking at implementing methods that return different columns, these will have to be in a method of type `GenericInvoker`.

❑   There are various columns that will cause the search to fail completely if they are returned in your `SpecificFinder` method. From my experience so far, these are SQL fields that store any data in a binary format such as `VarBinary`.

❑   Ensure that your Default content access account has access to your back-end data source.

❑   If you are writing your application definition files by hand, SPD is a great tool to use. If you have XML that is not formatted in a very readable layout, try selecting it all in SPD, right-clicking it, and choosing Reformat XML from the context menu.

❑   If you have a site that is allowing anonymous access, and you are using pass-through authentication in your application definition file, ensure that the account the IIS application pool is running under has read access to your back-end data source. This may mean running the application pool with a domain account if your SQL Server is not on the same machine that MOSS is running on.

❑   The log files are your friend. If you are having problems, be sure to check them out. If you used the default installation path, they can be found at the following:

```
C:\Program Files\Common Files\Microsoft Shared\Web Server Extensions\12\Log
```

❑   They seem to be cached slightly, so you sometimes have to wait a minute for the log information to appear for your particular error. For BDC errors, they are great because you get details of the SQL string that was attempting to be executed, parameters passed in, and, quite often, a lengthy ADO.NET error message that often points you in the right direction.

❑   If you are creating associations and the necessary method to describe an association query, ensure that this method is in the entity that is acting as the parent. Also, ensure that this entity comes after the child entity in the application definition file. If you don't stick to these two guidelines, you'll get an error when trying to import your application definition file.

Creating Web Services to Use with the BDC

The BDC can connect to standard databases such as SQL Server and Oracle. If you want to connect to a legacy back-end system that cannot come straight through an ADO.NET layer, or your data is perhaps in a remote location, the BDC could still make use of this data via Web services.

Writing application definition files for SQL Server is relatively easy, once you get your head around the different parts that make up the XML structure. The difference with the Web service route is that you may well be writing the application definition file and the Web services.

What you will quite often want to do is create Web methods that behave in similar ways that application definition methods require. For example, for an entity called `Customer`, you may have to create three separate methods:

❑ *A Web method that acts like a `Finder` method* — You have no parameters necessarily to pass in, and you have simply a list of `Customer` objects returned.

❑ *A Web method that acts as an `IdEnumerator`* — Remember, all that is required by an `IdEnumerator` is a list of IDs that you want the search service to index.

❑ *A Web method that acts as a `SpecificFinder`* — A parameter is required for this Web service because the `SpecificFinder` method should only return a single instance of an entity. Because it should only return one instance, this parameter is very usually the ID of the entity.

The BDC can only integrate with first-generation Web services, so currently this means Windows Communication Foundation (WCF) will not be compatible.

BDC Meta Man

At one of the first conferences where Microsoft was able to demonstrate a lot of MOSS 2007 functionality, I was waiting with baited breath for them to announce a tool to help users create application definition files without having to manually type them into Notepad. To many people's surprise, Microsoft announced that it wouldn't be releasing such a tool, but that it would be a good opportunity for a community or third-party tool.

The aim of the BDC Meta Man tool (Figure 10-18) is to make it possible to create application definition files by using your database's table structure. By navigating through the columns of a table you want to create as a BDC entity, and determining which column is a primary key, you are able to generate all the XML you'll need to be displaying that back-end data in MOSS 2007. Once you have a couple of entities created, you can also create associations between them by picking which primary key you want linked with which foreign key in the child entity. A nice relationship line is created between entities, which follows them around as you drag and drop the entities on your design surface.

The tool also has support for creating application definition files for Oracle databases as well as Web services.

BDC Meta Man is available from `www.bdcmetaman.com`.

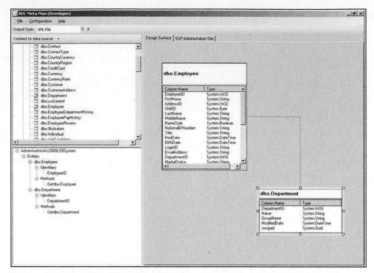

Figure 10-18: BDC Meta Man tool

Completing the Data Life Cycle

You may have noticed that I have only mentioned reading data from the back-end data source so that it can be displayed in MOSS 2007. What about when users want to edit their data or add new records?

The BDC has been designed only for the purpose of reading data from your back-end systems. Some of you may have thought that because you use SQL SELECT strings to get data from a data source, you could easily add UPDATE and INSERT SQL statements, and pass in the necessary parameters for these statements to execute. Though this is possible, it is not the recommended approach, because sending data through the BDC this way to be inserted or updated may be bypassing important business logic and rules that may exist in the current system used for these tasks.

Following are a couple of options available to you to allow users to create and edit data in a back-end system that links to the data being displayed in MOSS:

❑   If your back-end system has information added and edited by a Web site, it could be possible to add a custom action for an entity so that the actions drop-down provides users with the option to edit that particular row of data. Upon selecting the action, the URL will link to the administration Web site of the back-end system, and possibly be able to pass the primary key ID of the entity selected as a query string parameter. This way, the back-end system knows exactly which record of data to retrieve to edit.

❑   You could create an InfoPath 2007 form that is browser-enabled to edit and add data to the back-end data source. Again, to use this form, a custom action could be created for an entity with the ID value being passed to the InfoPath form as a query string parameter, so the form is aware of which record to edit. By using InfoPath, business logic and validation can be re-created on the client side, and the InfoPath form can be displayed through MOSS 2007 so that the user doesn't have to leave the SharePoint environment to be able to work with data through the various stages of its life.

Summary

The BDC is a new part of MOSS 2007 that enables you to integrate back-end systems of data with SharePoint with a no-code solution by creating application definition files. Once you've created the application definition files and imported them into your SSP, you can make use of the out-of-the-box Web Parts, crawl and search business data, include business data fields in document libraries, and use the data for user profiles, as well as create custom Web Parts and solutions.

Out-of-the-box BDC can import data from systems such as SQL Server and Oracle. But, if you have an old legacy system, or you have data in a system that is in a remote location but available over the Internet, you can create your own Web service interfaces that can make the information available to become part of the BDC.

The MOSS 2007 SDK and other sources go into the specifics of creating application definition files. Throughout this chapter, I've passed on some of the things I've learned about the BDC from building MOSS 2007 solutions and the BDC Meta Man tool.

11

Using Excel Services

by Luis Du Solier Grinda

Since SharePoint 2003, significant enhancements have been made related to the interaction with Microsoft Office Suite applications. You can now better share information generated with Office applications using a SharePoint collaboration Web site. The files stored in a SharePoint document library can be edited and shared with the rest of your coworkers using the Office family (for example, a Word client). This not only allows you to work with documents, but also to use your SharePoint team Web sites for sharing team calendars, creating and assigning tasks to other team workers, chatting with team workers, creating surveys, creating discussion forums, and keeping your team informed about any important activities.

These capabilities provide you with great functionality and interaction when using Word, Excel, PowerPoint, or Access. And, of course, when using a browser, team members can interact with their information and collaborate with other people on the same (or other) projects. The idea is to do more (or even have the capability to do much more) with the same applications and knowledge you and your people already have, with the purpose of being more productive.

Microsoft has introduced significant enhancements with Office 2007 and Microsoft Office SharePoint Server 2007 (MOSS 2007). This chapter focuses on Excel Services, which is included with MOSS 2007 as the server-side component of the client-server relationship. With Excel Services, you can now share your workbooks, and let your team interact online with the data worksheets using a Web browser and Excel Services.

Let's begin this chapter by taking a look at some great enhancements Microsoft has made with Office Excel 2007, which represents the client-side component of Microsoft Office.

Excel 2007 Improvements and Features

What has changed since Excel 2003? Table 11-1 shows the improvements between Excel 2003 and Excel 2007.

Table 11-1: Excel 2003 versus Excel 2007

Feature	Excel 2003	Excel 2007
Total number of available columns	256	16,000
Total number of available rows	64,000	1 million
Total amount of memory that Excel can use	1GB	Maximum allowed by Windows
Number of unique colors allowed a single workbook	56 (indexed color)	4.3 billion (32-bit color)
Number of conditional format conditions on a cell	3 conditions	Limited by available memory
Number of levels of sorting on a range or table	3	64
Number of items shown in the Auto-Filter drop-down menu	1,000	10,000
The total number of characters that can display in a cell	1,000 (when the text is formatted)	32,000, or as many as will fit in the cell (regardless of formatting)
The number of characters per cell that Excel can print	1,000	32,000
The total number of unique cell styles in a workbook (combinations of all cell formatting)	4,000	64,000
The maximum length of formulas	1,000 characters	8,000 characters
The number of levels of nesting that Excel allows in formulas	7	64
Maximum number of arguments to a function	30	255
Maximum number of items found by the "Find All" feature	65,472	About 2 billion
Number of rows allowed in a PivotTable	64,000	1 million
Number of columns allowed in a PivotTable	255	16,000

Continued

Table 11-1: Excel 2003 versus Excel 2007

Feature	Excel 2003	Excel 2007
Maximum number of unique items within a single PivotTable field	32,000	1 million
Length of the Multidimensional Expressions (MDX) name for a PivotTable item (also the string length for a relational PivotTable)	255 characters	32,000 characters
The length at which labels of fields are truncated when added to a PivotTable (also includes caption length limitations)	255 characters	32,000 characters
The number of fields (as seen in the field list) that a single PivotTable can have	255	16,000
The number of cells that may depend on a single area before Excel must do full calculations instead of partial calculations (because it can no longer track the dependencies required to do partial calculations)	8,000	Limited by available memory
The number of different areas in a sheet that may have dependencies before Excel must do full calculations instead of partial calculations (because it can no longer track the dependencies required to do partial calculations)	64,000	Limited by available memory
The number of array formulas in a workbook that can refer to another (given) workbook	65,000	Limited by available memory
The number of categories that custom functions can be bucketed into	32	255
The number of characters that may be updated in a non-resident, external workbook reference	255	32,000
Number of rows of a column or columns that can be referred to in an array formula	65,335	Limitation removed (full-column references allowed)
The number of characters that can be stored and displayed in a cell formatted as Text	255	32,000

You can find some interesting numbers about Excel 2007 on the Microsoft Excel Official Blog at `http://blogs.msdn.com/excel`.

Now that you've seen some of the improvements to the client side of this relationship, let's begin examining Excel Services (the server side) and discuss its relationship with SharePoint.

Overview of Excel Services

Excel Services is a new server technology included in MOSS 2007 that provides a Web-based user interface (UI) for sharing workbooks through a browser. Excel Services extends the functionality of Microsoft Office Excel 2007 by enabling users to share their workbooks securely across an enterprise when using any browser. There is no need for ActiveX, nor does the Microsoft Office Excel client need to be previously installed. Users can interact with shared information, and even present information from external data sources.

> Note that Excel Services is not the Excel client application hosted on a server, nor is it a workbook authoring or creation application. Rather, Excel Services is a brand new technology that comes with MOSS 2007 Enterprise Edition — and only with it. If you have only Windows SharePoint Services 3.0 (WSS v3.0), you'll need to implement MOSS 2007 Enterprise Edition as well.

A programmatic user interface (Excel Web Services) provides a Web Service API for access. With it, other applications can access the data to obtain granular information and business logic results. You can also specify which sort of data you would like to publish into a SharePoint document library, even if you do not want to publish the entire worksheet or workbook.

The Web-based UI is called Excel Web Access (EWA). It enables users to interact with (but not edit) existing data by using the browser they are already familiar with.

> Using Excel Services, you can only interact within the information shared on the SharePoint Web site. You cannot change the original file only using the Excel Web Access Web Part. The author of the original file must download the file, make the necessary changes, and republish it again, or automate updating by Excel Web Services.

Unsupported Features in Excel Services

Some features are not supported in this version of Excel Services 2007 when you publish an Excel 2007 worksheet on to the SharePoint server (which was already configured with Excel Services). Any workbook incorporating an unsupported feature will not load on the server. (This does not mean, however, that you couldn't have this functionality working just fine on the client side.)

So, before creating and publishing your worksheet, be aware of the following unsupported features:

❑ Spreadsheets with code, including spreadsheets with Visual Basic for Applications (VBA) macros, forms controls, toolbox controls, Microsoft Excel 5.0 dialogs, and Excel macro (XLM_ sheets)

❑ ActiveX controls

❑ PivotTables based on "multiple consolidation" ranges

❑ External references (links to other spreadsheets)

❑ Spreadsheets saved in formula view

- ❑ Data validation

- ❑ Query tables, SharePoint lists, Web queries, and text queries

- ❑ Spreadsheets that use spreadsheet and sheet protection

- ❑ Embedded pictures or clip art

- ❑ Cell and sheet background pictures

- ❑ AutoShapes and WordArt

- ❑ Organization charts and diagrams

For the complete list, you can check the Excel Team Blog at `http://blogs.msdn.com/excel/` `archive/2005/12/01/499206.aspx` *if you need more information.*

Now, let's dig deeper into Excel Services architecture and functionality.

Excel Services Architecture

As part of the MOSS 2007, Excel Services is built on ASP.NET and Microsoft Windows SharePoint technologies. It works with three crucial components:

- ❑ Excel Web Services

- ❑ Excel Web Access (EWA)

- ❑ Excel Calculation Server (ECS)

For a better understanding of how these work together, think of them as grouped in two layers (Figure 11-1):

- ❑ The Web Front-End (WFE) where EWA and Excel Web Services reside

- ❑ The application server where ECS resides and where all the calculations are made

Let's take a look at each component:

WFE Layer

As mentioned, this layer includes both Excel Web Services and EWA. This layer is used for the user presentation when all the content and information is rendered originating from the application layer where the calculations are made.

Excel Web Services

This component allows you to programmatically calculate, set, and obtain specific values within the data stored in the published worksheet. Using Excel Web Services, you can automate workbook updates, integrate data with other applications, and make the interaction more useful and productive with your SharePoint data.

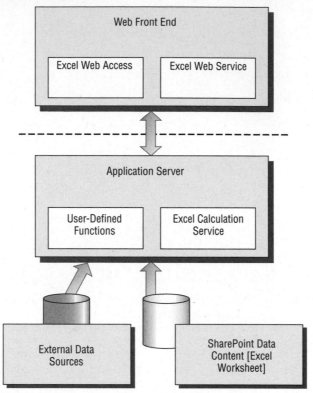

Figure 11-1: Excel Services architecture

Excel Web Access

This component enables the user to interact with the information published from an Excel worksheet that is stored in the SharePoint databases. EWA is a Web Part included with MOSS 2007 Enterprise, and it enables a user to render content as HTML. Because of this, there's no need to have the Microsoft Office Excel client or any other Office application installed to see and interact with the original worksheet.

For example, Figure 11-2 shows a simple Excel 2007 worksheet that includes a graphic. Figure 11-3 shows what is displayed when the data is shared through a SharePoint Web site using the EWA Web Part.

When you publish the worksheet, you can also specify which data (that is, a datasheet or even a data object) you would like to share. You can also publish the worksheet with preset parameters so that the users can interact with the EWA Web Part once the worksheet has been published.

Later in this chapter, you learn more about filtering (setting parameters for display of the worksheet) and the publishing steps involved.

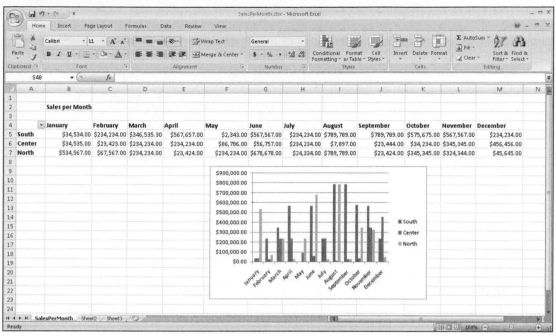

Figure 11-2: A simple Excel 2007 worksheet (data and graphic)

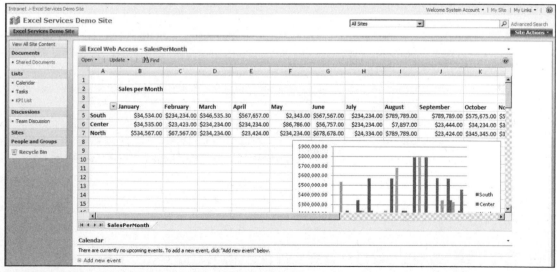

Figure 11-3: Worksheet displayed in the EWA Web Part

Application Server Layer (ECS)

In large implementations where companies distribute SharePoint with front-end Web servers and back-end application servers, the Excel Calculation Services (ECS) is hosted on the back-end, which will be responsible for loading workbooks, making the required calculations, and calling previously coded user-defined functions (UDFs) — all of this using the Excel Services Shared Service Provider (SSP) configuration. The ECS will also be responsible for maintaining the session state of the user interactivity. This session state is held by each user, and will be closed when the user closes the browser or a time-out occurs. Although the recommended architecture is to have a Front-End Layer and an Application Layer to balance the workload, it's also possible to have the three components in the same box. This should be dependent on the number of users who will be working with Excel Services capabilities. So, for big enterprises with a lot of users, you should have the ECS on the separated Application Layer.

A special API is provided for developers so that they can implement custom code. Developers can call the API to render content and make some data calculations on demand. Microsoft has provided a list of what you can do with the ECS and the API to establish a connection with the Excel Web Service.

Following are some of the included API functions:

❑ `GetApiVersion` — Get a version string of the installed Web service API build.

❑ `GetSessionInformation` — Get a few properties of the server session, primarily the language context of the session.

❑ `GetCell` — Get a value out of a cell. The two regular addressing options are available. You can either get formatted string values, or the raw binary values.

❑ `SetCell` — Set a value into a cell on one of the workbook's sheets. Two possible options exist for this method. One takes a cell address (for example, "B52") or a named range (for example, "Interest"), and the other accepts integer coordinates (for cases where it is more convenient for your code to use them). Typically, this is used when you have indexes in the code and want to use them to index the sheet.

❑ `SetRange` — Same as `SetCell`, but used for setting values in an entire contiguous range. The same two options are available.

❑ `Calculate` — Recalculate the formulas in a specific range or in the entire workbook. Useful when the workbook author has turned off automatic calculation. This also has two possible options (using a string or using integer coordinates to refer to a range), much like in the `Set` methods.

You can check the Excel Team Blog at `http://blogs.msdn.com/excel/archive/2005/11/17/493962.aspx` *if you need more information.*

Enabling and Configuring Excel Services

By default, Excel Services does not run after installing MOSS 2007 Enterprise. So, you must first enable Excel Services and configure it to tell SharePoint which document libraries will be able to host the worksheets to share with the team through a SharePoint Web site. These document libraries are *trusted file locations,* which means that if you publish worksheets on document libraries that are not configured as a trusted file location, the worksheet will not be allowed to be rendered in the browser.

Enabling Excel Services

To enable Excel Services in a MOSS server farm environment, follow these steps:

1. Go to SharePoint 3.0 Central Administration by clicking Start ⇨ Programs ⇨ Microsoft Office Server ⇨ SharePoint 3.0 Central Administration.

2. On the Central Administration Home page, click the Operations tab.

3. In the "Topology and Service" section, click the "Services on Server" link.

4. From this screen, you can enable or disable services for a selected server. Be sure the server you want to enable the service for is selected. If not, click the name of the desired server and select the Change Server option. Next, a window appears and you can click the name of the desired server.

5. Click the Start Action button for Excel Calculation Services. You should enable this service on an application server rather than a front-end Web server (for better performance and load-balancing calculation purposes). Of course, if you only have one server or one box on which to enable all the services, you can use that server, and the enabling will work. Finally you'll see a screen showing the service has been started, as shown in Figure 11-4.

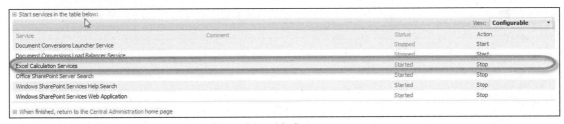

Figure 11-4: Excel Calculation Services Started (enabled)

After you have enabled Excel Services, you are ready to begin configuring. To do so, you must go directly to the SSP Home page. If you haven't already created an SSP, you must first create one.

If you have an SSP already created, you can skip the following section and go directly to the section, "Configuring Excel Services," later in this chapter.

Creating a Shared Services Provider

Let's talk a little bit about how SharePoint has evolved to better understand how it provides its services in the 2007 version. SharePoint 2003 consisted of Windows SharePoint Services 2.0 (WSS v2.0), which provided the capability to create collaboration Web sites for groups of people working on a project, and SharePoint Portal Server 2003 (SPS 2003), which added some powerful capabilities to the WSS collaboration experience (such as audiences, personal sites, advanced search, and site directory). SPS 2003 has been transformed into MOSS 2007, and part of the transformation included the introduction of the SSP.

Using the SSP, SharePoint now provides services to any collaboration Web site, regardless of whether the Web site is a team site, a meeting site, or even a portal site. In turn, these services are available to all the Web sites related to a specific SSP. That means you could have more than one SSP on your SharePoint farm, and each SSP would have related SharePoint Web sites. That translates into distinct audiences between SSPs. For example, an enterprise group may consist of a lot of companies, and each company could have an SSP for any number of team Web sites belonging to that company. So, the SharePoint farm can provide some services to some site collections (from some enterprise on the group), and different, distinct services to others.

The SSP needs at least one Web site for hosting its administration Web pages. Microsoft recommends at a minimum to use two Internet Information Server (IIS) Web sites: one for the SSP pages and another one for the My Site hosting pages. So, when creating a new SSP, you must specify the two Web sites that have already been created, or create the necessary IIS Web sites to host the administrative Web pages for the SSP and My Site path.

> **If you decide to use the same Web site to host both, you should specify a virtual directory to the My Site URL when you are configuring the My Site direction on the SSP creation process.**

For MOSS 2007, the IIS Web sites are called *Web applications*. Thus, you will have a Web application for the SSP Administration Web pages, a Web application for hosting My Site (the recommended approach), and a default Web application (probably using the Default Web Site) to host as many Web sites as you need.

> *You could also create new Web applications to host several Web sites using different security configuration, polices, and so on.*

Let's take a look now at how you create an SSP and the needed Web sites. As part of this process, you will specify a new Web site, as well as a new Web application.

To create the first SSP, follows these steps:

1. Open the SharePoint 3.0 Central Administration Home page.

2. Click the Application Management tab.

3. On the Application Management Home page, click the "Create or configure this farm's shared services" link, located in the Office SharePoint Server Shared Services section.

4. Click the New SSP button (located on the navigation options menu bar).

5. SharePoint presents a page where you must specify some important information. First, you must specify the name of the SSP, as shown in Figure 11-5. Then, you select an existing Web site, or you can create a new one that hosts the new SSP. Be careful that you do not select an existing Web site that uses Network Services as the Application Pool account.

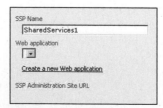

Figure 11-5: Specify a new name for the SSP

If you are deploying a farm implementation, and you select an existing Web site, this Web site must exist on every IIS front-end Web server in the farm. (You must be sure that every Web site from each server has the same description.) However, if you choose to create a new Web site, SharePoint creates the Web site on each server in the farm.

6. If you decide to create a new Web application, click the link "Create a new Web application."

7. Specify the name of the IIS Web site to be created. For this example, name the Web site `SharedServices1`, and specify a port other than 80.

8. Next, you will see the security configuration section for the new SSP. Here, you choose the required authentication provider: Kerberos (recommended for Integrated Windows authentication) or the basic Windows NT LAN Manager (NTLM). Select NTLM.

9. You also have the option to specify if you want to allow anonymous access for the Web sites that you plan to create over this Web application (an IIS Web site managed by SharePoint). Select No.

10. For the choice to have Secure Socket Layer (SSL) configured on your Web application for secure connections, select No.

11. At the Load Balancing URL section, don't change anything because SharePoint has already calculated the required information from the details previously provided by you.

12. On the next section, you must specify the Application Pool that will be used by the new Web application you are creating. You should have a separate Application Pool for SSP, so let's create it. Use your SharePoint Administrator account (domain\username and password). Microsoft recommends having a separate account for each Application Pool you'll use (SSP and My Sites Web application). You don't have to worry about giving them any special permission to the accounts used, because SharePoint will take care of that.

13. Leave the Reset Information Services section as it is.

14. On the next section, "Database Name and Authentication," you must specify the database server. The Database Name field corresponds to the name SharePoint will create. In this case, do not change the database name SharePoint has suggested.

15. Leave the remaining sections set with the defaults and click OK.

Once you've created the Web site for the SSP, you are returned to the page used to create the SSP. Now, let's continue with the My Site Web site locations.

1. On the My Site Location URL section of the page, you specify a Web application where My Site and user Profiles will be hosted (Figure 11-6). As mentioned, Microsoft recommends using a different Web application to host My Site so that you can back up and restore this independently from other Web applications. Let's create another new Web application.

Figure 11-6: The Web application details for My Site

2. When configuring the SSP, you should specify a virtual directory (such as /MySites). Even If you're using a separate Web application, you can also specify a virtual directory.

3. Click the "Create a new Web application" link to produce a page similar to the one you used for creating the new Web application for the SSP (Figure 11-7). Choose another port, but select a similar authentication configuration for this new Web application.

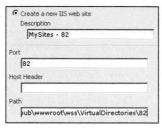

Figure 11-7: The Web application details for My Site

4. On next section, Database Name, you must specify the database server. You could change the database name to the one the new Web application will use. At the last section of the page, SharePoint suggests a name, but you could enter some other name that would help you identify the content stored there (such as WSS_Content_MySites).

Remember, this discussion has examined using a Web application and an Application Pool for the SSP, and another one for My Site. But this could change. If you use the same Web application for hosting the SSP and My Site, just be sure to specify some name (as a virtual directory) when you configure the My Site Hosting. (It shouldn't be at the Web application's root, so specify any number as a virtual directory.)

Now that you've created the first SSP and My Site Web applications, you must complete a few final steps to finish the creation process:

1. Return to the New Shared Services Provider Configuration Web page. At the middle of the Web page, you will see the SSP Service Credentials section. Here you must provide the SharePoint Administration account and password.

2. Leave the SSP Database section as it is and do the same for the Search Database configuration section.

3. On the Index Server configuration section, select the server that will crawl the content from all the Web applications associated with the SSP. Then, specify the location for the server when the physical index is going to be stored on the file system.

4. For the option to configure SSL for secure communications between Web Services and SSP, the default value is No. Choose Yes only if you plan to use SSL with Web Services.

One you have finished creating the SSP, you can continue configuring Excel Services.

Configuring Excel Services

Once you've enabled Excel Services on SharePoint 3.0 Central Administration, and you've also created the SSP, you are ready to configure Excel Services.

To configure Excel Services on the SharePoint server, you need to go to the SSP Home page. Once there, you'll need to find the Excel Services Settings. To go to the SSP Home page, follow these steps:

1. Go to the Shared Services Provider Home page by clicking Start ➪ All Programs ➪ Microsoft Office Server ➪ Central SharePoint 3.0 Administration.

2. At the Central Administration Home page, click the Application Management tab.

3. On the Application Management page, click "Create or configure this farm's shared service" in the Office SharePoint Server Shared Service section.

4. On the "Manage this Farm's Shared Services" section, position the mouse over the SSP previously created. You should see a small arrow. Click the arrow and select the third option from that drop-down list, Open Shared Service Admin Site.

5. On the Shared Services Administration Home page, you see the services grouped, as shown in Figure 11-8.

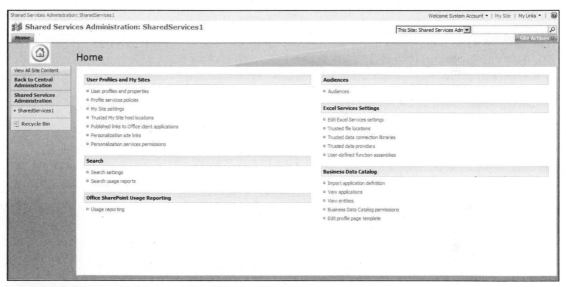

Figure 11-8: The Shared Services Administration Home page

On the right side of the screen, you see the Excel Services Settings section. Underneath that heading, you see links for the following:

❑ Edit Excel Services settings

❑ Trusted file locations

❑ Trusted data connection libraries

❑ Trusted data providers

❑ User-defined function assemblies

Let's take a look at each of these in a bit more detail.

Edit Excel Services Settings

In this section, you can configure a variety of settings, including the following:

- ❑ The file access method used by ECS to obtain the data worksheets from all non-WSS trusted file locations.

- ❑ The maximum user Session connections available (the default is 25 connections)

- ❑ The maximum limit for connection lifetime (such as 1,800 seconds)

- ❑ The Windows user credentials used for WSS to connect to external data connections.

Trusted File Locations

Here you can configure the following settings:

- ❑ *Location* — Here you can set the following:

  - ❑ *Address* — This is where you specify the document library Web address that will contain the worksheet you would like to render on the browser.

  - ❑ *The location type* — This refers to the type of container where the worksheets will be. This could be a WSS document library, a UNC, or an HTTP path. This means that you are not restricted to only using SharePoint document libraries for hosting a worksheet. Instead, you can use the same file system shared folders, or even Web hosting, and take advantage of Excel Services to render that content on a browser using a SharePoint site without moving any content or information.

  - ❑ *Trust Children* — This setting is used if you would like to enable Excel Workbooks that are in folders or subfolders from the specified root of the document library to render on the Web browser.

- ❑ *Session Management* — This section contains options to configure session time-outs.

- ❑ *Workbook Properties* — This section is used to specify the maximum workbook size (in megabytes) that ECS should be able to render. The default values go from 10 MB through 2000 MB (that would be 20 GB), and the default specified is 10 MB

- ❑ *Calculation Behavior* — The section specifies the distinct modalities that ECS can provide (File, Manual, or Automatic).

- ❑ *External Data Options* — This section enables you to specify certain configuration settings for external data rendering by Excel Services. This includes information that is presented to the user using the EWA, but is not static Excel data (but rather is from another data source).

- ❑ *User-Defined Function* — This section enables the use of UDFs so that ECS can call them when rendering content. You can code specific functions and embed them into .NET assemblies. Then, configure a trusted file location to enable the use of those UDFs to interact with the worksheets hosted on the document library already configured in the trusted file location. To do this, you must enable the use of UDFs before assigning them to a certain trusted file location. You should do this in the Excel Services User-Defined Functions Assemblies section at the SSP Home page.

Trusted Data Connection Libraries

You may encounter situations when you need EWA to render content from external data sources (SQL Server, for example). Those situations require a certain connection configuration to access the external data. This is where the settings for trusted Data Connection Libraries (DCLs) come into play.

You must have a specific connection string that the worksheet will use to connect to the data source. This is called the Office Data Connection (ODC) file. However, the ODC that specifies the connection string should also be a trusted location defined for Excel Services Settings.

You could also create another kind of SharePoint library, the DCL. In this kind of SharePoint library, you must upload the ODC that your worksheets will use. The DCL must be "trustable," so that's why you must add DCLs in the "Trusted data connection libraries" section of Excel Services Settings.

Only the ODC that has DCLs defined will have permissions to connect to its data source.

Trusted Data Providers

In this section, you define the allowed trusted providers that Excel Web Services could use (for example, SQLOLEDB, SQL Server, MSOLAP, OraOLEDB.Oracle.1, Oracle in OraHome92, and IBMDADB2). The trusted data providers are used to specify specific providers that Excel Services can use to connect to external data sources and to use the Excel Web Access Web Part to present and render that content to the users by Web browsers.

User-Defined Function Assemblies

User-defined functions (UDFs) are functions that are specified or created by the user to interact within the data that Excel Services renders via the browser. If the user needs certain specific or complex calculation operations, UDFs make it possible to extend the Excel Services functionality. Administrators enable UDFs on the trusted file location that points to where the worksheet resides. Administrators must register UDF assemblies in this section of Excel Services Settings, "User-defined function assemblies."

To enable UDFs, follow these steps:

1. Go to the Shared Service Provider (SSP) Home page.

2. Once there, click the UDF assembly link in the Excel Services Settings section.

3. Add the new UDF assembly you would like to enable. Specify in the Assembly textbox the string name or full path of the assembly that contains the UDF.

4. Specify the location of that assembly by indicating whether it's defined as a Global Assembly Cache (GAC) or on a file path.

5. Ensure that the Enable Assembly checkbox is checked. You can also provide a description about the UDF, but this is optional.

Once you have completed these steps, you must enable UDFs for the workbook on the trusted file location. To do so, click the "Edit trusted file location" link on the SSP Home page (in the Excel Services section). Once there, the last section labeled Allow User-Defined Functions must be enabled, as shown Figure 11-9.

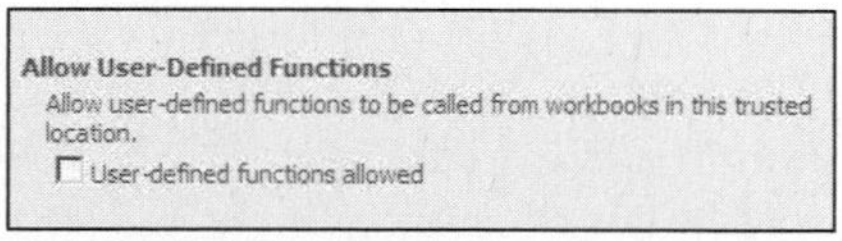

Figure 11-9: Enabling UDFs on the trusted file location

Publishing Data

Imagine that you've already created the Excel workbook you want to share with your team. Let's say that you open it in Office Excel 2007, and that you opt to insert some business logic to highlight some data.

To share this worksheet with your team, you must first publish it. To publish an Excel workbook, you must be using Excel 2007, because that version provides the option to publish to an Excel Services Server (contained with MOSS 2007), as shown in Figure 11-10.

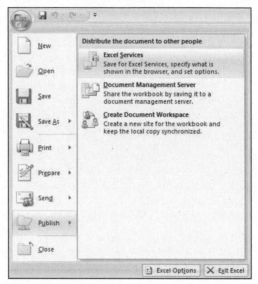

Figure 11-10: Publish to Excel Services option in Excel 2007

> If you don't see an option to publish to Excel Services, it may be that you don't have a version of Office 2007 that has the option to publish to Excel Services. Only Office Professional 2007 Plus, Office 2007 Enterprise, and Office 2007 Ultimate have the bits needed to publish to Excel Services.

Once you select the Excel Services menu option, you'll see a window that asks you for the corresponding URL to the previously saved workbook and publish it after that. You can choose some document library from within the SharePoint Site you are working on.

If you would like to select a certain object or worksheet to share with the team, you click the Excel Services option (Figure 11-10) to open a new window. As shown in Figure 11-11, this window allows you to specify objects from the workbook that you would like to publish and share with the team so they might interact when using the browser.

As you can see in Figure 11-11, you can specify an object or sheet that you would like to publish. Also, you can specify parameters so that users can interact with the information published and provided by the Excel Web Access Web Part.

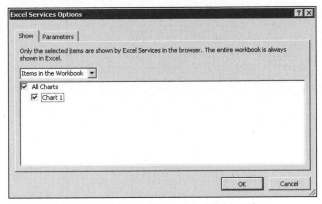

Figure 11-11: Specifying options at publishing time

For example, let's say that you had a Sales Report workbook with some formulas to calculate sales or commissions. You could save the workbook to a SharePoint site and then publish it, adding the corresponding fields from an Excel 2007 sheet that you would like to make available so that users could enter some values and recalculate using some Excel formulas.

Now, there are a couple of ways to publish data to Excel Services:

❑ *Static* — You could publish static worksheet data, which wouldn't have any external data source connections.

❑ *Dynamic* — You could publish a worksheet that connects to an external data source (thus presenting dynamic information stored on a database), or even connected worksheets on the Web site (to filter information depending on many factors).

You could use the Publish Parameters option to interact with a dynamic worksheet published to Excel Services, and interact directly with the information rendered by the Excel Web Access Web Part, which would access the external data source.

You can also use the file format compatibility kit to publish an Excel 2003 workbook without importing it into Excel 2007 to be saved as 2007 format. Once you have downloaded and installed the kit, you only need to change the extension from the Excel 2003 file to the corresponding 2007 file (.xlsx).

Finally, you could enter the SharePoint document library and select the Upload option. Select the Excel file, and once on the document library, if you mouse over and select the View on the Browser option, you'll see the data as though you'd added and configured the Excel Web Access Web Part.

Following are two primary limitations if you publish Excel 2003 files, however:

❑ You won't be able to specify or restrict some objects from being viewed by users.

❑ You won't be able to add parameters for user interaction.

Publishing Static Worksheets

To show you how to publish an existing or a new worksheet, let's use the Sales Report example just introduced. Figure 11-12 shows the worksheet as it appears in Excel 2007.

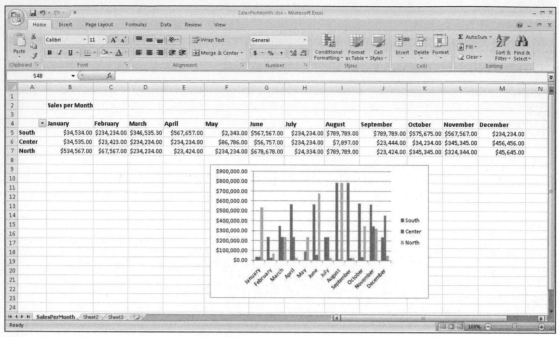

Figure 11-12: Sales Report Excel 2007 worksheet

Let's first incorporate a filter for every month. Once this worksheet has been published, a user could interact with the data by using the filters. To incorporate the filters, click "Sort & Filter" from the Ribbon located at the top of the page, as shown in Figure 11-13.

Remember that you can choose to publish the entire workbook, only a specific worksheet, or even a specific object.

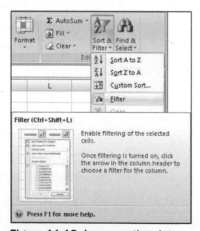

Figure 11-13: Incorporating data filters to worksheet columns so users can interact with the information

To publish the worksheet, click the Office Icon up in the left corner of the worksheet. Select the Publish option and then Excel Services.

Publishing Dynamic Worksheets

Now that you've seen how to publish and share static Excel worksheets with your work team, let's say that you now must share information that resides on an external data source (for example a SQL Server database). To accomplish this, you could use the Excel Web Part and Excel Web Service as an intermediate layer so that users could interact (read-only) with the database data.

To do this, you must connect Excel to the external data source. Once you have done this, the generated connection must be saved as an ODC. This ODC must also be stored on a trusted DCL (within your SharePoint site), and this trusted DCL must also be added to the SSP trusted connection libraries.

So, on one side, you'll have a document library that will contain the worksheets (which will also have configured the ODC as a connection string) that you want to be rendered on the browser. This is where the EWA Web Part will take those files from and render the content as HTML.

On the other hand, the ODC will be on a trusted DCL, which will have permissions from the SSP to allow and establish the corresponding data source connections.

> If you must connect to data servers on which Windows authentication is not supported, you should consider configuring the Single Sign-On (SSO) service to provide the required credentials for establishing a connection to the data source. In those cases, an encrypted database created by the SSO service will hold the credentials that WSS uses to sign to the data source, so users won't be prompted for a username and password when they access the data through a browser. Thus, in the Authentication Settings for the Excel Services connection, you would choose the SSO ID and specify one configured on the SSP.

For more information on this, there are some resources you might check: "Manage settings for single sing-on" (http://technet2.microsoft.com/Office/en-us/library/cd4f4a25-e393-4e1b-9c26-a0bed175d3a21033.mspx?mfr=true), *and "Plan external data connections for Excel Services"* (http://technet2.microsoft.com/Office/f/?en-us/library/7e6ce086-57b6-4ef2-8117-e725de18f2401033.mspx).

For more information about planning a recommended Excel Services configuration, see "Plan access to Excel spreadsheets" (http://technet2.microsoft.com/Office/en-us/library/93f576a4-e549-4675-b083-7fe4f145ac591033.mspx?mfr=true).

Let's open a worksheet that has already connected to the external data source. In this example, let's use the AdventureWorks database that Microsoft often uses in its examples.

To see how to install and configure this example database, browse to http://msdn2.microsoft.com/en-us/library/aa992075(VS.80).aspx. *It can be configured with either SQL Server 2000 or SQL Server 2005.*

As you can see in Figure 11-14, a filter has been added to the Row Labels column (Column A), as indicated by the down arrow appearing in the right side of Row 2. A user could use this filter to select what product to see from all the available information.

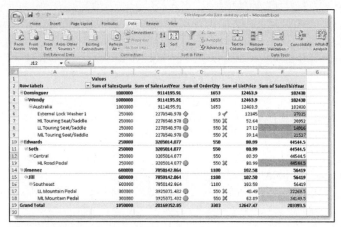

Figure 11-14: Sales Report Excel workbook connected to the external data source

Before publishing the worksheet and making it available for the team, you must extract the ODC that has the connection settings to the external data source, and upload it to a trusted DCL. To do this, follow these steps:

1. To extract the ODC, click the Data tab from the Excel 2007 Ribbon and select Properties, as shown in Figure 11-15.

Figure 11-15: Connection data source Properties

2. From the Connection Properties window shown in Figure 11-16, choose the Definition tab. Here, you specify and edit the query to the data source. You could build a query to search in any table, view, or even system tables. Clicking Authentication Settings at the bottom of the window enables you to configure the SSO ID as previously discussed.

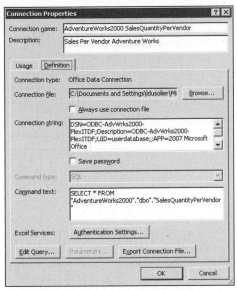

**Figure 11-16: Selecting the Definition tab in
the Connection Properties window**

3. Click the Export Connection File button toward the bottom of the Connection Properties window. From the resulting screen, you could export and save the file to a folder on your local machine, to a shared folder, or to a trusted DCL, as shown in Figure 11-17.

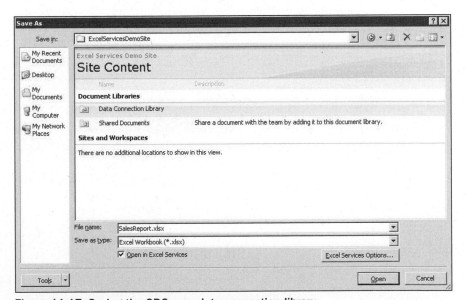

Figure 11-17: Saving the ODC on a data connection library

4. Once you've saved or uploaded the file to the trusted DCL, you must approve that connection file. To approve the DCL, just put the mouse over the text that appears on the "Name" column and click the arrow that appears on the right side of the file. Select the Approve/Reject option, and then click the Approved option (the first one from the option list). Click the OK button. If you want, you can add a comment. After that, you'll return to the DCL and you'll see the status at the last column as "Approved" (meaning that you can now use that DCL file).

5. The trusted DCL must be configured as a trusted address (if it isn't already a trustable DCL). Thus, you must add it to the trusted DCL list from your SSP. If you haven't done that, you'll need to copy the ODC URL from the DCL where you uploaded it. So, go back to the DCL and then right-click the ODC file you are working with. Click the "Copy Shortcut" link. You can now go to the SSP Home page and click Trusted Data Connection Libraries. Click the "Add trusted data connection library" link. In the Address textbox, type or paste the DCL that has the ODC.

6. Before publishing, you should verify that the connection file that your workbook will use is specified in the workbook connection properties. To do so, go back to the Microsoft Office Excel workbook, and click the Data Menu option from the Ribbon. On the Connections section, select the connection you've been working with. Click the Properties button from the right side of the Workbook Connections window. Click the Definitions tab to configure the connections properties. Click the Browse button next to the Connection file and browse to the ODC file. Select it. Click the OK button. Verify that the Web address of the ODC file appears in the Connection file textbox.

7. Select the "Always use the connection file" checkbox.

8. After that, you can click OK to save the configuration and proceed to publish the worksheet.

9. If you want to publish only a selected sheet, an object, or a graphic from the worksheet, click the Excel Services Options button in the lower right of the screen. This opens a new window with two tabs, as shown in Figure 11-18. If you click the Show tab, you can specify what you are going to publish and share with the team. If the sheet contains parameters to interact with the data, you could click the Parameters tab and define which ones you would like to publish.

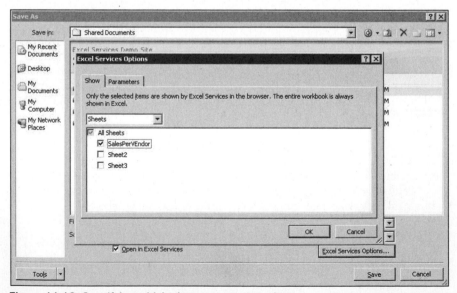

Figure 11-18: Specifying which sheet you want to share

10. In Excel 2007, click the Publish option (remember that the Publish option appears once you click the Office icon at the top-left corner of Excel 2007). Select Excel Services, and select the corresponding document library to save the worksheet.

Each time you publish a worksheet, the "Open in Excel Services" checkbox is checked by default. You can uncheck this option if you don't want Excel Services to open for you in a Web browser. Figure 11-19 shows how the worksheet displays in a Web page rendering the content, using the ODC from the allowed DCL.

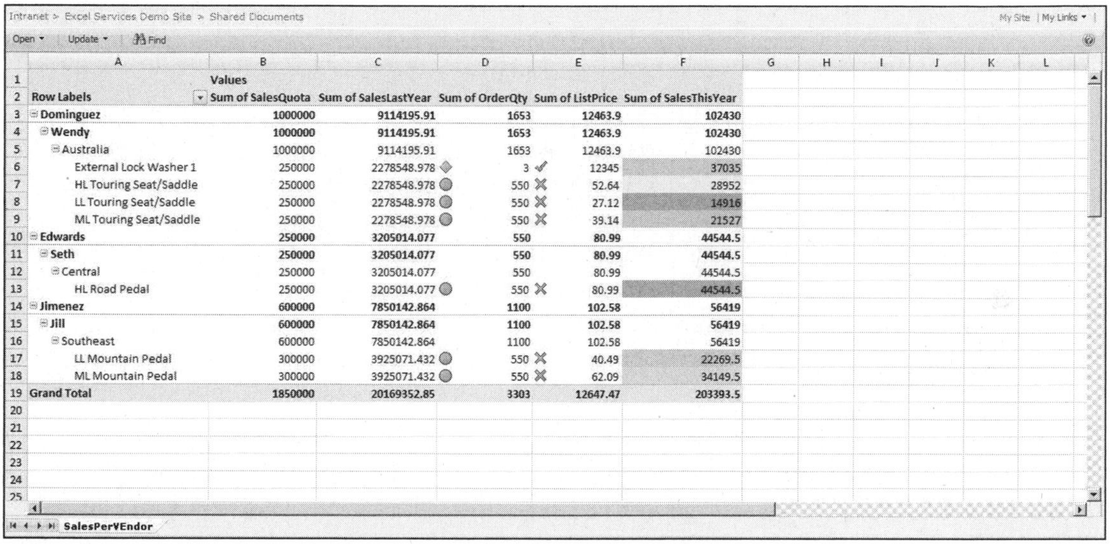

Figure 11-19: The Excel Web Access rendering data as HTML content

As you can see in Figure 11-19, only the sheet titled "SalesPerVendor" has been published. In this case, the author of the workbook must have specified to only publish and share this one sheet.

If you were to publish this worksheet with a specified filter, each user could load this data from a browser and, in real time, perform whatever kind of data filtering is allowed. Because every user session is independent from another, the application of a filter for some condition by one user does not affect other users.

For example, let's say you would like to filter the Sales Report worksheet by Product. On the right side of Row 2 in Column A in Figure 11-19, you see a down arrow. Clicking this arrow produces a drop-down menu. Select Product ➪ Filter, and you are presented with a dialog box such as the one shown in Figure 11-20. In this window, you select the Product name for which you want to apply the filter. When you are finished making your selection(s) and click the OK button, you see the content after the external data source has been re-queried, but this time only the data that matches the filter specifications is displayed (Figure 11-21).

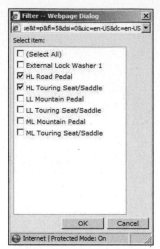

Figure 11-20: Specifying a certain filter

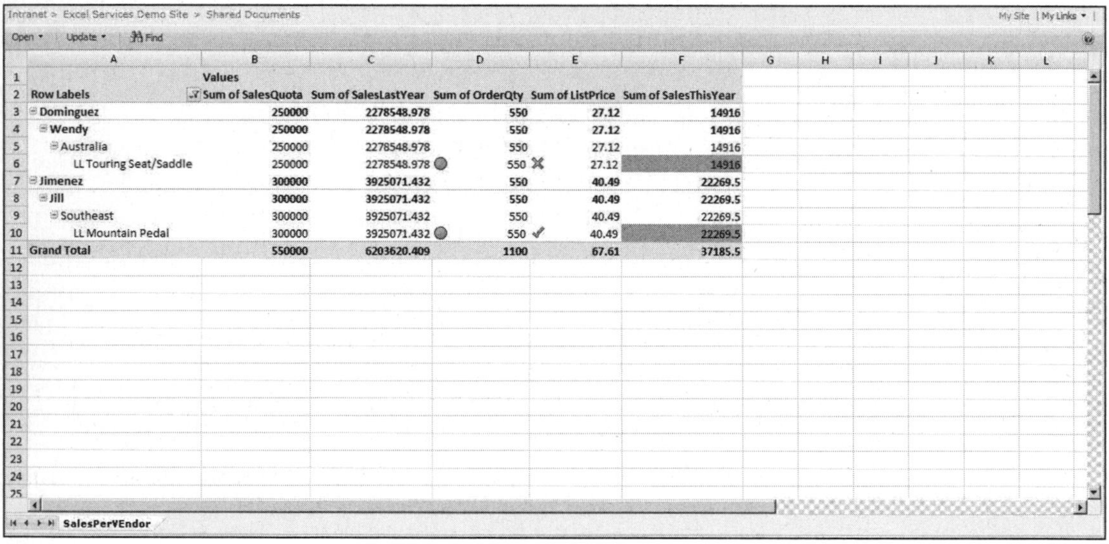

	A	B	C	D	E	F	G	H	I	J	K	L
1		**Values**										
2	**Row Labels**	Sum of SalesQuota	Sum of SalesLastYear	Sum of OrderQty	Sum of ListPrice	Sum of SalesThisYear						
3	Dominguez	250000	2278548.978	550	27.12	14916						
4	Wendy	250000	2278548.978	550	27.12	14916						
5	Australia	250000	2278548.978	550	27.12	14916						
6	LL Touring Seat/Saddle	250000	2278548.978	550	27.12	14916						
7	Jimenez	300000	3925071.432	550	40.49	22269.5						
8	Jill	300000	3925071.432	550	40.49	22269.5						
9	Southeast	300000	3925071.432	550	40.49	22269.5						
10	LL Mountain Pedal	300000	3925071.432	550	40.49	22269.5						
11	**Grand Total**	550000	6203620.409	1100	67.61	37185.5						

Figure 11-21: Filtering data and recalculating numbers

Now that you have a basic understanding of Excel Services and what it has to offer, let's check out the EWA Web Part to see what it has to offer.

Using the EWA Web Part

With the EWA Web Part, you can do plenty of things, depending on what type of information you would like to show. For example, you could add a new MOSS 2007 Web Part called Choice Filter Web Part, which could use parameters from an EWA Web Part to render certain data. This section highlights some of the many things you can do with the EWA Web Part.

Finding Information

You can search and find information by first clicking the Find icon in the EWA toolbar. For example, if you wanted to find some product name or number, just click the Find link and type your search query, as shown in Figure 11-22. Automatically, the EWA Web Part points to the result, as shown in Figure 11-23.

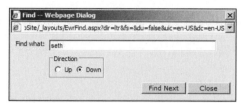

Figure 11-22: Specifying a word to search

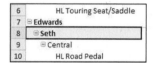

Figure 11-23: Result shown
by the Excel Web Access
Web Part

And once you specify the word you're looking for, you'll see the results in real time as Figure 11-23 shows.

Updating Data

By clicking the Update link in the toolbar and selecting Calculate Workbook, you can choose from some options to recalculate the information rendered by the EWA Web Part if the data has been updated.

This will reselect the information already rendered, and review if there's a change previously made by the workbook author, so the Web Access Web Part always presents actualized data.

Opening a Local Copy

Users with reader permissions (viewers may not) have the option of downloading a local copy of a worksheet as a snapshot to work with the data. This is accomplished by selecting Open ➪ Open Snapshot in Excel. The advantage of this feature is that these users would only see plain data, and not the business logic or formulas contained within the worksheet.

Creating a KPI List

Let's say that you would like to share the business intelligence in the Sales Report example as Key Performance Indicators (KPIs) through a Web site. With KPI Lists and Excel Services in MOSS 2007, you can accomplish this without any third-party tools. By using Excel 2007 from the client side (and with MOSS using Excel Services to present the information in a browser from the server side), this can be achieved with actual Excel files just by importing them into Excel 2007 and publishing them.

So, you can create a KPI list from the data rendered by an EWA Web Part. MOSS 2007 ships with a certain type of list called the KPI List.

To create a new KPI List, follow these steps:

1. Begin by clicking Site Actions ➪ Create ➪ KPI List to produce the screen shown in Figure 11-24. Click the KPI List link found in the fourth column from the left, near the middle of the column.

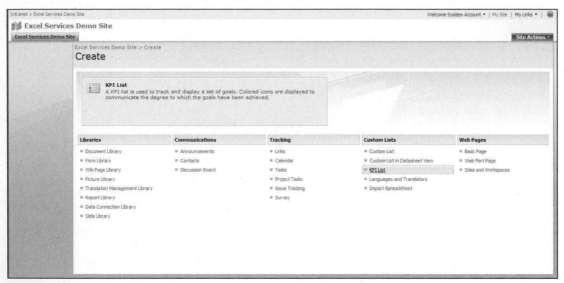

Figure 11-24: Create a KPI List

2. From the resulting screen shown in Figure 11-25, select "Indicator using data in Excel workbook."

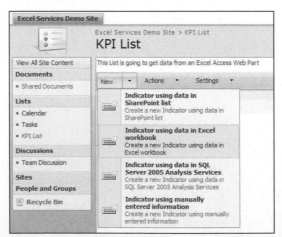

Figure 11-25: Creating a KPI List using distinct data sources

3. You can now begin configuring the KPI List from the screen shown in Figure 11-26. First, you must specify the name of the KPI List.

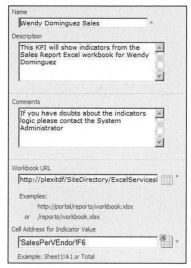

Figure 11-26: Specifying certain data for the KPI List

4. Next, enter a description and any comments you have about the KPI List.

5. For the Workbook URL, enter the corresponding URL of the worksheet you are using. After you have entered the workbook URL, click the Excel icon just to the right of the field to specify which column from the selected workbook will be used to make the calculations for the business logic that you define.

6. Enter a value for the cell in the worksheet that will serve as the indicator value.

7. In the lower portion of the configuration screen (Figure 11-27), you specify business roles for the Excel workbook.

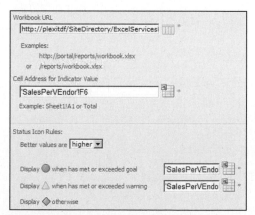

Figure 11-27: Specifying the business roles for the KPI

Figure 11-28 shows how the KPI List will display the information. In the same list, you could also have different KPIs from different sources and different people.

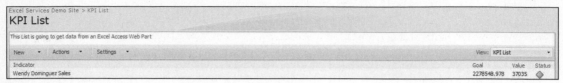

Figure 11-28: How the KPI List will display the information

Now that you've seen the potential of the KPI Lists, you can create them in any site collection or subsite. There are also two Web Site templates that come with an already created KPI and Dashboard structure:

❑ The Collaboration Portal Template [Publishing Templates]

❑ The Report Center [Enterprise Templates]

These two templates are very similar, and have a few sections that will help you to construct KPI lists and a great dashboard to start with.

If you click the Reports Center from the Collaboration Portal, or go into the Home page of a Report Center, you'll first see an introduction that discusses how to use the Report Center. In this Web page, you'll see a KPI sample with some custom data and graphical indicators that you can personalize to better understand how they work.

You'll also see a brief introduction to dashboards, as well as a link to access an already existing sample. This sample has some graphical indicators and KPIs bound to an Excel worksheet that has been published to a reports library contained within the Report Center.

These samples provide a great start to designing and constructing KPIs with dashboards related to having a complete Report Center for a company, complete with filters and different views so that distinct users may see only the data they're interested in.

For More Information

If you need more information about Excel Services, Wrox offers a couple of excellent books on this topic:

❑ *Beginning Excel Services* by Liviu Asnash, Eran Megiddo, Craig Thomas (Wiley Publishing, Inc., 2007)

❑ *Professional Excel Services* by Shahar Prish (Wiley Publishing, Inc., 2007)

You can find descriptions of each of these at www.wrox.com.

Summary

This chapter presented some interesting information related to Excel Services, which represents one of the great improvements of MOSS 2007. With Excel Services, you can share workbooks, worksheets, objects, data, and business logic so that users can interact with them. Instead of sending workbooks by email, you can use Excel Services for rendering content through a Web browser, and always present the final version of your data. With that capability, you can share financial data to have dynamic sales reports and statistics, insurance formulas, budget calculations — just about anything you want! This chapter also discussed the capabilities Excel Services provides in developing custom applications to obtain more business value for your company.

12

Securing SharePoint Communication

by Adam Buenz

Just as with all other Web-based applications, SharePoint is subject to electronic malicious actions of assorted types. Securing SharePoint is arguably one of the most unique and significant tasks that you will undertake when rolling out an initial SharePoint deployment, or securing a previously deployed SharePoint instance. The scope of securing SharePoint for your organization is considerable, from implementing transport layer security on the pipe to practicing appropriate Business Continuity Planning (BCP) strategies. By ensuring that all layers of security for SharePoint are accounted and planned for, you can mitigate numerous risks that would otherwise prove disastrous for your SharePoint infrastructure.

Fortunately, there are various avenues that you can exploit to procure effective SharePoint hardening mechanisms and security practices. Beyond the beneficial position that implementing appropriate SharePoint security practices will provide you and your organization, industries are subject to various business and governmental legal regulations that are generally federally mandated, therefore making securing SharePoint not an elective task.

The Breadth of SharePoint Security

The accessible techniques you can use to achieve a secure SharePoint information state range from built-in Windows Server 2003 and SharePoint security instruments to implementations of Microsoft sister server platforms that help you to procure secure Web application publishing, and provide stateful packet inspection of your SharePoint traffic. Following your implementation of these appropriate security standards, tools, and strategies, SharePoint can be used in a variety of circumstances within various industries, ranging from building influential custom facing business-to-business (B2B) extranets, to compelling internal intranets connecting your organization's information workers.

The security of SharePoint spans a wide assortment of technologies, attributable in part to the fact that SharePoint (albeit enhanced) is fundamentally an ASP.NET 2.0 Web application. Generally, when people plan for the security of SharePoint, it is common that they only arrange the security of the Web application itself, while ignoring some or all of the associated technologies. This fallacy, however, procures a false secure mindset that negates architecting a truly secure collaboration environment.

The security of SharePoint houses many layers, starting at the machine level all the way to the subsequent pages served per user requests. Therefore, the security of SharePoint encompasses technologies such as Internet Information Server (IIS), ASP.NET, SQL Server, and associated server platforms assimilated into overall SharePoint operations. Consequently, when you are planning, designing, and hardening a SharePoint environment, you must consider, account, and integrate each of these correlations into your overall SharePoint security program.

Steps to SharePoint Security

Defining a universal security approach to execute with SharePoint is not feasible. To properly secure your SharePoint environment you must study, scrutinize, and strategize the variety of ways that you will leverage SharePoint. The results of this analysis should then be used as parameters to the building of the overall SharePoint security program. For different implementations, distinct security attributes must be implemented. However, no global standard can be defined, because it is an individual organizational decision.

> *In any discussion of network security, it is often helpful to use the standard OSI Reference Model when describing levels of communication. Figure 12-1 shows the seven layers of this model.*

For example, let's say that you are deploying a small internal SharePoint implementation that allows users to collaborate on holiday planning events. In such an environment, you may deem transport-level security undesirable for the required effort of the IT team and performance overhead that it incurs because of handshaking negotiations. Furthermore, if the implementation is not heavily used, you may believe a very robust Disaster Recovery (DR) solution might not be required, because you consider the holiday planning data to be disposable.

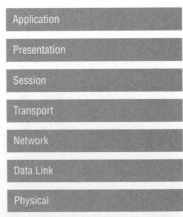

Application

Presentation

Session

Transport

Network

Data Link

Physical

Figure 12-1: OSI Reference Model

On the other end of the spectrum, let's say that you are deploying an extranet acting as business-to-business partner portal, serving large quantities of content to other companies through the inherent SharePoint Web Content Management (WCM) features. The extranet being publicly available may be more easily subject to malicious information interception and other forms of attack. Therefore, you must implement transport-level security routines to protect your information in transit. Also, if your vital extranet information is being stored on an internal, detached SQL server, you must put a well-defined DR solution in place, practice it, and update it frequently to absorb new technology and inevitable realizations in your organization.

Although a universal security constant is not possible, you can take steps to harden your SharePoint environment, each binding to a tier that defines the inclusive SharePoint architecture. Although these steps are not completely comprehensive in what you should include in an overall SharePoint security program, they provide you with some foundational buildings blocks that are generally found in most properly sheltered collaboration environments, as shown in Figure 12-2.

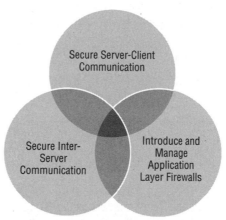

Figure 12-2: Foundational building blocks of SharePoint security

First, you will see how you can secure the communication layer to mitigate any type of information transmission compromise. This generally involves implementing security protocols when serving requests to clients through the use of Secure Sockets Layer (SSL), and securing communication between the relevant SharePoint servers (inter-server) involved in farm communication through IPSec.

Second, you will see how to protect the network layer through the use of a Microsoft Internet Security and Acceleration (ISA) Server application firewall to build a DMZ (Demilitarized zone). The outcome of placing ISA Server in front of your internal network firewall will result in stateful packet inspection of your SharePoint traffic, thwart security bypassing, provide connectivity monitoring, and avert operational incidents such as denial-of-service (DoS) attacks. Using intuitive programmatic objects provided by the ISA API, you will see how to rapidly develop small applications and scripts that will streamline administrative tasks related to an ISA instance.

Approaching the securing of SharePoint in a layered manner (whereby each segment is analyzed) you will form a security blueprint known as *threat modeling*. Using threat modeling, the assets that build up SharePoint are identified and inventoried, the systems architecture is considered and disseminated, and threats to your SharePoint environment are measured for all of the analyzed individual levels. Throughout this chapter, you dive into some of these layers and examine solutions to harden each.

Secure the Communication Layer

You must take into account numerous considerations when you are beginning to secure the communication layer that SharePoint is employing to serve user requests. The communication stack is the backbone of how SharePoint will serve content to your users, providing the first line of defense, coupling with the network layer, building up how requested SharePoint information packets are eventually served.

Although it is feasible to group both the communication layer and network layer into one aggregate collection (because several technologies that each encompass tend to overlap), there are distinct differences between the two that you must take into account.

Characteristically, implementing encryption at the communication layer is the minimum level of security that an organization should consider for implementation, because it is commonly the least expensive, easiest to apply, and provides the most essential security attributes that should be included in a fundamental SharePoint security approach. There are two communication encryption protocols that you should take into consideration, one dedicated to securing client requests and another related to securing inter-server communication.

Differences Between SSL and IPSec for SharePoint

When deciding on an encryption technology to protect traffic in transit, there are generally two types that are found within a SharePoint environment: Secure Socket Layer (SSL) and IP Security (IPSec). Several differences between the two make implementing either an attractive option for organizations. The choice basically breaks down to your organizational security needs, mandated corporate security standards, and how much effort you are willing to put forward. Optimally, a combination of both technologies can be leveraged to produce a mixed-mode environment that highlights requirements with the strength of each technology, notably using SSL for handling secure client requests for SharePoint content and IPSec for inter-server SharePoint farm communication encryption.

Architectural Differences Between SSL and IPSec

There are copious differences between IPSec and SSL that affect the decision of whether to implement either one of the technologies as a standalone encryption piece, or whether to employ a powerful mixed-mode environment. The most straightforward method to use when making the decision is to inspect the variations between the two encryption technologies, and to look at how each functions architecturally.

The principal architectural difference between SSL and IPSec is how each protocol is instantiated on an arbitrary server within a SharePoint farm. IPSec is instantiated as a machine layer setting because it is an IP layer protocol, existing at the layer three (network level) of the OSI stack (see Figure 12-1). Because of this low-level placement, it can be packaged into something very granular, such as the machine kernel using Bump-In-The-Stack (BITS), or offloaded outside the machine using Bump-In-The-Wire (BITW).

SSL, as opposed to the machine-level existence of IPSec, is a higher-level setting within the application layer of the OSI model. Therefore, it is instantiated on a per-application basis. SSL resides on the request stack above the actual information packet, deriving its plumbing from TCP/IP (however, below higher-level protocols such as HTTP). Because SSL is implemented on a per-application contract, SSL allows individual connections to be established, isolating security incidents as they occur. This differs from the IPSec protocol as far as which packet requests pool to a singular connection stream because of the machine-level configuration that IPSec exercises.

Because of these architectural dissimilarities, for your SharePoint environment, it is important to realize that IPSec is generally not considered a replacement for SSL. Because of where it sits on a machine, IPSec is meant to encrypt communication between two distinct servers, such as between your SharePoint Web Front-Ends (WFEs) and back-end SharePoint SQL databases. SSL, however, is meant to serve an arbitrary number of client requests, and, therefore, is the recommended encryption solution to use on your WFEs (because the number of users that will request content is generally not known). SSL in terms of IT team effort and required security knowledge is also much less complex and much quicker to put into production.

It is possible to force SSL protocol encryption between server communications using certificates, such as between the SharePoint WFE and back-end SQL database. However, there are performance considerations to take into account when you make that decision that make IPSec your wisest choice for inter-server communication.

SSL and IPSec tend to be very similar in terms of actual encryption performance, because the encryption routines that each provide tend to be identical, and, therefore, the scrambling processes tend to consume the same amount of computing cycles. However, the handshaking process that occurs between both services tends to be slightly faster when using IPsec. Furthermore, IPSec supports compression algorithms leveraging IP Payload Compression Protocol (IPComp), whereas with SSL, this is generally absent.

To function, IPSec will also use packet injection, because it modifies routed packets by placing a new TCP header onto the original packet. This is meant as a means to support other types of protocols such as UDP because SSL supports only TCP transmissions, and, therefore, slightly bloats the routed information.

Using a Mixed-Mode IPSec and SSL Solution

The most constructive way to set up your traffic encryption solution for a SharePoint farm is to utilize a mixture of SSL with IPSec, where you can leverage both technologies for their unique strengths. You can use SSL to secure client requests. However, you can secure the communication layer for inter-server SharePoint farm communication between specific servers providing functionality (such as Web application services, indexing, other search-related activities) and enterprise features (such as Excel Services and Forms Services that may run on other delegated machines) by using the machine-layer security settings provided by IPSec.

By using specific IPSec modes, you can ensure that the transmissions are secure by mandating that all machine-to-machine communication instantiated between two SharePoint farmed servers is using the IPSec protocol. This is accomplished by using an IPSec policy to prevent communication sniffing with blatant source and address parameter rules. Using this technique allows you to build an architecture known as *no fallback machine or server isolation.* This means that a network silo is fashioned between the IPSec-enabled machines, isolating them from the non-isolated machines by ignoring subsequent machine requests, crafting a proper, secure network segment for SharePoint operations.

For users requesting content off the SharePoint farm, you can then use SSL to encrypt the data that is being sent to users by using the functionality provided by Microsoft Certificate Services (MCS), SelfSSL (provided with the IIS 6.0 toolkit), or a public Certificate Authority (CA). This can be implemented alongside some of the inherent ASP.NET 2.0 provider and authentication functionality. Although basic authentication is generally the most used in regard to SSL, it is a best security practice to use the inherent provider functionality coupled with SharePoint Forms Based Authentication (FBA), because expiration-controlled cookies can then be used that are both tamper-proof and encrypted by default.

Although the influential encryption benefits of inter-server IPSec communication are the main purpose for its employment, there are also numerous other benefits that can be realized when implementing the proposed server isolation solution. Because there are going to be certain flagged attributes describing source and destination data when using IPSec, there is another layer of security introduced that allows you to verify packet reception and destinations between SharePoint farm servers. Furthermore, IPSec integrates directly in with Kerberos authentication, which provides distinct advantages over Windows NT LAN Manager (NTLM) authentication routines. You see how to disseminate, examine, and approach Kerberos authentication later in this chapter.

Setting Up IPSec No Fallback Isolation Between SharePoint Servers

When you enable IPSec with SharePoint, you generally will be configuring the encryption protocol between the SharePoint servers participating in the SharePoint farm, as well as the server incorporated as the domain controller (DC). This is done by generating an IPSec policy (consisting of appropriate filters, actions, and rules), and then assigning the policy you create to the participating farm members (such as the SharePoint Index and Search servers by exporting the IPSec policy). You can best think of a proper IPSec implementation as a subscription-based architecture, whereby each server that is participating in the overall IPSec scheme subscribes to the IPSec standard in order to communicate with each other, and within the policy, attributes assigned can control how that inclusive service communication happens.

Table 12-1 shows IPSec no fallback isolation policy elements.

Table 12-1: IPSec No Fallback Isolation Policy Elements

Element Name	Element Description
Create IP Filter List	The IP filter list will define the protocols and interface elements that establish access control to the SharePoint servers
Create IP Filter Actions	Determines how security is handled for both IPSec-enabled and non-IPSec-enabled machines
IPSec Policy	Determines the aggregate IPSec configuration and is used for deployment

Creating IPSec Reusable Batch Files

Although it is viable for you to establish IPSec filter lists, filter actions, and summative policies through the IPSec interface, it is often advantageous to script the required logic in reusable batch files to promote reuse throughout other SharePoint instances that you might be responsible for. To do this, you can use the netsh.exe command-line tool provided with Windows Server 2003 to create reusable .CMD scripts to consume whenever applicable, even for other server objects such as SQL clusters. As you will see, the Netsh IPSec context is a powerful option for quickly managing and configuring IPSec.

The first task is to create a policy object that will hold the policy name that is passed in as a string value. The policy is not immediately allocated because of the assign=no flag, which is intentional, because there are various attributes that still have to be added to the policy before it is consumed. The default value for this is also no. Therefore, to assign the policy, you must directly call this attribute out in your script, as you will see at the end of the script:

```
netsh.exe ipsec static add policy name="SharePointIsolationPolicy" assign=no
```

Once the `policy` object has been defined with a name, it is possible to subsequently add the appropriate filter lists and filter actions. First, you must define a filter list and give it a case-sensitive name. Executing the following command will instantiate an empty filter list, which can optionally take the description parameter as an argument if you want to specify more information about the filter list:

```
netsh.exe ipsec static add filterlist name="SharePointTraffic"
```

Once the filter list is identified, you can add the appropriate filters to the filter list to describe the source addresses, describe destination addresses, provide a brief description of the filter, describe the protocol that it is running under, describe subnet masks, and provide the relevant port information to define the interface requirements.

For example, you could create two filters to handle the most common protocols for SharePoint, HTTP and HTTPS. IPSec can handle any number of protocols (such as ICMP, TCP, UDP, RAW, or port-based protocols) because of where it exists in the machine stack. (IPSec modifies routed packets by placing a new TCP header onto the original packet.) Thus, it is possible for you to handle all acceptable protocols by setting `protocol=any`. The source and destination addresses that are being specified are fairly loose in the following example because they are accepting any source address and setting the destination address as the server that the SharePoint server is running on:

```
REM Create a filter to handle port 80 protocols (HTTP)
netsh.exe ipsec static add filter filterlist="SharePointTraffic" srcaddr=any
dstaddr=me description="HTTP"  protocol=TCP srcport=0 dstport=80

REM Create a filter to handle port 443 protocols (HTTPS)
netsh.exe ipsec static add filter filterlist="SharePointTraffic" srcaddr=any
dstaddr=me description="HTTPS" protocol=TCP srcport=0 dstport=443
```

> The two most confusing parameters in these commands tend to be `srcaddr` and `dstaddr`, because they can take arguments besides concrete IP addresses. There are five arguments that can be passed into this parameter, depending on how your SharePoint environment is architected:
>
> `Me` — *Current machine*
>
> `Any` — *Any machine*
>
> `IPAddress` — *Concrete source IP address*
>
> `DNSName` — *Source or Destination DNS Name*
>
> `ServerType` — *Communication protocol used, either WINS, DNS, DHCP, or gateway*

Then, you can define the relevant filter actions, which are exercised afterward when defining the applicable access rules. This will also be the place where encryption routines can be defined. There are some arguments that you can use with the `filteraction` parameter that may appear to be confusing:

❏   The `qmpfs` argument defines whether to enable Perfect Forward Security (PFS), a cryptography concept targeted to eliminate unnecessary and unauthorized key reuse.

❑ The `inpass` argument specifies whether incoming packets can be non-secured in interception when relaying must be secured. This is generally an acceptable option, because the inter-server SharePoint farm communication can be locked down when outgoing from the server.

❑ The `soft` parameter is a failsafe measure that allows IPSec to go unsecure if other SharePoint farm servers don't support IPSec. This is undesirable, because inter-server communication should be encrypted between all of the servers in your environment. So, the attribute of `soft` should be set to no.

❑ The `qmsec` (quick mode security settings) argument holds the main security arguments of the method. The `qmsec` parameter will specify the relevant encryption algorithms that are used when a new session key is `creating` (declared in the first parameter in kilobytes), and the session key `lifetime`.

In the following example, MD5 is used first, and then SHA1 is used:

```
netsh.exe ipsec static add filteraction name="SharePointOnly" qmpfs=yes soft=no
inpass=yes action=negotiate qmsec="SP[MD5]:100000k/1000s SP[SHA1]:100000k/1000s"
```

More general filter actions can be defined and offered for later consumption (such as common allowing and blocking) by setting the `action` flags to either `permit` or `block`:

```
REM Add a filter action that will allow all users (permit all)
netsh.exe ipsec static add filteraction name="Allow" action=permit

REM Add a filter action that will deny all users (block all)
netsh.exe ipsec static add filteraction name="Block" action=block
```

After the filter actions are defined, you must restrict the relevant traffic so that the source address and destination addresses are set to receive from the relevant SharePoint server. The rules declaration makes it possible for you to define whether the rule should leverage Kerberos authentication by using the `Kerberos=yes` flag and defining whether keys are shared.

```
REM Add the appropriate static rules for IPSec

REM Define the permit all rule
netsh.exe ipsec static add rule name="Allow HTTP" policy="
SharePointIsolationPolicy " filterlist="SharePointTraffic " kerberos=yes
filteraction=Allow

REM Define the block all rule
netsh.exe ipsec static add rule name="Block All"  policy="
SharePointIsolationPolicy " filterlist="SharePointTraffic "  kerberos=yes
filteraction=Block

REM Define the rule with the encryption previously defined
netsh.exe ipsec static add rule name="" policy=" SharePointIsolationPolicy "
filterlist="SharePointTraffic " psk="SharePointSharedKey"
filteraction=SharePointOnly
```

Now, the `policy` object contains all the relevant assets that are required for deployment, including the filter lists, filters, filter actions, and rules. For you to leverage the policy, the `set` method can be used against the `policy` object, and the `assign` attribute can be flagged with a `yes` value (which was previously flagged with the no value during the initial instantiation of the policy object). If you do not assign the policy, it will still be available from the policy store; however it will have no applicability.

```
netsh.exe ipsec static set policy name="IIS_Server_Policy" assign=yes
```

Once the policy is set, you can verify it in the IPSec Microsoft Management Console (MMC) snap-in or through more scripting. To verify the new policy through MMC, open the MMC snap-in and add the IP Security Monitor option, which should currently define the specific filters that were just created. To view the policy through scripting, you can use the following command:

```
REM Show the new policy in the policy store
netsh.exe ipsec static show all
```

Once the destination and source address values are set within the IPSec settings, if the servers are not called out within the policy settings, there will be no communication allowed except the values that were explicitly set.

After creating an IPSec policy, you may need to export and import the policy to other servers. For example, you may create a batch file that targets securing your search and index machines, because indexing typically is offloaded in SharePoint farms to siloed servers and its communication with the search servers is generally not encrypted. To export a created IPSec policy to all of the search computers, you can use the exportpolicy and importpolicy commands, which take the file paths to the IPSec policy as arguments, as shown here:

```
REM Export an IPSec Policy (.ipsec)
netsh.exe static exportpolicy c:\SharePointpolicy.ipsec
REM Import an IPSec Policy (.ipsec)
netsh.exe static importpolicy c:\SharePointpolicy.ipsec
```

Using this technique, you can select the servers that should subscribe to the policy within the SharePoint farm, and the communication that occurs between them can be restricted by the use of the IPSec policy, ensuring that any inter-server conversation happens with encryption.

Kerberos Authentication in SharePoint

As explained earlier, IPSec integrates directly with Kerberos authentication, which you have seen in the netsh.exe commands when creating a new static IPSec rule with the kerberos=yes argument set. Kerberos is commonly the best security selection for an authentication routine within a SharePoint intranet environment, although it tends to be put into practice less frequently because it is more complex to implement in comparison to NTLM (which doesn't require much architect interaction).

Several benefits inherent to Kerberos authentication make it a very attractive choice for SharePoint intranet authentication.

Kerberos authentication tends to provide much more rapid processing for the concrete authentication routine because of the unique ticketing architecture that builds its backbone. This is because each requesting entity on the SharePoint network can request an authentication ticket, known as a Ticket to Get Tickets (TGT) from the Key Distribution Center (KDC). The ticket is granted by one of the main services that Kerberos provides, the Ticket-Granting Service (TGS), which constructs the ticket with specific parameters such as time-to-live fields (TTL), session keys encrypted against the hashed user password, and aggregate authorization information. Once the TGT is given to a user, it can be given to the KDC to generate service tickets for specific machines, which are then cached on the client machine. This means you can allow your users access to all the resources that exist within a specific, declared domain, such as to servers offering data from Microsoft sister server systems (such as SQL Analysis Services, Reporting Services, or others) without concern for double-hop authentication problems.

This is contrary to how NTLM authentication works. When one of your user requests is submitted for a specific resource that exists on a domain, it requires that the domain controller (DC) be contacted to verify the user credentials. Kerberos bypasses this inefficiency because the ticket that is being issued negates the need to communicate back with the DC to provide access to various domain resources, thereby increasing the performance of the overall authentication process.

The native encryption options that are offered to you with Kerberos are much more attractive as well. NTLM uses only symmetric cryptography, whereas Kerberos supports both asymmetric and symmetric cryptographic routines, thus increasing the overall options of confidentiality. NTLM also only supplies client authentication, whereby the client will request a resource of the server, the server will challenge the client, the client inputs the relevant information, and the server then validates the information that is submitted from the client. Kerberos does not work in this limited fashion. Kerberos supports both client and server authentication.

One of the most intrinsic segments of Kerberos authentication is the use of *delegation* (also known as *authentication forwarding*), which ties directly back into the concept of ticketing through the use of the KDC. Delegation is exceedingly significant when examining the features of multi-tiered authentication routines, which are increasingly common within SharePoint environments that tend to aggregate various business systems. Within any .NET application, when a user frequently accesses a specific resource, there is generally a small impersonation routine leveraged for an arbitrary user to act as a specified service when requesting an explicit resource. This is accomplished by calling the `WindowsIdentity` class and then using the `Impersonate()` method to impersonate the service Windows user.

Kerberos takes this concept a step further. A user is not granted access to a specific resource on behalf of the service account. Rather, with authentication forwarding, the service can get access to specific resources based on the identity of the user. Therefore, when a user enters a SharePoint environment and tries to gain access to a secondary database server that gets its relevant information from another server, the user can grant the relevant access to the secondary server that uses the user identity to give rights to the services. The user can then gain access to the third server, as opposed to using the service account for representation for authentication.

Setting Up Kerberos Authentication for SharePoint

To set up a SharePoint server for Kerberos, your first step is to set the relevant Web application (IIS Virtual Server) to use Kerberos as opposed to NTLM authentication (because NTLM is generally the default authentication routine in most environments). This can be done in three ways. Using any of these methods produces the same results.

Your first option occurs when creating or extending a new Web application through SharePoint Web Central Administration (WCAM). You are offered the option of changing the Web application authentication type between NTLM and Kerberos authentication.

For pre-existing applications, switch your authentication on an existing SharePoint Web application in WCAM by selecting Authentication Providers in the Application Management interface, and change the IIS Authentication Settings to use Negotiate (Kerberos) Outside of the main SharePoint interface. You can also use the `adsutil.vbs` script using the `set` method:

```
cscript adsutil.vbs set w3svc/SharePointSiteId/root/NTAuthenticationProviders
"Negotiate,NTLM"
```

Lastly, you can also directly edit the IIS Metabase to change this property. Directly editing the IIS Metabase offers the greatest insight into the back-end operational structure of your SharePoint Web server. To change the authentication property within the IIS Metabase, first stop the IIS services, unless you have the "edit-while-running" feature enabled (direct Metabase edit configuration). Once the IIS service is stopped, navigate to the IIS XML Metabase file located in the `\system32\inetsrv\` directory that contains the `metabase.xml` file. Before you make any changes, it is advisable to make a backup copy of the Metabase XML file. Because the Metabase file in IIS 6.0 is built upon well-formed XML, it is possible for you to directly edit it within your favorite text editor, such as Microsoft Notepad or Microsoft Visual Studio .NET.

The object in the Metabase that you need to locate is the `IISWebServer` object that specifies properties of each virtual server on the SharePoint machine. One of the child elements of the `IISWebServer` object is the `NtAuthenticationProviders` Metabase property, which specifies the attributes that should be associated when integrated authentication is being used for the virtual server (Integrated Authentication being the most common Virtual Server authentication setting that exists for SharePoint instances targeting an intranet deployment).

Whatever solution you are using to enable Kerberos, the `NtAuthenticationProviders` element should have the appropriate Kerberos string, as shown here:

```
NTAuthenticationProviders="Negotiate,NTLM"
```

What this IIS property is saying is that, first, Kerberos negotiation should be attempted when passing in the authentication header. If the negotiation fails with Kerberos (either because of the requesting user not providing enough authentication information, or the involved applications not supporting Kerberos authentication), then NTLM authentication is used to provide you with an authentication fallback.

Once the SharePoint Web application is set up to use Kerberos authentication using any of the described methods, the next step is to configure the SharePoint machine to be trusted for delegation, which allows a service to impersonate the user account to access various resources that exist across a network. Once this setting is enabled, the SharePoint service can access other network resources on the network by impersonating the user. This is done by opening up the Active Directory MMC snap-in, locating your SharePoint server, and, under the delegation properties of the server, checking the Trust Computer box under the Delegation tab.

Because it is common for SharePoint service accounts to run under domain accounts, you must also configure the service account to be trusted for delegation as well (so that it will be allowed to impersonate relevant users, no matter what account is running under the SharePoint Application Pools). To do this, follow the same method described to trust the SharePoint server for delegation. However, simply use the `users` container in Active Directory to enable the same setting for the relevant service account.

Finally, you must configure the resources that you want the account to impersonate to have the relevant Service Principal Names (SPNs). When registering an SPN, you are essentially specifying how the Kerberos authentication routine will authenticate to the relevant service, and then leveraging it. This is done by using the `setspn.exe` command, as shown here:

```
setspn -A HTTP/ServerName Domain\UserName
```

It is a best practice when you are setting up the SPN for Kerberos that the DNS and the NETBIOS names are both set for SharePoint through `setspn`, because it will provide coverage for all names that the user may specify (assuming that the NETBIOS names are unique across an environment). If this is generally not the case within your environment, it is best to instead just use the fully qualified DNS name to make the authenticated connections. If the naming conventions are unique, this setting is much more comprehensive, as shown here:

```
setspn -A SharePointService/SharePointMVP.com SharePointMVP\Adam

setspn -A SharePointService/SharePointMVP SharePointMVP\Adam
```

Certificate Solutions for Serving Clients

To harden SharePoint packet transmissions when serving SharePoint content to your clients, the pipe off of which your SharePoint instance is serving requests must be secured to encrypt the communications occurring between the requesting client machines and the SharePoint server farm. When enabling SSL, there are a variety of certificate architectural considerations that you must consider, including the following:

❑   Using a mutually trusted public CA certificate issuance (such as Verisign or another public CA)

❑   Using the embedded certificate solution that Microsoft provides through the use of MCS

❑   Issuing a mutually untrusted certificate through SelfSSL out of the IIS 6.0 toolkit

The most cost-effective way to approach using SSL is to either utilize an existing MCS infrastructure (because it is built into Windows Server 2003 as an available Windows Service) or to use SelfSSL (because it allows the quick creation and destruction of certificates because the SharePoint server administrator becomes responsible for the certificate life cycle). The MCS solution is typically an enterprise-based implementation, because the architecture of MCS is somewhat more complicated than the simpler SelfSSL self-certificate issuance option.

Using and Understanding Microsoft Certificate Services

When leveraging the embedded MCS certificate solution options, your appropriate organization PKI representatives or delegated certificate administrators typically have the option to deploy and revoke digital certificates that can be assigned for use with your SharePoint instances.

As shown in Table 12-2, MCS offers four modes of operation, allowing it to act as different CA types.

Table 12-2: Microsoft Certificate Services Modes of Operations

CA Type	Description of Type
Stand-alone root CA	Exists at the root of a disassociated network.
Stand-alone subordinate CA	Belongs to an established disassociated network. Obtains CA certificates from the stand-alone root CA, but can issue certificates in subordinates.
Enterprise root CA	Exists on an associated network at the root of the domain and is considered to be the most trustworthy. Has access to Active Directory.
Enterprise subordinate CA	Belongs to an associated network as a member of an established CA hierarchy. Obtains CA certificates from the stand-alone root CA, but can issue certificates in subordinates. Has access to Active Directory.

The implementation of MCS is not such a relatively straightforward task and requires a granular level of planning and design, because it equates to setting up an enterprise CA that signals the beginnings of a formal PKI infrastructure. Furthermore, MCS management and administration can become relatively complicated because it offers its own interfaces for development, using either the `CryptoAPI` interface (called `CAPICOM`), or leveraging the `IISCertObj` object to build the relevant scripts.

If you have an internal CA that is currently activated within your domain, to get a certificate for the SharePoint server, you are going to use the certificate Web enrollment site, or contact the appropriate Public Key Infrastructure (PKI) representatives. To begin the certificate request for your SharePoint server, you must follow these steps using embedded Windows Server 2003 functionality:

1. Open the IIS manager (Start ⇨ Run, and type **inetmgr**) and expand the Server Name node.
2. Expand the Web Sites node. Right-click the SharePoint Virtual Server and select Properties.
3. Click the Directory Services tab.
4. Select Server Certificate.
5. Click "Create a New Certificate" and click Next.
6. Select "Send The Request Immediately to an Online Certification Authority" and click Next.
7. Choose a friendly name for the certificate, do not adjust the bit-length from 1024, and select Next.
8. In the Organization Information window, the Organization and Organization Unit Name textboxes should have relevant organization information. Click Next.
9. In the Common Name window, enter the fully qualified domain name (FQDN) for the SharePoint server. This will default to the name of the machine off of which you are requesting the certificate.
10. In the Geographical Information window, enter in your country/region, state/province, and city/locality from where you are requesting the certificate.

11. Select the SSL port that the SharePoint application will use. The default for the port is 443, and it is not recommended to change this setting.

12. In the Certification Authority window, select the internal CA responsible for processing your certificate request.

13. The last window will allow you to finalize your request. Ensure that all the settings displayed in this window are correct.

14. Click Finish when you are done with the certificate request.

15. You can view your certificate on the View Certificate option within the Virtual Server properties under the Directory Services tab.

When you are requesting a certificate, some organizations mandate that the certificate Common Name that you are requesting must match the name of the host name of your SharePoint server. If you are using host headers to display your SharePoint site, this can cause a certificate mismatch error in a user's browser. To get around this error, you can use the Subject Alternate Access (SAN) certificate extension to specify multiple names that the certificate can be accepted for. Although Windows Server 2003 does not natively support this, the CA responsible for your certificate request can adjust some flags to manipulate the certificate policy using the `certutil` command, as shown here:

```
certutil -setreg policy\EditFlags +EDITF_ATTRIBUTESUBJECTALTNAME2
```

This will change the behavior of Certificate Services so that your PKI infrastructure can issue certificates appropriately.

Because MCS becomes relatively involved when quickly trying to deploy a certificate solution, you can instead use a self-certificate issuance, which tends to be a quicker, self-manageable solution that provides a high level of self control. Self-issued certificates are an ideal option when you are setting up a development environment or staging environment.

Using SelfSSL to Create Self-Signed Certificates for SharePoint

If there is not an enterprise certificate architecture within your organization (either through the use of a public CA or through a corporate MCS implementation), you can create and issue a certificate easily through the use of SelfSSL, which is provided with the IIS 6.0 toolkit. Although using SelfSSL will allow the creation of a certificate for use with a SharePoint environment, if you are having more than a few internal employees access the site, it is best to request the certificate from a CA that all requesting parties can trust. However, using the SelfSSL utility is a good method to avoid the complications, cost, and corporate standards that come with the use of MCS or public CAs, and requires very little interaction from you as the SharePoint administrator.

To use `SelfSSL.exe`, you must first acquire some of the arguments that will be needed for the executable to function. The most difficult and obtrusive of these is the ID of the virtual server that the certificate is going to be run on. You can acquire this either through a user interface or programmatically through C# code.

To acquire the virtual server ID through a user interface, it is possible to use another tool out of the IIS toolkit called the Metabase Explorer, which will allow you to browse through the `ServerBindings` property from the IIS Metabase. Because the Metabase Explorer simply wraps the `metabase.xml` file with a UI client application, you could optionally open the `metabase.xml` file in a text editor to acquire the same information.

You can also explore the `ServerBindings` programmatically through managed code by creating a small iteration using the `DirectoryEntry` class out of `System.DirectoryServices` to represent an object in IIS and the `ServerBindings` property. Coupled with `PropertyValueCollection`, it is possible to house the relevant values of the `ServerBindings` properties, as shown here in C#:

```
DirectoryEntry mySharePointServer = new DirectoryEntry("IIS://localhost/w3svc/" +
websiteID );

PropertyValueCollection serverBindings =
mySharePointServer.Properties["ServerBindings"];
        for (int count = 0; count < serverBindings.Count ; count++)
          {
              (serverBindings[count]);
          }
```

Once you have the virtual server ID harvested to pass as an argument to the SelfSSL tool, the certificate can be generated by using some command-line executions that will create and assign the certificate to the SharePoint instance. SelfSSL, by default, will attempt to gather all the default values for the default Web site to give you a general idea of what the statement should look like. Table 12-3 shows the SelfSSL parameters.

Table 12-3: SelfSSL Parameters

CA Type	Description of Type
T (Trusted Certificate)	Add the certificate being created into the trusted certificates list, which will allow the certificate to be immediately consumed from the local browser.
N (Common Name)	This is the Common Name of Certificate. Ensure that this matches the FQDN of the site that SharePoint is running on; otherwise, you will encounter several certificate errors throughout the user experience.
K (Key Size)	The cryptographic key length, which is generally kept at the default of 1024.
V (Validity Days)	How long the certificate will be valid for (specified in days).
P (Port)	The SSL port for the certificate to bind to, which is generally kept to the default of 443.
Q (Quiet Mode)	Will overwrite any SSL settings that may be affected by the SelfSSL process. If not flagged, you will get a prompt asking you whether you wish to overwrite the SSL settings for the virtual server ID specified.

When building the SelfSSL statement to execute, it should look like the following:

```
selfssl.exe /N:CN= <Common Name>/K:<Key Length> /V:<Days>/S:<VID> /P:<Port>
```

Once the SelfSSL statement is executed, you can browse to the deployed SharePoint site by using the `https://` as opposed to the `http://` prefix with the URL configured for the SharePoint Web application. SelfSSL will take care of most of the default settings (such as calling the default 443 SSL port).

When executing SelfSSL, the process will overwrite any of your SSL settings for the target SharePoint Web application, so execute the command with care. If you are requiring SSL and 128-bit encryption for connections in your Virtual Server Secure Communications configuration, these settings must be manually set, and are not automated by SelfSSL.

You can require SSL for your SharePoint Web application within the IIS virtual server properties. This will force SSL encryption for all of your SharePoint traffic, not allowing the use of the HTTP protocol. This is generally a good option, because a user will not often be diligent enough to type in the `https://` prefix when navigating to your SharePoint site. To force SSL encryption, follow these steps:

1. Open the IIS manager (Start ➪ Run, and then type **inetmgr**) and expand the Server Name node.

2. Expand the Web Sites node. Right-click the SharePoint Virtual Server and select Properties.

3. Click the Directory Services tab.

4. In the Secure Communications group box, select "Require secure Channel (SSL)" and optionally select "Require 128-bit encryption."

5. Click OK.

> Though the SelfSSL tool provides a simple, intuitive process that allows bypassing the requirement for an internal CA infrastructure or commercial public CA certificate to SSL-enable a SharePoint instance, it is important to realize that the certificate being generated is not coming from what is considered to be a trusted source. Because the certificate is self-generated and not mutually accepted for all parties that may negotiate a connection to the SharePoint site, the browser may display a certificate error. When you are looking at permanent certificate options that will be facing actual clients in a production environment, it is better for you to use a universally accepted certificate solution (such as an enterprise certificate issued from MCS or a trusted public-issued certificate).

ISA Server and SharePoint

Because of the potential high costs of security breaches within a compromised SharePoint environment (in addition to the requirements to maintain compliance with business and legal regulations), it is often prudent for you to introduce more advanced security solutions. These can include application layer firewalls with stateful packet inspection, chained authentication, packet filtering, and reverse proxies through the use of Microsoft Internet Security and Acceleration Server 2006 (ISA Server).

In a SharePoint environment, the benefits of ISA Server include the use of an application firewall (that promotes application-layer filtering with stateful interrogation of SharePoint packets) and SSL bridging (that provides an end-to-end encryption solution). By using stateful interrogation against SharePoint traffic, the typical inspection of packets is enhanced. Legacy methods of packet inspection firewall technology will generally only inspect the header of a packet and the destination port, whereby the actual information payload is not scanned. However, ISA Server includes mechanisms that provide intelligent decisions to determine whether the traffic should be considered to be legitimate or malicious in intent.

There are three main tasks that you should perform in regard to ISA Server with SharePoint:

❑ Securely publishing your SharePoint server through the use of SSL bridging to support stateful inspection of traffic

❑ Configuring link translation to ensure that your sensitive and unintentional server names aren't returned in SharePoint objects like the Core Search Results Web Part

❑ Setting up connectivity verifiers to monitor your SharePoint server to ensure communication between ISA Server and your SharePoint server

Of course, several other tactics and approaches can be exploited using ISA Server. The following basic three options are the ones most commonly found in an enhanced ISA Server environment with SharePoint (targeted at small to medium enterprises). Similar to the reusability introduced with IPSec through the use of scripts, the ISA Object Model allows you advanced capabilities to tap into its unique objects to streamline advanced tasks through two methods:

❑ Scripts for reusable code to automate administrative ISA tasks

❑ Using managed languages to build applications against ISA Server

With the SharePoint Publishing Rule Wizard, introducing ISA Server into your SharePoint environment has also never been easier. The wizard greatly eases the process of securely publishing your SharePoint Web applications.

Setting Up SSL Bridging with ISA Server for SharePoint

SSL bridging is one of the many ISA firewall features that promote a high level of security for SharePoint traffic on SSL-enabled pipes. Unlike advanced hardware firewalls (which can perform stateful inspection on solely HTTP traffic), ISA Server provides the alternative to inspect even encrypted SharePoint SSL traffic. SSL bridging supports this scenario, because the packets are decrypted on reception by the ISA Server, and then re-encrypted when the packet is then forwarded to SharePoint.

Two methods of SSL bridging configuration are supported by ISA Server and can be leveraged, depending on the SharePoint security environment needs:

❑ *SSL-SSL bridging* — This is the most comprehensive security solution because the traffic is SSL-encrypted from the point of origin to reception by the SharePoint server, covering all the related network endpoints. Stateful inspection of the traffic can occur as well, because the packet can be decrypted upon reception on the ISA Server interface before being re-encrypted again.

❑ *SSL-HTTP bridging* — This provides encryption of the traffic between the requesting SharePoint user and the ISA Server. Afterward, the transmission between the ISA Server and SharePoint is sent in plain-text, therefore credentials can be intercepted on the internal network.

Programmatically, you can access these types through the `SecureProtocolRedirection` and `NonSecureProtocolRedirection` properties of the ISA Administrative Object Model. These properties control how requests are forwarded when they are piped in through both a secure and unsecure connection. These types are also accessible through the `PublishedServerType` property, which will determine how piped requests are handled by a related Web Publishing Rule. Programmatic manipulation of ISA Server administration objects is discussed later in this chapter, along with an examination of how exploiting such objects can ease complex administration tasks.

SSL-SSL bridging is undoubtedly the most secure SSL scheme that you can implement for SharePoint. This is because the entire transmission process from creation of the client request to final content service by SharePoint is encrypted. This particular bridging process encompasses an SSL session between the client and external ISA Server interface, and a subsequent SSL session between internal ISA Server interface and the SharePoint server. The overall sequence that builds up SSL bridging is relatively straightforward, and once understood, the benefits of implementing a complete end-to-end encryption solution are immediately evident.

Although there are several granular sequences that go into an endpoint-to-endpoint encryption solution, some of the principal ones forming the foundation are shown in Table 12-4.

Table 12-4: SSL Bridging Sequence of Events

Process Name	Process
Initial Request	A client will request the SharePoint instance with the `https` prefix to establish a preliminary SSL session between the client and external ISA interface.
SSL Connection Is Established	The SSL session is established between ISA Server firewall and the client. Data transmission that occurs between the client and the ISA Server is encrypted.
Web Publishing Rule Query	Web Publishing Rules are queried as to whether there is one that contains a destination set with the requested FQDN of the passed request argument. The Web Publishing Rule contains the listener reference to the aliased server certificate in the ISA Server machine Trusted Root Certification Authorities.
Matched Destination Set	If a matching destination set is found, the request will be forwarded according to the instructions that are included in the Web Publishing Rule.
Packet Decryption and Inspection	ISA Server decrypts the SharePoint traffic and inspects it to determine whether or not the traffic is considered legitimate.
Create SSL Connection To SharePoint	ISA Server will then instantiate a new secure connection to the SharePoint server by using the ISA Web Proxy Service to act as the requesting client on the internal ISA Server interface.
Traffic is forwarded to the SharePoint server	Following the secure line establishment to the SharePoint server from the ISA Server interface, SharePoint packets are forwarded in encrypted format.

> There are two main types of proxy modes that ISA will allow you to use.
>
> A transparent (reverse) proxy is when the client is not aware that there is a proxy in between the SharePoint server and its machine, so requests appear to be coming from the SharePoint server (such as edge firewalls). This is best for heterogeneous clients where browser software is not known. In this configuration, traffic is not optimized because the client can't optimize requests against a proxy server.
>
> The other type of proxy is a *forwarding proxy*, which places the proxy information in your user browsers within a domain generally through the use of a Group Policy Object (GPO) through the Group Policy Management Console (GPMC). If deploying outside of a domain, a forwarding proxy is usually enabled through the use of Auto discovery through either Dynamic Host Configuration Protocol (DHCP) or the Domain Name System (DNS). The benefits of a forward proxy are increased performance, user- and group-based access controls, and the ability to use Web Proxy chaining, whereby ISA firewalls and proxies can be connected to each other.

To enable SSL bridging, you must complete several Windows Server, SharePoint, and ISA configuration steps, each of which plays an intrinsic role in the overall communications process. Some of the steps are required to set the stage for the proper functioning of the ISA Server.

Setting Up Alternate Access Mappings (AAM)

The first of these groundwork steps is for you to set up Alternate Access Mappings (AAM) to ensure that your appropriate SharePoint URLs resolve to the correct content. There are two ways to configure Alternate Access Mapping Settings for the appropriate incoming and outgoing zones: using STSADM .exe or through WCAM.

This is an important step, because during the publishing of the SharePoint server, ISA Server will ask you whether or not you have achieved this task. ISA requires this information because SharePoint can be accessed from multiple URLs or locations, and still provide the same content to the user through the use of zones. AAM helps to resolve this issue by providing the means for appropriate URL resolution, so that users can type in the address http://www.sharepointmvp.com and they can be redirected to http://dmz.sharepointmvp.com. This step is pretty important, so it is better to have this done before starting the ISA Server publishing process.

The first way to implement AAM is through the use of the stsadm commands addzoneurl and addalternatedomain. The addzoneurl command will take the zone name that you are configuring for as a parameter, as well as the zonemapedurl, which takes the URL that the client will be requesting.

```
@ECHO ON

REM Adding an outgoing zone
stsadm.exe -o addzoneurl -urlzone extranet -zonemappedurl https://www.sharepointmvp
.com -url https://dmz.sharepointmvp.com

REM Adding an incoming zones
```

The `addalternatedomain` command is arguably where you might run into some trouble, because it will tie more into how you configure ISA Server. It takes in the `incomingurl` parameter, which represents the URL of how the site will be requested (the URL of the SharePoint server). By default, ISA will forward the original host header when using the SharePoint Publishing Wizard. So, the `incomingurl` parameter should match the URL you are publishing that your users will request. For some reason, if after ISA is configured and you do remove this option, you must ensure that the `incomingurl` parameter matches the address that you configure ISA to forward.

```
stsadm.exe -o addalternatedomain -urlzone extranet -incomingurl
https://www.sharepointmvp.com -url https://dmz.sharepointmvp.com
```

You can also set up the relevant AAM settings through WCAM. In the Operations tab in WCAM, under the Global Configuration group box, select Alternate Access Mappings. In the Alternate Access Mappings screen, you can edit existing URLs for zones and edit the Public zone URLs. When you are in the AAM WCAM interface, select the SharePoint Web application that you are publishing through ISA Server (typically in the Internet or Extranet zone). In this screen, ensure that the public URL that is being published by ISA Server is assigned to the Extranet zone, and add the internal URL (the DMZ URL) that will be used to forward the request. When you are finished, your AAM settings should have two URLs in the Extranet zone: the DMZ URL and the URL that people are using to request the site externally.

Using an Exported SSL Certificate

In an SSL bridging scenario, the ISA Server will sit in front of your SharePoint server, impersonating the SharePoint machine for user requests. For an SSL bridging scenario where packets are decrypted, inspected, and re-encrypted prior to routing, two certificates are required.

The first certificate will essentially impersonate the SharePoint server by using an exported SSL certificate from the SharePoint server or obtaining a properly configured certificate from a public CA. The certificate that sits on ISA should have a Common Name that corresponds to the SharePoint server so that it can intercept the client requests as requests traverse in for the SSL bridging to perform properly. The Common Name on the certificate that is installed on and is being presented by the ISA Server interface should match the FQDN of how people are requesting the SharePoint server. The SSL certificate on the SharePoint server should match the FQDN or IP Address that ISA is using to access the SharePoint server. Usually, when getting this certificate, it is best to procure it from an internal CA, because the ISA machine must be configured to trust the issuing source CA (which, in most organizations with an existing PKI infrastructure, is already configured as such).

Once the certificate is in ISA Firewall's Machine Certificate Store, you will be able to bind the certificate to a Web Listener, which will be consumed by the Web Publishing Rule responsible for relaying the appropriate SharePoint requests presented to the ISA Server.

Getting the required exported certificate into the ISA Firewall's Machine Certificate Store is a relatively straightforward task that can be achieved using some of the available Windows Server 2003 embedded wizards.

The first task is to export the certificate from the SharePoint server using the embedded certificate wizard provided with IIS 6.0 in Windows Server 2003. This certificate will be used to decrypt the SSL

SharePoint packets that are intercepted from ISA Server. You can easily do this through the IIS Virtual Server Directory Security tab that offers management of the related SSL certificates:

1. From the Directory Services tab for the SharePoint Virtual Server, select View Certificate.

2. In the Certificate window, select the Details tab.

3. Select "Copy to File."

4. Once the export process has begun, fill in the relevant details.

When exporting the certificate, it is very important to ensure that you are also exporting the private key (Figure 12-3). Otherwise, the SSL bridging configuration will fail. Be sure you note the password that is being used to protect the exported certificate, because this will be required later when adding the certificate to the ISA Firewall's Machine Certificate Store. Once you have exported the certificate, you will have a new `.pfx` file that represents your exported certificate.

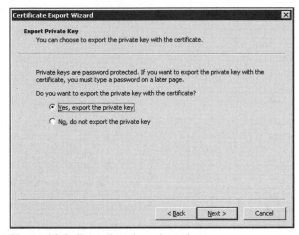

Figure 12-3: Exporting the private key

> **Protect your** `.pfx` **file with the utmost caution and care, especially when the** `.pfx` **file is being moved from server to server. If the** `.pfx` **file is compromised, your encrypted SharePoint communication could become compromised by a malicious user by intercepting and decrypting sensitive content.**

Once the certificate has been exported through the certificate wizard, it can be added into the ISA Firewall's Machine Certificate Store by first bringing up the certificates MMC snap-in. Follow these steps:

1. Bring up the Run dialog by selecting Start ⇨ Run. Once the Run dialog box appears, enter **MMC** and click OK.

2. In the MMC console, select File and click Add/Remove Snap-in.

3. In the Add/Remove Snap-in dialog, click Add.

4. In the Add Standalone Snap-in dialog (Figure 12-4), click Certificates, and click Add.

Figure 12-4: Add Standalone Snap-in dialog

Once the certificates snap-in has been added to MMC, it is possible to import the certificate into the ISA Firewall's Machine Certificate Store. One of the tasks available in the MMC certificates snap-in is to import a pre-existing certificate into the Certificate Store.

To import the certificate, open the Personal Certificate Store, right-click the Certificates node, and select Import. On the "File to Import" window, browse to the exported certificate, and enter in the relevant password you set previously to import the certificate. Once the certificate is placed within the Personal Certificate Store, it can then be moved to the Trusted Root Certification Authorities by cutting and pasting the certificate from the Personal container to the Trusted Root Certification Authorities container.

Once the certificate is placed within the Trusted Root Certification Authorities Store, the next step is to construct the appropriate Web Publishing Rule that will assimilate the certificate that was just imported into the Trusted Root Certification Authorities Store through the use of a Web Listener. Fortunately, generating these objects to securely publish your SharePoint server can be done with functionality provided by ISA Server through the use of the SharePoint Publishing Rule Wizard.

Creating a Publishing Rule through the SharePoint Publishing Wizard

Creating a Publishing Rule for a SharePoint server has never been easier with the introduction of the SharePoint Publishing Wizard. A Publishing Rule in essence is meant to define whether an allowance or denial rule should be executed when handling attempted user connections. This will become increasingly evident when modifying the properties of the Publishing Rule that the SharePoint Publishing Rule Wizard provisions out through the ISA Management Console. This is because, within the ISA Management Console, there is the option to Allow or Deny connections being established.

1. Open the Microsoft Internet Security and Acceleration Server 2006 management console.

2. Expand Arrays, and expand the relevant SharePoint Array.

3. Select the Firewall Policy node.

4. Select the Tasks tab.

5. Select Publish SharePoint Sites.

6. On the Welcome to the SharePoint Publishing Rule Wizard page (Figure 12-5), enter a friendly name in the rule name textbox.

Figure 12-5: SharePoint Publishing Rule Wizard page

Once the friendly name is entered for the SharePoint rule that you want to create, ISA Server will want to know whether you want to "Publish a single Web site or load balancer," "Publish a server farm of load balanced Web servers," or "Publish multiple Web sites." Which option to choose depends on your SharePoint implementation.

The most frequently used of these is to "Publish a single Web site or load balancer," because it is common that an organization pushes a single SharePoint portal instance through the ISA firewall. ISA Server does provide facilities for server farms that allow proper load balancing using session affinity or IP affinity, server health status supervision that couples with the related balancing algorithms, and draining of servers so that requests currently handled by a server can continue to be served while future connections are ignored.

For a simple SSL bridging scenario to secure a single SharePoint instance, the first option, "Publish a single Web site or load balancer," is the option that you should select, as shown in Figure 12-6. Click Next.

On the following window, you must make ISA Server aware of how encryption should happen for the communication layer. Because it is desirable to use SSL bridging to ensure that credentials are never forwarded in clear text (when ISA receives or forwards a request), select "Use SSL to connect to the published Web server or server farm," as shown in Figure 12-7. Click Next.

On the Internal Publishing Details window (Figure 12-8), you must supply the details for how the internal SharePoint site is going to be resolved through the ISA server proxy (see Figure 12-7). If you are publishing the SharePoint site by using the internal site name, it is best to verify that ISA can resolve this name by doing a simple ECHO request by executing a ping command from the ISA Server machine to the SharePoint machine. Ensure that, if doing an ECHO request, the internal interface is being called from the SharePoint machine as well; otherwise, communication will fail between the two servers. If ISA cannot resolve using the internal name, the "Use a computer name or IP address to connect to the published server" option must be checked. The entries that you place on this page must match the Common Name that is placed on the certificate bound to the SharePoint site on the SharePoint front-end Web server. Click Next.

Figure 12-6: Selecting "Publish a single Web site or load balancer"

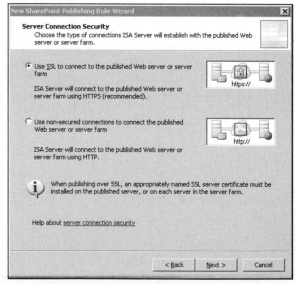

Figure 12-7: Selecting "Use SSL to connect to the published Web server or server farm"

Next, you must specify the Public Name Details that the Web Publishing Rule requires to contact the back-end SharePoint server (Figure 12-9). When applying this setting, you are allowed to accept requests for either a specified domain or for any domain. By very careful when selecting the "any domain name" option because this option promotes a low level of security.

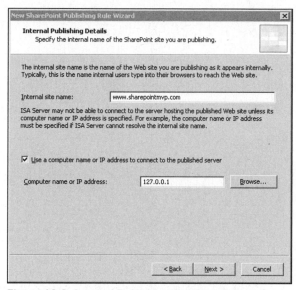

Figure 12-8: Internal Publishing Details window

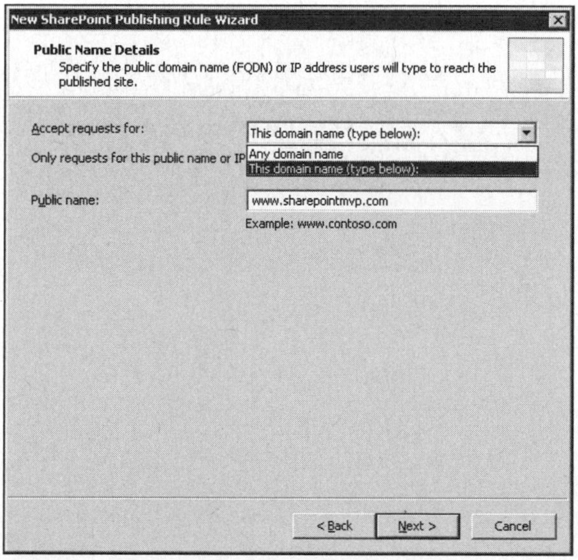

Figure 12-9: Public Name Details window

The reason that this is a very poor security option is that the Web Publishing Rule will accept incoming requests using any IP address or FQDN that can reach the IP address used by the Web listener for the Web Publishing Rule. All requests will be believed to be valid requests, thereby increasing the playing field for attacks. Limiting the requests to a specific domain greatly restricts the names that a user can request against the ISA Server for resolution. It is very important that the friendly name that users use in order to access the SharePoint instance be used in this textbox corresponding to its relevant DNS A record, and that the entry match the Common Name that is appended to the certificate being used. Enter the relevant domain name and click Next.

The next option in the SharePoint Publishing Wizard is to select a Web listener to use with the publishing rule that you are creating. A Web listener is a programmatic asset that essentially provides the relevant network objects (such as IP addresses, port information, and SSL settings) that will listen for requests as they are intercepted by the ISA Server on any number of interfaces. For a SharePoint server, if an extranet implementation is being resolved to www.sharepointmvp.com, then a Web listener is required to translate the relevant IP address and port number to the friendly name www.sharepointmvp.com.

If a Web listener is already defined, you can edit the properties of the listener from this window. If you haven't previously created a Web listener (as is the current case), you are afforded the option of creating one to correspond to your SharePoint Web Publishing Rule, which will allow the binding of a new Web listener to the certificate you imported.

To create a new Web listener, on the "Welcome to the New Web Listener Wizard" window (Figure 12-10), define a friendly name for the Web listener for systems administrators and architects to use. It is best to put the internal name of the machine that you are publishing in this textbox, along with the port name, supplementing it with any other information that may assist other administrators if they have to perform troubleshooting or leverage the specific Web listener that you are creating.

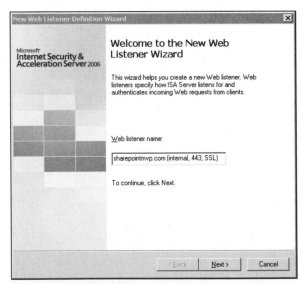

Figure 12-10: "Welcome to the New Web Listener Wizard" window

Once the Web listener has a friendly name, on the Client Connection Security window (Figure 12-11), ISA needs to know whether the listener requires SSL to communicate with requesting clients. Because a certificate has already been installed on the machine to supplement the listener with this option, check "Require SSL secured connections with clients." Using the other option of "Do Not Require SSL secured connections with clients" is very atypical, because the external interface will be allowed to establish lines that may transmit plain text, and this is generally only explored when using a uni-homed firewall for branch offices.

On the Web Listener IP Addresses window (Figure 12-12), ISA must be responsive to the requests that should be listened for. Generally, when placing an ISA Server in front of SharePoint, you are facing the external network to the world. Therefore, the External adapter should be selected. If there are specific IPs that should only be listening for requests on the External adapter (which houses multiple IP addresses), you can select the relevant IP addresses for the specific adapter in the Select IP Addresses window.

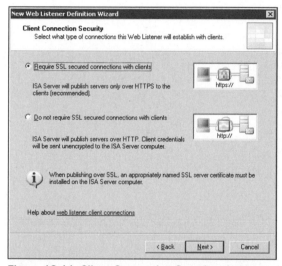

Figure 12-11: Client Connection Security window

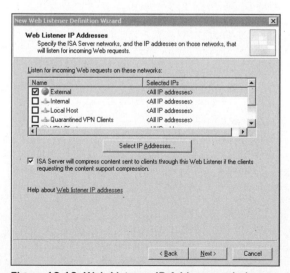

Figure 12-12: Web Listener IP Addresses window

It is important to use this option wisely, and to take advantage of the fact that you can select specific IP addresses. Because the adapter is bound to a range of IP addresses, when binding an SSL certificate to the adapter range as a whole, it will become restrictive for creating new listeners, because the SSL socket will become bound to all the addresses.

On this same page, remember to keep "ISA Server will compress content sent to clients through this Web Listener if the clients requesting the content support compression" checked, which will allow HTTP compression to work hand-in-hand with the ISA Server cache features. Although the caching features are not discussed here, the inherent ISA caching functions and Content Download Jobs can greatly increase SharePoint speed-to-reception time. If you want both internal and external users to have access to the SharePoint instance, both of the adapters should be selected in this window. Select the relevant adapter and IP addresses, and then click Next.

Because, in the Client Connection Security window (Figure 12-11), SSL was chosen as being required, the certificate to use with the listener must be defined. If the certificate was brought over using the Certificates MMC snap-in, it can be chosen on the Listener SSL Certificates screen by using the Select Certificate button, which will allow the display of all the valid certificates that can be bound to the Web listener being created, and that are currently trusted by the ISA machine. If you specified several IP addresses in the interface chosen in the Web Listener IP Addresses screen (Figure 12-12), you can assign a certificate to each of the IP addresses. The certificate interface is also very useful when inspecting whether any certificate you imported is set for expiration soon, whom it was issued by, if it was installed correctly, and other related metadata. Select the certificate that was imported from the SharePoint server and click Next.

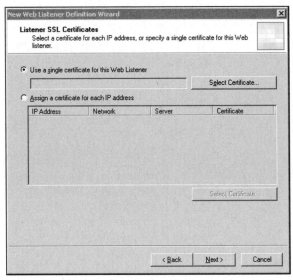

Figure 12-13: Listener SSL Certificates screen

In the Authentication Settings window, you are required to inform ISA of how clients requesting SharePoint content will specify the credentials that ISA Server should use, and how those exact credentials will be validated. A variety of options are available here, including the following:

- ❑ HTML Form Authentication
- ❑ HTTP Authentication
- ❑ SSL Client Certificate Authentication
- ❑ No Authentication

There are also a variety of ways to validate the credentials that the client is passing, including the following:

- ❑ *Active Directory* — Used if ISA belongs to a domain
- ❑ *Active Directory via LDAP* — Used if ISA does not belong to the domain, but you want ISA Server to tap into Active Directory
- ❑ *RADIUS (OTP)* — Used if you are using a one-time RADIUS password scheme
- ❑ *RADIUS* — Used for remote RADIUS authentication, most commonly found in use by network appliances
- ❑ *RSA SecurID* — Used if you have the relevant two-factor authentication schemes and hardware tokens

For an extranet environment that will have the logins stored within a medium such as Active Directory, the option to choose would be HTML Form Authentication (not be confused with SharePoint 2007 Forms Based Authentication, which is instead provided by the ASP.NET 2.0 pluggable framework) and Active Directory via LDAP.

By using the HTML Form Authentication option, there are many facets that are provided to you, such as the use of ISA Server Single Sign-On (SSO), not to be confused with SharePoint Single Sign On (SSOSrv) provided by MOSS, which is managed from the Services MMC console. However, authentication credentials are not cached, but rather housed within a temporary cookie.

On public computers, this becomes a concern. However, the option for users to select how they are connecting is provided on the ISA login form. The concept of this cookie (which can be found with an ISA* prefix) becomes important with load balancing for a farm when using a cookie scheme as opposed to source-IP based schemes, because the same server in round-robin load balancing will generally continue serving requests based on the GUID presented by the cookie (so that session affinity is maintained).

On the Single Sign On Settings window (Figure 12-14), select "Enable SSO for Web sites published with this Web listener" option and enter the relevant domain. In the provided example, www.sharepointmvp.com is being published, and therefore the sharepointmvp.com domain must be entered. The listener is then created and appended to the Web Publishing Rule. Click Next.

On the Authentication Delegation window (Figure 12-15), you must tell ISA Server how you would like communication to be authenticated with the back-end server. Table 12-5 shows several options, each of which can be leveraged by an organization, depending on corporate security standards and your SharePoint server needs.

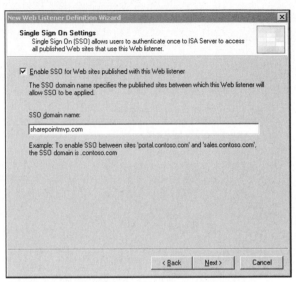

Figure 12-14: Single Sign On Settings window

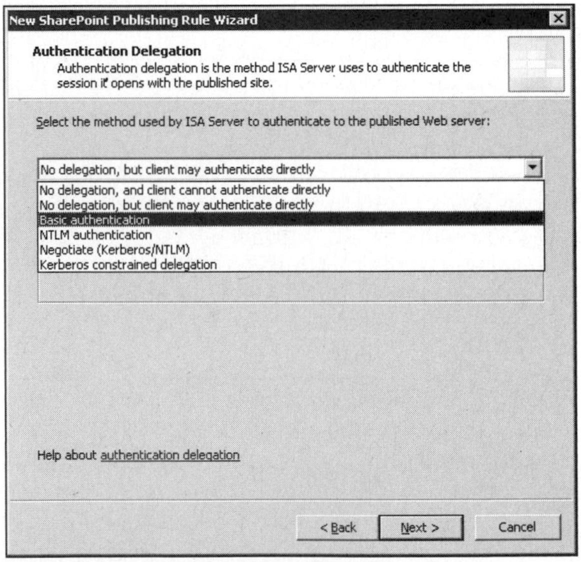

Figure 12-15: Authentication Delegation window

Table 12-5: Authentication Delegation Routines

Process Name	Process
No delegation, and client cannot authenticate directly	Essentially, this means that no credentials will be forwarded past the ISA Server to the SharePoint server that is being published, so the SharePoint content will not be accessible. Only use this if the SharePoint user base is accessing the ISA Server and not the serving SharePoint machine.
No delegation, but client may authenticate directly	The ISA Server will not forward the credentials to the SharePoint server. However, if the client is prompted for credentials for the Web server, the SharePoint machine can consume them.
Basic authentication	The ISA Server will simply forward the credentials to the SharePoint server using the basic authentication routine. If you are using basic authentication, then you must deploy an SSL bridging scenario, because the credentials will be forwarded in plain text to the back-end SharePoint server, along with whatever content is requested off the SharePoint server in the authentication header.
NTLM authentication	If NTLM is used throughout the corporate environment, the credentials can be forwarded using it, which would introduce domain controller verification, bypassing direct contact between the internal ISA interface and the SharePoint machine. If you are using NTLM for your SharePoint authentication as opposed to Kerberos, this is typically the most-used option.
Negotiate (Kerberos/NTLM)	A negotiation can happen where Kerberos or NTLM is used. This is frequently used when the appropriate IIS Metabase objects mirror the same setting.
Kerberos constrained delegation	If Kerberos is set up in the environment, and the ISA machine has been trusted for delegation of credentials (similar to how the SharePoint machine was set up previously for delegation of credentials through the Active Directory MMC), then a user certificate can be presented to authenticate to the SharePoint machine. Optimally, this is the most secure setting. However, it is more complex to set up, because it involves Kerberos authentication.

Given that SSL bridging is being used to authenticate to the SharePoint server, you can simply use basic authentication because the risk of tampering with the communication lines are rather low with an encrypted transmission. The most secure method is generally the use of Kerberos authentication, but, as mentioned, this requires extra configuration. When not using SSL for security, the most common setting is to "No delegation, and client cannot authenticate directly." Select "Basic authentication" because SSL is being used. Click Next.

On the ensuing Alternate Access Mapping Configuration window (Figure 12-16), you must tell ISA Server whether AAM has already been set up. This was previously accomplished through the use of the STSADM commands `addalternatedomain` and `addzonemap` or the WCAM Alternate Access Mappings Web inter-face. Therefore, select "SharePoint AAM is already configured on the SharePoint server." Because of how ISA will forward name requests, the appropriate entries must be added in the extranet URL list. Click Next.

On the User Sets page (Figure 12-17), you see the option to bind the rule that is being created to a specific user set. If there are groups that were previously created in Active Directory, you can produce custom groups to add into the user sets to provide a more granular, applied rule for access requests. If this isn't a particular concern, and you want to simply apply the rule to all users who are passing through the ISA Server, you can just accept the default rule of All Authenticated Users. Select All Authenticated Users and the click Next.

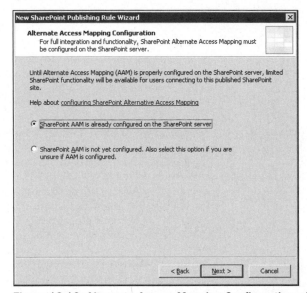

Figure 12-16: Alternate Access Mapping Configuration window

Figure 12-17: User Sets page

The last page on the SharePoint Publishing Rule Wizard is the "Completing the New SharePoint Publishing Rule Wizard" window, which allows confirmation of the edits made through the entire wizard process. If everything is acceptable, click Finish. You will notice that the new SharePoint publishing rule pointing to your SharePoint server is then available under the Firewall Policy Rules repeater within the ISA Server Management Console. To manage the new Publishing Rule, you can bring up the properties of it by right-clicking it and selecting Properties.

Because the additions haven't been committed to the ISA array, you must select Apply in the upper portion of the ISA Management Console for the relevant changes to take effect. Afterward, the SharePoint publishing configuration can be tested to see if other adjustments to ISA Server are necessary, based on your network configuration.

ISA and Link Translation

One of the principal benefits of using ISA Server in front of SharePoint is the option for link translation. Link translation in ISA Server is facilitated through the use of a filter, known as the *Link Translation Filter* (LTF), which is essentially an orthodox ISA firewall Web Filter. When you are facing a SharePoint environment externally in a proxy-based Web publishing scenario, oftentimes your sensitive machine names, absolute URLs, or non-standard port assignments commonly become available to your external users (which is mutually puzzling to your users and non-functional from an operational standpoint). This is frequently found in environments that begin to assimilate content from file shares and orphaned Line of Business systems into SharePoint (particularly evident within returned SharePoint search results in the Core Search Results Web Part provisioned in the SharePoint Search Center).

Link translation rides on a Web Publishing Rule, and, when the LTF is implemented, a default dictionary that will take care of HTTP to HTTPS, obscure port, and computer name translation is also provisioned. The first of these is particularly important, because, when using a SSL connection to SharePoint, all subsequent interactions from the user must follow the SSL protocol. Therefore, by default, in the link translation dictionary, the required HTTP to HTTPS entries are provided when one of your users initiates a connection with SSL. All subsequent requests will follow the HTTPS protocol maintained even when your SSL connections use a non-standard port designation.

If the default dictionary does not contain the required entries to properly facilitate your required link translation, or you find skews in the links being translated, it is possible to add custom dictionary entries to granularize how link translation occurs by appending explicit entries.

> **Don't assume that the default link translation that ISA provides is sufficient for your SharePoint implementation. SharePoint contains many embedded URLs and hard links to content throughout its application architecture. Ensuring that your AAM settings are correctly configured will help to eliminate several of these problems. When investigating link problems within your SharePoint site, make certain to not only examine the link translation libraries, but also to investigate your AAM settings!**

This is a powerful option to exploit when, after viewing the effective link translation rules that ISA provisions, there are still antiquated links not being parsed correctly at any point throughout the environment.

Because the link translation occurs on a Web Publishing Rule basis, modifying it is done through the properties of the Web Publishing Rule.

1. Select the relevant Web Publishing Rule and select the Tasks tab, which allows the option to Edit Selected Rule.

2. On the Link Translation tab, select "Apply link translation to this rule."

3. Select Configure and click the Add option.

4. In the Locally Defined Mappings dialog box (Figure 12-18), enter in the "Replace this text" entry the name of the string you want replaced in returned links, which corresponds to the explicit string that was erroneous before. Enter the value you want to replace the string in the "With this text" entry.

5. Click OK.

If, at some point, you want to verify the Global Site Mappings that have been implemented on the ISA machine, you can use the configuration box to build out a friendly report for records management purposes. This can be done by expanding the Configuration node and, under the General tab, selecting Global Link Translation. Because each array will maintain a store of the URLs that are being translated through within a relevant Web Publishing Rule, under the Global Mappings tab, all of the implicit and explicit dictionary entries can be examined, as shown in Figure 12-19. Because various arrays can exist throughout an enterprise that is using ISA Server, you should be aware that link translation can be spread across all arrays. Therefore, arrays can share link translation information in order to maintain conformity across ISA Server farms.

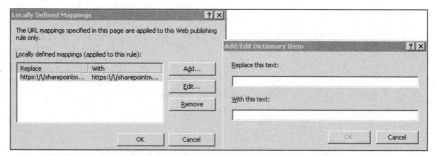

Figure 12-18: Locally Defined Mappings dialog box

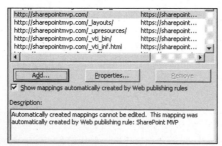

Figure 12-19: Implicit and explicit dictionary entries

Creating Connection Verification for SharePoint Server Health Monitoring

Within ISA Server, you can constantly validate the connections being established between a SharePoint site and the internal ISA interface to gauge your relevant uptime, and to ensure that your required SharePoint content is available to users. This is done through an ISA asset called *connectivity verifiers*, which will allow a variety of protocols to be used to verify connectivity. The following three connectivity verifiers are provided by default:

❑ Internet Control Message Protocol (ICMP) ECHO_REQUEST (Ping)

❑ TCP connection attempts

❑ HTTP GETs

Also available are varieties of groups that you can place a SharePoint connectivity verifier in (such as DNS, DHCP, and Active Directory) in order to organize the connectivity verifiers that you create.

The first step for you to establish the monitoring of connectivity is to create the actual connectivity verifier. Because this is considered in the ISA Management Console as a Monitoring Activity (because you are monitoring the SharePoint server health), select the Monitoring node. Once you are in the Monitoring interface, select the Connectivity tab and under the Tasks tab, select Create New Connectivity Verifier. When creating a new verifier, the SharePoint site must be presented as an argument. In the address textbox on the Connectivity Verification Details window, place the FQDN of the SharePoint site, because the verifier will exist to service the internal interface, as shown in Figure 12-20.

For this connectivity verifier, you are simply going to check whether the ISA Server sees the SharePoint instance as alive. This can be done by simply using an ECHO request. In the method used to verify the connection, select "Send a Ping request," and select the "Web (Internet)" group. If you would like to specify a time-out value to use, you can specify that count in milliseconds, and ISA can optionally send you an alert when this threshold is met. The connectivity verifier will generally run every 30 seconds while sending the request, and will wait for 5 additional seconds before responding by directing requests to a subsequent machine (based on the load-balancing algorithm).

Figure 12-20: Connectivity Verification Details window

When creating a connectivity verifier that conflicts in communication with a publishing rule, you will be informed that a new rule must be created in order for the ISA interface to send the request. By doing this, there will be the creation of a system policy rule that must be enabled for the connectivity verifier to function correctly. Click the Apply button in the ISA Server Management Console, as shown in Figure 12-21.

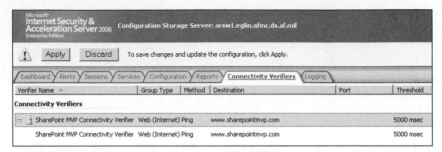

Figure 12-21: Clicking the Apply button in the ISA Server Management Console

After the connectivity rule has been implemented, there are a variety of interactions that can be performed with it. It is possible to modify, disable, delete, import, or export connectivity verifiers from this window in the ISA Server Management Console. In the monitoring dashboard view, the connectivity verifier will show relevant metrics in the Status column in order to report if something wrong does occur.

Managing ISA through Scripts

Though it is feasible for you to manage and administer an ISA instance providing SharePoint through the use of the ISA Management Console, in the spirit of creating reusable assets to use throughout your environment, it is sometimes helpful to instead place ISA routines within reclaimable scripts and applications. Besides automating repetitive, dull administrative tasks, you can position frequently called, difficult, complex tasks into scripts that allow you quick execution of assignments that would otherwise prove to be complicated and lengthy.

The ISA Server Administration Object Model allows quick programmatic access to the necessary ISA objects that can be used to vastly extend and ease the available ISA administration options, automating tasks that would otherwise prove to be very complicated to reproduce and execute several times. Several of the objects are even SharePoint-specific, such as the `FpcPublishedServerApplication` enumerated type (which contains a Publishing Rule flag for a SharePoint) and the `AlternateAccessMappingConfigured` property (to help to determine whether AAM is configured for a SharePoint server, which as demonstrated previously is important to ISA Server configuration when securely publishing SharePoint).

By using the Component Object Model (COM) objects, it is possible to tap into and control any other ISA Server arrays that may affect your SharePoint environment. Typically, ISA administration scripts are written in Visual Basic Scripting Edition (VBScript), because they can quickly be constructed within Notepad. However, you can also use a variety of languages such as Visual C++ or Microsoft Visual Basic (VB) to complete the same types of tasks within familiar development environments such as Microsoft Visual Studio .NET. Later in this chapter, you will see how to use a managed language (VB.NET) to perform tasks against the ISA Server as well to build client applications.

To use scripts to make any changes to ISA Server, you must first tap into the root `FPC` object, which will allow you the use of children `FPC` objects that are in the remaining object hierarchy. Before doing any pertinent scripting logic, you must create and set the root object. Because the script being developed is using VBScript, you can create the root object by using the `CreateObject` method. Once the root object is created, you can subsequently tap into the ISA Server Object Model. For example, you could perform something as simple as getting the current ISA Server Name by using the `GetContainingServer` method, as shown here:

```
Function ReturnTheIsaServerName()
    Dim FPCobject
    Set FPCobject = CreateObject("FPC.Root")
    GetIsaServerName = FPCobject.GetContainingServer.Name
End Function
```

Then, you could push the output from the function using `WScript` with an `Echo` method and calling the function name, as shown here:

```
WScript.Echo ReturnTheIsaServerName()
```

To further understand how you can utilize VBScript to automate generally repetitive, complex tasks for an ISA instance, consider one of the most common tasks that you may perform if you are responsible for maintaining the ISA environment: modifying existing rules that are associated with your SharePoint environment (either by enabling ones that are already created, or disabling ones that are currently in effect).

For example, an experimental ISA environment may experience frequent problems with an implemented Web Publishing Rule preventing access to your SharePoint environment. Because it is a development environment, a batch file to repeatedly execute rule management would be preferred over manual intervention, since adding a rule string into a script is much quicker than having to navigate through the ISA Management Console interface.

When you are creating more complicated scripts (such as one that taps into rule functionality), it is best to first test whether the object has already been created (as opposed to just directly creating the root object). Then, if the object hasn't been created, you can subsequently create and set the root object for tapping into other ISA children objects.

```
Set FPCobject = CreateObject("FPC.Root")
If Not IsObject(FPCobject) Then Set FPCobject = CreateObject("FPC.Root")
```

Once you have created the root object, you can begin to do more relevant ISA actions. When you are working with Web Publishing Rules, you must pass in a string parameter into the function specifying the rule name — in this example, `RuleNamestring`. Then, you can use the `FPCPolicyRules` collection to get the related rule name before activating or deactivating the rule.

```
Set PolicyRuleobject = FPCobject.GetContainingArray.ArrayPolicy.PolicyRules
.Item(RuleNamestring)
```

The `FPCPolicyRule` object has a property that allows the setting of whether or not a rule is enabled. You can use this to test whether a rule is currently enabled, and the `stringAction` parameter can be used to either enable or disable the relevant rule.

```
If Left(LCase(Actionstring),1) = "e" Then Stateboolean = True Else Stateboolean =
False
If PolicyRuleobject.Enabled = Stateboolean Then EnableorDisable = True
```

```
Exit Function
PolicyRuleobject.Enabled = Stateboolean
PolicyRuleobject.Save
```

Although managing Web Publishing Rules is a powerful option to use through scripts, a variety of other ISA administration objects can be tapped into to construct powerful administrative scripts. Let's consider another example.

ISA Server plays very heavily into subnets using private network IDs, and you can also manage subnets through the use of scripts by using FPCRuleElements, which has a Subnets property that allows the return of all the subnets within the ISA network or array.

For example, because the Subnets property allows the return of a collection of all subnets that are defined in an array, by declaring the root FPC object, the array, and the FPCsubnet object and collection, you could accomplish something such as simply displaying a list of subnets that are available on a specific ISA array, as shown here:

```
Dim FPCobject
Dim IsaArrayobject
Dim Subnetscollection
Dim Subnetobject
Set FPCobject = CreateObject("FPC.Root")
Set IsaArrayobject = FPCobject.GetContainingArray
Set Subnetscollection = IsaArrayobject.RuleElements.Subnets
```

Once Subnetscollection has the appropriate values, you can loop through the returned values by using a For Each loop on each Subnetobject in the Subnetscollection and parse out the variable subnets within a window using WScript. You can extend this concept further for tasks such as adding or deleting a specific subnet on an array.

Deleting a subnet can be accomplished by declaring a new DeletePassedSubnet() function and passing in the subnet parameter. You can then use the Remove() method out of the FPCSubnets collection to delete the specified subnet.

```
Function DeletePassedSubnet(SubnetNamestring)
    Dim FPCobject
    Dim IsaArrayobject
    Dim Subnetscollection
    Set FPCobject = CreateObject("FPC.Root")
    Set IsaArrayobject = FPCobject.GetContainingArray
    Set Subnetscollection = IsaArrayobject.RuleElements.Subnets
    Subnetscollection.Remove(SubnetNamestring)
    Subnetscollection.Save
End Function
```

You could also delete all the relevant subnets by introducing a For Each loop with the Remove() method.

```
For Each Subnetobject In Subnetscollection
        Subnetscollection.Remove(Subnetobject.Name)
    Next
```

Careful planning should go into running a script such as this, because it will drastically modify your ISA array, deleting all subnets that meet the condition. Research the ISA objects that you are using before your execute any ISA script!

Using a Managed Language with ISA Server Development

If you are a .NET developer you may find the use of scripts to be rather frustrating, because they are often constructed in text editors that don't offer the rich feature set of the Visual Studio integrated development environment (IDE). It is possible, however, to use managed .NET code against an ISA array to perform intuitive administration and management tasks. You will find this option to be very useful when writing WinForm client applications that provide functions like reporting and monitoring your ISA instance.

The main thing you must do when setting up your Visual Studio project is reference the FPClib object, because it provides all the methods of interaction that are required to interact with ISA Server. The FPClib object is located on your ISA Server in msfpccom.dll in C:\Program Files\Microsoft ISA Server\. Once this reference has been made, you can call the FPClib object by creating an imports directive for FPClib at the top of the relevant class file. Because most of the frequently created code for ISA Server at this level is in Visual C++ or Visual Basic for Applications (VBA), the following code examples are provided in VB.NET. Therefore, the similarities to those provided in the previous discussion on scripting should be relatively consistent.

Previously, you learned how to programmatically work with the rules that ISA Server is using to control access to the SharePoint server. This same type of functionality can be achieved in VB.NET. Most of the methods being called are very similar to those that were introduced in VBScript. By implementing such code, this method (frequently placed in a WinForms custom management console or Console Application) would be able to provide the capability to quickly add access rules to the ISA array by binding it as an event handler to something such as a button control.

The overall strategy can be accomplished by using the FPCPolicyRules collection and the AddAccessRule method to create a new FPCPolicyRule object, which will allow the creation of the relevant access rule. By doing a complex task such as adding an access rule, different concepts are introduced that would otherwise require user interaction to harvest the relevant information (such as using the AccessProperties and SourceSelectionIPs properties of the IFPCPolicyRule object to supply the necessary metadata to create the new rule). These don't necessarily have to be set to static values, however. They can be expanded to include user-entered information.

You can see that these set properties are being applied to the rule because the FpcIncludeStatus enumerated type is being set to fpcinclude so that the reference is established. The FpcPolicyRuleActions enumerated type is being used to say that the rule that is being created is going to deny the request (because rules, as discussed earlier, will either allow or deny access to the relevant SharePoint resources) by using the fpcPolicyActionDeny property.

```
Dim array As FPCArray
Dim fpcob As FPC = New FPCClass
Dim rules As FPCPolicyRules = array.ArrayPolicy.PolicyRules
Dim rule As FPCPolicyRule = rules.AddAccessRule()
rule.AccessProperties.DestinationDomainNameSets.Add(Conversions.ToString(),
FpcIncludeStatus.fpcInclude)
rule.AccessProperties.UserSets.Add("All Users", FpcIncludeStatus.fpcInclude)
rule.SourceSelectionIPs.Networks.Add("Internal", FpcIncludeStatus.fpcInclude)
```

```
rule.Action = FpcPolicyRuleActions.fpcPolicyRuleActionDeny
rule.Enabled = True
rules.Save(False, -1)
```

Along the same lines, you can add or modify other ISA network objects. For example, you could select a domain set by using the `DomainNameSets` property to get a `FPCDomainNameSets` collection, and use the `Add()` method to add a select domain set. This is a powerful option if the network that ISA is riding upon is frequently changing and subject to domain shifts.

```
Dim array As FPCArray
Dim fpcobj As FPC = New FPCClass
Dim rules As FPCPolicyRules = array.ArrayPolicy.PolicyRules
Dim sets As FPCDomainNameSets = array.RuleElements.DomainNameSets
Dim num As Integer = sets.Count
sets.Add()
sets.Save(False, -1)
sets.Refresh()
```

By introducing managed code into your ISA Server development environment you can greatly extend the possibilities when quickly developing client ISA tools to manage the overall SharePoint security infrastructure using a development environment that is familiar to .NET developers. Developers can interact with a development environment that they are familiar with, and tap into the ISA Administrative Object Model to quickly construct powerful methods to automate and extend the overall functionality of ISA.

Summary

The sphere of concepts that SharePoint security entails are exceptionally expansive. Starting at the foundational communication layer and extending to construction of intuitive and insightful applications and scripts that facilitate analysis, reporting, and managing security objects, there are several security considerations for you to take into account. Furthermore, because the realm of SharePoint security extends to all parties involved in your SharePoint environment (from system architects who will set up communication and architecture security, to the developer who is responsible for building both secure applications and security-related tools), each piece of your organization plays an intrinsic role in the overall security program.

A majority of the tools that are required for an appropriate implementation of SharePoint security are built directly into SharePoint, or into the Windows Server 2003 platform. Communication-layer concepts such as IPSec for inter-server communication and SSL for providing client-line security don't require the introduction of sister server platforms into the environment. To enhance security of SharePoint with more enhanced security attributes, using software appliances such as ISA Server allow the use of advanced security concepts (such as secure Web application publishing) and provide stateful packet inspection of SharePoint traffic.

The security concepts introduced in this chapter can promote a high level of reusability through the use of scripts, batch files, or managed code. Through proper exploitation of things such as the ISA Administrative Object Model, advanced management functionality can be procured, which will vastly enhance the security options that are available for an arbitrary organization, and will ultimately lead to a collaboration environment that people can trust.

13

Using Information Rights Management

by Jason Medero

Information Rights Management (IRM) is quickly becoming a must-have for any organization looking to protect its intellectual property to ensure that sensitive data is not accessible by unauthorized individuals. Windows Rights Management Services (RMS) is a Windows Server 2003 technology that works with applications to secure digital content. With the introduction of Microsoft Office SharePoint Server 2007 (MOSS 2007), these two technologies now work together so that information workers can collaborate on documents and still be confident that, when they take these documents offline, the documents are still secure.

In the first part of this chapter, I introduce you to Windows RMS — more specifically, how to go about planning, designing, and implementing RMS and MOSS by utilizing best practices that I recommend and have used in real business scenarios. I go into some of the functional architecture of RMS and how it integrates with MOSS 2007, explaining some of the key components that make up the RMS infrastructure. Throughout this chapter you will gain an in-depth understanding of how RMS and MOSS 2007 can be integrated together and used in your own organization.

IRM can be activated within document libraries and also for list attachment files. This feature can be controlled on a per-document library/list level. When IRM is configured, RMS-enabled files stored within that document library are encrypted and permissions to these files vary. The permissions within SharePoint document libraries and lists can become very granular, all the way down to the item level. In this case, certain users may have elevated rights to certain specific files.

This chapter is not a complete step-by-step guide on how to implement RMS and MOSS. Rather, this chapter looks into how these two technologies can work together to secure digital information within your organization.

If you would like to find some more documentation on IRM integration with MOSS 2007, the following links will provide you with a good starting point for collecting information about IRM. Also included in the list is a white paper that will guide you step-by-step through setting up your RMS environment.

- ❏ `http://www.microsoft.com/windowsserver2003/evaluation/overview/technologies/rmenterprise.mspx`

- ❏ `http://msdn2.microsoft.com/en-us/library/ms458245.aspx`

Laying the Foundation

Later on, this chapter examines a real business scenario. This scenario will depict how the integration of RMS with MOSS 2007 solved a growing challenge among organizations today — protecting internal confidential digital information from malicious use or mishandling. Organizations are finding out the hard way why confidential digital information must be kept inside the walls of an organization. Increased digital information thefts, combined with recently enacted legislative requirements, have forced companies to look at how they are currently handling digital information within their organizations.

In every organization, computers are used on a daily basis to create and handle this digital content. The problem lies in the amount of different avenues that are available to transfer this digital data outside of an organization. With the advent of external connections into an organization's private network, and increasingly popular small storage devices that can hold large amounts of dynamic data, have made securing this confidential data a very difficult task. Confidential data can be a number of things within an organization (such as a simple internal email message from the CEO, a document that contains research data, or database-driven financial reports). This is the type of data that must first be identified when planning for an implementation such as Windows RMS.

Planning Rights Management Services

When planning your RMS implementation, you should begin by first identifying what confidential content you want (and need) to protect. Some classic examples of files that you would like to protect are emails, confidential project documents, company confidential reports, financial workbooks, strategy planning documents, and many others. These files are normally shared in an assortment of ways. The most common ways are most likely through emails and file shares.

Organizations may want to also keep some files from being readily available to users internally, as well. These include personal health records, employee salary information, or employee performance reviews. For example, the CEO might send out an email to all internal employees that contains some confidential information. The CEO would like to lock down this email so that it cannot be printed, copied, or even forwarded, and so that the email has an expiration policy set for 48 hours. This is all possible by protecting that email through RMS.

RMS out-of-the-box can be used with any RMS-enabled application, including Microsoft Word, Excel, PowerPoint, and Outlook. The versions of these applications must be 2003 or later. If the user does not have the correct version of the application (or the application at all), the user will still be able to consume the information through an RMS-enabled browser. For example, the browser can be Microsoft Internet Explorer (IE) with the free Rights Management add-on. Furthermore, RMS has a Software Development

Kit (SDK) for the server and client components, which includes a set of tools, documentation, and some sample code. This enables software developers to customize their RMS server environments and create RMS-enabled applications.

The biggest question that I get is whether RMS can protect PDF files out of the box. The short answer is that PDF is not an RMS-enabled application out-of-the-box, and must be developed, or there are third-party add-on products that can be purchased to fill this gap.

> When using IE and the RMS add-on for IE, users cannot author new RMS-protected content; they can only consume this content. Authoring can only be done with an RMS-enabled application such as Microsoft Office 2003 editions and later.

Now that I have provided a clear example of some of the capabilities of Windows RMS, let's take a look at what is needed to get RMS up in your environment. Let's first take a look at the somewhat modified hardware and software requirements that I have come up with and refer to. These requirements were based on what Microsoft normally recommends, but I have added in some areas that I have seen to be required in real-life scenarios that are always dynamic. Table 13-1 shows the hardware requirements that I recommend for any RMS installation.

Table 13-1: Hardware Requirements for RMS

Requirement	Recommendation
Personal computer with one Pentium 4 processor (1,000 MHz or higher)	Personal computer with two Pentium 4 processors (1500 MHz or higher)
512MB of RAM	1GB of RAM
20GB of free hard disk space	60GB of free hard disk space
One network adapter	One network adapter

The most important requirement is hard disk space, because the RMS logging database can grow somewhat rapidly. From my experiences, RMS can quickly become a business-critical application. Keeping RMS working with 99.9 percent uptime is going to be critical because, if a user attempts to open up an RMS-protected document and the server is down, that user will be blocked from accessing the document until the RMS server is restored. This scenario could potentially be disastrous. With that in mind, an RMS cluster is always recommended, along with normal disaster and recovery planning.

Table 13-2 shows the software requirements for running RMS in your organization.

Note that Microsoft offers a free RMS trial service that can be used to author and consume content such as documents and email. This service does have its constraints in that it requires all users of this free trial service to have a Microsoft .NET Passport account. Of course, the major limitation is that, at any time, Microsoft could end this free service, leaving you with only a three-month time frame to re-secure your digital content. The only time I would recommend using the free trial service from Microsoft is if your company is evaluating the possibility of implementing RMS in its current production environment in the near future. The free trial, for the most part, works just as if you had it in your environment, minus the server-side RMS configurations that can be made when running it in your environment.

Table 13-2: Software Requirements for RMS

Software	Requirement
Operating system	The Windows Server 2003 family of operating systems.
File system	The Windows NT File System (NTFS) file system is recommended.
Messaging	Microsoft Message Queuing (MSMQ) that is included with the Windows Server 2003 family. To support logging, Active Directory Integration must be enabled.
Web services	This includes Internet Information Services (IIS), the Web services that are provided with the Windows Server 2003 family. ASP.NET must be enabled.
Active Directory directory service	RMS must be installed in an Active Directory domain in which the domain controllers are running Windows Server 2000 with Service Pack 3 (SP3) or later. All users and groups who use RMS to acquire licenses and publish content must have an email address that is configured in Active Directory.
Database server	RMS requires a database and stored procedures to perform operations. You can use Microsoft SQL Server 2000 with SP3a or later. For testing or other single-computer deployment, you can use Microsoft SQL Server Desktop Engine (MSDE 2000) with SP3.

To activate the free trial service, follow these steps using an Office 2007 application:

1. Click the Office Orb button in the top left of the Office application.
2. Click Prepare.
3. Click Restrict Permissions.
4. Click Restrict Access.
5. A dialog box is displayed, as shown in Figure 13-1.
6. Select "Yes I want to sign up for this free trial service from Microsoft."
7. The ensuing steps will ask you to either use your current .NET Passport account, or register a new .NET Passport account.

Once you receive your RMS certificate, you can then begin authoring restricted content and specifying who can access this content by using the user's .NET Passport account email address.

Following are major points that must be considered when planning your RMS implementation environment:

❑ RMS must be installed within an Active Directory domain. This is somewhat of a disappointment for smaller environments. A great example of this may be smaller law firms that do not use or need Active Directory services, but have plenty of confidential documents that get passed around and are susceptible to theft on a daily basis.

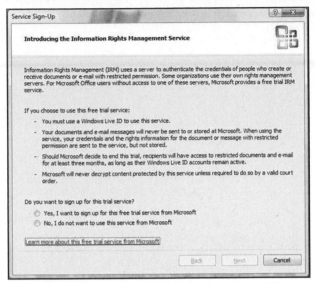

Figure 13-1: The free trial RMS service used with .NET Passport service

❑ When deploying RMS in an environment that consists of multiple Active Directory domains or forests, Active Directory Universal Groups must be used for replication to take place across all global catalogs.

❑ The domain functional level must be at least Windows 2000 Native and Windows Server 2003 at the forest functional level. This means that RMS *cannot* be deployed in an environment with a domain functional level of NT 4 domain.

❑ Larger organizations planning to use RMS and SQL Server clustering for maximum redundancy must use the Enterprise edition of SQL Server because the Standard edition does not support clustering.

❑ No additional services or sites should be run on the RMS server, because doing so could cause unwanted security risks.

❑ RMS logging will be disabled by default if ASP.NET v1.1.4322 is not installed and allowed within the IIS Web extensions. If ASP.NET 1.1 is installed and allowed, RMS logging can be enabled from the RMS global administration Web site.

❑ RMS cannot use Kerberos authentication. Once RMS has been provisioned on a Web site, Kerberos authentication is disabled for that server.

❑ RMS should *not* be provisioned on the same Web site as any of the SharePoint services, including Windows SharePoint Services (WSS) or MOSS.

Identifying RMS Client Technologies

As mentioned, this chapter is not meant to cover all aspects of RMS, and only covers the topics that are pertinent to understanding how RMS and MOSS work together seamlessly. The discussion now focuses on using RMS-enabled applications such as Microsoft Word, Excel, or PowerPoint. This is also known as Information Rights Management (IRM) when dealing with RMS-enabled applications.

In a nutshell, IRM allows end users and administrators to granularly specify permissions to many difficult file types. Out-of-the-box, these files include documents, worksheets/workbooks, and presentations. Everyday users are exchanging these types of files, some of which may be confidential. This confidential information is a great security risk if it falls into the wrong hands. IRM can be applied to files by using an RMS-enabled application, as described in this section. When discussing IRM, I am referring to the client-side component, and when I talk about RMS, I am referring to the server-side component.

The following examination will help you to gain comprehensive knowledge surrounding the RMS infrastructure and how it is tied into the client side of things. Once you have an understanding on how the RMS works, you will then be able to easily grasp how to utilize this technology in your environment with MOSS 2007.

RMS Machine Certificates and Lockboxes

In order for the RMS-enabled application to communicate with the RMS server, an RMS client must be installed and activated on each desktop. The RMS client is automatically activated upon installation. The installation creates a *lockbox* for RMS certificates, as well as a unique machine certificate that contains the computer's public key so that the RMS certification server can identify that machine.

> *If you change your hardware you will need to synch back up to the RMS server to receive a new lockbox. This will only be a problem if you are trying to access an IRM-protected file for the first time on that hardware. This is not a number that you can find and is generally hidden.*

The lockbox that is issued when the client is installed plays an essential role in identifying a computer or device that is trusted by RMS. The issued lockbox contains the computer's private key, which is used for the encryption and decryption process. The lockbox is unique to the computer that it is installed on, because it is built on a hardware identifier. The computers do *not* need to be a member of an Active Directory domain to receive a machine certificate or lockbox.

Rights Account Certificates/Client Licensor Certificates

The *rights account certificates* (RACs) that are distributed by the RMS *root certification server* are what identifies a trusted particular user in the RMS system. RMS issues the RACs that are associated with a user's account with a specific computer. The RAC will be included when the user requests a *client licensor certificate* (CLC) and *use licenses* (ULs). The client licensor is very important because this enables users to publish RMS-protected content (such as an email, for example) when they are *offline* (that is, not connected to the corporate network). In order for the computer to obtain a CLC, a user must first initiate a *client enrollment* request.

Following are the two types of RACs:

❑ *Standard* — RMS system administrators can specify the validity period in terms of days. This is set to 365 days by default. I like the default value because organizations may have many road warriors who might not have the capability to connect to the network for prolonged periods of time. If this certificate expires, this will disable that user from publishing any new IRM-protected content.

❑ *Temporary* — The temporary account certificates have a validity period that can be specified in minutes, with a 15-minute default value. This type of certificate allows users to temporarily consume IRM-protected content from a computer that they do not normally use.

The RMS client enrollment consists of the client computer signing and issuing the publishing license, which basically holds all of the permissions information for the IRM-protected content from that specific computer. Following are the client enrollment steps:

1. The user wants to RMS-protect a document, so he or she creates the document and elects to restrict permissions.

2. Simultaneously, in the background, the client computer sends the user's RAC in an enrollment request to the *publishing service* that runs on the licensing server or root certification server, both of which can be clustered. (The RMS service that is responsible for issuing the CLC is the RMS publishing service.)

There can be only one root certification server per Active Directory domain.

3. The RMS server validates that the RAC is not on the exclusion list.

4. The publishing service creates a key pair for the client computer that originally requested to restrict permissions.

5. The publishing service creates a CLC, places the public key in the certificate, and encrypts the private key with the RAC public key. To complete the public and private key handshake, the publishing service takes the encrypted private key and places it in the CLC.

6. The publishing service then issues the CLC to the client computer.

This entire process is transparent to the user and happens in a matter of seconds.

RMS Licenses

There are two core licenses that RMS uses to publish content and consume the rights-protected content. These two licenses are the *publishing license* and *use license* (UL). Because the publishing license generates the UL, let's first go over what a UL is.

First of all, to use any IRM-protected content, a UL is required. The UL specifies the permissions that a user has for the IRM-protected file. The UL for the protected content is issued by the server that originally issued the corresponding publishing license. A user who is named as a user in the publishing license for that content can request a UL for that specific file. The RMS application communicates with the RMS server to read the content, and enforces the permissions that come with the content.

Let's break down the process that is involved when acquiring a UL. For this scenario, let's name our user "John" and our protected file will be called Financials.

1. John receives a document called Financials from a co-worker who has IRM-protected this document because it contains confidential information.

2. John opens up the Financials file with Microsoft Excel (which is an RMS-enabled application). John does not have a rights account certificate (RAC) on the current computer he is using to open up this Excel file.

3. In the background, Excel is sending a request to the RMS server that issued the publishing license for a UL for the `Financials` file. The request includes John's RAC, which contains the public key that is used to decrypt the data that is intended for John. Because John has never opened up this Excel file on this computer, he must get issued an RAC for the specific computer that he is using in order to access the file.

4. The licensing server or the root certification server (in single RMS server implementations) validates that the user is authorized, and that John is named within the publishing license that is attached to the IRM-protected file.

5. Once the validation is complete, the RMS server will then create a UL. Simultaneously, the server validates John's RAC, which determines what permissions John has been granted to that document. The RMS server uses the server's private key to decrypt the symmetric content key. It then encrypts the file with John's public key that is attached to the publishing license, which is then finally enclosed to the file itself.

6. When the validation process is complete, the RMS licensing server sends the newly created UL to John's computer.

In this process, the only manual step that the user (John) must complete is opening the document in the RMS-enabled application. From there, the RMS-enabled application takes over and handles the entire client-to-server communications.

The entire process is completely transparent to the user because all the user sees is a small RMS popup window like the one shown in Figure 13-2. This popup box will show the first time an RMS-enabled file is opened. Users can select the "Don't show this message again" checkbox and it will not show again. Users with slower network connections might also receive a popup box that shows two computer icons communicating between each other. Most of the time, this window will not even pop up. I have seen this popup normally not last for more than 2 to 5 seconds. In most cases, users will see the IRM-protected file almost immediately after opening it. In extreme cases such as in larger organizations (1000+ users) where RMS is consistently being used, the wait time may be 5 to 10 seconds. This wait time can be greatly improved by adding a licensing server to your RMS cluster.

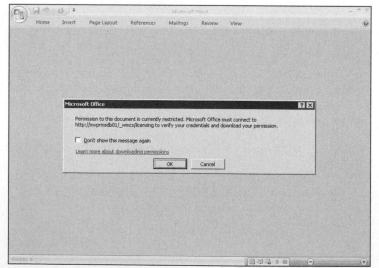

Figure 13-2: RMS popup box that users will see when opening an IRM-protected file for the first time

The following step-by-step scenario demonstrates the entire process of an author publishing an IRM-protected document all the way down to a consumer using an RMS-enabled application to consume the content when both parties are connected to the corporate network:

1. A user creates a new file through an RMS-enabled application in which the user has the capability to specify specific rights for that file. In doing so, the user creates a publishing license for the file which is now encrypted and which contains all the necessary information that the RMS server needs in order to verify and lock down the file accordingly. The publishing license is now bound to the file.

2. This right-protected file is then sent to a consumer who has read permissions on the file.

3. The RMS-enabled application the consumer uses to open the content sends a request. This request includes the consumer's RAC to the RMS server (the same server that issued the publishing license) to request the second UL for the file.

4. The RMS server then validates the user's credentials.

5. If the user's credentials are valid, a UL is generated and returned to the RMS-enabled application on the consumer's computer.

6. The RMS-enabled application that user is running opens the file. The user will be granted rights to that file, as defined in the UL.

Offline publishing (meaning authoring content that is outside of the corporate network) is different from online publishing (within the corporate network). The difference lies within the way the publishing process takes place. When the author restricts permission on a file, and then saves the file while offline, the CLC that is stored within the lockbox on the computer allows the device or computer to issue and sign the publishing license and bind it to the file.

> *The offline publishing process will not allow a device or computer to issue and sign a publishing license for any files until the author acquires a CLC. To acquire a CLC, a user must go through the RMS client enrollment process, explained earlier in this chapter. If the user is authoring IRM-protected files from multiple computers offline, each computer or device must go through the client enrollment process.*

The flowchart in Figure 13-3 shows the process flow that takes place when publishing IRM-protected content offline. Figure 13-4 shows the process flow that takes place when publishing IRM-protected content online.

The publishing license stores the usage rights that specify who can view the content, and edit it, as well as how the content can be distributed (printed, copied and pasted, and so on). The publishing license can be issued by the RMS-enabled application itself, the RMS licensing server, or the root certification server. Think of the publishing license as a component that stores what rights users have for that specific file.

Once the file is published with its associated publishing license bound to the actual document, this file is rights-protected and can be consumed. The publishing license parameters (rights to the file) are stored within the RMS server's database. When a consumer with rights to the file opens the file with an RMS-enabled application, the publishing license generates a UL that defines the user's rights for that file.

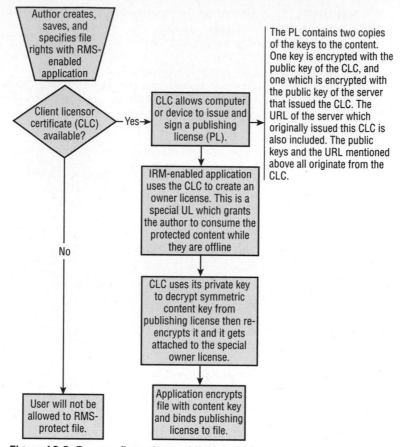

Figure 13-3: Process flow when publishing IRM-protected content offline

RMS Client Deployment

Each user account on the desktop activates a completely new RMS client the first time the user attempts to use an RMS capability. The client can be installed by simply pushing the software through a Group Policy software push. Or, this client can be deployed via an enterprise systems management piece of software such as Microsoft Systems Management Server 2003 (SMS). For larger deployments, I highly recommend using software such as SMS to deploy the RMS client. This will give you a good idea of who has the client already installed for inventory purposes.

If the client has not been installed on the computer, and a user tries to RMS-protect a document, the RMS-enabled application will detect that the client has not been installed. A message box will then pop up explaining to the user that, in order to use any rights-management features, the client must first be installed. If the user has appropriate permissions on the computer, the user can download and run through the install wizard very easily. In literally four simple clicks, the user will be run through the installation wizard and, if all goes smoothly, the user will see an RMS dialog box like the one shown in Figure 13-5.

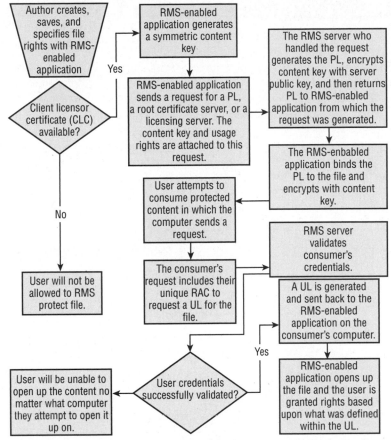

Figure 13-4: Process flow when publishing IRM-protected content online

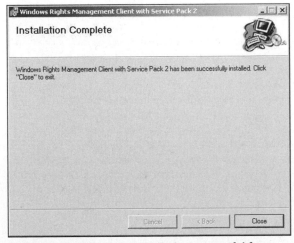

Figure 13-5: RMS client installation successful for manual install

Managing Your RMS Server

Once you have provisioned your first RMS server, you will have access to the Global Administration page shown in Figure 13-6. This page cannot be accessed from the browser on a remote computer unless you use Secure Sockets Layer (SSL) for the RMS Web site that is running RMS. Within the Global Administration page, a user can access the RMS administration page, which provides administrators with information about the RMS server or cluster. Administrators who have access can also change the RMS service account and uninstall the IIS Web site that RMS is using.

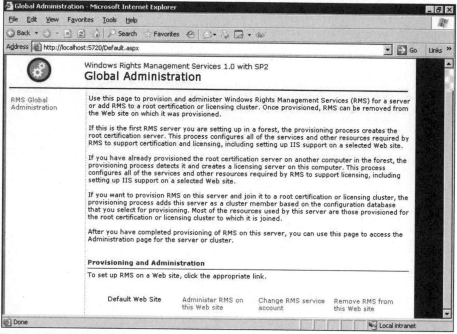

Figure 13-6: Global Administration page

The RMS service account is critical because it is a part of the RMS Service Group. The RMS Service Group has all of the appropriate permissions on all of the resources that are required for RMS to operate properly. The RMS service account should be unique and *only* used for RMS. For security reasons, it should serve no other purpose. This special account should only be changed as a last resort. When and if the RMS service account is changed, it cannot be the same domain account that was used to install RMS.

> *This chapter does not cover the step-by-step installation instructions for provisioning an RMS server or cluster. Refer to the Microsoft Windows Server TechCenter Web site for RMS, which you can find at* `http://technet2.microsoft.com/windowsserver/en/technologies/featured/rms/` `default.mspx`. *In the featured articles section, there should be an "Installing Windows Rights Management Services with Service Pack 2 step-by-step guide."*

Administering the RMS Server

The administration page for administering RMS is immediately available after provisioning RMS on a server. The Home page of the RMS Administration page displays information about your RMS deployment, as shown in Figure 13-7. At the top of Figure 13-7, you will notice such information as the cluster URL, the name of your configuration database, and what server it resides on. Another important information piece to note is the server licensor certificate expiration date. The server licensor certificate is what grants the RMS server the rights to issue licenses and certificates. This certificate is received upon the first provisioning of the root certificate server of your RMS implementation. When additional servers are added (optional), those servers will use the same licensor certificate.

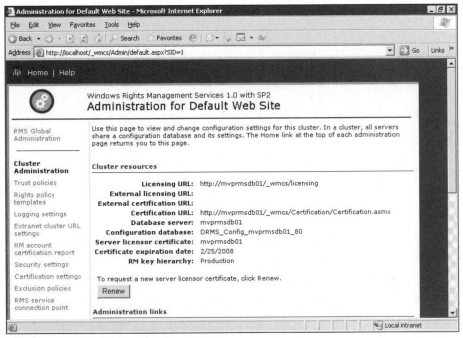

Figure 13-7: RMS Administration Web site

The default value given to the server licensor certificate is 365 days. The certificate can easily be renewed by clicking the Renew button (also shown in Figure 13-7). You can renew the server licensor certificate either online (if the RMS server has Internet access) or offline (if the server does not have Internet access). When renewing offline, you must first export the renewal request to a file, and then go to a Microsoft Web site on a computer that has Internet access. Once you receive the new server licensor certificate, you can import it, and your server licensor certificate will be renewed. If you click the Renew button on the Administration Web site, it lists the steps for renewing the certificate offline.

Let's briefly cover some of the administration options that can be exercised from the Administration Web site. Table 13-3 reviews some of the different administrative options that can be configured from the left side of the Home page of the Administration site.

Table 13-3: Administrative Options Configurable from the Administration Page

Administrative Option	Function
Trust policies	Ability to add trusted user domains to allow RMS servers in other domains to authorize requests. You can also specify to trust .NET Passport RACs.
Rights policy templates	Create and centrally manage rights policy templates for your entire organization. These templates can be chosen when RMS-protecting files with an RMS-enabled application.
Logging settings	Turn RMS server logging on or off, and view the logging database information.
Extranet cluster URL settings	This option provides the capability to add an externally available URL to support extranet users, and the capability to add a dedicating licensing server for extranet users.
RMS account certification report	This report shows you how many total certified users to date have used or are currently using RMS features.
Security settings	Selecting this link provides access to the following: reset the RMS server private key password, decommission the RMS server, and specify a Super users group. Users in the Super users group have full rights permissions on all IRM-protected files. You can also add proxy server parameters, if needed.
Certification settings	Specify the validity period for RACs and select an administrative contact for requesting additional rights on files. This option is only available on the root certification server.
Exclusion policies	Capability to set up different policies to exclude earlier lockbox versions, specific RACs, certain RMS-enabled applications, and earlier Windows operating system versions. All of these options give more granular control over security.
RMS service connection point	Administrator can unregister and register different service connection points (SCPs) from this administrative site. An enterprise administrator or equivalent is required to complete the registration process.

Securing Your RMS Server

Managing the security of your RMS server should be precisely planned out and carefully implemented. If a Super user account or database account is compromised, all of your protected content is at risk. For example, if a user from the RMS Super user group is compromised, then the person who has access to this

Super account would have full control access to *all* RMS protected content. Once a Super user account has been compromised, the RMS protected content is at high risk. All measures should be taken when locking down all components of your RMS server.

Protecting Your RMS Databases

The RMS databases are where all of your encryption information is stored. These contain critical pieces such as certificates, keys, Active Directory group membership queries, and the entire user logging information. A total of three databases hold all of this information: directory services, logging, and (most importantly) the configuration database. The configuration database is by far the most important and critical to everyday operation of your RMS server because it contains all of the certificates and keys that users authenticate against when publishing and consuming content. These three databases should be backed up and be treated as mission-critical. This should be done along with a major disaster and recovery option (which should be made available in appropriate situations).

The security for these databases is provisioned upon the creation of your first root certificate server, which will be the first server that is provisioned in your cluster. By using SQL Server 2005 as your database server for RMS, you are taking the first correct step in increasing the overall security of your RMS environment. Using the SQL 2005 surface area configuration wizard, you can explicitly manage your software's surface area and, in turn, leave fewer ways to attack your databases. RMS supports the use of SQL Server 2000 with Service Pack 4, but I would hands-down recommend SQL Server 2005 because of the pure security enhancements and control you get out-of-the box with the product.

Database access should be restricted to only those who should have rights to it. In many organizations, I see the Active Directory security group Domain Administrators added to the server upon server build. This is not a very good security practice because the RMS server should be locked down as tightly as possible with restricted access.

Following are some other RMS security best practices:

❑ The only databases that should be on the RMS database server are the three RMS databases.

❑ Do not run any unnecessary or additional services (such as additional IIS Web sites) or install WSS on the same server.

❑ Restrict physical access to the RMS database server.

❑ Lock down the virtual directories of the Web site that is used to administer RMS.

❑ Use caution when editing the RMS database permissions and the discretionary access control list (DACL).

❑ When configuring your SQL server, refrain from using SQL Server Authentication (SA), unless you are using some form of multi-protocol encryption or TLS to secure communications between your RMS server and your database server. If you are not planning on going through the extra steps to protect your database server, you should use Windows authentication because credentials are passed in plain text when using SA.

❑ The connection between the RMS client and the RMS server should be required to communicate through encrypted channels via SSL or Internet Protocol Security (IPSec).

❑ The connection between the RMS server and the SQL server should be encrypted through secure channel via SSL or IPSec. For more information on how to accomplish this task please check out the following two links:

```
http://msdn2.microsoft.com/en-us/library/aa302414.aspx
http://msdn2.microsoft.com/en-us/library/aa302413.aspx
```

❑ Enable SQL auditing on your SQL server. This will provide additional security for your RMS installation because it keeps track of activity and changes that are made to your databases.

Managing RMS Accounts and Groups

During the provisioning of your RMS root certificate server, RMS creates a special "full-control" Super users group. Users who are a member of this group have full owner control over all rights-protected content. These users will have access to any and all documents as if they had authored the files themselves. Users of this group can also change RMS permissions and decrypt content if they choose to.

At first glance, this group seems to be more of a security risk than anything, but it has a very practical use as well. A scenario in which an employee who has published some IRM-protected content gets terminated from an organization is a great example. Because the terminated employee is the author of this content, and that employee is the only user who has full control over this document, the Super group user can open this document and change the associated IRM-protected file permissions.

When deploying RMS in any environment, I always recommend to the customer that, if possible, two people should be dedicated with full control when publishing IRM-protected content. Then, if a user is terminated from the organization, there is always another user who can manage the IRM-protected file. The Super users group is empty by default, and users should be added to this group with the utmost caution. I generally recommend that there only be two individuals who have this special permission in order to minimize the security risk.

Active Directory (AD) accounts and the RAC for an AD account that is in the RMS configuration database are not synched. This unfortunately means that when an administrator deletes an account in AD, the associated RAC that is in the user key table in the RMS configuration database is *not* deleted. This can cause issues with the growth of the user key table because new keys are added, but old ones are never deleted. A recommended way to maintain your RMS configuration database is to implement a stored procedure that will delete a user key by its security identifier (SID) each time its associated user account is removed from AD. This will ensure that your user key table in your configuration database does not grow out of control.

If you are implementing RMS across multiple AD forests or domains, you must use Universal Groups so that group membership gets replicated across all global catalog servers.

IRM Integration

This section examines IRM integration and includes the following topics:

❑ Configuring IRM within SharePoint

❑ IRM integration into SharePoint document libraries and lists

- ❑ Developing custom IRM protectors
- ❑ The IRM protection process within SharePoint
- ❑ Sample IRM integration with SharePoint scenarios

Configuring IRM Within SharePoint

Let's first take a look at configuring a document library to utilize the IRM features. To use the IRM integration features in SharePoint, you must already have RMS configured properly in your environment. The steps in the following discussion outline not only how to configure IRM in your SharePoint environment, but how to best manage it as well.

To put this into perspective, let's take a look at a real-life business problem (scenario) that was solved with the integration of IRM and MOSS/WSS. For privacy purposes, I will assign the fictitious organization the name "Fabersoft." To set the stage a bit, let's take a look at a high-level overview of the organization.

Fabersoft is a company that is in the healthcare sector and is responsible for doing a ton of research to find potential cures for terminal diseases. Each year, this company spends millions of dollars on research, and the key to all this research is its documentation. These documents contain critical information that has been put there by researchers who have put many hours into this documentation. Fabersoft is competing against other major organizations to eventually come up with a drug to cure a variety of illnesses.

This documentation must be kept secret from competitors so as not to give them any advantage in such a competitive sector. In a sector such as healthcare, where research and development can cost companies millions of dollars, keeping this documentation locked down no matter where it is transported is the challenge. The company has MOSS 2007 deployed in its environments, and is mainly utilizing the product's collaboration capabilities to provide a place for all of the research teams. It has an RMS single server cluster in its environment and has been evaluating it for some time now. Fabersoft was extremely unhappy with what is required to RMS-protect large numbers of files. The company was also not very pleased with the management of these protected documents.

To overcome the issues it was having with RMS itself, we decided to take advantage of the integration between the two products. This will enable Fabersoft to RMS-protect documents as they are uploaded or created within an IRM-enabled document library or list (attachments). This would overcome some of the hardships that were involved with setting up RMS policy templates for each research team and specifying permissions per file. The IRM capability can be activated on a per-document library or list basis. In the case of lists, IRM pertains to the attachments that can be added to list items. The second concern about the management of these protected files would also be addressed with this integrated solution. The protected files are associated to the IRM policy of document libraries and, therefore, can all be centrally managed (from a permission standpoint) from the access control list (ACL) of the document libraries.

To configure an environment to integrate RMS and MOSS, you can follow the steps outlined here. This will prepare your environment so that you can enable the IRM feature on document libraries and lists as you see fit within your organization.

The following step-by-step configuration applies to a MOSS environment only:

1. Add your RMS server (http://servername) to your MOSS server's trusted sites.

2. Add your SharePoint server to your RMS server's trusted sites (`http://SharePointServerName`).

3. Install the RMS 1.0 with SP2 client on all SharePoint Web front ends (WFEs).

   You can download the latest RMS client from `http://go.microsoft.com/fwlink/?LinkId=67736`.

4. Double-click the RMS 1.0 w/ SP2 client and run through the quick install.

Next, you must log on to RMS server as an administrator of the server. The following steps explain how to add the SharePoint server(s) and the RMS Service Group to the RMS cluster Certification Pipeline. This will allow your SharePoint server(s) to communicate with your RMS server(s).

1. Log on to your RMS server that has local admin rights.

2. Click Start ⇨ My Computer.

3. Navigate to `C:\Inetpub\wwwroot\_wmcs\Certification`. The page should look like Figure 13-8.

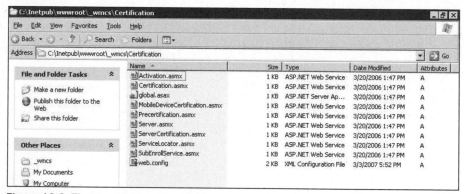

Figure 13-8: The `Certification` **folder**

4. Right-click `ServerCertification.asmx`, click Properties, and then click the Security tab.

5. Click Add.

6. Click Object Types, select the Computers checkbox, and then click OK.

7. Type your SharePoint server(s) names and click OK.

8. Click Add.

9. Click Object Types, select the Groups checkbox, and then click OK.

10. Type **"RMSServerName"\RMS Service Group** and click OK.

11. Click OK to close the `ServerCertification.asmx` Properties dialog box.

Next, follow these steps to enable IRM in your MOSS environment:

1. Log on to your SharePoint server and browse to Central Administration.

2. Click the Operations tab, then Security Configuration, and click the Information Rights Management link.

3. You will have navigated to a screen that looks like Figure 13-9.

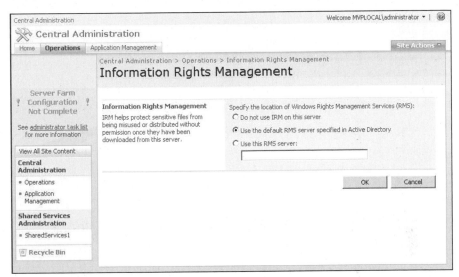

Figure 13-9: IRM page within Central Administration

4. The IRM page (Figure 13-9) displays your options for specifying your RMS server that MOSS is going to use when issuing licenses for files. Most of the time, if you have specified a Service Connection Point (SCP) in your RMS configurations, you can select "Use the default RMS server specified in Active Directory."

5. Click OK.

Now you must create an IRM permissions policy on a document library or list. The following steps pertain specifically to setting up a policy within a document library:

1. Navigate to a document library of your choice (preferably a non-production document library where you can run some tests).

2. Navigate to the document library settings for that document library.

3. Under the Permissions and Management heading, click Information Rights Management.

4. Select the "Restrict permission to documents in this library on download" checkbox. When configuring these settings, you should see a site that resembles Figure 13-10.

In the IRM configuration screen, you are actually configuring an IRM policy for the specific document library to which you have navigated. Including an appropriate and meaningful title and IRM policy description is very important, because this policy title and description will be attached to all files that have an associated RMS-enabled application for the specific file type. From this configuration screen, administrators can dictate a variety of different options for RMS-supported file types. You can choose whether to allow users to have copy/paste functionality when opening RMS-supported files from the document library. This will, of course, depend on whether the user has full control over the document, or just Contributor permissions.

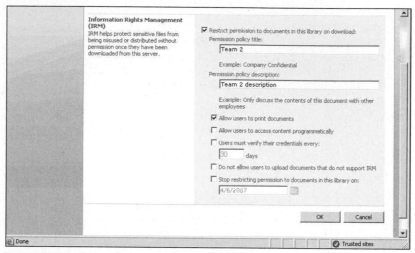

Figure 13-10: IRM policy configuration for a document library

Later in this chapter, I discuss how IRM-enabled document libraries and lists permissions map to which rights RMS gives the user upon file download.

Another option that is important to mention is the ability to control the duration in which users must verify their credentials with the RMS server. A recommendation for the duration depends on who is using the document library. Is the document library being used by users who are not normally connected to the internal network? Is your RMS server set up to provide access via an externally accessible URL?

The duration may also have to take into consideration any security policies that are currently being followed in your organization. If you have users who are accessing this document (for the most part) internally, or have access into the corporate network, setting the policy to 30 days or more will not be an issue. But, if you are dealing with users who are constantly on the road and do not always have access to the internal corporate network, or you have users who are strictly external, I would recommend enabling this option on a case-by-case basis. The reason is that when users must verify their credentials, they are essentially receiving a renewed UL for the file they are accessing. This requires communication with the RMS server in order to acquire a renewal of the UL.

Another great configuration option is the ability to limit file types that do not support IRM. To be more specific, once this option is checked off, users of that document library will only be able to upload file types such as Word, Excel, and PowerPoint. A table will be provided to show which file types are manageable out-of-the-box with IRM. This option is very powerful, because files that are not IRM-compatible will be denied when uploading to the document library, therefore making all RMS-supported files in the library encrypted and protected upon download.

IRM Integration into SharePoint Document Libraries and Lists

Let's now take a look at what is going on behind the scenes. Once IRM is enabled for a specific document library or list, all RMS-supported file types within it are protected. The component that actually is responsible for encryption and decryption of the file within the document library or list is called a *protector*. When a file is uploaded into an IRM-enabled document library or list, the file is not encrypted at that point. Actually, when a file is downloaded from the IRM-enabled document library or list, the file is encrypted and a special UL is given to the user for consumption of content.

The IRM protector (more commonly known simply as the protector) is associated with the document's file type. There are different protectors for different file types. So, when that user downloads that file from the library/list, it's SharePoint's job to determine which protector to use based on the file type. If the appropriate protector is registered and is considered an integrated protector, SharePoint will generate an issuance license (IL) for the file.

The IL is composed of the file's private key that is specific to that document, and used to encrypt the data in the rights-managed document. The IL also consists of a list of users (the ACL), which holds information about these users and their corresponding permissions to the file. Lastly, the UL includes the GUID of the document library or list from which the document was downloaded.

The GUID that is attached to the UL plays a key role in knowing where the file came from, as well as the permissions that are attached to that file. Recall the configuration options in Figure 13-10, the IRM policy configuration page for a document library. The policy title and description that was specified in the policy configuration page will follow the file around. In the case of a Word document opened up in Office 2007, the policy description and title will be shown in the document information panel (DIP), as seen in Figure 13-11.

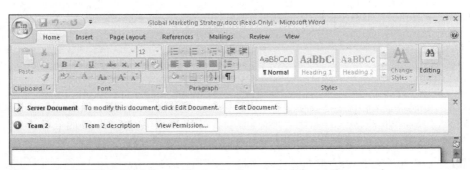

Figure 13-11: IRM policy information in the document information panel

Even if the file is downloaded from an IRM-enabled document library and then uploaded into another IRM-enabled document library, the file will retain the original IRM policy that the file came from.

It is also important to note that the file will also retain permissions wherever the file is taken. When the file is downloaded from the SharePoint library, the permissions of the user who has opened the file correspond to the ACL entry of that user for that document library. Table 13-4 shows each of the different users' permission levels in the ACL and the corresponding IRM permissions that will be enabled for that user. I recommend taking a good look at this table and memorizing the corresponding permissions because this will be extremely crucial when configuring custom permission levels for use within your document library or list.

Table 13-4: Permissions Level and Corresponding IRM Permissions

List Permission Level	Site Permission Level	Corresponding IRM Permissions
	Manage Web site	Users have full control over the files once opened in the client application, including read, edit, copy, save, and modify current permissions.
	Manage permissions	
Edit list items	Add and customize pages	Users of these levels will have the ability to edit, copy, and save permissions. User will have print capabilities if specified in IRM policy.
Manage list		
View list items		User will have read-only permissions and will not be able to copy, edit, or save content locally. User can only print if specified in the IRM policy for that document library.
All other ACL rights settings	All other ACL rights settings	All other rights are not valid and do not correspond to any IRM permissions. Users will be denied access when opening file.

Custom IRM protectors can be developed for managing file types that are not enabled out-of-the-box. For example, a developer might have a need to create an IRM protector for . PDF file types. This will most likely be a common request and one that third-party organizations may make available for purchase. But, if the developer wanted to create a custom IRM protector, that is definitely possible as well. By using the extensible IRM architecture in SharePoint, developers have the ability to create custom IRM protectors that will convert the custom file type(s) into rights management formats when downloaded from a document library. The custom IRM will also be responsible for converting the file types back to non-encrypted format when the user uploads them back to the document library.

Developing Custom IRM Protectors

Two types of IRM protectors can be developed that integrate with the IRM framework in SharePoint: *integrated protectors* and *autonomous protectors*.

Integrated IRM protectors use SharePoint (MOSS/WSS) to access the RMS server. These types of protectors rely on SharePoint to communicate with the RMS platform to encrypt and decrypt rights-managed files. When using this protector, SharePoint will automatically create the RMS metadata associated with the protected content. One caveat for using an integrated protector is that it requires an RMS-aware application (that is, one that is aware and capable of viewing the rights-managed content). If you are interested in possibly developing a custom RMS-aware application, you should first consult the Windows RMS SDK, which is available online or as a download from Microsoft.

An autonomous protector should be custom-developed if you want the protector to have complete control over how the protected file type is to be rights-managed. The autonomous protector has full control of the rights-managed process and is not limited to use the Windows RMS platform. It is important to note that the autonomous protector and the client application must use the same rights-management platform.

You can install both types of protectors within the same SharePoint installation without any issues. Each IRM protector can only be registered to a particular corresponding file type.

Once you have completed the process of developing your custom IRM protectors, you must register them with MOSS/WSS. Once the IRM protectors are registered, they will then become available for document libraries to use. If you are using multiple WFEs in your environment, each IRM protector must be properly registered on each WFE.

Following is a brief overview of the IRM protector registration process:

1. Register IRM protector as a Common Object Model (COM) object so that WSS/MOSS can reference each of the protector's different functions.

2. Create a registry key in the Web server extensions path:

   ```
   HKLM\SOFTWARE\Microsoft\Shared Tools\Web Server Extensions\"IRM Protector Name"
   ```

3. Set up the required registry subkeys in the `IrmProtector` path:

   HKLM\SOFTWARE\Microsoft\Shared Tools\Web Server Extensions\12.0\ IrmProtectors key

   a. *Name* — The `ClassID` of the IRM protector (which must be the same `ClassID` that was used to register the protector as a COM object)

   b. *Value* — The name of the IRM protector

   c. *Type* — String

There are also some highly recommended registry keys that should be added, which contain specific metadata that will enable you to easily identify the protector. The registry keys should be set in the following path:

HKLM\SOFTWARE\Microsoft\Shared Tools\Web Server Extensions\"IRM Protector Name" key

❑ Registry subkey:
  ❑ *Name* — Product
  ❑ *Value* — Name of the protector
  ❑ *Type* — String
❑ Registry subkey:
  ❑ *Name* — Extensions

- ❑ *Value* — Comma-separated list of file extensions that this protector converts
- ❑ *Type* — String
❑ Registry subkey:
- ❑ *Name* — Version
- ❑ *Value* — Version number of the protector
- ❑ *Type* — String

The following is a small code sample that gives you a good idea of how to associate file formats with your custom IRM protector. The example is a `.wxs` file that registers an IRM protector as a COM object, which also contains the correct registry keys and their values.

```xml
<?xml version="1.0" encoding="UTF-8"?>
<Wix xmlns="http://schemas.microsoft.com/wix/2003/01/wi">
  <Fragment>
    <DirectoryRef Id="STSBin">
      <Component Id="Your_Custom_IrmProtector" DiskId="1">
        <File Id="YourCustom.DLL_0001">
          <TypeLib Id="JK101003-7C38-6DL5-859C-7863869353J0"
            Advertise="no" Language="0" MajorVersion="1">
            <Class Id="6K3849SL-62F9-1846-C3K8-B576H399O679"
              Description="IrmProtector Class" ThreadingModel="both"
              Context="InprocServer InprocServer32">
              <ProgId Id="IrmProtector.Protector.1">
                <ProgId Id="IrmProtector.Protector" />
              </ProgId>
            </Class>
          </TypeLib>
        </File>

<Registry Id="IrmProtector.1" Root="HKLM" Key="SOFTWARE\Microsoft\Shared Tools\Web
Server Extensions\12.0\IrmProtectors" Name="{6K3849SL-62F9-1846-C3K8-B576H399O679}"
Value="YourCustom.Irm.Protector" Type="string" />

<Registry Id="IrmProtector.2" Root="HKLM" Key="SOFTWARE\Microsoft\Shared Tools\Web
Server Extensions\IrmProtector" Action="createKeyAndRemoveKeyOnUninstall" />

<Registry Id="IrmProtector.3" Root="HKLM" Key="SOFTWARE\Microsoft\Shared Tools\
Web Server
Extensions\IrmProtector" Name="Extensions" Value="XYZ,PDQ,FOO"  Type="string" />

<Registry Id="MsoProtector.4" Root="HKLM" Key="SOFTWARE\Microsoft\Shared Tools\
Web Server Extensions\IrmProtector" Name="Product" Value="PdfProtector"
 Type="string" />

<Registry Id="IrmProtector.5" Root="HKLM" Key="SOFTWARE\Microsoft\Shared Tools\Web
Server Extensions\IrmProtector" Name="Version" Value="1" Type="string" />

      </Component>
    </DirectoryRef>
  </Fragment>
</Wix>
```

The IRM Protection Process Within SharePoint

There are four components that go into the entire process when documents get downloaded from an IRM-protected document library. Because I have already discussed the first one (IRM protectors), let's take a look at the other three before jumping into some user scenarios:

❑ *Windows Rights Management Services (RMS)* — When using integrated IRM protectors (either custom-developed or out-of-the-box), RMS is used as the authentication provider. This means that IRM can use RMS for the entire authentication process, including creating licenses (issuance, Server EUL), authenticating users, and encrypting file content.

❑ *SharePoint (WSS/MOSS)* — SharePoint is responsible for managing the process of requests when a user is uploading or downloading documents.

❑ *Client application* — After the initial requested file is downloaded, in order for the user to open an IRM-protected file, the user must use an RMS-enabled application. The application is responsible for decrypting the file so that it is accessible to the user. The RMS-application will communicate with the RMS server directly and request an EUL for the file.

A flowchart of the process in which files get protected when using integrated and autonomous protectors can be found in the Windows SharePoint Services SDK. I would highly suggest downloading the SDK, because then you can easily search across it. By simply typing in the keyword "IRM," you will come up with an abundance of results pertaining to IRM. The SDK will be especially helpful for users who are looking for more information regarding the custom development of IRM integrated and autonomous protectors.

Before wrapping up this chapter with some real-world business scenarios, let's examine all of the file types that you can protect out-of-the-box with RMS and SharePoint. Table 13-5 shows the Microsoft Office applications and the corresponding file types/extensions that can be IRM-protected.

Table 13-5: File Types with Extensions That Can Be IRM-Protected Out-of-the-Box

Application/File Type	Extensions
Microsoft Word	
Document	.doc
Document	.docx
Macro-enabled document	.docm
Template	.dot
Template	.dotx
Macro-enabled template	.dotm

Continued

Table 13-5: File Types with Extensions That Can Be IRM-Protected Out-of-the-Box

Application/File Type	Extensions
Microsoft PowerPoint	
Presentation	.ppt
Presentation	.pptx
Macro-enabled presentation	.pptm
Template	.pot
Template	.potx
Macro-enabled template	.potm
Show	.pps
Show	.ppsx
Macro-enabled show	.ppsm
Office theme	.thmx
Microsoft Excel	
Workbook	.xls
Workbook	.xlsx
Macro-enabled workbook	.xlsm
Template	.xlt
Template	.xltx
Macro-enabled template	.xltm
Non-XML binary workbook	.xlsb
Macro-enabled add-in	.xla
Macro-enabled add-in	.xlam

Sample IRM Integration with SharePoint Scenarios

Files that are uploaded to a document library that has an IRM policy applied to it will immediately inherit the document library's IRM policy. This means that no matter where a file is taken to, that IRM policy will persist throughout the life of that file. For example, let's say that someone with Contributor rights to the document library were to download and save a document locally. The user then places that saved document into a user's network share. The user of this network share only has read permissions on this document, which have been defined within the document library permissions where the original document was downloaded and saved locally. Because the user of the network share only has read permissions, the user will not be able to open up that document or move it in any way. The only option that the read permissions user has over this document is to delete it from the network share location. The user will be forced to go to the document library where the file resides and open it up from there.

The reason for this is that the document has licenses attached to it that are specific to the user who downloaded them in the first place. These licenses are forever bound to that document while it lives outside of the document library. Once the document is uploaded to the specific document library where the document was originally downloaded from, it will then inherit any new permissions that have been set on that document library.

This brings to mind another scenario. What happens if, for example, user John has Contributor permissions within a specific document library and downloads "File A" from that library and saves it locally? Then, an administrator changes John's permissions to Reader within the SharePoint item level security of "File A" after John has already downloaded "File A" and saved it locally. Will those changes immediately reflect the file that has been saved locally to that user's computer?

The answer is "no," because the new changes will not take effect until the user downloads a new copy of "File A" from its respective document library where the changes were made. By the same token, John will not be able to make changes to "File A" that he has saved locally, and then upload and overwrite "File A" that is currently being stored in the document library. Because John has Contributor access to the document library, he can make changes to "File A" that was saved locally on his computer, and then upload it to the document library with a different filename.

If that administrator had changed permissions at the document library level from Contributor to Reader, John would no longer be able to add, view, update, or delete. When the permissions on a specific document library are changed, they take effect immediately. This means that when John returns to the document library where he originally was a Contributor and downloaded "File A" locally to his computer, he is now a Reader and will *not* be allowed to download, save, or edit files from that document library in any way.

So, how does the IRM policy that is set up within a document library attach itself to all files stored within the document library? What's the process for attaching a new IRM policy to a file that has an IRM policy attached to it?

Files from IRM-enabled document libraries carry that document library's policy wherever they go, no matter if they are downloaded locally, emailed to another person, taken off the computer with a storage device (flash drive), or uploaded into another IRM-enabled document library with different permissions. For example, if I download and save a file onto my desktop computer from an IRM-enabled document library, and then upload that file to another document library that is IRM-enabled, the IRM policy from the document library where the file was originally downloaded from will still be applied. The only way I can force that file to inherit the IRM policy into which it's been uploaded is if the previous restrictions are first removed. Once restricted rights are shut off for that file, I can then upload that document into another IRM-enabled document library in which the document will inherit the policy for its corresponding document library.

Summary

This chapter explained some of the core concepts and components of RMS, and its integration with MOSS 2007 and WSS 3.0. Enabling IRM to be used in conjunction with SharePoint document libraries and lists will most definitely relieve the nightmare of just simply using RMS to protect each file through the RMS client application.

Even though this feature seems somewhat easy to set up and begin to play with, much planning should, of course, be involved before going to production. Following are some questions that should be brought up:

❑ What kinds of file types are you looking to protect?

❑ How will you control which document libraries/lists will be IRM-enabled?

❑ How will you educate users to leverage this functionality?

❑ What is your disaster-recovery plan if something were to go wrong with the RMS server?

All of these questions should be considered when you are enabling this feature within SharePoint. Once your organization is ready to use this feature, the amount of control that you have over your organization's digital content is greatly improved, not only for your internal users, but for confidential data that you make available to external users as well.

14

Upgrading from SPS 2003 to MOSS 2007 Using the Gradual Method

by Shane Young

It was a dark and stormy night. I had just talked myself into sitting down long enough to take screenshots for my next blog posting when my phone rang. The call was from Big Ideas! — you may have heard of them, but probably not. Their ideas are Big, but their products haven't caught up yet.

Microsoft Office SharePoint Services 2007 (MOSS 2007) had just hit the streets and Big Ideas! had heard enough about the new features to make them believe it was a must-have upgrade. The ability to enforce checkouts, workflow, more powerful search, item-level security, security-trimmed user interface, a built-in recycle bin, the business data catalog — these were big items that Big Ideas! had to have in their organization as soon as possible, and they wanted me to make it happen.

Step back for a minute to understand why Big Ideas! wanted someone to review their upgrade plans. Upgrading a major enterprise platform such as SharePoint isn't like upgrading a favorite screensaver. Microsoft has spent a lot of time and money to make sure the upgrade process scales through the whole range of SharePoint users. Small organizations that only use a single server install must have a way to move their megabytes of data to a new system, and Microsoft itself needs a path to upgrade its terabytes.

Three different plans for upgrading were built into the MOSS 2007 installation, and each one is right for certain situations:

❑ In-place upgrade

❑ Gradual upgrade

❑ Database migration

The next few sections discuss each upgrade option in a little more detail, giving both the pros and cons of each approach. Keep your environment in mind as you read, and imagine how you would apply each procedure in your situation.

In-Place Upgrade

The automated in-place upgrade is perfect for small environments that have made no changes to the default SharePoint 2003. These customers installed SharePoint, created a site or area for a few departments, set up a document library or two, never took the shrink wrap off of their copy of FrontPage 2003, and use only the Web Parts that came with SharePoint.

This method is by far the simplest. You go to your SharePoint Portal Server 2003 (SPS 2003) server, pop in the MOSS 2007 CD, run through the install, click a couple of buttons in the wizard, get a cup of coffee, and SharePoint is upgraded. Enjoy!

The simplicity of this approach is both its greatest advantage and biggest fault. There is no undo. Once you tell it to upgrade, you are stuck with it. That's not a very comforting feeling if SharePoint is crucial to your organization. The only way to go back is to uninstall everything and recover from your SPS 2003 backups. You did do a backup, right?

Notice that, in the installer, Microsoft also notes that the in-place method is best for content databases that are less than 30GB. Among other reasons, this is because an in-place upgrade will take your entire environment offline until it is finished. Another key thing to keep in mind is that the more data you have, the longer it will take to upgrade. Instead of that cup of coffee, you could be in a situation where you need gallons to make it through.

At this point, you are probably thinking "Ok, I have 23GB of data in SharePoint. How long will my upgrade take?" Unfortunately, the answer for everyone is different, so I refuse to even guess anymore. I have done this upgrade process a couple hundred times, and I can tell you that they are all different. The only good news is if you do a test upgrade, the times on the same hardware tend to be very consistent. So, if you time your test upgrade, you will have a number to plan against.

Are you ready for another challenge? If you do have unghosted pages or custom site definitions, you only get one chance to deal with their upgrade. Later in this chapter, I discuss the use of upgrade mapping files for custom definitions. You can use these in this upgrade method, but, once again, you get one try. If you mess them up, you are stuck with your mistake. No fun.

So, the in-place option may be the simplest to use, but it is truly only for environments that are very vanilla. If you have used custom site definitions, unghosted any pages by editing them in Front Page 2003, or have done anything else unusual (you just never know), this method is not for you.

SharePoint Unghosted Pages

Do you know what an *unghosted page* is in SharePoint? Do you have any in your environment? Are you sure? Do you have a list of all of these pages? For those of you who are humming the "Ghost Busters" theme right now and wondering what those crazy guys have to do with SharePoint, maybe a quick explanation might help to understand ghosting in SharePoint.

The very simple, imperfect explanation is as follows. When you load a site, SharePoint caches the template for that site. Each page it serves to you is made up of that template and the unique information for that page contained in the database. This is normal behavior for SharePoint. In this uncustomized state, a page is "ghosted." In a sense, it doesn't exist as a single item in the database; only as a combination of the template and the unique content. This is normal behavior for SharePoint.

Now, if you edit a page with FrontPage and click "save," a copy of the entire page is saved in the database. That page is no longer able to use the cached template information. These customized pages are referred to as being "unghosted." They now exist as a single item in the database and are independent from the template. Every time you request the page, it must be retrieved from the database and sent through a special compiler. There is a slight performance penalty for rendering these pages.

If this is a new concept to you, I encourage you to spend a couple of minutes searching the Web for more information. You will find it is a very complex topic, and none of the experts even agree about the pros and cons. For the purpose of upgrading, you just need to understand them enough to know where they came from, and that the upgrade deals with each one differently. You will need to individually review each unghosted page once the upgrade process is complete.

As a final note, the official terminology is "customized/uncustomized," instead of "ghosted/unghosted." Though this may be the way Microsoft documentation addresses the topic, the community still generally uses the latter terms, especially when researching v2 environments.

Gradual Upgrade

The gradual upgrade method is the most flexible of all of the solutions. If you have a server that is already up to the new hardware specifications of SharePoint 2007, and you didn't get around to warning your aspiring Web developers not to go crazy with FrontPage, this is your road forward.

The gradual upgrade process is much better-suited to most environments than the in-place upgrade. It addresses several of the shortcomings of the in-place upgrade, giving you a little more room for dealing with some of the issues you may face on the road to MOSS.

The first thing that the gradual upgrade gives you is SPS 2003. You can upgrade a single site collection at a time, and if the upgrade doesn't go the way you hoped it would, you can revert back to your original. This means that you can test your upgrade mapping for a custom definition as many times as you like. If it doesn't work out, you can go back to the drawing board and try again. The same goes for sites that have unghosted pages. SPS 2003 keeps running right alongside MOSS 2007. You get all the functionality of both while you work out every detail of your upgrade.

As if that weren't helpful enough, the ability to upgrade one site collection at a time means that you can minimize the downtime needed for your upgrade dramatically. If your company has 4.3 terabytes (TB) of data in SharePoint in use almost 24 hours a day, being able to make the upgrade in small pieces can be a huge benefit.

Are you wondering what the catch is? Well, there are a few details you need to be aware of.

The first thing you need to know is that if you are using Scalable Hosting Mode or Active Directory Account Creation mode, you cannot use the gradual method. (Sorry I got your hopes up — move on to the database migration section.)

The next issue is something you were probably already thinking about. The amount of space it takes to create an upgraded version of a site collection while keeping your original isn't trivial. You may be thinking that you need twice as much space to have this luxury, but the truth is, you need more. In some of its documentation, Microsoft indicates that you need three times the space required to store the original site collection. But, in my experience, it is possible you will need up to six or seven times. Before you panic, let me explain.

During the upgrade of the site collection, SQL must make a duplicate of the original site. At the same time, a transaction log is created, which is usually as big as the site collection itself. After the copy is made, MOSS begins upgrading it, which requires more space and another transaction log. Without going into too much detail, the whole process can *temporarily* peak at six or seven times the size of the original site collection your are upgrading. But once the dust settles, you will only be using a little more than twice the amount of space of the original site collection. If your SharePoint system has lots of site collections, this is usually not too much of a problem. As long as you have three times the total amount of SQL space your SPS 2003 install used, you should be fine. If your SharePoint system only has one big site collection, you may need to take a careful look at your available space to ensure that you can handle that big peak.

There is another possible issue to be aware of with the gradual method. To keep the original SPS 2003 sites available, MOSS must use some redirection. I explain this in more detail later in the chapter, but for the moment, you just need to be aware of the implications of this redirection. If your users have a lot of bookmarks to different locations in SharePoint, they may not all work correctly until the upgrade of a site collection is finalized. Also, some applications (the Microsoft Office Suite, for example) don't interact well with this redirection.

Clearly, the gradual upgrade method isn't perfect, but it has a good mix of features for dealing with customizations and limiting downtime. If you need some flexibility in your upgrade plan, you have found your option.

Database Migration

In some Microsoft documentation, you will find that there are only two upgrade methods mentioned: in-place and gradual. Database migration (DB migration) is sometimes left off the list. Because it is an advanced and drastic procedure, DB migration should be attempted only if you have a special circumstance that makes it necessary.

Essentially, this process requires a fresh server farm to be created to house the new MOSS system. Once a new server farm has been built, a backup is made of the SPS 2003 content database. The backup is then "restored" to the MOSS farm. You then attach the databases to MOSS, and then all of your content is upgraded automatically.

Just like the in-place upgrade method, you only get one shot. If you have any custom site definitions, you must deploy your mapping files before attaching the databases. Sounds simple doesn't it? That part may be, but what about all the other pieces? Things like profile connections, audiences, and search must be reconfigured. Their settings were in the registry in 2003, so they didn't get brought over by the database backup/restore process. Do you have any custom or third-party Web Parts? You must manually install them in your new farm. Lots of little things like this, though not difficult, will require tremendous effort to identify and redo in your new environment.

A major pro for DB migration is that it is the fastest method for upgrading your sites. If you compare how long it takes gradual upgrade to upgrade 20GB of data versus the DB migration approach, DB migration wins hands down. You still have to go back and do all of the manual steps, so the speed gain may not be worth losing all the things the gradual upgrade does for you. (For example, the gradual upgrade method upgrades your search content scopes for you, but DB migration doesn't.)

The DB migration method is an advanced option. If this is your preferred method, it is probably because you have no other choices (for example, farms that are using Scalable Hosting Mode or Active Directory Account Creation mode, or those that are outgrowing their current hardware). The other possibility is that you are the kind of person who would enjoy building your own house out of stones you carried from the river bank. Much like building your own home, the DB migration process gives you maximum control at the cost of maximum labor.

If you would like more information on any of the methods just discussed, check out `http://technet2.microsoft.com/Office/en-us/library/396c85d9-4b86-484e-9cc5-f6c4d725c5781033.mspx?mfr=true`.

The Big Ideas! Portal

Before making any rash decisions about performing the Big Ideas! upgrade, I knew that I had to take a closer look at the portal. A little analysis now will save a lot of trouble later, and provides a good idea of where the areas of concern are. Big Ideas! has done a few things with its portal that would figure into the process of choosing an upgrade plan. I utilize a similar review for each upgrade I perform. By looking at the modifications that have been made to your environment, you can better prepare an upgrade strategy.

Branding

Although it is a functional tool for most companies, the desire to build and display an organizational brand causes many to make a few modifications to the default look of SharePoint. Big Ideas! was no exception. The changes made for the Big Ideas! branding were not extensive — simply the addition of the company logo at the top of the page. Even a change as simple as this must be given some consideration, such as backing up the graphical elements and altered CSS files in case you need to adjust them later. In some organizations, branding is done using FrontPage, which, as discussed earlier, will create unghosted pages. Big Ideas! took a much simpler approach that can be re-created in MOSS with little effort. The branding of this site doesn't look like it will create a large obstacle.

Navigation "Enhancements"

Big Ideas! is a forward-thinking company, and because of this, it has kept up with some of the trends in how to efficiently present and organize information. Through heavy use of topical areas and the Area Contents Web Part, Big Ideas! has managed to implement a "faceted browsing" interface for its portal. Faceted classification allows Big Ideas! to organize its information more efficiently, but the heavy reliance on areas/sub and the Area Content Web Part will require some attention after the upgrade because the Web Part will lose all the extensive configuration changes needed to create the functionality. And, areas no longer exist in MOSS 2007. Did I get your attention there? Keep reading. I will explain, I promise.

My Sites

Big Ideas! allowed its people to create My Sites. Why does this matter? It may not, but it is always worth the trouble to look at all the content in SharePoint when considering an upgrade. In this case, the My Sites look fairly innocent — users may have added pictures, created discussions, filled in the About Me, and contact info. As long as they have stayed with the core functions of SharePoint and haven't used FrontPage to make their My Site look like a `myspace.com` page, it shouldn't cause any trouble.

The Portal Site Directory

Because of its modern ideas about informational organization, Big Ideas! has customized some of the metadata in the Portal Site Directory to allow users to browse by different categories. This is another item that may not cause a problem, but because there are some structural differences in MOSS 2007, some things may need to be rethought.

Custom FrontPage Site Template

Before reading a few articles about the implications of using FrontPage to make changes in SharePoint, one of the designers at Big Ideas! used it to make a Custom Site Template and made it globally available. That template was used to create a top-level site for their Customer Relationship Management (CRM) Software Evaluation Team. Even though this template was created and used very early on in the implementation of SharePoint in the Big Ideas! organization, I still must plan for how it affects us now.

Custom Site Template

One of the things that Big Ideas! felt it needed was a Team Site for each of its large clients. To reduce the amount of work required to create a site for a new client, the Big Ideas! designers worked out a Client Team Custom Site Definition. These are the sites I mentioned before that can be translated to MOSS 2007 with the assistance of custom mapping files. Are you still curious about how a custom mapping file works? Good! Keep reading.

Sales Administration Site with a List Application

The Big Ideas! salespeople have been using a Sales Call Tracking List Application to track all of their phone contact with customers. They did this by creating a custom list definition in a custom site definition. Yikes! This application is a vital process of their sales process, and I must deal with it straight away. The system utilizes multiple lists, lookups, lots of views, and calculated fields to do its job. This is number one on the sales team's list of items that must continue to work after the upgrade.

Office Web Components

Number two on the sales team's "must-have" list are a couple of additions to the Sales Administration site. No one remembers how these were added, and questions about whether or not they were unghosted were met with blank stares. One of these pages is a Sales Dashboard that uses the PivotChart Web Part connected to a list in the site. The navigation bar on this page looks like FrontPage was used to alter it, but that shouldn't have unghosted it.

Dataview Web Parts

Another added Sales Administration page was a Customer Activity page with three connected dataview Web Parts. It is possible to create a page containing dataview Web Parts without unghosting it, but it is also very easy to make a mistake and accidentally unghost it. So, I had to keep an eye on this one.

That's not All!

Just a manual inspection turned up the list of items just discussed, along with some additional items that warrant special attention, such as the following:

- ❑ A top-level Windows SharePoint Services (WSS) site with three subsites, cross-site groups, and unique permissions
- ❑ Pages that make extensive use of the Web Capture Web Part
- ❑ A Volume Document site
- ❑ Search customizations:
  - ❑ Custom content sources for the index
  - ❑ A file share added to its own index
  - ❑ A search scope added for network files
  - ❑ A search scope added for external Web sites
- ❑ Alerts
- ❑ Audiences based off of a user property rule

You may have noticed that, in a lot of cases, I pointed out items that had been modified, or that appear to have been, without really saying how I planned on dealing with them. Often, in an upgrade, you won't know how to deal with an item until you upgrade it and see how it turns out. In many situations, you will find that no one knows exactly what was done to make a change. In your manual inspection, you want to note any modification you find so that you have the opportunity to carefully check how the upgrade may have altered it.

Using a Couple of Analysis Tools

After digging through the Big Ideas! portal, I identified the issues just discussed with only a visual inspection. At this point, I must perform an analysis using some real tools.

The SharePoint Utility Suite v2.5 is a collection of tools that Keith Richie created while he was working as a Premier Support Engineer at Microsoft. One of the tools in the suite is called `spsitemanager`. This tool has an amazing number of uses, but only one is directly relevant to the situation being examined here. The `analyze` option can look at the current SharePoint environment and identify any sites or lists that violate the capacity guidelines set out by Microsoft.

You can find the SPS 2003 capacity guidelines here for reference:

```
http://office.microsoft.com/en-us/sharepointportaladmin/CH011725111033.aspx.
```

To download the SharePoint Utility Suite v2.5, go to this address:

```
http://www.microsoft.com/sharepoint/downloads/components/download.asp?a1=724
```

Once you download the ZIP file, extract the contents to your file system. Then, navigate to the `sputilsuite/wss/spsitemanager` folder. In this folder, you will find `SpSiteManager.doc`, which will explain how to build the tool. In that same document (around page 24), you will find more information on the `analysis` command and its proper usage.

For Big Ideas!, I ran the command as follows:

```
Spsitemanager -o analyze -allvs -sdd dump.xml -analysislevel 3
```

This created an output file called `dump.xml` that could then be reviewed. In this file, I found entries such as the following:

```
<site url="http://portal.abc.local" databaseserver="W2K3"
databasename="Portalfo1_SITE" usercount="44"
id="0d6eef35-7fc3-459b-9ecb-789796e673ae" webcount="72" storage="7929002"
quotaid="0" quotastoragemax="0" quotastoragewarn="0" readlocked="False"
writelocked="False">
```

This identified that the portal site collection had 44 users, 72 subsites (or areas), using roughly 8MB of storage (the number `7929002` is in bytes), and the site had no quota or locks. That's all good news. The dump file contains one of these entries for every site collection in the farm.

Also, the most important part of the file is the top, where it lists warnings such as the following:

```
<warning url="http://portal.abc.local/sites/finance" description="This web contains
the List at /sites/finance/Lists/Contacts/AllItems.aspx that has a total number of
2376 items. Greater performance can be achieved by reducing the number of
individual items below 2,000." />
```

This says the Finance site has 2,376 items in the contacts list, which violates the capacity guidelines. These are the spots where the upgrade process has the greatest potential for timing out or causing other errors. The general recommendation is to find a method for bringing the item in question back to guideline levels, if at all possible. In the case of this list, Big Ideas! had been complaining for months that the list was very slow while opening or editing. Breaking the list into two separate items, one for customer contacts and one for vendor contacts, solved the problem.

Some customers want a way to find all of their unghosted pages. I strongly support this idea. The tool that some customers choose to use is the Ghost Hunter Web Part, which is part of the Web Part Toolkit created by Maurice Prather. You can find this tool at the following URL:

```
http://www.bluedoglimited.com/Downloads/default.aspx
```

Once you add the Ghost Hunter Web Part to your site, it allows you to query your site for unghosted pages. Once it discovers unghosted pages, you can then even choose to re-ghost them (setting them back to the way they were before FrontPage was used).

For the Big Ideas! project, I decided not to use Ghost Hunter. I have found that the upgrade handles each page so differently that it is easier to upgrade them and see what happens. When you use a tool like Ghost Hunter, it will just remove all customizations you made with FrontPage and send you on your way. The upgrade process will do its best to keep customizations that it understands, thus reducing the amount of changes you must redo.

No matter what tool you choose, it is necessary to know which pages are unghosted so that they can be reviewed during the upgrade. Later in this chapter, I discuss a built-in MOSS upgrade tool called prescan .exe that will allow you to make a list of all the unghosted pages you must look at. If you are using the gradual approach, you can then review the original unghosted version of the page and the upgraded, re-ghosted version at the same time. Being able to see each version makes it very easy to quickly compare differences, and ensure that you have not lost any critical modifications.

Now, it's time to make the decision about what upgrade process is best for this project.

Performing the Upgrade Using the Gradual Method

Big Ideas! took to SharePoint very quickly, and has used it effectively for a few years, so the chances that its portal would be a good candidate for the in-place upgrade were pretty low. After taking the time to look around, the in-place upgrade was definitely out of the question. Too many items were vital to the day-to-day operation of Big Ideas! to risk the one-shot in-place upgrade. If something went wrong, the entire portal would have to be restored, and the upgrade would have to be started all over.

A DB migration wasn't a good solution for this project either. Besides the fact that DB migration shares many disadvantages of the in-place upgrade, Big Ideas! has planned ahead, and its server is more than capable of handling the requirements for MOSS 2007. Big Ideas! also doesn't use Scalable Hosting Mode or Active Directory Account Creation Mode either, so there is no compelling reason that would force the option.

Even if Big Ideas! had wanted to transition to new hardware, I would have chosen to use the gradual approach. I feel that moving hardware and doing an upgrade at the same time introduces too many changes to wade through in the case of errors. I would have done the upgrade on their current hardware and then confirmed all was well. Then, I would have moved the fully upgraded environment to new hardware. This is not exactly by the book, but it is what makes me most comfortable.

What this upgrade needed was an approach that ensures that all of the small changes made over years of day-to-day use don't break. The ideal is to have the ability to upgrade a site, test if it is functioning correctly, and then revert to the original if there are problems. Big Ideas! must be allowed to keep working with as little disruption to its business as possible.

This sounds to me like the perfect candidate for gradual upgrade.

Making the Choice

For all of the customers I have upgraded to this point, I have used the gradual upgrade. Why? I just like the flexibility. Even if my intentions are to sit down and upgrade the entire environment today, and the customer has little or no customization, I still use gradual. The flexibility just can't be beat.

I like being able to only do a couple of site collections at a time. I like knowing exactly how big each collection set that I am upgrading is. I also like to be able to show my clients the 2003 version of the site.

More than once, I have received a phone call two days after an upgrade from a customer convinced that the upgrade was responsible for some lost data or broken piece of functionality. I then connect over to the 2003 version of the site that I leave running for at least a month and look at the item in question. Every time, the issue the customer is blaming on the upgrade exists in the 2003 version of the site. Without that proof, no one would have ever figured out the true cause of the issues. They would have just blamed it on SharePoint.

If you are at all on the fence about which method to use, I strongly recommend the gradual upgrade.

A Rundown of the Gradual Upgrade Process

For this section, I am going to let Big Ideas! have a break. From my years of writing training material, I have found that the more generic the instructions, the better for you to follow along at home. But don't worry. Once we get through the procedural stuff, it's back to the story.

Once you have decided to use the gradual upgrade process, you should be aware of some important steps. Before you jump right in with an upgrade, let's first take a look at what must happen:

1. You will need to install MOSS and all of its prerequisite software.

2. You must run configuration wizard to specify the type of upgrades and the basic settings to get Central Administration up and running.

3. Navigate to Central Admin and specify the services and their appropriate settings.

4. Now, you can begin the upgrade. Here you must specify a temporary URL that will host your previous version content. This can either be a different host header URL (http://portal_old) or a different port (http://portal:8080); either works fine and you get to specify the URL.

5. Now that the upgrade is configured, you upgrade site collections, either one at a time, or many at a time. Keep in mind that you must upgrade the root site collection first. Generally, this is your portal.

6. Once everything has been successfully upgraded, you have worked through any issues, and you sure that you are finished with the upgrade, you can finalize the upgrade.

7. Finally, you uninstall SPS 2003, WSS v2, and delete any leftover databases.

Fundamentals of Redirection

How does redirection work? I am glad you asked. For Big Ideas!, the 2003 portal was hosted at `http://portal.abc.local`. When we began the upgrade, we told MOSS that Big Ideas! wanted the old content hosted at `http://portal.abc.local:8080`. If a user navigated to `http://portal.abc.local` and that site hadn't been upgraded, MOSS would respond with a `302` message that redirects the user's browser to the appropriate spot on `http://portal.abc.local:8080`. If that site had been upgraded, MOSS would simply render the page in 2007 at the current URL.

Now, you have to be careful with this redirection thing. Although most browser software understands a `302` response and will go to the correct page, most application software will not.

For example, Microsoft Word doesn't understand the redirect, so if you clicked `http://portal.abc.local/sites/hr/document library/policy.doc` in your "recently used files" list in Microsoft Word, the program would try to open the document from SharePoint. If that site has not been upgraded, SharePoint responds with a `302` redirect response, which Word does not understand. Word responds by presenting you with a `file not found` message.

If you plugged that same path into Internet Explorer, it would redirect to `http://portal.abc.local:8080/sites/hr/document library/policy.doc` and open the document with no problem. None of my customers have had any major issues with this, but it is something to keep in mind.

Server Requirements

The first thing I did after determining that I wanted to use the gradual approach for the Big Ideas! upgrade was to confirm that the hardware was within spec. I went out to `http://technet2 .microsoft.com/Office/f/?en-us/library/4d88c402-24f2-449b-86a6-6e7afcfec0cd1033 .mspx` and found the minimum requirements for a MOSS server.

The Big Ideas! server had two dual-core processors at 2.5GHz and 2GB of RAM, well within the minimum. After some debate, it was decided that upgrading the RAM to 4GB would be helpful. This minimal expense would ensure that the server didn't have growing pains any time soon.

If you have much experience with SPS 2003, you know that the product was pretty hardware-friendly. In most small and medium environments, the only bottleneck encountered was RAM. In MOSS 2007, you will find this is no longer the case. Though RAM can still be an issue, the amount of CPU cycles the product consumes has increased tremendously. Why? Thanks to the additions of a security-trimmed user interface and item-level security, the amount of processing SharePoint needs has greatly expanded. Keep this in mind as you plan your upgrade and examine your hardware. How much CPU is your server using today? What does your memory consumption look like?

SPS 2003 was already installed at Big Ideas!, so most of the core software requirements were already in place. The two new additions to this list were the Microsoft .NET Framework 2.0 and 3.0. The 3.0 version of the Framework provides all of that fancy workflow stuff that makes tackling this upgrade so worth it.

After evaluating Big Ideas! configuration, I discovered that the .NET 2.0 Framework was installed. That was good, I needed it, but there was a problem. Even though .NET 2.0 was installed, it was not listed in IIS Manager under Web Server Extensions. This can happen if you install .NET 2.0 and then install IIS. If this is the case in your environment, you have a special command you need to run. Running this command doesn't hurt anything, so you could also run it to be sure, even if everything looks fine.

1. Open a command prompt.

2. Change directories to `c:\windows\Microsoft.NET\Framework\v2.0.50727`.

3. Run the command `aspnet_regiis -i` as shown here:

```
C:\WINDOWS\Microsoft.NET\Framework\v2.0.50727>aspnet_regiis -i
Start installing ASP.NET <2.0.50727>.
............................
Finished installing ASP.NET <2.0.50727>.
```

4. Now, open IIS Manager and confirm that ASP.NET v2.0.50727 is Allowed, as shown in Figure 14-1.

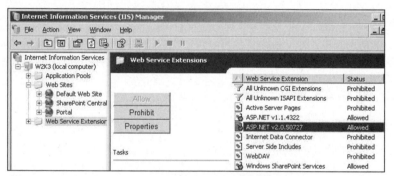

Figure 14-1: Confirming that ASP.NET v2.0.50727 is Allowed

This will not be a common scenario, but is worth confirming before you go forward. Those who have been hung up on this issue have spent hours trying to figure it out, and to no avail.

If you navigate back to your portal, you should still see things just the way you left them. If, after navigating back to your portal you get a message such as the following, this means that, while you were installing .NET 2.0, it took over your virtual server in IIS:

```
ERROR: This Windows SharePoint Services virtual server has not been configured for
use with ASP.NET 2.0.50727.42. For more information, please refer to Knowledge Base
article 894903 at http://go.microsoft.com/fwlink/?LinkId=42660.
```

To fix this, open IIS, click Web Sites, right-click your portal's site, and choose Properties. Now, click the ASP.NET tab, change the ASP.NET version back to 1.1.4322 (or whatever is the appropriate 1.1 version number for your server), and click OK. Your portal should display fine now.

Installing .NET 3.0 Framework is pretty straightforward and I will not consume pages in this chapter on how to do this. Keep in mind that there are separate versions of the Framework, depending on if you are using a 32-bit or 64-bit platform. You can download them from here:

```
http://www.microsoft.com/downloads/details.aspx?FamilyId=10CC340B-F857-4A14-83F5-
25634C3BF043&displaylang=en
```

As a side note, there are two types of installers available for the .NET 3.0 Framework. One will download the bits you need as setup runs (which is a very hands-off approach if the server you are deploying it on has fast Internet and you aren't in a hurry). The other is the redistributable installer package that contains all the needed parts in one file. Generally, I know what version I want to install, and I don't want every server in my farm downloading the bits. In this case, I download the redistributable packages. They are bigger, but this way I can copy the whole file to my server and click Install. The server no longer has to go out to the Internet to bring in the files. Much faster.

Installing MOSS

Let's see where you should be if you were following along with the steps I followed to perform the Big Ideas! gradual upgrade. Hardware requirements met? Check. Software requirements installed? Check. Time to install MOSS? Check.

Now, let's walk through the MOSS installation steps you must follow for performing the gradual upgrade:

1. Do a backup!!! Ensure that you have completely backed up SPS 2003 and you know how to restore it, just in case. I haven't had to go to a backup yet, but I always feel better knowing that it is available.

2. Pop in the DVD and wait to be greeted by the "Enter your Product Key" screen. If you didn't get the screen, you may need to manually run setup.exe.

3. Now, enter your Product Key and click Continue.

4. Read that big, long License Agreement, check the box if you accept, and click Continue.

5. You now see a screen that asks about upgrading earlier versions (Figure 14-2). You have three choices: Gradual, In-place (default selection), or "No, do not upgrade." For Big Ideas!, I chose "Yes, perform a Gradual upgrade." You may be asking, "Why doesn't DB migration show up?" That is because, if you were doing DB migration, you would build a clean install of MOSS 2007 on fresh hardware, and then manually move the databases over. You would not install anything on your current server. In gradual and in-place upgrades, you install MOSS on your existing hardware.

6. If you want, you can navigate over to the File Location tab and change where MOSS gets installed to. For Big Ideas!, I left the defaults for all of the other tabs.

7. Once you have made any other modifications, click Install Now.

8. When the install finishes, you will see a screen that says to complete the install, you must "Run the SharePoint Products and Technologies Configuration Wizard now." Do not click Close yet. There is another step first. (If you have already clicked Close, the world will not end. You just don't follow instructions well.)

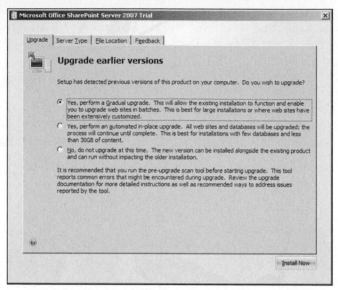

Figure 14-2: Confirmation screen that you want to upgrade

9. Now that the install portion is finished, you must run prescan.exe.

    a. Open the command prompt.

    b. Navigate to c:\program files\common files\Microsoft shared\Web server extensions\12\bin.

        Enter **prescan.exe /c preupgradescanconfig.xml /all** and press Enter (Figure 14-3). This will create a file called PreupgradeReport_<guid>_Log.txt and place it in your local settings\temp folder. You can now review this file for possible issues SharePoint will have during the upgrade. Also, keep in mind that you cannot run prescan against a site collection that is locked, over quota, or otherwise non-writable. That is one of the reasons for running spsitemanager earlier.

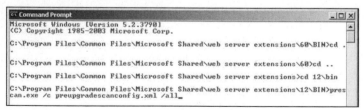

Figure 14-3: Running prescan.exe from the command prompt

prescan.exe will list custom site definitions you have used, unghosted pages you have created, and any other random problems you may have. William Baer has written an excellent article explaining many of the errors that may appear in this report, and how to deal with them. You can find the article at http://blogs

.technet.com/wbaer/archive/2006/12/22/prescan-errors-what-they-mean.aspx. The most common source of errors seems to be orphaned sites. No fun. Luckily for Big Ideas!, its prescan logs were clean as a whistle.

    c. Once you have reviewed everything and made any necessary updates, close the command prompt and any other windows you may have accessed.

10. Go back to your finished screen from earlier and click Close.

11. The "Welcome to SharePoint Products and Technologies" screen should open. Click Next.

12. You will receive a warning box letting you know that some services will be restarted. Click Yes.

13. Another warning message appears, letting you know that if you use language packs, now is the time to install them. Big Ideas! does not use any language other than English, so I could safely click OK.

14. At the "Connect to a server farm" screen shown in Figure 14-4, you want to choose "No, I want to create a new server farm" and then click Next. This has caused confusion for several people. Even though you may have an existing SharePoint Portal Server 2003 farm, you do not want to connect to it. Instead, you would create a new 2007 farm. If you were adding an additional server to the farm, you would choose "Yes." (Big Ideas! just has one SharePoint server.)

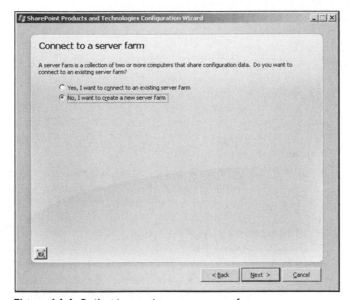

Figure 14-4: Opting to create a new server farm

15. On the Specify Configuration Database Settings screen, you must enter the Database Server name and password for your account, and then click Next.

16. On the "Configure SharePoint Central Administration Web Application" screen, you can specify a specific port number for Central Administration to run on if you choose. I left the default. You can also choose whether the farm will use Windows NT LAN Manager (NTLM) or Kerberos authentication. If you have never heard of either of these, choose NTLM (the default) and click Next. If you are Active Directory savvy and you have configured your environment to use the ticket-based system of Kerberos, then go for it. I stress that the default of NTLM is what most users will use.

17. Take a moment to confirm all of your settings are correct and then click Next.

18. Now, the configuration wizard will run 11 steps. Go get a drink and chill for a couple of minutes.

19. Once you get the "Configuration Successful" message, click Finish. If you do not get the success message, you need to check the logs. They are located at `c:\program files\common files\Microsoft shared\web server extension\12\logs\`. Start with `upgrade.log` and see where it takes you. Hopefully, you have no issues, and this was wasted ink.

MOSS is now installed and running beside SPS. Before continuing, let's look at what has happened.

If you navigate to your portal in the browser, everything should still be normal SPS 2003.

If you look at your SQL Server, you will see that a couple of new databases have been created. One is called `SharePoint_Config`, which is the new configuration database created when you established a new farm. The other database is `SharePoint_AdminContent_<guid>`, which was created to house the Central Administration site collection. This is one of the first changes that you encounter between 2003 and 2007. Central Administration is no longer this crazy `aspx` page full of links and more links; it is now an actual SharePoint site collection. Very cool.

If you open IIS, you will see that there are two new sites: SharePoint Central Administration v3 and Office Server Web Services. Both are self-explanatory. I just want to make sure you realized that you have new sites. And, while we are on the topic of sites, let's discuss a terminology change.

These "sites" or "virtual servers" in IIS will now be called Web applications. Anywhere in SharePoint you see a reference to a Web application, SharePoint is referring to the actual site within IIS. Once you get the hang of this idea, it makes navigation and research much easier.

> *Let me insert one last tidbit of knowledge here. For Big Ideas! to install .NET 2.0 and 3.0 Framework, install MOSS, and run the configuration wizard, the organization consumed about 1.2GB of space on its server — just in program files. As I went through the rest of this process, I continued to keep an eye on drive space.*

Configuring MOSS

Well, as you probably noticed when you closed the configuration wizard, it took you to Central Administration. Now that you have arrived at Central Admin, there are several small tasks to do before trying to perform an upgrade.

The first step is establishing the services on the server. Big Ideas! only has one MOSS server, so all services will run on this one server. If your environment has several servers in your SharePoint farm, you must activate the appropriate services on each server in the farm. You can find guidance on building larger farms at `http://technet2.microsoft.com/Office/en-us/library/776589ed-aba4-47eb-8c4d-86905ac11a511033.mspx?mfr=true`.

1. Click the Operations tab.

2. Click "Services on Server" under "Topology and Services." You will be taken to the screen shown in Figure 14-5. At the top, you will notice the different roles that can be selected for the server. Each one simply highlights the services recommended for that particular role. They serve no other purpose. The key is to ensure that all of the required services are turned on somewhere in your server farm. In this case, there is only one SharePoint server; so click "Single Server or Web Server for small server farms" so that you can ensure that you have enabled all of the necessary services.

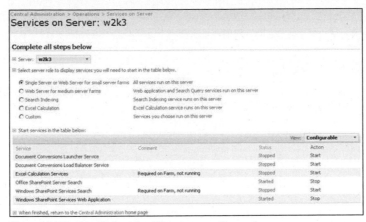

Figure 14-5: Specifying the "Services on Server"

3. Click the Start button located next to Document Conversions Load Balancer Service.

4. Once the update finishes, click the Start button next to Document Conversions Launcher Service.

5. Specify the Load Balancer Server and click OK.

6. Click the Start button next to Excel Calculation Services.

7. Click the Start button next to Windows SharePoint Services Search.

8. Specify the necessary accounts and passwords on this screen. For the service account, you should use the same account you are running your other SharePoint Services as. For the Content Access Account, you should specify a special new account. For Big Ideas!, I created a domain user called `MossSearch`, with a complex password, and set the password to never expire. I then only used the account for the search access account. MOSS then set up this account with read access to the entire farm, so it could crawl all content. This is another change from SPS 2003. In order for the account to crawl the farm in 2003 and get all of the user access rights loaded, the account required administrator permissions. Not anymore. Once you finish filling out this screen, click Start.

> **Another very common mistake I am seeing in the field occurs when setting up accounts in MOSS. People are not entering the `domain\username`, but rather just the `username`. This will cause you so many headaches. Be certain that, anytime you are providing MOSS setup or configuration with account information, you are providing the `domain\username` format.**

9. Now, your Services on Server screen should have everything listed as started. If so, it's time to move on to configure email. Click the Operations tab.

10. Click "Outgoing e-mail settings" under Topology and Services.

11. Fill out your email server and the address you would like the emails to come from. Click OK.

If you don't know these settings, you can open up SPS Central Administration v2 and get the information by clicking "Configure e-mail server settings."

Your server is now ready to rock and roll. Next, let's discuss the process of upgrading sites to see the fruits of all of this labor.

Upgrading Your Sites

The moment of truth is here. You are ready to actually start upgrading some of the site collections. Other than a couple of random IIS resets, nothing that has happened to this point has affected users. That is about to change. So, the next move is to set up a communication strategy.

Big Ideas! is a small company with less than 50 users, so this was a pretty simple process. I put out a note one week in advance informing the user population that, over the weekend, I would be upgrading from SPS 2003 to MOSS 2007, and that they could expect some changes come Monday morning. I also provided many (if not all) with either a preview of MOSS (using lunch meetings) or with access to a playground. Some of the key users were given basic MOSS training in advance so that they could hit the ground running with the new features.

The Big Ideas! portal is set up so that, in each major group, there is a SharePoint "owner" who is responsible for security and content in his or her sites. That way, if someone in Finance wants a subsite created for a special project, that person could go to the Finance site owner and make the request, not to IT. I have found that having people take ownership of SharePoint has really helped with adoption.

As part of the upgrade, I also coordinated with these site owners, arranging a time when their sites would be upgraded so that they could review the results. I wanted to confirm everything was working properly, and who better than the people responsible for the content to tell me that we were good to go?

> There is something else to consider at this point. I have found that it is worthwhile if you can schedule a time to reboot the server between doing all of this installation, configuration, and upgrading. Installation has managed to consume a lot of RAM that you could use to speed up the upgrade process. This step is not required, but helpful if you have the ability.

Enough exposition, let's get back to the task of upgrading:

1. Navigate back to SharePoint Central Administration v3 if you aren't still there.

2. Click the Operations tab.

3. Under Upgrade and Migration, click "Site content upgrade status."

4. You are taken to a screen shown in Figure 14-6 that will list all of your SharePoint site collections. Find the one for your portal (or whichever portal you would like to start with) and click "Begin upgrade."

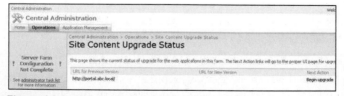

Figure 14-6: Site Content Upgrade Status screen

5. Now, you are taken to the Set Target Web Application screen shown in Figure 14-7. On this screen, you must tell SharePoint on which URL it will host the 2003 sites. For Big Ideas!, I chose to use the same host header (`portal.abc.local`), but moved to a different port (8080 instead of 80). Most of the Microsoft documentation recommends using a different host header (`portal_old.abc.local`). The only challenge there is that you must then have a new DNS entry created for `portal_old`. In some companies, this is easy to get done; in others, this can take two weeks to get the paperwork through. Make your decision and enter the Port and Host Header as applicable.

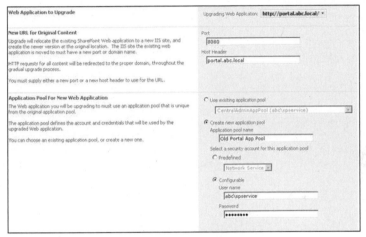

Figure 14-7: Set Target Web Application screen

6. Under Application Pool For New Web Application, choose "Create new application pool" and assign it a Name, User name, and Password. Remember to specify `domain\username`. The temptation is to use an existing application pool, but this generally will not work. Your 2003 portal will need to run as .NET 1.1 and your MOSS sites will need to run as .NET 2.0. A .NET1.1 and 2.0 Web application cannot exist in the same application pool. So, create a new application pool for your 2003 Web application.

7. You can have IIS reset automatically, or wait for you to do it manually, as shown in Figure 14-8. This is only relevant in multiple farm scenarios.

8. For Security Configuration, use the appropriate setting for you. The default is NTLM. Modify this only if you have taken the appropriate steps to use Kerberos authentication.

9. For the content database, I generally let SharePoint choose the name for me. If you want to specify names, go ahead.

10. SSP Database Settings is where you specify the SSP Database Name and Search Database Name. These are the databases in which the Shared Service Provider (SSP) will host the audiences, profiles, search information, and so on. MOSS is nice enough to set all of this up for you when you do a gradual upgrade. For Big Ideas!, I named the database `Portal_SSP_Content_DB` and `Portal_SSP_Search_DB`. If you don't provide a name, the server will create these database names for you. It will use the naming convention `name_PROF_SBS` and `name_SERV_SBS`. I prefer names that make a little more sense than that.

11. Finally, leave the index information on default and click OK.

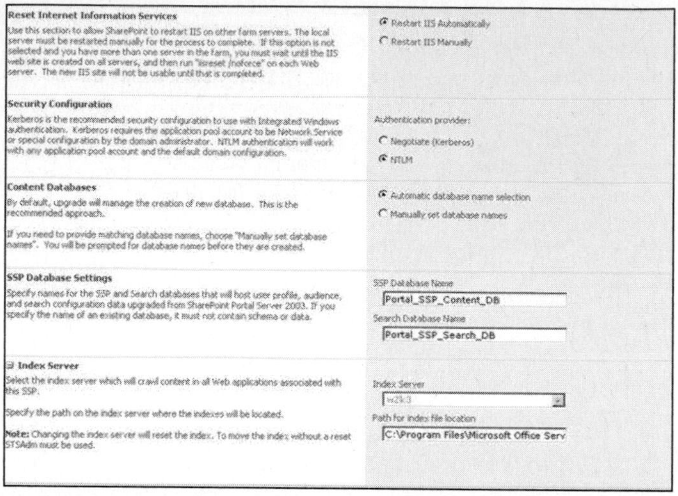

Figure 14-8: Selecting how to reset IIS, the security configuration, naming content databases, SSP database settings, and index server settings

This process takes several minutes to create the new SSP, move the portal Web application, create the new Web application, and the applicable databases. When it finishes, you will find four new databases: two for the SSP, one for the new Web application you created called `name_site_Pair`, and, finally, the WSS Search database created back when you were turning on services. If you look in IIS, you will see just one new Web application (or site, or virtual server, depending on your terminology) listed called `Name_Pair`. This is the new MOSS 2007 Web application.

In the gradual upgrade of Big Ideas!, I noted that another .13GB of data was placed on the Big Ideas! server, resulting in a grand total of 1.57GB of storage consumed — and I still hadn't upgraded the first site.

Take a moment now to navigate to your portal and see what happens. You should be immediately redirected to the Web application you specified earlier. Users at Big Ideas! enter `http://portal.abc.local` in the browser and are instantly sent to `http://portal.abc.local:8080/default.aspx`. The typical end user probably will never notice this redirection even happened.

OK, let's get back to the upgrade. It is finally time to upgrade the first site.

1. On the Site Collection Upgrade screen shown in Figure 14-9, select the site collections you would like to upgrade by checking the box to its left and clicking Upgrade Sites. You must upgrade the root site (the one specified with a /) first. You can do other site collections with it, but it must be in the first batch. For Big Ideas!, I just upgraded the root site collection by itself first by choosing / and clicking Upgrade Sites.

2. On the Sites Selected for Upgrade screen shown in Figure 14-10, you can note the size of the collection(s) you are about to upgrade and then click Upgrade Sites.

Let me insert just a couple of notes on what is happening now. SharePoint is now copying the entire site collection from its current home to a database called `WSSUP_Temp_<guid>`. Once the entire site collection is there, it will run the upgrade against this database and put the upgraded content into the `name_site_Pair` database. Once the upgrade is completed, it will then delete the `WSSUP_Temp_<guid>` database.

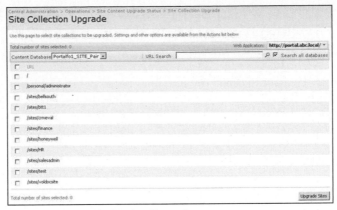

Figure 14-9: Site Collection Upgrade screen

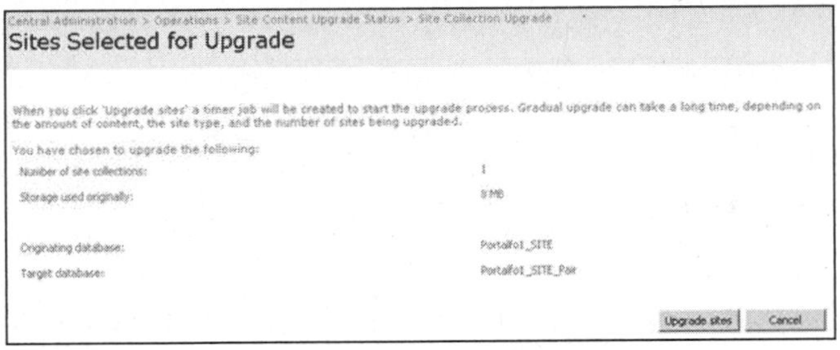

Figure 14-10: Sites Selected for Upgrade screen

You could sit and stare at the upgrade-running screen and click Refresh a lot, but it doesn't help. Though you will see numbered steps and think "Oh, it got to 100 of 135, it must almost be done..." Nope. There seems to be no rhyme or reason as to which steps are slow and which are fast; just know that you are going to watch paint dry for a while. Very exciting. It is worth noting that the root site collection always takes longer to run than the other site collections. This is probably because it is establishing the structure. Either way, a 1GB root site collection takes longer than a normal 1GB site collection.

Eventually (and hopefully), you will get a screen that says, "No upgrade job pending. Upgrade succeeded on Date Time." If you do, congratulations, you have just upgraded your first site collection.

If you wanted to see an overly detailed log of what just happened, you can navigate to `c:\program files\common files\Microsoft shared\Web server extensions\12\logs` and look at `upgrade .log`. This is often the best place to start looking for errors if you have received any during the upgrade process. If you start at the bottom of the file and navigate up a couple of lines, you will find the text `Elapsed time migrating [SPMigratableSiteCollection Parent=SPManager]: Time`. This time is the total elapsed time from the beginning to the end of the upgrade. This is much easier to use than trying to keep notes on when you start and finish. There are other `Elapsed time` entries, but those are for individual site collections.

Navigate in your browser back to your portal URL. You should now see the portal has been upgraded to MOSS 2007 and you are no longer redirected to the new URL. If you wanted, at this point you could type in the URL to the old site collection and still access it. So, now you could have two browser windows open, one pointing at the 2007 version of your site and one pointing at the 2003 version of your site. Your job of comparing what the upgrade has given you is a lot simpler this way. After I finished upgrading all of the Big Ideas! site collections, I looked for "inconsistencies" that I needed to deal with.

At this point, consider manually locking the v2 site collections you have just upgraded. Though most users will never see them again, you know that some will find a way. That is what users do: find ways to undermine your hard work. Some call it "a pain in the butt"; I call it "job security." Either way, I highly recommend locking the old sites. You can either do this from SharePoint Central Admin v2 or through a command-line tool like spsitemanager.exe that was downloaded earlier in the process. Because I just had one site collection to do for Big Ideas!, I used the GUI. Let's take a look at that.

1. Open SharePoint Central Admin v2 (Figure 14-11).

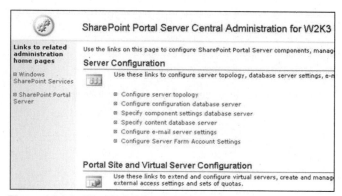

Figure 14-11: SharePoint Central Admin v2 screen

2. In the left-hand column, click Windows SharePoint Services to be taken to WSS Central Admin.

3. Under Component Configuration, click "Manage quotas and locks."

4. Now, click the link for "Manage site collection quotas and locks" to produce the screen shown in Figure 14-12.

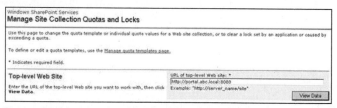

Figure 14-12: "Manage Site Collection Quotas and Locks" screen

5. Under Top-level Web Site, enter your v2 URL (for Big Ideas!, this was http://portal.abc .local:8080). Click View Data.

6. You might get a message in red that says, "The site name entered is invalid: YOUR URL Please enter the URL of the site as http://siteurl." This means that you have probably entered in the v3 URL instead of your v2 URL.

7. Under Site Lock Information, choose "Adding content prevented," enter a reason why you are locking the site, and click OK.

8. Now, you can close Central Admin v2. This can be confusing. You click OK and you stay on this same page. Either way, you are now good to go, and users can't accidentally enter information on the v2 copy of the site.

Now, even if users find their way to the pre-upgrade version of the site, they cannot make changes. Sadly, if you did allow them to make changes here, there is no easy way to move that content from the old to the new.

That's enough of this v2 stuff. Let's get back to upgrading to v3.

1. Open Central Administration v3 again.

2. Click the Operations tab.

3. Click "Site content upgrade status" under Upgrade and Migration.

4. Click "Continue upgrade" beside your portal Web application.

5. Now, you could continue upgrading site collections at whatever pace you want. For the Big Ideas! upgrade, I decided to just upgrade all of the site collections at once by checking all of the boxes and clicking Upgrade Sites.

6. Now, on the Sites Selected for Upgrade screen, you get some handy information: the number of site collections and storage used. This would be a good time to confirm that you aren't about to upgrade 2TB of data or something random like that. If the numbers look reasonable to you, click the button "Upgrade sites."

7. This is the point in the process where you may choose to watch paint dry. For me, I chose to eat French toast and drink a Mountain Dew. What a yummy breakfast!

8. Once you get the "upgrade successful screen," you are finished. Hooray!

Now, if you navigate back to the portal in your browser you should see nothing but beautiful MOSS 2007. No more being randomly redirected to SPS 2003. Yuck!

Reviewing the Upgraded Portal

I suppose this is the moment of truth. It's now time to browse from site to site and see what has happened. If I were sitting with the people from Big Ideas!, I would be telling them about all of the new features and capabilities of MOSS 2007. I am going to assume you already know about the new stuff and you really just want to fix the broken stuff. Fine, be that way! So, fast-forward through the happy, fluffy stuff (where I tell a really good joke that you don't get to hear) and start pointing out the broken stuff. This will be a pretty long list, but don't get discouraged, because it is all fixable.

The Serious Consumption of Disk Space

Remember way back in the beginning of the chapter when I discussed how this upgrade process chews up some serious disk space? The Big Ideas! upgrade provides a perfect example.

Upgrading a batch of sites, 257MB in size, consumed a total of 0.7GB of space when finished. That's reasonable. At the peak of the upgrade process, they consumed 1.8GB of storage space from the server. Yikes! This is a combination of log files, temp files, database storage, and transaction logs. When you are working with a client such as Big Ideas! where all of the files are on one physical disk, this is very easy to see. If you are in a more typical environment where the server and storage is spread out, the consumption may not be as readily noticeable, but it will happen.

As long as I'm discussing disk space, I should point out one more spot where you can get back a whole bunch of disk space: transaction logs on the SQL databases.

What are they? Anytime you write to a SQL database, it keeps a log of all of the transactions that take place. That way, you can recover or roll back changes if you are really talented with SQL Server. Normally, the database maintenance plans that run on the SQL Server will back up and then purge these logs from your disk. I have seen more than one customer, though, who never has this process take place, often because they are using a third-party tool for the database backups. Nonetheless, you can manually purge these files if you want to free up disk space, and now would be the perfect time.

The Big Ideas! database has 370MB of data in the database and another 418MB of data in transaction logs. Wow! I could see where I could get back almost half a gigabyte of storage and, considering I only burned up 0.9GB of storage upgrading the Big Ideas! sites, that would leave me with roughly .5GB of consumed space for this portion of the upgrade. Sounds like a win for me.

If you have SQL 2000, you can access the Knowledge Base article at `http://support.microsoft.com/kb/272318`, or if you have SQL 2005, use `http://support.microsoft.com/kb/907511`.

Branding Is Gone

The first thing the folks at Big Ideas! noticed was that the branding was gone. Throughout the portal, Big Ideas! had used a custom icon and CSS file to give it a little more of a company feel. Unfortunately, the upgrade had no way of bringing those changes over, so the portal was set with the default icon and CSS file. Big Ideas! could just jump right back in, upload and attach the correct image file, and create a new CSS to get back to something like it had previously, and this would require little work. Even better, Big Ideas! could explore the new possibilities of branding that are available to them. These are called *master pages*, and are covered in Chapter 6.

Themes are another victim of the upgrade. Even if you used one of the out-of-the-box themes, your changes are gone. The good news is that you can quickly go back to your site and choose from one of the new out-of-the-box themes. Though this will require a little effort, I don't consider it critical to a successful upgrade. Those users who took the time to play with this on v2 of the site can spend their Monday morning playing with this in v3.

Changes Unique to the Portal

A couple of changes will only affect your portal site collection. One of these changes is that all of your areas have been upgraded to Publishing sites. This is a good thing, but does need to be looked at. Any portal areas that were in what are called *buckets* (where, in the case of Big Ideas!, the URL was `http://portal/c1/sales`) have been converted to the proper URL (`http://portal/sales`). If there are any conflicts, MOSS will automatically append a number to the URL starting with 0. MOSS will also handle the redirecting of requests to the old bucket location at the site's new home. Now, that's pretty slick.

When you start using the upgraded site and you click Site Actions ⇨ Create Site, you will notice that you are only allowed to create Publishing sites below the site you are in. This is because portal areas in 2003 were configured this way so that the behavior got upgraded. If you would like to be able to create other types of sites below your upgraded portal sites, check out an article I wrote (`http://msmvps.com/blogs/shane/archive/2007/02/08/moss-after-an-upgrade-you-can-only-create-publishing-sub-sites.aspx`) that will tell you how to create any type of subsite you would like.

Did you use a lot of listings in SPS 2003? Big Ideas! did. If you recall, there were two types of listings in SPS 2003, listings that were little more than a link to content and listings that were built up with text. During the upgrade, each type is handled differently. The link-based listings are upgraded to new links lists called listings and are rendered on the page using the Content Query Web Part. The text-based listings are converted to news pages, and for each one, it is now a `file.aspx` stored in the `pages` folder. They are also exposed via the Content Query Web Part.

Unfortunately, most of my customers have found that this butchers the structure or look-and-feel they created for navigating information. You should really plan on looking at this portion of your upgrade. You might have to re-engineer your whole layout to use the new tools available to you. If you are finding that you are using the Content Query Web Part a lot, then reading the article from the Microsoft ECM team blog at `http://blogs.msdn.com/ecm/archive/2006/10/25/configuring-and-customizing-the-content-query-Web-part.aspx` should help. It discusses how to customize the Web Part and make it do some tricks that SPS 2003 did out-of-the-box.

The site directory has also undergone some modifications. The most drastic of these changes is that when you click Create Site, you now are creating a subsite instead of a new site collection (as in SPS 2003). Why? As you look at the portal, you are going to find that it has lots of fancy new "roll up" style Web Parts, such as the Content Query Web Part, which can look through your whole *site collection* for all documents (or any other content type) that meet certain criteria. Though this can be very helpful in designing your portal, these Web Parts can iterate through the current site collection, but not all site collections. If you want these Web Parts to look in other sites, they have to be subsites, not separate site collections.

So, you are thinking, "Great, I will just keep everything in one big site collection." That would work fine for Big Ideas! because it only has 10GB of content in its entire portal. All of that data will live in one database with no problem. What if you are more like Microsoft and you have close to 10TB of data in your portal? Do you want one database with 10TB of data? Not if you would like to ever back up or manage that database.

Everything in a site collection must live in the same database. You must break things into separate site collections using multiple content databases. Unfortunately, the query Web Parts (and other things) can't function across those boundaries. This is a real challenge you with face with MOSS 2007 if you have lots of data. I wish I could give you some magical answer that would make everything better, but I can't. Be aware of the limitations of both approaches, and try to manipulate them to fit your needs.

Be aware of the fact that all of the sites you upgraded from 2003 are separate site collections. If, after reading all of those plusses and minuses, you would like to move all of those site collections to be sub-sites of your "portal," you can. I wrote a handy article on how to do that posted at http://msmvps .com/blogs/shane/archive/2006/11/14/consolidating-site-collections-after-upgrading-sharepoint.aspx.

Conversely, if you would like to change the default behavior of the Site Directory to create separate site collection in 2007 (like it did in 2003), you can. Joel Oleson wrote a quick blurb on the subject at http://blogs.msdn.com/joelo/archive/2006/08/18/705157.aspx.

Finally, here's the big bummer part of this process. All of your portal alerts were lost in the upgrade. In SPS 2003, you had two types of alerts: portal alerts (which were search-based) and WSS site alerts (which were timer-based). In MOSS 2007, you only have timer-based alerts. All of the search-based alerts that you upgraded no longer function. Users must manually resubscribe to any Publishing sites they want alerts for. I know, this is not good news, but it's better that I tell you, and you tell your users, rather than waiting three months for the users to find out on their own.

Search

So, Microsoft has made some changes to the way search is done in 2007. The really good change is that WSS sites and portal sites now use the same search engine. That means no more of the portal having its own search engine and WSS relying on SQL full text indexes. There's now one search engine across the board.

This search engine is now handled by the SSP. You no longer have to click Site Settings ➪ Configure Search and Indexing to manage the search. You will need to navigate to your SSP and manage search from there. The easiest way to find the SSP (if you are wondering) is to open SharePoint Central Administration v3 and click the link below Shared Services Administration on the left-hand side of the page.

Search also has become a lot better at providing more relevant results. A lot of this can be attributed to the Microsoft Live search team. The SharePoint guys stole some of their research and put it into the search engine, leaving us with some changes. One is that you now only use one content index. In 2003, you had two indexes by default and you could create additional indexes as you saw fit. Not anymore, because you have one index for everything. Don't worry, though, because this index can safely store millions of documents with no problems.

Also, to help you get more accurate results, the way scopes are built has changed. Creating search scopes is radically different, and a big plus. Now, if you want to create a scope that points to just a specific document library, you can (in 2003, this was nearly impossible). The down side to this is that all of the scopes you had in 2003 are gone after the upgrade. You will have to revisit this topic and manually re-create them.

Speaking of things that are gone, your index is currently empty. During the upgrade, all of your content sources and crawl rules got upgraded and attached to the new index with no problems. The only issue is there is no default crawl schedule. So, until you go to the SSP, click Search Settings, click "Content sources and crawl schedules," and click "Start all crawls" on the left, you will have no data in your index. I recommend this as an early step once your upgrade is complete. While you are here, you may want to define an index schedule for each of your content sources, unless, of course, you want to come in every day and manually do this.

While we are discussing search schedules, this also a good time to go in and disable the index schedule in your 2003 portal. Because we all know that indexing is the most processor-intensive task SharePoint does, relieving it of the unnecessary burden of indexing the v2 portal will help lighten the load.

I encourage you to allocate some time and really look at the new power of search. It is my favorite feature in MOSS 2007 and worthy of an entire chapter of its own. Look at the flexible scopes, using the 11 search-related Web Parts to make some awesome solutions. Search reports are very powerful for finding out what your users are searching for, and are or are not finding. Specify authoritative pages to really help weight your search results, and, finally, revisit keywords and best bets. This is too much fun!

Also related to search, SharePoint still uses iFilters to crawl custom file types. The best example of this is adding the Adobe PDF iFilter that most administrators did in SPS 2003. Also, you probably remember adding the `pdf16.tif` icon, so that when looking at a document library, you had a pdf icon instead of the untitled icon. Well, during the upgrade, the icon does get moved to the proper new folder, but its custom entry in the new `docicon.xml` file is not there. So, you must navigate to `c:\program files\common files\Microsoft shared\Web server extensions\12\template\xml\` and add the entry again for your custom icons. This is not crucial, but just another little thing that needs to be done.

Security Confusion

All of your security comes over in the upgrade; nothing to set up or fix there. Depending on how you defined security in v2, you may find that some of your administrators can no longer access sites they could before the upgrade. This is not an error, but rather done by design.

In v2, all administrators of the server automatically had access to all sites in SharePoint. As a result, in many environments, these users were never added to the sites they needed access to. In v3, local administrators no longer automatically have access, so, after the upgrade, you could be getting phone calls from your fellow administrators complaining about access issues.

At this point, you have two choices: add them specifically to the necessary sites (my recommendation), or go to the Web Application policy and give them full access to everything again. If you choose the latter approach, there is a quick article I wrote to help you do this located at `http://msmvps.com/blogs/shane/archive/2007/01/21/become-administrator-of-the-entire-Web-application.aspx`.

Unghosted Pages

If I navigate to the Big Ideas! Sales Administration site, I discover an example of an unghosted page. Using FrontPage 2003, Big Ideas! modified this page to have three connected dataview Web Parts (Figure 14-13). These connected Web Parts were used to track the activity of Big Ideas! customers. The biggest giveaway that the page is unghosted is the fact it looks just like a v2 page (Figure 14-14), even though the other pages in the site look like v3.

What I did was to revert this site to definition to see what happens. To do this, follow these steps:

1. Navigate to the page and copy its URL.
2. Now, go to the Home page of the site and click Site Actions ➪ Site Settings.
3. Under Look and Feel, click "Reset to site definition."
4. Under "URL for the page," paste in the captured URL and click Reset.
5. At the popup warning, click OK.
6. Now, navigate back to the page and see what has happened (Figure 14-15).

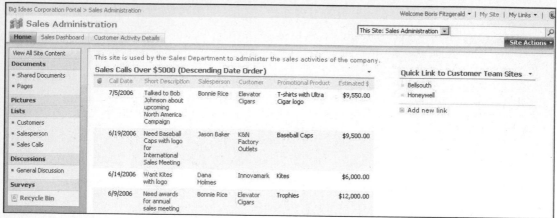

Figure 14-13: Unghosted page

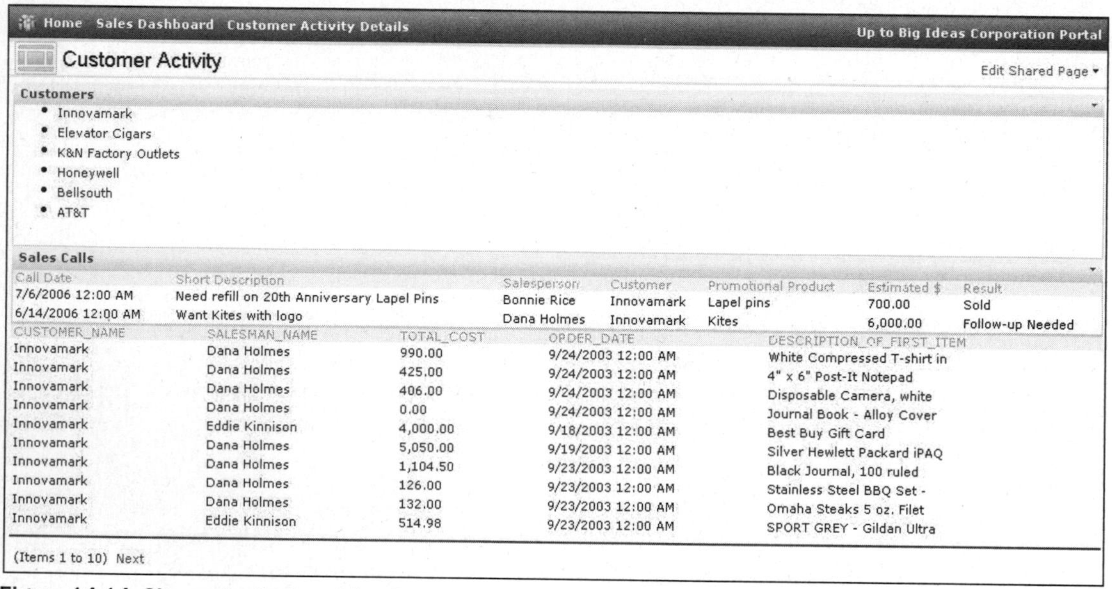

Figure 14-14: Site page displayed in v3

You can see that the page now has the navigation elements and features of a v3 site. What you may also notice, though, is only two of our four Web Parts made it over in the conversion process. You must now open SPD and re-create the full functionality. Unfortunately, that process is too detailed to go into in this text. Keep this in mind: Every page that you reset to site definition will have a unique challenge, which is why I choose not to re-ghost them all at once.

When starting the upgrade of site collections, there is menu item called Upgrade Settings on the left-hand side of the page. Here, you could choose to have the upgrade process automatically reset all pages to their original definitions. Doing that would be more convenient, but then odds are that you never would notice in a quick glance that part of this page might be missing. Use the option to reset all pages with caution.

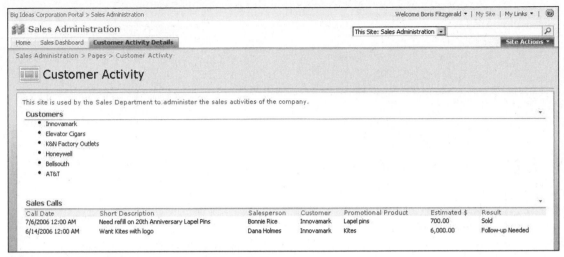

Figure 14-15: Result of reverting the site to definition

At this point, you should use the list of unghosted pages (provided in the prescan.exe log) and deal with each page one at a time. Big Ideas! was a small environment with only a couple of unghosted pages, so I quickly dealt with the issues. You could have hundreds or thousands of pages to look at, though. This is why, in the planning stage, you want to identify all of these pages and determine the best method for you to handle yours.

Custom Definitions

Another major challenge to deal with is the handful of sites that are built using custom site definitions with custom list definitions. If you navigate through your portal and come to one of these sites, you would see the site exactly the way it was in v2 — no security trimming, no Site Actions button, no 2007 features at all. Instead, you have a v2 site just the way you left it. That's no fun.

The reason this site looks just like v2 is because SharePoint didn't even try to upgrade it. When the upgrade process encountered the site, it checked to see what definition it was built from. It found the site was built from "Custom Customer Site Definition." Then, SharePoint went to a folder that contains all of the mapping files for converting from a v2 site to a v3 site, and looked for one matching "Custom Customer Site Definition." When it didn't find one, it just skipped the upgrade process for the site and moved it as is.

For every site definition that came with SPS or WSS v2, Microsoft has included a mapping file in the folder c:\program files\common files\Microsoft shared\Web server extensions\12\config\upgrade. This XML file essentially maps every list and functionality over to its equivalent in v3.

For Big Ideas!, I had to go back to the original developer of the custom site and list definitions and have her create a v3 equivalent. The custom list became a custom feature in v3. Once the functionality was re-created, she then had to create an XML mapping file to put in the upgrade folder. This file would have the map from things like custom lists in v2 site to features in v3 site. I then installed the custom feature, deployed the new site definition, and put the mapping file in the appropriate folder. Now, I was ready to try upgrading the site again.

When you encounter a site that hasn't upgraded in a satisfactory way (such as one that used a custom definition), you can quickly revert it back to its v2 form by following these steps:

1. Open SharePoint Central Administration v3.

2. Click the Operations tab.

3. Under Upgrade and Migration, click "Site content upgrade status."

4. Click "Continue upgrade" beside your Web application.

5. On the left, under Actions, click "Revert site."

6. Beside Site Collection, click No Selection and then Change Site Collection.

7. Click the site collection you want to revert and click OK.

8. Check the site collection at the top and ensure that it is the site collection you want to revert back to v2. Click Continue.

9. This is your last chance to double-check. If you are sure, click OK at the warning popup.

10. The revert happens almost immediately. This is because it is just updating its internal pointer to redirect users who navigate to that site collection back to the previous version URL. In the Big Ideas! site, I reverted `http://portal.abc.local/sites/CMReval`, so now when a user goes to that URL, the user is redirected to `http://portal.abc.local:8080/sites/CMReval` until I am ready to upgrade it again.

11. Now, deploy the custom definition, the list feature, and the mapping file onto the server as instructed by your developer.

12. From the Site Collection Upgrade screen, you see `/sites/cmreval` listed. You can check the box beside the site and click Upgrade Sites.

Now, you get to watch paint dry again. Didn't you miss it? Once the upgrade is successful, you should be able to navigate to the site again and see how well the developer did. Big Ideas! was the first site my developer had to create all of these pieces for. It took her several tries to get all of the pieces of the puzzle lined up, so don't get frustrated while your developers work through the process. Upgrading and reverting a site collection is fairly easy for administrators. This is exactly why I prefer the gradual process. It makes it very easy to work on one piece at a time.

Web Parts

You may or may not have noticed, but some of your custom or third-party Web Parts may not be available in the upgraded portal. What has happened here is that the Web Parts installed to the Global Assembly Cache (GAC) when you originally deployed them are still available after the upgrade. The Web Parts that you deployed to the `bin` are not automatically upgraded and will need to be redeployed. Bin vs. GAC? Yeah, I was confused the first time I heard this too. What it means is that when you were installing them using `stsadm.exe`, you either deployed them directly to a Web application or you chose `-globalinstall`. If you did a global install, then you put them in the GAC. If you went directly to a Web application (or virtual server, as it used to be called), then you installed them to the `bin` directory.

You also need to ensure that all of these Web Parts work correctly in MOSS 2007 and its ASP.NET 2.0/3.0 Framework. There are also a couple of deprecated Web Parts that come to mind: "My Alerts" (which was used on My Sites to display all user alerts) and all of the "Grouped Listings" Web Parts. The "My Alerts" Web Part will just show up as an error on any page it was added to. The "Grouped Listings" Web Parts have been converted to Content Query Web Parts.

Finalizing the Upgrade

So, after a few weeks or maybe even a month or two, it is time to start considering finalizing the upgrade process. Why wait so long? As I pointed out earlier in the chapter, it is very helpful for you, the SharePoint administrator, to be able to reference the v2 sites for a while — to help you confirm functionality, to check out how that old branding looked, even to make sure the unghosted pages work as expected. Knowing users the way I do, I know it could very well be a month or longer before they navigate back to some sites and truly test everything out. If your server has the capacity to host both v2 and v3 for a while, and it isn't causing you issues, I wouldn't be in a hurry to move on.

The Finalizing Process

OK, so now you have decided it is time to let go of the past. What do you do now? It is pretty straightforward. Just follow these steps:

1. Open SharePoint Central Administration v3.

2. Click the Operations tab.

3. Under Upgrade and Migration, click Finalize Upgrade.

4. Ensure that, on the Finalize Upgrade screen, there are no actions listed. If none is listed, click Complete Upgrade.

5. Click OK at the warning popup.

This will remove all temporary files that were used by the upgrade process. It will also remove your ability to do any upgrading or reverting, so I hope you were really ready.

Removing the Old

Well… you don't need that 2003 stuff anymore so let's get rid of it also. What follows are just overview steps; I will leave the details to you. (Remember, no matter how excited you are to remove the old program, using a sledge hammer on a computer is never a good idea.)

1. Uninstall SharePoint Portal Server 2003 from Control Panel Add ⇨ Remove Programs.

2. Uninstall Windows SharePoint Services 2.0.

3. Back up all of your databases. (Seriously! You are about to go in and delete a handful, and I will feel better if you had a way of recovering in case your clicker finger gets out of control.)

4. Delete all of your SPS 2003 databases. By default, this should be `SPS01_Config_db`, `<name>_PROF`, `<name>_SITE`, and `<name>_SERV`. *If you are not 100 percent sure, don't delete any databases until you are sure.*

5.   Now, navigate to IIS and delete the old sites. Old Central Admin should be already gone as a result of the uninstall. In the case of Big Ideas!, I only had only one Web application to delete called portal. To confirm, I looked at the properties and saw that it used a host header of `portal.abc.local` and ran on port 8080. The one running on port 80 is where MOSS lives today; I didn't want to delete that!

6.   Now, reboot the server and ensure that MOSS is completely accessible. If so, you are ready for a well-deserved break. Congratulations!

As a final note, our friends at Big Ideas! took a look at disk space at this point. They found that, after the upgrade was completed and all of the v2 stuff was removed, their net drive space use was about 1.2GB greater. That tells me that overall MOSS is just a little bit fatter than SPS. I'm not saying this is the net change you will see in your environment, just what Big Ideas! saw.

Summary

The gradual upgrade is by far the most versatile upgrade option for SharePoint. In some cases, it may be necessary or desirable to use one of the other options, but the blend of flexibility and control provided by the gradual method makes it my pick for the go-to method anytime you have a choice.

As a final reminder, before attempting any of the steps in this chapter, be sure you have both a good backup and a plan for rebuilding your v2 system if anything goes wrong. You can never be too careful.

You may have noticed in several places that I urge you to involve your user community in the upgrade process. SharePoint is a collaboration platform that, when used to its fullest potential, involves all the members of your organization. Use the ideas and experience of your user pool to make your upgrade more reliable, and you will be doing yourself a big favor. The keys to a successful upgrade are knowledge and planning. Hopefully, I have helped you find one and create the other. Good luck!

Index